CONSTITUTIONAL JUSTICE, EAST AND WEST:

**Democratic Legitimacy and Constitutional Courts
in Post-Communist Europe in a Comparative Perspective**

Law and Philosophy Library

VOLUME 62

CONSTITUTIONAL JUSTICE, EAST AND WEST

Democratic Legitimacy and Constitutional Courts in Post-Communist Europe in a Comparative Perspective

Edited by
WOJCIECH SADURSKI
European University Institute, Florence
and
University of Sydney

KLUWER LAW INTERNATIONAL
THE HAGUE – LONDON – NEW YORK

Published by
Kluwer Law International
P.O. Box 85889, 2508 CN The Hague, The Netherlands
sales@kli.wkap.nl
http://www.wkap.nl

Sold and distributed in the USA and Canada by
Kluwer Law International
101 Philip Drive, Norwell, MA 02061, USA
kluwerlaw@wkap.com

Sold and distributed in all other countries by
Kluwer Law International
Distribution Centre, P.O. Box 322, 3300 AH Dordrecht, The Netherlands

DISCLAIMER: The material in this volume is in the nature of general comment only. It is not offered as advice on any particular matter and should not be taken as such. The editor and contributing authors expressly disclaim all liability to any person with regards to anything done or omitted to be done, and with respect to the consequences of anything done or omitted to be done wholly or partly in reliance upon the whole or part of this volume without first obtaining professional advice regarding the particular facts and circumstances at issue. Any and all opinions expressed herein are those of the particular author and are not necessarily those of the editor or publisher of this volume.

A C.I.P. Catalogue record for this book is available from the Library of Congress.

Printed on acid-free paper

ISBN: 90-411-1883-7

© 2002 Kluwer Law International

Kluwer Law International incorporates the imprint Martinus Nijhoff Publishers.

Printed and bound in Great Britain by Antony Rowe Limited.

Table of Contents

Acknowledgments

Constitutional judicial review poses intractable problems for constitutional lawyers and legal theorists alike. Notwithstanding the conventional wisdom that higher courts armed with justiciable bills of rights are a desirable, if not necessary, feature of democratic rule, lively debates continue to probe this assumption. How can the judicial assessment, and occasional invalidation, of laws passed by elected legislatures be reconciled with our intuitions of a democratic society?

Such issues are brought into particularly sharp focus in the practices of contemporary Central and Eastern Europe where activist constitutional courts have assumed a prominent role in public governance. By evaluating various aspects and interpretations of judicial review in the context of both the jurisdictions where this practice has been developing for a long time, in North America and several Western European states, and in those which are relatively new to this phenomenon, in postcommunist states of Central and Eastern Europe, this book attempts to provide material for a new assessment of the functions and rationales of a robust constitutional adjudication.

This study has been undertaken within the framework of a project sponsored and funded by the European University Institute in Florence: I am grateful to the Institute and to its Research Council for their generous financial and institutional support. Almost all the authors of the chapters included in this volume met at a workshop at the European University Institute in May 2000 to discuss the first drafts, and we all benefited from the input of those scholars who have not contributed to the volume but who participated actively in the discussions: Philip Alston, Adam Czarnota, Bruno De Witte, Alessandro Pizzorusso and Cheryl Saunders, among others. I am grateful to a number of my collaborators who provided research and editorial assistance at various stages of preparation of the workshop and of this volume: Navraj Ghaleigh, Victoria Jennett, Andrew Johnston, Sejal Parmar and Ania Slinn. My special thanks go to Marlies Becker for her excellent secretarial work which has displayed a unique mix of efficiency and skill.

List of Contributors

Sergio Bartole, Professor of Constitutional Law, University of Trieste

Klaus von Beyme, Professor Emeritus of Political Science, University of Heidelberg

Miroslav Cerar, Assistant Professor at the Law Faculty of the University of Ljubljana and an adviser on constitutional issues to the National Assembly of the Republic of Slovenia

John Ferejohn, Carolyn S.G. Munro Professor of Political Science and Senior Fellow of the Hoover Institution, Stanford University and Visiting Professor of Law and Politics at New York University

Venelin Ganev, Assistant Professor of Political Science, Miami University of Ohio

Leszek Lech Garlicki, Judge of the European Court of Human Rights, former Judge of Polish Constitutional Tribunal and Professor of Constitutional Law at the University of Warsaw; now Judge of the European Court of Human Rights

Nida Gelazis, Research Associate at Robert Schuman Centre, European University Institute, Florence

Tania Groppi, Professor of Public Law, University of Siena

Gábor Halmai, Professor of Constitutional Law and Human Rights at the Szechenyi University in Gyor, Hungary, and Director of the Hungarian Human Rights Information and Documentation Centre

Darina Malová, Associate Professor of Political Science at Comenius University, Slovakia

Pasquale Pasquino, *Directeur de recherche* at CNRS, Institut Jean Nicod – EHESS, Paris, and Professor at the Global Law Program of New York University

Marie-Claire Ponthoreau, Professor of Public Law, University of Limoges, France

Jiří Přibáň, Professor of Jurisprudence and Sociology of Law at the Faculty of Law, Charles University, Prague and Lecturer at the Cardiff Law School, University of Wales

LIST OF CONTRIBUTORS

Giancarlo Rolla, Professor of Public Law, University of Siena

Wojciech Sadurski, Professor at the European University Institute, Department of Law, and the University of Sydney, Faculty of Law

Martin Shapiro, James W. and Isabel Coffroth, Professor of Law, University of California at Berkeley

Jeremy Webber, at the time of writing, Professor and Dean, Faculty of Law, University of Sydney; now holder of the Canada Research Chair in Law and Society, Faculty of Law, University of Victoria

Renate Weber, Lecturer on international human rights, National School of Political Science and Administration, Bucharest; Chair, Open Society Foundation, Romania

Kataryna Wolczuk, Lecturer in Ukrainian Studies at Centre for Russian and East European Studies (CREES), the University of Birmingham

Jacques Ziller, Professor of Public Comparative Law and Head of the Law Department, European University Institute, Florence, and Professor of Public Law, University of Paris-1 Panthéon-Sorbonnne

Constitutional Justice, East and West: Introduction

Wojciech Sadurski

A distinguished constitutional scholar recently remarked:

> Given the vitality of both constitutional and statutory review in Western Europe and a few other assorted foreign places, it has gotten harder and harder for constitutional law scholars, both lawyers and political scientists, to take a completely American view. So long as judicial review was a peculiarly American phenomenon, it seemed sensible to try to explain it in peculiarly American terms. Why did Americans let their judges get away with a level of policymaking that no other people in the world would tolerate? Now we have to ask, why do so many people in so many parts of the world entrust so much of their governance to judges?[1]

Why indeed? Today, the question posed by Martin Shapiro is nowhere as valid and urgent as in the new, post-communist democracies of Central and Eastern Europe (CEE). One of the most striking features of the ongoing transitions to democracy in these societies is the spectacular growth in the role and prominence of constitutional courts and tribunals in shaping the new constitutional order.

Before the fall of communism there existed only two constitutional tribunals in CEE: in Yugoslavia since 1963 and in Poland since 1985.[2] While they were not exactly sham institutions, their position was far from one that allowed the exercise of a robust constitutional review. Quite apart from legal definitions of their competence, the genuine powers of both were inevitably subject to the restrictions stemming from the Communist party rule. The position today is that all the post-communist countries of Central and Eastern Europe have

---

[1] Martin Shapiro, "The Success of Judicial Review", in Sally J. Kenney, William M. Reisinger & John C. Reitz (eds), *Constitutional Dialogues In Comparative Perspective* (London: Macmillan 1999), pp. 193–219 at p. 218.

[2] It was actually in 1982 that the constitutional amendment creating the Polish Constitutional Tribunal was passed but not until 1985 that the statute on the Constitutional Tribunal, which established a specific basis for that body, was enacted. The Tribunal began its operations in January 1986. For the sake of completeness, mention should also be made of the Czechoslovakian Constitutional Court of the interwar period, although it was a rather feeble affair, see Herman Schwartz, *The Struggle for Constitutional Justice in Post-Communist Europe* (Chicago: University of Chicago Press 2000), pp. 29–30.

Wojciech Sadurski (ed.), Constitutional Justice, East and West, 1–18
© 2002 *Kluwer Law International. Printed in Great Britain.*

constitutional courts,[3] and while the effectiveness of these tribunals varies, they have everywhere made a strong mark on the process of constitutional transition. Many of them have performed a wide range of constitutionally prescribed roles, including overseeing elections and referendums, deciding upon the prohibition of political parties and adjudicating on the conflicts of competences between state institutions. The most significant impact of constitutional tribunals however has been in that area which is the central focus of this book: the review of enacted law. Evaluating statutes for their consistency with the constitution is probably the most significant – and undoubtedly the most controversial – function that constitutional courts perform in CEE, and elsewhere in the world.

At least some of the constitutional courts of the region have dealt with national legislation in a manner contrary to the wish of the parliamentary majorities and governments of the day. Important aspects of laws on abortion,[4] the death penalty,[5] "lustration" (the screening of officials suspected of improprieties under the auspices of the *ancien regime*),[6] criminal prosecution of former communist

---

[3]   A partial exception is Estonia where, rather than setting up a conventional Constitutional Court, a separate chamber of the Supreme Court (the National Court) has been established, called the Chamber of Constitutional Control.

[4]   See, e.g., Decision of the Polish Constitutional Tribunal of 28 May 1997, no. K. 26/96, in *Orzecznictwo Trybunału Konstytucyjnego, Rok 1997 [Case Law of the Constitutional Tribunal, 1997]*, (Warszawa: C.H. Beck 1998), pp. 173–246. This decision was reprinted in *East European Case Reporter of Constitutional Law* 6 (1999), pp. 38–129. The decision invalidated certain amendments of June 1994 to the Penal Code which liberalized abortion rights. See also the decision of Hungarian Constitutional Court of 17 December 1991, no. 64/1991, reprinted in László Sólyom & Georg Brunner, *Constitutional Judiciary in a New Democracy: The Hungarian Constitutional Court* (Ann Arbor: University of Michigan Press 2000), pp. 178–203.

[5]   The abolition of the death penalty was decided by the constitutional courts in Lithuania, Albania, Ukraine and Hungary. For the text of the Hungarian Court's decision declaring capital punishment unconstitutional (decision 23/1990 of 31 October 1990) see Sólyom & Brunner, *op. cit.*, at pp. 118–38; the decision was also reprinted in *East European Case Reporter of Constitutional Law* 1 (no. 2) (1994) at pp. 177–205.

[6]   For example, in Hungary the Constitutional Court found a number of constitutional problems with the law on lustration passed by the Parliament early in 1994 (decision no. 60/1994, of 22 December 1994, reprinted in *East European Case Reporter of Constitutional Law* 2 (1995) pp. 159–193). In order to comply with the Court's decision, the Parliament had to rewrite the law which it did by July 1996. The new law (passed by the Parliament dominated by a different majority from that in 1994) greatly reduced the scope of lustration. For a discussion, see Gábor Halmai & Kim Lane Scheppele, "Living Well Is the Best Revenge: The Hungarian Approach to Judging the Past", in A. James McAdams (ed), *Transitional Justice and the Rule of Law in New Democracies* (Notre Dame: University of Notre Dame Press 1997), pp. 155–84 at pp. 177–8. Lustration laws were also struck down, or substantially weakened, by Constitutional Courts in Albania and Bulgaria, see Ruti Teitel, "Post-Communist Constitutionalism: A Transitional Perspective", *Columbia Human Rights Law Review* 26 (1994), pp. 167–90 at pp. 180–82.

officials responsible for crimes against the people during the communist period,[7] economic austerity measures,[8] fiscal policy,[9] citizenship requirements,[10] personal identification numbers for citizens,[11] indexation of pensions,[12] have all been struck down. It is no coincidence that the Hungarian Constitutional Court figures so prominently in this list of examples. It is perhaps the most activist constitutional court not only in CEE but also in the world.[13] More importantly for present purposes, according to one of its leading commentators, "[i]t serves

---

[7] In a Decision 11/1992 of 5 March 1992 the Hungarian Constitutional Court struck down *An Act Concerning the Right to Prosecute Serious Criminal Offences committed between 21 December 1944 and 2 May 1990 that Had Not Been Prosecuted for Political Reasons* of 4 November 1991. The effect of the statute would have been to extend retrospectively the statutory period of limitation during which offences occurring in the 1956 massacres could be prosecuted. The decision is reprinted in László Sólyom & Georg Brunner, *Constitutional Judiciary in a New Democracy: The Hungarian Constitutional Court* (Ann Arbor: University of Michigan Press 2000), pp. 214–28.

[8] For example, the Hungarian Constitutional Court struck down important aspects of a number of laws which were meant to constitute a package of austerity measures introduced by the Government in 1995; see e.g. decision 43/1995 of 30 June 1995 on social security benefits, reprinted in Sólyom & Brunner *op. cit.* at pp. 323–32.

[9] See, e.g., the decision of the Polish Constitutional Tribunal; no. K 8/97 of 16 December 1997 striking down a number of provisions of the tax statute of 26 July 1991, reprinted in *Orzecznictwo Trybunału Konstytucyjnego, Rok 1997 [Case Law of the Constitutional Tribunal, 1997]*, (Warszawa: C.H. Beck 1998), pp. 545–59.

[10] In Slovenia, the Constitutional Court decided Case No. U-I-206/97, annulling on 17 June 1998 part of a law on the amendments to the Law on Foreigners. The amendments would change the required period before an immigrant could apply for permanent resident status from three to eight years. See Constitution Watch, *East European Constitutional Review* 7 no. 3 (1998) pp. 36–37.

[11] On 13 April 1991, the Hungarian Constitutional Court declared the use of uniform personal identification numbers unconstitutional, decision 15/1991, reprinted in Sólyom & Brunner *op. cit.* at pp. 139–50.

[12] The Croatian Constitutional Court invalidated in 1998 a provision of the 1993 Code on Equating Retirement Incomes on the basis that the code demanded that pensions increase relative to changes in the cost of living rather than relative to the increase of average incomes, see "Constitution Watch", *East European Constitutional Review* 7 no. 3 (1998), p. 9. The Polish Constitutional Tribunal ruled on 17 July 1996 that a 1995 law which would suspend the indexation of pensions in the forth quarter of 1996 was unconstitutional, Decision K. 8/96 in *Orzecznictwo Trybunału Konstytucyjnego, Rok 1996 [Case Law of the Constitutional Tribunal, 1996]*, vol. 2 (Warszawa: C.H. Beck 1998), pp. 46–65.

[13] This is the view of Wiktor Osiatynski, "Rights in New Constitutions of East Central Europe", *Columbia Human Rights Law Review* 26 (1994), pp. 111–166 at p. 151; see also Jon Elster, "Constitution-Making in Eastern Europe: Rebuilding the Boat in the Open Sea", *Public Administration* 71 (1993) pp. 169–217 at p. 199.

as the exemplar for every new Constitutional Court in Central Europe".[14] Some of these decisions have had enormous financial and budgetary implications; some transgressed clear and strong majority feelings and others rode roughshod over delicately crafted political compromises. There have been decisions taken on the basis of perceived irregularities in law-making procedures and in the constitutional divisions of powers among the lawmaking bodies, but far-reaching decisions have also been based on the constitutional justices' interpretations of vague and unclear constitutional substantive provisions on which reasonable people may disagree.

Constitutional discourses in and about CEE – that is, accounts and analyses of constitutional developments, produced by scholars, observers, lawyers and politicians – have not failed to recognize the momentous importance of constitutional tribunals. Indeed, in much of the scholarly discussion those courts have been credited with playing *the* central role in the constitutional transition from authoritarianism to democracy. They have been described as the promoters and defenders (often, nearly the only promoters and defenders) of the values of constitutionalism, the rule of law and human rights in political and legal environments contaminated by legal nihilism and marked by a disregard for individual rights and the lack of a tradition of *Rechtsstaat*. The following observation by Herman Schwartz, a distinguished American scholar and a perceptive student of post-communist constitutionalism, is fairly typical of the literature:

> The performance of some of [the East European Constitutional] courts so far shows that despite the lack of a constitutional court tradition, men and women who don the robe of constitutional court judges can become courageous and vigorous defenders of constitutional principles and human rights, continuing the pattern shown elsewhere in the world.[15]

This is a heart-warming, feel-good story. It is a story about the courageous, principled, enlightened men and women of integrity who, notwithstanding the risks, take on the corrupt, ignorant, populist politicians. This is a story of the court as a noble "forum of principle" to be contrasted with the elected branches and their practices of horse-trading, political bargains and opportunistic deals. This is a story about impartiality against bias, selflessness versus self-interest. This is a story about respect for paramount values, announced in a Constitution, but which are not to be seen by every mortal, as they often

---

[14]   Spencer Zifcak, "Hungary's Remarkable, Radical, Constitutional Court", *Journal of Constitutional Law in Eastern and Central Europe* 3 (1996), pp. 1–56 at p. 26.

[15]   Herman Schwartz, "The New East European Constitutional Courts", in A. E. Dick Howard (ed.), *Constitution Making in Eastern Europe* (Washington, D.C.: Woodrow Wilson Center Press 1993), pp. 163–208 at p. 194.

remain "invisible".[16] The story is all the better since it is linked – as in the passage from Professor Schwartz – with a global story. The men and women who don the judicial robes in Central and Eastern Europe are not alone. They belong to a small but distinguished community of constitutional judges around the world. And, consistently with "the pattern shown elsewhere in the world", they will see to it that noble Constitutionalism will prevail over dirty politics.

It is a nice story but is it the whole story and is it an entirely accurate story? To be sure, among some of the most vocal opponents of constitutional tribunals in CEE were people like President Lukashenka of Belarus or ex-Prime Minister of Slovakia Meciar – not exactly paragons of democracy. But the nastiness of your opponents does not necessarily render you beyond any criticism. For all the importance of the emergence and growth of post-communist constitutional courts, the phenomenon has remained strangely under-theorized. Constitutional review has been applauded, celebrated and embraced with enthusiasm by constitutional observers and actors, within and without the region, but rarely have the difficult question of democratic legitimacy of those tribunals been raised.

And yet, one would think that these questions must arise whenever an unelected body exercises the power of annulling the decisions of electorally accountable bodies in a democracy, and that the best strategy for the courts themselves would be to face the problems of legitimacy squarely and openly. After all, as Alec Stone Sweet proclaims in his recent book on four powerful constitutional courts in western Europe: "When the court annuls a bill on rights grounds, it substitutes its own reading of rights, and its own policy goals, for those of the parliamentary majority".[17] This applies to Western *and* to Central/Eastern European courts alike, and not just to annulments on "rights grounds" but also on the grounds of inconsistency with such general constitutional clauses as "social justice" or "democratic state based on law". However, the implications of this statement for the democratic theory and practice of post-communist polities have rarely been articulated in the discourse on constitutional tribunals.

In particular, rarely have the intransigent issues of political legitimacy, institutional competence, and possible infringements of the political rights of citizens been discussed. These three dimensions are, however, obviously invoked whenever the last word on the issue of rights protection or policy-setting are placed in the hands of a body which is not accountable to the electorate in the way

---

[16]   The concept of "invisible constitution" was coined by the (then) Chief Justice of the Hungarian Court, László Sólyom, see Sólyom & Brunner *op. cit.* at p. 41, see also Zifcak, *op. cit.* at pp. 5–6.

[17]   Alec Stone Sweet, *Governing with Judges* (Oxford University Press 2000), at p. 105. Note that the phrase by Stone Sweet is not made in a critical context, and is not accompanied by an attempt to question the legitimacy of the "annulment" which is referred to in the quoted passage.

parliaments (and governments controlled by parliaments) are. Electorally accountable bodies presumptively enjoy the paramount legitimate authority to decide on issues of policy on which members of society disagree. The judiciary – including constitutional courts – is notoriously ill-equipped to evaluate options and choices on some issues, such as socio-economic policies with important financial implications. Finally, placing the protection of certain rights and other political values (such as "social justice") in the hands of constitutional courts simultaneously removes these spheres from the agenda of the elected bodies, and consequently restricts the capacity of citizens to participate in political decisions which affect the contours of such rights or political values. While, in itself, this is not a conclusive argument against such an institutional transfer of competence, a reduction in the enjoyment of political rights of citizens calls for a strong defense for such an institutional arrangement.

No such defenses have been forthcoming from constitutional discourse in CEE, and the unproblematic character of the constitutional review of laws as exercised by constitutional courts has been, more or less, taken for granted.[18] It has been assumed that if there is an interpretative clash concerning constitutional rights between the parliament and the constitutional court, the parliament must be wrong and the court must be right. Somehow it has become conventional wisdom that a majority of judges of the constitutional court (which may be as few as five)[19] necessarily knows the "true" meaning of a constitutional right better than a majority of the parliamentary chamber. Consequently, the only significant critical voices about the institutional position of constitutional courts in post-communist systems have argued that they are not powerful enough, not independent enough, not secure enough in the finality and enforceability of their judgments.

Why has the legitimacy of constitutional courts been taken for granted? Why have so few dissenting voices[20] arisen in the constitutional discourse of CEE?

---

[18] E.g., with respect to the Constitutional Court of the Czech Republic, Pavel Holländer reports: "The scope of the Constitutional Court's powers, as defined by the Constitution, is not subject of a discussion in legal theory", "The Role of the Czech Constitutional Court: Application of the Constitution in Case Decisions of Ordinary Courts", *Parker Sch. J.E.Eur. L.* 4 (1997), pp. 445–65 at p. 447.

[19] Constitutional Courts in Albania, Bosnia-Herzegovina, Lithuania, Macedonia, Romania and Slovenia have nine judges. Even smaller Courts exist in Moldova (6 judges) and Yugoslavia (7 judges).

[20] These exceptions include Stephen Holmes, "Back to the Drawing Board", *East European Constitutional Review* 2 no. 1 (1993) pp. 21–25 ("To overlegitimate the [constitutional] court is to diminish the [parliamentary] assembly in the public's eyes and to help discredit the nascent idea of representation through periodic elections", *id.* at 23) and Andras Sajo, "Reading the Invisible Constitution: Judicial Review in Hungary", *Oxford Journal of Legal Studies* 15 (1995) 253–67 and "How the Rule of Law Killed Hungarian Welfare Reform", *East European Constitutional Review* 5 no. 1 (1993) pp. 31–41.

One could perhaps be forgiven for offering simple answers formulated in terms of vested interests and self-aggrandizement. After all, the constitutional discourses have been primarily produced by those who stand to gain the most from the theories supporting a strong role for constitutional courts: academic constitutional lawyers and constitutional judges themselves (the latter being largely drawn from the former). Self-congratulatory rhetoric supports both the position of the constitutional judiciary and law professors owing to their symbiotic relationship. Strong constitutional review strengthens the status of academic constitutional lawyers (they get more material to work on – not just the text of constitutional acts but also the case law, and also may hope to be cited in the judgments and – the ultimate reward – find themselves one day on the bench), while the supportive doctrines produced by constitutional lawyers elevate the position of constitutional judges *vis-à-vis* political branches. Both phenomena are mutually sustaining.

Nothing in the preceding paragraph is restricted to CEE. Martin Shapiro has noted how the emergence and growth of constitutional review in Western Europe has affected favorably the fortunes of academic constitutional lawyers: "European constitutional law teachers went from the bottom of the pecking order of teachers of something like Freshman civics, to near the top of the order as constitutional judicial review came to flourish on the Continent. And just as that particular body of law made more of them, they made more of it".[21]

This shift has been recognized – though rarely – by Western Europeans academic constitutional lawyers and judges, too. Bernhard Schlink, who combines both these professional roles, has caustically noted the relationship between the German Constitutional Court and the constitutional academia in his country: "*Karlsruhe locuta, causa finita* – this remark creates an image of this new situation, in which the *Bundesverfassungsgericht* speaks ex cathedra and representatives of dethroned constitutional scholarship stand at its feet".[22] He further remarked that constitutional scholarship has adapted to the BVG "as a sort of junior partner", and that many constitutional law professors have behaved "as loyal compilers and systematizers of [BVG's] decisions, even as possible candidates for future positions on the Court ... Constitutional scholarship would like to participate in power, and it realizes that the courtiers are rewarded for their service to the royal court by being allowed to influence it".[23] And Schlink himself is scarcely an anti-establishment revolutionary. It is significant that this mutually reinforcing relationship between the academic (mainly constitutional) community and the courts exercising constitutional review is a quasi-universal phenomenon,

---

[21] Shapiro, *op. cit.* at p. 214. See also, similarly, Stone Sweet, *op. cit.* at pp. 146–9.

[22] Bernhard Schlinck, "German Constitutional Culture in Transition", in Michel Rosenfeld (ed.), *Constitutionalism, Identity, Difference, and Legitimacy: Theoretical Perspectives* (Durham: Duke University Press, 1994), pp. 197–222 at p. 219.

[23] *Id.* p. 220.

which can be ascertained not only in European legal systems but also in countries as remote from the continental model as Canada[24] or New Zealand.[25]

There are, no doubt, also more profound reasons for the uncritical approaches to the constitutional courts in the region. The very high social standing of those courts, compared to other public institutions,[26] is a consequence of, and contrast with, the general disenchantment with political branches of the government. Not unlike post-war Germany,[27] "politics" was largely discredited after the fall of Communism, and there has been a widespread, cynical conviction that politics is a dirty business. Being novel institutions (with the exceptions of Poland and Yugoslavia), constitutional courts did not have to bear the same general opprobrium as those tainted by their complicity in non-democratic practices. Further, in at least some post-communist countries (for instance, in Hungary), they were viewed by the then anti-communist, democratic opposition as one of very few institutional checks, agreed upon at the Round Table negotiations, upon the power of less-than-legitimate Parliament and government, dominated as they were by the Communists and their successor parties. Further, the two professional groups which provided the pool of candidates for judges of the constitutional courts – legal academics and the judiciary – were popularly regarded as less "compromised" than the "political class". (Even though the latter was largely composed of new people, the pervading cynicism and lack of trust in politicians inherited from the *ancien regime* affected all politicians during the transition). Notwithstanding that legal academics – and most of the justices of the post-communist CCs have been law professors (in particular, constitutional law professors) – were among the most conformist in academic circles of communist states, this truth has somehow not contaminated their reputation – perhaps due to the relatively high prestige enjoyed in CEE by academics generally. As for the judiciary, only a few judges in the Communist era were directly involved in politically sensitive trials, and it would be correct to say that the bench was not held in disregard in most of the countries of the region – at least, compared to other public figures. It would be perhaps most realistic to say that the senior judiciary have been and remain relatively unknown figures (with few exceptions,

---

[24]   See F. L. Morton, "The Charter Revolution and the Court Party", *Osgoode Hall Law Journal* 30 (1992) pp. 627–52 at pp. 641–2.

[25]   James Allan notes that "there has been a good deal of encouragement for the judiciary from the academy when the courts give themselves more power [to review statutes] under the [Bill of Rights] Act [of 1990]", James Allan, "The Effect of a Statutory Bill of Rights where Parliament is Sovereign: the Lesson from New Zealand", in T. Campbell, K. D. Ewing & A. Tomkins, eds, *Sceptical Essays on Human Rights* (Oxford: OUP 2001), pp. 375–90 at 384–5 (footnotes omitted).

[26]   See, e.g., on Hungary, Halmai & Scheppele, *op. cit.* at p. 181, Figure 1. In 1995 support for the Constitutional Court was 58%, for the Parliament: 36%, and for the Government, 35%.

[27]   See Schlinck, *op. cit.*, at pp. 210–211.

such as a high-profile Chief Justice Zorkin of the Russian CC in years 1991–93), unburdened by any special liabilities related to their professional membership.

There is a broader reason for the relatively uncritical approach to constitutional courts within the post-communist world. While – as it will be argued – these courts are essentially political institutions, engaged in wide-ranging law- and policy-making,[28] they escape the social criticism endured by other political and legislative institutions thanks to their ability to draw upon the appearance of neutrality enjoyed by courts. The traditional paradigm of the judicial process is of a neutral umpire adjudicating between two parties and dispassionately dispensing justice. This description may fit contractual disputes but is scarcely an apt description of courts seised of constitutional disputes. When engaged in abstract review, constitutional courts rather act as an additional legislative chamber which may, often on the basis of vague and eminently controversial constitutional pronouncements, strike down legislation enacted by another body, which is also committed to implementation of the same constitutional norms. However, the paraphernalia of the judicial process – elaborate procedural requirements, the aura of reasoned debate, courtroom symbolism – create an air of majesty and dignity that other political institutions do not possess. The actual character of constitutional courts is substantially obscured by their very practices. The judicial costume lends an extra legitimacy and respectability to these institutions.

This is not to say that constitutional courts are indistinguishable from legislative bodies, but then, no two law-making bodies are identical either. In bicameral systems, the role of the second chamber is usually quite different from that of the "lower" one. For instance, in Poland, the role of the Sejm (the lower chamber of the Parliament) is significantly broader than that of the Senate.[29] These infirmities of the Senate do not render it non-legislative, and if in someone's view they do, that would be an odd semantic convention. The same applies to Constitutional Courts. The fact that they operate under a number of restrictions on their law-making activity does not undermine their legislative character. In the end, there is not much that turns on the semantic (whether to characterize these bodies as essentially "judicial" or "legislative") distinction.

It is more interesting to note, on the one hand, that there are important differences between these Courts and the paradigmatic judicial institutions, and on the other, that their part in lawmaking is informed by a number of constraints (differing from country to country) which do not apply to the parliament. For example, they operate under procedures which borrow greatly from courtroom

---

[28]   This characterization applies only to the most mature post-communist democratic systems.

[29]   It is only the Sejm that enacts statutes. The Senate can make amendments or reject the bill in its entirety but these decisions of the Senate can be overturned by the Sejm with an absolute majority. If the Senate does not express its views about a bill in the thirty days, the bill is considered to be adopted by the Parliament in the Sejm's version.

procedure and symbolism in that they usually are not self-activated (but then, sometimes they are,[30] and in a system in which a large number of important laws are brought before the constitutional court for review, the significance of that distinction between the court and the legislature is greatly diminished anyway).[31] Further, they are more of a "negative" than "positive" legislator, to use a classical distinction by Hans Kelsen (but then, they sometimes issue affirmative pronouncements about the specific ways in which the defective laws have to be repaired, and in any event, the distinction between "positive" and "negative" is unclear).[32] Finally, they are compelled to argue in ways which use the structure of legal syllogism, meaning, in effect, that when they wish to invalidate a law of which they disapprove, they must argue that it is inconsistent with their understanding of the Constitution – either a specific provision, or a more nebulous "constitutional value". Certain types of arguments in favor or against a given law which are available to the members of parliament (for example, about the degree of societal support for a proposed move) are normally not available to justices of the Constitutional Courts.

Much as these courts try to establish themselves (often, in good faith) as neutral interpreters of the allegedly self-evident meaning of the constitution, commentators need not take these assurances at face value. The rejection of a judicial paradigm liberates commentators to ask questions about the legitimacy of constitutional courts' role in lawmaking and in the displacement of the will expressed by other institutions, notably, the parliaments. It is not that, at the end of the day, legitimacy is to be doubted on the simple basis of a lack of electoral pedigree. But, if the role of the constitutional courts is to be maintained or even enhanced, their legitimacy has to be argued for, rather than simply assumed.

The absence of such a reflection in the post-communist settings is all the more glaring once one considers the debates in Western liberal democracies about the limits and justifications of judicial constitutional review. The gap is puzzling. An institution has been straightforwardly imported into post-communist systems from the West but the ideological and theoretical controversy surrounding that institution has not. If there has been a degree of angst caused by the activities of constitutional courts in the countries which served as models to new democracies, then there is no reason to refuse to ask similar questions with respect to their progeny.

To be sure, the longest and the deepest habit of challenging active constitutional review has developed in the country which influenced the establishment

---

[30] Constitutional Courts in Hungary and Poland (though only in exceptional circumstances) can act on their own initiative.

[31] See, similarly, Michel Troper, *La Théorie du droit, Le droit, L'Etat* (Paris: PUF, 2001), pp. 244–5.

[32] See *id.* at p. 18.

and development of CCs in CEE to a very modest degree, namely, the United States. A tradition of doctrinal and judicial warnings about the dangers of enthusiastic judicial lawmaking has been famously punctuated by, among other things, James Thayer's influential essay of 1893 calling for judicial restraint in the name of the goal of self-government, Alexander Bickel's celebration of "passive virtues" that the Court displays in avoiding excessive exercise of its reviewing powers, John Hart Ely's defense of judicial review only insofar as it remedies political malfunctions of representative democracy, and – most recently – Cass Sunstein's plea for "judicial minimalism".[33] The very title of a recent book by Mark Tushnet – *Taking the Constitution Away from the Courts*[34] – expresses well the strength of a doctrinal challenge to the principle of judicial supremacy and finality of judicial articulation of constitutional norms. Tushnet calls for a "populist" constitutional law in which the courts (including the Supreme Court of the United States) do not occupy any privileged position – *vis-à-vis* political branches – in authoritative pronouncements about the meaning of the Constitutional provisions.

It is not only the commentators but also the justices themselves who have long been reminding themselves of the requirements of proper deference to democratically elected bodies, and for recognizing the presumption of constitutionality of statutes. Even if these reminders have often been only rhetorical, and if they served often as a disguise for activism, the very fact that the Supreme Court's judges have felt a need to justify themselves in that way is significant. But often the argument about the proper respective roles of the legislature and the Court served as a justifying reason for refusing to invalidate legislation, as, for instance, in the decision refusing to invalidate legislation prohibiting doctor-assisted suicide, the Supreme Court declared: "By extending constitutional protection to an asserted right or liberty interest, we, to a great extent, place the matter outside the arena of public debate and legislative action. We must therefore 'exercise the utmost care whenever we are asked to break new ground in this field' ...".[35]

A similarly sceptical attitude towards activist judicial review has been articulated by many observers of the Canadian Supreme Court after thoroughgoing, rights based review was instituted there with the entrenchment of the Charter of Rights and Freedoms in 1982. As one legal scholar notes: "Over the two

---

[33] James B. Thayer, "The Origin and Scope of the American Doctrine of Constitutional Law", *Harvard Law Review* 7 (1893) pp. 129–56; Alexander M. Bickel, *The Least Dangerous Branch* (New Haven: Yale University Press 1962); John Hart Ely, *Democracy and Distrust* (Cambridge: Harvard University Press 1980); Cass R. Sunstein, *One Case at a Time: Judicial Minimalism on the Supreme Court* (Cambridge: Harvard University Press 1999).

[34] Princeton: Princeton University Press 1999.

[35] *Washington v. Glucksberg*, 521 U.S. 702. 720 (1997) (quoting *Collins v. Harker Heights*, 503 U.S. 115, 125 (1992)).

decades that judges have given concrete meaning to abstract rights, celebration of constitutional rights has turned to scepticism and the institutional legitimacy of the courts has been threatened".[36] This, by no means, is the only attitude to the rights review that is registered in academic or political circles in Canada, and it should be noted that the public prestige of the Supreme Court among the Canadian population is very high. Still, interestingly, a 1999 survey showed that the Canadians were divided evenly on the proposition that "the right of the Supreme Court to decide certain controversial issues should be reduced".[37] The issue of the institutional competence of the Court, and its legitimacy to strike down laws adopted by the state and federal parliaments is certainly on the agenda in Canada. Its sharpness is perhaps somewhat weakened by (theoretical at least) availability of the "notwithstanding" clause of the Charter which allows the parliaments to enact a particular measure, notwithstanding its possible inconsistency with the Charter rights. The clause, however, has been rather conspicuous by its non-use (with a few exceptions, relating mainly to the special issue of Quebec), and it has not been generally a great success in academic writings or in the community at large as an example of a compromise between parliamentary supremacy and judicial review.[38]

In contrast to the Supreme Court of the United States (and, *mutatis mutandis*, the highest appellate courts of Canada and Australia), European constitutional adjudication has not developed a tradition of self-doubt, agonizing, and "exercising the utmost care" whenever "breaking new ground" in constitutional matters. This may be due to a number of factors. For one thing, there is a much stronger tradition and habit of deference to the highest bodies of government (and this includes the judicial branch) in Western Europe than in the United States. More importantly, constitutional adjudication, in an abstract form, has been introduced explicitly in the Constitutions, rather than implicitly and only by the doctrine developed by the court itself, as was the case of the USA.[39] Continental

---

[36] Judy Fudge, "The Canadian Charter of Rights: Recognition, Redistribution, and the Imperialism of the Courts", in T. Campbell, K. D. Ewing & A. Tomkins, eds, *Sceptical Essays on Human Rights* (Oxford: OUP 2001), pp. 335–58 at p. 335.

[37] *Id.* at p. 336.

[38] One commentator even suggests that, except for the francophone majority in Quebec, the notwithstanding clause "has now ... generally assumed the mantle of being constitutionally illegitimate", Janet L. Hiebert, *Limiting Rights* (Montreal: McGill-Queens University Press 1996) at p. 139.

[39] This contrast is not as sharp as this sentence suggests, regarding, for instance, France, where the dramatic extension of the authority of the Constitutional Council was a result of decisions of the Council itself rather than of a prior constitutional design. In a watershed decision of 1971, the Council "incorporated" the set of unwritten principles into a constitutional package (known by the doctrine as *le bloc de constitutionnalité* on the basis of which the constitutional review of laws is conducted). The Council did it by announcing its reliance on, among other things, "*les principes fondamentaux reconnus par le lois de la République*" *(P.F.R.L.R.)* [Fundamental Principles of the Laws of the Republic] even

constitutional courts do not, therefore, feel any special reasons for anxiety about its legitimacy when deciding about the constitutionality of statutes. The general constitutional design of these institutions locates them in a special position, not comparable to that of ordinary courts. An American observer is right to note that "German, French, and other continental constitutional tribunals have neither hesitated nor apologized when issuing wide-ranging decisions on basic constitutional issues, often drawing on unwritten or historical principles and values".[40]

But one should not overstate that point. While the strength and the vigour of criticism of constitutional courts is nowhere near as formidable in Western Europe as in the United States, it is not quite absent. The critique of Schlink, referred to above, is one example. Similarly, consider France where the tradition of warning against "*le gouvernement des juges*" well precedes the establishment of the *Conseil constitutionnel* and goes back to a 1921 book by Edouard Lambert who addressed his criticism to the US Supreme Court's role.[41] More recently, Bernard Chantebout concluded that the power of constitutional interpretation is by its very nature political, and that "it raises a problem of the compatibility of constitutional review with democracy".[42] Earlier, in an impassioned article, René de Lacharrière argued that review of constitutionality has no constitutional basis in France, and went on to say, with sarcasm, of the concept of "*le gouvernement des juges*" that

[i]t is in reality neither government nor judges but something much better: a supreme censure which, without giving any traditional guarantees provided by a high jurisdiction, and while usurping powers which are not allocated to it by constitutional texts or even are explicitly denied, dominates from now our entire political edifice.[43]

---

though the *P.F.R.L.R.* were not even mentioned by the Constitution in force (of 1958) at the time, much less specified. However, the Council gave legal weight to the (unenumerated) PFRLR because they were mentioned in the Preamble to the 1946 Constitution which, in turn, was mentioned by the Preamble to the 1958 Constitution. These principles, the value of which was found to be equal to those of the Declaration of Rights of Man and Citizen of 1789, were said to be discernible (by the Council itself, naturally) in the legislation in place up to the fall of the republican system in France, i.e. up to July 1948. See Georges Burdeau, Francis Hamon & Michel Troper, *Droit constitutionnel*, vol. 26 (Paris: L.G.D.J. 1999) at pp. 714–15.

[40] H. Schwartz, *supra* note 15 at p. 165, footnote omitted.

[41] Edouard Lambert, *Le gouvernement des juges et la lutte contre la législation sociale aux Etats-Unis; l'expérience américaine du contrôle judiciaire de la constitutionalité des lois* (Paris: Giard 1921).

[42] Bernard Chantebout, *Droit constitutionnel et science politique* (Paris: A Colin 1997), at p. 60, quoted by Troper, *supra* note 31 at p. 237 [The translation of this, and the following, passages from French are mine – WS].

[43] René de Lacharrière, "Opinion dissidente", *Pouvoir* 13 (1980), pp. 132–150, at p. 139.

He also laments that the "enterprise of the *Conseil constitutionnel*" provides an extreme illustration of a "divorce that occurred between the French people and their politics" and that the only remedy is to "reintroduce ... a little more real democracy to our institutions".[44]

But is it legitimate to draw an analogy between the Constitutional Courts in transitional states and those in more "developed" and "mature" systems, and to replicate the arguments about the proper judicial role forged in those more mature systems? It is sometimes claimed that such an extrapolation is unjustified and that the relevant differences between the states which have only just emerged from authoritarianism and those in established democracies should lead us to suspend criticisms of strong judicial review which would otherwise be justified in the West. A careful student of post-communist legal transformation, Ruti Teitel, suggests that the usual doubts about the legitimacy of judicial lawmaking simply do not apply to a transitional legal environment: "Our ordinary intuitions about the nature and role of adjudication relate to presumptions about the relative competence and capacities of judiciaries and legislatures in ordinary times that simply do not hold in unstable periods. ... In periods of political change, the very concerns for legitimacy and democracy that ordinarily constrain activist adjudication may well support such adjudication as an alternative to more politicized uses of the law".[45]

In my view, there are good reasons to resist reliance on the exceptionalism of transitional states as a means to suspend the objections which we might have elsewhere to the institutional anomalies. As the post-communist states of CEE become more mature and stable, so the objections against judicial lawmaking which are pertinent elsewhere in the democratic world apply with equal force to CEE. In particular, there is little or no reason to suspend "our ordinary intuitions" about democracy and legitimacy with respect to countries such as Hungary, Poland or Slovenia, the very countries where the constitutional courts are particularly activist. In many relevant respects these states fully resemble mature democracies, exhibiting as they do developed and pluralistic party systems, a free and diverse press, well-educated and politically aware electorates and independent judiciaries etc.

Moreover, there would be a certain irony in the use of exceptionalism to defend the role of the activist CCs since some of the most activist Courts themselves actually refer to the "normalcy" of the democratic systems in which they operate to justify some of their most activist decisions. The rhetoric of transition and extraordinariness is actually strongly resisted by the constitutional courts themselves. In an important decision of December 1994 declaring the lustration law (vetting of political figures) unconstitutional on various grounds,

---

[44]   *Id.*, at p. 150.

[45]   Ruti Teitel, "Transitional Jurisprudence: The Role of Law in Political Transformation", *Yale Law Journal* 106 (1997), pp. 2009–2080 at p. 2034.

the Hungarian Constitutional Court relied partly on an argument that a successful transition to a democratic system has actually occurred without a need to change the personnel through a lustration; the upshot was that the alleged purpose of the challenged law (namely, to secure a successful transition) could not apply. The principles to be applied to assess the lustration provisions had therefore to be those applicable to a democratic state based on a principle of rule of law. The Court drew a clear contrast between the past and the present, separated as they are by "the transition as a historical fact".[46] It made clear that the lawfulness of the "lustration" laws should be judged not by reference to unusual circumstances of transition but rather by appeal to balancing of the rights and interests at issue.

Apart from anything else, exceptionalist arguments resonate with the attitude that Central and Eastern European societies are as yet too immature for democracy.[47] As an example of such arguably patronizing attitudes, consider the views of John Gray who believes that democratic institutions are not well suited to post-communist societies, and that – at least to many of them, including Russia – "authoritarian political institutions, buttressed by indigenous cultural traditions, seem to offer the best matrix for the emergent civil society".[48] Gray's prescription is largely based on his diagnosis that a decisive role in shaping political life in these societies is played by pre-Communist traditions which are "hardly those of Western liberal democracy".[49] But there are three problems with his prescription of "authoritarianism plus free markets", *based on that particular diagnosis*. First, at least some of these societies had a pre-Communist past not less democratic than the pre-World War II systems of many Western European societies which now have unimpeachable democratic credentials. Second, the democratic aspirations of peoples in countries of the region have been greatly influenced by the universal rise of democratic beliefs in recent decades – so that the explanatory power of the pre-Communist past has now a very limited application. Third, the prescription of authoritarianism may be a self-fulfilling prophecy if the policies of the West are shaped by it. This would be a truly regrettable effect of Gray's prescription.

As an aside, we may note that the exceptionalism of post-communist states has been used also for an opposite purpose to that mentioned above – not to mitigate our common misgivings about strong judicial role but to amplify them. Writing about Hungarian constitutionalism, Andrew Arato remarks: "[J]udicial review does raise problems from the point of view of democratic legitimacy in

---

[46] Decision no. 60/1994 of 24 December 1994, reprinted in Sólyom & Brunner, op. cit, pp. 306–15 at p. 312.

[47] I should emphasize that I am not attributing such an attitude to Ruti Teitel.

[48] John Gray, "From Post-Communism to Civil Society: The Reemergence of History and the Decline of the Western Model", *Social Philosophy and Policy* (1993), pp. 26–50 at p. 46.

[49] *Id.* at p. 27.

a normally functioning liberal democracy. These problems, moreover, are inevitably exacerbated by the unavoidable activism in the context defined by *the weak democratic legitimacy of the constitutional document*".[50] But this point has a very limited application. Hungary provides the only example of a post-communist state having a constitution adopted by a non-democratically elected parliament.

Constitutional adjudication in Central and Eastern Europe has been mainly influenced by post-World-War II constitutional tribunals in Western Europe. But it has not been unaffected by the American example, either. For one thing, American constitutional lawyers were very active in Central Europe after the fall of Communism, sharing their views, knowledge and experience with their Central European counterparts. As a leading American constitutionalist observed, perhaps not very generously but realistically: "American constitutional lawyers ... were happy to cheer the fall of the Berlin Wall and to celebrate the rise of world constitutionalism with an orgy of junketeering to far-off places in need of legal lore".[51] For another thing, the emergence and growth of constitutional courts in Western Europe after World War II undoubtedly can be traced, to some extent, to inspiration from the United States. This has led some American experts to the conclusion that Americans themselves can learn something, for the purpose of perfecting their system of judicial review, from experiences elsewhere. As Professor and Judge Guido Calabresi remarked in one of his judicial opinions:

> At one time, America had a virtual monopoly on constitutional judicial review, and if a doctrine or approach was not tried out here, there was no place else to look. That situation no longer holds. Since World War II, many countries have adopted forms of judicial review, which – though different from ours in many particulars – unmistakably draw their origin and inspiration from American constitutional theory and practice. These countries are our "constitutional offspring" and how they have dealt with problems analogous to ours can be very useful to us when we face difficult constitutional issues.[52]

Calabresi's remarks explain the structure of this book. It attempts to confront

---

50 Andrew Arato, "Constitution and Continuity in the Eastern European Transitions: The Hungarian Case (part two)", in Irena Grudzińska Gross (ed.), *Constitutionalism & Politics* (Bratislava: Slovak Committee of the European Cultural Foundation 1994), pp. 271–88 at p. 274, emphasis in the original, footnote omitted.

51 Bruce Ackerman, "The Rise of World Constitutionalism", *Virginia Law Review* 83 (1977), pp. 771–97 at p. 772. See also A. E. Dick Howard, on American experts in Central Europe: "Traffic is heavy between the United States and the emerging democracies. ... Americans who travel to consult on new constitutions are sometimes dubbed 'constitutional Johnny Appleseeds'", "How Ideas Travel: Rights at Home and Abroad", in Howard, *op. cit.*, pp. 9–20 at p. 10.

52 *United States v. Then*, 56 F.3d 464, 469 (2d Cir. 1995) (Calabresi, J., concurring) (citation omitted).

the experience of constitutional review in the key Central and Eastern European countries (especially those where constitutional courts established themselves as reasonably independent, active and innovative bodies) with constitutional review in North America – the United States and Canada – and Western Europe. The thought is that both sides can learn something from this comparison. The comparison is preceded by a more theoretical paper by Pasquino and Ferejohn which offers a general perspective on what they call "deliberative institutions" of which constitutional courts are prominent representatives.

The general focus in this book is on the issues which relate to the legitimacy of constitutional courts in a system of constitutional parliamentary democracy. No general presupposition in favour of, or against, strong and activist judicial review is adopted nor indeed has a common perspective been expected from the various contributors to this book. However, if there has been one broad idea which has suffused the editing of this book, it could be summarized as follows: the existence of strong, activist constitutional courts, empowered to strike down parliamentary statutes on the basis of their inconsistency with broadly worded constitutional rights, is a matter of institutional choice rather than of the very principle of respecting constitutional rights. It is an "institutional" choice rather than a matter of principle, in that it posits a disagreement between two high political bodies – the majority of the legislature and the majority of the Court – as to a proper articulation of the broad, and by necessity vague, rights provisions of the Constitution. Since reasonable people may often disagree as to the "correct" implications of an abstract right for a specific controversy, the true choice for constitution-makers is about which of the two institutions, when disagreeing, should have the last word. This is a matter for institutional design, and should be based on issues such as the comparable skills, qualifications and mandates of the respective bodies rather than be solved by an appeal to an abstract principle.

This highlights the importance of the dimension of legitimacy in this institutional design. As a prominent student of Western European constitutional courts wrote:

> It would be a mistake to dismiss parliamentary adjudication of rights as inherently less meaningful or less 'judicial' than the deliberations of a constitutional court. Parliament and the court are doing more or less the same thing, speaking in more or less the same language and working through more or less the same normative material. ... When the court annuls a bill, it substitutes its own reading of rights, and its own policy goals, for those of the parliamentary majority.[53]

The decision about allocating authority should always based on a *comparison*

---

[53] Alec Stone Sweet, "Constitutional Dialogues: Protecting Rights in France, Germany, Italy and Spain", in Kenney et. al (eds.), *supra* note 1, pp. 8–41 at p. 26.

of the relative virtues and vices of different institutions, rather than on looking at various institutions one at a time. Even if we are sceptical about the competence of the legislative process in the rights context, this is not enough to support a shift to the judiciary. We first must be satisfied that the judiciary will provide a superior alternative to the legislature.[54] And in making such an assessment, it is important to guard against a temptation of comparing an *ideal* picture of judicial review with a *non-ideal* world of legislative decision making.[55]

Such a judgment will hinge on a great number of variables, and on their relevance to an institutional ability to discern the meaning of rights. These variables include, among other things, such matters as the procedures of selection and recruitment of members for a given body, the conditions of job security of the decision makers, the flexibility in determining one's agenda, whether they are self-activating or not, the access to information and empirical studies on matters affected by a decision, requirements for giving reasons for one's decisions and defending them against critics, patterns of responsibility for unpopular decisions, etc. Any of these variables may be considered relevant to the relative institutional competence in the area of rights protection. But these considerations cannot be substituted by easy and simple pronouncements that judicial review automatically follows from constitutionalism's restricting role *vis-à-vis* majority rule.

It may be that parliaments are often defective instruments for respecting the rights enshrined in constitutions – but it is question-begging to declare that the judiciary is *automatically* better qualified to determine the best interpretation of general constitutional rights provisions. This may sound banal. But then, it cuts so markedly across the broad consensus of contemporary constitutional theory in Central and Eastern Europe, and in much of Western Europe, that it may be useful to make these arguments from the outset.

---

[54] For a forceful expression of this view, see Neil K. Komesar, "Taking Institutions Seriously: Introduction to a Strategy for Constitutional Analysis", *Univ. of Chicago Law Review* 51 (1984), pp. 366–446 at p. 376.

[55] See Stephen M. Griffin, *American Constitutionalism: From Theory to Politics* (Princeton: Princeton University Press 1996) at p. 123.

Constitutional Justice in the Established Democracies

1. Constitutional Courts as Deliberative Institutions: Towards an Institutional Theory of Constitutional Justice

John Ferejohn and Pasquale Pasquino

The collapse of the communist empire coincided with a new wave of constitution making. All the Eastern European countries included in their new constitutions an organ in charge of constitutional adjudication that is modeled on what we define below as the Kelsenian type. This was neither surprising nor original. The same phenomenon occurred in Southern Europe about 20 years ago, after the collapse of fascist authoritarian regimes in Greece,[1] Portugal and Spain. Likewise, after the Second World War, a similar process took place in Austria, Italy and Germany. For this reason the following discussion of constitutional justice in post-authoritarian regimes is pertinent to the recent developments in Eastern Europe.

This institutional revolution can be understood in terms of a simple and more or less unified model.[2] The idea is straightforward: each of the European states is committed to maintaining parliamentary authority over the executive and judicial departments. And, as a matter of sociological fact, each of the post-authoritarian states exhibited distrust either of the judiciary (in the post fascist states) or the parliament (in France) or both. Each therefore chose to introduce a model in which constitutional review of parliamentary actions would take place in a specialized court, outside the judicial system. That model, because it puts some legislative policy making in the hands of constitutional courts (and not merely negative legislative authority as Kelsen himself was forced to admit[3]), places the additional burden of legitimation on those courts. To some extent the burden of legitimation can be addressed by insulating the justices from political

---

[1] Greece has been familiar with judicial review since the 19th century; it is interesting though to note that only the constitution enacted in 1975 at the end of the military regime introduced (art. 100.1e) a *Special* [and specialized] *Supreme Tribunal* overarching the diffuse system of judicial review.

[2] It may be useful, in making sense of the success of the Kelsenian model, to separate parliamentary sovereignty theory with its hierarchical doctrine of the separation of powers naturally hostile to any judicial review, from sociological expectations, like the distrust of the constitution makers towards judges educated in authoritarian regimes, or the distrust towards parliaments that have a record of complicity with fascism or communism.

[3] See 'Wer soll der Hüter der Verfassung sein?' (1931), Italian translation in: H. Kelsen, *La giustizia costituzionale* (Milano: Giuffrè 1981), p. 260.

Wojciech Sadurski (ed.), Constitutional Justice, East and West, 21–36
© 2002 *Kluwer Law International. Printed in Great Britain.*

pressure and by permitting them to craft procedures (such as holding sessions in private, issuing opinions on behalf of the court, etc) that produce impartiality or the appearance of impartiality. But, beyond these more or less structural assurances, constitutional courts need to provide reasoned justifications for their decisions. We argue, in short, that constitutional courts face special and demanding deliberative expectations. In fact, to some extent, these expectations are embodied in the constitutions that created these courts. For example, the organic law of the Fifth French Republic regulating its procedures requires that the Constitutional Council provides a reasoned justification for its holdings.[4]

In *Political Liberalism*, John Rawls described courts as exemplary deliberative institutions – forums in which reasons, explanations, and justifications are both expected and offered for coercive state policies.[5] The authority of courts is supposed, on this view, to rest in large part on the qualities of judicial reasoning – reasons linking court decisions to legal or moral authority – especially since courts as institutions lack democratic credentials and often lack the means to implement their decisions. So, deliberation and reason-giving seem especially valuable (and familiar) aspects of adjudication. If, therefore, we are trying to locate the institutions where reasoning and deliberation play an important role in public life, it is apt to begin with courts and especially with courts dealing with constitutional issues.

In this chapter, therefore, we compare European and American constitutional courts as deliberative forums. We argue that constitutional courts are very differently situated in various political systems. They are asked different kinds of questions by different political actors, and are faced with different expectations, histories and cultural and political constraints. In view of this diversity of circumstances it is to be expected that constitutional courts adopt different kinds of deliberative practices even when treating quite similar issues. Still, despite the diversity, we think there is an important sense in which each of the constitutional courts we examine – the French, German, Italian, Spanish and U.S. courts – have retained the exemplary deliberative character that Rawls describes.

1. DELIBERATIVE EXPECTATIONS

What kind of deliberation are courts asked to undertake? Aristotle's conception of deliberation puts the main emphasis on the requirement that deliberation

---

4   'The Constitutional Council shall give a reasoned decision' (Ordinance no. 58–1067 of
     7 November 1958 incorporating an Institutional Act on the Constitutional Council; art. 20).
     See also, concerning Italy: Law no. 87 of March 11th 1953, The composition and procedures
     of the Constitutional Court, Art. 18: 'Judgements are issued "In the name of the Italian
     people", and set out the reasons for the decision...'.
5   John Rawls, *Political Liberalism* (New York: Columbia University Press), pp. 231–36: 'The
     Supreme Court as Exemplar of Public Reason'.

aims at critically evaluating, and perhaps changing, goals or preferences. In deliberating, people come to recognize and embrace reasons for action that they may not have understood previously. In public deliberation, moreover, the kinds of goals or preferences that agents might be expected to bring to the forum are especially likely to be subject to revision insofar as, at least within a liberal legal system, private and public purposes must fit together in complex ways.

But whether goals or purposes actually change as a result of deliberation, or whether they merely remain open to revision, the way that deliberation changes or reinforces goals or purposes is by giving reasons or arguments. Deliberation in this sense is participating in the process of reasoning about public action. This entails being open to reasons – that is, being willing to alter your preferences, beliefs or actions if convincing reasons are offered to do so – and being willing to base attempts to persuade others on giving reasons rather than threatening coercion or duplicity. Rather than asking, like Aristotle, whether minds are changed, we would ask only whether public action is conducted through reasoning. Minds may rarely actually change as we suspect they seldom do on the American Supreme Court, at least not at the level of deep political commitments. Nevertheless, even if its members remain quite fixed in their general purposes, the Court is nonetheless a forum of reason and deliberation in another sense. The fact that court decisions have effects on real or hypothetical cases, and are aimed at deciding what can or should be done in concrete settings, permits judges who disagree about fundamental principles to find agreement on more concrete levels. While abstract ideas may not be open to revision, ideas about particular cases may be much more flexible and pragmatic.

Moreover, high courts, unlike other political institutions, do not simply publish orders or decisions. They are expected also to publish plausible rationales for their holdings: arguments that others can be expected to respect and embrace, whether or not their own interests have been vindicated. The expectation that courts explain their holdings can be seen as a deliberative expectation in two senses. The first, just given, is that reasons are given that can be understood and embraced as, in some normative sense, *our own* reasons for action. Courts offer, in Rawls' idiom, public reasons for action – reasons of a kind each of us can be expected to embrace from our own moral vantage point. Secondly, since courts are collegial institutions, these reasons are arrived at through an internal process of deliberation, guided by the particular court's decision-making norms. This process may or may not be regulated by a shared expectation that the court will publish a single opinion or that multiple opinions will be published as well. A court's published reasoning is, in this sense, negotiated within a normative framework ranging from consensus seeking to majoritarian.[6]

---

[6]   The changing practices of the U.S. Supreme Court regarding the (increasingly frequent) publication of dissents and concurring opinions is an example of the historical flexibility of these decision-making norms. Perhaps, in an increasingly pluralist culture, there are good reasons to offer multiple rationalizations for holdings and that is the best explanation for why the Court's normative practices permit them.

Reason-giving seems especially important for the authority of courts in two respects. The first we might term *democratic*: because (most) judges are not electorally accountable, the reasons offered in their decisions – especially if some of those reasons are rooted in the (positive) acts of electorally accountable bodies – can provide indirect democratic justifications for public actions. And even if judicial deliberations are not traceable to legislative acts, if they are rooted in (constitutional or moral) principles that in some way underlie democratic government or that are presupposed by a democratic people, judicial reasons can still be seen as indirectly or transitively democratic. Judicial opinions and decisions are, in this respect, the working out of democratic principles in new circumstances and in particularities of specific cases.

In this sense, deliberative judges may actually enhance the powers of democratically elected officials by offering them a more flexible and intelligent system to implement and refine their own legislation and public ordinances. If this is what legislators expect of judges, it should follow that democratic legislators would be eager to expand the judiciary and enlarge judicial powers, purely in the pursuit of empowering the democratic branches, and in enlarging the people's capacity for collective action. Alternatively, insofar as they are acting on constitutional or moral principles, deliberative judges may enhance the authority of the people (either as a collectivity or as individuals) as distinct from their democratic representatives. Rawls' own account of public reason might be seen as emphasizing the democratic character of judges in the sense that public reasons are reasons that we can all, whatever our comprehensive views of the good, be expected to endorse. Public reasons, on this view, have a kind of (non positivistic) democratic character at least insofar as most citizens adhere to one or another comprehensive view of the good. But, of course, judicial deliberations have risks for the legislature as well. Judges, acting on reasons, can modify or nullify democratic commands, and demand of the pattern of legislation a kind of coherence or *rationality* that forbids elected officials from making certain kinds of policies, however politically attractive they may be. But whether such risks are to be seen as pro or anti-democratic depends on connections between the legislature and the polity, amongst other things.

The second way in which reason-giving is important for judicial authority is the way that judicially provided reasons allow others – state officials, other judges, lawyers, ordinary citizens, etc. – to anticipate the implications of the current decision for future cases. Reason giving, in this sense, is *efficiency* enhancing: it plays a predictive or coordinating role rather than a justificatory one; it helps to permit others to choose their actions intelligently in light of their likely consequences. It helps to perfect the rule of law in light of experience. Reason giving in this second sense aims at a certain kind of efficiency – permitting courts to channel or coordinate lots of private and public actions without too much wasteful litigation. Of course, efficiency can be a justification as well. If the deliberative activity of courts permits society to more effectively coordinate actions and to achieve important common purposes, there is more to be said for according respect and allegiance to courts. But this kind of justification has nothing to do with democracy and would be available to courts in any legal system.

While deliberation and giving reasons are important sources of legitimacy for judges in any legal system, they seem to bear particular weight in democracies. The expectation or demand that political authority be seen as flowing, directly or indirectly, from the people together with the notion that democratic institutions must respond to popular demands places judges in a peculiarly weak position. This is, of course, at the root of the worries over the countermajoritarian aspects of judicial review.

2. DEMOCRATIC DELIBERATION

In contrast to what we expect from courts, we do not demand as much by way of reason-giving from our other, more evidently democratic, institutions. True, we might expect that unelected bureaucrats provide some rational connection between their decisions and those of the legislature. Such a demand arises because of the weak democratic pedigree of public agencies: their connection with ordinary voters is remote, operating through a chain of election and delegation that is only as strong as its weakest link. In any case, at least as things have evolved in the United States and most western democracies, we do not demand that rationales for bureaucratic action be either clear or convincing. Administrative actions should be reasonable in the sense of using means more or less proportional to legislated ends, as interpreted by the executive or the agency itself. Usually we trust that the fact that agencies are at least indirectly accountable to voters permits us to rely on their exercise of authority, without always demanding extensive deliberation or reason giving.[7]

Still less do we ask that the legislature itself provide reasons for its actions, at least not in any legal forum. Citizens in most democracies expect political parties to elucidate some kind of thematic program that might serve to explain or justify the legislative program they would push if given the chance. But such manifestos or platforms fall very far short of providing closely reasoned justifications for actual legislative proposals. In any case, the only recourse for a poor justification is subsequent electoral rejection at a more or less distant time and

---

[7] Obviously, the extent to which such trust is placed in administrative decisions depends on the nature of the administrative actions in question. When agencies are judging individual claims concerns with due process lead to deliberative expectations of the kind imposed on courts. Where they are setting general or abstract policies, such expectations tend to be displaced to the electoral process. If voters think that the current administration is not being vigorous in protecting environmental values, they can replace agency leaders by installing another administration.

in circumstances in which the reasons for electoral failure are likely to be obscure. We may expect to see, but hardly demand, a preamble before a legal text, but the content of that preamble is seldom taken as seriously as the actual provisions of the law that follows. Almost never is the understanding of the law itself seriously modified by such preambular expressions. While some legal scholars urge that legislative actions be held to some kind of deliberative test – as a way of forcing legislative deal-making to be responsive to public rather than private values – as things stand neither the courts nor the general public have been willing to establish or enforce such expectations. Thus, in spite of some hand-wringing by legal scholars, we permit the legislature to engage in logrolls, build checkerboard statutes, enact Christmas tree bills and make other kinds of bargains pretty freely and we impose legal restrictions only where there is a conflict between the final legislative action and a constitutional value or norm.

Finally, when it comes to electoral decisions, far from requiring deliberation or reason giving, our public norms seem to forbid it. In this context we are thinking specifically of the secret ballot, and restrictions on campaigning near polling booths, but the more general endorsement of the *one-person-one-vote view* of electoral democracy and the growing efforts to regulate and restrict campaign contributions and spending, work to make democracy at the electoral level a matter of numbers, independent of reasons or reasoning. Moreover the reluctance of courts to look behind electoral results (including popular initiatives and referenda) to probe for inadmissible *intent* of the kind that would routinely be sought in legislative records is another suggestion that we take the ballot box to be a reason free zone – at least in the sense that the exercise of the franchise ought not to depend on the capacity of the voter to give or have good reasons. She just has the right to vote and is free to use it however she wants. In effect, if reasons are to be reflected in the electoral process, they must *work through* the individual voter, by persuading her to cast her ballot based on one set of considerations rather than another. But in the end, however they choose to cast (or not cast) their votes, it is numbers and not reasons that count.

The reasons for such limitations are pretty obvious. Theorists since Plato have worried about the corruptibility of public deliberation. They feared that ordinary citizens would be too easily swayed by seductive rhetoric, or by bribes, or that they would be intimidated by public officials or private interests. Such fears historically led to a deep suspicion of political parties, interest groups, or other formations that could overwhelm the ordinary citizen. Rousseau and Madison, to take two prominent examples, regarded the public arena as sufficiently corruptible that they went to great lengths to seek institutional reforms capable of channeling these powerful tendencies. Rousseau, in the *Social Contract*, would prohibit the formation of parties and other factions if possible, and prohibit legislative proposals from addressing private individuals and groups. And while he deplored the need for the Romans to have adopted secret balloting, he recognized that the corruption of the Republic was too advanced to permit open expressions of the franchise. Madison, who was more sceptical of limiting or regulating private interests directly, proposed multiplying them in the interest of limiting their influence in the public forum. It took another hundred years for Americans to adopt secret balloting as a way of limiting the corruption of the franchise.

We have sketched a rough range of deliberative expectations of institutions in a democracy. The most democratic institutions, in the sense of closeness to the people, are not expected to be deliberative at all and, indeed are surrounded with impediments to deliberation, whereas the least democratic decision -making institutions are expected to be conducted as more or less pure forums of public reason. There are several possible explanations for these divergent expectations.

In one sense, deliberation or reasoning might be regarded as a substitute for more directly democratic legitimacy. If you have the votes, you don't need to persuade others to follow you because they have essentially already promised to do that by electing you to office. If not, persuasion and reasoning is the only way to go. Deliberation and reason-giving are, in this sense, ways in which non -democratic institutions can go about getting people to go along with their decisions. In this sense, deliberating and giving reasons are special burdens that courts and agencies must bear if they are to make authoritative decisions.

Another possible interpretation is that, built deeply into western democratic traditions is the suspicion that deliberative requirements are somehow anti-democratic or elitist. To tell the people or the legislature that having a majority is not enough and that you must also have good reasons to act is to disable or weaken something essentially important in democratic life. This position is not necessarily anti-deliberative, but it is sceptical about the imposition of deliberative requirements on majority action. If reasons and deliberations are to play a role in shaping the law, they must operate through the votes of citizens and their representatives. If reasons are good, then they will sway majorities one way or the other and be reflected in their votes, at least if the tendencies to corruption are limited. If not, well, the reasons must not have been very good in the first place. Reasons, in a democracy, should not get counted twice.

A third possibility is this: in a constitutional democracy, public policy choices take place within a hierarchy of norms – moral and constitutional norms that appropriately limit democratic choices. When engaged in regulating the boundaries between such norms and democratic choices, reason-giving and deliberation is especially important. After all, what is being contemplated in such regulation is telling the people or their representatives that a certain policy may not be permitted. Courts and administrative agencies (when acting like courts) therefore are burdened with deliberative expectations in precisely those areas where constitutional values may be at stake. The legislature, insofar as it acts as a constitutional interpreter, would face similar deliberative expectations, but not when it is engaged in making policies of the kind that are safely within the bounds of constitutional acceptability.

3. CONSTITUTIONAL COURTS IN MODERN DEMOCRACY

Roughly speaking, we may describe the institutional position of constitutional courts as situated along a single dimension, with pure parliamentary sovereignty regimes, such as Britain or the French Third and Fourth Republics at the left and a Montesquieuian separation of powers regime on the right. Between these two poles are a variety of constitutional systems that mix aspects of legislative supremacy with other more or less independent institutions. Parliamentary sovereignty regimes by definition regard both the executive and the courts as subordinated to the legislature, with their role being to implement and enforce the legislator's commands. The notion of judicial review of legislation is, for this reason, completely alien to such legal regimes and, as a result, the way in which legal institutions can lead to statutory revision takes on a particular institutional form in such settings.

In general, parliamentary sovereignty regimes must place constitutional review inside the legislature. Otherwise parliament would not be sovereign. This implies that in parliamentary sovereignty regimes constitutional review can only be *a priori* – prior to the promulgation of a legislative proposal as law – and *abstract*, in the sense of involving only the comparison of legislative and constitutional texts. Moreover, in such systems, while advice as to constitutional principles may be widely sought, the authority to invoke constitutional principles will have to be concentrated in a small number of hands internal to the legislature. Thus, in Britain, France, Finland and Sweden (until very recently) whatever constitutional review takes place occurs wholly inside the legislature. Traditionally, this review may be concentrated in an upper chamber, which may have some kind of negative legislative authority (such as a suspensive veto), or a judicial committee of some kind, or perhaps in a separate institution such as the French Conseil d'Etat, which can advise the legislature on constitutional issues. More recently, the French Fifth Republic has devised what may be termed a third legislative body – the *Conseil Constitutionel* – that can modify or veto proposed legislation.[8] This institution was originally invented by the Gaullists as a way of *rationalizing* or controlling parliament, but it has evolved in such a manner as to permit general constitutional review of governmental legislative proposals.[9] But wherever the review or advice originates, the authority to apply constitutional principles to legislation rests with the legislature itself.

---

[8] Alec Stone, *The Birth of Judicial Politics in France* (Oxford: Oxford University Press), 1992, and John Bell, *French Constitutional Law* (Oxford: Clarendon Press), 1992.

[9] This transition occurred at two critical moments in recent French history. First, in 1971 the *Conseil* asserted the authority to strike down governmental legislation based on broad (and uncodified) constitutional principles (the so called *bloc de constitutionnalité*). In this particular case, the *Conseil* asserted that there was a right to free association that could be discerned from the 'fundamental principles underlying the republic.' In the same opinion the 1789 Declaration of the Rights of Man and the preamble to the 1946 Constitution were elevated to the status of constitutional norms that could be used to overturn legislative

Division of power regimes, again by definition, hold the legislative, executive and judicial powers to be separated horizontally rather than vertically, and such regimes tend to attribute constitutional authority to institutions exercising each of these powers. Montesquieu, of course, famously defined despotism as a circumstance without separated powers, arguing that undivided powers inevitably produced arbitrary and unpredictable rule. He thought it particularly important that courts, when applying law to particular cases, were not legislating in any important sense. The judicial power was in this sense a *pouvoir nul*. But this did not mean that judges (or, perhaps more precisely, juries) exercised no discretion in applying the laws. A court could refuse to apply a law to a particular case if its application would produce injustice. This would not nullify or abolish the law but would set its effects aside in that particular case. This kind of review authority, the power to interpret law and facts in application, produces a characteristic kind of judicial review that is quite distinct from that found in parliamentary sovereignty regimes. Review authority is dispersed throughout the judiciary – any court must interpret the law, constitutional or statutory, in order to apply it. It is exercised in the context of concrete cases and is neither abstract nor a priori. Finally, it is not legislative in the sense that laws are not abolished but only refused application to the case (and, depending on the legal system to *similar* cases).[10]

As an example, Article III of the U.S. Constitution places the Supreme Court at the head of the federal judicial department, permits constitutional review of statutes to arise only out of genuine cases or controversies, and permits any court to engage in such an inquiry.[11] The U.S. system of constitutional adjudication is, in this respect, completely different from the French and most other European models. Courts, in applying statutes must always read them in view of the Constitution, and never apply them in ways that would violate constitutional protections. In view of this requirement statutes are often given interpretations fitting them into the constitutional scheme and are occasionally given no authority at all. While such actions may have something like legislative effects,

---

proposals. The second critical moment occurred in 1974 when the government, fearing electoral defeat, successfully urged a constitutional amendment permitting any 60 members of the legislature to refer legislation to the *Conseil Constitutionel*. Thus, after 1974, the *Conseil* focused increasingly on reviewing governmental initiatives with the powerful constitutional tools it created in 1971.

10 The *non-legislative* character of judicial review is a theoretical idea. Judicial systems with dispersed review will typically give order and predictability to judicial actions by devising methods of hierarchical control of lower courts that create coherent rules or doctrines out of diverse decisions. The effect of such developments is to make judicial action more legislative as statutory rules are supplemented with judicially crafted ones.

11 In many respects, the Norwegian system of constitutional adjudication resembles the American in that such review takes place in concrete cases and is dispersed throughout ordinary courts.

they do not formally change or eliminate statutory texts in the manner of the French system. Unconstitutional statutes are not repealed or eliminated. They are simply given no application to particular disputes. Putting matters this way emphasizes the judicial rather than legislative aspects of judicial review.

While most European legal systems have parliamentary sovereignty traditions – in the sense that both the executive and the judiciary are subordinated to parliament – developments in the twentieth century, particularly following the two world wars, have tended to erode these commitments. Thus, Austria after WW I,[12] and Germany and Italy after WW II (and Spain and Portugal after the collapse of fascist regimes), adopted constitutions that departed from the hierarchical parliamentary model in important ways. For convenience, we may call all of these regimes Kelsenian, after the eminent Austrian jurist who invented its distinct institutional form. Each of the European constitutions reflect, in various ways, Kelsen's central idea that constitutional adjudication is more of a legislative than a judicial function. When a constitutional court strikes down a statute it is not only legislating in the negative sense of abolishing a law, but insofar as it must reconstruct the legal situation before the statute, it is legislating positively as well.[13]

Kelsen's notion of constitutional adjudication emphasized this legislative aspect by conceiving it as involving a comparison of a statutory and a constitutional text. Such abstract review arises not out of a fact specific case with real (harmed) litigants claiming rights, but as an a priori and abstract comparison of texts. Constitutional adjudication seen this way seems inherently political, in the sense that a constitutional court must deliberate and choose from among alternative normative rules for regulating social conduct. As a result, Kelsen thought that constitutional courts should be placed outside the judiciary as well as the other governmental departments. Their powers were to be exercised by politically appointed judges, usually drawn from people particularly competent at making abstract comparisons among texts, and with the capacity to deliberate

---

[12] Austria was the first country on the European continent to introduce in 1920 a Constitutional Court. Hans Kelsen played a crucial role in establishing this institution. It is important to take into account that historical antecedents of such an organ were courts adjudicating conflicts between the central government and the *Länder* in the Austro-Hungarian Empire as in the Holy German Empire (*Reichskammergerich*).

[13] This is even more obviously the case when a constitutional court construes a statute in light of constitutional values. Kelsen himself hesitated in defining the role of the Constitutional Court. At the beginning he spoke of 'negative legislation', but later on, answering C. Schmitt, he accepted, in his book *Wer soll der Hüter der Verfassung sein?* (1931), that the Court plays a positive legislative function. See P. Pasquino, 'Gardien de la constitution ou justice constitutionnelle? C. Schmitt et H. Kelsen'; in *1789 et l'invention de la constitution*, sous la direction de M. Troper et L. Jaume (Paris: Bruylant – L.G.D.J.), 1994, pp. 141–152.

about norms and explain decisions, and not necessarily from those with judicial experience.

3.1. Constitutional Adjudication in Post-Authoritarian Regimes

Kelsen's ideas have proved especially attractive to post-authoritarian regimes. Not only were they adopted in Austria, Germany, Italy and Spain, but they have also taken root throughout Eastern Europe after 1989. Each of the post-authoritarian constitutions put in place institutions of constitutional adjudication that permitted constitutional review of legislative, and sometimes of executive and judicial acts. But in each of these cases, the very fact that there was a transition under way from an old and distrusted regime to a new one, meant that judges were viewed with particular suspicion, as potential holders of constitutional review authority.[14] As a result, there were powerful political reasons to place constitutional adjudication outside the judiciary – in effect the reviewing body was placed above each of the other institutions in position to review any governmental action from a constitutional perspective – and given to a specialized and politically appointed body.

While Kelsen emphasized abstract constitutional review, all of the modern post-authoritarian constitutional courts have concrete a posteriori review powers as well. Access to these courts is controlled not only by governments and political minorities, but also by ordinary litigants in the context of specific cases, or, as in Italy, by ordinary law courts. Thus courts may be asked, in a Kelsenian fashion, to compare constitutional and statutory texts abstractly (by direct referral of a constitutional issue), or they may be presented with a constitutional issue that arises in an ongoing case before a lower court, or they may be presented with a whole decided case (as happens in both Spain and Germany).[15] In any of these situations, the actual authority to nullify or modify legislation is generally concentrated in the constitutional court and not dispersed throughout the judiciary. If an ordinary court doubts the constitutionality of a law, it must stay the proceedings before it and refer the question to the constitutional court for determination.[16]

The makeup of these constitutional courts is distinctive as well. Because the

---

[14] The judiciaries of each of these systems are essentially closed career hierarchies that are particularly insulated from outside influence. This extreme insulation of judges made it even less likely that important additional powers would be vested in them following the collapse of authoritarianism.

[15] This is the traditional practice also for appeals to the European Court of Human Rights in Strasbourg, which reviews cases only after litigants exhaust domestically available remedies. With the incorporation of the European Convention on Human Rights, domestic courts increasingly give direct application to human rights law.

[16] Courts applying European Community Law follow the same practices.

separation of powers systems tend to have dispersed and concrete review, ordinary judges can be expected to develop competence in constitutional adjudication. In post-authoritarian systems, however, where constitutional review is concentrated and often abstract, ordinary judges have no special claims to authority. Moreover, because of their authoritarian past, judges in these systems were at least initially distrusted as arbiters of constitutional and democratic values. Thus, in all of the post-authoritarian systems, law professors tend to occupy many of the seats on the court together with some judges.

3.2. A Special Case: the French Conseil Constitutionel

The institution of constitutional review in the French Fifth Republic is worth considering separately. The French republican tradition is solidly in the parliamentary sovereignty tradition and, it has been hostile to constitutional adjudication since the Revolution.[17] But De Gaulle and his supporters insisted on placing institutional restraints on parliament and one of these was the *Conseil Constitutionel*. Within the parliamentary sovereignty system, the only way that this could be done was to place the court effectively within the legislature. Thus, to a greater extent than Kelsen recommended, this placement emphasized the *Conseil*'s legislative function. It is permitted to review statutes only prior to their promulgation, and then only on referral from the government or (since 1974) significant political minorities of deputies or senators. Thus, legislative proposals cannot become law if the *Conseil* strikes them down. But, the *Conseil* has no capacity to review a statute after it has become law, and regular courts are not empowered to undertake constitutional review in the course of ordinary litigation. In the French view, the statute law is sovereign and subject to no external checking, certainly not by judges, and neither by a constitutional court. Rather, the constitutional court, by becoming part of the legislature itself, plays an essential role in preserving the idea of sovereignty of the law. Legislative action cannot occur in the presence of an objection by the *Conseil*, but once it takes place, is unchecked by constitutional mechanisms.

Because French legislative proposals cannot become law in the presence of *Conseil* refusal, if it is requested (and this is virtually always at the request of a political minority appealing against government sponsored legislation) constitutional review must take place immediately after the legislative action and in the face of a sitting government whose proposed law has been challenged. This means such review has to happen quickly and, in view of the majoritarian nature of French political institutions and political culture, in a potentially politically charged situation. By contrast, constitutional challenges to U.S. statutes must await a case raising the issue in a genuine manner and this often occurs long

---

[17] In 1795 the post-Jacobin *Convention* unanimously rejected a proposal presented by Sieyes to introduce a *jury constitutionnaire*.

after the legislature that enacted the statute has disappeared. In post-authoritarian systems, such as Germany, Spain and Italy, constitutional courts cannot prevent a law from taking effect, even while review has an abstract character. Thus, unlike the French situation, since the government is enforcing the disputed law, there is not much political pressure to resolve constitutional issues quickly (indeed, political pressures might work in the opposite direction), and so abstract review may take place after the heat of political battle is somewhat dissipated.

Perhaps because of its placement within the legislature, the makeup of the *Conseil* is comparatively quite distinctive. Those on the court only occasionally have substantial legal or judicial backgrounds and there are also few law professors. Rather, the *Conseil* is dominated by political allies of the appointing authorities. This is not to say that the members are unable to understand or make legal arguments, but only that a high value is placed on their political judgement. This seems especially crucial in view of the urgency with which they must reach decisions.

4. DELIBERATION IN CONSTITUTIONAL COURTS

The argument in this section is that the three distinctive systems of constitutional review produce three separately identifiable deliberative patterns. In separation of powers systems, in which constitutional review takes place in ordinary courts, there is a great need for coordination and communication among judges. Such systems tend to develop open forms of deliberation with public hearings, published opinions and votes, and doctrines of precedent. In the Kelsenian model, with concentrated constitutional review powers in a specialized tribunal, clarity of constitutional decisions is crucial if ordinary courts are to be able to apply them, so such courts tend to speak with a single voice and to articulate reasoned rationales. Such systems rarely have public hearings or published dissents. In parliamentary sovereignty regimes, constitutional review is a part of the legislative process aimed at ensuring that legislation conforms to constitutional requirements. How exactly this is done depends on the particular way in which constitutional review is integrated into the legislative process.

In France, the parliamentary sovereignty system with the most institutionalized system of constitutional review, the court deliberates in secret session, without public hearings or presentations, over the legislative proposals that are placed on its docket. The important feature of French constitutional review is that the statute voted by parliamentary majority cannot be promulgated until the *Conseil* assents to it. So there is an enormous time pressure on the review process (the delay is normally one month, but 'this period shall be reduced to eight days where the Government declares the matter urgent').[18] The Conseil issues its

---

[18]   Art. 25 of the Ordinance no. 58–1067 of November 1958.

opinions in the name of the court, with no reported votes or published dissents. Its opinions are typically very brief and do not elaborate constitutional objections to legislation in any great detail. Instead, the Conseil may report that the proposed legislation is, in whole or part, constitutionally objectionable in view of several sources of constitutional law: the 1789 Declaration, the Preamble to the 1946 Constitution and to the 'Fundamental Principles underlying the laws of the [Third] Republic.'[19] Not surprisingly, many of the most far-reaching decisions concern themselves with overly broad or unconstrained delegations of authority to administrative agencies.[20] Typically, in the face of such concerns,

---

[19] Representative in this perspective is the very important opinion of July 16, 1971 that rules on the right of association and modifies substantially the role of the Council. The decision is not only short, but it did not really spell out the reasons for including the *bloc de constitutionnalité* among the sources for constitutional adjudication:

In the light of the Constitution and notably of its Preamble;

In the light of the *ordonnance* of 7 November 1958 creating the organic law on the Conseil Constitutionnel, especially chapter 2 of title II of the said *ordonnance*;

In the light of the *loi* of 1 July 1901 (as amended) relating to associations;

In the light of the *loi* of 10 January 1936 relating to combat groups and private militias;

Considering that the *loi* referred for scrutiny by the Conseil constitutionnel was put to the vote in both chambers, following one of the procedures provided for in the Constitution, during the parliamentary session beginning on 2 April 1971;

Considering that, among the fundamental principles recognized by the laws of the Republic and solemnly reaffirmed by the Constitution, is to be found the freedom of association; that this principle underlies the general provisions of the *loi* of 1 July 1901; that, by virtue of this principle, associations may be formed freely and can be registered simply on condition of the deposition of a prior declaration; that, thus, with the exception of measures that may be taken against certain types of associations, the validity of the creation of an association cannot be subordinated to the prior intervention of an administrative or judicial authority, even when the association appears to be invalid or to have an illegal purpose;

Considering that, even if they change nothing in respect of the creation of undeclared associations, the provisions of the art. 3 of the *loi*, the text of which is referred to the Conseil before its promulgation for scrutiny as to its compatibility with the Constitution, is intended to create a procedure whereby the acquisition of legal capacity by declared associations could be subordinated to a prior review by a court as to its compliance with the law;

Considering that, therefore, the provisions of the article 3 of the *loi* are declared not to be compatible with the Constitution ...

(English trans. by J. Bell, *French Constitutional Law* (Oxford: Clarendon Press, 1992), pp. 272–73).

[20] See the vehicle search cases (J. Bell, *op. cit.*, p. 141 and 308–09) and the Nationalization decisions. The 1971 decision that *discovered* that freedom of association was a constitutional principle was also of this form. Implicitly, a group could be made illegal if there were principled reasons relating to public security that could be produced.

the government can re-draft the legislation by including some standards governing subsequent administrative actions.

While the French Constitutional Council has invalidated legislative proposals with some frequency, it has more often held parts of proposed laws offensive to constitutional principles,[21] and has increasingly issued opinions suggesting that a law would be constitutionally valid only if it is interpreted in a particular way.[22] This last strategy is particularly problematic in view of the separation of the *Conseil Constitutionel* from the judiciary. How can the *Conseil* offer any assurance that a promulgated law will be interpreted in a constitutional fashion? As there are no formal mechanisms or doctrines (such as *stare decisis*) to ensure this, the only guarantee is the persuasiveness of the reasons offered by the *Conseil* either to the ordinary courts, the *Cour de Cassation* or to administrative agencies. There is some evidence that agencies, perhaps seeking clear guidance from a tribunal that can be troublesome, have tended to use *Conseil* decisions in formulating internal guidance to their personnel. And, ordinary courts, seeking legal stability have frequently taken up *Conseil* interpretations as authoritative.

In the Kelsenian or post-authoritarian systems, the courts typically deliberate in secret, only rarely hold public hearings, and opinions are issued in the name of the whole court without recorded votes. Few of these systems permit the publication of dissenting opinions. Those courts that permit direct access to litigants (such as Spain and Germany) usually institute an internal division of labor (meeting in panels for considering such cases). Some of these courts permit or encourage subject matter specialization (commonly in Italy but opposed in Germany). All of these courts are *internally* deliberative in the sense that they do much of their work in a collegial and face to face fashion where real attempts are made to convince others and produce a collectively reasoned decision. This is especially so in Italy where the court aims at, and usually achieves, consensual decisions (as far as can be told from discussions with justices and other observers).

The deliberative practices on the US Supreme Court are quite different and we may term them *externally* rather than internally deliberative. In part this is made necessary by the fact that the Court has no monopoly on constitutional interpretation and mostly acts to regulate the process by which the Constitution is applied by other courts. This coordinating or regulatory role forces the Court to do its work in a public and transparent manner that permits other agents – judges, agencies and lawyers – to anticipate clearly and (mostly) successfully how the Court itself would rule on cases not yet before it. Moreover, the notion that statutes may raise constitutional issues as they are applied rather than on

---

[21] From 1981 to 1993, about 50% of the referred laws have been censured by the Council; see A. Stone, 'Constitutional Politics and Malaise in France', in J.T. Keeler and M.A. Schain (eds.), *Chirac's Challenge* (New York: Saint Martin 1996), p. 65.

[22] Alexandre Viala, *Les réserves d'interprétation dans la jurisprudence du Conseil constitutionnel* (Paris: L.G.D.J. 1999).

their face, sometimes leads the Court to permit or encourage experimentation in lower courts, rather than seeking an immediate resolution of the constitutionality of a statute restricted to the text itself. Obviously, this strategy is available only in systems permitting concrete review and can arise in Kelsenian systems only in considering constitutional complaints (*amparo* and *Verfassungsbeschwerde*).

The American Supreme Court acts publicly in several senses. First, access to its docket is open to litigants generally and its decisions on whether to take a case are public. On rare occasions members of the Court even announce their individual views on this issue. Secondly, public hearings are the norm, at least for the most important part of the Court's docket, votes are recorded and dissenting (and concurring) opinions published. The Court rarely tries to speak with one voice, apparently preferring to let conflict and disagreement ferment. On most accounts the actual level of internal deliberation on the court may be low, in the sense that the Justices do not spend very much time in conference deliberating specific issues in cases (observers usually report that justices interact mostly with their own clerks and less often with other justices and rarely with the aim of actually changing minds or votes). Internal deliberation seems mostly to take place after the initial voting has taken place in conference, when the justices decide whether they can agree in whole or part with the opinion written for the Court. Such deliberation takes place in writing for the most part and not through face to face interaction. But this very fact permits the deliberative process to be much more transparent to outsiders than face to face deliberation would be. The public manner of conducting its business puts the Court at the center of wider deliberative processes within the judiciary, the legal, and political communities.

2. Some Conditions for the Success of Constitutional Courts: Lessons from the U.S. Experience

Martin Shapiro

In recent years we have been experiencing a global flourishing of constitutional courts wielding the legal authority to declare legislative and executive acts unconstitutional. Such judicial review has flourished even in nations whose legal culture was long thought to be antithetical to it such as France. It occurs even in a few non-Western nations such as Korea, India and Japan. It occurs in Israel which does not have a written constitution. It occurs in trans-national settings such as the European Union and the European Convention on Human Rights system. It has now appeared in states that have emerged from former Soviet domination.

Yet very clearly to encounter the legal forms of judicial review is not necessarily to encounter successful judicial review, granting that in this instance success is difficult to define or measure. My definition of success is a purely institutional one involving whether a constitutional court has achieved acquiescence in its judgments by other public and private institutions, organizations and individuals. I do not concern myself at all with issues of the goodness or justice of the policies pursued by such courts. At a minimum successful judicial review would require that constitutional judgments are routinely, if not always, obeyed by both governmental and private actors, and that relatively significant acts of government are judicially invalidated on constitutional grounds, at least occasionally. Measurement difficulties occur along a number of dimensions. Even constitutional courts that are usually considered highly successful have experienced extended periods of massive disobedience to some of their decisions even while being routinely obeyed as to others. The U.S. Supreme Court, for instance, encountered long resistance by autonomous local government authorities and even state governments to its school prayer and desegregation decisions.[1] Its judicially pronounced national code of police conduct is frequently evaded by police perjury and other misconduct.[2] Yet that code generally has been effective in changing police conduct; school prayers are not said in many places where they would be in the absence of Supreme Court decisions; legally sanctioned

---

[1] Stephen Wasby, *The Impact of the U.S. Supreme Court* (Homewood, Ill. Dorsey Press, 1970); Gerald Rosenberg, *The Hollow Hope* (Chicago: University of Chicago Press 1991).

[2] Wayne La Fave, *Search and Seizure: A Treatise on the Fourth Amendment* (1978). (St. Paul: West 1996).

Wojciech Sadurski (ed.), Constitutional Justice, East and West, 37–59
© 2002 *Kluwer Law International. Printed in Great Britain.*

apartheid has disappeared even if many American schools have student populations consisting entirely of minority children.

Along another dimension it is possible at least in theory to imagine successful review systems in which only specific applications of law to particular individuals are constitutionally invalidated rather than statutes themselves. Few would argue, for instance that German administrative courts are less successful at administrative, as opposed to constitutional, review than are French administrative courts because one may only quash individual applications while the other can also quash entire administrative rules.[3]

Finally and most importantly is the problem of anticipated reaction. The French constitutional court now engages in abstract, pre-enactment review of virtually every important French statute. In that sense it would appear to be among the most successful judicial review courts in the world. Yet it has actually struck down very, very few French legislative acts. Should we conclude that its review powers largely are a sham? There is a substantial amount of evidence that so few statutes are struck down precisely because the French Assembly is so mindful of the Constitutional Council's pronouncements, and the Council so explicit in stating its future intentions, that French statutes are rigorously tested constitutionally before the Assembly approves them by what amounts to a constitutional dialogue between the Assembly and the Council.[4] Similarly at the level of administrative judicial review, British judges today claim to be engaging in rigorous review. When it is pointed out to them that, except in immigration matters, there have been only a handful of instances in which they have invalidated decisions of central as opposed to local government authorities, their response is that the ministries are so mindful of and obedient to judicial decisions that they almost never make unlawful decisions.[5] In these circumstances a certain amount of skepticism about the level of real judicial power necessarily arises.

The clearest example of the form of judicial review not necessarily corresponding with reality occurs not even in the old Soviet Union but in the continuing practice in nearly all of Latin America. In most Latin American states the writ of *amparo* or its equivalent provides every citizen direct access to the courts to complain of any unconstitutional act of government even minimally imposing injury on that individual, and courts have broad powers of constitutional review. Yet in reality constitutional judicial review is a dead letter in most of Latin America even in those countries where thousands of writs of *amparo* are filed

---

[3]   See Jürgen Schwarze, *European Administrative Law* (London: Sweet and Maxwell, 1992), pp. 261–277.

[4]   Alec Stone, *The Birth of Judicial Politics in France* (New York: Oxford University Press 1992).

[5]   See Susan Sterett, *Creating Constitutionalism?* (Ann Arbor, University of Michigan Press 1997).

every year. It remains very questionable whether even such highly esteemed constitutional courts as that of Japan ought to be regarded as successful.[6]

Along a final dimension even a constitutional court that manages to bring off major interventions in its polity's political system or public policies may be deemed substantively unsuccessful, that is to have moved its policy in wrong directions. Thus the Mongolian Supreme Court has fundamentally altered what had been intended to be a parliamentary system of government into one in which cabinet officers cannot serve in Parliament. This judicial incursion may have gravely reduced the chances for success of the whole Mongolian constitutional system.[7] Hungarian judicial interventions in the nation's international economic arrangements have been extremely popular, and indeed may be the basis for what is widely seen as the great success of constitutional judicial review in Hungary,[8] but they may have to be almost entirely evaded if Hungary is to be admitted to the European Union. American scholars are in substantial agreement that the U.S. Supreme Court has been quite successful in fostering free trade among the American states[9] but are in bitter disagreement about whether other Supreme Court interventions or refusals to intervene in economic policy matters have been good or bad for the American economy.[10] Of course even a generally highly successful constitutional court may experience marked lack of success on a particular question at a particular time. Thus clearly the U.S. Supreme Court hoped to end political controversies over abortion by turning the issue into one of constitutional law and resolving it by a constitutional compromise, the famous trimester system in which pro-abortion forces win the first three months of pregnancy, anti-abortion forces the last three and the middle three remain indeterminate. Even such an exactly 50–50 judicial compromise served only to exacerbate rather than end political controversy. Clearly the Court as an institution would have been better off if it had stayed entirely out of the controversy.

Even with all this said, however, there clearly has been enough successful constitutional judicial review in enough places that we may begin to speculate on the causes and conditions of success. Before doing so in general, however, it

---

6   See Lawrence Beer, *Constitutional Case Law of Japan, 1970–90* (Seattle: University of Washington Press 1996).

7   Thomas Ginsberg, *Growing Constitutions: Judicial Review in New Democracies* (Dissertation, University of California, Berkeley 1999).

8   See Laszlo Solyom, 'The Hungarian Constitutional Court and Social Change', *Yale Journal of International Law* 19 (1994), pp. 223–237.

9   Vincent Blasi, 'Constitutional Limitations on the Power of State to Regulate Goods in Interstate Commerce', in Terrance Sandalow and Eric Stein, eds. *Courts and Free Markets* (Oxford: Oxford, University Press 1982), pp. 247–281.

10 See Martin Shapiro, 'The Supreme Court's "Return" to Economic Regulation', *Studies in American Political Development* (New Haven: Yale University Press 1986) vol. 1, pp. 91–141.

might be well specifically to consider the case of the United States whose experience surely has inspired much of the global movement toward review.

1. AMERICAN EXPERIENCE: DEMOCRATIC AND REPUBLICAN VERSIONS

Americans themselves, and certainly non-Americans, are heavily dependent on scholarly evaluations of American judicial review, and American scholarship on that subject is longstanding, massive and very distinguished. It is also highly and deeply partisan, quite literally partisan in the sense that there are really two bodies of scholarship, one Republican and the other Democratic. And this partisanship is very heavily disguised under claims of scholarly and/or professional and/or judicial neutrality that are absurd. Since the 1890's American writing on judicial review and the Supreme Court has been consistently dominated by the American left, bearing in mind that the American left is far to the right of the European left, at least until the recent move to the right of the European left. Since the 1930's the overwhelming bulk of the American words written about the Supreme Court have been written by liberal, New Deal Democrats and have been written deliberately in the interests of Democratic Party electoral prospects and policy positions although there is an endless amount of lying and some self-delusion about all this among the participants. The fundamentals of this situation are not really altered by the minor incursions of Robert Bork, the Chicago school and/or the 'originalists' although these voices do add a slight counterpoint to the Democratic anvil chorus of the 1930's through the 1960's. Nearly all the 'authoritative' writing on the Supreme Court from which outsiders draw their knowledge, the casebooks, treatises, classic law review articles and distinguished volumes of constitutional commentary, have been written by liberal Democrats for liberal Democratic purposes. The fact that a few of the writers and Supreme Court justices involved were nominally Republicans should not confuse us about all this. The California Republicanism of Earl Warren was always a peculiar form of liberal Democratic politics in disguise.

Given the unity of its sources and purposes, it might appear somewhat surprising that American constitutional writing appears to feature a great divide between two schools, that of judicial self restraint and that which labels itself constitutional rights and others label judicial activism. The debate across this divide has colored much of the world's thinking about constitutional judicial review so that its specific origins within American liberal Democratic Party politics is worth pursuing even for non-Americans.

There are two dimensions to this judicial activism versus judicial self-restraint debate, one tactical, the other generational. Let us proceed one at a time.

As we all know from American constitutional history, again a field of scholarly writing dominated by liberal Democrats, in 1932 the New Deal came into office with an overwhelming mandate to deal with the Great Depression and quickly proceeded to do so by joint Presidential-Congressional action. Whereupon a still Republican dominated Supreme Court sought to thwart the New Deal. This conflict led to a 'Court Crisis' which was resolved in 1937 by a surrender of the Supreme Court to President Roosevelt and company. While this liberal Democratic history leaves out, covers over and/or distorts various things, it is close enough for our purposes, which after all is to understand the thinking of Democrats who necessarily believed their own story.

If the Supreme court was indeed a Republican fortress defending a laissez-faire economic theory against Democratic, pragmatic, regulatory intervention to alleviate the rigors and failures of the market, then once the Democrats captured the fortress in 1937, two opposing courses of action were available to them. When a frontier fortress is captured the victors either level it to the ground or take it over for their own defense. One group of Democrats, which for a time totally dominated academic commentary, counseled destruction. The Court ought to declare that it would no longer exercise a constitutional veto over legislation. Judicial self-restraint became the orthodoxy of the American law schools.[11] Within the fortress itself Justice Frankfurter became the most influential proponent of this strategy.[12] Never again should non-elected judges thwart elected legislators and political executives, who presumably would, for the foreseeable future, if not forever, be Democrats.

To another group of Democrats, however, it seemed foolish to destroy the fortress just when it could be turned from favoring Republican interests to favoring Democratic ones. Recall the composition of the winning New Deal Democratic coalition. It was composed of the poor, that is the unpropertied; Catholic and Jewish, largely urban, immigrants; northern blacks; the Southern whites who prevented Southern blacks from voting at all; labor union members and intellectuals, that is people who earned a living by talking and writing. The new Democratic Court could protect the unpropertied by ignoring the property rights guarantees of the Constitution which the old bad Court had used to protect the haves against the have nots. It could defend religious minorities against old line-largely Republican-Protestantism by emphasizing the religion clauses of the First Amendment. It could defend intellectuals by judicial activism in favor of free speech. It could favor unions by a judicial self-restraint, rejecting the old Court's interventions against government wages and hours regulation. The basic New Deal strategy toward labor, however, was not to turn the guns of the Supreme Court on its enemies but instead to exclude all federal courts from labor cases and create a new pro-labor, special court, the National Labor Relations Board. That court was called a 'board' not a 'court' as a gesture toward the sensibilities of those who believed that courts should be independent

---

[11] See e.g. Alexander Bickel, *The Least Dangerous Branch* (Indianapolis: Bobbs-Merrill 1962).
[12] Wallace Mendelson, *Justices Black and Frankfurter, Conflict in the Court* (Chicago: University of Chicago Press 1961).

and neutral. The NLRB was to be a little bit independent and neutral but not really. It was imbedded in heavily pro-union legislation and charged with enforcing that legislation. And like most so-called 'independent regulatory commissions' in the U.S. it was both prosecutor and judge and had been set up to be captured by one of the set of interests it regulated.

As to African-Americans, however, the Democrats faced a terrible problem. The Democratic Party depended upon a large block of Southern Democratic Congressmen and Senators to maintain the Congressional majorities needed to enact Democratic programs. That southern Congressional block and the voters behind it were dedicated to apartheid. Northern blacks were largely Southern refugees from apartheid, and they were a significant voting resources for the Democratic urban machines that supplied the huge, and liberal, block of Northern Democratic Congressmen and Senators. In the face of this dilemma the Democratic Supreme Court simply remained silent from 1937 until the 1950's when acute pressure from the NAACP finally forced it into reluctant action.

The move to shift the guns of the fortress to Democratic defense was embodied in the famous *Carolene Products* case[13] with its celebrated Footnote Four. The Court announced that hence forth it would presume the constitutionality of economic legislation, that is essentially that it would read the word property out of the Constitution thus abandoning the defense of the propertied against the unpropertied. The ambiguous concept 'presumption' was used precisely because the word property was so clearly there in the Constitution. A presumption is a legal conclusion of a court held without regard to whether what is being presumed is true or not. The Court would presume there were no property rights in the Constitution even though there really were. This presumption is announced in the text of the Court's opinion. In the celebrated footnote exceptions are stated in which the court will not presume constitutionality but will instead be judicially active. The exceptions are simply a list of the members of the Democratic coalition. The Court is to be active in defense of freedom of speech, that is intellectuals, and religion, that is Jews and Catholics, and it is to defend 'discrete and insular minorities.' Here again the words are very carefully chosen. Jews and Catholics thought of themselves as discrete and insular minorities, and they should surely be served by the Court. So, of course, did those who were then called Negroes. But it is preferable not to be too specific about Negroes, given the needs of the party for Southern votes in Congress and in the Presidential electorate. Northern Negroes could see themselves as the prime discrete and insular minority, and Southern whites would not be affronted by a specifically racial reference.

Thus *Carolene Products* announces judicial self restraint as the Court's response when Republicans seek the Court's help and judicial activism when Democrats seek it. All Democrats, and thus nearly all the great American

---

[13] *United States v. Carolene Products* 304 U.S. 144 (1938).

authorities on constitutional law, have agreed on judicial self-restraint for Republican constitutional claims. Democrats have split on *Carolene Products*, Footnote Four, claims. Some have argued for completely tearing down the fortress, not using it even to defend Democrats. Others have accepted footnote four as a clever way of turning the guns of the fortress against Republicans.

At this point a brief, esoteric excursion is necessary. Besides Justice Frankfurter, an ardent New Dealer, the most prominent proponent of extreme judicial self-restraint, of tearing down the fortress, was Learned Hand, a distinguished judge who never reached the Supreme Court although everyone agreed he should have. The official composer of the Carolene Products decision was Justice Stone, and, later, the most ardent spokesman for judicial activism was Chief Justice Earl Warren. All three were Republicans, not Democrats. But all three were very peculiar Republicans. Hand and Warren were 'Progressive' Republicans. The Progressives believed in government regulation of the economy. They had split the Republican Party in 1912 leading to the presidential election victory of the Democrat Wilson. Indeed Hand never reached the Supreme Court because Democratic presidents passed him over as a Republican and Republican presidents passed him over as a Republican traitor. Warren was from such a deviant Western Progressive Republican wing that under the then very peculiar California system of elections he had once won both the Republican and Democratic nominations for the state's governorship. Indeed he had reached the Supreme Court as part of a deal in which main line Republicans had bought off the left wing of the party in order to secure the nomination of Dwight D. Eisenhower. Justice Stone also came from the liberal wing of the party, and footnote four was not written by Stone but by his law clerk, an ardent New Deal Democrat.

2. TWO GENERATIONS

The first of our two stories, that of Democrats and Republicans, is now told. The second story is about generations.[14] Contemporary thinking about the Supreme Court has been shaped by two generations of constitutional scholars. For the first the New Deal 'court crisis' was the defining moment of their lives. At that moment the elected, that is Roosevelt and company, were good, and the Court was in the hands of the devil. The solution could only be to shut down the constitutional business of the Court. Edward S. Corwin was the doyen of the writers on constitutional law. Paul Freund[15] was the pope of the law professors in the Vatican of the Harvard Law School, and Herbert Wechsler at

---

[14] See Martin Shapiro, 'Fathers and Sons: The Court, the Commentators and the Search for Values', in Vincent Blasi, *The Burger Court* (New Haven, Yale University Press 1983), pp. 218–238.

[15] See Paul Freund, *Supreme Court and Supreme Law* (Cambridge, Mass.: Harvard University Press 1954).

Columbia was the Archbishop of Canterbury. The last great prophet of the group was Alexander Bickel at Yale. All four and their army of colleagues were ardent New Dealers and ardent proponents of judicial self-restraint. Corwin was really the constitutional spokesman for the Roosevelt presidency both before and after the great President's death.[16] Both Bickel and Freund were constantly touted as prospective appointments to the Court of Democratic presidents although neither made it for personal and private reasons that had nothing to do with their Democratic allegiance. Wechsler was so committed to judicial self-restraint that he could not accept even *Brown v. Board of Education*.[17] Freund wrote little, but he persuasively taught one Harvard class after another that a Court that did least was best.

In this world of self-restraint, the selective activism of preferred position kept its head above water in the writing and teaching of certain First Amendment, that is freedom of speech and religion specialists, like Thomas I. Emerson and Leo Pfeffer who were New Deal enough on property but followed Footnote Four.[18] Indeed in certain very influential scholars whose age put them just at the boundary between the two generations, most notably Jesse Choper and John Hart Ely, preferred position became the dominating orthodoxy, but always very carefully in defense of the interests of the American moderate left.[19]

The second generation, roughly those born after 1940, experienced the great civil rights crisis precipitated by *Brown v. Board*[20] as their defining moment. Or rather starting with *Brown* they experienced an almost unbroken stream of Warren Court and even Burger Court victories for 'human rights' and for whoever succeeded in claiming underdog status in American society. The Warren Court was best, of course, with desegregation, rights of accused, and keeping religion out of schools (which, given the way American schools are governed, meant keeping locally dominant religion out of the schools and local minority religion protected). The Burger Court was not so different; gender discrimination condemned, abortion rights announced, death penalty procedurally hedged. There were disappointments, but mostly only in the Court not going quite far enough in serving the left. The push toward constitutionalizing welfare entitlements was blunted.[21] Inter-district desegregation remedies which would have

---

16 See Edward S. Corwin, *The President: Office and Powers*, 4th ed. (New York: New York University Press 1957).

17 Herbert Wechsler, 'Toward Neutral Principles of Constitutional Law', *Harvard Law Review*, 73 (1959), pp. 1–37.

18 See Thomas I. Emerson, *The System of Freedom of Expression* (New York: Random House 1970); Leo Pfeffer, *The Liberties of an American* (Boston: Beacon Press 1956).

19 Jesse Choper, *Judicial Review and the National Political Process* (Chicago: University of Chicago Press 1980); John Hart Ely, *Democracy and Distrust* (Cambridge, Mass.: Harvard University Press 1980).

20 347 U.S. 483 (1954).

21 *San Antonio Indep. School District v. Rodriguez*, 411 U.S. 1 (1973).

thwarted 'white flight' from judicially imposed school integration were refused.[22] The death penalty was not ended.[23] The Court was very good to speakers of obscenity[24] but very mixed on protecting those accused of communist speech.[25]

The first generation had feared judicial activism because it had seen the old Republican judicial activism in favor of property. It was tempted by preferred position but haunted by the fear that if the guns of the fortress were kept unspiked and turned to fire in favor of the rights of Democrats, they might some day be turned in the other direction again. The second generation had lived their whole lives with the guns firing against property and in favor of Democrats. They could hardly conceive of them firing any other way.[26] At worst they would not fire often and far enough. It would be time enough to retreat to judicial self-restraint if and when some highly unlikely catastrophe should occur and the Court should rediscover property rights.

Today the dominant orthodoxy of the American constitutional academy is preferred position with a heavy emphasis on judicial activism in favor of "rights," that is of left political interests. The first generation of New Dealers has largely left the scene. Even the bridge group is reaching retirement age. The second generation, whose only complaint can be that the Court has not been quite active enough, is now firmly in control. Among the very thin rank of Republican scholars, most do not even have the nerve to openly proclaim property rights but hide in the side show of propounding "originalism" against policy oriented constitutional 'interpretation.' Only a few desperately shop among the constitutional clauses to find some way of bringing property back in.[27] In response the new doyens of the New Deal successor generation, notably Bruce Ackerman, construct elaborate barriers to assure that property cannot be brought back in but openings remain for further expansion of Democratic 'rights.'[28] At the moment, however, the Supreme Court is giving little comfort to either those who would restore judicial protection of the "old" property or those who wish for the judicial construction of constitutional welfare rights.

22　*Milliken v. Bradley* 418 U.S. (717) (1974).

23　*Gregg v. Georgia*, 428 U.S. 153 (1976).

24　*Miller v. California*, 413 U.S. 5 (1973).

25　Cf. *Dennis v. United States*, 341 U.S. 494 (1951) with *Yates v. United States*, 354 U.S. 298 (1957).

26　See e.g. Michall Perry, *The Constitution, the Courts and Human Rights* (New Haven: Yale University Press 1982).

27　See Richard Epstein, *Principles for a Free Society: Reconciling Individual Liberty with the Common Good* (Reading, Mass.: Perseus Books 1999).

28　Bruce Ackerman, *We the People* (Cambridge, Mass: Harvard University Press 1998).

3. FEDERALISM

Let me now, briefly, integrate my story of 1932 to 2000 into the longer American historical picture. The early history of the U.S. Supreme Court is a curious mixture of caution and successful boldness. It is well known that the Court's boldest move was its self-endowment with the power of judicial review which is not explicitly provided in the Constitution itself. That great achievement of John Marshall is not quite as bold as it looks. It occurs when most of the framers of the Constitution are still alive, and a majority of them probably favored some kind of judicial review. *Marbury v. Madison*,[29] the case establishing the Court's review powers, nominally is a challenge to Congress because it declares a Congressional statutory provision unconstitutional. But the provision declared unconstitutional is a minor technical provision of a statute about the judiciary. For all its later expansive interpretation, *Marbury* is actually an announcement of the narrowest form of judicial review most likely to have been intended by the framers. It is self-defense review by the Court to protect its own independence from Congress as one of the three great branch of the national government. Moreover, as is well known, *Marbury* entailed no risk of disobedience by Congress or President. In *Marbury* the Court denies itself a power, the power to issue a writ of *mandamus* given to it by Congress. Thus the only government officers called upon to obey the Court's decision are the justices themselves who have ordered themselves not to issue such writs. *Marbury* was decided in 1803. The Court does not again declare a Congressional statute unconstitutional until 1857.[30] Nor did it declare any action of the President unconstitutional during the pre-Civil War period.

In the pre-civil war period the great bulk of the Supreme Court's declarations of unconstitutionality were directed against state statutes and were mostly in the service of implementing free trade among the states which had clearly been one of the major purposes of the Constitution. It might appear at first glance that this campaign of interventions against the states was an extremely risky one. The Court proclaims itself as the arbiter of clashes between state and national regulatory authority when it itself is a part of the national government.[31] This looks dangerously like the Court acting as judge in its own case, and this danger is surely at its greatest when the Court strikes down a state statute for conflicting with a statute of its 'own' government, that is a national statute enacted by Congress. Here the Court calls on two cultural resources. First, the Constitution itself and the dominant political philosophy of the time proclaimed the virtues of "separation of powers." The very essence of American constitutional

---

[29]   1 Cranch 137 (1803).

[30]   *Dred Scott v. Sanford*, 19 How. 393 (1857).

[31]   John Schmidhanser, *The Supreme Court As Final Arbiter of Federal State Relations* (Chapel Hill: University of North Carolina Press 1958).

thought was the separation of the three great branches. Thus when the Court struck down a state encroachment on Congressional authority, it was not seen so much as favoring its "own" government over that of a state as acting as a referee between a state and the Congress from which the Court was entirely separated. Second, this appearance of constitutional independence and neutrality of the Court toward Congress was reinforced by the general, accumulated cultural capital that the Supreme Court inherited from the British and colonial courts. The Supreme Court bore the name and appearance of a court. In the English speaking world the very defining characteristic of courts was supposed to be their independence and neutrality.[32] One of the ultimate achievements of the English civil war had been the acknowledgment by the Crown of that independence, and the colonists had always insisted on the independence of their own courts during their struggle with the Crown and Parliament.[33] Thus the apparent anomaly that an integral part of Party A was setting itself up as a judge of clashes between Party A and Party B did not appear to be an anomaly to people who believed that the Supreme Court justices were separated from and independent of the rest of that government of which they were a part. This vision was reinforced by the circumstance that neither the state nor the national government were usually the named parties in the Supreme Court cases involving the boundary between their authorities. Usually such cases were lawsuits of one private party against another.[34]

Even more fundamentally "federalism" cases provide the intrinsically most favorable ground for successful judicial review. Federalism is actually a kind of cartel of the member states. In a cartel the most favorable position for any one member is that all the other members obey the cartel rules while it itself is free to break them. That is why most cartels are short lived. To succeed cartels need some strong method of discipline to constrain members each of whom has strong incentives to violate cartel policies. The second best position for each cartel member is that all members, including itself, obey the rules. Then the purposes for which all the members joined the cartel will be achieved. Thus cartels pose a typical prisoners' dilemma problem. It might appear superficially that when any member state of a federalism is caught cheating by a federal court, the other member states would say, "There but for the grace of God go I," and would side with their fellow member state against federal authority. Each state knows, however, that if it supports its fellow member state against the federal discipline imposed by a federal court, the federalism will soon be destroyed and the

---

[32] Martin Shapiro, *Courts, A Comparative and Political Analysis* (Chicago: University of Chicago Press 1981), Ch. II.

[33] Stanley Katz, 'The Politics of Law in Colonial America: Controversies over Chancery Courts and Equity Courts in the Eighteenth Century', in Donald Fleming and Bernard Bailyn, eds., *Law in American History* (Boston: Little Brown 1971), pp. 257–286.

[34] See e.g. *Gibbons v. Ogden*, 9 Wheat. 1 (1824).

advantages gained from the cartel will be lost. So as any member state cheats and is caught, its fellow member states will tend to opt for the second best position and side with the federal court seeking to bring all states into compliance with the cartel agreement. Of course, where the court decides in favor of a member state's authority against national authority, the there-but-for-the-grace-of-God-go-I phenomenon will work. The rest of the central government may oppose the central court, but all the member states are likely to support it.

Until the issue of slavery created a situation in which individual member states saw themselves not as one member among many, each seeking to maximize its own interests, but instead as components of one of two conflicting alliances of members, the Supreme Court was successful in its federalism decisions. It was successful because it provided the necessary disciplinary mechanism for achieving the second best, but only stable, solution to the cartel prisoners' dilemma problem confronted by each member state. As the Court policed one or another offending member, the others at least tacitly supported the Court not their fellow members.

It is primarily for this reason that nearly all the early successes of judicial review come in federal or quasi-federal systems: the USA, Canada, Australia, Germany, the European Convention of Human Rights, the Council of Europe (armed with the ECHR) and the European Union. That the very earliest successes are in the English speaking world may be a result of the inherited cultural vision that federal courts, while "in" the central government, are sufficiently separate and independent to act as neutral arbiters of clashes between central government and the member states.

Finally it must be noted that the success of the Marshall Court in establishing judicial review essentially as a method of policing a federal free trade cartel depended in large part on the Court itself adopting a very intermediate and balanced position in the central government- member state tension. In general the Court announced the doctrine of "enumerated powers." The general power to govern remained with the states. Only those powers explicitly enumerated in the Constitution were to be exercised by the central government. Yet the Court also looked favorably on the 'necessary and proper' clause to allow considerable expansion of national authority.[35] This intermediate position is even more explicit in the interstate commerce cases themselves which are at the heart of federalism. In the famous case of *Gibbons v. Ogden*[36] the Court strikes down a state act in conflict with a Congressional statute regulating commerce 'among' the states. Marshall suggests that the interstate commerce power may lie exclusively in the central government, but carefully and explicitly avoids such a conclusion. In one of his last, and less well-known, opinions, however, *Willson v. Black-Bird*

---

[35] The classic statement of both these principles is *McCullock v. Maryland*, 4 Wheat. 316 (1819).

[36] *Op. cit. supra* note 34.

Creek Marsh Company,[37] Marshall explicitly acknowledges that states retain some authority even over interstate commerce. In the better known case of *Cooley v. Board of Port Wardens*,[38] Marshall's successor, Chief Justice Taney, crafts an extremely elaborate compromise between state and Congressional commerce authority and one that appoints the Court itself as the ultimate watch dog over the cartel. The *Cooley* rule provides that when Congress has not acted on an interstate commerce matter the states may act, but that, even when Congress has not acted, the Supreme Court may independently strike down state laws too seriously hampering interstate commerce.

It should be remembered that the commerce clause of the U.S. Constitution is not a free movement clause like that of the European Union treaties but merely gives regulatory authority to Congress. If it wishes, Congress may limit interstate commerce or authorize the states to do so. Congress may block state regulation by passing conflicting commerce laws of its own which, under the supremacy clause, will take precedence over state laws. Why then could the Court be a successful alternative to Congress in policing state commerce regulation, a task that Congress was empowered to do itself by exercise of its own power to make supreme commerce laws? Here contrasting institutional capacities is the answer. Congress, particularly the early Congress which was without staff resources, was not a good surveillance instrument. It could not be expected to even be aware of, let alone make decisions about, the numerous laws of the numerous states that impinged upon interstate commerce. Neither, on its own, could the Supreme Court which was even more without staff resources. The Court, however, could easily mobilize the powerful private litigation market to do its surveillance for it. Once the Court announced it was available to strike down state laws impinging upon interstate commerce, private parties whose own businesses were suffering from such laws could easily mount lawsuits to bring them to the Court's attention. That indeed is how both *Gibbons* and *Cooley* arose. Thousands of potential clients and thousands of lawyers stood vigilantly watching state legislation and forwarding to the Court those state laws that might hamper the free market.

Of course commercial interests could always approach Congress for new legislation correcting state interferences with commerce. But it is far easier, quicker and cheaper to win a Supreme Court case than to push legislation through Congress. Moreover frequently such issues are raised collaterally in civil litigation by parties whose interest is in wining their case by any possible argument rather than in maintaining the cartel. Thus in true Adam Smith fashion, private greed becomes the engine for bringing state incursions on interstate commerce to the attention of the central government. So long as the Supreme Court did not stray too far from the policies of Congress, Congress

---

[37]   2 Pet. 245 (1829).
[38]   12 How. 299 (1852).

was more than pleased to leave the state surveillance task to the Court, particularly because the Court could shift most of the costs of surveillance onto litigating parties.

The other area in which the early Supreme Court appeared to be active and successful involved the contract clause of the Constitution. The famous cases are *Dartmouth College v. Woodward*[39] and the Charles River Bridge Case.[40] These cases appear to be judicial interventions against state authority in favor of private property and, as such, figure heavily in various Marxist or other economic interpretations of U.S. constitutional history. Actually these cases, particularly Charles River Bridge are really much misunderstood. In reality they expand the economic development resources of the state governments at a time when, as the governments of 'developing' economies, the states were vitally concerned with building their economic infrastructures.[41] The Court, however, benefited from the appearance of championing private property.

The experience of the Supreme Court with slavery and the Civil War is really of little importance to our story. The Court failed, but so did all the other American institutions, not only the institutions of government but of society more generally including organized religion, the press, the market, and the political parties. No lesson about the potential for success of a single institution like a constitutional court can be learned from the breakdown of an entire society. If the constitution itself fails, of course the constitutional court will fail. The Supreme Court can be, and has been, criticized for a Quixotic attempt to pull the slavery issue out of politics in the Dred Scott decision[42] and for the racist substance of that decision. In fact a majority of the justices would have preferred to avoid the major issue in Dred Scott and were pulled into the maelstrom by the overweening ambition of one of their number. But the Court did no worse than Congress, the President and the state governments.

4. THE SUPREME COURT AND ECONOMIC REGULATION

The next great period of judicial activism begins about 1890. This period is the subject of much myth making by the New Deal Democratic constitutional scholars we looked at earlier. Like many myths, these Democratic myths contain much truth but truth conveyed by extreme, imaginative exaggeration. The myths create the dreaded two-headed monster of 'substantive economic due process'

---

[39] 4 Wheat. 518 (1819).

[40] 11 Pet. 420 (1837).

[41] Martin Shapiro, Introduction to, Charles Warren, 'The Charles River Bridge Case', *Green Bag* 2d, 3 (1999), pp. 75–78.

[42] *Dred Scott v. Sanford*, 19 How. 393 (1857).

and 'dual federalism.'[43] The due process clauses,[44] of course, say that they are about process. Neither the federal government nor the states may deprive a person of life, liberty or property without due process of law. So presumably they may deprive a person of life, liberty or property with due process of law, that is under a properly enacted general statute and after a fair hearing. The Supreme Court turned the process clauses into substance clauses. In effect they held that government could not take life, liberty or property *unreasonably* no matter what process it employed.

So much is certainly true. The mythic part begins with the Democratic assertion that there is something particularly evil about the Court's substantive due process move.[45] The trouble for American liberals is that once Democrats took over the Supreme Court in 1937 the Court employed substantive due process, and its twin, substantive equal protection, to protect and extend many constitutional 'civil rights and liberties' whose judicial extension liberals applaud. The Supreme Court's abortion decisions, and its free speech decisions for instance, depend largely on such a substantive approach. Thus liberal commentators have had to denounce not 'substantive due process' but 'substantive *economic* due process,' that is the protection of property rights by courts but not their protection of "human rights." The difficulty is that the Constitution provides that persons may not be deprived of 'life, liberty or *property*' (emphasis added) without due process of law. Why should substantive due process be a good thing when employed by liberal justices in behalf of life and liberty interests and a bad thing when applied by conservative justices to protect property interests?

The other part of the myth is that from about 1890 to 1937 the Court used substantive economic due process to block all attempts by government to move beyond laissez-faire. In reality, in this period state and national government engaged in massive amounts of economic regulation most of which was not struck down by courts. A 'reasonableness' standard allowed courts great discretion. Courts invented exceptions, distinctions and multiple, conflicting lines of precedents that allowed them to uphold some regulation and strike down other. The Supreme Court did seriously obstruct minimum wage and maximum hours legislation but gradually gave ground on both. It is hard to say how much legislation was not enacted because of anticipated findings of unconstitutionality. Ultimately, however, the Supreme Court's balance between laissez-faire and intervention was somewhat to the right of those of legislators and the electorate but not very far to the right.

---

[43]   See Martin Shapiro, 'The Supreme Court and Economic Rights', in M. Judd Harmon, ed., *Essays on the Constitution of the United States* (Port Washington, N.Y.: Kennikat Press 1978), pp. 74–99.

[44]   Amendment V and XIV of the U.S. Constitution.

[45]   Cf. Frank Strong, *Substantive Due Process of Law* (Durham, N.C., Carolina Academic Press 1986) with Bernard Siegan, *Economic Liberties and the Constitution* (Chicago: University of Chicago Press 1980).

About the same can be said of 'dual' federalism. The myth is that whenever states regulated the economy, the Court held that they were unconstitutionally trenching on federal commerce powers and whenever the federal government enacted economic regulation, it was held to be invading the reserved powers of the states. In reality large amounts of both state and federal regulation survived judicial federalism tests. For instance the Supreme Court struck down some state railroad regulation but upheld federal regulation. Here again the Court's record was mixed, ambivalent and changed over time. Here again its record was more anti-regulatory than the stance of elected officials and of the voters but not much more.

Nevertheless, viewing the Supreme Court from its beginnings until 1937, we can certainly say that it first served the propertied, commercial and financial interests that wanted a national economy and then served developing corporate business that sought to avoid those government regulations that appeared detrimental to its interests. In doing so, however, the Court never adopted a totally national versus state stance nor a totally laissez-faire versus regulatory stance.

5. THE SUPREME COURT AND RIGHTS

What the Court did after 1937 was to turn the legitimacy it had gained through a long record of moderate service to nationalizing, capitalist, economic interests to the service of the socially, economically and politically less powerful. The American lesson is not that a constitutional court that vigorously champions "human" or minority" or "underdog" rights can be very successful for that very reason. The lesson instead is that the American Supreme court eventually was successful at serving the have nots because it had built up a very long record of successful, moderate service to the haves and more particularly that it was, from its origins and for a very long time, basically identified with the forces of economic development in a nation that has experienced miraculous economic development. When the Supreme Court did successfully shift from serving the most powerful to serving the least powerful, it did so not alone or in opposition to other parts of government but as part of a New Deal coalition that enjoyed overwhelming national political support.[46]

If other countries believe they can simply emulate the "human rights" successes of the Warren court, they must take into account that the post-1937 successes of the Supreme Court in behalf of the downtrodden were very much the fruit of a long, carefully calibrated, judicial investment in the fortunes of the "uptrodden". Moreover, even the Warren Court was forced by political pressure to act with careful strategic calculation, choosing to protect some rights of some categories of persons while withholding protections from other rights. The Warren Court

---

[46] Robert Dahl, 'Decision-Making in a Democracy: The Role of the Supreme Court as a National Policy-Maker', *Journal of Public Law*, 6 (1958), pp. 279–94.

may have been the pinnacle of judicial activism in the United States, but it was selected and guarded activism. Even the Warren Court while advancing to protect the rights of racial and religious minorities, accused persons and some speakers sharply retreated from earlier attempts to protect the speech rights of those accused of Communist leanings.

More specifically the American story shows a very strong correlation between the success of judicial review and federalism and a far more problematic one between judicial review and "rights." The Court has a continuous record of adjusting federal relationships in ways that moderately but increasingly favor national over state perspectives. Its rights record is more intermittent, and, if you are willing to count property rights as rights, one in which there have been major retreats as well as advances.

6. SEPARATION OF POWERS

American experience with division of powers between member state and national governments and with individual rights leads us to what is sometimes a third major aspect of constitutional judicial review, the division of powers among institutions of the central government, what Americans call "separation of powers." It may well be that constitution makers divide what they fear most. The American founders feared the legislature most and divided it into two houses as well as dividing it off from the executive. Post-Leninist states are likely to fear the executive most and so may be inclined to divide it. Paradoxically, however, the executive comes to be divided in some countries in order to strengthen executive leadership in the face of legislative paralysis. Thus the divided French executive occurs because of a desire to strengthen executive authority by partially separating it from parliamentary control. Similar suggestions have been prevalent in Italy. A number of states have moved to a directly elected presidency or otherwise sought to strengthen the office of the president in what formerly had been essentially parliamentary systems with titular, head of state, presidents.[47] Where such shifts occur the result is a divided executive, divided between the newly enhanced presidency and the long-existing prime ministership.

Obviously party systems are crucial in determining these developments. In polities with many parties and resulting coalition cabinets and weak prime ministers, an elected presidency divides the executive but is designed to strengthen it. In polities with a few strongly disciplined parties, parliamentary government turns into prime ministerial government. If a strong Presidency is introduced into such a system, the intent is surely to weaken executive power.

Whatever the intention, a divided executive or an executive divided from the

---

[47]   A further variant is the direct election of the Prime Minister as in Israel.

legislature or any combination of the two quite naturally calls forth judicial review for the same reasons federalism does. If constitutions divide powers it can be anticipated that boundary disputes will arise between the power holders. The judicial triad is a routine solution to two party disputes. Why not a constitutional court to resolve constitutional boundary disputes between legislature and executive or the two parts of a divided executive? This logic is so compelling that even the French who had sworn never to have judicial review succumbed to it when they divided their executive.

Yet a constitutional court that takes on division of powers between two parts of its own central government is in a far more dangerous position than one that handles federalist divisions between central and member state governments. It does not have the advantage of providing the mutually second best solution for all players. Instead of leading the way out of a prisoners' dilemma, it becomes the potential decider of winner and loser in a zero sum, two person game. And both the players are far more powerful than the judicial decider. Against such executive and legislative players, or rather constitutionally coequal branches of government, the only real enforcement powers a constitutional court possesses is the power to publicly announce that one of them has violated the Constitution. How effective a sanction that is depends on the degree to which the constitution and the court enjoy politically effective support.

It is unlikely that a constitutional court will succeed nearly as well at enforcing separation of powers between coequal branches of national government as at enforcing federalism boundaries. Under most circumstances it would seem unwise for courts to provoke constitutional crises with coequal branches. Of course in rights cases too a constitutional court is saying no to some powerful government actor, but often it is saying that a very subordinate government agent has acted wrongly, and the winner is not a rival government actor but usually a single individual. Even so rights cases are dangerous for courts but often not as dangerous as separation of powers cases.

Thus in the United States, in France and in Korea, constitutional separation of powers within the executive or between executive and legislature is one of the factors initially generating judicial review, but the constitutional court in fact intervenes in relatively few separation of powers disputes. The argument here is not that federalism, separation of powers or individual rights concerns are necessary or sufficient conditions for successful judicial review. Moreover, even in those polities where it can be argued that federalism or separation of powers motivated the initial adoption of review, a constitutional court subsequently may do little federalism or separation of powers business and turn largely to rights. Rather what is being argued here is that federalism and separation of powers jurisdictions, all other things being equal, tend to strengthen the institutional position of constitutional courts because a constitutional court appears to be an institutionally convenient means of dealing with the boundary problems endemic to such division of powers systems.

Similarly if allegiance to individual rights is sufficiently deep and broad in the politically relevant population, a constitutional court may rest the legitimacy of its policymaking role on the perceived necessity of having judicial review in order to protect rights. In each instance the question is whether the political dedication to federalism or separation of powers or rights is strong enough, and the perception of the necessity of courts in order to achieve federalism or separation of powers or rights is strong enough to successfully counter whatever opposition to judicial review is aroused by the constitutional court's policy making. And, of course, the three factors may be additive. That is a court that supports two or three of them may be in a stronger position than a court that supports only one of them.

In addition to federalism, separation of powers and rights, another factor appears to have been important in the initiation of constitutional judicial review in some countries. Some states, most notably Italy and Hungary, passed through changes of regime in which it was inconvenient to throw out the old legal codes and have the new legislatures enact new ones. By establishing constitutional rights judicial review, the new constitutional courts could instead gradually purge the old codes of their objectionable provisions without the necessity of major efforts by the new legislatures. This special function for rights review then serves as a firm foundation for subsequent rights review even of statutes enacted by the new legislature.

7. RULE OF LAW

The dangers that judicial challenges to other major governmental actors entail suggest a final point that has been brought forcefully to my attention by the work of one of my graduate students, Javier Couso who has been studying the Chilean constitutional court. This point involves the "rule of law." There is vast literature on the rule of law and the subtle differences between it and its cousin, the *Rechtsstaat*, which I have neither the qualifications nor the space to analyze. Crudely put there is a primitive and an advanced version of rule of law. The advanced version piles various natural law, human rights and equality features into the concept. The more primitive simply requires that government itself obey its own existing laws unless and until it chooses to enact new ones and obey those. Such a rule of law does not eliminate discretion but requires that discretions be created and constrained by law. One of the major current problems of constitutional development is that many polities with weak traditions of rule of law in this more primitive sense are anxious immediately to move to rule of law in the more advanced sense. Such a movement may be premature. It involves the risk of losing everything as a result of seeking too much too fast.

If the pursuit of rights is dangerous for a constitutional court because it generates conflict with politically powerful legislative and executive government actors, then the pursuit of rights infused rule of law by constitutional courts is equally dangerous. And just as these dangers may escalate if the constitutional court has not laid up a long record of serving the haves before beginning to serve the have nots, so it may escalate if rule of law in the more primitive sense has not been well established before rule of law in the more sophisticated sense is pursued. Moreover rule of law in the more primitive sense is prerequisite to rule of law in the more sophisticated. The judicial proclamation of constitutional rights is meaningless if there is not an effective obligation on the part of government to obey legal rules. Indeed under certain political conditions primitive rule of law may be sufficient to guarantee the rights which would be built into more sophisticated rule of law. Thus the German constitutional requirement that speech may not be limited except by a general law may be as effective for Germany as the American constitutional requirement that there may be no laws abridging freedom of speech is for the U.S.

The problem that Mr. Couso raises is whether a court system laboring to strengthen primitive rule of law in a polity in transition from non-democratic to democratic politics ought also to intervene against governmental action threatening constitutionally established rights. Ultimately the law making powers, including the constitutional law making powers, of courts rest on a subtle relationship between their institutional reputation as independent, neutral law appliers and the reality of their law making. It is of course precisely for that reason that lawyers and judges consistently substitute the word "interpretation" for the word "making." Courts say they interpret the law or interpret the constitution when what they mean is that courts make the law and make the constitution. Everyone admits that legal and constitutional change occurs as a result of judicial interpretation but no law person is prepared to say openly that the judges make these changes. The changes apparently occur without anyone making them. Indeed the basic reason that so much effort is taken in constructing the sophisticated version of the rule of law is that it non-obviously conflates law making with law enforcement in ways that the more primitive version does not. Using the advanced version judges may make constitutional rights while asserting that they are only enforcing the rule of law.

Viewing the American experience it can be argued that the greatest achievement of the Marshall Court was not the self-proclamation of its power of judicial review but the conversion of the U.S. constitution into U.S. constitutional law.[48] Today it is extremely difficult to get American law students to read the constitutional document although they dutifully plow through hundreds of Supreme Court decisions. All Americans know that the constitution is not what the constitution says it is but what the Supreme Court says it is. But that conversion of constitution from textual to case law was achieved through the widespread acceptance of long strings of Supreme Court decisions serving national economic

---

[48] See Sylvia Snowiss, *Judicial Review and the Law of the Constitution* (New Haven: Yale University Press 1990).

integration, economic development and corporate interests. Only after the eleva-
tion of judicial law over the text of the constitution was achieved in this way,
did the constitution come to mean what the Supreme Court said it meant about
the rights of the less powerful.

Cases in which a constitutional court affirms the existence of individual rights,
even the rights of the socially and economically powerful, against the actions of
government are the cases most likely to publicly spotlight the law and constitution making activities of courts. That revelation is highly dangerous for those
courts and most dangerous for constitutional courts in polities where there is
not a long established, wide spread understanding that the government must
obey the law. For a constitutional court can only succeed at constitutional law
making if it can clothe its making as law and everyone thinks that government
ought to obey law.

Where a single court or a court system has both constitutional law and
administrative law judicial review powers, and where rule of law traditions are
weak, may it not be better at least initially that judges concentrate on administrative law review rather than constitutional review? Administrative law review
is fundamentally about rule of law in the more primitive sense. It requires that
in the exercise of discretion granted to them by statute, administrators obey the
procedural and substantive requirements of the statutes, in short that the government obey its own laws. And administrative law, no matter how much disguised
judicial law making it contains, limits government in a context that proclaims
that the judge is enforcing the will of the legislature and that judges will
themselves obey any commands issued by the legislature. Unlike constitutional
review no judicial challenge to the overall powers of government occurs. In
reality there may be as much or more political or policy intervention by judges
in administrative review as in constitutional review but it is far less open,
dramatic and broad brushed. In polities where primitive rule of law is still at
risk, courts need to call on all their prestige as independent and neutral law
finders to successfully defend it. Constitutional "rights" and separation of powers
decisions are most likely to bring that independence and neutrality into question.
Should courts risk undermining their capacity to build primitive rule of law by
making constitutional judgments before rule of law has been fully established?

In many nations emerging from authoritarian regimes of various sorts, the
judiciary might well feel that its priority chore should be the building up of
support for the rule of law in the more primitive sense.[49] That priority may be
justified simply because for most individuals in their daily lives it is actually
more important that government obey its own rules whatever they are than that
individual rights be judicially protected against legislatures. The priority might

---

[49] Cf. Mark Brzezinski, Herbert Hausmaniger and Kim Scheppele, 'Constitutional
"Refolution" in the Ex-Communist World; the Rule of Law', *American University Journal
of International Law and Policy* 12 (1997), pp. 87–116.

also be justified on the grounds that the general institutional power of courts fundamentally depends on primitive rule of law and that only courts enjoying a firm primitive rule of law base eventually will be strong enough to challenge statutory rights infringements. It may finally be justified on the grounds that immediate constitutional rights interventions by courts will too much expose judicial law (constitution) making too soon, before the courts have built up sufficient institutional legitimacy to sustain it. In contrast administrative, primitive rule of law review will avoid direct political challenges to government and portray judicial law making as judicial service to elected legislatures rather than pursuit of judges' own values.

What is being tentatively argued is that the constitutional courts of polities recently emerged from authoritarian government ought not embrace the Warren Court model too eagerly. Instead such courts might contemplate an initial period of service, not necessarily to dominant interests, but to the rule of law in the primitive sense. Such a period of service would not only be valuable for its own sake but as a means of building up judicial legitimacy before taking on the risky business of constitutional rights making. I have said that the argument has been made tentatively. Any general argument of this sort must be tested against the particular circumstances of particular polities.

8. CONCLUSION

The ultimate 'lessons' for the new Central European constitutional courts taught by the American experience are essentially cautionary ones. The American success story is of little comfort to constitutional courts whose *initial raison d'etre* is the protection of individual and minority rights against majority legislation. For the U.S. story is one of a Court whose eventual service to rights rests on two previously, slowly and cautiously built, foundations, one systematic, the other historical. One foundation is a tacit bargain struck between court and majority in which the court essentially says to the majority something like the following: 'You have chosen a system of constitutionally divided powers. Such a system must inevitably breed conflicts among the various power holders. Courts are a convenient instrument for resolving conflicts. If you wish to empower a court to resolve such conflicts, you, the majority, must be prepared to pay for that convenience by accepting at least occasional anti-majoritarian judicial interventions in favor of rights.' The historical foundation is the Supreme Court's more than century-long, legitimacy building service to the most powerful political and economic interests in American society before it turned that long and slowly established legitimacy to the service of individual rights.

Eastern European constitutional courts bent on anti-majoritarian, rights protecting interventions cannot rely on either of these foundations. Instead they must base themselves on the most dangerous ground, that of an open anti-majoritarianism. They must say: 'Knowing your own propensity to unwisely sacrifice long-term human rights in which you yourself believe to your own short-term preferences, you, the majority, actually want us, the constitutional court, to protect you against yourself, by thwarting your own anti-rights moves.' American experience is 19th and early 20th century experience. Late 20th and early 21st century experience *may* be one of sufficiently universal, strong and deep majority commitment to human rights that the new constitutional courts can achieve success through delivering this message. The absence of the American foundations, however, suggests that new constitutional courts ought to choose carefully the occasions on which they resort to such a message. Even with those foundations the U.S. Supreme Court has been relatively cautious about challenging majorities. Moreover in this whole analysis I have deliberately left aside the central normative question: under what circumstances, if ever, *should* courts substitute their own policy preferences for those of the majority?

3. Institutional Dialogue between Courts and Legislatures in the Definition of Fundamental Rights: Lessons from Canada (and elsewhere)

*Jeremy Webber**

1. INTRODUCTION

In recent years, a number of commentators have used the concept of dialogue to capture the relationship between Canadian courts and legislatures in the judicial review of constitutionality.[1] As long as dialogue is treated sceptically

* My thanks to Eric Ghosh for his able research assistance and to Eric, Janet Hiebert, Peter Hogg, Rod Macdonald, and Andrew Petter for their trenchant comments on an earlier draft of this paper.

1 Peter Hogg and Allison Bushell, *'The Charter Dialogue Between Courts And Legislatures (Or Perhaps The Charter Of Rights Isn't Such A Bad Thing After All)'* Osgoode Hall Law Journal 35 (1997), pp. 75–124; Janet Hiebert, *'Why Must a Bill of Rights be a Contest of Political and Judicial Wills? The Canadian Alternative'* Public Law Review, 10 (1999), pp. 22–36 (hereafter, Hiebert (1999a)); Janet Hiebert, *'Wrestling with Rights: Judges, Parliament and the Making of Social Policy'* Choices, 5(3) (1999) (Institute for Research on Public Policy), pp. 1–36 (hereafter, Hiebert (1999b)); Kent Roach, *The Supreme Court on Trial: Judicial Activism or Democratic Dialogue* (Toronto: Irwin Law, 2001). Hiebert prefers the term 'conversation'. For criticisms of the idea of dialogue, see Jamie Cameron, *'Dialogue and Hierarchy in Charter Interpretation: A Comment on R v. Mills'* Alberta Law Review, 38 (2001), pp. 1051–1068 (who rejects the idea of dialogue, at least within section 1 of the Charter, because it undermines the supremacy of constitutional interpretation, without the procedural sanctions of section 33) and, at the other end of the spectrum, Christopher Manfredi and James Kelly, *'Six Degrees of Dialogue: A Response to Hogg and Bushell'* Osgoode Hall Law Journal, 37 (1999), pp. 513–536 (who argue that Hogg and Bushell exaggerate the extent to which there is true dialogue). There is a rejoinder in Peter Hogg and Allison Thornton, *'Reply to "Six Degrees of Dialogue"'* Osgoode Hall Law Journal, 37 (1999), pp. 529–536. See also: Mark Tushnet, *'Policy Distortion and Democratic Debilitation: Comparative Illumination of the Countermajoritarian Difficulty'* Michigan Law Review, 94 (1995), pp. 245–301. The courts themselves have begun to refer to dialogue. See, for example: Vriend v. Alberta (1998) 156 DLR (4th) 385 at 438–439 (per Cory and Iacobucci JJ); Corbière v. Canada (MINA) (1999) 173 DLR (4th) 1 at 63 (per L'Heureux-Dubé J); R v. Mills (1999) 180 DLR (4th) 1 at 19–20 and 37–38 (per McLachlin and Iacobucci JJ); Little Sisters Book and Art v. Canada (2000) 193 DLR (4th) 193 (SCC) at 294 (per Iacobucci J). Hogg and Bushell are chiefly concerned with a less demanding form of dialogue than that which is the focus of this paper: the ability of legislatures to adapt

Wojciech Sadurski (ed.), Constitutional Justice, East and West, 61–99
© 2002 *Kluwer Law International. Printed in Great Britain.*

and is not assumed to describe an ideal conversation, the idea of dialogue can provide a useful perspective on human rights protections generally, for it emphasises the extent to which both courts and legislatures have valuable things to say about rights, directs our attention to the ways in which the two institutions interact, and provides tools for evaluating the remarkably broad range of mechanisms that can be used to protect rights.

This paper reviews a spectrum of means by which such 'dialogue' over rights can be structured in a constitutional system. It then focuses in more detail on three specific forms of rights protection and evaluates the institutional balance achieved in each:

- the finding, by the courts, that constitutional provisions dealing with other matters contain implicit rights guarantees, so that rights come to be addressed through the adjudication of provisions having little ostensibly to do with rights (an 'implied rights' approach);
- the entrenchment of a bill of rights in the constitution, backed by judicial review, but subject to express derogation by legislative action (the approach contained in section 33 – the 'notwithstanding clause' – of the *Canadian Charter of Rights and Freedoms*[2]); and
- the declaration of rights in an ordinary statute, lacking constitutional status but protected by a requirement that derogation occur in a specified manner and form (the 'statutory bill of rights' approach).

Each of these mechanisms has been used in Canada. In this paper I will draw primarily on Canadian experience, although I will also discuss the Australian jurisprudence on implied rights and refer to approaches to rights taken in a number of other chiefly Anglo-American jurisdictions.

The notion that rights guarantees are characterised by 'dialogue' between courts and legislatures may strike the reader as both counter-intuitive and normatively inappropriate. We generally think of judicial review in much simpler and monological terms. Parliament passes laws, and courts either uphold them or strike them down on the basis of their interpretation of the constitution. Any sense that political actors influence the courts' interpretation of the constitution seems incompatible with judicial independence and the rule of law; we assume that courts should come to their own conclusions as to constitutionality, without reference to what political actors like or dislike. Some legal realists have emphasised that political actors do have an impact on judicial review. But this

---

their legislation to withstand constitutional scrutiny, once a law has been declared invalid. This paper concentrates not on legislatures' responses to judicial decisions, but on legislatures' impact on the interpretation and application of the rights themselves.

[2]   Canadian Charter of Rights and Freedoms, Part 1 of the Constitution Act, 1982, being Schedule B to the Canada Act 1982 (UK), 1982, c 11 (hereafter Canadian Charter of Rights and Freedoms or, simply, Charter).

impact is generally treated by the realists themselves as incompatible with claims of judicial independence.[3]

In this paper, I will deal with principled justifications for legislative participation in the definition of rights only *en passant*, as part of the evaluation of the balance struck by various rights instruments.[4] I should note, however, that institutional dialogue over rights is much more common than is often acknowledged – indeed is, to some extent, universal.

In Canada, the claim that judicial review involves dialogue has special credence because of two distinctive aspects of the *Canadian Charter of Rights and Freedoms.*

First, the Canadian *Charter* contains an express limitation clause, section 1, which states that its rights and freedoms are 'subject only to such reasonable limits, prescribed by law, as can be demonstrably justified in a free and democratic society.' This clause recognises not only that rights are subject to limits, but also, implicitly, that government should have the burden of justifying those limits.[5] Second, the Canadian *Charter* permits legislatures to derogate from some of the rights it enunciates. Section 33 provides that legislatures can insulate a statute from certain forms of *Charter* review by expressly declaring that the statute shall operate notwithstanding certain sections of the *Canadian Charter of Rights and Freedoms.* When this occurs, judicial review is excluded. Both these provisions suggest that the legislature may actively participate in the definition of constitutional protections.

Although these clauses are distinctively Canadian, there are functional parallels in virtually all constitutions. Other bills of rights contain express limitation clauses.[6] But even if they do not, it is generally conceded that all rights are subject to limits. Those limits may not be conceived as restrictions of an otherwise unlimited right; they may be conceived as aspects of the definition of the right. And there may be no clear understanding that government has the burden of justifying limits; it may simply be assumed that the courts will determine the limits. But these distinctions make little difference for our purposes. The rights

---

[3] Although he is not generally considered a legal realist, this was essentially the argument put so effectively by Robert Dahl in his classic article, '*Decision-making in a Democracy: the Supreme Court as a National Policy-maker*' Journal of Public Law, 6 (1957), pp. 279–295.

[4] I address some of the issues in '*Constitutional Reticence*' Australian Journal of Legal Philosophy, 25 (2000), pp. 125–155.

[5] R v. Oakes [1986] 1 SCR 103 at 136–137. As Hogg and Bushell emphasise in above n. 1, pp. 87–90, other Charter rights contain their own internal qualifications which have, within a more restricted compass, a similar effect.

[6] For limitation clauses that apply, like Canada's, to the rights instrument generally, see: New Zealand Bill of Rights Act 1990, No. 109 (NZ), section 5; Constitution of the Republic of South Africa 1996, section 36. Other instruments have limitations clauses applicable to specific rights. See, for example: International Covenant on Civil and Political Rights, article 19(3); European Convention on Human Rights, article 10(2).

are, in any case, subject to limits; and when a statute is subjected to judicial review, any government will seek to justify a measure that it wishes to retain.

The Canadian *Charter*'s 'notwithstanding clause' appears more strikingly original than the limitation clause, but even it has functional parallels elsewhere. Virtually every constitution is subject to amendment by some legislative process, onerous though it may be.[7] The distinctive characteristic of the Canadian provision is really the ease with which the rights guarantees may be set aside, and the implicit message that it may be legitimate to do so.

All of this suggests that there is something of broader significance to the notion of dialogue between courts and legislature in judicial review. At the very least, it emphasises that constitutional review is about a complex relationship between legislatures and courts. Judicial review is not simply about laws enacted and then subjected to the guillotine of judicial nullification. There is considerably more potential for – indeed presence of – to-and-fro between legislatures and courts. Or, to put it another way, the interpretation and enforcement of rights by courts always operates within a zone of tolerance created by the relative difficulty of legislative override (whether the override would occur by ordinary legislative process or by constitutional amendment). The control of the courts over legislative action is always conditional, dependent on the degree of institutional friction within the system. This means that it is possible for framers of a constitution to structure the institutional relationship in a variety of ways to achieve a desired balance in legislative and judicial roles.

One final comment. Throughout this paper I use 'political' in contrast to 'judicial' to refer to the broad spectrum of public debate, decision-making and action outside the courts. Of course, judges are also political actors in a broad sense. Moreover, I accept that there is no sharp distinction between the kinds of reasons employed by judges and those employed in political discourse generally (although there are significant differences in the weight given to particular kinds of reasons). My choice of terminology is merely a matter of convenience. In this paper I am concerned with the manner in which judges enter into dialogue with broader political processes (especially with governments and legislatures) in their administration of rights guarantees. Those broader political processes are wide and various; it is simplest to use the catch-all 'political' to describe them.

---

[7] See, however, article 79 of the Basic Law of the Federal Republic of Germany, which purports to prohibit amendments to substantial sections of the constitution. The Supreme Court of India has also held that the basic structure and framework of the Indian Constitution is unamendable, even though the express terms of the Constitution impose no such limitation: RC Bhardwaj (ed), *Constitution Amendment in India*, 6th ed (New Delhi: Northern Book Centre 1995), pp. 10–13.

2. CLEARING THE UNDERBRUSH

Before plunging into the mechanisms for dialogue, it is worth setting out a series of assumptions that underlie my discussion of bills of rights. First, I do not accept a simple 'checks-and-balances' – or libertarian – justification for constitutional review, in which judicial review is defended purely and simply because it limits government, regardless of the grounds of limitation. On the contrary, the ability to participate actively in government to achieve societal goals is a key dimension of freedom. A corollary of this is the vesting of a measure of trust in democratic institutions – a commitment to their efficacy, as the most representative of governmental institutions. All other things being equal, democratic institutions should be permitted to make decisions and carry them into effect. The nullification of statutes through judicial review therefore requires specific justification.

Second, the choice of whether to have judicial review of rights guarantees is not a straightforward choice between having rights or not. Legislatures too are concerned with rights, although sometimes in different ways from courts. Indeed, institutional characteristics mean that both courts and legislatures have strengths and weaknesses in the definition, interpretation, and application of rights, to which I will return below. One can therefore be a strong supporter of rights without supporting judicial review on the basis of a constitutionalised bill of rights. Support for judicial review requires an additional premise: a reason why that particular institutional form is appropriate.

I do not want to appear disingenuous about this. I do have concerns with the extent of hegemony of the discourse of rights and about its tendency towards simplification, uniformity of treatment, highly symbolic argumentation, and resistance to compromise, all of which I have explored elsewhere.[8] Scepticism towards or opposition to a constitutionalised bill of rights is often founded upon opposition to the peculiar role of rights discourse under such a regime, and this paper is no exception. But for the purposes of this paper, it is sufficient to note that scepticism with respect to judicial review may have little to do with support for or opposition to rights. One can be for rights, but consider other means of protection to be preferable.

Third, constitutional bills of rights often serve a variety of ends; the substantive protection of individual rights and freedoms is not their sole function. They have often played an important role, for example, in national consolidation. They have established a common basis of citizenship, affirmed that all citizens are subject to the same governmental authority, or sought to enunciate the fundamental values of the nation. This national symbolic role may align closely with

---

[8] See Webber, above n. 4; Jeremy Webber, *'Tales of the Unexpected: Intended and Unintended Consequences of the Canadian Charter of Rights and Freedoms'* Canterbury Law Review, 5 (1993), pp. 207–234.

the protection of rights but the two functions are not identical. There can be points at which they diverge. There may, for example, be very good reason on grounds closely linked to human-rights concerns for recognising a measure of diversity within the public institutions of the state. It may be perfectly appropriate, for example, for cultural minorities (indigenous peoples; linguistic minorities; gypsies) to have access to their own institutions (schools; social programs; even governmental structures, especially in the case of indigenous peoples). Yet those very demands have often been resisted in the language of equality derived from constitutional guarantees, for reasons that have little to do with individual liberty but a great deal to do with a desire for national consolidation.[9] It is important, then, to be clear on the functions to be served by a bill of rights. In this paper I will focus entirely on the human rights dimension of bills of rights, although noting complications posed by their national symbolic role.

Fourth, it is important to pay attention to the real issues that are likely to be dealt with under a bill of rights. Many justifications for bills of rights rely upon a parade of horribles; the rights guarantees are justified on the basis of the need to prevent the grossest of human rights violations. But in most societies with strong democratic cultures, bills of rights are not used to prevent gross violations. They are deployed at the margins. They define the rights' outer limits, or rule upon their implications in situations in which judgements of right and wrong are highly complex and disputed. Under the *Canadian Charter of Rights and Freedoms*, for example, the Supreme Court of Canada struck down the federal government's legislation regulating tobacco advertising on the basis of freedom of expression; it has struck down provisions that prohibited interprovincial law firms or required lawyers to be Canadian citizens.[10] Granted, it has made some decisions that have had an important impact on the rights of individuals. This is true, for example, of its early judgement striking down Canada's abortion law on procedural grounds, or its more recent decision extending Alberta's *Individual Rights Protection Act* to include discrimination on the basis of sexual orientation.[11] But in the vast majority of cases there have been strong arguments on each side of the issue; the ultimate decision has been a matter of fine determination.

If the rights culture in a particular country is sufficiently strong that gross

---

9   See Webber (1993), *ibid*, at 230–231; Jeremy Webber, *Reimagining Canada: Language, Culture, Community, and the Canadian Constitution* (Montreal: McGill-Queen's University Press 1994), especially pp. 141–144 and 234ff; and, more generally, Jeremy Webber, 'Constitutional Poetry: The Tension Between Symbolic and Functional Aims in Constitutional Reform' Sydney Law Review, 21 (1999), pp. 260–277.

10   RJR – MacDonald Inc v. Canada [1995] 3 SCR 199; Black v. Law Society of Alberta [1989] 1 SCR 591; Andrews v. Law Society of British Columbia (1989) 56 DLR (4th) 1 (SCC).

11   R v. Morgentaler [1988] 1 SCR 30; Vriend, above n. 1.

violations of rights never come before the courts, then one has to ask whether judges must have the last word. If judicial review does nothing more than substitute the reasoned opinion of a judge for the reasoned opinion of the legislature on a matter of real doubt as to what justice requires, why bother? Of course, the situation is rarely that simple. Legislatures can lose sight of rights considerations in their rush to achieve a social objective. Unpopular minorities can find themselves disadvantaged by measures that individually may not amount to much, but that cumulatively impose a significant and debilitating burden. The point is that there are many ways in which rights protections can be achieved. One may structure the institutional relationship differently depending on the matters likely to come before the courts.

This in turn suggests that different forms of rights protection may be appropriate in different contexts. One may need entrenched bills of rights most in societies that lack an established democratic or human-rights culture, where the symbolic affirmation of rights serves an important role and political power must be forcefully constrained. They may be less necessary in societies in which human rights already form an important strand in political debate.

3. INSTITUTIONAL DIALOGUE AND THE STRUCTURE OF HUMAN RIGHTS PROTECTIONS

What elements determine the scope for dialogue in the enforcement of human rights protections? They are remarkably diverse. When taken together, they define a broad range of options for the institutionalisation of human rights. It will be useful to address them under three headings: 3.1) Extent of Entrenchment; 3.2) Strategy of Judicial Review; and 3.3) Mechanisms for Legislative Involvement in the Definition of Rights.

3.1. Extent of Entrenchment

We commonly think of constitutional entrenchment as being all or nothing: rights are either enshrined in the constitution, exempt from legislative tampering, or they are left to the mercy of the legislature. Entrenchment is a much more relative concept than this suggests, however. In essence, it is concerned with the degree to which rights provisions have a controlling impact on legislation, and the ease with which the provisions can be changed. There are a wide variety of means by which rights can be pursued, each postulating a different relationship between legislature and courts. Often these are cumulated within one legal system. Canadian law sports a particularly rich selection. Here I canvass the possibilities in order of increasing constraint.

(a) Non-binding Declarations of Rights

Some rights have no binding force within the domestic legal system. The protections operate by virtue of their moral force alone. Their impact can nevertheless be substantial, inducing legislatures to amend their laws to bring them into conformity. The most common example occurs in the case of international norms. In countries descended from the British constitutional tradition, international norms created by treaty have no direct force within domestic law. They need to be incorporated into legislation in order to take effect domestically. In formal terms, then, the rights are at the mercy of the domestic legislatures and can exercise no direct constraining effect.

The international instruments can nevertheless have a substantial impact. In Canada, for example, a decision by the United Nations Human Rights Committee held that the definition of 'Indian' in the federal *Indian Act* contravened article 27 of the *International Covenant on Civil and Political Rights*, because the *Act*'s gender-specific structure (under which Indian women who married non-Indian men lost their status, but Indian men who married non-Indian women did not) unjustifiably denied Aboriginal women the right to enjoy their culture in community with other members of their group. The *Act* was amended, even though the measure had previously been upheld by the Canadian courts under the *Canadian Bill of Rights* (a statutory bill of rights pre-dating the adoption of the *Canadian Charter of Rights and Freedoms*) and even though a number of First Nations disagreed vehemently with the change.[12] Similarly, in Australia, a decision of the Human Rights Committee prompted the Commonwealth Parliament to adopt legislation overriding Tasmania's criminalisation of sex between consenting homosexual adult men.[13] And until the incorporation of the *European Convention on Human Rights* into British law by the *Human Rights Act 1998*, that *Convention* too had no direct force within domestic British law (except as an aid to interpretation). Yet it nevertheless had a significant impact, leading to a number of amendments to British law.[14]

There are also 'programmatic rights' in international law and some national constitutions. These rights are similarly exempt from judicial review. Their implementation is left entirely to the discretion of the legislature.[15]

---

[12] Lovelace v. Canada, Communication No 24/1977 (30 July 1981) UN Doc CCPR/C/OP/1 at 83 (1984); An Act to amend the Indian Act, SC 1985, c 27 (Bill C-31); Canadian Bill of Rights, SC 1960, c 44; A-G Canada v. Lavell [1974] SCR 1349.

[13] Toonen v. Australia, Communication No 488/1992 (4 April 1994) UN Doc CCPR/C/50/D/488/1992; Human Rights (Sexual Conduct) Act 1994, No 179 (Cth); Croome v. Tasmania (1997) 71 ALJR 430 (HCA).

[14] Human Rights Act 1998, c 42 (UK). For the impact of the Convention prior to the adoption of the Human Rights Act 1998, see David Kinley, *The European Convention on Human Rights: Compliance Without Incorporation* (Aldershot: Dartmouth 1993).

[15] See, for example: International Covenant on Economic, Social and Cultural Rights, article 2(1); Constitution of the Republic of Ireland, article 45; Constitution of India, Part IV.

(b) Interpretive Conventions Based on Implicit Norms

Human rights can also have an impact on the law through interpretive conventions, under which courts strive to interpret legislation in a manner consistent with rights. Here, the rights considerations have no independent constraining effect. They cannot be used to strike down legislation. They simply shape the judge's interpretation of the law, so that the law is rendered as consistent as possible with human rights norms.

These human rights norms can sometimes be a matter of general principle, with no authoritative legislative expression. One good example is found in the Supreme Court of Canada's decision in *MacKeigan* v. *Hickman*.[16] There, the relevant statute provided that a Commission of Inquiry could summon 'any persons' to give evidence as a witness. The Court held that this very general language should not be taken to override a principle as important as judicial independence; it therefore held that the statute did not permit a Commission to compel a judge to testify as to their reasons for decision in a particular case. Another example is the requirement of compensation when property is expropriated in Canada and the United Kingdom. There is no express guarantee of compensation. The courts simply presume that compensation is to be paid unless the legislature stipulates otherwise.[17]

Here again the impact can be substantial even though ostensibly one is merely in the realm of statutory interpretation. There is always considerable latitude in interpretation. If courts insist upon an extraordinary degree of clarity before they interpret a statute so that it constrains rights, the protection can be very great indeed. It can amount to a requirement that to impair rights, a legislature must do so explicitly.

(c) Interpretive Conventions based on Explicit Norms

In some cases, legislatures enact express norms, which are then used by courts in their interpretation of other statutes. This method of rights protection works much like that described in the previous section: the courts do not invalidate legislation, but they do interpret it restrictively in order to avoid an impairment of rights. As in the previous section, the effect can be significant; the courts can require a very high degree of clarity before they find that rights have been restricted.[18]

The difference is the involvement of the legislature in the specification of the norms. This creates real give-and-take between courts and legislature. The legislature sets the norms, sometimes enshrining them in a statutory bill of rights;

---

16   [1989] 2 SCR 796.
17   A-G v. DeKeyser's Royal Hotel [1920] AC 508 (HL); Burmah Oil v. Lord Advocate [1965] AC 75 (HL); Manitoba Fisheries v. The Queen [1979] 1 SCR 101.
18   See, for example: Winnipeg School Division No 1 v. Craton [1985] 2 SCR 150 at 156.

the courts take those norms and use them to interpret other laws, construing those laws so that they respect the legislature's norms. This differs from the situation described in the previous section, in which courts are responsible both for the articulation of the norms and for their use in interpretation.

This form of interpretation was one of the ways in which the statutory, pre-*Charter, Canadian Bill of Rights* was understood to work – although how well it worked is another question: the weakness of the *Canadian Bill of Rights* – its lack of constraining effect – was fiercely criticised by human rights advocates.[19] A more successful example is the *New Zealand Bill of Rights Act 1990*. That act cannot be used to invalidate legislation, yet it has nevertheless had a significant impact on criminal procedure and the common law of defamation.[20] Interpretation is also one strategy used by the United Kingdom's *Human Rights Act 1998*, which incorporates the *European Convention on Human Rights*. That act, however, goes well beyond interpretation (i) to invalidate subordinate legislation; (ii) to bind public authorities; (iii) to permit courts to declare that primary legislation is incompatible with the *Convention* (although that declaration does not affect the statute's validity); and (iv) to permit a Minister of the Crown to make amendments to bring the statute into conformity.[21]

In each of these examples, the human rights norms are enacted by the same legislature whose statutes are then subject to scrutiny. But judicial interpretation sometimes draws on norms articulated by other legislatures than the one scrutinised. Indeed, this is one way in which treaty norms can have an impact on domestic law, even without the incorporation of the treaty into domestic statutes. The courts interpret domestic law so that it is, as far as possible, consistent with international law.[22]

---

[19] Canadian Bill of Rights, SC 1960, c 44. See: Walter Tarnopolsky, *The Canadian Bill of Rights*, 2nd ed (Toronto: McClelland and Stewart 1975).

[20] New Zealand Bill of Rights Act 1990, No. 109 (NZ). See: K.J. Keith, ' *"Concerning Change": The Adoption and Implementation of the New Zealand Bill of Rights Act 1990'* Victoria University of Wellington Law Review, 31 (2000), pp. 721–46; James Allan, *'Turning Clark Kent into Superman: The New Zealand Bill of Rights Act 1990'* Otago Law Review, 9 (2000), pp. 613–632.

[21] 1998, c 42 (UK), especially sections 3, 4, 6, and 10. Australia's Racial Discrimination Act 1975, No 52 (Cth) has also been used to interpret later legislation. For example, there was considerable discussion when the Native Title Act 1993, No 110 (Cth) was enacted, and when that act was amended in 1997–98, over whether it should be made expressly subject to the Racial Discrimination Act 1975 so that any provisions offending the Racial Discrimination Act 1975 would be rendered inoperative. On both occasions, Parliament ultimately settled on language that merely invited the courts to use the Racial Discrimination Act 1975 to interpret the Native Title Act 1993. See: Frank Brennan, *The Wik Debate: Its Impact on Aborigines, Pastoralists and Miners* (Sydney: University of New South Wales Press 1998), pp. 69–71, 73–74, and 85.

[22] For an example that had considerable prominence within Australia, see: Minister of State for Immigration and Ethnic Affairs v. Teoh (1995) 183 CLR 273.

(d) Rights Guarantees Protected by a Manner and Form Requirement

In the mechanisms examined thus far, the rights norms do not bind the legislature. At least in theory, the legislature could set them aside, as long as it did so with sufficient clarity to overcome the court's interpretive presumptions. In Canada, however, legislatures have enacted rights norms, binding those very legislatures, through the imaginative use of manner and form requirements. To understand how these requirements work, it is important to realise that in the British tradition legislatures generally cannot bind themselves. The doctrine of parliamentary sovereignty requires that at any point, the legislature can change its mind, passing laws that contradict its earlier enactments. Whenever there is inconsistency, the former laws are repealed to the extent of that inconsistency. Among other things, this principle operates as an important bulwark of democracy, for it means that legislators can always repeal the work of their predecessors; a government facing defeat cannot bind its successor.

Manner and form requirements operate as a limited exception to this principle, at least in Canada. Although legislatures cannot bind themselves as to substance, Canadian courts have held that legislatures can bind themselves as to process. They can stipulate a particular procedure – a specific 'manner and form' – by which enactments must be made. Until repealed, these stipulations (as long as they are genuinely procedural and do not amount to a disguised limit on substance) must be followed by the legislature's successors.[23] These requirements can be used to offer a qualified protection to human rights norms. Instead of attempting to impose the norms directly, the legislature enacts, in the rights instrument, a distinctive procedure by which restrictions must be adopted. Because it is purely procedural, the requirement binds the legislature's successors.

In Canada, the stipulated requirement is usually that, to set aside the rights guarantees, the legislature must state explicitly that the statute is to apply notwithstanding the rights guarantees. This does not bind as to substance; the legislature can always set aside the protections, by an ordinary majority, as long as it does so explicitly. But it does guard against inadvertent restrictions of rights, and it also plays a very important signalling function: any government seeking to set aside the guarantees must do so explicitly, and that will in turn tend to generate a vigorous public debate, forcing the government to justify its actions. The manner and form requirement serves, in other words, as a trigger to the democratic process, by providing clear notice that a rights issue has been raised.

In Canada's federal system, statutory bills of rights of this kind only bind legislation of the level of government that enacts them.[24]

---

[23] See: R v. Drybones [1970] SCR 282; Ford v. Quebec (1988) 54 DLR (4th) 577; Reference Re: Canada Assistance Plan (1991) 83 DLR (4th) 297 (SCC) at 322–324.

[24] It is possible, depending on the nature of the federal regime, for a statutory bill of rights enacted at one level to bind legislation enacted by the other level. This is the case in Australia with the Racial Discrimination Act 1975, No 52 (Cth), adopted under the

This was the principal approach adopted in the *Canadian Bill of Rights* – the statutory bill of rights enacted by the Parliament of Canada in 1960. Although its role in rights protection has largely been overtaken by the *Canadian Charter of Rights and Freedoms* (a constitutional instrument), the *Canadian Bill of Rights* remains in force. In 1985, it was used by three judges of the Supreme Court of Canada to strike down the refugee determination process in Canada's *Immigration Act*.[25] Alberta employed a similar approach in the *Alberta Bill of Rights* of 1972.[26] Quebec did so as well in the *Charter of Human Rights and Freedoms*, a statutory bill of rights enacted in 1975.[27] In 1988, the Supreme Court of Canada relied on the Quebec *Charter* to strike down a section of Quebec's language legislation that banned the use of English on commercial signs. The decision had a very significant political impact. The Quebec National Assembly re-adopted the sign law in modified form (popularly known as Bill 178), this time protecting it from the *Canadian Charter of Rights and Freedoms* (but not the Quebec *Charter of Human Rights and Freedoms*) through the use of a 'notwithstanding clause'. As I discuss further below, that action provoked vigorous criticism from English-speaking Canadians. This reaction contributed to the ultimate defeat of a package of constitutional amendments (the 'Meech Lake Accord') supported by Quebec.[28]

The effectiveness of manner and form requirements is therefore well established in Canadian law. They are used to give qualified force to statutory rights guarantees. I return to the value of these instruments in structuring institutional dialogue below.

(e) Constitutionally Entrenched Guarantees

Of course, when we think about bills of rights we usually think of instruments subject to full constitutional entrenchment. Even here, however, there is more variation than might at first appear.

First, the nature of the entrenched norms can be very different, with important consequences for the scope of judicial review. Occasionally, decisions that are

---

Commonwealth's external affairs power to incorporate the International Convention on the Elimination of All Forms of Racial Discrimination into Australian law. Because it benefits from the paramountcy of federal legislation over inconsistent state legislation, it binds the states without any need to resort to manner and form requirements. See Koowarta v. Bjelke-Petersen (1982) 153 CLR 168.

[25] Canadian Bill of Rights, SC 1960, c 44; Singh v. Minister of Employment and Immigration [1985] 1 SCR 178 (the remaining three justices came to the same conclusion on the basis of the Charter).

[26] SA 1972, c 1.

[27] SQ 1975, c 6.

[28] Ford, above n. 23; An Act to amend the Charter of the French Language, SQ 1988, c 54 (Bill 178); Webber (1994), above n. 9, at 138ff.

(one suspects) primarily based on rights considerations are framed in language that has little to do with rights. This was a familiar phenomenon in Canada prior to the adoption of the *Canadian Charter of Rights and Freedoms* where, in a few celebrated cases, decisions with a strong human rights element were based on the federal/provincial division of powers.

In some cases, this was bona fide division-of-powers reasoning, in which the rights concern was genuinely tied to the nature of the particular power in issue. Thus, in Canada, criminal law is a federal matter. The criminal power was interpreted to cover a number of legislative aims that had strong potential to impair individual rights, such as the suppression of sedition or the enforcement of religion (an interpretation with some justification, given the purposes to which the criminal law had historically been put). Provincial laws dealing with these matters were struck down as infringing upon federal authority.[29] At other times, one had the impression that division-of-powers reasoning was being distorted in order to attain a rights objective. This may have been the case in *McKay* v. *The Queen*, for example, in which by-laws enacted under provincial authority to regulate signs were held not to apply to federal election signs.[30]

In any case, although provisions dealing with the division of powers have on occasion served the ends of human rights, their potential has been limited. The protection they afforded was minimalist, for the court had to find a plausible hook within division-of-powers reasoning on which to hang its decision. In principle the decisions were only concerned with who could infringe rights; if the measures of one level of government were struck down, it was always open

---

29 Switzman v. Elbling [1957] SCR 285; AG Ontario v. Hamilton Street Railway [1903] AC 524 (PC); Henry Birks & Sons v. Montreal [1955] SCR 799. The celebrated Australian case, Australian Communist Party v. Commonwealth (1951) 83 CLR 1, also used division-of-powers reasoning in the service of human-rights ends. There, the High Court considered the validity of the Communist Party Dissolution Act 1950 (Cth), which attempted to rely on the defence power or on an implied power to defend governmental institutions to declare the Communist Party unlawful and prohibit Communists from serving in the Commonwealth government and in certain unions. The Court held that the statute was beyond the scope of both powers. Similarly in Adelaide Company of Jehovah's Witnesses Inc v. Commonwealth (1943) 67 CLR 116, the High Court struck down a wartime regulation purporting to dissolve a Jehovah's Witnesses organisation on the grounds that it went beyond what was necessary for the prosecution of the war and was therefore beyond the scope of the defence power. This last decision is especially interesting for there is an express guarantee for freedom of religion in the Australian constitution (section 116), which the court decided would not have been violated by the regulation. This preference for division-of-powers reasoning may reflect the fact that at least until recently, judicial review on division-of-powers grounds had more legitimacy than review on the basis of rights, perhaps because judgements based expressly on rights challenge legislative policy much more directly.

30 McKay v. The Queen [1965] SCR 798.

to the other level to adopt them. Finally, the simple fact that these decisions relied on surrogate arguments meant that it was impossible to develop a coherent and explicit rights jurisprudence.

A second type of entrenched rights consists of implied rights. These rights are not explicitly set out in the constitution, but instead are derived from other provisions that ostensibly have little to do with rights. They differ from the division-of-powers judgements in that the court uses the language of rights in its reasoning, finding that a particular right is implicit in the constitution. The notion of implied rights has had a large hurdle to clear. There is a strong commitment to parliamentary sovereignty in the British tradition. That has generally meant that constitutional restrictions are read narrowly, especially if (as in the case of rights) the effect of the restriction would be to prevent all levels of government from enacting the measure.

There are many ways in which rights might plausibly be implied. The ones that have attained the most currency, however, are founded on constitutional provisions that establish democratic structures of government. The argument is that democratic institutions cannot operate without free political debate. Some protection of freedom of speech must therefore be implied.

Although certain Canadian judges flirted with the implication of rights guarantees prior to adoption of the *Charter* (and indeed after), this reasoning had not found its way into the reasons for judgement of the majority of the Supreme Court of Canada prior to the adoption of the *Canadian Charter of Rights and Freedoms*. Instead, the majority had always rested its decision on alternative grounds. Ironically, however, Canadian musings about an 'implied bill of rights' did contribute to the development of a vigorous implied-rights jurisprudence in Australia.[31] I will return to this form of protection below.

Third, there are explicit rights guarantees. I need say little about them here for they are by far the best known. I simply note that they too can vary considerably in their constraining effect, depending on how they are drafted.

Indeed, not all express rights are justiciable. So-called 'programmatic' rights – often rights to services that would impose onerous financial obligations on government (housing; education; social welfare; environmental protection) – serve merely as directions to government to make those aims a legislative priority. The courts have no role in their enforcement.

Entrenched rights also differ in the extent to which they are insulated from legislative impairment or change. There are at least three different ways in which rights protections can be subject to legislative restriction: First, all rights are

---

[31] Canadian cases often considered to open the door for implied rights include: Re Alberta Statutes [1938] SCR 100 at 133–134 (per Duff CJ); Saumur v. City of Quebec [1953] 2 SCR 299 at 354 (per Kellock J) and 363 (per Locke J); Switzman v. Elbling [1957] SCR 285 at 328 (per Abbott J); OPSEU v. Ontario [1987] 1 SCR 2 at 57 (per Beetz J). For the Australian decisions, see below, nn. 55–58 and accompanying text.

subject to limitations; the very process of definition, through judicial interpretation, involves a delineation of limits. When scrutinising a statute impugned on human-rights grounds, the courts will attempt to determine whether a legislature has over-stepped those bounds. In this process, political actors too play a role. They can discuss rights considerations at the time of adopting legislation, offering rationalisations that in turn influence the courts.[32] They can, through their lawyers, offer further justifications when the matter goes to court. Thus, at least through the exercise of persuasion, political actors can have an impact on the scope of the rights. In Canada, this role is contemplated in section 1 of the *Charter*. Second, charters of rights can expressly permit legislative derogations. As already mentioned, that is the case in section 33 of the Canadian *Charter*. I explore section 33 in detail below.

Ultimately, rights guarantees can always be set aside by constitutional amendment. The ease of amendment differs from constitution to constitution. Some constitutional provisions, in some countries, are amendable by ordinary majority. In Canada, this was the case with guarantees for the use of French originally applied to the North West Territories and inherited by the provinces of Alberta and Saskatchewan upon their creation. These provisions had fallen into disuse prior to the provinces' creation, without being formally repealed. When, in 1988, the Supreme Court found that they were still in force, the legislatures of the two provinces immediately repealed the guarantees and validated previous acts passed in violation of the requirements.[33]

Generally the mode of amendment is considerably more difficult than this. It may be so difficult as to be functionally impossible. Indeed, it has been argued that some provisions of some constitutions are unamendable (although this is very rare). Even those constitutions, however, can be overthrown by revolution.[34] It is preferable, then, not to treat entrenchment as though it rendered constitutional provisions untouchable. In the last analysis, all constitutions are open to change. The sanctity of rights protections therefore depends, always, upon the dynamic relations among institutions in the political order. Entrenchment is always a matter of degree.

---

[32] Hogg and Bushell, above n. 1, pp. 101–104, give a number of examples where legislatures or government agencies explicitly state, sometimes in the preamble to an act, why the measure constitutes a reasonable limitation within the meaning of section 1 of the Charter.

[33] R v. Mercure [1988] 1 SCR 234; The Language Act, SS 1988, c L-6.1; Languages Act, SA 1988, c L-7.5.

[34] See above n. 7. Indeed Dicey argued, with real justification, that the fact that a constitution was unamendable might actually encourage revolution, citing the rapidity with which supposedly unamendable French constitutions had been replaced: Albert Dicey, *Introduction to the Study of the Law of the Constitution*, 10th ed (London: Macmillan 1959) at 128–131.

3.2. Strategy of Judicial Review

The extent of institutional interaction – including the extent to which legislatures participate in the definition of rights – is also affected by the judges' conception of their task. Their definition of the content of rights can either foster legislative action or foreclose it.

(a) Rights Guarantees as Minimum Guarantees

First, room for legislative action can be preserved by courts approaching constitutional provisions on the basis that they are meant to provide minimum guarantees, not to confer on courts the power to regulate everything having to do with the subject matter of particular rights, such as expression or religion. Such a restrained interpretation has the merit of coinciding with most justifications for judicial review on rights grounds. These justifications tend to focus on rights guarantees as minimum guarantees – as ensuring a basic minimum level of respect for individual freedom and equality.[35]

Constitutional texts rarely take such a minimalist form, however. They speak in ringing language, proclaiming the need to respect 'freedom of expression' or 'equality before the law', without hedging those concepts about with qualifications. Constitutional provisions do not speak of a 'necessary minimum of free expression' or a 'fundamental baseline of equality'. Courts, faced with the rights' broad language, can be tempted to give it full rein. They can start with the abstract concepts of expression and equality and seek to define exhaustively their scope and meaning in a liberal society. The role of judicially enforced rights as minimum guarantees can fall away, the concepts come to be defined in plenary terms, and all legislative restrictions compelled to pass rigorous constitutional standards.

This seems to be what has happened in Canada with freedom of expression. The Supreme Court of Canada defined expression broadly to cover any attempt to convey meaning, from commercial advertising to 'the imagery of a sexual

---

[35] This approach to interpretation and that in the next section also allow more room for the kind of dialogue emphasised by Hogg and Bushell, above n. 1–legislative responses to judicial decisions that meet legislative aims and yet conform to judicial decisions – for more latitude is permitted to legislative action. For an example, see Roach, above n. 1, pp. 271–273. It is puzzling, however, that Hogg and Bushell cite (at 85–87) situations in which the courts direct how legislation might be redrafted to remain within constitutional bounds as examples of the potential for dialogue. To the extent that the court dictates how a legislature must respond, the relationship hardly seems one of dialogue but rather one of compliance (as indeed Hogg and Bushell acknowledge, though half-heartedly, at 98). See Hiebert (1999b), above n. 1, pp. 10–15, for discussion of one particular instance, and Manfredi and Kelly, above n. 1, generally.

gadget'.[36] All expressions are accorded, at least ostensibly, equal constitutional protection. Thus, the constitution is taken to have entrenched the right of the tobacco company, RJR-MacDonald, to advertise tobacco in the same terms as it protects the citizen's right to criticise her government.[37] Even if commercial expression has social utility (and it undeniably does), what compelling reason is there to subject its regulation to constitutional constraints normally reserved for political or artistic expression? If the rights are taken as minimal standards, some dimensions of expression can be left to unencumbered legislative control. The constitutional rights can be defined as basic guarantees, not all-encompassing codes of expression.

(b) Judicial Deference to Legislature or Executive in the Limitation of Rights

Courts can also leave room for legislative or executive participation through judicial deference, the courts deferring, on some questions, to the judgement of the legislature or executive. Under this model, a court does not insist that the legislature conform in all respects to the judge's own opinion. The court recognises that there can be legitimate differences of view, and allows the legislature some latitude. This kind of deference is common in judicial review of administrative action, where courts have often recognised that administrative tribunals, as the primary decision makers, should be permitted to develop their own interpretations of law. After all, legislatures have conferred decision-making power on the tribunals, often because the tribunals possess special expertise. The courts have expressed this deference in a variety of ways, depending on the drafting of the legislative regime. But a common formulation is that the courts should not intervene unless a tribunal's decision is manifestly unreasonable.

Deference is controversial in the area of rights protections, however. Human rights are generally considered to be supervening norms that should stand beyond all legislative or executive control. Their very purpose is to constrain government. It makes no sense (on this view) for courts to defer to their judgements. The Supreme Court of Canada has, for example, distinguished between constitutional and legislative norms in describing its deference towards administrative tribunals, holding that it wants to hear what administrative tribunals have to say about constitutional issues, but it will in the end make up its own mind.[38]

At the same time, the Court has indicated that it will exercise some deference towards the legislatures in its judgements on limitations of rights, when those limitations involve the evaluation of sociological fact or the balancing of multiple interests, on the grounds that legislatures are equally or better placed to make

---

[36] Irwin Toy v. Quebec (1989) 58 DLR (4th) 577 (SCC) at 606–608; R v. Butler (1992) 89 DLR (4th) 449 (SCC) at 472.

[37] RJR – MacDonald, above n. 10. See the critique in Hiebert (1999b), above n. 1, at 10–15.

[38] Cuddy Chicks v. Ontario (LRB) (1991) 81 DLR (4th) 121 (SCC) at 129–130.

those judgements. This has compensated, to some extent, for its expansive definition of such rights as freedom of expression. The rights may be defined broadly, but legislatures are given latitude in their limitation.[39] Using this deference to compensate for an over-broad interpretation generates tensions, however, for on the one hand it appears to weaken the protection of things that genuinely should be rights, and on the other it continues to treat things that should not be rights as though they were worthy of constitutional protection. In Canada, that tension came to the fore in *RJR-MacDonald*, where the Supreme Court drew back from the previous extent of its deference to limitations on advertising.[40]

Nevertheless, significant deference continues. The Court has even upheld legislation that was consciously framed, by Parliament, on the basis of the judgements of dissenting, not majority justices, in a previous *Charter* decision. In the first decision, the Supreme Court had divided 5–4 on the circumstances in which a person accused with sexual assault must, in the preparation of his defence, have access to the records of rape counsellors who had supported the victim in the aftermath of the alleged assault. The dissent had argued for a much stricter scope of disclosure. Parliament clearly preferred the dissenting judgement, and framed legislation that departed in material ways from the majority's position. In a subsequent challenge, the Supreme Court upheld that legislation, on the grounds that *Charter* decisions always left open a range of permissible responses, and that Parliament was entitled to listen to the voices of parties other than the courts (in this case, those vulnerable to sexual violence) when framing their responses. The Court focused primarily on the seriousness with which Parliament had considered the rights concerns, and specifically invoked the idea of dialogue in justifying that degree of deference.[41]

(c) Framing Norms

The interpretation of rights usually proceeds upon the assumption that one can, in theory, describe precisely what rights require and what they proscribe. It may

---

[39] See, for example: Irwin Toy, above n. 36, at 625–630; McKinney v. University of Guelph (1990) 76 DLR (4th) 545 (SCC) at 665–673. Hiebert (1999a), above n. 1, p. 28, rightly notes that the Court has rarely held the legislative objective to be insufficient to justify limiting the right. Judgements have, with very few exceptions, been decided on the proportionality of the measures.

[40] RJR-MacDonald, above n. 10, at 88ff.

[41] R v. O'Connor [1995] 4 SCR 411; An Act to amend the Criminal Code (Production of records in sexual offence proceedings), SC 1997, c 30; R v. Mills, above n. 1, especially pp. 19–20 and 37ff. For background, see Hiebert (1999b), above n. 1 pp. 16–25. Jamie Cameron has criticised the decision in Mills on the basis that it grants the legislature licence to ignore the courts' interpretation of the Charter, undermining the supremacy of the courts in constitutional review. Moreover, Parliament can do this without paying the institutional price demanded in section 33. See Cameron, above n. 1.

well be impossible to do so in advance – adjudication tends to elaborate norms case by case, as the court is confronted with the circumstances in which the norms operate – but in principle rights are susceptible of detailed statement. This assumption may not hold true of all guarantees, however. Some rights may be incapable of detailed elaboration. Their normative content may operate at a purely abstract level, compatible with a wide range of detailed instantiations. These norms are called 'framing norms', for they provide a framework of entitlement without specifying precisely what that entitlement entails.[42]

One of the best examples of a framing norm is the indigenous right to self-government, which has been widely discussed but not yet recognised in Canada.[43] It is unrealistic to think that self-government could ever be reduced to a highly specific set of requirements enforced by the courts. Its elements remain irreducibly abstract: the ability of indigenous peoples to participate in institutions that govern their communities; the right to have governmental institutions reflect norms determined in the community; the capacity of the community to control matters central to indigenous identity. The precise means by which these objectives could be achieved are as various as the communities themselves. Judicial review of such norms therefore takes a distinctive character. Instead of seeking to render the requirements progressively more explicit, it begins with the legislative measures under review, considers them in the light of the broad standards implicit in the norm, and decides simply on the basis of the broad standards whether they conform or not.

Framing norms are not as uncommon as they might appear. Indeed, to some extent all norms have an element of framework about them, for no matter how explicit they are made through the process of interpretation, they never address a specific case in all its particularity. At the last stage of any judgement, the judge must decide how the case falls in relation to the rule, using much the same approach as that described above. The difference between framing norms and other norms lies in the fact that in the former, one no longer expects to be able

---

[42] Jeremy Webber, '*Beyond Regret: Mabo's Implications for Australian Constitutionalism*', in Duncan Ivison *et al* (eds), *Political Theory and the Rights of Indigenous Peoples* (Cambridge: Cambridge University Press 2000), pp. 60–88 at 75–76.

[43] See, for example, the form of the right in the failed set of constitutional amendments known in Canada as the Charlottetown Accord: proposed sections 35.1ff of the Constitution Act, 1982, Charlottetown Accord, Draft Legal Text (9 October 1992), sections 29ff. An inherent right of self-government was recognised, but its instantiation was to be determined through negotiations supervised by the courts. The Corbière decision, above n. 1, evinces a similar spirit. It too concerned the design of indigenous governmental institutions (although not under an inherent right). There, a statutory provision denying non-resident band members the right to vote was ruled invalid under the Charter. But the declaration of invalidity was suspended for 18 months in order to permit a replacement provision to be developed.

to render the norms increasingly concrete. Rather, one accepts that they will remain permanently abstract and one is content to work with that abstraction.[44]

The recognition of a class of 'framing norms' does make a difference. To take one example, in a series of cases in the late 1980s the Supreme Court of Canada held that the *Charter*'s guarantee of freedom of association included no special protection of the right of workers to bargain collectively. The court came to this decision even though freedom of association had commonly been used, in international conventions, to refer to workers' rights of collective action. The principal reason for the court's decision was its concern that the phrase, 'freedom of association', could not have been intended to constitutionalise Canada's highly detailed collective bargaining regime. It noted that other countries had adopted very different forms of workers' control.[45] This reasoning is right as far as it goes. It would indeed be inappropriate to hold that the labour relations regime of the 1980s had been frozen in constitutional stone. But at the same time, the court's decision deprived freedom of association of one of its principal contemporary elements. The problem may have lain in the court's assumption that *Charter* rights had to be interpreted in a manner that progressively developed a single, precise, determinate content to the right, and that only that content could have normative force. Instead, freedom of association, insofar as it relates to workers' collective action, may be best conceived as a framing norm, establishing a principle at a level of abstraction only, leaving wide latitude to legislatures as to how the right might be fulfilled.[46]

Framing norms have become much more familiar in recent years as a result of the development of the European Union. The European Commission's directives take this form. They do not stipulate the measures that governments must adopt. They establish broad objectives and leave to governments how those objectives might be achieved.

For the purposes of this paper, the chief significance of framing norms is that they presuppose a substantial measure of collaboration – of dialogue – between courts and legislature in the practical definition of rights. The courts set the framework; the legislature determines the means.

(d) Nonjusticiable Norms

Finally, courts may simply find that some norms are not susceptible to judicial review and leave them entirely to the political process. Some norms (such as the

---

[44] It is important, however, that framing norms are limited to situations in which norms genuinely are incapable of further precision. Otherwise, court decisions can leave legislatures in an invidious position, having little sense of how legislation might be redrafted in order to render it valid.

[45] Re Public Service Employee Relations Act [1987] 1 SCR 313; PSAC v. Canada [1987] 1 SCR 424; RWDSU v. Saskatchewan [1987] 1 SCR 460; ILO Convention (No 87) concerning Freedom of Association and Protection of the Right to Organise (1948).

[46] That said, there are reasons to be grateful for the non-recognition of collective bargaining under the Charter: Webber, above n. 4, pp. 141–142.

commitment to equalisation payments between governments in section 36 of Canada's *Constitution Act, 1982*) may expressly set aside judicial review; these are the 'programmatic rights' discussed previously. But it is also possible that the courts might find that other provisions do not give rise to judicial review, either because a different remedy is specified or because the subject matter of the right is held simply to be inappropriate for judicial determination.[47] In either case the definition of the right would be left within the legislative realm.

3.3. Mechanisms for Legislative and Executive Involvement in the Definition and Enforcement of Rights

Finally, there are many mechanisms by which the legislature and executive can themselves shape the meaning of rights.

(a) Democratic Participation

Most importantly, the very existence of democratic government and popular participation serves to protect rights. Constitutional lawyers tend to think of rights entirely in terms of constraint – and specifically constraint of the legislature – but without doubt, the most powerful bulwark of rights in a democracy is broad participation by an engaged citizenry in the business of government. That participation contributes to the articulation of rights through the prominent role that rights play in parliamentary debate and executive decision-making. The ability to petition, to question one's government, and to seek to change governments constitute powerful means of challenging abusive conduct and vindicating rights claims. It is profoundly wrong – indeed dangerously so – to believe that rights must operate only by constraining democratic action.

(b) Legislative/Executive Enforcement

Moreover, the responsibility to enforce constitutional protections has at times been conferred directly on the legislature and executive, rather than courts. This is true, for example, of the guarantees in the Canadian *Constitution Act, 1867* with respect to religious schools. Although schools are normally under provincial jurisdiction, those guarantees provide that an appeal from any act or decision 'affecting any Right or Privilege of the Protestant or Roman Catholic Minority of the Queen's Subjects' lies to the federal Governor-in-Council (the federal

---

47 Canada's denominational schools guarantees in the Constitution Act, 1867 (below, n. 48) have been analysed as having two dimensions, one enforceable by both the courts and the federal executive and legislature, the other enforceable only by the latter: Tiny Separate School Trustees v. The King [1928] AC 363 (PC) at 369–370. Canadian courts have rejected the 'political questions doctrine', under which certain ostensibly constitutional questions would be deemed non-justiciable: Operation Dismantle v. The Queen [1985] 1 SCR 441 at 472 (per Wilson J).

cabinet). If the cabinet's order is not obeyed, the federal Parliament is empowered to pass remedial legislation. The Fourteenth Amendment to the Constitution of the United States (adopted following the Civil War to entrench the equality of the former slaves) also provided for Congressional action to enforce its terms.[48] Legislative enforcement is particularly useful when trying to protect the rights of minorities within complex public institutions, where judicial remedies may prove inadequately flexible or incapable of creating detailed remedial administrative regimes.

Legislatures have also pursued rights within their own jurisdictions, enacting declarations of rights and establishing commissions for their enforcement. Undoubtedly, in Canada, the practical impact of these measures on the lives of individuals has far outstripped the effect of the *Charter*, for they apply to private as well as public action, and guard against discrimination in employment, in housing, and in a host of other day-to-day contexts. The doctrines developed under these regimes have also had a significant impact on the interpretation of the *Charter*, notably in the concept of discrimination adopted by the courts.[49]

(c) Prior Examination and Review

Constitutional bills of rights also stimulate a measure of self-scrutiny on the part of the legislature and executive. This helps to ensure that legislation is kept within constitutional bounds. It may also furnish careful discussions of rights, which may in turn influence the courts if the legislation is subsequently challenged. The self-scrutiny can occur in myriad places – in law reform commissions, administrative tribunals, the decisions of ombudsmen, and so on. In Canada, there has also been a structured process for reviewing legislation to ensure compliance with the *Charter*. In the period immediately following adoption of the *Charter*, existing legislation was examined and amended to bring it into conformity with the law officers' understanding of the *Charter*'s requirements. Indeed, the entry into force of the equality guarantee in the *Charter* was delayed for three years to allow this process to occur. Now, as part of the regular

---

[48] Constitution Act, 1867, section 93(3) and (4); Constitution of the United States, 14th Amendment. This is also one of the strategies used by the Human Rights Act 1998 c 42 (UK), section 10, to get around the limitations imposed by parliamentary sovereignty; Ministers are empowered to amend legislation to bring it into conformity with the European Convention on Human Rights if there are 'compelling reasons' to do so. The power of the Canadian government to disallow provincial statutes – now in disuse, but used actively during the first decades of Confederation – was also exercised using quasi-judicial forms, and often with rights concerns as the basis for review (although in this case the concerns often related to property). The power is contained in Constitution Act, 1867, section 90.

[49] For a clear example of the impact of these regimes, see: Andrews, above n. 10, at 16–19 (per McIntyre J).

procedure for drafting new legislation, each law is scrutinised to ensure it conforms.[50]

The standards applied internally can be more demanding than those applied by the courts, the law officers taking a more expansive definition of the rights. This can happen haphazardly, as law officers make the wrong guess as to the interpretation that will ultimately be adopted by the courts. But sometimes governments purposely disagree with the court's interpretation. A good example occurred in relation to Ontario's Sunday-closing legislation. That law prescribed Sunday as the common day of rest in the retail sector. There were exceptions, notably one designed to accommodate individuals whose religious beliefs specified a day of rest other than Sunday, although this exception was restricted to stores under a certain size. The Supreme Court of Canada upheld the restriction as establishing an acceptable balance between the proprietors' beliefs and the interests of the employees. Yet, under a new government, the Ontario legislature amended the law so that the religious exemption was no longer limited by the store's size.[51]

(d) Arguments in Justification

As already noted, the Canadian *Charter* itself implicitly invites governments to justify their legislation as part of *Charter* challenges. They sometimes do this in anticipation. They do it in argument before the courts. Legislatures have also, in substance, re-enacted legislation that has been invalidated by the Supreme Court of Canada, or have enacted legislation that appears at variance with the reasons of the majority of the Court, advancing renewed justification under section 1. They have thereby expressed their disagreement with the Court's decision and forcefully re-engaged the debate over justification. Of course, by declining to use section 33 and relying instead on section 1, they have left the ultimate decision on validity to the courts. But in at least one such case – the enactment of provisions to limit the circumstances in which an alleged victim's

---

50   Department of Justice Act, RSC 1985, c J-2, section 4.1. For a discussion of this process, see: Hiebert (1999b), above n. 1, pp. 6–9. See also Brian Slattery, 'A Theory of the Charter' Osgoode Hall Law Journal, 25 (1987), pp. 701–747; Janet Hiebert, 'A Hybrid-Approach to Protect Rights? An Argument in Favour of Supplementing Canadian Judicial Review with Australia's Model of Parliamentary Scrutiny' Federal Law Review, 26 (1998), pp. 115–138. For similar requirements, see Canadian Bill of Rights, SC 1960, c 44, section 3; New Zealand Bill of Rights Act 1990, No. 109 (NZ), section 7 and the discussion in Keith, above n. 20, pp. 731–735; Human Rights Act 1998 c 42 (UK), section 19.

51   R v. Edwards Books and Art [1986] 2 SCR 713. The legislation was amended by SO 1989, c 3. Hogg and Bushell, above n. 1, pp. 104–105, give another example of the same phenomenon, where the Canadian Parliament revised legislation dealing with the tax deductibility of child support payments, even though the government had won the previous Charter action.

rape counselling records would be released to the accused (discussed above) – Parliament's arguments have been successful.[52]

Government consideration of rights concerns, as part of its exercise in justification, can therefore have an impact, at times dramatic, on the practice of judicial deliberation.

(e) Political Pressure on Judicial Decision

Finally, there is one last set of mechanisms by which governments can influence the interpretation of rights: direct political pressure. We generally think of these mechanisms as being plainly antagonistic to rights, not contributing to any sort of 'dialogue'. They often strike us as illegitimate exercises of power, almost certainly impairing the rights of individuals. This caution is wise. Judicial decision making is distinctive in its acute attention to the individual case, so that decisions are made in a manner sensitive to the situation, thereby doing justice (as far as human fallibility permits) to the interests of the individuals concerned. Political argument rarely attends so carefully to the individual case. If legislatures or executives made all the decisions, we would run the risk of losing sight of individuals' interests in our rush to achieve a social aim. Our defence of judicial independence and due process is therefore a profoundly important principle.

But the fact remains that mechanisms for political pressure do exist, and they are deployed (among other things) in disputes over the meaning of rights. They include fierce political criticism, pressure on the resources of the courts, the packing of courts, physical intimidation, forced removal, and ultimately constitutional amendment. Some of these mechanisms are legitimate in the sense that they are expressly contemplated by the constitution – such as powers of judicial appointment, or the requirements for constitutional amendment. Nor are their effects always bad. They are sometimes used, it appears in retrospect, on the side of the angels. This was true, for example, of Franklin Delano Roosevelt's court-packing plan, which may well have influenced the US Supreme Court to overturn its doctrine of substantive due process, thus paving the way for the New Deal legislation.[53] Their contribution, then, is not unremittingly negative, although we generally do well to assume the worst.

---

[52] See above, n. 41, and text accompanying that note. The substantial re-enactment of provisions declared invalid occurred in response to R v. Daviault [1994] 3 SCR 63. The subsequent legislation is An Act to amend the Criminal Code (Self-induced intoxication), SC 1995, c 32. There has yet to be a definitive ruling on the constitutionality of that legislation largely because, even if valid, it would only apply in very special circumstances. Those decisions that have considered its validity, all by lower courts, are divided: R v. Vickberg (1998) 54 CRR (2d) 83 (BCSC); R v. Brenton (1999) 180 CLR (4th) 314 (NWT SC); R v. Dunn (1999) CRDJ 441 (Ont SCJ).

[53] Laurence Tribe, *American Constitutional Law* vol 1, 3rd ed (New York: New York Foundation Press 2000), pp. 14, 1360–1361.

But despite the evil or ambivalence of their effects, we should remember them. They bring home the fact that no matter how we insulate the judicial role, the relationship is one of institutional interaction, not complete autonomy. Realising that, we can work to structure the interaction in the most appropriate manner, including establishing protections for judicial autonomy.

Moreover, in a backhanded way, recognising the existence of these forces relativises and clarifies our claims about judicial review. I noted at the beginning of this paper that justifications for judicial review frequently rely on the need to guard against the grossest of abuses. There is a real question, however, whether judicial review is much of a bulwark when a political system decays to such a desperate degree. Even if the courts do stand up (and history shows that they often do not[54]), the political process has levers at its command to overcome the courts if the democratic ethic of rights protection is absent. This is not an argument for ignoring the potential for abuse, nor is it an argument against human-rights adjudication in normal times. But it does suggest that the remedies to gross abuses lie within a broader social/political approach, and that judicial review needs to be justified in terms of its relative contribution in normal, not abnormal times. This too drives us back upon the analysis of interaction, relationship and balance.

4. DIALOGUE IN THREE STRATEGIES FOR HUMAN RIGHTS PROTECTION

There are therefore a wide array of mechanisms to provide for institutional dialogue in the definition and enforcement of rights. Nor is this account exhaustive. The reader will doubtless have added his or her own examples.

In this section, I will examine in more detail three of these mechanisms – all employed in Canada, one in Australia – to assess their strengths and weaknesses as strategies for rights protection. The mechanisms are:

(a) implied rights;
(b) express constitutional guarantees, subject to legislative derogation; and
(c) a statutory bill of rights, protected by a manner-and-form requirement.

I will focus primarily on the second and third, citing the first principally by way of contrast.

---

[54] The US Supreme Court's acceptance of the internment of Japanese Americans during World War II is often cited: Korematsu v. United States 323 US 214 (1944). Institutional mechanisms within the public service can sometimes be more effective. In a seminar at the Faculty of Law, McGill University, based on his book, *In the Highest Degree Odious: Detention Without Trial in Wartime Britain* (Oxford: Oxford University Press 1994), Brian Simpson noted the institutional ethic of the British Home Office in the defence of the liberties of the subject, and the relative strength of this branch of the public service, in contrast to the courts, in the protection of the rights of detainees during World War II.

4.1. Implied Rights

As mentioned above, this mechanism involves the determination that certain rights are implicit in the constitution. Commonly, the rights are founded upon constitutional terms that establish democratic institutions (from which rights to political free speech are derived) or establish the courts (from which norms to protect judicial independence are derived).

Among jurisdictions with which I am familiar, a jurisprudence of implied rights is most developed in Australia. There, the High Court of Australia has recognised a right of free political expression, working off the provisions establishing representative government in the Australian Constitution (notably sections 7 and 24, which state that members of the Senate and House of Representatives are to be 'directly chosen by the people'). In the first of these cases, Brennan J (as he then was) summarised the essential argument:

> ...where a representative democracy is constitutionally entrenched, it carries with it those legal incidents which are essential to the effective maintenance of that form of government. Once it is recognized that a representative democracy is constitutionally prescribed, the freedom of discussion which is essential to sustain it is as firmly entrenched in the Constitution as the system of government which the Constitution expressly ordains.[55]

This right was used to strike down laws that prohibited criticism of members of the Industrial Relations Commission and that limited television advertising in elections. It also prompted the High Court to revise the law of defamation insofar as it applies to criticism of public officials.[56]

Other rights too might be implied from the constitution. In Australia, there was some discussion over whether a state's constitution required rough equality in the determination of electoral boundaries (so that each person's vote would be of approximately equal value). The court refused to find such a requirement.[57] The High Court has declined to hold that a general right of equality can be derived from the federal constitution.[58] But other principles with strong rights implications have been implied. In both Australia and Canada, the courts have developed constitutional guarantees of the independence of the judiciary, from which additional limitations have been derived: in Canada, judicial review of

---

[55] Nationwide News Pty Ltd v. Wills (1992) 177 CLR 1 at 48–49 (per Brennan J). See also: Australian Capital Television Pty Ltd v. Commonwealth (1992) 177 CLR 106.

[56] Nationwide News, ibid; Australian Capital Television, ibid; Theophanous v. Herald & Weekly Times Ltd (1994) 182 CLR 104; Lange v. Australian Broadcasting Corporation (1997) 145 ALR 96.

[57] McGinty v. Western Australia (1996) 186 CLR 140.

[58] Leeth v. Commonwealth (1992) 174 CLR 455; Kruger v. Commonwealth (1997) 146 ALR 126.

the jurisdiction of administrative tribunals has been constitutionalised on this basis; in Australia, the principle of the separation of powers has been used to strike down a law designed to keep a named offender in preventative detention beyond the end of his original sentence.[59]

Implied rights involve the finding that rights have been constitutionally entrenched, but do so in a particularly confined way. They do not directly promote dialogue between legislature and courts – they do not involve any special interaction between court and legislature in the definition of rights – but they do tend to leave substantial latitude to the legislature.

Implied rights are confined by the very fact that they are based on implication. There is no general, unambiguous statement of the rights. The courts must, above all, establish that the rights are entrenched, even though the document makes no reference to them. There is often disagreement over the standard to be applied when finding an implied right: does the right have to be necessary to any reasonable interpretation of the text, or is it sufficient that it be broadly congruent with the constitution's principles? There is the problem of distinguishing between, on the one hand, a mere assumption on which a constitutional provision is based and, on the other, a true implication, in which the assumption itself is constitutionally protected.[60] Moreover, the very fact that an implied right is not express, yet has such a significant impact on legislative authority, encourages judicial restraint. Courts are less likely to fall prey to one common

---

[59] The Canadian decisions tend to use section 96 of the Constitution Act, 1867 as the foundation for the protection of judicial independence in Canada although judicial independence has recently been recognised as a general unwritten principle: Re Remuneration of Judges [1997] 3 SCR 3. Section 96 is, on its face, merely a power of appointment, although it is the first in a set of provisions that enshrine the Act of Settlement, 1701 (UK) in Canadian constitutional law. For discussion of the implications based upon it, see Peter Hogg, *Constitutional Law of Canada*, 3rd ed (Scarborough: Carswell 1992) at 184ff. For the constitutionalisation of judicial review of administrative jurisdiction, see: Crevier v. A-G Quebec [1981] 2 SCR 220. For the separation of the judicial power in Australia, see Leslie Zines, *The High Court and the Constitution*, 4th ed (Sydney: Butterworths 1997) at 161–218. For the derivation of individual rights from the separation of powers, see: Zines, *ibid*, at 202–212; Chu Kheng Lim v. Minister for Immigration, Local Government and Ethnic Affairs (1992) 176 CLR 1; Kable v. Director of Public Prosecutions (NSW) (1996) 138 ALR 577.

[60] Australian Capital Television, above n. 55, at 135 (per Mason CJ). A good example is section 92 of the Australian Constitution, which provides: 'On the imposition of uniform duties of customs, trade, commerce, and intercourse among the States ... shall be absolutely free.' For many years, this section was interpreted as prohibiting a range of government measures, especially nationalisation, that would interfere with free markets. In 1988, however, the High Court in Cole v. Whitfield (1988) 165 CLR 360 ruled that the section only prohibited trade barriers, such as tariffs. The framers of section 92 may have assumed the existence of private ownership, but they did not intend to set it in constitutional stone. See Zines, *ibid*, at 108–153.

hazard of constitutionalised charters of rights – the temptation towards maximal rather than minimal definitions of rights.

Finally, an implied right always depends upon cues in the text, and this limits the range of rights that can be implied. The rights tend to be political, strongly tied to the integrity of public institutions. Hence, they protect political speech (on the basis that the constitution establishes representative government) but not artistic speech. In Australia, an implied guarantee of equality foundered precisely because the right claimed was general and sweeping, lacking a clear constitutional touchstone.[61]

Implied rights therefore have a restricted scope, tightly tied to the express provisions of the constitution. They tend to be focused solely on political freedoms. And because the rights are inferred, because they are derivative, never primary, and because they are the product of complex interpolation, there is always the potential for adjustment into the future. These limitations are virtues if one believes that constitutionally entrenched guarantees should be restricted to truly fundamental principles, dealing with the citizen's political relationship to the state.

4.2. Express Rights, Subject to Derogation

Under implied rights, judicial review has a restricted role simply as a result of the allusive and ambiguous form in which the rights are expressed (or unexpressed). In the second mechanism for rights protection examined here – express rights subject to derogation by the legislature – the rights are stated just as they are in any constitutionalised bill of rights, but they are then subject to legislative derogation: the legislature can choose to override them in a manner expressly provided in the constitution.

The *Canadian Charter of Rights and Freedoms* is the principal example of this strategy. Section 33 of the *Charter* reads in part:

(1) Parliament or the legislature of a province may expressly declare in an Act of Parliament or of the legislature, as the case may be, that the Act or a provision thereof shall operate notwithstanding a provision included in section 2 or sections 7 to 15 of this Charter.
(2) An Act or a provision of an Act in respect of which a declaration made under this section is in effect shall have such operation as it would have but for the provision of this Charter referred to in the declaration.

Certain conditions limit the use of the override, although the section itself keeps these to a minimum and the courts have been reluctant to find that more exist by implication. First, the override is only applicable to certain rights (those found in sections 2 and 7 to 15). Paradoxically, these tend to be the most broadly

---

[61]   Above n. 58.

accepted rights, including freedom of religion, freedom of association, freedom of expression, rights arising in the context of criminal proceedings, and equality. The chief exclusions are rights to vote and, significantly, mobility rights and official languages. The last two exclusions give a clue to the rationale underlying the choice to include or exclude. Mobility rights and language rights were highly controversial among a number of provinces at the time of the *Charter*'s adoption, the former because of potential interference with provincial policies with respect to economic development and absentee ownership, the latter because of Quebec's desire to require the use of French in certain contexts. At the same time, the federal government was intensely committed to both sets of provisions as ways of requiring both economic integration and bilingualism. The override excluded precisely those rights most likely to be subject to derogation.

Secondly, any invocation of section 33 is subject to a five-year sunset clause. At the end of five years, the derogation lapses (although it can be re-enacted indefinitely). This requires that derogations be justified repeatedly, at periodic intervals. Five years was chosen as the period because that coincides with the maximum term of any government.[62]

Superficially, section 33 of the Canadian *Charter* is similar to the 'notwithstanding' clause in the *Canadian Bill of Rights*, the statutory bill which I introduced above and will discuss further below. Each clause apparently permits the legislature to derogate, and in each case, derogation must be express in the derogating act itself, in order to trigger a popular debate in which the government will be compelled to justify its actions. Indeed, in this respect the *Canadian Bill of Rights* served as the model for section 33 of the Canadian *Charter*. But in another respect, the two instruments are very different. In a statutory bill of rights, it is the very ability to derogate that renders the bill effectual; that capacity transforms the bill from what would be an invalid constraint on the substance of legislation to one of procedure only. Paradoxically, then, it is the very ability to set the rights aside that renders the statutory instrument binding on later legislation. In the *Charter*, on the other hand, the rights are constitutionally entrenched; they control, of their own force, all legislation. There, the notwithstanding clause does nothing but allow the legislature to set the rights aside.

In the *Charter*, section 33 was a compromise between parliamentary sovereignty – the British constitutional doctrine that treats the legislature as the supreme branch of government – and judicial review. At the time of patriation of the Canadian constitution in the early 1980s, the governments of Saskatchewan and Manitoba opposed the inclusion of an entrenched charter of rights precisely because they believed it would shift decision-making from the legislature to the

---

[62]   The limitations on the use of the clause are all found in Canadian Charter of Rights and Freedoms, section 33. For the refusal of the courts to imply more restrictions, see text accompanying n. 69 below.

courts. Saskatchewan's left-leaning government cited the US constitutional doctrine of substantive due process (which had impeded the adoption of much social legislation up to the 1930s), as a reason for limiting the powers of judicial review. Those provinces agreed to the *Charter* only on condition that it include a clause permitting legislatures to derogate from its guarantees. Section 33 was therefore adopted precisely because of misgivings, among some governments, about rights review.[63] The section has been seen by many (not least in Canada), as inconsistent with the very idea of a charter of rights. Some have argued that it should be removed.[64]

Such a stark opposition is unfortunate, however. There is a justification for the notwithstanding clause – perhaps the best justification – that sees it as establishing an appropriate balance between courts and legislature, through the facilitation of dialogue between those institutions with respect to rights. According to this view, section 33 is not anti-rights; it simply allows the legislature to participate in their interpretation and application.[65]

The justification starts from the premise that there can be legitimate differences over the definition of rights. There is reason, then, to provide an outlet through which alternative understandings of rights can be advanced and defended. This is especially true when, under entrenched charters of rights, courts' interpretations can be very difficult to correct (the usual mechanisms being revision by the courts themselves or constitutional amendment).

It also recognises that different types of institutions carry different advantages – and different biases – in rights definition.[66] Courts excel at the sober analysis of specific claims in a manner that pays close attention to individuals and that is isolated (though only in relative terms) from broader political concerns. They are especially effective where all considerations relevant to a particular dispute are well defined, so that interests are crystallised and the parties implicated are known and represented. They depend, in their procedure, on parties appearing

---

[63] 'Patriation' is the term coined in Canada to describe the creation of a domestic amending formula for the Canadian constitution (prior to 1982, the principal constitutional document was simply a statute of the British Parliament, amendable only by that Parliament). As part of patriation the constitution was significantly amended, notably by the introduction of the Canadian Charter of Rights and Freedoms. For discussions of the process leading to patriation, see: Roy Romanow et al, *Canada ... Notwithstanding: The Making of the Constitution 1976–1982* (Toronto: Carswell/Methuen 1984); Webber (1994), above n. 9, pp. 99–120.

[64] See below n. 76.

[65] For influential arguments in favour of the clause, see: Paul Weiler, *'Rights and Judges in a Democracy: A New Canadian Version'* University of Michigan Journal of Law Reform, 18 (1984), pp. 51–92 at 79–92; Peter Russell, *'Standing Up for Notwithstanding'* Alberta Law Review, 29 (1991), pp. 293–309.

[66] See the more extensive discussion of institutional strengths and weaknesses in Webber (1993), above n. 8, at 218ff and Webber, above n. 4, at 137–144.

before them and arguing all relevant considerations. They have great difficulty dealing with issues in which interests are widely distributed, so that no one party has sufficient interest to appear and the only viable procedural approach would involve inquiry and investigation. Courts focus overwhelmingly on protection against government interference, not positive action by government to advance the interests of individuals or groups, for judicial review is conceived (rightly) as a restraint on government action, rather than the assertion of an alternative or complementary governmental authority. The net effect of this, however, is that judicial review tends to privilege private over public action, for only the latter is subjected to *Charter* scrutiny. Finally, courts do best when the interests are simply aligned – when the dispute takes a bipolar (with two opposed positions) rather than polycentric form (where a multitude of competing interests need to be balanced). The former accords most closely to courts' adversarial procedures, in which, paradigmatically, two parties contend, marshalling their own sets of evidence. Indeed, because of their adversarial procedure and their bias towards the restraint of government, courts are prone to simplify rights claims so that they conform, as closely as possible, to a bipolar form – the individual pitted against the state – even when the state may simply be serving as a stand-in for the broadly distributed interests of individuals in society at large.

Legislatures have strengths and weaknesses that broadly correspond to those of courts. They are much better at dealing with polycentric issues and with widely distributed interests. They have procedures well adapted to investigation and inquiry. They are able to act positively, deploying resources to attain ends rather than standing back to let the situation be determined by the play of private forces. Those advantages come with disadvantages. Legislatures can respond to a perceived balance of interests – or to a strongly articulated majority interest – in a manner that has insufficient regard for minorities or individuals. Because they work by majority rule, they can weigh all individuals' self-defined interests equally, when some interests may deserve added weight because of their fundamental character (religious beliefs; freedom of expression; the freedom to associate; mobility rights). In their pursuit of general social interests, they can lose sight of the particular situation of individuals.

Section 33, it might then be argued, achieves an appropriate balance between the benefits of the legislature and those of the courts in the definition of rights. It provides for judicial review on a full array of rights concerns, but it also allows legislatures to have the last word if they disagree fundamentally on how rights have been defined and applied. Even then, rights concerns are highlighted because of the requirement that the legislature be explicit in its intention to override the constitution's declaration of rights. This triggers democratic scrutiny, which only the strongest justification is likely to surmount.

This may be the best justification for section 33, but in practice the section has been less than successful at fostering a productive dialogue. It has been used in seventeen situations (although in one the act was never proclaimed in force).

The experience has been decidedly mixed. The use of section 33 has been concentrated in few hands. The province of Quebec was responsible for fourteen of the seventeen instances; although other jurisdictions have from time to time vehemently disagreed with *Charter* decisions, all except Alberta have tended, in recent years, to shy away from section 33 and to use renewed justification under section 1 instead. Moreover, in a great many instances, the use of section 33 has escaped public notice almost entirely. Were it not for the recent work of Tsvi Kahana, thirteen of those instances would have remained in utter obscurity.[67]

Quebec was the first jurisdiction to use the clause. In June 1982, soon after the proclamation of the *Charter*, it passed a law invoking section 33 with respect to all existing Quebec statutes. It then proceeded to insert a comparable clause in each subsequent act. This was done to protest against the patriation of the constitution over Quebec's objections. The Quebec government, under the *indépendantiste* Parti québécois, had participated in the negotiations leading up to patriation, but had ultimately rejected the package agreed to by Ottawa and the other provinces. Quebec took the position that it should be able to veto constitutional reform, given that it was the only province with a French-speaking majority. When patriation proceeded regardless, it opted out of the new *Charter* to the maximum extent possible.[68]

This use of the notwithstanding clause was highly unusual, focused as it was on the legitimacy of the constitutional order as a whole. The blanket use of the clause was challenged in *Ford* v. *Quebec*,[69] the plaintiffs arguing that the wording of section 33 contemplated a more precise or explicit derogation. They suggested that a valid derogation should occur only after the courts had ruled on the rights concerns, should identify precisely what rights were to be set aside, or should specify the aspect of the law to be protected from scrutiny. They argued that this interpretation was justified by the signalling function of the notwithstanding clause; if there were no express identification of the rights in question – if the invocation of the clause simply exempted all statutes from rights review – no sensible debate over the issues could be joined. This may have been right, but the Supreme Court saw that such requirements, once established, were likely to become disguised substantive limitations on the ability of the legislature to invoke section 33. It declined to start down that road and instead upheld the blanket invocation of the notwithstanding clause. In so doing, it confirmed that

---

[67] See Tsvi Kahana, '*The notwithstanding mechanism and public discussion: Lessons from the ignored practice of section 33 of the Charter*' Canadian Public Administration, 44 (2001), pp. 255–291, who describes in detail each of the uses of the clause. I am grateful to Janet Hiebert for bringing the pending appearance of this article to my attention.

[68] The blanket override was An Act Respecting the Constitution Act, 1982, SQ 1982, c 21. For the circumstances leading to its adoption, see: Webber (1994), above n. 9, especially at 113ff.

[69] Above n. 23.

section 33 was a recognition of parliamentary sovereignty within the rights context, one that was not to be hedged about by judicially imposed restrictions.

In the Quebec provincial election of 1985, the federalist Liberal Party defeated the Parti québécois. The new government stopped invoking section 33 in every piece of legislation, but it did not repeal previous invocations. Instead, it let them expire as they reached the five-year limit. This exposed, for the first time, Quebec's legislation to full *Charter* review. Since then, Quebec has invoked section 33 on thirteen occasions. Twelve concerned highly complex legislative regimes dealing with pensions (raising concerns of gender discrimination), the role of religion in education (freedom of religion), and agricultural development (age discrimination). These twelve instances received no public attention.[70] The reasons are obscure, but are probably due to the arcane nature of the legislative regimes, the limited legitimacy of the *Charter* in Quebec (in each case the first use of the clause occurred shortly after the blanket invocations were discontinued), and the fact that in the education acts, the provisions were closely related to constitutionally entrenched guarantees of religious school boards.

In 1988, however, there was a very public and highly contested use of the clause. This occurred in response to the decision in the *Ford* case noted above. That decision had struck down provisions of Quebec's language law that required that commercial signs and company names be in French only. Ironically, the most important sections were invalidated on the basis of Quebec's own, statutory, *Charter of Human Rights and Freedoms*, not the Canadian *Charter*, for the sign law provisions were protected from the Canadian *Charter* by a still subsisting notwithstanding clause.

Ford generated a fierce political controversy in Quebec. Most francophone Quebecers might have been willing to relax the province's language laws, but they did not want relaxation to be dictated by the Supreme Court of Canada, in a manner that removed control from Quebecers' elected representatives. Quebec therefore re-enacted the sign law provisions, in modified form, this time protecting them against the Canadian *Charter* through the use of the notwithstanding clause.[71] Here, the clause was used precisely in the manner contemplated in the 'best justification' for section 33 offered above; a legislative majority set aside rights review on the basis that freedom of linguistic expression, in commercial signage, was outweighed by other public considerations.

The Quebec government paid a significant price for its use of the clause. Anglophone members of the government resigned, many Quebec anglophones left the provincial Liberals, and an English-speaking protest movement took hold. Most importantly, anger in the rest of Canada over Bill 178 (as the act was known) contributed to the defeat of the Meech Lake Accord, a set of

---

[70] Kahana, above n. 67.
[71] An Act to Amend the Charter of the French Language, SQ 1988, c 54 (Bill 178).

constitutional amendments designed to address Quebec's constitutional griev-ances. The events demonstrated, then, that broad popular debate could be generated by the use of section 33 and that governments could incur heavy costs as a result – even when, as in Quebec, they retained the support of majority opinion within the province. Five years later, once passions within the province had cooled, the Liberal government again amended the sign law so that it fell within the limits set by the Supreme Court of Canada and allowed the notwith-standing clause to lapse – although by that time, much of the damage had been done.[72]

The notwithstanding clause has only been used on three occasions outside Quebec. The first was in the Yukon Territory in 1982. This provision, never proclaimed in force, was designed to protect aboriginal nominations to the Land Planning Board, It received no public attention and was almost certainly unne-cessary given the distinctive treatment of indigenous peoples in the Canadian constitution.[73] In 1986, Saskatchewan used the clause to protect a statute adopted to end a strike. This was ultimately proven unnecessary when the Supreme Court held, in a separate case, that the right to strike was not protected under the *Charter*'s guarantee of freedom of association. The invocation of the clause elicited real critical debate, although the Supreme Court's subsequent decision took some of the force out of that discussion.[74] In 2000, the Alberta legislature amended its Marriage Act to define marriage in exclusively heterosexual terms, invoking section 33. Again, there was public opposition, although muted, perhaps because capacity to marry falls within federal jurisdiction and Alberta's enact-ment would therefore have been purely symbolic. In 1998 the Alberta government seriously contemplated the use of section 33 in two other circumstances that would have had a material effect on legal rights. In each case it retreated, in one instance in response to a very strong public reaction.[75]

Thus, the clause has been invoked very rarely outside Quebec, and even in

---

[72] An Act to Amend the Charter of the French Language, SQ 1993, c 40. For the Bill 178 controversy generally, see Webber (1994), above n. 9, at 138ff.

[73] Land Planning Act, SY 1982, c 22, s 39(1); Kahana, above n. 67, at 258 and 266.

[74] SGEU Dispute Settlement Act, SS 1984–85–86, c 111, section 9; Kahana, *ibid* at 269–270. The Supreme Court's decision was RWDSU, above n. 45.

[75] Marriage Amendment Act, 2000, SA 2000, c 3; Kahana, *ibid* at 268–269. The circumstances in which Alberta contemplated but refrained from invoking the clause were in a proposed statute to limit the damages payable for the forced sterilisation of certain classes of disabled people under previous provincial legislation, and the province's response to the decision in Vriend, above n. 1. In the former case, strong public outcry forced the government to withdraw the bill. In the latter (which would have reversed the Supreme Court of Canada's extension of the Alberta's Individual's Rights Protection Act, RSA 1980, c I-2 to ban discrimination on the basis of sexual orientation), the government itself decided not to use the clause, despite demands from its supporters. See Hiebert (1999a), above n. 1, at 30 and 34.

Quebec most of its uses have been buried in highly complex regimes, in six cases closely related to existing guarantees of religious school boards. Indeed, it is fair to say that section 33 has achieved very little legitimacy outside francophone Quebec, with the partial exception of Alberta. It was fiercely criticised by many rights advocates at the time of the *Charter*'s adoption. There are still forceful calls for its removal, as well as periodic demands that stricter conditions be placed on its use.[76] Legislative intervention under section 33 tends to be seen as plainly and simply anti-rights, not as a means by which legislatures can insist on their own interpretations of rights.

Section 33 has, in the end, made very little difference to the way in which rights are conceived under the *Charter*, at least in English-speaking Canada. The mythology of judicial review on rights grounds remains very strong – the sense that courts protect rights, unproblematically defined, against legislative or executive oppression. There is little conscious weighing of the strengths and weaknesses of legislatures and courts as interpreters of rights. I suspect that this is due in large measure to the fact that the rights are still enshrined in a constitutional text. Regardless of whether the constitution invites legislative participation – as the Canadian *Charter* arguably does in section 33 – the very context of the clause suggests that when it is invoked, fundamental rights are set aside. Constitutions carry a powerful symbolic charge. They are perceived to be basic laws, setting out the premises on which society should be governed, with a measure of fixity and permanence that is beyond politics. Against this backdrop, section 33 looks very odd indeed, introducing variability and the will of a transient majority into the very application of the constitution.[77]

4.3. A Statutory Bill of Rights, Protected by Manner and Form Requirements

This brings us to the last strategy of rights protection examined here: the declaration of rights in statutory form, protected by a manner and form require-

---

[76] Russell, above n. 65, at 301–302; Michael Mandel, *The Charter of Rights and the Legalization of Politics in Canada*, revised ed (Toronto: Thompson Educational Publishing 1994) at 87ff; Hiebert (1999a), above n. 1, at 31–32. It is indicative of section 33's shaky legitimacy that following the decisions in Daviault, above n. 52 and O'Connor, above n. 41, Parliament did not use section 33 but instead relied on a renewed argument under section 1. See above nn. 41 and 52.

[77] There is an argument that section 33 may have had an indirect impact on dialogue by rendering the courts more deferential to vigorous claims of justification under section 1. On this view, section 33 provides support for the legitimacy of a legislative role (and a possible option for a frustrated legislature) that may lead courts to enter more readily into dialogue. (I am indebted to Eric Ghosh for this argument.) It is of course very difficult to assess whether there has been such an affect. I suspect that it is absent or modest, given the existence of vigorous arguments between courts and legislatures over rights definition in all countries, the avenue to express such arguments under section 1 of the Canadian Charter, and section 33's own perceived illegitimacy.

ment. I have already described the nature of this mechanism above. The rights are expressed in an ordinary statute. They can be set aside, however, by the legislature expressly stating that an act applies notwithstanding the bill of rights. That ability to set the rights aside transforms the act from a substantive to a procedural limitation, permitting it to bind the legislature for the future. Statutory bills of rights are binding (in Canada), but only in relative terms. In fact, there are two ways in which their effect can be modified or displaced: 1) a legislature can stipulate that an act applies notwithstanding the bill of rights; or 2) it can amend the bill of rights itself, changing the very expression of the rights (and indeed there have been a number of such amendments in Canada).

The *Canadian Bill of Rights*, adopted by the federal Parliament in 1960, was the first example of this legislative method, although the same approach was adopted in Quebec and Alberta. The record of the *Canadian Bill of Rights* was not particularly noble. Prior to the adoption of the *Charter*, it was used to strike down only one legislative provision. For much of its history, there was some question whether it rendered legislation invalid or merely provided standards to be applied when interpreting legislation. It was prone to inconsistent, timid, and downright poor interpretations.[78] This has sometimes been blamed on its statutory, not constitutional, character. Although this character may have played some role, one suspects that the problem was more general: the *Canadian Bill of Rights* was adopted at a time when justiciable rights were uncommon outside the United States, and Canada's legal culture and legal education were ill adapted to rights review. Judicial interpretation of statutory bills of rights and of human rights codes (which are applicable to particular types of services and do not purport to bind the legislature) has been much bolder and more sophisticated in recent years, suggesting that it was legal culture rather than the *Canadian Bill of Rights'* statutory character that determined that instrument's weak interpretation. Indeed, the interpretation of the *Canadian Bill of Rights* itself has improved.[79]

Because of the inadequate interpretation of the *Canadian Bill of Rights*, and because all of Canada's statutory bills of rights have, since the early 1980s, largely been displaced by the Canadian *Charter*, it is difficult to draw satisfactory conclusions. I strongly suspect, however, that statutory bills of rights have

---

[78] The one decision striking down legislation prior to the Charter is Drybones, above n. 23. For experience under the Canadian Bill of Rights, see Tarnopolsky, above n. 19.

[79] For suggestions that the weakness of the Canadian Bill of Rights was due to its non-constitutional character, see R v. Big M Drug Mart [1985] 1 SCR 295 at 333 and 341–344 (per Dickson J). However, this is probably best understood as the most obvious point of distinction between the Bill and the Charter for a Court seeking to distance itself from the previous case-law. For interpretations subsequent to the Charter, see: Singh, above n. 25; MacBain v. Lederman [1985] 1 FC 856 (CA). Keith makes an argument similar to mine in relation to the New Zealand Bill of Rights Act 1990 in above n. 20, pp. 730–731 and 737.

advantages that are worth revisiting, especially for those nations, like Australia, that do not have constitutionalised bills of rights and are considering adopting them. In particular I believe that statutory bills of rights may provide a better framework for dialogue between legislature and courts.

As argued above, one of the chief obstacles to dialogue under the *Canadian Charter of Rights and Freedoms* has been the symbolic force of a constitutionalised charter, which drives a deep gulf between the constitutionally protected rights and all other interests. The rights assume a superordinate importance, resistant to balancing. Any attempt by the legislature or executive to define rights or determine their application is viewed with extreme scepticism, as an illegitimate attempt to impair fundamental liberties. The ability of legislatures to derogate in section 33 becomes virtually unusable.

Statutory bills of rights escape some of these evils. The act itself, as an ordinary statute, carries nothing like the same symbolic charge. It is therefore less susceptible to the view that the rights as defined by the courts are immutable, to be kept exempt from any legislative tampering. On the contrary, the statutory rights are emphatically the product of legislative action. The legislature is a collaborator in their adoption and definition, not an antagonist. It has a manifest claim to share in their continued definition, not only through express derogation but more importantly through the amendment of the statutory bill itself (which clearly involves redefinition, not just the setting aside of the rights). There is thus a viable avenue through which the particular strengths of legislatures – the weighing of dispersed social benefits; balancing in polycentric issues; the ability to inquire and investigate; an understanding of the positive value of state action in promoting social welfare – can make themselves felt in rights jurisprudence.

Moreover, the statutory form avoids some problems with the interpretation of constitutional rights, precisely because the statutory rights are not set apart in a sacrosanct document. The rights can be considered in relation to other interests without an exaggerated gulf between the two. Moreover, their application is less likely to be distorted by the high symbolism and nationalistic aims that sometimes afflict constitutional instruments.

Yet, because of their relative binding force, the statutory provisions do continue to protect against inadvertent or surreptitious legislative impairment of rights. They do this not by removing a swath of decisions from political debate, conferring them exclusively on the courts (as constitutional provisions tend to do). Rather they work by stimulating debate, warning that rights may be in peril and thereby prompting (one hopes) vigorous popular engagement in the issues. In short, through the adjudication of the rights themselves, statutory bills of rights provide an opportunity for the kind of careful, individualised and relatively dispassionate analysis of rights concerns that we expect of the courts. That analysis has real effect: the courts can invalidate legislation, certainly protecting against inadvertent impairments and even providing some protection against purposeful rights infringements. Yet they do this in a way that relies upon provisions that are defined by the legislature, and they expressly depend upon the support of an engaged citizenry for their ultimate efficacy. Thus, they feed the democratic process, rather than detracting from it. Statutory bills of rights are therefore most compatible with the view, which I accept, that democratic institutions are an indispensable bulwark against repressive conduct – a bulwark which, once eroded, cannot adequately be replaced by judicial institutions, for the courts themselves ultimately depend upon a measure of popular support for their efficacy.[80]

5. CONCLUSION

The range of institutional mechanisms for rights protection is therefore considerably broader than we generally think. Even in jurisdictions most committed to judicial review, rights protections involve a complex interaction among institutions. When addressing issues of constitutional design, there are a variety of ways in which that interaction can be structured.[81]

My own preference, in societies with a strong rights culture like Canada or Australia, is for mechanisms that permit a continued role – even a predominant role – for the legislature. There are many reasons for this preference, some of which have been evident in this paper and which I have discussed further elsewhere. But one essential one is that in such societies, the principal rights issues do not involve gross violations, but rather difficult issues of judgement. I cannot see why the legislature should have no legitimate part in those decisions.

Section 33 of the *Canadian Charter of Rights and Freedoms* may be best justified in these terms, but it has not fulfilled that promise, for it still participates in the high symbolism of a constitutionalised bill of rights, which forcefully impedes institutional dialogue. Section 33 may have served as a pressure valve at the time of adoption of the *Charter* and may continue to do so as long as there is extensive dissatisfaction with the Canadian constitution in Quebec, but

---

[80] For discussion of this 'democratic deficit', see Webber, above n. 4, pp. 141–144. It is important to be clear on the nature of the public support necessary for the courts. It is not support for each and every decision. If this were necessary, there would be no advantage whatever (other than spreading the workload) in having courts separate from the legislature. Judicial independence truly would be a mirage. A studied and institutionalised inattention to popular opinion is a critical dimension in the judicial role. Without it, the courts are disabled from exercising precisely the kind of deliberation we expect of them. There does have to be popular support for them as institutions, exercising independent judgement, however. We cannot afford to neglect the public culture of rights and liberties and the institutional safeguards that sustains them.

[81] For a stimulating argument along similar lines, see Roderick Macdonald '*The New Zealand Bill of Rights Act: How far does it or should it stretch?*' in *(1993) Proceedings of the New Zealand Law Conference.*

it is unlikely to provide a continuing mechanism for dialogue. Surprisingly, the strongest examples of institutional dialogue under the Canadian *Charter* have occurred within the framework of arguments over justification under section 1.

Statutory bills of rights have a better chance of capturing the appropriate balance. There, the courts retain a role, but it is a role focused upon the area where courts undeniably have a strong institutional advantage: the application of general norms to particular situations, in a manner that maximises the chance that the particularity of those situations will not be overlooked or overpowered in the rush to achieve a general object. The use of an ordinary statute does mean that rights are vulnerable to a cynical or repressive legislative initiative. There are institutional impediments to this, through the promotion of political debate and the opportunity for judicial pronouncement. But at the end of the day a determined majority can have its way. The peremptory control of a constitutionalised bill of rights may be appropriate in some contexts, then, especially where there are permanent political minorities, or where the weakness of a country's rights culture makes strong constitutional statement desirable.

But it is important to realise that a capacity to overpower rights does not necessarily mean that rights are in jeopardy. On the contrary, maintaining legislative responsibility can foster a broader and more inclusive rights debate, one that reinforces a concern for rights within the popular milieu generally. Nor should we exaggerate the efficacy of judicial review. It too can be swayed by an inflamed public. It too can lose its nerve.

In countries with a strong rights culture, questions of rights serve as prompts to reflection and institutional self-restraint – as occasions to confront once again the difficult mediation between individual and society. They serve only very rarely as the occasion for heroic stands against oppression. Structures that are more nuanced than constitutionalised bills for rights – structures that provide for a genuine dialogue between the courts and the democratic process – may well be most appropriate.

4. The German Constitutional Court in an Uneasy Triangle between Parliament, Government and the Federal Laender

Klaus von Beyme

1. THE RISE, ORGANISATION AND ELECTION OF JUDGES

The founding fathers of the German Basic Law were motivated by two concerns in creating the new 'watchdog of the constitution' which has no precedent in German history – one was the concept of the legal state, the other was to create an institution which could mediate in the first true federalist system in German history. As to the former, the positivistic interpretation of constitutional law had capitulated without resistance before Nazi illegality, since law was conceived in the main formalistically, in terms of 'due process', but not materially in terms of the legal principles on which the Weimar Constitution rested. In post-war Germany, the Constitutional Court was to control whether or not laws principally conformed to the values of the Basic Law.

It was not easy to build the principle of judicial review into a system so deeply shaped by Roman law tradition, in which the principle of judicial review developed in the tradition of the common law countries was not known. The authoritarian tradition in Germany, moreover, denied to judges the authority to override the laws of the state. The German concept of the legal state, the *Rechtsstaat*, was conceived as apolitical and neutral towards the issue of power. It did not presuppose political principles such as parliamentary sovereignty in Britain or judicial review in the United States.

After 1945, a fundamental change was planned by the founders of the new system. The competences of the Constitutional Court were far more extended than in most systems. In many respects it differed from its model, the Supreme Court of the United States, which was also an appellate court in civil and penal matters for federal courts. Judicial review was highly centralised in Germany which created new dangers not sufficiently anticipated by the founding fathers. In Germany, the monopoly of judicial review in one body creates greater dangers on encroachment on the other constitutional powers in the system than in the United States. Moreover, the US Supreme Court only has jurisdiction in matters of concrete judicial review and it does not interfere in conflicts between institutions to the extent of the German *Organstreit*[1]. Foreign observers have called

---

[1] "The Constitutional Court interferes in cases of disagreements or doubts on the ... compatibility of state law and federal law" (Grundgesetz Art. 93, 1, No. 2).

Wojciech Sadurski (ed.), Constitutional Justice, East and West, 101–118

the German Constitutional Court the 'most original and interesting institution in the West German system' (Alfred Grosser). It was shaped not only by progressive motives. The deficiencies of a democratic tradition, and the German tendency to emphasise legal principles more strongly than political participation certainly played a part when the new institution was created.

The Constitutional Court has a position superior to that of the five Supreme Federal courts mentioned in Article 95 of the Basic Law. It is autonomous and independent of the other institutional powers (§ 1 of the Law on the Constitutional Court). In the first years of its existence, the organisational implications of this law were neglected. Only in 1953 was the Constitutional Court entitled to have full self-administration and its budget was no longer incorporated in the budget of the Ministry of Justice. In spite of this innovation, the Constitutional Court has been called a 'lame constitutional institution'[2] since it has no formal procedure of its own and its organisation is not regulated by the Constitution but by ordinary legislation. More important than these formalities is the actual power of the Court, which contradicts the conclusion that the Court did not become an independent equivalent of the other constitutional powers.

The Constitutional Court is composed of two panels or 'Senates'. Each Senate has an exclusive sphere of jurisdiction: the first over the control of norms and constitutional complaints concerning Articles 1–17 of the Basic Law; the second with jurisdiction over problems of the civil service, military service, appeals, the execution of punishment and prisons, conflicts between institutions, the outlawing of parties and complaints about electoral procedure. The first Senate, therefore, has been called the 'Senate of Civil Rights', and the second, the 'Senate of Constitutional Law'. In cases of doubt over which Senate has jurisdiction, a committee of six judges (President, Vice-President and two judges from each Senate) decide. The judges and the respective Senates are not interchangeable; the judges are elected exclusively to serve in one Senate. Originally, there were 12 judges in each. In 1956 the number was reduced to 10 and in 1963 to 8. The fact that judges are not interchangeable together with the fact that they have permanent positions can create problems for a quorum, since at least six judges have to be present. In order to prevent the Senates from being blocked by excessive litigation on the 'partisanship of judges', 'The Law on the Constitutional Court' has made sure[3] that former activities of prospective judges in legislation and the publication of scholarly opinions or membership of a political party is no reason to exclude judges from participating in a decision by the Senate.

In spite of the attempts to avoid political manipulation of the judiciary, the election of judges itself is not without political implication. In some countries,

---

[2]   Christian Starck, *Das Bundesverfassungsgericht im politischen Prozeß der Bundesrepublik.* (Tübingen, Mohr 1976), p. 31.

[3]   BerfGG Bundesverfassungsgerichtsgesetz (Law on the Constitutional Court) § 18.

co-optation by the supreme judges from the status group of judges is provided for. In some other countries, the executive nominates or co-operates in the appointment process with the legislature which has a veto power (e.g. the US Senate). Germany deliberately chose the election of judges by Parliament (the Bundestag), in order to give the court the maximum possible democratic legitimation. The federalist legitimation also had to be included. Therefore the electoral committee of 12 people in the Federal Diet elects only half of the judges, the other half being elected by the Federal Council, the representatives of the Länder, by a two thirds majority. There is a danger of politicisation since the parliamentary groups *de facto* negotiate the candidates. This has sometimes aroused bitter controversies in public. Since the increasing conflicts in the polarising party system, the two different forms of democratic legitimation for the judges is becoming increasingly problematic[4] and the need for a uniform procedure to elect all the judges is being debated among lawyers.[5] Politicisation is mitigated during the elections by the two thirds rule which requires a broad consensus among the parties and gives the opposition some weight in every decision.

Moreover, the premises for attaining the highest office in the German court system are defined rigorously enough to prevent an influx of incompetent politicians into the Constitutional Court. The limitation of office to 12 years excludes problems of senility (sometimes to be found in the US Supreme Court) and the impossibility of being re-elected strengthens the independence of the judges who are never invited to do any favour for the parties for this reason. Party politics cannot be denied, but the party ties among the judges are fairly equally distributed. On the whole, there has been a slight majority of pro-CDU judges, which can be explained by the number of judges who gave up their offices or died and were replaced during the time of the CDU-government.

The political proportional arrangements are limited since other proportional considerations also have some bearing on the election of judges. There is an attempt to balance the regions and denominations between centralisers and federalists. Special care was taken to ensure that no former Nazis came into the Constitutional Court. The Catholics are somewhat underrepresented, though most of the candidates proposed by the CDU were Catholics. The regional proportions are fairly balanced; for there is only a slight over-representation of the south-west for the simple reason that Karlsruhe, the seat of the court, is located in Baden-Württemberg. Also foreign observers have testified that the general quality of the judges is high, most of them are not dogmatic on a liberalism-conservatism scale, and that they have proved to be pragmatic in their views. The divisions between the judges have not always been identical

---

4   W. Billing, *Das Problem der Richterwahl zum Bundesverfassungsgericht* (Berlin, Duncker & Humblot 1969), p. 291ff).

5   Christian Starck (ed.), *Bundesverfassungsgericht und Grundgesetz* (Tübingen, Mohr, 2 vols. 1976), vol. 1, p. 79.

with party lines and the alliances within the Senates have changed according to the issues at stake.[6] 'Enlightened' public opinion among the German elites, with the exception of the party officials, university professors and the top bureaucrats, rates the work of the Constitutional Court very highly.

2. THE JURISDICTION OF THE CONSTITUTIONAL COURT

The Constitutional Court does not act at its own initiative, but only when called upon. Its role as a 'guardian of the constitution' is deliberately passive, since an active role would endow the Court with excessive weight over the other constitutional powers.

The quantitative importance of its competences differ. Constitutional complaints form the bulk of proceedings (1951–99: 122, 256). Proceedings on the control of concrete norms are second in importance (1951–99: 3, 121 see Table 1).

The constitutional complaints made in 1969 have been integrated into the Basic Law by amendment (Art. 93, section 1, no. 4a). This is the most important part of the court's activities for the individual citizen. Citizens who feel that their civil rights have been violated can initiate a constitutional complaint, although *their own* rights have to be violated by a governmental act – there is no popular complaint on behalf of a third party, as is provided for in the Bavarian Constitutional Court. The number of those entitled to a constitutional complaint has sometimes seemed to increase so rapidly that the efficient protection of civil rights was endangered and the Constitutional Court degenerated to an appellate court for many proceedings with many far-fetched justifications. A good many of the constitutional complaints do not find their way to the Court but are filtered out by a special committee of both Senates (consisting of three judges). The most important reasons for the refusal to hear cases are the passing of time limits and that complaints do not fall within the Court's jurisdiction but under that of the ordinary courts of justice. The judicial review of norms below the constitutional level comes under the competence of the Constitutional Court only when it rules that subordinate courts violated or ignored constitutional norms concerning civil rights. Only a small proportion of the proceedings finally lead to laws being overridden or to the annulment of court sentences and administrative decrees.

The object of protection is not the persons or institutions who sue for their rights. The legislature is to be protected against the possibility that courts obviate or ignore its laws.[7] Only the Constitutional Court can review laws (Gesetze), whilst decrees can be reviewed by any court below the constitutional court level. In no other sphere has the Constitutional Court respected the principle of 'judicial restraint' so much and so strictly scrutinised petitions. In no other

---

[6] Donald Kommers, *Judicial Politics in West Germany.* (London, Sage 1976), p. 155..

[7] Bettermann, Starck, above, n. 3, vol. 1, p. 328.

Table 1 Workload of Federal Constitutional Court (1951 – 31 December 1999)

Proceeding	Cases filed	Cases decided	Cases terminated without decision
Forfeiture of basic rights (Art. 18 GG)	4	3	1
Prohibition of parties (Art. 21 ABS. 2 GG)	5	4	1
Election disputes (Art. 41 ABS. 2 GG)	138	93	24
Presidential impeachment (Art. 61 GG)	–	–	–
Conflicts between high federal organs (Art. 93 Abs. 1 Nr. 1 GG)	128	60	57
Abstract judicial review (Art. 93 Abs. 1 Nr. 2 GG)	140	81	50
Federal Land conflicts (Art. 93 Abs. 1 Nr. 3 GG)	33	19	12
Other public law conflicts (Art. 93 Abs. 1 Nr. 4 GG)	73	35	35
Judicial removals (Art. 98 Abs. 2 u. 5 GG)	–	–	–
Constitutional disputes within Länder (Art. 99 GG)	20	13	3
Concrete judicial review (Art. 100 Abs. 1 GG)	3121	972	1958
International law disputes (Art. 100 Abs. 2 GG)	15	7	7
State constitutional court certifications (Art. 100 Abs. 3 GG)	8	5	3
Disputes concerning the continued validity of federal law (Art. 126 GG)	151	19	132
Interlocutory order and other proceedings (32 BVerfGG)	1070	728	336
Constitutional complaints (Art. 93 Abs. 1, Nr. 4a u. b GG)	122256	100031	15672
Total	127162	102070	18291

Source: Unpublished statistical summary prepared by the Constitutional Court, Karlsruhe 2000.

sphere of the Constitutional Court's jurisdiction is the discrepancy between the number of decisions and of proceedings ended by a withdrawal as striking as in the case of jurisdiction over concrete norms.

Proceedings for abstract judicial review, which can be called on by the Federal Government, state government or at least one third of the members of the Federal Diet, independently of a concrete impending case, are mainly perceived as an instrument for protecting minorities and the opposition. Bavaria and Hesse are the outriders in the application of this means in the name of their respective oppositions in the Bundestag. Since 1969 and the growing polarisation of parties, the control of abstract norms has mainly been used by the Christian Democrats. Particularly prominent decisions have included those on the German treaty

(Deutschlandvertrag 1952),[8] the question of the Saar,[9] party finance in 1966,[10] the supervision of telephones in 1970,[11] the basic treaty between the two German states *(Grundlagenvertrag)* in 1973,[12] the decision of the Federal Council[13] and abortion in 1975.[14] Recent criticism that the Constitutional Court has abandoned the principle of judicial restraint is mainly related to the proceedings on abstract norms. Criticism is growing since the court has sometimes mixed up the different types of proceedings. A decision concerning the sessional expenses of Deputies[15] has rightly been called a quasi-control of abstract norms disguised as a constitutional complaint.

Federal-state conflicts have been of less importance than originally expected, but the rare cases have had far-reaching political implications. The decline in importance of the Länder, the growing interlacing of the parties on national and state level, the administrative controls which rarely admit cases of federal supervision of acts initiated by the Länder, have all contributed to a decline in this form of litigation. Some of the cases were not typical pieces of litigation between the Federation and the Länder, but controversies between the government and the opposition parties disguised under the procedural form of the federal-state conflict (e.g. Referendum on atomic armament in Hesse,[16] TV litigation.)[17]

Conflicts between high federal organs have also been rare (73 decisions by the end of 1999). One of the reasons for this was the overlap with the proceedings on the regulation of abstract norms, which in case of doubt was considered the more promising form of litigation. On the other hand, the Court was inclined to postpone decisions in these conflicts so that these cases lost their urgency. The proportion of withdrawals by parties was, therefore, particularly high. In the sphere of electoral law, parties were even able to act as litigants, as happened in the proceedings on party finances and the five-percent clause.

The remaining sphere of jurisdiction is the outlawing of political parties. This has happened only twice so far, in the 1950s. In 1952 the neo-fascist SRP was proscribed[18] and in 1956 the Communist Party, KPD, was similarly treated.[19]

---

8   BVerfGE Bundesverfassungsgerichtsentscheidungen (the collection of the decisions of the Constitutional Court), 1, p. 396.
9   BVerfGE, above, n. 7, 4, p. 157.
10   BVerfGE, above, n. 7, 20, p. 56.
11   BVerfGE, above, n. 7, 30, p. 1.
12   BVerfGE, above, n. 7, 36, p. 1.
13   BVerfGE, above, n. 7, 37, p. 363.
14   BVerfGE, above, n. 7, 39, p. 1.
15   BVerfGE, above, n. 7, 40, p. 296f.
16   BVerfGE, above, n. 7, 8, p. 122f.
17   BVerfGE, above, n. 7, 12, p. 205f.
18   BVerfGE, above, n. 7, 2, p. 1.
19   BVerfGE, above, n. 7, 5, p. 58.

3. JUDICIAL REVIEW OF LEGISLATION

Legally, Parliament can participate in the proceedings of the Constitutional Court in several ways:

- as complainant;
- as defendant (§ 63, Law on the Constitutional Court);
- as co-complainant in a judicial procedure which the Bundestag has not initiated (§ 65.2, Law on the Constitutional Court);
- as witness or adviser (§ 94.1, § 23.2 Law on the Constitutional Court).

The Court is in a strong position vis-à-vis the Bundestag. Parliament may have the first word, but the Constitutional Court has the last one. Three types of proceedings are available:

- judicial review of norms;
- challenges to the law's constitutionality brought by citizens;
- disputes between state agencies in front of the Court.

The sentences of the Constitutional Court can have serious *ex post facto* consequences for legislation. They have, however, an impact even *ex ante* because the legislators frequently act in a kind of 'anticipatory obedience' to the Court. Oppositional threats 'to carry a Bill to Karlsruhe' are quite normal in parliamentary debates.

Three indicators reveal the influence of the Constitutional Court on legislation:

1. the number of laws which have undergone judicial review;
2. the number of laws invalidated by the Court;
3. the preventive threat of taking a case to Karlsruhe in the parliamentary debates.

The impact of the Constitutional Court on legislation is not reflected in the statistics of the Court. It is treated as a kind of 'political question' – left to political scientists, who have in the main only conducted selective studies on some laws.[20] There is only one study which selected most of the key decisions from 1949 to 1994[21] which casts some light on the role of the Constitutional Court on the transformation process. In the following ways, these studies falsify the common prejudice that the Constitutional Court is a 'cemetery of important parliamentary laws':

- Since the fifth legislature (1965–69) the number of *laws declared null and void* has decreased on an annual basis. In this case the norm has to be substituted.

---

[20] Christine Landfried, *Bundesverfassungsgericht und Gesetzgeber.* (Baden-Baden, Nomos 2nd edition 1996).

[21] Klaus von Beyme, *The Legislator: German Parliament as a Centre of Political Decision-making* (Aldershot, Ashgate 1998).

- A milder form of critique of the legislator can be manifested in the form of words that a law is *incompatible with the Basic Law*. In this case the legislator has various options by which to correct its work and the norm cannot be applied. The judgment on the 'Law on Allowances for Deputies' showed, however, that the room for manoeuvre is not much greater than in the case of a law being declared null and void.[22]
- *The request to keep to a mode of interpretation of the law compatible with the constitution* apparently binds the hands of the legislators least. For innovative treaties (for example, Moscow, Warsaw, Maastricht) the Constitutional Court used to take resort to this kind of intervention. It respects the prerogative of Parliament but, since there is no political questions doctrine (that is, refusal of a case because it is not judicial but political and thereby falling under the auspices of another institution) accepted in Germany, it means no further interpretation or amendment of the regulation is considered constitutional. In such a case, the Court detailed instructions on which application of the law is the only legal one. This type of intervention is also increasing in other countries – for example, in France with the *déclaration de conformité sous reserve*.[23]
- In foreign policy the Court's impact is limited. In domestic decisions it can immobilize forthcoming amendment policy, as in the case of the codetermination judgments. In foreign policy issues the Court – normally liberal in matters of basic rights of the citizens – has sometimes shown a conservative attitude. If we compare judgments which renounced territories which were formerly part of the German Empire, the judgment of the Saar statute sounded as though it was expressing confidence in Adenauer's foreign policy, whereas the judgment on the treaty with the GDR and Poland sounded rather like a vote of censure against Brandt's *Ostpolitik*.
- Most of the key decisions which underwent judicial review were declared *compatible with the Basic Law*, among them far-reaching innovations such as the 'Reform of the Penal Law' (1969) or the 'Law for Promoting the Labour Market' (1969).
- In rare cases the indirect control of norms on the basis of a challenge to the constitutionality of a law has led to the *quashing of the judgment of a lower court* (3 out of 108 judgments).

The Constitutional Court has intervened in the legislative process since 1951. If we look at the statistics of laws which have been declared null and void or incompatible with the Basic Law, a clear hierarchy of policy arenas is visible: social, finance and legal policy attract most of the interventions (Table 2). The

---

[22] Landfried, above, n. 6, p. 49.

[23] Louis Favoreu in Christine Landfried (ed.), *Constitutional Review and Legislation. An International Comparison* (Baden-Baden, Nomos 1988), p. 100.

key decisions which attracted the Constitutional Court's interventions is an indicator for legislative conflicts: 40% of the key decisions were confronted with the Court. The Constitutional Court issued 108 judgments concerning 60 laws. An important question is to what extent the oppositional parties use the Constitutional Court for their veto politics: 27.7% of all the judgments preclude an action by the oppositions because they were issued in later legislatures. Later judgments normally add amendments to a law, although not necessarily only those parts which have recently been amended.

Table 2 Policy fields in which laws were declared null and void or not compatible with the Basic Law (1951–91)

Social Policy	61
Tax and fiscal policy	35
Legal policy	29
Regulations among the state agencies	25
Economic policy	12
Transfer policy	9
Educational policy	7
Labour market policy	6
Health policy	4
Environmental policy	1
Military policy	1
Others	7

The Constitutional Court has hardly ever prevented a key decision, although the whole or parts of 14.8% of the laws were declared null and void. In one-fifth of the cases (19.4%) the law was declared as being incompatible with the Basic Law. The judgments containing a negative intervention against the legislator are most frequent in legal policy (21.8%) and social policy (19.4%). In both fields the opposition cannot be blamed for the interventions because the laws were passed with large majorities, thus including most of the votes of the opposition. The size of a majority does not protect, however, against unconstitutionality of a law (for example, the Party Law 1967). There were even unanimous decisions ('acceleration of the procedure for asylum-seekers' 1978) which failed to be accepted by the Court in Karlsruhe.

Extensive laws which created new rights and possibilities for the citizens most frequently underwent judicial review (64.7%), followed by *regulative* measures (42.4%). The latter were most frequently among those laws declared null and void (21.7%), followed by the *redistributive* laws (18.1%). *Protective* measures most frequently ended by being declared as incompatible with the Basic Law (35%), although the decision in Parliament in this type of regulation tended to be less conflict-ridden than others, since the federal units often drive the issue to the Court because they have to implement it and costs are involved. *Extensive* measures were most frequently earmarked with the clause that the interpretation has to be strictly within the limits of the Constitution (33.3%). Judgments were quashed exclusively in legal policy.

3.1. Ex-ante Impact of the Constitutional Court

The *ex-ante* impact of the Constitutional Court has contributed to the fact that the legal control of a bill has been shifted from the Ministry of Justice to informal steering bodies. In the parliamentary stage of the decision-making ex-justices of the Constitutional Court have often been invited to parliamentary hearings, not because they were experts on the substance of the law, but only to hear their opinion on the possible reactions of the Constitutional Court.

In many debates the threat to take the issue to Karlsruhe is present – even in 12% of those 'key decision' laws for which this ultimately did not happen. The 'Karlsruhe astrology' sometimes developed strange forms. Entire constitutional mandates were interpreted in some judgments. In other cases, opinions of judges were constructed without recourse to a specific decision.[24] Over-interpretation of judgments are used to functionalize the Court. Individual phrases of judgments are discussed without evaluating the context and considering whether the phrase was taken from the basic reasons of a judgment or merely *obiter dicta* which are increasingly invading the Constitutional Court's judgment.

The *ex-ante* impact of the Constitutional Court has three variations in the parliamentary debates:

- threat and counter-threat in the struggle between parties;
- hidden conflict in the governmental coalition;
- the development of an inter-party consensus.

3.2. Threat and Counter-threat in the Struggle between Parties

Since Almond's and Verba's civic culture study,[25] Germany has been renowned for her legalistic culture. Political conflict is unpopular. Most Germans would prefer to settle disputes through the courts. An early example of this attitude was exemplified by the conflict about the 'European defence community' (1954). The Christian Democrats tried to sue the SPD opposition. The Court turned this down.[26] The SPD opposition tried to outlaw the treaty but the Court ruled that a Bill – not yet passed by Parliament – could not be subject to judicial

---

[24] For example, 12th BT Deutscher Bundestag (parliamentary minutes) 30.6.1994, pp. 20949C, 20958A.

[25] G. Almond and S. Verba, *The civic culture: political attitudes and democracy in five nations* (Princeton: Princeton U P, 1966).

[26] BVerfGE, above, n. 7, 2, p. 145.

review.[27] The Court, at this early stage of consolidation of democracy, had to teach the political parties the lesson that the majority and the minority of Parliament are not entitled to act as complainant and were directed back to the road of political settlement of disputes[28] instead of asking for a preventive control of norms which did not yet exist.

In later cases Parliament began to perceive that the threat of the Court was no substitute for a political decision.[29] Sometimes the opposition's attempt to terrorize the government with these threats were met with humour, as in the case of the 'Law on the Promotion of Vocational Training' (1981):

> In the future each Federal minister will have to carry the Constitution day and night under his arm to make sure that not a minor paragraph of the Bill can be found which serves as pretext that the Constitutional Court tries to enter into political decisions.[30]

Threats by a conservative *Land*, like Bavaria, were countered with irony: 'They did not vote for the Constitution, but they use it as a base to sue the government'.[31]

The Green Party as a new opposition initially criticized the conservative judgments of the Constitutional Court but, as soon as they realized the usefulness of the strategy, they also used threats of the Court – even in matters which did not consider only the constitutionality of the Bill, but also its feasibility.[32] In other words, judicial activism was criticized, but invited when it seemed to benefit the party's strategy.

3.3. Hidden Conflict in the Governmental Coalition

Occasionally a dissent in the coalition was rhetorically taken to Karlsruhe as in the case of the 'Second Law for Fortune-Building' for all citizens.[33]

3.4. The Development of an Inter-party Consensus

In some cases, the interventions of the Constitutional Court were so substantial that an inter-party consensus grew in order to avoid repeated sanctions from the Constitutional Court, as in the case of the regulations of abortion.[34]

---

[27]   BVerfGE, above, n. 7, 1, p. 396.
[28]   BVerfGE, above, n. 7, 2, p. 144, 170f, 178.
[29]   9th BT, above, n. 21, 26.5.1981, pp. 2057B, 2058B.
[30]   9th BT, above, n. 21, 1.10.1981, p. 3190A.
[31]   *Ibid.*, p. 3195C.
[32]   10th BT, above, n. 21, 26.9.1985, p. 119231.
[33]   4th BT, above, n. 21, 5.5.1965, p. 90051.
[34]   12th BT, above, n. 21, 25.6.1992, pp. 8241B, 9960ff.

Opposition against the 'counter-captains of Karlsruhe' sometimes entered the debate.[35] Not all the cases where parliamentarians and their juridical experts launched constitutional defeatism against a Bill ended up before the Court (for example, the 'Law on Chemicals' 1980). Moreover, experts were hardly ever unanimous even on the legal aspects. In a hearing on the 'Codetermination Bill' in December 1974, six experts thought that the Bill was constitutional, whereas five others raised doubts on this (Minutes of the hearing, 19.12.1974: 36). Only rarely did a constitutional lawyer admit that 'all the jurists also conduct legal policy'.

In some cases the counterarguments against the anticipatory obedience to the Court were those of time: the Court in the meantime will have noticed that there had been a change in the legal mood of the population which it would be unable to ignore in a future decision.[36] In other words, a historical change of values was set against the assumption of permanent values on the basis of a natural right doctrine in the Court.

When certain Deputies took the Court's judgment for granted without admitting the right of politicians to criticize them, the opposition made clear that it is close to the essence of democracy that even 'a criticism which turns out to be wrong has a right to be uttered' (H-J. Vogel: 8th BT, 8.6.1978: 7562C). In some of the crucial laws, the constitutional misgivings were launched by the interest groups concerned. When the majority chose to ignore them (12th BT, 9.12.1992: 10915B) as in the case of the 'structural reform of the health system' (1992) it was a victory of the political decision, no longer intimidated by Court judgments which had been functionalised by vested interests.

The all-party consensus to agree on the necessity of political decisions against a narrow legalism sometimes developed because the Constitutional Court expanded its competences:

- The Court's *statement of facts* was increasingly transformed into a prognosis of future development;[37]
- The Court developed a tendency to *regulate a whole complex* instead of confining itself to the issue at stake. The judgment on the 'Allowances of the Parliamentarians'[38] was thus transformed into an 'abstract review of a norm' even though only a very concrete challenge to its constitutionality was on the judges' table. The Court increasingly leaves judgments on legality and enters into the political feasibility of policies. There is a danger that the Constitutional Court starts from the assumption that it has greater wisdom than Parliament, even in political matters.

---

[35] 7th BT, above, n. 21, 7.9.1975, p. 13885B, 12th BT, 26.5.1994, p. 19971C.

[36] 12th BT, above, n. 21, p. 8250D.

[37] K.J. Philippi, *Tatsachenfeststellungen des Bundesverfassungsgerichts.* (Cologne, Heymanns 1971), p. 193.

[38] BVerfGE 40, p. 296.

- The Court's judgments are full of restrictions for political actors in the future. The *obiter dicta* – which are only loosely related to the issue – are proliferating. Since the 1970s decisions increasingly make appeals for action to the legislator. This was sometimes necessary to protect such human rights as in the 'equalization of legitimate and illegitimate children.' In many other key decisions, however, as in the Party Laws, the decisions on education, abortion or in the 'basic treaty with the GDR' (1973), the sentences put Parliament under the tutelage of the Constitutional Court.

Negative consequences of the expansion of competences of the Constitutional Court are:

- the *retardation of political decisions* because the legislator waits until the judgment is issued;
- *further devaluation of the Deputies' judgment;*
- *strengthening of the influences of bureaucracies and parties outside parliament.*

In the 1970s judicial activism was directed against the Social Democratic government and caused much criticism. In the 1990s a series of judgments was directed against the conservative government and provoked wide criticism even among the most conservative constitutional lawyers who normally refrain from criticizing the Constitutional Court. The propaganda for a 'lean state' threatened to turn into a promotion of an 'opulent judicial review'. The waves of judicial activism and judicial restraint will probably never find a balance acceptable to all parties and politicians.

4. THE ROLE OF THE CONSTITUTIONAL COURT IN THE PROCESS OF CONSOLIDATION IN UNIFIED GERMANY

Germany is the deviant case in transition studies and hardly mentioned in comparative volumes. West Germany has exported its model to the East. The majority of the voters invited Bonn to do so. They wanted quick unification, not because of nationalist feelings – though they had a more traditional patriotism than the West Germans if we trust the surveys[39] – but because of DM-Nationalism as Habermas called it, with moral disappointment. Even the former communists wanted unification – only more slowly, more confederative and closer to a 'third road' between market economy and planned society.

The first function of the Constitutional Court fortunately did not have to be used: it was the living guarantee of reunification – even against the will of a parliamentary majority in the West. As in Ireland the preamble in the Basic Law required reunification as a kind of moral duty. If the Bundestag had declined

---

[39] Bettina Westle, *Kollektive Identität im vereinten Deutschland.* (Opladen, Leske & Budrich 1999).

the offer of the GDR for an immediate 'Anschluss', the East German government could have complained in Karlsruhe and the Court would certainly have imposed unification on the legislator. This hypothetical 'worst case scenario' did not happen – but it shows already that the mere existence of the Court has anticipating motivating power in the political arena. The normal threat in the debates reads: 'your opinion is not 'Karlsruhe proof'. This scenario, however, might have happened if the legislator knew the costs. Most economic experts calculated 200 billion DM and did not anticipate that West Germany has to pay almost this sum every year.

The Constitutional Court was the institution with the highest reputation, especially in times when Parliament and the parties were discredited because of their egotism or their inactivity. The reputation of the Court was far above Parliament, Government and even the churches.[40] The Court had an important function as guardian of 'due process' in a transition which in some respects resembled the age of gold-digging crowds which overran the new Laender. The Court protected the chances of smaller East German parties by ruling that the five-percent-threshold during the first all-German elections should not apply to the whole territory but that the votes should be counted separately in East and West. Many commentators thought that the former communists would disappear soon but this was a fundamental error because until 2002 they obtained about one fifth of the Eastern votes. In the meantime they even entered into a formal coalition in regional governments (Mecklenburg-Pommerania, Berlin). The PDS benefited most from this decision because all the other Eastern parties disappeared in the meantime. The Greens also benefited because they were the only 'non-colonizers' and decided not to form a list of alliance between the parties in the two territories. Because the Greens in the West failed to pass the threshold, only the Eastern Greens were represented from 1990 to 1994 in the Bundestag. This would not have been possible without the decision of the Federal Constitutional Court. The PDS did not win all the trials it initiated. In its attempt to keep the money of the former state party SED the Court ruled against the former communists.[41]

The image of the first 'liberal' Senate of the Court was challenged when it ruled that former GDR employees who had been suspended after unification because their institutions had been abolished, according to the Court's opinion were legally dismissed. For six months (9 months for older people) they got 70% of their former salary. 309 Eastern citizens had complained, arguing that they were discriminated because of the 'collective lay-offs'. The Court, however, did not recognize a violation of 'human dignity' in the collective lay-offs. But it ruled

---

[40] See Oscar W Gabriel (ed.), *Politische Orientierungen und Verhaltensweisen im vereinigten Deutschland.* (Opladen, Leske & Budrich 1997).

[41] BVerfGE, above, n. 7, 84, pp. 304ff.

that for women with children, the handicapped and elderly people certain improvements have to be envisaged in order to avoid poverty.[42]

After the 'counterrevolution' of 1990 many conservatives and liberals thought they could reverse all the decisions of the former communist government. The expropriations were highly disputed. Only those implemented by the Soviet Military Administration (SMAD) were recognized because they were beyond German control at that time and even the Basic Law was not yet valid in the West (and East because since 1949 the Western constitution claimed to be valid for all the Germans). The government argued that Gorbachev had exchanged this recognition for his agreement to reunification. After his resignation in 1991 he publicly challenged this opinion. In April a new case was pending against the 'compensation law' (EALG) passed by Parliament in 1994. The complainants argued that the Federal Government wanted to finance reunification by the expropriation of former owners in East Germany. The law was based on the device of 'restitution before compensation' but admitted numerous exceptions. The former owners who challenged the law asked to call Gorbachev as a witness. The Court declined the demand.[43] This was justified because previous decisions from 1991 to 1996 were not based on the argument that the Soviets had interfered but rather on arguments of justice and feasibility.

It is doubtful that Gorbachev had asked for such a clause to preserve the status quo of Soviet expropriations in Germany. But there was no doubt that the last communist government under Modrow (until March 1990) had pressured for such a clause. The issue affected mainly the owners of great estates above 100 hectares and certain owners of industrial enterprises who were allegedly guilty of war crimes – a notion which the Soviets in 1946 used quite often against everybody whose political opinions they resented. The recognition of these expropriations until 1949 were written down in the treaties with the GDR even under the new democratic government de Maizière (March-October 1990). The Court obviously followed the government's 'reason of state' in external and domestic affairs.

Even the Christian Democrats in their majority did not want a complete reversal of all property relations in East Germany. The state run factories were handed over to a parastatal trusteeship organization (*Treuhand*) which had to square the circle by expelling the 'devil of state monopoly' by the 'beelzebub of a parastatal centralized monopolistic institution'. The Treuhand did successfully so until the end of 1994. Also in this decision[44] the Government was granted wide scope for manoeuvring. The reconstruction of East Germany – according to the Court's majority – should be 'just and fair' but should not entail huge costs by private restitutions and endless litigation. The reconstruction of the

---

[42]   BVerfGE, above, n. 7, 85, pp. 167ff.
[43]   Frankfurter Allgemeine Zeitung: 12.4.2000: 1.
[44]   BVerfGE, above, n. 7, 84, pp. 90ff.

'*status quo ante*' was not considered as feasible. This wise compromise was facilitated by the fact that West Germany had also recompensated East Germans who came as refugees to the West (about three and a half million) for their losses of property in the GDR – as Adenauer had done before with the Germans expelled from the Oder-Neisse-territories.

The Constitutional Court had to interpret the Unification Treaty twice. In both cases it did so with great 'judicial restraint'. Before 1990 the Court was frequently criticized that it lacked judicial restraint by its moralizing approach to many issues. It was now blamed for decisions which did not show any moral compassion for the injustice suffered by the East Germans under communist rule.[45] In both cases the Court did not challenge the '*indemnity clause*' of the Unification Treaty (II.4.5) which changed Article 143 of the Basic Law and provided that GDR law may deviate from the Federal Law until the end of 1992. Frequently the Court was also accused of ignorance about the situation in the East. The problem was not easily to be cured because hardly any jurist -who had not cooperated with the state security – could be found on Eastern territory. So the new Laender for a long time remained without representation on the Court.

Judicial politics in Germany was always built on the '*spirit of consensus*'. Leftists suspected that this meant '*adaptation to power*'.[46] This was certainly more true after 1990 than before. But nevertheless the Court acted as a mediator between East and West and on the whole was highly respected even in the Eastern Laender. The Round Tables of the democrats – including former communists – had no alternative. If the GDR would have persisted, the model of Karlsruhe would have been copied in East Berlin as the drafts for a new GDR constitution showed. This consensus has been called '*meta-law*' or '*constitutional patriotism*' which guided the unification process much more than ethnic nationalism. This consensus – comprising many citizens with the exception of those who want radical majority decisions – led to the *apolitical climate* in which many citizens prefer a 'neutral' decision from Karlsruhe to a 'partisan parliamentary decision' in Bonn or Berlin. There was always in the German tradition a certain distrust for majority decisions and a *legalism* which was already discovered by Almond and Verba in their seminal study on 'Civic Culture' (1963). This function of mediation has sometimes been abused by the parties in Parliament, as in the case which the liberals (FDP) carried to the Constitutional Court, asking for a decision whether Germans should serve on AWACS aeroplanes on behalf of the UN.[47] The decision was used by the plaintiff as a 'sham trial' for a '*political*

[45] Friedrich K Fromme, Wer bestimmt? *Frankfurter Allgemeine Zeitung*, 14 February 1996, p. 1.
[46] Ulrich K Preuss, Politik aus dem Geist des Konsenses. Zur Rechtsprechung des Bundesverfassungsgerichts. *Merkur* (1987), pp. 1–12.
[47] BVerfGE, above, n. 7, 90, pp. 286ff.

question' – in a situation where the liberals were in the very government which had decided to support the United Nations in military actions. After the Nazi illegalism, the American doctrine of political question was not accepted. The Germans want a *'lückenlosen Rechtswege-Staat'* – a system in which no governmental act is exempt from judicial review. Indeed, in the Weimar period another doctrine still prevailed, the doctrine of *'justizfreie Hoheitsakte'*, e.g. that certain government actions, in foreign and military affairs and in internal security matters, were exempt from judicial review. The consequence of this ultra-legalistic concept in the Federal Republic is, however, that the Court is frequently drawn into political quarrels which the American Supreme Court would bluntly refuse to consider. Most of the conservative constitutional lawyers agreed: in this case the Court should have refused to accept the matter.[48]

The danger of abusing the Court for political matters came to the fore when in a decision on 'freedom of opinion' the Court had to decide whether soldiers may be called 'murderers' by their leftist critics,[49] or when the Court had to liberalize the prosecution of 'sit-ins' in front of nuclear power stations or military establishments.[50] Widely discussed was also a decision which ruled that GDR spies were not liable, as long as they had respected GDR law.[51] German courts have sentenced GDR soldiers who killed refugees from the GDR at the wall in most cases 'on probation'. They were free because it was clear that they would never be able to do it again.

An important issue was abortion. The GDR had far more liberal provisions than West Germany with its considerable share of Catholic population – almost absent in the East (5%). The Western majority imposed its restrictive laws on the new Laender. The Constitutional Court in the abortion cases[52] departed from its normal moderation. The legislator was trimmed by detailed prescriptions as to how the compromise should read and probably exceeded the Court's competences. The peaceful revolutionaries of the GDR in many cases were deeply disappointed. One of their leading figures, Bärbel Bohley, put it bluntly: 'We wanted justice – but we got only the legal state'. It will need a certain time of socialization in Western culture to recognize that their is no justice *per se* – and that the legal state is the best one gets on earth.

German reunification caused much international turbulence – but for the West Germans themselves the *Europeanization* process after the Maastricht Treaty had much more impact, excepting the financial burden caused by unification.

---

[48] Rupert Scholz, Das Bundesverfassungsgericht: Hüter der Verfassung oder Ersatzgesetzgeber, *Aus Politik und Zeitgeschichte* B 16 (1999), pp. 3–8, p. 8.

[49] BVerfGE, above, n. 7, 92, pp. 1ff.

[50] BVerfGE, above, n. 7, 92, pp. 1ff.

[51] BVerfGE, above, n. 7, 93: 1.

[52] BVerfGE, above, n. 7, 88, pp. 203ff.

20% of all parliamentary decisions are already mere implementations of 'guide-lines' or 'decrees' issued in Brussels. The European Court of Justice in Luxemburg effectively streamlines the legal systems in Europe. The German Constitutional Court became worried by this development. In a Maastricht decision it tried to set limits to Europeanization, a naive and probably futile attempt. The Court ruled – linguistically Germano-centered – that Europe is neither a 'confederation' nor a 'federation' but something in between which was dubbed 'Staatenverbund', an untranslatable monsterword which only the Swedes can accept (statsförbun-det). There is simply no word for this German construction and will inevitably be translated as 'confederation' or 'federation'.[53]

Germany used to be the 'obedient disciple' of Europe after war. But in the meantime, under the pressure of the double financial burden of reunification and of the highest contributions to the Community which certainly exceed any fair calculation of the per-capita inputs in comparative perspective, the Germans are no longer the 'good guys' and try to calculate the costs of further integration. Because they have -among the bigger countries – by far the highest proportion of foreigners and asylum seekers, they started to find restrictions. The Court tried also to build up barriers against too much of a 'multicultural society' and challenged electoral rights for foreigners.[54]

Other cases of judicial activism had little to do with the process of consolida-tion. A laicist minority found it unacceptable that a crucifix is required in every class room in Bavaria. The Court accepted that this custom contradicted Art. 4 of the Basic Law on freedom of religion. This sentence – acceptable in a postmodern society – was nevertheless a flop because the Court did not work carefully enough and had to issue a second version of the guidelines of its decision in order to clarify the matter.

On the whole the Constitutional Court has acted in a very responsible way since 1990. It should, however, consider more judicial restraint in order not to delegitimize itself, if it wants to retain the highest degree of popular trust vis-à-vis the other institutions of the Federal Republic.

---

[53] BVerfGE, above, n. 7, 89, pp. 155ff.
[54] BVerfGE, above, n. 7, 83, pp. 37ff.

5. The Experience of the French Conseil Constitutionnel: Political and Social Context and Current Legal-Theoretical Debates

Marie-Claire Ponthoreau and Jacques Ziller

This chapter explores the experience of the French constitutional court, the *Conseil Constitutionnel* and in particular the most recent debates concerning its role and legitimacy (Part 2) after considering some of the most characteristic features of the system (Part1). The purpose of this investigation is to provide the basis for drawing lessons from this experience and consequently how it may apply to other countries, especially those in transition towards democracy.

1. EXPORTING THE MODEL OF THE CONSEIL CONSTITUTIONNEL?

1.1. A Tentative Survey of Relevant Contextual Elements

Constitutional review is nowadays presented as a prominent feature of the French system of rule of law (*l'Etat de droit*).[1] However the system is quite peculiar. Most of its mechanisms are probably well known to foreign readers, but it is worthwhile to review some of its most characteristic aspects and some of the seemingly anecdotal elements concerning the way it was established, in order to understand how such an institution although very remote from French legal tradition is solidly rooted in the French political system and society.[2]

1.2. The Asence of an Explicit Constitutional Charter of Fundamental Rights

In order to understand the role, and function of the French Constitutional Council and especially in order to draw some lessons from the debates surrounding it, one specific feature has to be stressed, a feature that highlights an important formal difference between the French system and other European legal systems: it is the absence of an explicit constitutional charter of fundamental rights which is a familiar feature of other post World War Two constitutions.

---

[1] See Jacques Chevalier, *L'Etat de droit* (Paris: Montchrestien 1992).

[2] One of the best sources with a comparative perspective is John A. Rohr, *Founding Republics in France and America – A Study in Constitutional Governance* (Lawrence: University Press of Kansas, 1995).

Wojciech Sadurski (ed.), Constitutional Justice, East and West, 119–142
© 2002 *Kluwer Law International. Printed in Great Britain.*

This is due to a series of political circumstances not concerning the issue of constitutional review.

The first draft constitution of 1946, adopted by the National Assembly – where the three major parties were the Communists, Socialists and Christian-Democrats – contained such a catalogue of rights as did the Italian constitution of 1947 and the German fundamental law of 1949. But this draft constitution was rejected by a negative referendum in May 1946; this was due to the opposition of General de Gaulle, who had retired from government in January 1946, and a large number of Christian-Democrats from the *Mouvement Républicain Populaire* (MRP). A new amended version was adopted during the summer on the basis of a consensus amongst the three major parties. The charter of rights included in the first version could have been adopted with small amendments, but for an unresolved battle about freedom of education. In the French context free schools means catholic education, and the tradition of the political left has been very much opposed to religious education since the beginning of the XXth century, as the Church was seen as a major opponent of Revolution and democracy.[3] As no agreement was possible on this major and very sensitive issue, the Assembly decided to adopt only a Preamble, recognising a number of new rights on a declarative mode in addition to the old Declaration of 1789. The Preamble also referred to "the fundamental principles recognised by the Republic's laws" (*principes fondamentaux reconnus par les lois de la République*), an ambiguous sentence which obviously was referring mainly to the freedom of the press Act of 1884 and the freedom of association Act of 1901, but also, for the left, it referred to the Act of 1905 separating the Church and State, whilst some Christian democrats had in mind some sentences of other statutes which provided for financial support for "free" schools.

This might seem anecdotal at the end of the XXth century, but it reveals a lot about the political and ideological context of French constitutional review. In 2000 it is still not possible to say that the "school issue" (*querelle scolaire*) is totally outdated; it is still a very controversial and divisive issue in French politics: probably the most controversial of all the issues concerning fundamental rights. All projects that have attempted to write down a 20th Century charter of fundamental rights have failed due to the persistence of such divisions. This has two consequences.

From a political perspective this means that there is still a lack of consensus between the democratic political parties on the content, or even the scope of fundamental rights. More importantly, it means that fundamental rights are still potentially a pretext to debates based on party-politically based interpretations, far more so than in a country like Germany. This gives a highly political content

---

[3]   See Marcel Morabito, *Histoire constitutionnelle de la France – 1789–1958* (Paris: Montchrestien, 2000, 6th ed.).

to all debates on the interpretation of the Constitution, even in legal doctrine (see section 2).

Technically speaking the only means by which France can claim a list of constitutionally protected rights under the 1958 constitution is through the very short paragraph 1 of the Preamble according to which "the French People solemnly proclaims its faithfulness to the rights of man and to the principles of national sovereignty as defined in the Declaration of 1789, confirmed by and with additions from the Preamble of the Constitution of 1946". According to the established interpretation, this refers to three elements: the Declaration of Human rights of 1789, a list of 17 articles, finely and clearly drafted and very representative of the first generation of rights, the Preamble of the constitution of 1946, a list of 16 paragraphs of a declaratory nature, and representative to a large extent of the third generation of rights, and the famous fundamental principles recognised by the Republic's laws (*principes fondamentaux reconnus par les lois de la République: PFRLR*)[4] for which there is not the slightest indication of content, and even less a list, and which very typically covers a number of the rights of the second generation. The only formal limitation to the concept of the Republic's laws is in the word Republic, so it cannot refer to statutes adopted before 1793, or during the periods 1799–1848, 1852–1870 or 1940–1945. French doctrine refers to these texts as the "constitutional bloc", e. g. the texts and principles that have constitutional value even if they are not directly embedded in the document called "*Constitution de la République française*". There is a continuing debate about the precise limits of this bloc (see Section 2) In addition, a very small number of relevant sentences are to be found in the rest of the text, for instance the principle of equality and non discrimination in article 1.[5]

1.3. The Shift of Tradition in Matters of Parliamentary Sovereignty

From the Revolution of 1789 onwards and for about 160 years, French public law has been dominated by two fundamental concepts: the general will is the only source of law (*la loi, expression de la volonté générale*[6]), and the principle of representative democracy. The first concept induced a sacred character of statute law, without much attention being given to the difference between the constitution and acts of parliament. A century later, with parliamentarianism

---

4   See Rohr, above n. 2, p. 141.

5   "France shall be an indivisible, secular, democratic and social Republic. It shall ensure the equality of all citizens before the law, without distinction of origin, race or religion. It shall respect all beliefs." (Translation by National Assembly on: http://www.assemblee-nationale.fr/english/8ab.asp).

6   The expression is usually quoted from Jean-Jacques Rousseau, *Du Contrat social ou principes du droit politique*, 1762 (Paris: Flammarion [Gf Philosophie], 2001).

firmly rooted, the second concept led to a monopoly on decision-making by members of parliament, through a combination of two supposedly opposed theories of sovereignty. According to the theory of *souveraineté nationale*[7] the only sovereign was the Nation, embodied by its representatives – allowing for a role for the King and for restricted suffrage. According to the theory of *souveraineté populaire*[8] the People was the only sovereign, and expressed itself through its elected representatives and through direct consultation (*plébiscite*). Under the IIIrd Republic (1875–1940), the golden age of classical French constitutionalism, those concepts helped to support the unlimited power of the two houses of parliament. This was enhanced by the fact that the three "constitutional laws" of 1875 had been conceived as a transitional constitution and thus contained only arrangements for the functioning of state institutions. This firmly established parliamentary sovereignty and therefore French constitutional law was as opposed to the concept of constitutional review as British constitutional law. Parliamentary sovereignty was not a principle as such, only the result of the combination of the two dominant legal concepts. This theoretical limitation as well as political circumstances restrained the two supreme courts – the *Cour de Cassation* for civil and criminal courts and the *Conseil d'Etat* for administrative courts – from any attempt to develop a French version of *Marbury v. Madison*. Only a small part of legal scholarship tried to undermine theoreticallly this unlimited power of members of parliament: the most representative was Raymond Carré de Malberg, professor in Strasbourg after World War I. His influence was limited by the fact that he met quite some hostility from a number of colleagues who accused him of being too much influenced by German legal theory. He was rediscovered only in the sixties and is now considered as the main forerunner of modern French constitutionalism. In his pamphlet *La Loi, expression de la volonté générale* (1931),[9] he demonstrated how the initial revolutionary theories had been unduly diverted by politicians and recommended introducing elements of direct democracy and constitutional review in order to balance parliamentarianism.

Parliamentary instability during the last decades of the IIIrd Republic and even more during the IVth Republic (1946–1958) as well as the lack of courage of most members of parliament in 1940 – only a very small number of them voted against giving the full powers to Maréchal Pétain that enabled him to establish an authoritarian regime on a formally legal basis – were the grounds for a dramatic change which was prompted by the unsolved crisis of the Algerian

---

[7] Usually considered as due to Siéyès 'Qu'est-ce que le Tiers-Etat', 1789 in Emmanuel Joseph Sieyès, *Ecrits politiques* (Paris: Editions des archives contemporaines, 1985).

[8] Usually considered as due to Rousseau, above n. 6.

[9] Raymond Carré de Malberg: *Contribution à la théorie générale de l'Etat* (Paris: Sirey, 1920–1922 [reprint Paris: CNRS 1985]), and *La loi, expression de la volonté générale* (Paris:Economica, 1984 reprint).

war which helped General de Gaulle to come back into power in 1958. At that time there was an important consensus in doctrine and amongst politicians about the need to reduce the power of members of parliament. This resulted in the Constitution of 4 October 1958 which contained a number of technical constraints limiting the power of parliament, including a system of review of statute law by the newly created Constitutional Council. The aim of the system was clearly to avoid parliament going beyond the competencies which were distinctively attributed by the Constitution. The purpose was not to check how parliament exercised legislative power, but to see that it restricted itself to adopting statute law in the most important fields and did not interfere with the executive power of the cabinet.

This has two consequences. For more than ten years, there was hardly any link between the French system of constitutional review and fundamental rights, as these were not at stake in the numerous cases submitted to the Council. Furthermore, the Council developed as an institution which should not review statutes on merit, but only check if the right procedures had been followed – cabinet decision for executive regulation, parliamentary procedure for acts of parliament – setting hence the ground for the "theory of the pointsman" (*théorie de l'aiguilleur* – see Part 2 of this chapter).

The main problem with this change has been due to the fact that the whole system of mechanisms imagined in 1958 was designed to contain excesses of the continental type of non majoritarian parliamentarianism which had developed in France – as in Germany under the Weimar Republic, in Italy and in the Benelux countries.[10] The personality and charisma of General de Gaulle and the constitutional reform of 1962 providing for the direct election of the President of the Republic created the conditions for a majoritarian parliamentarianism on the Westminster model, and thus those mechanisms tended to become important weapons used by the government against the opposition. Until 1971 the Council was mainly seen as one of these mechanisms, thus not at all a guardian of fundamental rights, but possibly one of its enemies. This origin of the Council still accounts for an important part of the current debates about constitutional review in France.

1.4. Checks and Balances between Government and Opposition

After decades of governmental instability and weak Cabinets, France became, under the rule of General de Gaulle, a prominent example of governmental stability and a strong executive, with a dominant party (the Gaullist party UNR, than UDR replaced in 1976 by Chirac's RPR) which had no parliamentary tradition and thus little respect for the rights and status of opposition. Once De Gaulle had withdrawn from politics after having lost the 1969 referendum, the

---

[10]   See Philippe Lauvaux, *Le parlementarisme* (Paris: PUF, coll. Que-sais-je? 2nd ed. 1997).

opposition parties, and mainly those from the centre started using the constitution in order to develop better conditions for parliamentary democracy; the centrist politicians had stopped supporting de Gaulle when he put an end to the negotiations with the United Kingdom on its accession to the European Economic Community in 1962 and thus felt free to criticize him unlike during the period 1958–62, where solidarity in the Algerian war strongly limited the scope of opposition in parliament.

The first clear case where this happened was in 1971[11] when the President of the Senate took for the first time the initiative to ask the Council to review a bill on merit in a highly sensitive political context where the government was struggling for months with extreme left groups supported by the philosopher Jean-Paul Sartre. In order to stop post-1968 unrest, the bill tried to reform the famous Act of 1901 on freedom of association, a very important symbol of French democracy. The Senate had been strongly opposing General de Gaulle from 1962 to 1969 and the President of the Senate, Alain Poher, had been a candidate of the centre at the 1968 presidential election. In the same way as his predecessor, Gaston Monerville, he wanted to promote the image of the Senate as a defender of civil liberties. Monerville was very sceptical towards the Council – which had refused to acknowledge his request to review the 1962 Act instituting the direct election of the President on the basis that it had been adopted by referendum – although the procedure for constitutional amendment had clearly been violated. Alain Poher on the contrary seems to have been advised about the mood of the members of the Council at that time. Amongst them were François Luchaire,[12] a professor of public law from the centre left *Parti radical*, Paul Coste-Floret, a former Christian democratic minister of the IVth Republic, and François Goguel former head of the Senate's services. It was quite a surprise for public opinion to discover that there was an institution called *Conseil Constitutionnel* that was able to counteract government,[13] even when the latter had an overwhelming majority in the National Assembly. For legal scholarship, the surprise was just as great, as there seemed to be nothing in the constitution to prevent the amendment of the 1901 Act. The 1789 Declaration did not recognise any freedom of association: on the contrary the Revolution abolished all "intermediary institutions" (*corps intermédiaires*) as well as the system of corporatism which had been dominating professional life and obstructing the proper functioning of market mechanisms. One – or more – of the subtle legal

---

[11]   See Rohr, above n. 2, p. 141.

[12]   See François Luchaire, 'Souvenirs du 16 juillet 1971' in *La Liberté d'association et le Droit – Centenaire de la loi du 1er juillet 1901* (Paris: Conseil Constitutionnel, 2001), pp. 17–22.

[13]   Decision n° 71–44 DC of 16 July 1971 (*liberty of association*). Decisions of the Council are to be found on: http://www.conseil-constitutionnel.fr; the most important decisions are commented, with indications of doctrinal references, in Loïc Philip and Louis Favoreu, *Les grandes décisions du Conseil Constitutionnel* (Paris: Dalloz, 2001, 11th ed.).

124

minds amongst the members of the Council remembered the sentence about the fundamental principles recognised by the Republic's laws, of which the 1901 Act was the most prominent example. Interestingly the Council not only took a big risk in using such an unprecedented and extensive technique of interpretation, but also decided to quash the bill: obviously there were not only subtle legal minds but also some very sensitive political minds amongst the members of the Council, who knew that they would be supported by an important part of the political class, which stretched beyond the divisions between government and opposition.

It is quite clear that this case law would have remained quite exceptional without the political changes of 1974 where Valéry Giscard d'Estaing from the centre right *Républicains indépendants* won the presidential election, putting an end to Gaullist domination of the institutions. He very quickly prompted a series of reforms in order to modernise French political life by enhancing the status of opposition. One of those reforms was the change in the list of authorities allowed to refer bills to the Constitutional Council. In the 1958 Constitution only the President of the Republic, the Prime Minister, the President of the National Assembly and the President of the Senate could do so – only the latter could be close to opposition. From 1974 on, 60 members of the National Assembly or 60 members of the Senate could refer a bill to the Council, a change of procedure that opened the door for a quite extensive jurisprudence.[14]

The origins of the 1974 reform seem to be quite often forgotten in contemporary debates: whereas it accounts once again for the "theory of the pointsman" (see Section 2), it is of little help when it comes to legitimising the council and its jurisprudence. The lack of consensus on a possible charter of fundamental rights has always prevented a more comprehensive reform which would officially establish the Council as a major institution of the French system of rule of law. The constitutional sources of the institution point to a mechanism in the parliamentary checks and balances, any further role is based on the content of the council's case law which would probably not have developed as it did if France had not been familiar for a long time with a system of legislative review which provided for techniques to be taken up by the Council in reviewing acts of parliament.

1.5. *The Classical Possibilities of Judicial Review of General Norms*

Even French doctrine shows little awareness of the fact that judicial review of legislation pre-existed the 1971 decision and even the 1958 constitution. This is due to a specific concept in French public law that is intimately linked with the

---

[14] See Rohr, above n. 2, p. 143.

French concept of separation of powers and the institution of the *Conseil d'Etat*.[15] Since 1790 separation of powers means in French public law that the (ordinary) courts are not entitled to interfere with the work of the executive. The *Conseil d'Etat* had been established as the government's legal council in Bonaparte's constitution of December 1799. As such it advises governments on bills before they are presented to parliament, as well as on general regulations which governments adopt for the implementation of bills. As an administrative judge, the same *Conseil d'Etat* is entitled to review all governmental decisions – acting independently in the name of the people since 1872. Whereas the principle of separation of powers is deemed to prevent courts from interfering with government and from reviewing acts of parliament, nothing prevents the *Conseil d'Etat*, an independent institution within the executive branch, to review all decisions taken by the authorities of the executive branch, including delegated legislation and general regulations, be it only in order to make sure that governments act according to the indications of parliament.

Whereas in most European continental countries there are totally different remedies against administrative acts and against government regulations, the same remedies are available for both types of instruments in France.[16] As a consequence, review of government regulations developed in the *Conseil d'Etat's* jurisprudence during the XIXth century, as well as the possibility of quashing illegal regulations. Other European countries had to wait for constitutional review in order to apply this type of remedy; as long as there was no constitutional review of acts of parliament, the only reviewing systems on government regulation were based on the courts ability to suspend the application of a regulation in clear-cut *ultra vires* cases.

Furthermore, as the constitutional laws of the IIIrd Republic included provisions on substance, and in order to avoid debates on the legal status of the 1789 Declaration as well as a number of other former constitutional charters of rights, the *Conseil d'Etat* started referring to "general legal principles" (*principes généraux du droit*) during the last decades of the XIXth century. Unlike the principles of natural justice in English law, the French *principes généraux du droit* are not limited to procedural concepts linked to the due process of law, they include a number of substantive principles amongst which the principle of equality has a paramount position. What was new with the Constitutional council was the institution, created in 1958–with a forerunner with very limited powers under the 1946 constitution – and above all the fact that it could oppose the will of parliament; on the basis of a different and broader system of remedies, the

---

[15]   See L. Neville Brown and John S. Bell, *French Administrative Law* (Oxford:Clarendon Press, 5th ed. 1998, and John Bell, *French Legal Cultures* (London:Butterworths, 2001).

[16]   Jacques Ziller, 'Le contrôle du pouvoir réglementaire en Europe', *Actualité Juridique, Droit Administratif*, n° 9/199, pp. 635–644.

Conseil d'Etat was doing the same with norms adopted by the executive for a century in the framework of judicial review of government action.

1.6. The Legitimacy of the Members of the Constitutional Council

It is well known that no professional requirements are necessary in order to become a member of the French Constitutional Council, whereas in other European countries candidates usually need to be qualified lawyers from practice or academia.

A number of commentators stress the fact that the French system enables the appointment of experienced politicians to the Council, which might account for a fine-tuned political sensitivity.[17] As a matter of fact, more than two thirds of the 60 members of the Council to date have been active in politics before joining the Council, as members of government (about one third), members of parliament, or direct advisers of major politicians.[18] This has accounted for the acceptance of the Council's decisions by the political class, even in the very delicate matter of reviewing parliamentary elections, the field where it has encountered most political criticisms.

Some others commentators underline how few academics have been members of the Council, something which highly contrasts with the Italian experience, and also that of Germany or Spain for instance.[19] Only five members of the Council have been professors of public law: Marcel Waline, François Luchaire, Georges Vedel, Jacques Robert and Jean-Claude Colliard. Two out of nine members of the Council were members together between 1965 and 1971,[20] only one for the rest of the time and there was none of them in the periods 1959–1962 and 1974–1980. The number of career judges (magistrats) is even smaller, and they have obviously been appointed for political reasons much more than for professional ones. A much higher number have been advocates, but most of the latter very quickly started a political career. Clearly the authorities in charge of appointing the members of the Council – the Presidents of the Republic and of both Houses of parliament – have tried to send signals to society that legal technique should not be the most important element in the Council's reasoning.

The lawyers amongst the Council are not to be found amongst professors of public law, a characteristic that corresponds best to French public law tradition. Strikingly the number of former members of the Conseil d'Etat amongst the

---

[17] See for instance the handook by Jean Gicquel, *Droit constitutionnel et institutions politiques* (Paris: Montchrestien, 15ed. 1997), p. 747.

[18] These numbers are the result of a rapid evaluation based on the list of the members of the council (http://www.conseil-constitutionnel.fr) and biographies of most of them which are available on different sites of the Internet.

[19] See Gicquel, above n. 17.

[20] Waline and Luchaire.

Council is twice as high as that of professors of law. A number of very prominent members of the *Conseil d'Etat* have been appointed to the Constitutional Council, amongst them René Cassin – appointed in 1960 – who had a prominent role in drafting the 1948 UN Declaration of Human rights, and Yves Guéna – presently President of the Council – who drafted legislation for Michel Debré (also a member of the Conseil), De Gaulle's minister of justice in 1958 who drafted essential parts of the Constitution before becoming the first Prime Minister of the Vth Republic.[21] For a century, both members of the *Conseil d'Etat* and professors of public law have had a prominent role in the development of practice and doctrine in public law, and those who have appointed the members of the Constitutional council have been careful to keep this tradition alive. The *Conseil d'Etat* has always had a very specific role in French state institutions,[22] especially as it has served as a kind of retreat for prominent members of the opposition of the day. Léon Blum for instance has been famous with generations of students of administrative law for his influence on the jurisprudence of the Conseil d'Etat in which he served, while being known to the public as the socialist leader who won the 1936 elections and was the first Prime minister of the Popular front.[23] This phenomenon has for a long time contributed to increasing the legitimacy of the institution within parliamentary democracy. The prominent role of the *Conseil d'Etat* in 2000 may be illustrated by the following indications: the French judge at the Hague Court of International Law,[24] at the European Court of Justice[25] and at the European Court of First Instance[26] in Luxembourg, at the European Court of Human Rights[27] in Strasbourg are all members of the *Conseil d'Etat*; as are the Heads of the Legal services of both the European Commission[28] and the Council[29] of the European Union; as is the President of the French Constitutional Council Yves Guéna.

Furthermore the day to day running of the Council is controlled by the *Conseil d'Etat*: the Council has been installed in the *Rue Montpensier* in the same block of buildings as the *Palais Royal* where the Conseil d'Etat sits.; This

---

[21] See Olivier Duhamel and Jean-Luc Parodi (eds.), *La constitution de la cinquième République* (Paris: FNSP 1985).

[22] Jean-Paul Costa, Le Conseil d'Etat dans la société contemporaine (Paris:Economica, 1993).

[23] Léon Blum, see a short biography on http://www.conseil-etat.fr/ce-data/persos/blum.htm.

[24] Maurice Guillaume.

[25] Jean-Pierre Puissochet.

[26] As a matter of fact, the French judge at the Court of First Instance has always been a member of the Conseil d'Etat, with the exception of the period 1995–2001 with André Potocki an "ordinary" judge who afterwards became president of the Paris Court of Appeal.

[27] Jean-Paul Costa.

[28] Jean-Louis Dewost.

[29] Jean-Claude Piris.

may seem purely anecdotal but the Secretary general of the Council is traditionally a member of the *Conseil d'Etat*. He (the gendered pronoun is used deliberately as all Secretaries general have been so far male) is not only in charge of
the organisation of the council but it seems that he has a more and more
important role in the drafting of the Council's decisions. According to French
judicial tradition there are no separate opinions of members of the Council, only
one decision of the Council as a whole, without any indication about the number
of votes in favour and who has lead the drafting. One of the favourite games of
French doctrine is to try to find out who wrote what. A number of important
sentences of famous decisions have thus been attributed to Georges Vedel, one
of the most eminent professors of public law, but more recently it has become
fashionable to consider the Secretary General as the author of a number of
shrewd formulae. This has happened quite often with Olivier Schrameck, a
Conseiller d'Etat who was secretary general from 1994 to 1997, after having been
the main adviser (*directeur de cabinet*) of the then minister of education Lionel
Jospin; after the elections of 1997 he left the Council and became again the main
adviser of Lionel Jospin when the latter became Prime Minister. His predecessor
Bruno Genevois (1986–1994) is the author of one of the most authoritative
handbooks on the case-law of the Council.[30]

A more detailed sociological analysis of the Council would show how well it
has been inserted since the beginning in what the French call *l'appareil d'Etat*:
a set of public structures where the *grands corps*[31] – established groups of civil
servants like for instance the *Conseil d'Etat*, the *Cour des Comptes* (Cour of
auditors), or also the prefects and the big groups of state engineers – play as
important a role as the official decision making institutions, because they are
the key to the daily functioning of the latter. This has guaranteed the acceptance
of the Council's decisions by the French civil service long before the question
about the acceptance by courts started to matter, when the Council began to
use the technique of "congruency conditioned by interpretation" (see section 2.2.).

2. SOME DOCTRINAL DEBATES ABOUT THE FRENCH CONSEIL CONSTITUTIONNEL

Forty years after its birth, the Constitutional Council is still subject to heated
debates about the issue of its possible reform. In the seventies and eighties the
main doctrinal debate about the Council referred to its nature: judicial or
political? The discussion was unavoidable, be it only for the choice of the word
"Council" instead of "Court" when it was established. At that time, participating
in the debate meant taking a position on the development of a new kind of

---

[30] Bruno Genevois, *La jurisprudence du Conseil Constitutionnel – Principes directeurs* (Paris:
S.T.H., 1988).
[31] See Rohr, above n. 2, p. 29.

constitutional law in France.[32] Nowadays the judiciary nature of the Council seems to be admitted by a large part of doctrine, and the rise of new constitutional law resulting from constitutional review has been generally accepted by legal scholarship.

However insisting – as does Louis Favoreu[33] – on the fact that the Council is in line with the European model of Constitutional courts might reinforce the idea that law and politics are two totally separated worlds and that the Council only acts within the first of these. On the contrary acknowledging its specific character, as do Pierre Avril and Jean Gicquel,[34] helps to fully understand the interaction of both worlds. This remains true even if the objective is to transform the Council into a real court through the introduction of a system of preliminary ruling, as in the case of Dominique Rousseau.[35] The mere fact that doctrine unanimously supported the Council in order to protect the institution in the Dumas case shows how fragile its legitimacy still is: in 1998–1999 Roland Dumas refused to step down from his post of President of the Constitutional Council for almost one year whilst" being subject to criminal proceedings for corruption which related to his former duties as a Minister of foreign affairs. This case shed light on the absence of a fully-fledged constitutional status for the Members of the Council.

The old discussion on the Council's nature is still structuring contemporary doctrinal debates: According to Olivier Cayla,[36] the fact that constitutional lawyers strongly insist on its "scientific" – thus neutral – nature is intended to deny any political or axiological dimension in the way it functions. According to him "the Kelsenian positivist paradigm – as adapted to France especially by Eisenmann – is the privileged framework within which the legal phenomenon is being examined"[37] Within this conceptual framework, the doctrinal discussion has shifted from the mere existence of the Council to the way constitutional justice is being exercised.

In a very classical way, as happens in Germany or in Italy, the issues presently addressed are those relating to the conciliation of democratic theory and the exercise of constitutional justice. For the Constitutional Council these issues appear under three forms:

---

[32] François Luchaire, 'Le Conseil constitutionnel est-il une juridiction?', *Revue du droit public*, 1979, p. 27.

[33] 'Synthèse', in Guillaume Drago, Bastien François et Nicolas Molfessis (eds.), *La légitimité de la jurisprudence du Conseil constitutionnel* (Paris:Economica, 1999), p. 390; see also his remarks in *Le Conseil constitutionnel a quarante ans* (Paris: L.G.D.J., 1999), p. 200.

[34] Pierre Avril and Jean Gicquel, *Le Conseil constitutionnel* (Paris: Montchrestien, 1998), p. 139.

[35] Dominique Rousseau, in *Le Conseil constitutionnel a quarante ans*, above n. 33, p. 188.

[36] 'Le Conseil constitutionnel et la constitution de la science du droit', in *Le Conseil constitutionnel a quarante ans*, above n. 33 p. 106.

[37] Idem, p. 113.

How far may it go in the creation of norms necessary to its reviewing function?
How far may it go in reviewing the content of acts of parliament?
How far may it go in the protection of fundamental rights?

This paper concentrates on three main streams in contemporary French legal doctrine, best illustrated by professors Louis Favoreu – a kind of "bodyguard" of the Council –, Dominique Rousseau – also trying to protect the Council, but in a more global framework of constitutional democracy – and Michel Troper[38] – whose aim is not to defend the Council, but to understand what it is doing.

2.1. The Discussion on the Extension of Norms of Reference

This discussion has always been very vivid since the fundamental decision of 16 July 1971. It is often based on accusations, especially on the part of politicians, as shown by the following quotation from Prime Minister Balladur to the Congress in Versailles – the *Congrès*, in France is a plenary meeting of both houses of parliament – which convened for the first time in November 1993 in order to reverse a decision of the Council through constitutional amendment. "Since the Council has decided to extend the scope of its review to the Constitution's Preamble, this institution has been inclined to check the congruency of acts of Parliament with general principles which are sometimes more of a philosophical or political than a legal nature, sometimes contradictory, and furthermore conceived in times different of ours".[39] As explained in the previous section, unlike the Italian or Spanish constitutional courts the Council is not bound by a fully-fledged catalogue of fundamental rights. Even the most critical commentators note that the Council has to face a difficult alternative: "if the constitutional judge were to apply only the letter of the Constitution, its review would be inefficient and useless because the text only exceptionally gives an answer to the question put to the court. If on the contrary it tries to give life to the Constitution through a "constructive" interpretation, it will be accused of arbitrariness and of wanting to act as a government".[40] It is obvious that the Council has followed the second path in order not to be a useless institution. In this framework legal scholars are debating the margin of manoeuvre which the Council may enjoy while tracing the limits of the "constitutional bloc"[41](see above Part1)– the apparatus of constitutional norms of reference.

---

[38] See Michel Troper, 'La signature des ordonnances. Fonctions d'une controverse', *Pouvoirs*, n° 41, 1987, p. 75, a pioneer study in terms of legal sociology applied to this topic.

[39] Déclaration du Premier ministre devant le Congrès réuni à Versailles le vendredi 19 novembre 1993 quoted in *Le Monde* 20 november 1993, p. 10.

[40] Danièle Lochak, 'Le Conseil constitutionnel, protecteur des libertés?', *Pouvoirs*, n° 13, 1991, p. 42.

[41] Jean Michel Blanquer, 'Bloc de constitutionnalité ou ordre constitutionnel', in *Mélanges offerts à Jacques Robert* (Paris: Montchrestien, 1998) clearly shows how untidy these limits are.

Doctrinal positions on this question are quite clear. The trend led by Louis Favoreu and supported by Georges Vedel[42] tries to downplay the Conseil's power in order to avoid presenting it as "the master of sources of constitutional law". The purpose of such a position is to avoid the criticism of a government of judges. The debate on the limits of the "constitutional bloc" has been focusing on the "fundamental principles recognised by the Laws of the Republic" (PFRLR – see Part 1). Georges Vedel claims that the Council has set strict conditions to recognising such principles.[43] Louis Favoreu claims that even the principle of continuity of public services – a very important and specific traditional principle of French administrative law that guarantees the continuity of public administration and other policy implementing bodies – and that of the separation of powers which the Council calls "principles with constitutional value"[44] can somehow be linked to provisions of the Constitution, and that at any rate the Council does not use the expression "general legal principles" (*principes généraux du droit*).[45] This reasoning which leads to minimising the Council's power to establish principles is subject to two kinds of comments. First an unlimited belief in the constitutional text is being transferred on what the Council says, as if it were possible to lay down definitively the meaning of a provision of the constitution without having to repeat the interpretative reasoning at the moment where it is being applied. Second, it is still the Council who decides whether the conditions needed for the recognition of PFRLR are met.[46] By laying down more precise conditions the Council however puts limits to the development of its own interpretation, and its authority would suffer if it did not respect its own interpretation.

On the contrary Dominique Rousseau's thesis of democracy insists on the Council's power. All elements of the constitutional bloc are taken into account without trying to hide principles or other components for which the link to the constitution is not always clearly established, like "objectives of constitutional value", "constitutional requirements", "requirements of general interest" or "legitimate objectives". Rousseau even finds this constitutional bloc too narrow as he recommends departing from the 1975 jurisprudence by which the Council

---

[42]   Georges Vedel, 'Le précédent judiciaire en droit public', *Revue internationale de droit comparé,*, n° spl. *Journées de la société de législation comparée,* vol. 6, 1984, p. 283.

[43]   'Préface aux actes du Colloque de Rennes', in Drago, Bastien and Molfessis, above n. 33, p. XI et p. XII.

[44]   See Decisions 79–105 DC of 25 july 1979 for the first principle and 79–104 DC of 23 may 1979 for the second, above n. 13.

[45]   Louis Favoreu, 'Dualité ou unité de l'ordre juridique: Conseil constitutionnel et Conseil d'Etat participent-ils de deux ordres juridiques différents?', in *Conseil constitutionnel et Conseil d'Etat* (Paris: LGDJ-Montchrestien, 1989), p. 151.

[46]   See Marie-Claire Ponthoreau, *La reconnaissance des droits non écrits par les cours constitutionnelles italienne et française. Essai sur le pouvoir créateur du juge constitutionnel* (Paris: Economica-PUAM) 1994.

excludes reviewing statutes on the basis of their compatibility with international treaties.[47] His main motivation is that he thinks constitutional review might lose relevance if it lets stand statutes which would later be set aside by ordinary courts due to their incompatibility with an international covenant.[48] This is in line with his view that the Council takes part in a continuing creation of rights: through its exchanges with other institutions, social actors – like political parties, the doctrine and more globally with public opinion- the Council acknowledges new demands and concerns emanating from our ever-evolving society. This does not eliminate the Council's subjectivity but "forces it to let evolve the text and its jurisprudential arbitration" even if the author regrets that "the Council is sometimes too slow in accompanying this tread towards progress".[49] This doctrinal trend is paradoxically close to Favoreu's positions, who claims that constitutional review of acts of parliament by the Council is preferable to review by the judges in Luxembourg and Strasbourg.[50] Rousseau's logic is the same in refusing a competition which might lead to "marginalising the Council and its case-law".[51] This logic of constantly establishing rights and the attempt to see the Council as a vehicle of 'trendy ideas' (idées dans le vent[52]) are questionable; the danger is not that of a constitution with variable geometry but that of a judge who would be beholden to public opinion as expressed by mass media. The kind of public and reasoned use of opinion of the Siècle des Lumières to which D. Rousseau refers does not exist any more, and it is thus surprising that he tries to theorise a "continuous democracy" as being a "deliberative democracy (...) a sign of something beyond representative democracy" and thus as a new era of democracy in which constitutional justice would serve as a pillar.[53]

As opposed to those two trends in defence of the Council, Michel Troper adopts the point of view of legal science as a descriptive rather than prescriptive theory.[54] In developing what he calls a realistic theory of interpretation he tries

---

[47]   See decision n° 74–54 DC of 15 January 1975 (abortion), above n. 13.

[48]   See Dominique Rousseau, in Dominique Rousseau and Frédéric Sudre, Conseil constitutionnel et Cour européenne des droits de l'homme (Paris: S.T.H., 1990) recently restated in, 'Neuf années au Conseil constitutionnel. Débat entre Jacques Robert et Dominique Rousseau', Revue du droit public, 1998, p. 1763; and his remarks at the conference, Le Conseil constitutionnel a quarante ans, above n. 33, p. 189.

[49]   See Dominique Rousseau, Droit du contentieux constitutionnel (Paris: Montchrestien, 1999, 5th ed).

[50]   Louis Favoreu 'La légitimité du juge constitutionnel', Revue Internationale de droit comparé, 1994, p. 581.

[51]   above n. 49, p. 199.

[52]   Pierre Avril and Jean Gicquel, 'La Constitution est-elle devenue "ringarde"?', Le Monde, 1 July 1999.

[53]   'Introduction', in Dominique Rousseau (ed.) La démocratie continue (Paris-Brussels: L.G.D.J.-Bruylant, 1995).

[54]   'Justice constitutionnelle et démocratie', Revue française de droit constitutionnel, 1990, p. 32.

to explain what "interpreting" means and – within a doctrine that is not well versed in hermeneutics – helps to get rid of the idea that a legal provision needs only interpretation in a case where it is not clear.[55] On the basis of Kelsen's work Troper has popularised the idea that interpretation is a pre-condition to any application of rules.[56] He thus participated in explaining the formula according to which "interpretation is an act of will, not of knowledge".[57] The starting point here is radically different from that of Vedel and Favoreu. For Troper it is not the text itself, but the representation one has of the text – and thus the norms – which matters. All depends upon the image the Council wants to foster: that of "protector of civil liberties" – which was dominant in the seventies and eighties with the use of PFRLR – or that of "non yes this might seem strange but it is right: non-master of the sources of constitutional law" – which it started to promote in the 1980s. The descriptive approach recommended by Michel Troper should not deter from judging upon the value of constitutional decisions. In the case of one of the most sensitive decisions of the Council – that of 22 January 1999, about the ratification of the Treaty establishing the International Criminal Court – he did not hesitate to support an interpretation that was not based upon a developed written justification and that was based on an unorthodox view of article 68[58] of the Constitution, relating to the criminal liability of the President of the Republic.[59] The Council's interpretation, according to which the President is only accountable to the High Court of Justice – a special court for members of the Executive – during his mandate gives him a privilege of jurisdiction which ministers only enjoy for actions that are linked to their functions. Troper explained different interpretations of article 68 and by supporting the Council's solution he directly took part in the polemics that surrounded this decision, presented by part of the press as a suspicious exchange

---

[55] See for instance the discussions between Loïc Philip and Jean Foyer in, *Le Conseil constitutionnel a quarante ans*, above n. 33, p. 185.

[56] Hans Kelsen, *Théorie pure du droit* [translated into French by Ch.Eisenmann from the second edition of *Reine Rechtslehre*] (Paris: Dalloz, 1962), p. 403; Michel Troper, 'Le problème de l'interprétation et de la théorie de la supralégalité constitutionnelle', in *Mélanges Eisenmann* (Paris: Cujas, 1975).

[57] See Troper's preface to Jacques Meunier, *Le pouvoir du Conseil constitutionnel. Essai d'analyse stratégique* (Paris-Brussels: L.G.D.J.-Bruylant), 1994, p. 8.

[58] Decision n° 98–408 DC or 22 January 1999 (International Criminal Court), above n. 13. Art. 68 is stating:

"The President of the Republic shall not be held liable for acts performed in the exercise of his duties except in the case of high treason. He may be indicted only by the two assemblies ruling by identical votes in open ballots and by an absolute majority of their members; he shall be tried by the High Court of Justice." Above n. 13.

[59] Michel Troper made his views known through the press: 'Comment décident les juges constitutionnels', *Le Monde*,13 february 1999, later published in the *Revue française de droit constitutionnel* (1999, n° 37, p. 325).

between President of the Republic Jacques Chirac and and President of the Constitutional Council Roland Dumas. The Council's attitude of not justifying its position on such a delicate matter was lacking in prudence, but to Troper this is not important: the restraints put on the judge – including that of justifying his or her decisions – are extra-legal in the French contemporary system and thus without consequence if the judge decides not to accept them.[60] However, if the legal world is a world of representations, how does one explain that judges do not feel bound by an obligation to motivate their decisions in order to facilitate their acceptance by the community of interpreters?[61] The debate is shifting here to the more general problem of interpretation and argumentation in law and so it should, due to the fact that the judge's function is mainly an interpretative activity.

2.2. The Discussion about Extension of Reviewing Techniques

As soon as 1987–in the framework of a conference on the Constitutional Council and political parties, members of parliament started to question the technique of "congruency conditioned by interpretation" (conformité sous réserve d'interprétation). This method was described as "the Constitutional Council treading on the legislator's ground" (P. Clément, centrist party UDF) or leading to the "slippery path of injunction" (J.-C. Martinez, extreme-right party FN).[62] This technique of "congruency conditioned by interpretation" also used by the German and Italian constitutional courts, enables the Council to indicate to the Executive and the Judiciary what conditions are necessary to a constitutionally correct application of a statute. It may thereby subtract or add to the statutory text in order to make it congruent with the constitution. In his already quoted speech to the Congress in 1993, Prime Minister Edouard Balladur condemned the large power of interpretation taken up by the Council in indicating "to government and administrative courts how an Act of Parliament has to be applied, going even sometimes very far into detail". As a matter of fact, courts have tried to resist this "congruency conditioned by interpretation" because it limited their own power to interpret. They have even publicly criticised this technique through their unions.[63]

Constitutional doctrine is far less opposed to it,[64] as it is conscious that the

---

[60] Troper, above n. 54, p. 46.

[61] See Ponthoreau, above n. 46.

[62] See Louis Favoreu (ed.), Le Conseil constitutionnel et les partis politiques (Paris: Economica, 1988).

[63] Association professionnelle des magistrats in Le Monde, 8–9 august 1993.

[64] Some however are critical, see for instance Dimitri Georges Lavroff, 'Le Conseil constitutionnel et la norme constitutionnelle', in Mélanges Gustave Peiser (Grenoble: P.U.G., 1995), p. 352; Henri Roussillon, Le Conseil constitutionnel (Paris:Dalloz, 1996, 3rd ed), p. 74.

Council has to face a growing number of cases and thus needs to have a more flexible attitude towards congruency of a statute with the Constitution. Refusing to declare an act as void is not only motivated by the will to safeguard a text with high political content which includes questionable provisions, but is not contrary to the constitution as a whole. It is also a way of avoiding the discontinuity in norms which would result from quashing the text, a sanction which would be disproportionate because of the gap that would remain in the text of the statute if only some words or sentences of the statute had to be deleted. Private law doctrine, for instance François Terré[65] (*in* Drago, 1999) on the contrary tends to see this as "an astonishing expression of intellectual despotism" which leads to blocking "the mental mechanisms of the interpreters" and thus to channel or even tie up the Court of Cassation.

On this question, Louis Favoreu – who has for a long time been showing how all branches of law are being progressively constitutionalised[66] – tends to call upon comparative law to clarify the situation. German and Italian constitutional courts can use constraining mechanisms in order to impose their "conditioned interpretation". Favoreu points to the advantage of ex ante review as in France, which allows judges to inject a degree of constitutionality into statutes by means of "congruency conditioned by interpretation" even before they have been submitted to any other interpretation. This is as efficient as, but less cumbersome than, the Council acting before the courts act. He therefore prefers ex ante review and he claims that once ordinary judges become better informed and educated they will "naturally" follow this line. He also denies any criticism of fostering "hyper constitutionalism" and claims that "the expansion of constitutionality is not accompanied by a full cleaning up of the legal order as the constitutional judge will mainly constitutionalise [...] living law, that is solutions which have already been adopted by ordinary or administrative courts".[67] As the constitutional judge has had to review statutes concerning all fields (criminal law, labour law, budgetary law ...) all those disciplines have been constitutionalised to some extent: this is not the problem. It is rather the will to institute the constitutional judge as the only holder of constitutional truth, as expressed in the debate started by the *Koné* decision of the *Conseil d'Etat* in 1996, in which the supreme administrative court for the first time decided to recognise PFRLR which had not previously be discussed by the Council.

Nowadays, the old discussion about the submission of administrative law to constitutional law is being largely replaced by a dispute between private lawyers and constitutional lawyers that Georges Vedel tried to stop by indicating that

---

[65] Quoting Dean Carbonnier and concluding the Rennes conference, *La légitimité de la jurisprudence du Conseil constitutionnel*, above n. 33, p. 407.

[66] See 'L'apport du Conseil constitutionnel au droit public', *Pouvoirs*, n° 13, 1980, p. 17.

[67] Louis Favoreu, *Droit constitutionnel* (Paris: Dalloz, 1999), pp. 343–45.

"the Constitution has been built on law, and not law on the constitution".[68] The discussion thus is not really about the Constitutional Council, but more about the delimitation of different branches of legal science.

According to Dominique Rousseau the Council is competing with government and parliament in law making. In this competitive norm-making regime the Council has no privileged position as it is bound in practice by a series of constraints which allow for the participation not only of the other institutions but also of ordinary judges, doctrine and relevant pressure groups amongst others. Paraphrasing Habermas, Rousseau talks of judicial acting (*l'agir juridictionnel*): this is a meaning produced by several interpreters. The Council does not offer a guarantee of definitive or transcendental truth, thus keeping the way open for changes in case law or even departing from stare decisis.[69] In this view the technique of "congruency conditioned by interpretation" appears as a method adapted to consensus building in giving a meaning to constitutional provisions through the application of statutes". Thereby the technique loses its "despotic" character, and Rousseau recently described it as a technique "whereby the Constitutional Council registers the exchange of arguments which has been continued in front of it",[70] an expression which does not aim at being neutral. It means that the Council is not master of the mechanism. It should be noted that contrary to Louis Favoreu, Dominique Rousseau does advocate the creation of ex post review in order to install a dialogue between constitutional judges and ordinary judges when it comes to interpreting statutes and thus avoiding the Council being perceived as the master of the Constitution. On the other hand he follows the former in defending the constitutional discipline, and has proposed stopping the discussion about "pan-constitutionalism" through means of interdisciplinary co-operation.

As Michel Troper does not try to justify the democratic character of exercising constitutional justice, he did not comment specifically on the development of reviewing techniques, but more generally on the question of discretionary power of the Council. He has tried to indicate from the perspective of legal science what concept of democracy is compatible with such a power. He sets as a premise of the French political system that the Council has the quality of a representative institution, and that as such it participates in the expression of the general will as a co-legislator. In Troper's view, the general will does not correspond to the moment of adoption of a statute but to that of its implementation.[71] As "the true legislator is not the author of the text but its interpreter"

---

[68] In Bertrand Mathieu and Michel Verpeaux (eds.), *La constitutionnalisation des branches du droit* (Paris: Economica-PUAM, 1998), p. 16.

[69] Dominique Rousseau, above n. 49, p. 419.

[70] Preface to the thesis of Alexandre Viala, *Les réserves d'interprétation dans la jurisprudence du Conseil constitutionnel* (Paris:L.G.D.J., 1999), p. VI.

[71] Michel Troper, above n. 54, p. 47.

public institutions are not submitted to the Constitution: there is no hierarchy between the Constitution and the decisions of the Council. The latter is only submitted to its own will because only those norms that it originates exist. Therefore it is not only a co-legislator, but also the only true author of the constitution. Troper's theory tends to entirely dissolve the traditional distinction between law making (*législation*) and judicial decision-making (*juridiction*). It is indeed possible to think that the distinction between law production and law implementation is too rigid, but it is not a reason for totally distinguishing them: the legislator is free from bonds to the legal system and can act at the moment it decides to, whereas the judge can only act when asked to and cannot give random meaning to a legal text. Furthermore, whereas the judge has to justify his or her decisions, the legislator is not bound by any duty of that kind. Troper's conclusions go directly against the democratic theory according to which only the people are sovereign. But for him this is only a myth. At any rate representation and sovereignty are meta-legal concepts. Nevertheless the debates throughout the last decade shows that French doctrine is far from following this idea and tries on the contrary to understand what is the meaning of the concepts of sovereignty and representation.

2.3. *The Discussion about Reinforcing the Protection of Fundamental Rights*

One of the most debated issues of the last decade is that of supra-constitutionality. This formulation is specific to French doctrine and linked to a debate that originated under the IIIrd Republic (1875–1940). It was triggered by the formulation introduced into our constitutional law by the revision of 14 August 1884–still applicable –, according to which the republican form of government may not be amended. It points to natural law as being above the Constitution. The debate was very vivid in 1993 when the Government introduced a bill amending the constitution, which had the same content as a text which had been rejected by the Council's decision of 13 August 1993 concerning a bill on immigration. For the first time constitutional amendment was used in order to by-pass a decision of the Council. Prime Minister Balladur's already quoted speech to the Congress included all the criticisms about the Council. Far beyond the crisis and the attempt to by-pass the Council, the issue was whether constitutional-amending power could do whatever it wanted and thus possibly give constitutional status to provisions that would violate fundamental rights?

Doctrinal positions can be organised around the theory of the pointsman (*théorie de l'aiguilleur*), developed by Louis Favoreu as early as 1982.[72] According to this theory which rests upon Charles Eisenmann's work and which is also

---

[72] The theory has been fully developped in Louis Favoreu, 'Le Conseil constitutionnel et la cohabitation', *Regards sur l'actualité*, n° 135, 1987, p. 3; see also his remarks in *La politique saisie par le droit* (Paris: Economica, 1988), p. 30.

supported by Georges Vedel, any unconstitutionality – even on content – can be analysed as a lack of competence of the ordinary legislator as only the constitution making power could make the decisions which were quashed by the judge. Therefore the constitutional judge can only indicate which way ought to be taken at an unclear juncture: legislative or constitutional procedure. The powers that are instituted by the constitution (*pouvoirs constitués*) have to follow the will of constitution making power (*pouvoir constituant*). Thus the Council never goes against general will and the will of the nation's representatives. As Dean Vedel said: "If judges do not govern, it is because the sovereign can at any moment repeal their decisions as long as it appears in all its majesty of constitution making power".[73] The main aim of this theory is to legitimate the Council, but it does not solve the issue of majoritarian theory: abuse of power is not to be feared from the legislative, but from the constitution making power. The Council's decisions of 6 November 1962 and of 23 September 1992 whereby the Council refused competence for reviewing bills which have been approved by referendum point in the same direction.

It would be indeed anti-democratic for a judge to overrule a decision that has been taken by the people according to established procedures. However, is it possible to set aside any minimal review of the action of revision according to the ultra-democratic argument of the sovereignty of the power of revision? What happens then with the liberal argument according to which constitutional review has to protect the minority against abuse of power? With Olivier Beaud's writings, the discussion has been redirected in this way: what is at stake is not the protection of the constitutional judge but the preservation of the Constitution.[74] It is not necessary to admit *supra* constitutionality in order to give legal value to limitations of content to the constitution amending power. A constitutional limitation to amending power is only possible through a distinction between derived constitution making power (*pouvoir constituant dérivé*) and original constitution making power (*pouvoir constituant originaire*). Before Beaud recalled this old distinction which was already made before World War II by Bonnard, an important part of doctrine saw the constitution amending power as the expression of constitution making power and thus needed the concept of *supra* constitutionality in order to limit this power.

This also explains the strange formula of the Council's decision of 2 September 1992: "without prejudice of the limitations due to the periods where constitutional amendment cannot be undertaken or pursued (...) and with due respect to the provisions of article 89 paragraph 5 (...) the constitution making power is

---

[73] Georges Vedel, 'Schengen et Maastricht. A propos de la décision n° 91–294 DC du 25 juillet 1991', *Revue française de droit administratif*, 1992, p. 180.

[74] See Olivier Beaud, *La puissance de l'État* (Paris: PUF, 1994).

sovereign".[75] Doctrine has wondered whether the Council thus indicated that it felt competent to review whether these limitations had been acknowledged. Louis Favoreu has had difficulties on this point as comparative law is essential to him and as the German and Italian constitutional courts admit or even practice this kind of review. However according to him, admitting this review of constitutional bills "destroys the argument according to which the legitimacy of the constitutional judge derives from the fact that he does not have the last word".[76] This is also the reason why Georges Vedel strongly opposes such a review of constitutional amendments.[77] There is however confusion: nobody proposes to submit the original constitution making power to review and thus the constitutional judge cannot have the last word. The judge is not sovereign.[78] The constitution amending power derived from the constitution is empowered by the Constitution to modify the text only if the limits on time and content are acknowledged. In its decision of 1992 the Council only underlines the existence of limits, it doesn't claim competence.[79]

According to Dominique Rousseau, on the contrary, the Council has clearly claimed a competence to review the constitutionality of constitutional bills.[80] This extension of competence is in line with the concept of democracy which is supported by Dominique Rousseau: not a democracy of numbers (majoritarian democracy) but a constitutional democracy (democracy based on competition of views on fundamental values) the main values of which are fundamental rights and pluralism of opinion, and of which the Council is the guardian.

Michel Troper's position is also in line with his theory of interpretation: he rejects Olivier Beaud's argumentation as simply being "the old naturalistic justification of power".[81] For him the constitutional judge always has the last word. This idea according to which the constitutional judge has the last word is fully compatible with the wishes of the two other theories discussed here, namely their wish to enlarge the Council's competence not only to reviewing constitutional bills, but also to the constitutional review of decisions made by the President of the Republic – under article 16 about emergency powers – or

---

[75] Decision n° 92–312 DC (Maastricht II) above n. 13. Article 89 par. 5 is stating that "The republican form of government shall not be the object of an amendment". There is no consensus in French doctrine about the meaning of this sentence apart from a prohibition of the restauration of monarchy.

[76] Louis Favoreu, above n. 50, p. 581.

[77] 'Souveraineté et *supra* constitutionnalité', *Pouvoirs*, n° 67, 1993; see also his preface in Drago *et al.*, above n. 33.

[78] Olivier Beaud, 'Le Souverain ', *Pouvoirs*, n° 67, 1993, p. 43.

[79] Olivier Jouanjan, 'La forme républicaine, norme *supra* constitutionnelle?' in *La république en droit français* (Paris: Economica, 1996), p. 277.

[80] *Droit du contentieux constitutionnel*, above n. 49, p. 187.

[81] Michel Troper, "La notion de principes *supra* constitutionnels", *Revue internationale de droit comparé*, n° spl., journées de la société de législation comparée, 1993, p. 355.

a preliminary ruling on the interpretation of the Constitution. They come strangely together in supporting the idea of a "judiciary sovereignty".[82] However if one thinks about the numerous missing elements in the French system of constitutional review – let us add the most controversial one: the absence of a possibility to suspend the application of unconstitutional statutes – the Constitutional Council is far from having all the competencies of the German constitutional court and from having the same general influence on the function of institutions. Shifting from the former traditional French idolatry of statute law (*la Loi*) to that of constitutional decisions, a good deal of doctrine has opted to support the Council in order to complete the French system of Rule of Law, or just by submitting itself to *communis opinio*.

3. CONCLUSIONS

The members of the Constitutional Council, and especially its former President Robert Badinter (1986–1995) have invested a lot of energy in the 1990s in trying to help establish the rule of law (*l'Etat de droit*) in newly emerging democracies. They have established and reinforced relations with their counterparts in Constitutional Courts in Central and Eastern Europe. It is therefore especially important to evaluate the relevance of the French experience to those countries, but French lawyers – even if they are comparatist – may be the worst placed to do so. The following tentative conclusions should therefore be examined with great care.

France might seem to have an experience quite remote from that of emerging democracies, as it is one of the most ancient parliamentary democracies and the very specific charasteristics of the Constitutional Council which make it different from most other European constitutional courts might reinforce this impression. On the other hand, there may be useful lessons to learn from this last aspect.[83] The Council has not been established as a constitutional court, and certainly not as a protector of fundamental rights. But the conjunction of some initiatives of the political class – the reform of 1974–and those of its members have enabled its transformation into the latter type of institution. The fact that it has never be composed of a majority of professional constitutional lawyers and judges has not diminished its legitimacy, even with academics who debate about a number of issues which are known to their colleagues from other countries, and it has certainly helped its integration into the classical French system of state institutions. Last but not least, it shows how little the existence of a codified system of norms matters to the operation of judges: France is usually considered as a

---

[82]   In the wording of Olivier Beaud who criticises its validity, in 'Le souverain', above n. 78, p. 43.

[83]   The comparison between France and the United States might also be very useful. See Rohr, above n. 3 p. 138.

classical example of a system of "civil" or "written" law, in contrast to "common law" countries. In constitutional law – as already was the case with administrative law – it relies very heavily on judge-made law for reasons which are partly explained by political and historical circumstances, but also to a great extent by a longstanding legal tradition which has its roots in the two century old Conseil d'Etat, if not in more ancient institutions.[84]

---

[84] Tocqueville already pointed out that the French state tradition was based on quite some continuity, beyond the apparent disruption of the Revolution of 1789 in *L'Ancien Régime et la Révolution*, see Jacob-Peter Mayer (ed.), *L'Ancien Régime et la* Révolution de Alexis de Tocqueville (Paris: Gallimard 1985).

6. Between Politics and the Law: The Development of Constitutional Review in Italy

Giancarlo Rolla & Tania Groppi

1. BASIC FEATURES OF CONSTITUTIONAL REVIEW IN ITALY

1.1. Composition and Powers of the Constitutional Court

The Italian Constitution of 1948 demonstrates the important link between a democratic state governed by law, a rigid constitution and constitutional review. The framers of the Constitution, having opted for a "rigid" constitution entrenched by a difficult amendment process, designed a system of constitutional review that was ranked among the various 'guarantees of the Constitution'. In accordance with the dominant constitutional trends in postwar Europe (particularly as expressed by Hans Kelsen), they designed a system of centralized review, with the creation of an 'ad hoc' organ of constitutional justice separate from the judiciary.

The Constitutional Court's composition reflects an effort to balance the need for legal expertise, characteristic of a judicial body, against the acknowledgment of the inescapably political nature of constitutional review: Fifteen judges, chosen from among legal experts (magistrates from the higher courts, law professors, and lawyers with more than 20 years of experience) populate the Court, one-third of whom are named by the President of the Republic, one-third by Parliament in joint session, and one-third by the upper echelons of the judiciary.

The powers of the Constitutional Court, defined in article 134 of the Constitution, are typical of constitutional tribunals. The Court has the power:

(a) to adjudicate the constitutionality of laws and acts having force of law, issued by the national and regional governments;
(b) to resolve separation-of-power conflicts between organs of the national government, between the national and regional governments, and between regions;
(c) to adjudicate crimes committed by the President of the Republic (high treason and attack on the Constitution). Article 2 of Constitutional Law n. 1 of 1953 added a further power beyond those listed in the Constitution:
(d) to adjudicate the admissibility of requests for referenda to repeal laws, which may be sponsored by 500,000 voters or 5 regional councils pursuant to article 75 of the Constitution.

Wojciech Sadurski (ed.), Constitutional Justice, East and West, 143–159
© 2002 *Kluwer Law International. Printed in Great Britain.*

1.2. Limitations on the Powers of the Constitutional Court and the Importance of Certified Questions

Compared to other models of constitutional adjudication, especially the most recent ones, these powers seem notable for being so apparently limited and minimalist. On the one hand, the Italian Constitutional Court has no powers beyond constitutional adjudication (aside from adjudicating crimes committed by the President of the Republic) which are present in other systems of constitutional law, and which could almost be labeled political: for example, many systems involve powers relating to electoral issues, supervision of political parties, and ascertaining the incapacity of the President of the Republic.

On the other hand, with regard to the Court's main power of reviewing the constitutionality of laws, several limitations arise from articles 134–137 of the Constitution, Constitutional Law n. 1 of 1948, and Law n. 87 of 1953. These limitations concern the means of triggering constitutional review, the object that it reviews, and the types and effects of its decisions. First of all, access to constitutional review is rather circumscribed: The Italian system offers essentially *a posteriori* review, which arises out of a separate judicial proceeding. In order to submit a question to the Constitutional Court, a judge must explain why it is relevant and not patently groundless. As for the first requirement, the judge must establish that judgment in the pending case 'could not be reached independently of the resolution of the constitutional question.' In other words, the challenged law must be necessary and unavoidable for resolution of the lawsuit. With regard to the second requirement, the judge must entertain a plausible doubt about the constitutionality of the legal rule that must be applied to resolve the case at bar. The judge must not express an opinion about the constitutionality of the rule (that job belongs to the Constitutional Court) but must determine whether the challenge has any colorable legal basis.

The constitutional proceeding begins with a certification order, whereby the judge suspends all proceedings and submits the question to the Constitutional Court. In that order, the judge must indicate not only the relevance and plausibility of the question, but also the 'object' and 'parameter' of review: that is, he must identify the challenged law and the constitutional provision that it violates. The Constitutional Court's first task is to verify the existence of these elements, before turning to the merits. Neither private citizens nor parliamentary groups nor local (sub-regional) governments can directly invoke the Court's jurisdiction. Only regions can directly challenge national or regional laws they believe injure their own power, and the national government can do the same with regional laws. The keys that open the door to constitutional review are primarily in the hands of ordinary judges, who therefore perform the important function of screening the questions that the Court will be called upon to answer.

Secondly, the 'object' of constitutional review is represented exclusively by laws and by acts having force of law. On the other hand, constitutional review encompasses neither sources of law inferior to statutes, unlike many other constitutional systems, nor court judgments. Furthermore, the Court may not wander from the '*thema decidendum*' (that is, the object and parameter of review) identified in the certification to the Court. As stated in article 27 of Law n. 87 of 1953, 'The Constitutional Court, when it accepts an application or petition involving a question of constitutionality of a law or act having force of law, shall declare, within the limit of the challenge, which of the legislative provisions are illegitimate.' In other words, constitutional review is limited to the question presented, and occurs 'within the limit of the challenge.' Article 27 itself carves out an exception to this general principle: The Court may also declare 'which are the other legislative provisions whose illegitimacy arises as a consequence of the decision adopted.' At issue here is 'consequential unconstitutionality.'

Thirdly, there is a limited range of decisions that resolve the process of constitutional review. Aside from decisions that are interlocutory or reject a question on procedural grounds, decisions either *accept* or *reject* constitutional challenges, known respectively as *sentenze di accoglimento* and *sentenze di rigetto*. The consequences of these two sorts of decisions, including their temporal effects, are rather straightforwardly defined by law. Decisions that *reject* a constitutional challenge do not declare a law constitutional. They merely reject the question as it was raised. These judgments are not universally binding, that is, they are not effective *erga omnes*. Thus, the same question can be raised again, on the same or different grounds; only the judge who has certified the question cannot raise it again in the same lawsuit. For this reason, such judgments are said to be effective only as between the parties, that is, *inter partes*. On the other hand, judgments that *accept* a constitutional challenge are universally binding (or, put another way, are effective *erga omnes*) and are retroactive, in the sense that the constitutional rule cannot be applied beginning on the day after the judgment is published. This retroactivity is limited by what are called '*rapporti esauriti*,' which might be translated as 'concluded relationships.' For reasons of convenience and legal certainty, judgments do not affect situations that were already resolved by final judgments or claims that are barred by statutes of limitations or the like. Yet there is an exception to this rule where a final criminal conviction has been entered pursuant to the law now declared unconstitutional: The law provides that such a conviction and any related punishment should cease.

Moving from a simple list of the Court's powers to statistics about its activities, the limited nature of its powers becomes even clearer. The vast majority of the Court's activity is dedicated to the constitutional review of laws, overshadowing its other powers, in particular with regard to national-regional conflicts. Within this category of constitutional review, particular importance is assumed by 'incidental' review or certified questions, which, as the statistics indicate, has absorbed most of the Court's energy during its forty years, and which therefore deserves the bulk of our attention.

Table 1

	1956–65	1966–75	1976–85	1986–97	Total
Constitutional review (incidental)	808	1,636	2,102	5,658	10,562
Constitutional review (principal)	106	120	138	552	926
National-regional conflicts	87	126	108	336	710
Conflicts between state powers	1	9	5	41	56
Admissibility of requests of referenda	0	2	16	67	85

DATA (sources: Constitutional Court).

1.3. Judicial Nature of the Constitutional Court's Review of the Constitutionality of Legislation

The model of constitutional review of laws adopted in the Italian Constitutional Court is based on a qualitative distinction between judicial review and other non-judicial forms of reviewing the constitutionality of laws. The Italian Constitution provides several mechanisms for reviewing the decisions of the legislature. Especially important is the review performed by the President of the Republic in promulgating national laws (which can be sent back to the Chambers with a reasoned explanation, so that they can proceed to a further vote: art. 74 Const.), as well as that performed by the Government with regard to regional laws (which can be sent back, through the Government Commissariat, to the regional council for a new vote that must be made by absolute majority: art. 127 Const.). Judicial review differs from these proceedings, in that: a) it entails review performed by a body detached from the legislative process that enjoys guarantees of impartiality and professionalism; b) review occurs through a trial-like process; and c) the decision is reached by applying judicial methodology.

The Constitutional Court is therefore a true 'court,' though one separate from the judiciary. It is a special court, which decides issues submitted to it through defined procedures, as the Court itself has recognized on several occasions. Of course, this is a unique sort of procedure. The subject of the judgment is a law, or rather an act that is the result of the will of political actors, Parliament and the Government, with all of the consequences that entails. In this respect, one can speak of constitutional proceedings not primarily aimed at protecting individual rights, but rather at ensuring the conformity of statutory law with the text of the Constitution, and therefore at protecting a superior interest: the maintenance of the constitutionality of the laws.

Three elements make judicial review proceedings unique. First, although judicial review is aimed at guaranteeing the objective interest of the legal system in the constitutionality of the laws, this interest is joined with the desire to protect concrete rights that have been injured by the legislator. Safeguarding the legal system and protecting individual rights are complementary rather than opposite goals, especially when one considers that 'the more intensely and directly rights are defended, the more objective and just is the legal system.'

Second, constitutional review, unlike other judicial proceedings, is marked by a greater degree of procedural flexibility. This flexibility arises not from the lack of a dedicated set of rules, but from the Constitutional Court's freedom to interpret and apply its procedural rules. The Constitutional Court, unlike other Italian courts, possesses normative powers with respect to its own proceedings that find expression either in the adoption of formal procedural rules (that is, 'rules for proceedings before the Constitutional Court') or in simple procedural decisions. This room for maneuver allows the Court to modify its prior practice, or procedural rules themselves, in order to achieve a desired goal, or to more fully effectuate constitutional values. This 'discretion' enjoyed by the Constitutional Court has divided scholars: some authors claim that the Constitutional Court's activity should be subjected to established procedural rules that are spelled out with precision, while others believe that a certain measure of discretion is unavoidable, given the nature of judicial review. This disagreement mirrors the larger debate between those who emphasize the judicial nature of constitutional review and those who instead focus on its necessarily political nature.

Third, the Constitutional Court, besides being a court, is also an actor that 'creates' legal rules. Indeed, it has the 'last word' on the interpretation of the Constitution. This 'last word' binds all legal actors, much as precedent does. This aspect of judicial review gives the Court's decisions special weight, much different from the decisions of other judges: They produce effects like those of sources of law.

In light of these three features (judgments aimed mainly at guaranteeing the consistency of the legal system; discretion in applying procedural rules; and the normative value of its decisions) one must affirm the judicial nature of the constitutional review performed by the Constitutional Court. Yet one cannot neglect the unique factors that permit one to speak of a 'third way.' Independently of its judicial nature, the Court sometimes uses standards that belong to the political decision-making process. The Court itself has denied that it forms part of either the ordinary or the special judiciary, *tout court*, 'given the many and profound differences between the task assigned to the Court, without precedent in the Italian legal system, and those which are well known and historically well established as belonging to the judiciary.' (Judgment n. 13 of 1960; Order n. 536 of 1995). One should not forget, indeed, that 'a good system of constitutional adjudication is that which can identify a proper point of equilibrium' between politics and jurisprudence. This generally valid observation is especially appropriate in the Italian case, where the 'ambiguity' of the system has been fostered by the legislature itself (and intensified by the anomalies of the Italian political system).

2. EVOLUTION OF THE ITALIAN MODEL OF JUDICIAL REVIEW

2.1. The Centralized and Concrete Model of Constitutional Review

An analysis of the powers granted by the Constitution and a glance at the procedures used are indispensable for understanding the mechanics of the Italian Constitutional Court, yet they are not sufficient for comprehending the role it plays in the legal system. To this end, one must consider other aspects, taking account of history and considering the provisions governing constitutional review in the light of the dynamism of its jurisprudence. It is hard to understand the current system simply by looking at the statute books. Theory traditionally distinguishes between the North American model ('judicial review of legislation') which is diffuse, concrete, and binding as between the parties, and the Austrian model (*Verfassungsgerichtbarkeit*) which is centralized, abstract, and binding universally. Judged against this backdrop, the Austrian model clearly had the greatest influence on the framers of the Italian Constitution.

Undoubtedly, the implementation of our system has not maintained the purity of Kelsen's Austrian model, having introduced some features that approach the American model of judicial review. As an initial matter, the centralization of review has been mitigated by endowing ordinary judges with two important powers: first, the decision whether or not to raise a constitutional question; second, the constitutional review of rules that are subordinate to statutes (a power of review that belongs exclusively to ordinary courts). This peculiarity has a significant impact on how we classify the Italian system, since it indicates that it is not an absolutely centralized model of constitutional review, but rather a model with some features of diffuse review. Furthermore, the requirements that the question be relevant and explained by the certifying judge have introduced into the process features similar to those contained in systems of concrete review.

The hybrid nature of the Italian system is highlighted by the Court's practice which, in some phases, has helped to increase the degree of concreteness of its judgments. In this regard, one can emphasize the following developments:

(a) The recent and drastic reduction of time taken to decide a case and the consequent elimination of pending questions means that a constitutional decision increasingly has concrete effects for the parties in the case at bar;

(b) The Constitutional Court has increasingly employed its evidence-gathering powers before deciding questions. As a result, the Court can better understand the practical aspects of the question that gave rise to the constitutional challenge, the effects that would flow from the Court's judgment, and the impact of a judgment on the legal system;

(c) An interpretative continuum has arisen, in two respects, between the Constitutional Court and ordinary courts (in particular, the Court of Cassation and the Council of State). On the one hand, the legal principles and interpretations of the Constitution provided by the Constitutional Court acquire force for all legal actors, especially courts that must directly apply the Constitution or review rules that are subordinate to statutes. On the other hand, when resolving constitutional questions, the Constitutional Court tends to address the legal provision in question not in the abstract, but as it has been concretely applied. The Court tends to rule on the "living law," or the rule as it has been interpreted in case law. In this way, there seems to have been a tacit division of labor between the Constitutional Court and ordinary courts, so that each endorses and approves the other's interpretation within its own sphere. This tendency may be broken by the excessive speed of the Court in deciding cases: the object of the proceeding may very well be a statute for which the 'living law' has yet to be consolidated.

One can undoubtedly affirm that the Italian system has evolved in a direction that blurs the distinction between the two traditional theoretical models, giving rise to a 'third way' or, perhaps more accurately, to a hybrid system that is open to the influences of both great models. As shown above, the Italian system contains elements from various systems of constitutional review: The system is centralized for laws and acts having force of law, but diffuse when reviewing a subordinate rule; constitutional review is *a posteriori* in cases involving certified questions or when a region challenges a national law, whereas it is *a priori* when the national government challenges a regional law; finally, the decisions of the Court are universally binding when they strike down a law, but are binding only between the parties when they turn away a constitutional challenge.

2.2. "Interpretative" and "Manipulative" Judgments and Relations with Courts and the Legislature

The powers of the Italian Constitutional Court and the process of constitutional review were regulated in the years immediately after the entry in force of the Constitution and have not changed much since. Faced with this static legislative situation, the Court's case law has been extremely dynamic. During this period, the Constitutional Court has revamped its own procedural tools, primarily through interpretation rather than rulemaking. The Italian Constitutional Court has shown most creativity in the effects of its own decisions, especially in their effects on the legal system.

The Constitution and statutes govern only the structure and effects of judgments that accept or reject a constitutional challenge. The rich variety of judgments that characterize the Italian constitutional system arise from the creativity of the Court, which has found ways to solve problems not so much by drawing on abstract theory, but on the necessity to respond to specific practical needs. In particular, the various types of judgments arise from the necessity, recognized by the Constitutional Court, to consider the effects of its decisions and to calibrate their impact on the legal system and on other branches of government, in particular on Parliament and the judiciary.

This result was made technically possible by the theoretical distinction between 'disposizione' and 'norma,' or legal 'texts' and 'norms' A 'text' represents a linguistic expression that manifests the will of the body that creates a particular legal act. A 'norm,' on the other hand, is the result of a process of interpreting a text. By use of hermeneutic techniques, one can derive multiple norms from a single text or a single norm from multiple texts. This distinction between text and norm is particularly important in that it permits the separation of the norm from the literal meaning of the text, in a way cutting the umbilical cord that link them at the moment the text is approved. This distinction allows the system to evolve, facilitating the interpreter's creative activity and helping to reduce the 'destructive' activity of the Court, with its consequent gaps in the legal system, giving it the ability to operate with more surgical precision.

A. Relationship with the Courts

The need to establish a relationship with the courts, which are charged with interpreting statutory law, has led the Constitutional Court to issue two kinds of decisions, 'corrective' decisions and 'interpretative' decisions (which can come when the Court either strikes down or upholds a law). These two kinds of decisions have allowed a division of labor between the ordinary courts and the Constitutional Court and have mitigated conflicts that arose during the Court's early years.

(a) With its so-called 'corrective' decisions, the Constitutional Court avoids the merits of the constitutional question. It limits itself to stating that the statutory interpretation of the certifying judge is incorrect, in that he failed to consider either the teaching of other courts, a consolidated interpretation of the law in question, of the plain meaning of the text or, increasingly, of a possible interpretation that would conform to the Constitution.

(b) With 'interpretative' decisions, the Constitutional Court adopts one of the possible interpretations of the challenged text, choosing one that is either consistent with the Constitution (i.e., a sentenza interpretativa di rigetto) or one that is contrary to the Constitution (i.e., a sentenza interpretativa di accoglimento).

In particular, in the absence of 'living law,' the Court proposes to the courts an interpretation that would render the statute consistent with the Constitution, thereby saving it from unconstitutionality. With such an interpretative judgment that 'rejects' a challenge, the Court reaches the merits and declares the challenge 'unfounded' insofar as the law can be attributed a meaning consistent with the Constitution, which is different from the one given it by the certifying judge or the petitioner. Among the possible meanings of the text, the Court chooses the one that is compatible with the Constitution, putting aside those which could conflict with the Constitution. Such an interpretation offered by the Court is not, however, universally binding. It is effective only insofar as its opinion is persuasive or its authority as constitutional arbiter is convincing. A legal duty is created only in relation to the judge who raised the question. In the case at bar, the norm cannot be applied according to the interpretation initially proffered by the judge in the certified question.

(c) Faced with this tendency of judges to ignore legal interpretations offered by the Court, the Court has discerned a need to overcome the structural limits of interpretative judgments that *reject* a challenge. It has therefore issued interpretative judgments that *accept* a challenge. In such judgments, the Court chooses among the possible meanings of a norm and declares unconstitutional the one that is incompatible with the Constitution. All other possible meanings of the text remain available; the interpretative approach is similar to that of the kind of judgment discussed just above, but the practical effects are different. With interpretative judgments that *accept* a challenge, the Court does not eliminate the text from the legal system, but only one of the norms to which the text could give rise. The text, in other words, continues to be applied and is therefore effective, except for the norm deemed unconstitutional.

B. Relationship between the Court and the Legislature

While '*interpretative*' judgments seem designed to address the relationship between the Court and ordinary courts, other sorts of decisions have instead affected the relationship between the Court and the legislature.

(a) An especially delicate issue has been the use of '*additive*' judgments, whereby the Court declares a statute unconstitutional not for what it provides, but for what it fails to provide. In this way, the Court manages to insert new rules into the legal system, which cannot be found in the statutory text. This kind of decision runs contrary to Kelsen's model of constitutional review, according to which a constitutional court ought to be a '*negative legislator.*' With these judgments, the Constitutional Court transforms itself into a creator of legal rules, thereby playing a role that in our system belongs principally to Parliament. Yet in many cases, the mere nullification of an unconstitutional law would not solve the problem posed by the constitutional question, and the addition of a missing rule is the only way to remedy the violated constitutional value and, therefore, offers the only way for constitutional law to perform its task. A first effort to limit the creative impact of such judgments is the rule that they are appropriate only where it is said, to use a poetical metaphor, that the judgment inserts only '*rime obbligate,*' or 'obligatory verses,' into a statute. That is, the norm proposed by the Court is logically necessary and implicit in the normative context, thereby eliminating any discretionary choice.

(b) A second effort to eliminate the interference with the parliamentary realm implied by these judgments has led, in recent years, to the development of slightly different judgments, which are described as adding only 'principles' rather than norms. These are known as *'additive di principio.'* In these decisions, the Court does not insert new rules into the legal system, but only principles that the legislature must implement with statutes that are universally effective. In its opinions in such decisions, the Court indicates a deadline within which the legislature must act and sets forth the principles it must follow. In this way, a single decisional tool manages to combine the contents of an 'additive' judgment with a sort of 'delegation' order, in order to reconcile the immediacy of the Court's 'acceptance' of the constitutional challenge with the preservation of the legislature's discretion. These judgments pose greater problems with regard to their effectiveness *vis-à-vis* ordinary judges. Although in most cases it is considered that legislative action is needed to apply the principle, in some cases judges have considered themselves capable of applying the Court's decision to arrive at a rule governing the case at bar.

(c) Another type of decision born of the necessity of caution in relation to the legislature are the so-called 'admonitory' decisions or *'doppie pronunce'* – what one might call 'repeat or follow-up judgments.' The Court has resorted to these tools when it has faced highly politicized questions. In these cases, it has preferred to bide its time and hint at its decision that the challenged norm is unconstitutional, without explicitly declaring it so. The Constitutional Court has introduced a logical split between its judgment and its opinion: The former announces that the constitutional question is 'inadmissible'; the latter, however, clearly indicates that the constitutional doubts are well-founded. Structurally, *'doppie pronunce'* imply that in the first instance the Court will reject the certified challenge, asking the legislature to act. If Parliament does not act and the question is raised again, the Court will respond with a judgment that accepts the constitutional challenge, declaring the law unconstitutional.

(d) Finally, the highly political nature of some issues, combined with the need to balance the defense of social rights against the state's financial crisis, have obliged the Constitutional Court to modulate the temporal effects of its decisions that strike down laws as unconstitutional. In this way, the Court tries both to assure that the Government and Parliament have the time needed to fill the gap created by its nullification of a law, and to strike a balance between the constitutional rights central to the social welfare state and the scarcity of economic resources. This problem is not unique to the Italian legal system. Comparative law offers several solutions. The Austrian Constitutional Court can postpone the effects of a judgment nullifying a law for up to one year, thereby letting parliament regulate the area and avoid legal gaps. The German federal court can also declare laws simply 'incompatible' (*Unvereinbarkeit*), without declaring them nullified, or can declare that a law is 'still' constitutional. In that case, the law is declared only temporarily constitutional. The court retains its power to declare the law unconstitutional if the legislature does not modify the law to conform with the court's judgment.

In Italy, by contrast, the temporal effects of judgments that accept a constitutional challenge are rigidly established. The Constitutional Court has tried, through its case law, to spread over time the effects of its decisions in two ways. First of all, it has imposed limits on the retroactive effects of its decisions accepting constitutional challenges (in order, for example, to protect certain trial proceedings) through what have been labeled judgments of 'supervening unconstitutionality.' In these cases, the norm is not nullified *ab initio*, but only from the moment at which it becomes defective. The simplest example is when a new constitutional norm takes effect, but one could also imagine a change in the economic or financial environment, in social attitudes, or in a more general change in conditions that leaves a norm incompatible with the Constitution.

Finally, the Court can postpone the effects of a declaration of unconstitutionality (for example, where judgments lead to expenses for the public treasury), leaving the legislature a fixed amount of time to act before the statute is nullified. These are decisions of 'deferred unconstitutionality,' where the Court itself, based on the balancing of various constitutional values, pinpoints the date on which the law is nullified. Such decisions pose serious problems of compatibility with the Italian system of constitutional review, in that they do not affect the case at bar, thereby detracting from the concrete nature of review that characterizes the system.

3. THE MAIN STAGES OF DEVELOPMENT OF ITALIAN CONSTITUTIONAL REVIEW AND ITS INFLUENCE ON THE STRUCTURE OF GOVERNMENT

To evaluate the role played by the Constitutional Court in the Italian constitutional system, its relationship with other branches of government and with parliamentary democracy, one can delineate (at the risk of oversimplification) several stages in its development.

3.1. Promotion of Reforms

The first period (from the fifties to the early seventies) could be described as 'implementation of the Constitution' or 'promotion of reforms.' This period was characterized by the central role played by the Constitutional Court in the modernization and democratization of the Italian legal system, as well as in the affirmation of the values contained in the new republican Constitution. In this process of systemic reform, the Court acted as a stand-in for Parliament, which was slow and timid in modifying statutes inherited from earlier times. In this phase, the Constitutional Court took on what might be described as a 'didactic' function, in that it breathed life into the Constitution's principles and brought them to the attention of society, as well as a catalyzing function, as it renewed the legal system by eliminating norms contrary to the Constitution.

The Constitutional Court found itself constantly filling in for Parliament, which pursued statutory reform slowly and hesitatingly, and found itself in conflict with the highest levels of the judiciary, in particular with the Court of Cassation and the Council of State, according to whom programmatic constitutional norms did not provide grounds for judicially reviewing legislation. Beginning with its first judgment (n. 1 of 1956), which constitutes a landmark in Italian constitutional law, the Court affirmed the binding nature of all constitutional norms (thereby overriding the classic distinction between preceptive and programmatic norms), specifying their binding character not only in relation to the government, but also private parties, and reiterated its power to review laws that predated the Constitution. In this way, thanks also to the stimulus provided by progressive elements of the judiciary, which raised numerous constitutional challenges to laws enacted before the Constitution concerning liberty as well as social and economic rights, the Constitutional Court was able to purge the legal system of numerous unconstitutional norms dating to the nineteenth century as well as to the fascist era. Worthy of note are the Court's actions to protect personal liberty (such as its judgments in connection with the public security law of 1931 and the old system of unlimited pretrial detention), freedom of expression (which was purged of the worst lingering traces of fascism, the multiple permits to be obtained from the police), freedom of assembly (the Court declared unconstitutional a law that required prior notice for assemblies in public places, judgment n. 27 of 1958), and gender equality (the Court declared unconstitutional, in judgment n. 33 of 1960, a 1919 law that excluded women from a vast array of public positions).

In this initial phase, the Constitutional Court was considered, both by legal scholars and public opinion, the principal (if not the only) interpreter and defender of the Constitution and of the values it embodied. It is this stage that explains how the Constitutional Court garnered its authority and prestige within the Italian government, even though it was a body created out of nothing by the Constituent Assembly, and laid the foundations of its legitimacy.

3.2. Mediation of Social and Political Conflicts

The second stage ran from the mid-seventies to the mid-eighties and has been described as that of 'mediation of social and political conflicts.' This was a period in which, after the 'cleansing' of preconstitutional legislation, the object of constitutional review was no longer preconstitutional legislation, but recent laws that had been drafted and approved by the republican Parliament. For this reason, the Court took on a more politicized role characterized by balancing techniques–essentially in the search for equilibrium and mediation among the various interests and values involved in constitutional questions. The Court slowly changed the nature of its judgments. No longer was it simply a question of applying the traditional syllogism that compared an inferior norm to a superior one. Instead, it became a matter of considering all the constitutional values at stake, of weighing them and establishing not which would prevail, but what was the best balance possible among them. In sum, one can say that at this stage the Constitutional Court evaluated the choices of the legislature, its exercise of discretion, to determine whether it had adequately taken into account all the values and constitutional principles that might affect a certain issue. This operation was made technically possible by an evolving interpretation of the equality principle. From article 3 of the Constitution, according to which all are equal before the law, can be drawn a duty of reasonableness for the legislature, so that it not only must regulate different situations differently, but also must not use arbitrary criteria. In order for a norm not to be unconstitutional, one must avoid contradictions between the goals of a law and the concrete normative rules, between the objective pursued and the legal tools used to achieve it. In sum, one must avoid irrational contradictions between the goals of the law and the content of its text. In these years, the Court acted in numerous areas that characterize a secularizing society. It is enough to mention its judgments regarding divorce, abortion (see judgment n. 27 of 1975, which sought to strike the difficult balance between protecting the fetus and safeguarding the mother's health), church-state relations, family rights, the right to strike (the Court declared political strikes unconstitutional), and numerous issues connected with the right to work and social welfare. In this way, the Court struck down what it termed 'unjustified discrimination' in the salaries of public employees (judgment n. 10 of 1973), upheld the 'Workers' Statute' (judgment n. 54 of 1974), and issued innumerable additive judgments that increased state spending that aimed at equalizing (upward) the system of state welfare and wage payments. Emblematic of this stage are also the many decisions concerning radio and television, decisions in which the Court found itself hounding and scolding the legislature in the name of freedom of expression, yet without ever succeeding in completely guiding its choices into conformity with the Constitution (see, among the many decisions, judgment n. 202 of 1976, which definitively opened the doors to local radio and television broadcasting).

3.3. The Elimination of the Case Backlog

Paradoxically, the Constitutional Court's tremendous success during the first stage of its activity turned out to be one of the principal factors that rendered the system of constitutional review ineffective. The massive quantity of questions raised has made it rather difficult to issue decisions at an acceptable pace. The increase in the number of questions gave rise to a significant backlog and a prolongation of the process. This spiral threatened not only to swamp the Constitutional Court, but also to impair its institutional function. The time factor, the length of the proceeding, is crucial for the impact of constitutional decisions on the legal system. Fortunately, the members of the Court, aware of these risks, dealt with this problem in the late eighties through a series of reforms of the Court's procedural rules. These reforms gave rise to a third stage known as "operational efficiency" that ran from the mid-eighties to the mid-nineties. The main goal of this new phase was to reduce the time taken for a constitutional decision and the number of pending questions, through declarations of inadmissibility in summary orders (*ordinanze*) of a large number of questions that were obviously inadmissible or frivolous, as well as through the selection of cases on which to focus the Court's attention. To this end, the Constitutional Court adopted numerous procedural innovations (organization of work, streamlining of debate, deciding cases by summary order, etc.) that helped to reach these goals. At the beginning of the nineties, the number of pending questions was significantly lower and the length of constitutional review had become nine months.

In order to reach this result some sacrifices had to be made, as pointed out by scholars who during these years focused their attention on constitutional procedure. For example, the number of decisions increased, but often at the expense of more summary opinions. The method for organizing work reduced the collegiality of decision-making and the importance of the parties' contributions, simultaneously increasing the procedural discretion of the Constitutional Court. In sum, operational efficiency does not always equate to effective decision-making. Insufficiently explained opinions are less persuasive and carry the risk of reducing consensus, both among scholars and the public, about the decisions of the constitutional tribunal and, as a consequence, of reducing its legitimacy. Various procedural ideas have been advanced to promote more carefully reasoned opinions, in particular the introduction of dissenting opinions. Likewise, some have proposed allowing interested parties to participate in constitutional proceedings even though they are not involved in the lawsuit giving rise to the constitutional question, in order to offer the Court more viewpoints in evaluating constitutional claims. Yet none of these attempts has produced any change in constitutional procedure.

3.4. The Court During the Transition Years

Now that the case backlog has been eliminated, the Italian system of constitutional review has entered a new stage, whose features are still unclear. First, the brief time that passes between when a question is raised and decided means that the object of the Court's review is ever more frequently a law that has just been adopted: that is, laws that are supported by a current political majority. This rapidity has important consequences for the relationship between the Constitutional Court and Parliament as well as the judiciary. As for the former, the Court is inevitably drawn into current political conflicts. When politically and socially important issues are at stake, connected with recently approved laws that are often the result of delicate compromises and grand debates, it is unavoidable that the Court's decisions are politically influenced and that its legal judgments are viewed both by the public and scholars as decisions of mere political convenience. The difficulties in these cases are obvious. In order to preserve the decisions' authority, the Court's opinions take on special importance, particularly in their ability to persuade on the rhetorical rather than the logical level. As for the latter aspect, that of relations with the courts, the Court's rapid turnaround and the fact that it confronts 'new' laws means that the Court is forced to rule on the constitutionality of laws that have not yet received a consolidated judicial interpretation, the so-called 'living law.' The Court is therefore called upon to perform the task of interpreting the law subject to review–a task that belongs to the judiciary rather than the Constitutional Court. This raises afresh the problem of relations with the judiciary that the use of the 'living law' was thought to have overcome.

Second, the constitutional tribunal finds itself interpreting constitutional texts that embody principles of the welfare state, that is, that recognize social rights, in an environment marked by the financial crisis of the state and by economic austerity policies. The Court is trapped between Scylla and Charybdis: between the danger of abdicating its role of supreme guarantor of the Constitution and the rights it protects, and the danger of provoking serious economic repercussions with its decision. The Court's concern for the financial consequences of its decisions is readily perceptible from a survey of its activity. Indeed, it frequently issues evidence-gathering orders to acquire information about the costs of possible judgments striking down laws. It has created a special office to quantify the financial burdens of such judgments before they are adopted. Furthermore, a look at the Court's case law shows its tendency to significantly reduce, compared to the earlier stages, the number of decisions based on the principle of equality and designed to equalize unequal situations upward. On the contrary, on some occasions the Court has chosen the opposite path; faced with challenges raised in the name of equality, it has decided to equalize the situations downward, raising before itself *sua sponte* the question of the constitutionality of the baseline offered by the certifying judge (the *tertium comparationis*). This was the situation with regard to the personal income tax on pensions of parliamentary deputies. The favorable treatment only they received was invoked as the baseline due to all citizens in a case involving the income of employees. The Court did not hesitate to question *sua sponte* the favorable treatment accorded to pensions, and declared them unconstitutional. (Jmt. n. 289 of 1994).

In hopes of balancing these two goals–on the one hand to fulfill its role of constitutional guardian, in particular of social rights, and on the other not to directly create state budgetary burdens without adequate financial support–the Constitutional Court has in recent years developed the innovative decisional techniques mentioned earlier, in particular judgments that 'add principles' rather than norms. These decisions are aimed at recognizing rights, but leaving it to the legislature to choose the means for implementing them and the funds to meet their costs. Illustrative of this tendency is judgment n. 243 of 1993. In that decision, the Court declared unconstitutional norms that excluded cost-of-living adjustment from the calculation of severance pay benefits, but held that its decision could not take the form of the mere nullification of a law, or of an additive judgment. Rather, it fell to the legislature to choose the appropriate means, 'in view of the selection of economic political choices needed to provide the necessary financial resources.'

Third, the current stage of constitutional jurisprudence is occurring in an unstable political and institutional context characterized, since 1992, by the weakening of the established balance of political power, with the collapse of the old party system, the change in the electoral system, and the birth of alliances and alignments that have not yet sufficiently consolidated their positions. These elements, too, highlight the political role played by the Court. There has been an increase, both quantitative and qualitative, in the powers of the Constitutional Court with strong political ramifications, such as those related to conflicts over the attribution of powers among the branches of government and the admissibility of referenda to repeal laws. As a result, there has been a tendency to emphasize the Constitutional Court's role as an arbiter in political and constitutional conflict–a role from which the Court has not sought to extract itself. In this vein, it is worth noting its judgment concerning votes of no-confidence in individual ministers (which the Court found constitutional, even in the absence of express constitutional provisions, on the ground that they are inherent in the form of parliamentary government: judgment n. 7 of 1996); the cases regarding decree-laws (the Court went so far as to declare the unconstitutionality of reissuing them, in judgment n. 360 of 1996, because they violate legal certainty and would change the structure of government); and the case law governing the immunity of parliamentary deputies for statements made in the performance of their official functions (in this regard, after many years of uncertainty, the Court annulled a parliamentary vote of immunity deemed to have been adopted in the absence of any functional nexus between the declaration of the deputy and his parliamentary activity: judgment n. 289 of 1998).

The current stage is also marked by the need, more and more widely acknowledged, to modify the Constitution, which has sparked various attempts to amend the organizational portion of the Constitution, none of which have yet met with success. It is not easy to predict what role the Court will play in a period of transition toward new, and still unforeseeable, constitutional arrangements. The

Court could act as the stalwart defender of the current Constitution, by protecting the *status quo* and opposing all change, or it could unconditionally endorse all amendments proposed by Parliament. Somewhere between these two extremes seems to lie a better, third way: The Court could facilitate change while guaranteeing that it occurs with full respect for prescribed procedures and, if necessary, with the supreme principles of the constitutional order that animate our Constitution, govern the structure of the State, and ensure continuity.

Constitutional Justice in Post-communist Europe

7. Legitimacy and Reasons of Constitutional Review After Communism

Wojciech Sadurski

All the post-Communist countries of Central and Eastern Europe (CEE) have adopted a model of judicial review which borrows more – much more – from the Western European tradition than from the American one. A composite picture of the system of judicial review of the CEE countries would highlight that it is exercised by specially established constitutional courts which exclusively exercise the power to make authoritative decisions about the unconstitutionality of laws, and whose decisions – taken after the laws have entered into force – are made *in abstracto* (not in connection with any particular litigation) and are final (that is, can be overridden only by constitutional amendment).

There are some exceptions to this composite picture. In one country (Estonia) the task of constitutional review is entrusted to a department within the highest appellate court. In nearly all CEE countries (except the Ukraine), the constitutional courts exercise abstract review *alongside* "concrete" review although not in the sense in which the US Supreme Court exercises it (that is, when a determination of the constitutionality is part and parcel of a decision taken in the appellate process) but, rather, by answering questions on constitutionality asked of them by ordinary courts when those courts are presented with constitutional issues. In some countries, the constitutional courts have a power to decide about constitutionality *before* the law enters into force, but only when asked to do so by the State President (Poland, Hungary, Estonia), and in one country, abstract review can be exercised only before the promulgation of the law (Romania). Finally, in one country (Romania) invalidations resulting from an abstract review are not final and can be overridden by a qualified parliamentary majority.

These exceptions notwithstanding, one can broadly describe the model of judicial review adopted in the region as centralized, abstract, *ex-post* and final. Review of this sort runs into familiar problem of legitimacy: why should courts displace the preferences of representative bodies? To be sure, the question of legitimacy may be raised also with regard to a decentralized, concrete, *ex-ante* and non-final review but, under each of these four criteria (with the possible exception of the *ex-ante* feature) the legitimacy concerns are less pressing. And precisely because this model raises legitimacy concerns in their most extreme form, the question may be properly asked, why was this model of review chosen in the first place by constitutional designers?

Wojciech Sadurski (ed.), Constitutional Justice, East and West, 163–187
© 2002 *Kluwer Law International. Printed in Great Britain.*

These two issues inform the structure of this chapter. In part 1, I discuss the question of the legitimacy of constitutional courts (*qua* courts rather than *qua* legislative organs). Part 2 explores some of the reasons usually produced as explanations for the dominance of the abstract and centralized model of judicial review in the post-Communist constitutional systems. The two themes are then brought together in the concluding part.

1. THE PROBLEM OF LEGITIMACY OF CONSTITUTIONAL COURTS

Klaus von Beyme argued in his comparative study of constitutional review, written just before the collapse of authoritarianism in Central Europe, that "[j]udicial review works most effectively and intensely in those political systems in which the *Rechtsstaat* had been established before the advent of democracy, and where federal structures functioned as an obstacle to the majority principle dominating parliamentary democracies".[1] On the face of it, the experience of those constitutional courts in CEE which function "most effectively and intensely" seems to contradict this proposition. In the most successful democracies arising out of the fall of Communism in the region, democracy has arguably been established *before* the entrenchment of the practices of the *Rechtsstaat*. In addition, only one of the post-Communist European states is a federation (Russia), and it has not produced an obviously "effective and intense" practice of judicial constitutional review, at least not when compared to Hungary, the Czech Republic or Poland.

This departure from the rule discerned by von Beyme may be instructive: it suggests that judicial review may have a problem in CEE. The absence of a *Rechtsstaat* tradition prior to the establishment of democracy may explain why judges in CEE do not clearly demarcate between the judicial and the political functions of the state, and the absence of federalism may deprive the existing constitutional courts of at least one obvious *raison d'être*. For the most activist courts of the region, which happen also to be found in the most successful constitutional-democratic political systems arising out of Communism, this translates itself into a major problem of legitimacy.

It is obvious that those courts[2] – let us use as exemplary for the activist courts the constitutional tribunals of Hungary, Czech Republic and Poland – do *not* have a problem of legitimacy in at least two senses of the word: one sociological, the other formal and institutional. In respect of an institution, 'legitimacy' is sometimes used as an equivalent to its social standing and popularity. Clearly, constitutional courts in the region enjoy a high level of social acceptance and

---

[1]   Klaus von Beyme, "The Genesis of Constitutional Review in Parliamentary Systems", in Christine Landfried, ed., *Constitutional Review and Legislation* (Nomos: Baden-Baden, 1988), pp. 21–38, at p. 37.

[2]   Unless stated otherwise, all references to 'courts' are to constitutional, not ordinary, courts.

recognition, despite occasional disagreements and criticisms of its particular decisions.[3] Constitutional courts in CEE emphatically do not have a problem of legitimacy in the sociological sense of the word.

Further, these courts do not have a problem of legitimacy in the formal and institutional sense, which may be understood as compliance with the constitutionally recognized limits and working under constitutionally defined standards. They do not exceed the powers granted to them by the respective constitutions, by the statutes on Constitutional Courts or by other relevant laws of their respective jurisdictions. Even if one disagrees, on merits, with this or that decision, one must be careful not to frame the criticism in terms of a charge that the court acted *ultra vires*. If one alleges that a particular decision – or even a set of decisions – has been taken on grounds other than those explicitly provided by the constitution or the set of valid norms guiding the judicial review, this is precisely the sort of substantive disagreement about a decision which is to be expected in a society marked by profound disagreements about the matters which may become the subject of judicial review. A charge that a court decides on the (improper) grounds of the political or moral preferences of its judges as opposed to the (proper) grounds of inconsistency with the Constitution is a statement which reflects, rather than stands outside of, the substantive disagreement as to the wisdom, or otherwise, of a particular decision. Whether the court's decisions are genuinely based on constitutional principles rather than the judges' own policies and moral values is in itself a controversial matter, and the level of this controversy is no different from the controversy of the wisdom (or otherwise) of any other political decisions.

Of course, within any given bundle of powers granted to a particular institution, there is always some leeway for a more "expansive" or a more "prudent" course of action. A constitutional court when exercising judicial review of a statute may, without violating the rules of the game, adopt a mode of reasoning which is more or less likely to result in invalidation. It may be, therefore, within a recognized set of conventions governing its actions, more or less activist, or, using a different parlance, construe its authority less or more narrowly. But if it does opt for a broader construction and becomes more "activist", it does not *ipso facto* exceed the formal powers granted to it by the laws of the state.

And yet, from the mere fact that the Court remains *intra vires* and does not violate the formal, institutional rules of legitimacy of its decisions, it does not follow that the Court's actions are unproblematic from the point of view of legitimacy in a broader, critical sense of the word. The question then becomes *not*: "Is the Court authorized to take this type of decisions" but rather "*Should* the Court be authorized to take them?" The question of the *democratic* legitimacy of an institution is not exhausted by the fact that the institution acts within the constitutionally established limits and that the constitution itself has been enacted

---

[3]   See Wojciech Sadurski, "Introduction" to this book, text accompanying footnote 26 at p. 8.

democratically. There is no contradiction in terms if one claims that a constitutionally established device is undemocratic.[4] It is a commonplace that a democratic procedure for establishing an institution does not necessarily confer a democratic character on the institution itself. A democratically constituted constitutional convention, proceeding in a democratic manner may decide to establish a non-democratic, or imperfectly democratic, institution. The degree of democracy that the constitutional convention wishes to infuse into the institutions that it is about to set in motion is in itself a matter of free choice if the convention is to be truly democratic.

Just as there is no necessary connection between a democratic procedure of setting up an institution and a democratic character of that institution, so there is no necessary connection between the *un*democratic nature of an institution and its illegitimacy (even in a broader, critical sense of the word). A central bank, a civil aviation authority, the army or a national opera company are not "democratic" institutions (not just in the sense of their internal decision-making process but, more importantly here, in that their specific acts, or sometimes even the entire strings of acts, do not track the actual distribution of social preferences) but this does not render them illegitimate. More relevantly for our purposes, ordinary courts are not, and are not meant to be, democratic institutions and yet, in itself, it does not affect adversely their legitimacy. The main source of their legitimacy, as Martin Shapiro famously argued in his classic study on courts, derives from the "triadic" model in which two persons decide to call upon a third, neutral umpire, in order to resolve their disagreement. Shapiro argued further that "the substitution of law and office for consent" which distinguishes courts *par excellence* from go-betweens, mediators and arbitrators, introduces an important tension between the social logic of a triad (which is a source of a legitimacy of the court) and the actual operations of the court.[5] In particular, Shapiro argues that the courts' involvement in public law, their exercise of social control and their lawmaking functions importantly weaken their triadic, legitimizing structure. And yet, it is Shapiro's thesis that courts, as we know them, are not qualitatively different from more triadic institutions (such as mediators): they "are simply at one end of the spectrum rather than constituting an absolutely distinct entity."[6] The need to elicit some remnants of consent (revealed, for instance, by courts' reluctance to decide in the absence of one of the parties), their frequent pursuit of a compromise, and many other mediating

---

4   See Jeremy Waldron, "Precommitment and Disagreement", in Larry Alexander, ed., *Constitutionalism: Philosophical Foundations* (Cambridge University Press, Cambridge 1998), pp. 272–73.

5   Martin Shapiro, *Courts: A Comparative and Political Analysis* (University of Chicago Press, Chicago 1981), chapter 1.

6   *Id.*, p. 8.

components in judging, render them just a species of a broader family of triadic institutions.

It is important not to overstate Shapiro's point: much of his argument is devoted to showing that the traditional "prototype of courts" is not reflected in the actual operations of judicial bodies. And yet, it is important to retain his general conclusion that it is precisely the departure from the triadic structure that is a source of possible weaknesses of judicial legitimacy. "[F]rom [the triad's] overwhelming appeal to common sense stems the basic political legitimacy of courts everywhere,"[7] asserts Shapiro, but "[c]ontemporary courts are involved in a permanent crisis because they have moved very far along the routes of law and office from the basic consensual triad that provides their essential social logic."[8]

This tension between courts' claim to legitimacy and their non-triadic patterns of operation is further magnified when the procedure abandons all pretenses to adjudication of conflicting interests between two parties, and focuses instead on an abstract scrutiny of a legal text. If the scrutiny is unrelated to any particular conflict between two parties, the "triadic" sources of legitimacy of courts disappear altogether. This is the predicament faced by those constitutional courts whose functions include abstract judicial review. One could perhaps try to argue that a remnant of the triadic structure is there: there is a complainant (usually, the outvoted parliamentary minority, or the President), a respondent (the representatives of the parliamentary majority, or of the government), and a neutral umpire: the Constitutional Court. But this analogy is not apposite. The "triad" which underpins the prototype of courts is not constituted by two parties disagreeing about what social norms should be properly enforced in law, and a third party who resolves their dispute, which is the situation of the constitutional courts' adjudication. The conflict which is the stuff of a triadic judicial resolution revolves not around abstract ideas concerning rights but around the claim that one party's interests have been violated by another, under the existing valid rules. A better analogy to the conflict which lies at the heart of abstract judicial review is to the disagreement between a majority and the opposition about what law or policy is best for the society, under general and indeterminate constitutional provisions. Indeed, this is precisely what is at stake in the discourse within the abstract constitutional review of legislation. And in *this* discourse, the Constitutional Court is unable to rely on the argument that all it is doing is *applying* the existing law because it is precisely the rightness (under general constitutional standards) of the new law which is the subject of the controversy. As Jürgen Habermas has said, "[t]he legitimating reasons available from the

---

[7]   *Id.*, p. 1.

[8]   *Id.*, p. 8.

constitution are given to the Constitutional Court in advance from the perspective of the application of law – and not from the perspective of a legislation that elaborates and *develops* the system of rights in the pursuit of policies."[9]

While court-based legitimacy seems hardly applicable to abstract review, one can think of different types of democratic legitimacy that might support courts' authority to invalidate statutes. It is not unthinkable, and certainly not patently absurd, that a sort of "third chamber" (or a second chamber, in unicameral parliamentary systems) endowed with the task of taking another look at the bill, this time from the narrower point of view of constitutional values, can be given a justification based upon the general principles of democratic legitimacy. A combination of long tenure, immunization from direct societal pressures and from temptations of re-election with a degree of electoral pedigree (after all, judges of constitutional courts are appointed almost always by democratically answerable bodies) may be just the right mix to combine a good democratic mandate with the institutional incentives for a serious, principle-based review required from a "negative legislator". If what worries us (as it should) is the matter of the democratic mandate of a negative legislator, then this concern may be (partly, at least) met by the fact that members of constitutional courts are much more democratically appointed than ordinary judges. Indeed, one could make an argument that a constitutional court is an indirectly elected democratic (or near-democratic) "chamber of reflection", the purpose of which is to reconsider the bill in a more dispassionate manner, removed one step further from specific political controversies. This immunization from the passions of the moment need not necessarily deprive the constitutional court's task of its representative character: one may, for example, charge the court with the task of identifying (and giving effect to) whatever consensus can be found on a given issue (which has a bearing on constitutional interpretation) *in the light of* (rather than in isolation from) the actual, current moral and political views in the community. One can even appeal to the Rawlsian idea of "overlapping consensus" as a proper device upon which a constitutional tribunal should base its representative function.[10]

It is not my claim that such an argument is compelling. As a matter of fact, I do not think it is.[11] Apart from everything else, such a rationale would generate

---

[9] Jürgen Habermas, *Between Facts and Norms*, trans. William Rehg (Polity Press, Cambridge 1996), p. 262, emphasis in original.

[10] For such a conception of role of the Supreme Court of the United States, see Richard H. Fallon, "The Supreme Court, 1996 Term – Foreword: Implementing the Constitution", *Harvard Law Review* 111 (1997): 54–152, pp. 144–145.

[11] To see why not, consider this typical statement from a proponent of the idea of representative functions of the US Supreme Court: "Without surrendering its prerogatives of judgment or compromising its obligation to uphold constitutional values in the face of political opposition, the Court, in specifying the *meaning* of constitutional principles, must be accountable at least in part to manifestations of reasonable moral and political commitments displayed by the citizenry, both nationally and locally", Fallon *id.* at p. 145, footnotes

a number of questions: if we need a "negative legislator" whose task would be to test the bill from the point of view of constitutional mandate, should it be composed exactly in the way that actually-existing Constitutional Courts are composed? Why should its composition be limited to lawyers only – after all, legal skills are not decisive (and not the *only* relevant ones) for articulating the specific meaning of broad, value-based constitutional pronouncements? These are important questions but will not be pursued here. The only point being made is that a construal of constitutional courts as part of an institutional system of law-making is not incoherent and does not seem to raise impossible problems in supplying their democratic legitimacy. Certainly, the prospect of finding legitimating arguments for abstract review in terms of traditional representative democracy seems to be more promising than in terms of judicial function.

The paradox is that the constitutional courts themselves, and their most fervent doctrinal supporters, usually strenuously resist the characterization of their position in the political system as a second or third legislative chamber, and construct their own self-perception as "courts", albeit somewhat different from the "ordinary" courts. There has been a controversy among the constitutional lawyers of CEE as to whether Constitutional Courts should be classified as within the judiciary or as *sui generis* bodies. Further, the actual location of the provisions on the Constitutional Court in the structure of the respective constitutions varies somewhat from country to country. For example, in Slovakia the Constitutional Court is regulated in the part of the Constitution devoted to "[t]he judicial power"[12] and is characterized *inter alia* as "an independent judicial authority".[13] Similarly, the constitutional courts in Russia and in the Czech Republic are regulated in separate chapters while in Poland, the Constitutional Tribunal is regulated in the chapter generally entitled "Courts and Tribunals" but with its own subchapter. (But then, the Polish statute on the Constitutional Tribunal explicitly states, in its first article, that the Tribunal

---

omitted, emphasis in the original. For one thing, there is an apparent possibility of tension between the obligations proclaimed in the first and in the second parts of the sentence. What if "citizens' commitments" clash with "constitutional values" as understood by the justices? Second, the proviso that the only commitments which the Court must respect are the "reasonable" ones opens the gate to a number of "filtering devices" which will transform the actual conventional morality into something hardly recognizable by the citizenry, see Sadurski, Conventional Morality and Judicial Standards", *Virginia Law Review* 73 (1987) 339–97. Finally, an idea that the Court must be accountable to "commitments" rather than to the citizens themselves strikes me as fanciful. Accountability presupposes a possibility of censuring the agent by the principal – how can "commitments" do it? And yet the choice of words is not incidental because, naturally, there is no way in which the justices of the US Supreme Court can be "accountable" to the citizens in the ordinary sense of the word.

12 Part 7 of the Constitution of the Slovak Republic.
13 Article 124 of the Constitution of the Slovak Republic.

is a judicial body). By contrast, several other constitutions include provisions on constitutional courts in separate chapters or parts altogether, without including them in any broader subdivisions. For example, in Croatia the chapter on the Constitutional Court comes between chapters on "judicial power" and local administration, in Lithuania between the chapters on the Government and the Courts and in Hungary between the chapters on the President and the Ombudsman, etc. The approaches in these countries ranged between pigeon-holing Constitutional Courts in the "judicial" branch (which seems to be the dominant practice)[14] and characterizing them as *sui generis* institutions which is arguably an avoidance of characterization. For instance, the author of a chapter in the fundamental treatise on the Polish Constitution, who is a Constitutional Court judge himself, Professor Janusz Trzciński concludes that "the functioning of the CT [Constitutional Tribunal], as determined by the Constitution and by the Law on the CT, does not fit the accepted classifications [of branches of government into legislative, executive and judicial]."[15] To my knowledge, there have not been any strongly expressed views within the mainstream constitutional doctrine in the region (and certainly not by any of the Constitutional Courts concerned) that constitutional courts, when exercising abstract judicial review, belong to the *legislative* branch of the state.

The self-perception of those courts as part of the judiciary, broadly speaking, has been also endorsed by some friendly commentators from the outside. Owen Fiss announced that: "In the new democracies of the East ... the judiciary ... must give life and force to the idea of a constitutional court ... [to] convince their fellow citizens that law is distinct from politics, and that they are entitled to decide what the law is."[16] The characterization of constitutional courts *qua* courts is implicit in Ruti Teitel's view that the power of overriding the Constitutional Tribunal's decision by the Parliament in Poland (before the adoption of the 1997 Constitution) was a case of mixing judicial and legislative powers, and evidence that "the understanding of separation of powers is far from entrenched in the region."[17] The image is of a legislative body (the Parliament) intruding upon the functions of a judicial body (the Tribunal).

It may seem ironic that the doctrine which would offer perhaps the most promising path of legitimating the Courts in their exercise of abstract constitutional review is most decisively resisted by the Courts themselves, while the

---

[14] See Zdzislaw Czeszejko-Sochacki, Leszek Garlicki & Janusz Trzciński, *Komentarz do Ustawy o Trybunale Konstytucyjnym* (Wydawnictwo Sejmowe, Warszawa 1999), p. 8 who state that, in Poland, the majority of authors consider the Constitutional Tribunal as belonging to the judicial branch.

[15] Leszek Garlicki, ed., *Konstytucja Rzeczypospolitej Polskiej: Komentarz* (Wydawnictwo Sejmowe, Warszawa 1999), chapter 8, p. 10.

[16] Owen Fiss, "Introductory Remarks, Symposium", 19 *Yale J. Int. L.* 219 (1994).

[17] Ruti Teitel, "Post-Communist Constitutionalism: A Transitional Perspective", *Columbia Human Rights Law Review* 26 (1994): 167–190, p. 178.

doctrine which is patently unsuited to provide such legitimacy is the one most zealously defended by those Courts and their apologists. But the paradox is, of course, illusory. If one adopts a "third chamber" perspective on the exercise of abstract constitutional review, there is no justification whatsoever to stick to the current composition of the Courts consisting, as they are, of lawyers only. As Burt Neuborne once observed, "When substantive-review judges identify values and totally insulate them from majority will, the troublesome question of why judges are better than other officials in identifying and weighing fundamental values cannot be avoided."[18] Why indeed? Decisions about death penalty, abortion, defamation of public officials, etc. may be dressed in a legal garb but they ultimately hinge upon fundamental value choices on the making of which legal education has no bearing whatsoever. The fact that it is the Constitution rather than a non-textual moral or political theory which forms the direct basis for a scrutiny of a given law is no good reason to restrict the range of scrutinizers to lawyers.[19] After all, what constitutional review in such cases is about is not the detection of a "true" legal meaning of such constitutional concepts as the right to life, privacy or freedom of speech but rather a decision about what cluster of values is preferable in the articulation of a vague constitutional formula with reference to a specific problem unaddressed in determinate fashion by a constitutional text. It is precisely *because* the issue is a choice of a cluster of values rather than an exegesis of the legal concept that a representative task of the scrutinizers is being called for. But, at the same time, for that very same reason no necessary connection exists between legal qualifications of scrutinizers and the nature of scrutiny, and that is why the democratic legitimacy of Constitutional Courts, as they are constituted, is continually called into question.

And it will not do to attempt to legitimize the existing Constitutional Courts by pointing at less-then-perfect legitimacy of parliaments. "The conventional concern of the absence of democratic accountability posed by judicial lawmaking seems less apt in periods of political flux. In such periods, the transitional legislature frequently is not freely elected and, further, lacks the experience and legitimacy of the legislature operating in ordinary times."[20] Ruti Teitel makes this observation as a response to the charge of the lack of legitimacy of constitutional courts, in particular, in post-Communist transition. But the observation about the legislatures not being freely elected applies to some of the legislatures in the region only (for example, only to the post-Round Table election in Poland

---

[18] Burt Neuborne, "Judicial Review and Separation of Powers in France and the United States", *N.Y.U. Law Review* 57 (1982): 363–342, p. 368.

[19] This had been recognized in the design of at least one constitutional court outside the CEE, namely the French *Conseil constitutionnel*, the members of which do not have to have (and it actually happens that they do not have) any formal legal qualifications.

[20] Ruti Teitel, "Transitional Jurisprudence: The Role of Law in Political Transformation", *Yale Law Journal* 106 (1997): 2009–2080, p. 2033 (footnote omitted).

in June 1989): usually, only to the first term of legislatures after the transition. This observation has, therefore, now only historical value. In those countries where the freedom and fairness of election of legislatures is questionable (Belarus), the problem of "activist" Constitutional Courts does not arise in the first place. In turn, the most activist Constitutional Courts operate alongside fully mature, freely elected legislatures. Their "experience" may be put in doubt (but so may be the experience of new constitutional courts) but the remark about their "lack of legitimacy" is question begging. Anyway, even if the legitimacy of the parliaments is less than perfect, surely the remedy is not to supplant part of their power by bodies which have *even less* legitimacy to create law and determine policies.

2. WHY ABSTRACT/CENTRALIZED CONSTITUTIONAL REVIEW?

To ask why the CEE countries have adopted, without exception, a "European" model of abstract judicial review, concentrated in a specialized constitutional-review body, may sound foolish. After all, they *are* European countries, they *do* belong to a "continental" legal and constitutional tradition, and those same factors which determined the victory of the Kelsenian[21] judicial review (as opposed to the US model) on the continent, arguably must have informed the emergence of this very type of courts in the Central and Eastern part of the continent, when the circumstances for democratic development finally became ripe.

At the end of the day, this may be the correct answer, and yet I do not think that the consideration of this question is superfluous. Asking the simplest and the most naïve questions can sometimes be illuminating. I believe that this is the case here. For one thing, not all Western European countries have adopted any system of *judicial* constitutional review at all, and of those Western European countries that have adopted a Kelsenian model, at least one (Greece) came close to a dispersed, US-style model.[22] As Allan-Randolph Brewer Carias argued at

---

[21] "Kelsenian" is herein used as a short-hand to describe the Continental model of abstract and centralized review. I am however conscious that the model which emerged in Europe after the Second World War, in particular in Germany, but also in Italy, Spain, France etc, is not purely "Kelsenian" model because it envisaged, among other things, a rights-based scrutiny of constitutionality of laws, and contains important elements of "positive" legislation. In both these respects, Hans Kelsen expressed the opposite views when he advocated the establishment of the constitutional court in Austria. See Alec Stone Sweet, *Governing with Judges* (Oxford University Press, Oxford 2000), pp. 34–38.

[22] Under the 1975 Constitution of Greece (art. 95), all courts have the power not to apply legal provisions which they consider to be contrary to the Constitution. A diffuse system exists also to a certain degree in Switzerland (although only Cantons' laws, not the federal ones, can be judicially reviewed) and in Portugal.

length in his book, there is no necessary connection between the way constitutional review is designed (that is, whether it is centralized or diffuse) and the family of legal systems to which a given nation belongs (that is, whether it is a civil or common law system).[23] Second, even in some of the most emblematic systems of abstract and centralized review such as Spain, there have been proposals to establish a decentralized, American-style model, in which all courts would be authorized to review statutes under constitutional rights claims.[24] Third, we should be wary of explanatory determinism: after all, the emergence of the Kelsenian model in CEE may be *under*-determined by the factors usually referred to in this context. If this is the case (as I indeed believe with regard to a number of explanations discussed below), then the emergence of such a model may be seen to be a historical contingency, and a belief in a plausibility of an alternative scenario (in which the American-style model would have been chosen) may not be as absurd as it seems at first blush. And further, if that is the case, the usual *explanations* for the emergence of the current system may be better characterized as *justifications* for the maintenance of that particular system. They can therefore be seen more as legitimating the status quo than analyzing it dispassionately.

After all, the post-1989 constitutional and political scene in CEE was, partly at least, a laboratory in experimentation in which many of the decision-makers could have thought that they were making a fresh start. Of course no start is ever fresh. But the post-1989 scene was a mixture of embeddedness in the old traditions and experimentation with the new. There were many options on the menu, and the American-style solution on many constitutional arrangements was not out of the question. In addition, there was no shortage of American experts around, including constitutional experts, to provide advice and advocate the right solution. And it just happened that the solutions proffered by American constitutional experts were, most often, those corresponding to the liberal (in the American sense of the word) reading of the US constitutionalism – which included activist, US-style judicial review. Some of those American liberals explicitly urged the new activist constitutional courts (in particular, the Hungarian Court) to abandon abstract review altogether and, hence, to follow the US path.[25]

If we reconsider the question of why the CEE countries adopted the centralized and abstract model of review, *and* if as a result of this reconsideration we conclude that the usual explanations fail to fully account for the choice of the model (hence, they "under-determine" the model), *then* we can gain two things.

---

[23] Allan-Randolph Brewer Carías, *Judicial Review in Comparative Law* (Cambridge, Cambridge University Press, 1989), pp. 128–131.

[24] See Stone Sweet, *op. cit.*, pp. 120–21.

[25] See Bruce Ackerman, *The Future of Liberal Revolution* (Yale University Press, New Haven 1992), pp. 108–9.

First, we can help re-open the debate about the merits of US-style review and its future prospects in the region. (This, of course, is relevant only if we find that the US model has some advantages over the centralized and abstract model; something that I cannot even begin to argue here).[26] Second, we can debunk the usual explanations by showing that, to some degree (that is, to the degree that there *is* under-determination), they are *ex-post facto* rationalizations, and hence must be seen as legitimating ideologies.

Let us dispense first with what are arguably the two weakest explanations of the phenomenon of constitutional courts in CEE. The first one appeals to the willingness of the countries of the region to match the expected criteria which would facilitate their admission to the European Union, and those criteria are said to include a "European" rather than the US style of judicial review. It has been also said that the EU, generally, expected the candidate countries to set up a system of constitutional courts which would have a very strong position vis-à-vis legislatures: "[w]hile parliaments and presidents will predictably resist judicial interventions, they are painfully aware that highly visible confrontations with their domestic constitutional courts will gravely threaten prospects for early entry into the European Union, which is already looking for excuses to defer the heavy economic costs that admission of the East entails".[27]

This is sheer speculation, and improbable at that. I know of no evidence that accession to the EU figured on constitution-makers' minds when deciding about the system of constitutional review in CEE, and I do not know why it should. After all, the preparations for accession to the EU, even in the cases of the countries long considered the most obvious candidates, began well after the establishment of constitutional courts. And, on the other hand, I know of no evidence that the EU made it a part of its set of criteria for candidate states that they establish a system of constitutional review with a strong position of the courts vis-à-vis the legislature. In the first important decision of the EU which can be seen as setting the conditions for membership by post-Communist European states, the European Council in Copenhagen in December 1993 established that the candidate countries in order to be successful must display, among other things, "stability of institutions guaranteeing democracy, the rule of law, human rights and respect for and protection of minorities" but no specific institutional forms of attaining these conditions have been established. Apart from everything else, it would be hypocritical for the EU to expect, much less demand, that constitutional courts be established: there are members of the EU

---

[26] For my argument to this effect, see Wojciech Sadurski, "Judicial Review, Separation of Powers and Democracy: The Problem of Activist Constitutional Tribunals in Postcommunist Central Europe", *Studi Politici* 3 (1999): 93–117.

[27] Bruce Ackerman, "The Rise of World Constitutionalism", *Virginia Law Review* 83 (1997): 771–797, pp. 776.

whose democratic credentials are unimpeachable and who have no French- or German-style constitutional review.[28]

The second explanation which seems to me quite weak is that there is a correlation between the fact that a country has just emerged from a period of authoritarian rule and the fact that it has established a "Kelsenian" rather than the US-style model of constitutional review. One can see a certain logic in the question by Louis Favoreu: "How could an American system function in the Federal Republic of Germany, Italy, Spain, or Portugal, with judges from the preceding period of dictatorship named to the courts? Adopting judicial review in these countries would require "purification" on a massive scale of a corps of magistrates, while one could immediately find a dozen or so constitutional judges with no prior culpability during those periods, capable of carrying out their duties without mental reservations".[29] The argument about a generalized distrust of the judiciary as the state emerges from a period of authoritarian rule, is then extrapolated to the CEE post-Communist countries.[30] And yet, the reality of post-Communist regimes defies the simple dichotomy noted by Favoreu. Neither were the judges of Constitutional Courts in the region quite "purified" of their old habits and ideologies, nor were the ordinary judges as hopelessly immersed mentally in the "preceding period of dictatorship" as to offer no likelihood that they will dispense justice in accordance with the new axiology of the law.

One must not protest too much. Ruti Teitel certainly has a point when she observes that "as new forums specially created in the transformation [new constitutional courts'] very establishment defines a break from past political arrangements".[31] Indeed, a "concrete" system of review would most probably have to rely on the old judiciary and so the symbolic effect of novelty would be lost. But the explanatory power of this observation is limited. Even leaving aside the counter-examples of Poland and ex-Yugoslavia (where the establishment of constitutional courts was not coinciding with the transformation), there have been some "old" institutions (such as Presidency in Poland or Czech Republic) which quickly acquired a much more powerful symbolism as vehicles of transformative politics than the "new" constitutional courts. No doubt, Vaclav Havel or Lech Walesa were much more powerful symbols of the new, even though they occupied "old" offices, than the largely nameless and faceless judges of constitutional courts in Warsaw and in Prague.

---

[28] The United Kingdom and the Netherlands have no judicial constitutional review at all, while Denmark, Ireland, Greece and Sweden have adopted systems bearing resemblance to the US-style model of decentralized judicial review.

[29] Louis Favoreu, "American and European Models of Constitutional Justice", in David S. Clark, ed., *Comparative and Private International Law: Essays in Honor of John Henry Merryman on His Seventieth Birthday* (Duncker u. Humblot, Berlin 1990), p. 110.

[30] See, e.g. chapter 1 by John Ferejohn & Pasquale Pasquino in this volume, p. 31.

[31] Teitel, "Transitional Jurisprudence", *op. cit.*, p. 2032.

Perhaps the most significant explanatory power lies with the attachment of lawyers and constitution-makers in the region to the traditional "European" (as opposed to the US) tradition of separation of powers in which the role of ordinary judges is strictly confined to the application as opposed to the making of law. The adoption of the Kelsenian system seemed to disturb this tripartite structure of government to a lesser extent than allowing all the regular courts to check the laws for their unconstitutionality in the course of ordinary adjudication. The point made about the Western European systems, that the Kelsenian model "could be easily attached to the parliamentary based architecture of the state"[32] applies to the CEE countries as well. This has been certainly a frequent argument within the doctrine of these countries: that to authorize regular judges to declare the laws unconstitutional would place them above the legislature and would be inconsistent with the tripartite division of powers.[33]

These are plausible explanations, as far as the compatibility of any form of judicial review of constitutionality with "old constitutionalism"[34] is concerned. But much the same reasons which are being produced against the US-style judicial review, in terms of traditional tripartite separation of powers, can be used to attack abstract and centralized judicial review, as long as it is *judicial* rather than kept within the legislative branch. All the more so, it applies to the concrete judicial review exercised by constitutional courts, alongside with their power of abstract review. If a single ordinary court can initiate a review of a statutory provision by (what is seen to be) a court, albeit a special type of court, what is left of the traditional European separation of powers, with the dogma of the sovereignty of parliaments and a linked dogma of courts being confined to applying, as opposed to making, of the exiting law?

Perhaps a more relevant point is the *formal* absence of a doctrine of "*stare decisis*" in the continental legal tradition. In the "decentralized" model of judicial review, such as in the US, a strong precedent doctrine provides for a degree of consistency within the overall judicial system. When all the courts have to follow the *rationes decidendi* of the Supreme Court, and of the relevant higher appellate courts in their respective jurisdictions, the dangers of arbitrariness, uncertainty and lack of uniformity are minimized. But when there is no *stare decisis* (so the argument goes), a concrete-decentralized model threatens the unity of a legal

---

32 Stone Sweet, *op. cit.*, p. 37; see also Stephen M. Griffin, American Constitutionalism (Princeton University Press, Princeton 1996), p. 121.

33 See e.g. Andrzej Wasilewski, "Przedstawianie pytań prawnych Trybunalowi Konstytucyjnemu przez sądy (art. 193 Konstytucji RP)", *Państwo i Prawo* vol. 54, no 8/1999, pp. 25–39, at p. 29; Anna M. Ludwikowska, *Sadownictwo Konstytucyjne w Europie Srodkowo-Wschodniej w Okresie Przeksztalcen Demokratycznych* (TNOiK, Torun 1997), p. 21.

34 On "new constitutionalism" in Europe, contrasted to pre-World War II European constitutionalism, see Stone Sweet, *op. cit.*, p. 31, pp. 37–8.

system, and one can envisage an unwieldy situation in which some courts could find a particular law unconstitutional while others might uphold it.

But the distinction is one of a degree rather than of kind, and it cannot make all that much difference. The decentralized system yields a degree of uncertainty and inconsistency, regardless of the *stare decisis* doctrine. In the United States, unless and until the Supreme Court has pronounced on a given issue (which, under a certoriari system and due to the control of the Court of its own agenda need not be the case on every contentious constitutional issue tackled by lower appellate courts), there may exist a situation in which the Courts of Appeals for different circuits will come up with different solutions to one and the same constitutional controversy.[35] On the other hand, it is simply not the case that in continental European law a system of judicial precedent does not operate in fact. In that system, consistent decisions of the courts – especially, of the highest courts – are in practice treated as unquestionable sources of law.[36] Similarly, in the CEE countries it has been long accepted that, for instance, judgments of Supreme Courts have a role of binding precedents for all other courts, at least to the degree to which the written laws do not provide determinate solution to a particular controversy.[37]

The upshot is that neither the general "architecture" of the system of separation of powers, nor the significance (or otherwise) of the precedent, provide sufficiently

---

[35] This is not merely a theoretical possibility. Consider the current status of affirmative action, one of the most contentious issues in American constitutionalism. In 1996 the Court of Appeals for 5th Circuit invalidated an affirmative action plan implemented by the University of Texas Law School and held that the use of race as a factor in university admissions was constitutionally proscribed, *Hopwood v. Texas*, 78 F.3d 932 (5th Cir.1996). The other circuits follow the 1978 Supreme Court's decision *Regents of University of California v. Bakke*, 438 U.S. 265 (1978) which explicitly permitted certain forms of race-based preferences in admissions. The *Hopwood* court argued that it was not bound by *Bakke* precedent because Justice Powell's opinion (for the Court) did not garner a majority (in fact, the central part of Powell's opinion, though not an opinion in its entirety, *was* joined by the majority of judges). The Supreme Court denied *certiorari* in *Hopwood*, 518 U.S. 1033 (1996). I am grateful to Robert Post for this suggestion.

[36] This is so even if the doctrine explicitly rejects the idea of a precedent as a binding source of law. Consider this exposition of the French approach by two leading French theorists: "The courts very rarely cite precedents and must not base their decisions on them, because the only legitimate source of law consists of statutes. On the contrary, if one looks at the material that is in fact used, one realizes that precedents are the most important. ... Precedents, without being formally binding, may have force if created by a court superior to that where the case is pending. This simply reflects the hierarchical structure of the courts", Michel Troper & Christophe Grzegorczyk, "Precedent in France", in D. Neil MacCormick & Robert S. Summers, *Interpreting Precedents: A Comparative Study* (Dartmouth: Aldershot, 1997), pp. 103–140 at pp. 112–13 and p. 117.

[37] See, e.g., Lech Morawski & Marek Zirk-Sadowski, "Precedent in Poland", in MacCormick & Summers, *op. cit.*, pp. 219–58.

strong relevant reasons for opting for a Kelsenian as opposed to the US-style model of constitutional review. It may be seen more as an excuse than a convincing justification. In this, the establishment of abstract/centralized review after the fall of Communism resembles the establishment of abstract/centralized review in Western Europe where, as Alec Stone Sweet notes "a majority of political élites remained hostile to sharing policy-making authorities with judiciaries" and where the opponents of decentralized concrete review saw in such a scenario "the spectre of the dreaded 'government of judges'".[38] It may well be that such fear also weighed on constitutional decision-makers' minds in the CEE when they refused to consider the decentralized, US-style of constitutional review. But let us note a strange inconsistency between such an explanation and, on the other hand, another conventional reason given against the US-style judicial review in Europe, namely, about the low status, prestige and skills of continental judges as compared to the US. If indeed (as is largely the case) "the judiciaries of these new nations [sic] have very little institutional capital"[39] then the fear that these judiciaries will reach for the power amounting to a "government by judges" seems ill-founded. And perhaps Japan, which has a concrete/decentralized model within the context of a relatively low-status judiciary[40] shows that the fear of "government by judges" once the decentralized model of constitutional review is instituted is unfounded. And it is clear, upon reflection, why. Because the decentralized review carries with itself a whole set of doctrines of judicial restraint which are simply inapplicable to abstract constitutional review.[41]

But (it may be claimed) the reason for the priority of abstract and centralized review and hostility towards the decentralized is deeper than that. The United States – an emblematic case of decentralized/concrete review, has a tradition of free-market, anti-statist approach to law, officials and the state. In contrast, the CEE countries share with their Western continental counterparts a tradition of statist and centralized approach to the state in general, not just to the judiciary. The higher the role of the state in society and economy, the more tendency there is towards state-controlled review of constitutionality. Such an argument has been recently made by John C. Reitz who describes a close correlation between forms of review and the general approach to the role of the state.[42] In the US,

---

[38] Stone Sweet *op. cit.*, p. 40.

[39] Owen Fiss, "Introductory Remarks, Symposium", 19 *Yale J. Int. L.* 219 (1994).

[40] For a characterization of the Japanese system of constitutional review as "modeled very much after the American system of judicial review", see Itsuo Sonobe, "Human Rights and Constitutional Review in Japan", in David M. Beatty, ed., *Human Rights and Judicial Review* (Kluwer: Dordrecht, 1994), pp. 135–174, at p. 138.

[41] I develop this argument in my article, "Judicial Review", *op. cit.*

[42] John C. Reitz, "Political Economy and Abstract Review in Germany, France and the United States", in Sally J. Kenney, William M. Reisinger & John C. Reitz, *Constitutional Dialogues in Comparative Perspective* (Macmillan, Houndmills 1999), pp. 74–84.

where a market-centred approach prevails, only concrete review is available, with some residual aspects of abstract review (but not capable of being initiated by political actors). At the other extreme of the spectrum, in the most statist-centrist tradition, France, only abstract review initiated by political actors is allowed. In the mixed systems (e.g. Germany), we have a combination of abstract review, concrete review and constitutional complaint.

There seems to be an undeniable logic in this fit between abstract review and statism because various forms of concrete review (which normally have to be initiated by the subjects not directly controlled by politicians, such as ombudsmen, the judiciary, or, in the case of constitutional complaint, by the individuals) implicate a partial loss of control by the state of the initiation of constitutional review. The correlation seems to be supported by the other European cases *not* considered by Reitz, namely by Italy and Spain, which, on the spectrum ranging from statism to market-centredness can be located half way between the US and France, and where the judiciary (in the case of Italy) and the judiciary or the Ombudsman or the individuals concerned (in the case of Spain) can initiate the process of concrete review. But is there really such a correlation? Was Italy of 1948 so much less statist-oriented than France of 1958 as to account for the difference between the presence and the absence of concrete review? And similarly, was post-Franco Spain of 1978 as infused with non-statist, corporatist elements as Germany of early 1950's that the presence of concrete review which can be initiated even by individuals can be explained by the role of the state?

Perhaps. I am unable to pursue such an analysis in the framework of this paper. Only two observations are in order at this point. First, one should be careful not to take the very availability of concrete review as one possible *symptom* of the less statist approach to the role of the state (as public lawyers would probably tend to do) since the explanatory role of the state factor would be then nil. One and the same factor cannot at the same time be a result of and evidence for a proposed causal factor. Second, if the general approach to the role of the state is to explain the nature of judicial review in the CEE (something that Reitz is *not* doing) then we have a clear case of under-determination there. After the transition, the question of the tasks of the state in the society (and towards economy in particular) has been and still is one of the most contentious, unresolved issues in CEE.

But a more interesting question is, whether such a "fit" is present also at a deeper level, as Reitz suggests that there is a connection between the fundamental *values* underlying the model of review and those behind the model of the state? According to Reitz, the principal value which supports abstract review is "legal certainty". This is because an authoritative decision about the validity (constitutionality) of a new statute is taken even before (or soon after) the statute enters into force, and there is no period of uncertainty between the enactment and the review. In turn, such a period of uncertainty is necessarily produced by a form of review which is conditioned by a specific legal "case or controversy". So much is probably uncontentious: legal certainty may be indeed higher in the system of abstract as opposed to concrete review. I say "probably" because, once the system allows concrete review alongside abstract review, as all the continental systems of judicial review do, with the exception of France, and as all the CEE systems of judicial review do, with the exception of Ukraine, the effect of legal certainty related to the abstract review is lost. Indeed, the effect of legal certainty is assured only when a review is solely *ex ante*, so that once the law is ratified, there is no possibility of ever declaring it unconstitutional (as is the case in France). But *ex post* abstract review introduces an element of uncertainty. This element is related not so much to the abstractness but rather to the fact that review may be initiated (never mind by whom) already after the law entered into operation. And this kind of uncertainty can well be minimized by a simple technique of establishing a legal deadline by which a new law can be challenged.[43] If no such techniques are actually being used[44] it may be for the reason that the uncertainty resulting from abstract, *ex post* review has never been perceived as a major problem.

But even conceding, for the sake of argument, that abstract and centralized review provides for a higher level of legal certainty than the concrete and diffuse one, does it follow, as Reitz claims,[45] that abstract review is based on a degree of paternalism, while the US model of concrete review reflects strong anti-paternalistic stance of the American constitutional system? In Reitz's words: "The kind of citizen required by a system limited to concrete review is a 'tough' citizen, one who is willing to run significant risks deliberately in order to vindicate his rights, not one who waits for the paternalistic arms of the state to take care of him".[46] Now we may accept *arguendo* that the general hostility to paternalism is higher in American political culture than in Europe. It remains to be seen whether this higher American anti-paternalism can indeed explain reliance on concrete review only, and *a contrario* whether a relatively higher degree of acceptance of paternalism in Europe explains the European preference towards abstract review.

Taking the argument one step at a time, it *may* be true that paternalism (government knowing what is good for its citizens better than citizens do themselves) is inconsistent with a high degree of legal uncertainty: a paternalist

---

[43] In contrast, such a deadline regarding a challenge initiated in the course of concrete review (but not constitutional complaint) that is, occasioned by a concrete litigation, would be clearly pernicious. A person has no control when she can be brought to court under a particular law which she can then claim unconstitutionally violates her rights!.

[44] As one example of such a time limit one might mention the rule in Poland until 1997 that abstract review of statutes applied only to statutes enacted no earlier than 5 years before the date of the Constitutional Tribunal's decision (Article 24 of the Law of 29 April 1985 on Constitutional Tribunal). This limit has been abandoned by the new statute on Constitutional Tribunal, adopted 1 August 1997.

[45] Reith, *op. cit.*, pp. 80–81.

[46] *Id.*, p. 81.

government would like to signal clearly to the citizens its expectations about their behavior. But the link between paternalism and high legal certainty (which yields, as we have seen, abstract but also in particular an *ex ante* or limited-in-time review) is contingent and indirect at best. After all, any government interested in guiding the behavior of its citizens by clear rules, paternalist or not, has an interest in providing a high degree of legal certainty to citizens. This legal certainty (and thus, the efficiency of authoritative rules) clashes at times with other values, such as flexibility or individual self-determination, but it is not clear why the "paternalistic" attribute of rules would add an extra weight to the legal certainty side of the calculus. While the anti-paternalist might applaud opening the path for individuals through concrete review, it is question-begging that she should fear maintaining the path for abstract review at the same time, and so it is doubtful whether "[r]ejection of paternalism surely lies at the heart of ... the US rules on justiciability".[47]

The only reason why an anti-paternalist might disfavor abstract review would be that she would fear that the government (or any other official body endowed with the authority to initiate the review) could be tempted to exercise it in a paternalistic fashion, that is, on the basis of the alleged good of the citizens who might benefit from the success of the review, *even despite the citizens' views to the contrary*. For paternalism, strictly speaking, occurs only when the authority displaces the actual citizens' preferences while claiming that it is doing so for their own good. But such a depiction of the official motives behind the review strikes me as convoluted if not fanciful in most cases: in the emblematic examples of the exercises of review in the abstract-review-only situations, that is, in the famous decisions of the French *Conseil constitutionnel*, one would search in vain the cases which would fit such an account. And no wonder. When a French legislative minority successfully challenged the bills on media pluralism[48] or on nationalization of enterprises[49] they did not appeal to any paternalistic arguments but to their own political or ideological visions, different from those of the majority. This was a routine game of democratic politics, resolved by the *Conseil* in these cases in favor of the minority, but appeals to paternalism did not (nor did they need to) figure anywhere in the discourse. As a general speculation, it is hard to see why, *as a rule*, the initiators of abstract review would "become detached from the concerns of the individuals whose rights are immediately at stake" so at to risk a situation in which the citizens would be actually opposed to the goals underlying such an intervention.[50]

---

[47]   *Id.*, p. 81. See also Lea Brilmayer, "The Jurisprudence of Article III: Perspectives on the 'Case or Controversy' Requirement", *Harvard Law Review* 93 (1979), pp. 297–321 at p. 313.

[48]   See Stone Sweet, *op. cit.*, pp. 80–83.

[49]   See id., pp. 66–8.

[50]   The words in quotation marks are from Lea Brilmayer, "A Reply", *Harvard Law Review* 93 (1980), pp. 1727–33, at p. 1732, and they apply not so much to an abstract review initiated by political bodies but to the idea of public interest litigation launched by "altruistic plaintiffs".

But perhaps there is another type of link between paternalism and abstract review: a fear that the exercise of constitutional review by individuals concerned would be unwise, immature, detrimental to themselves. Such fear would certainly have strong paternalist undertones, and one can understand why, when defending the projects of fundamental reform of constitutional review in France in the early 1990s, the then President of the *Conseil* Robert Badinter warned: "on ne peut traiter indéfiniment les citoyens en *éternels mineurs*".[51] The main point of the proposed reform (which failed to gain the support of the Senate) was to endow each party to a legal process with a right to challenge the constitutionality of a statute (on the basis of an alleged violation of the party's fundamental rights), provided the *Conseil constitutionnel* had not pronounced on the constitutionality of this law before. The attitude attributed (no doubt, with good reasons) to the opponents of the reform by President Badinter indeed smacks of paternalism.

However, once there exists a path of concrete review (and, even more importantly, of constitutional complaint) available to individuals alongside the abstract review initiated by the political actors, the link between abstract review and paternalism disappears altogether. The French system *can* be therefore, perhaps, accused of (or only explained by reference to) the tradition of paternalism, but the German, Spanish, Italian etc. cannot. It is not that there is *less* paternalism in a mixed system which combines abstract and concrete review, rather it is the case that there is no link between paternalism and the constitutional model of review at all. So the possible link between the CEE model of review and a (putative) paternalistic tradition cannot be seriously upheld.

Perhaps a better explanation could be that concrete review is well suited to a narrow understanding of the role of the constitution (and, consequently, of constitutional review), namely, when the constitution's main purpose is seen as a safeguard of individual and minority rights against majoritarian oppression. This is very much a characteristically US model of constitutionalism. The tradition of seeing the protection of individuals against majoritarian oppression as one of the main purposes of the constitution has resulted in the well-established perspective on constitutional review seen as the last bastion of individual (and minority) rights against legislative intrusion. It is plausible that one who endorses this view of the constitution's purpose and this perspective on constitutional review may have a clear preference for a concrete, as opposed to abstract, constitutional review. This is because if the whole rationale of the review is based on distrust towards political institutions, then it would be odd to endow those very institutions with the task of initiating such a review. When individuals feel that their rights are violated by the legislative majority, they can look after themselves and press their claims in the court leading, hopefully, to constitutional

---

[51] Robert Badinter, quoted in Jean Gicquel, *Droit constitutionnel et institutions politiques*, 14th edn (Paris: Monthchrestien, 1995), p. 767 (emphasis in original).

review – so the argument goes. However, if we broaden our view about the proper realm of constitutionalism, and in particular if we incorporate socio-economic functions into the scope of the constitution (and, again, of constitutional review as a consequence), individual litigation is no longer an adequate mechanism to initiate constitutional review.[52]

This proposition could be plausibly defended on a number of grounds but the most obvious would be that the individual citizens do not ordinarily have (each taken individually) sufficient interests which would compel them to launch a constitutional litigation, or (what comes basically to the same thing), that their interest in winning such litigation is, at best, only indirect and remote. What is important is that the constitutional court is now seen not only as a protector of individual and minority rights against legislative majority but, more fundamentally, as a guardian of the constitution as a whole, including its separation-of-powers rules and socio-economic policy constitutional guidelines, when applicable. And in such a perspective it is only logical that the judicial review of legislative acts should be triggered by political actors in those cases when one would not normally rely on individual court suits.

This argument seems plausible, though one must not exaggerate the link between abstractness of review and the policy-oriented nature of the review. After all, in the constitutional systems which rely on concrete review only, such as the US, Canada or Australia, much review has a policy-oriented aspect, not reducible directly to the protection of individual rights against majority. It is significant that in a famous article about the Supreme Court's role, Robert Dahl had characterized the Court as a "national policy-maker" and showed that the dominant views on the Supreme Court have never been for long out of line with the policy views dominant among the lawmaking majorities of the time.[53] Under the relaxed rules of standing, not only individuals but also groups and associations can pick up various policy-based grievances and turn them into constitutional suits – in the US, they have standing to assert those interests of their members which are germane to the association's purpose.[54] An even broader test of standing was adopted in Canada where all that "a plaintiff in a suit

---

[52] See Reitz, *op. cit.*, pp. 81–84.

[53] Robert A. Dahl, "Decision-Making in a Democracy: The Supreme Court as a National Policy-Maker", *Journal of Public Law* 6 (1957): 279–295.

[54] See *Hunt v. Washington Apple Advertising Commission*, 432 U.S. 333, 343 (1977), discussed by Brilmayer, "The Jurisprudence of Article III", *op. cit.* at pp. 318–19. In this decision, the Supreme Court unanimously accepted the standing of a state governmental commission composed of representatives of apple industry (and thus treated it as analogous to a voluntary association) to challenge the constitutionality of a statute regulating the packaging of apples. This is as clear a case as they have come to the use of concrete review for a change of economic policy.

seeking a declaration that legislation is invalid" needs to show is that "he has a genuine interest *as a citizen* in the validity of the legislation...".[55] In India, another concrete-review country, the courts have been long used for public-interest legislation, and the standing to sue has been granted to any "member of the public having sufficient interest", where "sufficient interest" encompasses a genuine concern for the rights of others.[56] The concreteness of review does not seem to be such an impediment to policy-related complaints, after all.

But even if abstract review seems *better* suited to those exercises of review which are not directly related to a claim of a violation of individual right, this would only provide a partial explanation for the dominance of abstract review in CEE constitutional systems, for two reasons. First, even if one adopts a broader notion of constitutionalism, which encompasses a control by the constitution of large areas of policy-making, it still does not explain why one would want to involve a constitutional court into this control. Unless one equates the scope of the constitution with the scope of justiciability, and believes that any constitutional violation should be reviewed by a constitutional court, the argument for abstract judicial review is question-begging. In other words, it is of course undeniable that abstract review does involve the court in national policy-making to a much higher degree than concrete review. But it still does not follow that one *should* want to involve a court in policy-making. Second, the prevailing arguments in favour of establishing constitutional courts in that region were made precisely in terms of a protection of constitutional rights against legislative violations of those rights, that is, in terms which place themselves safely in the traditional, anti-majoritarian logic of a concrete review. This, to be sure, was not the only type of argument in the constitutional discourse of these countries but it was a dominant one. The leading courts in the region liked to emphasize that they saw their main role as the protector of individual rights. As the then Chief Justice Sólyom of the Hungarian Constitutional Court declared, "We always stress that we are activists in certain areas, namely, concerning fundamental rights, where the Court does not hesitate to decide 'hard cases'. But we are self-restrictive concerning the problems related to the political structure".[57] A commentator on the Hungarian Court could therefore accurately observe: "The Hungarian Constitutional Court has defined its own activity as that of the guardian of human rights in the midst of a quasi-revolutionary transforma-

---

[55] *Minister of Justice of Canada v. Borowski* [1981] 2 S.C.R. 575, 598, emphasis added.

[56] See Charles R. Epp, *The Rights Revolution* (University of Chicago Press, Chicago 1998), p. 86.

[57] Interview with Laszló Sólyom, *East European Constitutional Review* 6 (1) (1997): 71–77, p. 72.

tion ...".[58] And this was by no means limited to the Hungarian court only.[59]

That is why a general thesis by Martin Shapiro that the power of constitutional courts today derives from the fact that they are useful as arbitrators in division-of-powers disputes, so that they "keep the basic institutional processes running",[60] and consequently that the acceptance by these political actors of the rights adjudication as a necessary cost of having this instrument in place, does not apply easily to the phenomenon of the CEE constitutional courts. As the above quoted declaration of Justice Sólyom, among others, suggests, it is not the case that the main declared aim of setting up the constitutional court was to supply an umpire in division-of-powers disputes rather than to articulate rights. Neither is it the case that, in CEE, rights adjudication came later in time than division-of-powers adjudication, the trend that Martin Shapiro discerns with regard to other constitutional courts in the world. On the other hand, the fact that these courts tend to be more deferential to legislatures on separation-of-powers issues than on rights issues[61] seems to confirm a hypothesis that, in order to gain a necessary capital allowing the Court to be activist on rights, it must "shore up its party political and popular support"[62] by deferring to politicians on other issues which may affect the politicians' vested interests much more directly, namely on their powers and procedures available to them.[63]

3. CONCLUSIONS

There have been important reasons why the European continental tradition inclined the designers of the constitutional review in Western Europe towards a centralized/abstract model, imagined by Kelsen after the First World War in Austria, rather than towards the actually existing US model, and these reasons have had their impact on constitutional developments in CEE after the fall of Communism. What I have insisted upon throughout the second part of this

---

[58] Andrew Arato, "Constitution and Continuity in the Eastern European Transitions: The Hungarian Case (part two)", in Irena Grudzinska Gross, ed., *Constitutionalism & Politics* (Slovak Committee of the European Cultural Foundation, Bratislava 1993), p. 271.

[59] A judge of the Russian CC states that the goal of protecting and guaranteeing human rights is one of the three, equally important, tasks of the Russian CC, alongside with overseeing the federal-regional relationships and the relationships between the highest bodies of the Russian state, Interview with Boris Ebzeev, *East European Constitutional Review* 6(1) (1997), 83– 88, p. 86.

[60] Martin Shapiro, "The Success of Judicial Review", in Kenney, Reisinger & Reitz, *op. cit.*, p. 205.

[61] See footnote 57, above. See also Arato, *op. cit.*, pp. 272–3.

[62] Spencer Zifcak, "Hungary's Remarkable, Radical, Constitutional Court", *Journal of Constitutional Law in Eastern and Central Europe* 3 (1996), 1–56, p. 27.

[63] See, similarly, Wiktor Osiatynski, "Rights in New Constitutions of East Central Europe", *Columbia Human Rights Law Review* 26 (1994), 111–166, p. 151, at n. 185.

chapter, however, was that there is a distinctive air of under-determinacy about all these reasons, and that one should resist the temptation of a "geographical" determinism in understanding the emergence of robust constitutional review in post-Communist systems. In conjunction with the argument of the first part of this chapter, namely, that there is a persistent and chronic problem of democratic legitimacy of the abstract constitutional review, the usual explanations of why this rather than the other model of review has been set up in CEE may be seen as ideological rationalizations for a troubling *status quo*.

Consider this fundamental feature of the American tradition of constitutional thinking, arguably rendering it different from the "continental" tradition. As Stephen Griffin shows convincingly in his book on American constitutionalism, already in the early days of its operations, the Constitution of the United States became "legalized", that is to say, was placed within the framework of the common law, made subject to the interpretation by ordinary judges by the methods of interpretation of the ordinary law and made enforceable in ordinary courts of law and interpreted as any other legal document.[64] As Griffin further argues, this was strongly linked to the Federalist conception of the politics and to the faith in the enlightened élites. However, "[s]ince political actors would inevitably treat the Constitution instrumentally, the only source of constitutional meaning that was independent of politics was the impartial judiciary".[65] Admittedly, the *traditional* "continental" thinking about constitutionalism lacked the two ingredients crucial to Griffin's story, namely, the "legalized" constitution and the general distrust towards politicians (including the elected ones) combined with the high social prestige of the judiciary. But what applies to the old, 19th century and the pre-2nd World War European constitutionalism, does not apply to "*new* constitutionalism", as developed in the era between the fall of the Third Reich in Germany, Fascism in Italy and the end of the Franco era in Spain. Indeed, the two distinctive features of the new constitutionalism have been that, first, a constitution is a legal document, part of the legal system, and subject to all those rules of interpretation, implementation and enforcement as any other legally binding document (and not merely an emphatic political declaration of principles and goals), and, second, that there should be, at best, only a limited trust in the politicians' will and skill to protect constitutional values in good faith.

Both these features have been figuring very prominently in the constitutional discourse after the fall of communism in CEE. The former – "legalization" of the Constitution – was not only a reception of the now dominant "new constitutionalism" in Western Europe, but was also additionally, and powerfully, forged as a reaction against "socialist constitutions" of the bad old days, often not worth the paper they were written on.[66] The latter – distrust of political branches

---

[64] Griffin, *op. cit.*, pp. 17, 13.

[65] *Id.*, p. 17.

[66] See, e.g., Rett R. Ludwikowski, *Constitution-Making in the Region of Former Soviet Dominance* (Duke University Press: Durham, 1996), pp. 36–39.

of government – resonated with the remarkable (and saddening, to many) cynicism of the general population about the skills and motivations of the new political élites after the fall of Communism. Put together, you had the ingredients for entrusting the judiciary with the task of controlling the constitutionality of laws in the process of ordinary litigation. What *was* missing was the strong and powerful judiciary, but then, the constitutional designers in the post-Communist systems have never even begun a reflection about the institutional remedies of this problem in the context of a decentralized judicial review. The prophecy about the judiciary's inability to discharge this task was never tested, and became self-fulfilling.

Let us suppose that I am right about the under-determinacy thesis of the second part of this chapter. How, one might ask, does it tie up with the legitimacy problem of the first part of the chapter? After all, even if the abstract review system in the CEE has been "under-determined", an alternative system, one relying fully on concrete review in a decentralized fashion, might not have been any better a solution to the legitimacy problem.

Once we frame the question in these terms, the response is quite obvious: while any system allowing non-representative bodies (judges) to invalidate the laws enacted by democratic parliaments carries a serious potential for legitimacy deficit, such deficit is at its highest when the invalidation comes at a behest of an outvoted legislative minority launching an abstract challenge to law in terms of its alleged inconsistency with the broad constitutional terms. A concrete and decentralized system is not immune to such problems but it is at least capable of elaborating the doctrines aimed at the deliberate minimization of the direct clash of judicial review with the principles of democratic legitimacy of laws. Such doctrines – having to do mainly with the issues of justiciability – have no place (no necessary place, at least) in the system of abstract review. Alas, this proposition can only be asserted here, not defended.

8. The Hungarian Approach to Constitutional Review: The End of Activism? The First Decade of the Hungarian Constitutional Court

Gábor Halmai

1. "CONSTITUTIONAL REVOLUTION" IN HUNGARY

Constitutional development in Hungary took a different direction from that in other former socialist countries. The Hungarian approach is notable in that it emphasized continuity and this is certainly attributable to the fact that in Hungary there was no revolution to sweep away the constitution of the *ancien regime*. The changes in Hungary were not triggered by mass demonstrations as in Romania, the former GDR or Czechoslovakia. To use the language of the English historian Timothy Garton Ash, events in Hungary can be described as some sort of "refolution", understood as reforms of revolutionary significance interrupting the continuity of the previous regime's legitimacy without impacting on the continuity of legality. The paradoxical situation in this type of political transformation is reflected by the fact that, while the institutional structures of the Hungarian constitutional state have been developed and strengthened and fundamental rights and freedoms safeguarded, at the same time the constitution of Hungary, whatever significant changes and amendments may have been made, continue to be titled as if they were merely amendments to the first written constitution of 1949.[1]

Conceptions of how to reform the Stalinist Constitution of 1949 took shape ten years ago during the negotiations of the National Round Table. The participants in these negotiations were the members of the Opposition Round Table (EKA) and the representatives of the Communist Party. (There was a "third side" at the Roundtable consisting of the representatives of the mass organizations under communism, but they were quite inconsequential.) After the negotiations, the illegitimate Parliament had nothing to do but rubber stamp the amendments, which entered into force on the anniversary of the 1956 revolution, 23rd October 1989.[2] Notwithstanding a few modifications, this comprehensive

---

[1] For an account of Hungarian constitutional developments after 1989, see Halmai (1996). [Please note that footnotes refer to sources listed in the Bibliography at the end of this book.]

[2] Act XXXI of 1989 on the amendment of the Constitution.

Wojciech Sadurski (ed.), Constitutional Justice, East and West, 189–211
© 2002 *Kluwer Law International. Printed in Great Britain.*

amendment has been the fundamental document of the constitutional "change of system" ever since. The recently published minutes[3] of the EKA and national round table negotiations allow us a more accurate understanding of the intentions of the "founding fathers" and to observe their realization or modification.

There were several reasons why the notion of waiting for the constitution to be drafted by a new, democratically elected, Parliament was given up. Both the State Party and the opposition were motivated by the fear that they would lose in the first elections. Neither wanted to leave the formation of the new constitutional system to the new Parliament in the transition because they had no way of knowing how they would be represented in it. Thus, the amendments of 1989 gave new content to the old form of 1949. Notwithstanding its totalitarian skeleton, this constitution may still be called a document that shapes the rule of law.[4]

Partly because it was born during negotiations, this hybrid constitution incorporates a model of consensual Parliamentary democracy which is widespread in continental Europe. This model assumes the existence of more than two parties and the possibility of a coalition government. The constitution also knowingly rejected the presidential or semi-presidential systems which were preferred by the then Hungarian Socialist Workers' Party and were introduced later on in many post-communist states. The new Hungarian constitution also did not favor the pure form of (Westminster) Parliamentarism. Further, there are certain distinct features of the decision making model incorporated in the constitution of 1989–90 – special in contrast with the West-European continental model – such that the consent of the opposition may be required for certain important matters and that the executive is more closely checked because as it is counterbalanced by the opposition. This result obviously grew out of the 40 year heritage of a totalitarian regime. A good example of a distinctively Hungarian constitutional development is the requirement legislation on especially important matters needs to be passed by a two thirds majority. The stronger check on the legislation which limits the governing majority may be traced in the constitutional status of the President of the Republic, the Ombudsman and the Constitutional Court.

The "constituent fathers and mothers" of Hungary chose the Austrian-German model for the protection of constitutionality through the constitutional court. Famously, the Austrian constitutional court set up in 1868 was the first to work in this domain. From 1920 onward it also had the right to revise Acts of Parliament. The constitutional courts of Germany and Italy – and later of Spain and Portugal, also established in the Austrian model after World War II – were invested with openly political competencies to control and balance legislation

---

[3] Bozóki (1999).

[4] According to the new preamble, the revision was needed "in order to promote the peaceful political transition into the rule of law realizing the multiparty system, Parliamentary democracy and social market economy".

following the bitter experiences of the previous dictatorial regimes. The Hungarian Court continues in this tradition.

1.1. The Organization of the Constitutional Court

According to the above mentioned "republican" amendment of 23 October, 1989 and the *Act on the Constitutional Court* framed simultaneously,[5] the first Hungarian Constitutional Court started to function on 1 January, 1990. The Court was set up prior to the democratic Parliamentary elections to ensure the constitutionality of legislation during transition. Its establishment was urged primarily by the governing party (the Hungarian Socialist Workers' Party), as it had greater opportunity to install judges into the court before the elections than after. In compliance with the agreement concluded at the Roundtable talks, the successor party to the Hungarian Socialist Workers' Party could name two judges out of the first five to the court. A further two judges were nominated by the Opposition Roundtable, while the fifth was an independent judge accepted by all parties concerned. It has been much debated whether the newly formed body can be considered legitimate, having been constituted by a Parliament of dubious legitimacy. So when the *Act on the Constitutional Court* finally came into force in November 1989, it consisted of only five members, and the nomination of the five remaining judges was left to the Parliament elected in the spring of 1990. The five vacancies were to be filled by the Parliament at the time of the fifth year of the Constitutional Court's activity following a second general election. In late 1994 – prior to the election in question – the total number of the constitutional judges was determined to be eleven, through a proposal by the Constitutional Court agreed upon by more than two thirds of the Parliament.[6] The reduction took place because the experiences of the previous five years showed that a body of fifteen members would not be able to function well, and it would not be wise to set up two senates, as the failure of the German system showed.

The judicial selection process involves a nominating committee consisting of one member of each Parliamentary faction which puts forth a recommendation as to the nomination of the members of the Constitutional court. The fact that the committee is composed of an equal number of representatives from each of the parties in the Parliament reduces the dominance of the stronger parties in the nomination of the judges, thereby promoting the political neutrality of the Constitutional court. A further safeguard is that judicial nominees are put to a

---

[5]   Act XXXII of 1989 on the Constitutional Court.

[6]   Act LXXIV of 1994 on the amendment of the Constitution. At that time, however, the body consisted of only nine members, one of its former members having been elected judge of the International Court in The Hague. His post was not filled by the Parliament until 1996.

vote of all members of Parliament. The MPs consider the opinion of the constitutional committee of the Parliament and successful nominees require the approval of two thirds of Parliamentarians. Accordingly, any constitutional judge must have both the support of a majority of Parliamentary parties as well as the support of two thirds of the members of the Parliament, ensuring that there is broad consensus over judicial selection. The appointments are for nine years and can be renewed once.

To guarantee the independence of the Constitutional Court, the law defines cases of incompatibility. Accordingly, the judges of the Court shall not be members of Parliament, members of local administrative bodies, trade union leaders, members of any political party and shall not pursue any gainful occupation except for scientific, educational, literary, and artistic activity. The independence of the judges is guaranteed also by the fact that they enjoy the same immunity as the members of Parliament, an immunity that can be withdrawn only by a decision of the plenary session of the Constitutional court. The Constitutional Court judges appoint from among themselves the President and the vice-President of the court for a term of three years, whose activity in co-ordination and representation naturally does not affect the independence of the judges. The Constitutional Court makes its final and universally binding decisions by a majority of votes of those judges who hear the case. The more significant cases require a plenary session of all the judges, while governmental regulations and regulations of lower levels require chambers of only three judges.

1.2. The Jurisdiction of the Court

The Constitutional Court of Hungary has an exceptionally wide jurisdiction even in international comparison since it initially had to oversee the activity also of the former, less than legitimate, Parliament. At the time of the formulation of the separate *Act on the Constitutional Court* (summer of 1989), the opposition groups were not yet sure of the outcome of the democratic elections, they sought to build into the *Act on the Constitutional Court* guarantees also against the next Parliament and Government alike. It was, therefore, not by chance that the Constitutional Court was given a wide variety of functions to control both legislative and executive power in the new system of government, created by extensive amendments to the Constitution. The Court's position was further strengthened by the absence of other important institutions for the protection of law. In particular, there were no administrative courts and the Ombudsmen mentioned in the Constitution had not been elected yet, either. Should another type of Parliament (namely, a bicameral one) have been elected? A balancing approach to legislation may well have promoted a different approach on the part of the Constitutional Court. As it was, the Constitutional Court was the only state institution that had the power to challenge the unicameral Parliament, the majority coalition of which selected the government.

Until 1998 the Hungarian Constitutional Court had the power to review the constitutionality of a proposed bill in the Parliament before it was voted on, when a motion to this effect was submitted by the Parliament, its permanent committees, or a group of at least fifty MPs. Once the unconstitutionality of a bill or part of it had been established, those submitting the motion had to see to its being corrected. However, the Constitutional Court voluntarily renounced this right in 1991, saying that its exercise would mean interference with the legislative process. The decision was brought in connection with a motion of fifty-two opposition MPs against the first compensation Bill.[7] In 1998 the Hungarian Parliament wanted to eliminate the Court's power to engage in preventive norm control, the power to review laws before they were enacted. The Bill to change the *Constitutional Court Act* to this effect was challenged before the Constitutional Court itself, which ruled that it was not unconstitutional to abolish this jurisdiction. The elimination of jurisdiction over the preventive control of Bills passed but not yet promulgated can still be initiated by the President of the Republic. Once such an Bill is declared unconstitutional, the President cannot promulgate it before it is made constitutional by Parliament. This is what happened, for example, in the case of the *Compensation Act.*

Retrospective abstract norm control – the review of laws for constitutionality on the basis of a factual challenge after promulgation – is a sort of jurisdiction also possessed by the Hungarian Constitutional Court. The need to review systematically the constitutionality of the surviving elements of the old legal system has made this the main function of the Hungarian Constitutional Court. Retrospective norm control can be initiated by anyone, even if they are not affected by the regulation in question. So the unique method of the Hungarian Constitutional Court has made the citizens participants in the process of the transformation of the old legal system. Anyone can call the attention of the Court to a potentially unconstitutional law and the Court must examine any such law called to their attention. Such "popular actions" have led to several decisions by the Constitutional Court influencing decisively the organs of the state and the regulation of fundamental human rights. It was in the wake of such civic motions that the Administrative Courts were set up in Hungary, the death penalty abolished, the general use of the PIN number declared unconstitutional and the criticism of public officials allowed.

In such a motion the petitioner can suggest the full or partial nullification of the legal regulation or statute challenged. By such an *actio popularis,* any statute or even administrative regulations (for example, ministerial decrees) can be challenged. Retrospective norm control can be initiated also by judges of the ordinary court. Such judges can suspend any case pending before them and initiate proceedings before the Constitutional Court, if they consider the legal

---

[7]   Decision no. 16/1991. See the English translation in Sólyom/Brunner, pp. 151–158.

provision to be applied in the case unconstitutional. The decision to nullify a law generally applies only prospectively. One of the exceptions, however, occurs in criminal cases when people convicted under an unconstitutional law automatically have the right to have their convictions reviewed. This applies retroactively to all those whose convictions were generated under the-now unconstitutional law. In such cases the Constitutional Court is bound to prescribe a specific and constitutional revision of the criminal procedure.

This "self-triggering" mechanism of the Hungarian Constitutional Court manifests itself also in cases when the Parliament has created an unconstitutional situation not by sanctioning an unconstitutional regulation but by neglecting to carry out its legislative duties. Such a procedure can be initiated by the Court *ex officio* and also by any citizen of the country. This is the procedure that alleges a "constitutional omission" on the part of the Parliament. Once the omission has been established, the legislature has to comply with the request of the Constitutional Court to fulfill its duty and enact a law to fill a gap in the law or to correct a constitutional error. Such an omission happened, for example in the case of the *Media Act*, when the Parliament failed in its constitutional duty to enact a law regulating broadcast media.[8] It reveals the limitations of the authority of the Constitutional Court that the several Parliamentary terms went by before *Media Act* was passed finally in 1996.

Persons whose rights have been violated by the application of an unconstitutional legal provision may lodge a constitutional complaint for the violation of their constitutional rights to the Constitutional Court, having exhausted alternative legal avenues. In this respect however, the power of the Hungarian Constitutional Court is not as wide as that of other European constitutional courts. The Hungarian Constitutional Court cannot deal with direct individual complaints against an administrative or judicial decision in a concrete case if those direct complaints do not challenge the constitutionality of the norms on the basis of which the decision has been brought. Due to these limitations, the number of the complaints presented to the Hungarian Constitutional Court in the past ten years does not amount even to 1% of the total number of potential claims. The Hungarian constitutional judges have tried to breathe life into the lifeless institution of the constitutional complaint more than once in the past few years, and their first decision serving as a precedent did in fact annul a judgment in a concrete case.[9]

The Constitutional Court must interpret the constitution to settle specific matters of abstract review, but it is also authorized, on the petition of specified bodies, to interpret constitutional provisions abstractly, without reference to particular cases. In these cases, the Court may be called upon to interpret what a constitutional clause means in general, without a corresponding request to

---

8 Decision no. 37/1992. Ibid, Sólyom/Brunner, at pp. 239–245.
9 Decision no. 57/1991. Ibid, at pp. 171–177.

apply that interpretation in the course of reviewing a specific law. This is an unusual phenomenon in international comparison. Such abstract decisions, which are essentially advisory opinions, have been made in connection with the constitutional powers of the President of the Republic.[10]

2. THE ACTIVISM OF THE COURT IN THE FIRST NINE YEARS TERM

The first nine year cycle of the Hungarian Constitutional Court's proceedings came to an end in 1999. Of the various achievements of the Court in this period, it is very likely that these nine years will be known as the era of the Sólyom Court.[11] Judge László Sólyom was the President of the Court during this time, and the Court's jurisprudence and style very much reflected his leadership. As one of the brand new institutions within the newly formed constitutional regime, the Constitutional Court had to quickly establish its own legitimacy, and at the same time the legitimacy of the hitherto unknown institution of constitutional review. This legitimacy has a number of different aspects, which included the "quality" of the Courts' decision making, the independence of the judges elected in a politically divided Parliament, and the reputation these judges have established in the wider community.

The Constitutional Court, while relatively popular in the wider community, has sometimes been subject to strong criticism both from members of the government, Parliament as well as from academic commentators. The grounds of criticism have included the extent of the Court's intervention into the law making process and the (perceived) liberal bias of the decisions, but the censure can be primarily characterized as the cost of the Court's judicial activism in its first nine years. President Sólyom explained after the Court's first year of existence that its activism was based on the broad charter given to the Court, which gave much leeway to the judiciary in determining the part they would play in fashioning a new constitutional democracy. In the midst of political changes, the legislators who enacted the Court had but a vague conception of the functions of a constitutional court ... Owing to the historical context of its formation, the Constitutional Court had exceptional freedom to develop its place in a constitutional order. This included not only the political importance it would assume but also the legal character it would adopt ... We must be aware, therefore, that our fate (with all of its consequences for Hungarian democracy) is in our own hands.[12] Critics of the Sólyom Court claim that the Court has engaged in two types of activism: an activist interpretation of the Constitution on the one hand, and an activist interpretation of the court's own competences on the other.

---

[10] Decision no. 48/1991 (Ibid, at pp. 159–170.), and no. 36/1992.

[11] The author was fortunate enough to have served during the first six and a half years of the Court's life, as a colleague of László Sólyom.

[12] Cf. Sólyom (1991).

2.1. Activist Constitutional Interpretation

The criticism from the political actors stems from a familiar diffidence towards courts deciding cases involving highly charged political issues such as retroactive justice, lustration, access to the files of the communist regime, the competences of the President of the Republic and the Government's economic stabilization package. In 1994, an attempt was made to evaluate the first two years of the Court's caselaw which categorized the judges as "activist human rights fundamentalists" or "Parliamentary legal allies".[13] The essence of this attack on "fundamental law activism" was that the Constitutional Court's practice of striking down laws that are inconsistent with the constitution cannot be based on such "super abstract" legal formulations as the rule of law, human dignity or equal protection.[14]

2.1.1. Retroactive Justice

Hungary's first elected Parliament passed a law concerning the prosecution of criminal offenses committed between 21 December 1944 and 2 May 1990. The law provided that the period of statutory limitation recommence as of 2 May 1990 (the date that the first elected Parliament took office) for the crimes of treason, voluntary manslaughter, and infliction of bodily harm resulting in death – but only in those cases where the "state's failure to prosecute said offenses was based on political reasons." The President of Hungary, Árpád Göncz, did not sign the Bill but instead referred it to the Constitutional Court.

In its unanimous decision, 11/1992 (III. 5) AB, the Constitutional Court struck down the Parliament's attempt at retroactive justice as unconstitutional for most of the reasons that Göncz's petition identified. The Court said that the proposed law violated legal security, a principle that should be guaranteed as fundamental in a constitutional state. In addition, the language of the law was vague, not least because the formulation "political reasons" had changed so much over the long time frame covered by the law and the crimes themselves had changed definition during that time as well. The basic principles of criminal law – that there shall be no punishment without a crime and no crime without a law – were clearly violated by retroactively changing the period of limitation. The only sorts of changes in the law that may apply retroactively, the Court said, are those changes that work to the benefit of defendants. Citing the constitutional provisions that Hungary is a constitutional state based on rule of law and that

---

[13] Cf. Pokol (1994) ch. 5.

[14] Since the second half of the 1990's, the main proponent of this critique, Béla Pokol has acted as a constitutional expert for the Small Holders Party, and after the 1998 elections he became the head of the Parliamentary Standing Committee for Constitutional Issues. His critique is both legal *and* political.

there can be no punishment without a valid law in effect at the time, the Court declared the law to be unconstitutional and sent it back to the President.[15]

2.1.2. Lustration and Informational Self-Determination

After a long period of hesitation, the Hungarian Parliament passed a law early in 1994, which included a compromise solution to the issue of the secret agents of the previous regime's police. The law set up panels of three judges whose job it would be to go through the secret police files of all of those who currently held a certain public offices (including the President, Government ministers, Members of Parliament, Constitutional Court judges, judges of lower Courts, some journalists, holders of high posts in state universities or state-owned companies, as well as a specified list of other high officials). Each of these people would have to undergo background checks in which their files would be scrutinized to see whether they had carried out certain "lustratable" activities[16] under the previous regime. If they did, then the panel would notify the person of the evidence and give him or her a chance to resign from public office. Only if the person chose to remain in office would the panel publicize the information. If the person contested the information found in the files, then prior to disclosure, he or she could appeal to a court which would then conduct a review of evidence *in camera* and make a judgment in the specific case. If the person accepted a judgment against him or her and chose to resign, then the information would still remain secret.

After the law had already gone into effect and the review of the first set of Members of Parliament was already underway, the law was challenged by a petition to the Constitutional Court. The Court handed down its decision in December 1994,[17] in which parts of the 1994 law requiring "background checks on individuals who hold key offices" were declared partly unconstitutional. In its reasoning, the Constitutional Court held that the law violated the constitutional right of the citizens to access to information of public interest which is a part of the fundamental right of communication. The Court also ruled that the legislative attempts to deal with the problem of the files were constitutionally incomplete because they failed to guarantee that the rights of privacy and informational self-determination of all citizens would be maintained. Because the Parliament had not yet secured the right to informational self-determination, and first of all the right of people to see into their own files, the Court declared Parliament to have created a situation of unconstitutionality by omission.[18]

---

[15] Op. cit. Sólyom/Brunner, at pp. 214–228.

[16] The law classified the following activities as "lustratable": carrying out activities on behalf of state security organs as an official agent or informer; obtaining data from state security agencies to assist in making decisions; and being members of the (Fascist) Arrow Cross Party.

[17] 60/1994 (XII.24) AB. Op. cit. Sólyom/Brunner, at pp. 306–315.

[18] The new law, LXII/1996, was approved by the Parliament on July 3, 1996.

2.1.3. Competences of the President of the Republic

Political activism has at times arisen in respect to issues of governmental organization. Such were the decisions handed down in 1991–1992 dealing with the interpretation of the President of the Republic's legal sphere of influence under the Constitution. The motions for a constitutional interpretation – seeking to have the Constitutional Court decide a debate between the Prime Minister and the President – were jointly submitted by the Prime Minister and the majority of the ruling Party's ministerial and Parliamentary committees. Forced into a highly contention arena, the majority of the Court accepted the task of circumscribing the jurisdiction of the President when the constitutional text itself offered no explicit support for such a position.

The primary bone of contention among the Justices was the sensitive question of the President's legal sphere of appointment. The majority (led by Sólyom) determined that the President can only reject an appointment (that is, refuse to accept it as the Constitution specifies that he must), where there is an absence of a legal regulation governing the appointment or if in the course of investigating the person proposed for nomination, the President has substantial cause to conclude that appointing the person would seriously disturb the nation's democratic processes.[19] In their dissenting opinions, three Justices argued however that the Constitutional Court exceeded its jurisdiction in its interpretation, that the decision surpassed the interpretation of the Constitution's applicable regulations and that it belonged in the realm of Constitutional legislation.

2.1.4. Austerity Package

A series of decisions on elements of the government's economic stabilization package of 1995 effected a change in the Constitutional Court's interpretation of social rights. In its decision 43/1995 (VI.30) AB, the Court abolished numerous provisions of the austerity package statute on the basis of its interpretation of welfare benefits as acquired rights. The Constitutional Court determined that legal certainty, as the most important conceptual element of constitutional legitimacy and the primary conceptual basis for the protection of acquired rights, is of special significance from the perspective of stabilizing welfare systems. Although the legislature has the right to change the entire scheme of long term child welfare support, it could not so in violation of the Constitutional requirement of legal certainty. According to the Court, those affected by the new system were constitutionally guaranteed a certain amount of preparation time so as to adapt to the changed regulations and organize their family's household finances based on the new conditions. It was necessary for the Constitutional Court in its justification take a position such that in all cases of social security services where the element of security plays a part, the constitutionality of a decrease in

---

[19]   Decision cp. 48/1991. (IX.26.) AB. Op. cit. Sólyom/Brunner, at pp. 159–170.

services or their abolition is to be judged according to the criteria of preservation of property.[20]

2.1.5. "The General Rights of Personality"

According to its critics, the Court's decisive turn toward activism took place early in its history with the 8/1990. (IV.23.) AB ruling.[21] This decision judged unconstitutional the pre-transition regulation of the Labor Code, which empowered trade unions to represent workers – even if were not union members and perhaps even against their expressed will – without their separate power of attorney. The basis for nullifying this legal rule was the human dignity provision in the Constitution, which the Constitutional Justices (on the recommendation of Sólyom as the presenting Justice in the case)[22] in their justification of the decision considered an expression of "the general rights of personality". This right, which does not appear in the Constitution, is, according to Sólyom's view, "derived" from the right to human dignity. "The general right of personality is a 'mother right' – i.e., a subsidiary fundamental right which may be relied upon at any time by both the Constitutional Court and other courts for the protection of an individual's autonomy when none of the concrete, named fundamental rights is applicable for a particular set of facts".[23] At least one commentator (Pokol) considers this extract to be the "credo of activism," whereby even the constitutionally binding minimum on which to base the Constitutional Court's decisions has disappeared to be replaced by the merest sense of justice.

The criticism of course, correctly predicted that the avalanche of constitutional issues would gather momentum in the course of years to come. The Justices determined in ruling 57/1991. (XI.8.) AB that "the right to self-identity and self-determination is part of the 'general rights of individuals.'"[24] Further, this right includes each individual's personal right to discover their parentage. The following year, decision 22/1992. (IV.10) AB declared unconstitutional the requirement that enlisted officers request permission from their superiors to marry, on the basis that the right to marry, as part of the right to self-determination, is such a fundamental right that it stands under Constitutional guardianship. One can

---

[20] Ibid, at pp. 322–332.

[21] Ibid, at pp. 105–107.

[22] In the Hungarian Constitutional Court all cases are assigned to a judge by the President before they are discussed in plenary session. The assigned judge (usually assigned the case on the basis of prior specialties and competences) works out his or her own best solution to the problem, writes a draft opinion and then tries to convince the other judges of that outcome. In the first nine years President Sólyom assigned many of the "big cases" to himself, giving one more reason to speak of the Sólyom Court between 1990 and 1999. See the cases in Sólyom/Brunner.

[23] Op. cit. Sólyom/Brunner, at p. 107.

[24] Op. cit. Sólyom/Brunner, at pp. 171–177.

also include here the treatment as a birthright under the right of human dignity, Ruling 14/1995. (III.13.) AB of the right of gay and lesbian couples to live life in legally recognized partnership. In this case, the Court – based on Sólyom's presentation – unanimously decreed that there can be no categorical Constitutional differentiation between persons living together in emotional and material partnership on the basis of gender, because individuals must be judged based on the principle of equal dignity. In this case, the Court cited the Constitution's prohibition on discrimination and did not frame new legislation, but as Sólyom later commented, it could have done so.[25]

Ruling 9/1990. (IV.25.) on the constitutionality of positive discrimination, according to the criticism, carried the activist line further. Through the application of Dworkin's familiar formula on the requirements of "treatment as persons of equal dignity", it dissolved the contradiction between Paragraph 1., Section 70/A of the Constitution that formally declared equality under the law, and Paragraph 3 of that same section, which implies equality in content and requires the development of equal opportunity as a constitutional objective. Sólyom acknowledges "the Dworkin effect" in the *Fundamentum* interview. Moreover, he there expressly acknowledged his faith in the Dworkinian principle as the basis of activism and the moral interpretation of the Constitution. The first rulings with reference to positive discrimination seemingly follow [Dworkin's] argumentation verbatim, according to which in the final analysis we must reach a solution that in terms of usefulness to society creates equality, while as a tool, it is equipped with inequality at the same time. This is the philosophy of affirmative action. Dworkin provided reinforcement on behalf of precisely this issue of the system of morality; namely, how autonomous is the Court when it reaches a borderline case. In his view, within an unbiased neutral reading of the Constitution, numerous possibilities for interpretation exist, but the moment a person arrives at a border line in a "hard case," it is here that the judge's moral perspective and reading play a part.[26]

2.1.6. The Right to Life: the Death Penalty

Ruling 23/1990. (X.31) AB abolishing the death penalty[27] featured many concurring opinions revealing the peak of activism while at the same time presenting the first articulation of dissenting opinions by the "Parliamentary legal allies." Among the concurring opinions, Sólyom's demonstrates the unmistakable signs of activism in two respects. Firstly, the President of the Court recognizes its

---

[25] He stated in a *Fundamentum* interview that they could have designated as a separate right in the ruling (had they so desired), that a couple has the right to be recognized as such independent of their gender, p. 37. Ibid, at pp. 316–321.

[26] Ibid, at p. 32.

[27] Op. cit. Sólyom/Brunner, at pp. 118–138.

relationship to Parliament on the one hand and, to the Constitution on the other. In the former regard, the critic[28] of the court considered the following statement key to the Sólyom position: "Parliament may maintain, abolish or restore capital punishment at its discretion until the Constitutional Court renders a final decision on the constitutionality of this punishment".[29] This interpretation of the text understands Sólyom to be obviating the possibility of subsequent reinstatement of the death penalty by the Parliament, even by way of constitutional amendment, thus empowering the Constitutional Court with the right to declare a Constitutional Amendment unconstitutional. Of course, it is also possible to interpret Sólyom's text in a different way (and subsequent actions would rather support the interpretation that Sólyom thought exactly this), such that after a decision by the Constitutional Court, Parliament's ability to act as legislator ceased to exist with respect to reinstating the death penalty, but not Parliament's ability to act as constitutional law-maker. The 1994 decision seems to confirm this. In that case the Court, having determined its own lack of jurisdiction, rejected the motion that initiated a review of one of the statues within the Constitution.[30] Sólyom's words confirm the same in his *Fundamentum* interview, even if, in its articulation, it awakens certain doubts about his own opinion: "The majority of the Constitutional Court finds no need to examine the constitutionality of Constitutional Amendments, although theoretically it could be justified."[31]

The second disclosure associated with the 'Sólyom-type' activism, which has since become renowned because of the concurring opinion attached to the decision on the death penalty, is the concept of the "invisible Constitution". The Constitutional Court must continue its effort to explain the theoretical bases of the Constitution and of the rights included in it and to form a coherent system with its decisions, which as an 'invisible Constitution' provides for a reliable standard of constitutionality beyond the Constitution, which nowadays is often amended out of current political interests; therefore this coherent system will

---

[28] Pokol, *op. cit.*

[29] Op. cit. Sólyom/Brunner, at p. 125.

[30] Rule 23/1994. (IV.29.) AB. Antecedent to the issue was that the Constitutional Court in its decision 3/1990. (III.4.) AB declared unconstitutional that regulation of the law on the right to vote, according to which a citizen who was out of the country on the day of election would have been impeded in voting. Prior to the first democratically held elections Parliament did not wish to amend the law, for this reason it preferred to insert into the Constitution the limitation declared as unconstitutional by the Constitutional Justices. Prior to the 1994 elections, some Hungarian diplomats serving abroad attacked this constitutional passage at the Constitutional Court; the Court however, determining that it was outside its jurisdiction despite the fact that for as long as the regulation appeared only in the law and not in the Constitution, it declared its contents unconstitutional.

[31] *Fundamentum* interview, p. 34. Despite the phrasing's double meaning, he did not attach a concurring nor a dissenting opinion to the ruling referenced above.

probably not conflict with the new Constitution to be established or with future Constitutions.[32]

Although it is true that in subsequent opinions Sólyom did not repeat the expression that visibly irritated politicians, he never renounced its content, as confirmed in a 1997 interview. "Our Constitutional Court proceedings in the interest of coherency – especially in the 'hard cases' – modulate on the boundary of drafting a Constitution, I never denied this."[33] He reiterated in a separate interview in 1998, shortly before stepping down, in which he discussed the misconception by many of the concept of an 'invisible Constitution'. When confronted with the question of whether he would retract the metaphor, Sólyom replied, No. "What I have written, I have written. In those days, the Constitution was amended monthly, as daily politics happened to desire. It was precisely for this reason that I wanted to point out that the Constitution is of a higher order; it is not merely the strict order of technical regulations, but of principles. We had to discern these principles by our decisions, clarify, elucidate and apply them, because no one can determine them from mere one line paragraphs and simple sentences. Of course, it is possible to pass Constitutional Court decisions by retreating behind the letter of the law – there are examples in Europe and Asia as well."[34] The decision on the death penalty represented the first open difference between an activist understanding of fundamental rights by President Sólyom, and the position of the "Parliamentary legal ally" by the dissenters.

Although interpretation of the Constitution belongs under the sphere of jurisdiction of the Constitutional Court, dissolution of contradictory constitutional regulations is the right and obligation of Parliament [which is] vested with the power to enact constitutional legislation. The Constitutional Court cannot usurp this right.[35]

2.2. Jurisdictional Activism

Before addressing the question of whether the Sólyom Court had a tendency to extend its jurisdiction, it is worth analyzing the experience of those nine years from the perspective of the more important decisions on competences.

2.2.1. Preliminary Norm Control and the Process of Legislation
The first decision that revealed self-restraint[36] was presented by President Sólyom before the Court, and was supported unanimously. As mentioned before, the Court refused to comment on the constitutionality of a draft law currently before

---

[32] Op. cit. Sólyom/Brunner, at. p. 126.
[33] Ibid. p. 37.
[34] Mihalicz (1998), p. 438.
[35] Dissent by Justice Péter Schmidt.
[36] Ruling 16/1991. (IV.20.) AB. Op cit. Sólyom/Brunner, at pp. 151–158.

the Parliament, saying that to do so would interfere with the process of legisla-tion. In those times, the threat of interference was in fact a matter of a significance because, according to the House Rules one reading of an Act may be directly followed by another without the necessity for an intervening period for legislative correction. In essence, the Court's determination of cause meant that it also became impossible to submit the preliminary motion for constitutional examina-tion in such a way that it would satisfy the Court's requirements. That argument seems entirely acceptable. It would be a different matter if, as a result, the Constitutional Court was denied the exercise of its jurisdiction, as it was embod-ied in a law currently in force. Therefore, it was not simply a strict interpretation of jurisdiction, but rather, its *contra legem* interpretation. In 1998, as if acknow-ledging the Court's exercise in self-restraint, Parliament amended the law on the Constitutional Court and abolished the possibility of preliminary constitutional review of legal proposals.[37] As a result, the mechanism of preliminary examina-tion for constitutional compliance of recognized but not yet proclaimed laws became restricted to review initiated by the President of the Republic.

2.2.2. The Abstract Interpretation of the Constitution as an "Advisory Opinion"

The initial understanding of the Constitutional Court with respect to the abstract interpretation of the Constitution was determined by the self-restrictive character of Ruling 31/1990. (XII.18) AB. At the time the Constitutional Justices unanim-ously rejected the motion by the Finance Minister, in which he asked for an "advisory opinion" on the constitutionality of various governmental ideas about raising the interest on long-term housing loans that were earlier transferred at a preferred rate. According to the Constitutional Court's justification, if they were to interpret the powers to interpret the constitution in the abstract sense this broadly, it could easily lead to a situation where the respective legislative bodies could ask for a "constitutional interpretation" before the creation of not only legislation, but also governmental or even ministerial decrees. The Justices argued that this would lead to the Constitutional Court's assuming legislative or even executive responsibility, in clear conflict to the principles on government organizations embodied in the Constitution and could foreseeable result in a "Constitutional Court government."

2.2.3. The Constitutional Complaint, as Genuine Legal Remedy

The Hungarian Constitutional Court, charged with the most extensive jurisdic-tional competence in the world when it comes to ensuring abstract constitutional compliance – in contrast to the German, Swiss, Spanish and Austrian courts – was nonetheless not initially authorized to review the constitutionality of con-crete judicial and administrative decisions, at least not without having to examine

---

[37] Law I. 1998.

the constitutionality of the standard that served as a basis for the specific decision as well. The absence of a so-called "constitutional complaint" in Hungarian Constitutional Court jurisdiction, meant that the Constitutional Court complaint procedure codified in 1989 did not fulfill its actual function as a legal remedy. (Since this hybrid complaint solution was nothing more than a motion for the examination of abstract constitutional compliance in a specific matter, which had no effect on the solution to the given case whatsoever, such complaints accounted for only one percent of all submissions to the Constitutional Court.) Members of the Constitutional Court who wanted to enlarge the jurisdiction of the court attempted to breathe life into the lifeless institution of the constitutional complaint in Ruling 57/1991. (XI.8.) AB.

In a case involving a judicial procedure that was already legally in force, the majority ruled that it was unconstitutional for a law to conclusively divest a child from her/his right to know who her/his parents if such information was contained in public records. Further, this inability to be able to find out one's parentage resulted in infringement of the child's general individual rights. For this reason, the Constitutional Court determined that once a regulation was shown to be in violation of the Constitution in the matter under complaint, the Court could decisively overturn the judicial judgments queried. Moreover, the Court ordered birth certificate data, changed as a result of judgments that caused infringement of the constitution, to be reinstated to their original status. According to the justification, it was the only way that the unconstitutional situation could be remedied in a specific case and, as a result, the right of minors to self-determination and self-identity guaranteed under the Constitution was also correctly enforced. That is, it provided the opportunity that once they reached the age of adulthood, people could personally initiate clarification of their family status and origin of their blood line.

This rationale also attempts to explain on what basis the Constitutional Court took the step of overturning a concrete legal judgment in the matter. Clearly, while the law on the Constitutional Court does not completely regulate its manner of legal procedure, in certain cases the legal remedy for infringement of the law must be determined by the Constitutional Court itself. The ruling was met by stringent criticism both from the President of the Supreme Court, as well as sections the legal community who claimed that the Constitutional Court slipped into the forbidden territory of legal enforcement, thereby infringing the jurisdiction of the Supreme Court to pass judgment and determine the proper legal remedy.[38]

Dissenting opinions from the Constitutional Justices did not question the

---

[38] The President of the Supreme Court in a statement of protest cited Paragraph 70/K of the Constitution, according to which lawsuits in connection with violations of fundamental rights belong in the domain of regular courts. *HVG [Hungarian Newspaper Weekly]* 1998 May 1.

judgment but instead took issue with the elimination of the statutes that served as its basis. The majority opinion judged the statutes under attack to be in violation of the Constitution on the basis that judicial practice – adhering to the Supreme Court's interpretation of the law – applied these in a consistently unconstitutional manner. According to the majority reasoning, the Constitutional Court has interpretive jurisdiction only with respect to the Constitution's provisions, and has no independent power to interpret law. For this reason, the Constitutional Court had to examine the constitutional complaint against the text of the law to be applied from the perspective of understanding and content as it was applied – that is, the Court had to compare the "living law" with the content of the Constitution's provisions. But it was precisely this theory of "living law" that two Justices found unacceptable.[39] According to the dissent, the Constitutional Court has no jurisdiction to examine the constitutionality of the application of law in practice. Furthermore, the Court cannot "punish" the legislature because of unconstitutional interpretation of the law on the part of other state institution's application of the law by striking out a statute that under correct interpretation does not otherwise violate the Constitution. Beyond extending the realm of jurisdiction the Court also causes legal uncertainty if they consider the content of the legal regulation not according to the text as it appears in *Hungarian Official Gazette* but as that which it "attributes to the permanent and unified application of the law in practice." According to the reasoning of the two dissenting judges, the Constitutional Court should instead explain in the justification exactly which interpretations of a particular law would allow the law to be applied without constitutional problems. As we can see, it is here that the basis for the subsequent practice of the interpretation of constitutional conformity first appeared.

In connection with the conflict that emerged as a result of Ruling 57/1991. (XI.8.) AB between the Constitutional Court and the Supreme Court on whether the Constitutional Court's jurisdiction could be extended to assessing the constitutionality of interpretations of laws in concrete cases, a solution offered itself in the form of a compromise which emerged in the course of the preliminary preparations for a new Constitution in 1995. Under the interpretation of the proposal formulated by the two courts and presented to the preliminary drafters of the Constitution, the Presidents of the two courts agreed that in matters of fundamental law the final decisions would continue to be brought by regular courts. At the same time, in the case of infringement of rights guaranteed under the Constitution, it would be possible to request the Constitutional Court to take a theoretical position, which would subsequently bind the decision of the regular court in consideration of the matter at the time of passing judgment. Although with this solution the Constitutional Court would not have been

---

[39] See the dissenting opinions of Justices Kilényi and Schmidt. Op. cit. Sólyom/Brunner, at pp. 176–177.

authorized to be the actual final adjudicator of the complaint on constitutional legality, nevertheless, the Constitutional Court would have the ability to exercise binding influence on the fate of a specific case at issue with its assessment of the case-specific constitutional claims. With interruption of the process of drafting a preliminary Constitution however, enactment of this proposal also failed. The two courts, even in the absence of codification, nonetheless attempted a solution from among the existing legal possibilities. In the case in which the Supreme Court upheld the denial of the group registration in a case involving a gay rights association called "The Rainbow Partnership for Gay Rights," in the course of examining the petition, it turned to the Constitutional Court with a motion for constitutional interpretation on the more general constitutional claim of what to do in the case of a conflict between the right of association on one hand and the constitutional protection of children on the other. The Supreme Court in the end decided the case using the contents of the Constitutional Court's ruling.[40]

In the absence of a legislative solution and in the course of a complaint in a specific court case brought before the Constitutional Court in 1998, the Constitutional Court again had to address the constitutional problem in connection with application of the legal requirements in a successful constitutional complaint. Ruling 23/1998 (VI.9.) AB – referring in several instances to the 1991 decision – repeatedly emphasized that according to Paragraph 57(5) of the Constitution, the constitutional complaint has the quality of an actual legal remedy and for this reason its effectiveness depends upon having legal consequences. These legal consequences must extend to the examination of the merits of a legally closed case, since this is the only means through which the principal element of the legal remedy can succeed – namely by correcting the legal infringement. The unanimous decision determined that specifically allowing the constitutional complaint to carry with it a legal remedy does not follow necessarily from Paragraph 57(5) of the Constitution. But, if the legislature allowed the Court to have this jurisdiction, then it would be the Court's constitutional responsibility to create such procedural regulations through which the legal violation would in fact become remediable. If the Court failed to provide a remedy under this circumstance, it would be a violation of a person's general right to legal remedy. From another perspective, the failure of the Court to act would also violate of the principle of legal security. While the ruling passed by

---

[40] The fundamental justification for denial of the court registration was the fact that the founding regulations of the association did not exclude membership of those under 18 years of age. The motion, based on Article 67, Paragraph 1. of the Constitution, in connection with an interpretation of the state's tasks with respect to the physical, mental and moral development of children, asked for an answer to the question whether the right to association for those under 18 years of age, guaranteed under Article 63 Paragraph 1, could be restricted in a legal manner. For criticism of the Constitutional Court's ruling containing an affirmative reply, see Halmai/Scheppele (1997).

the Constitutional Court in the complaint case is binding on the ordinary court where the case is being adjudicated, the procedural regulations through which the ordinary court would be able to get the case before the Constitutional Court are missing. Based on the foregoing, the Constitutional Court determined that Parliament committed an unconstitutional omission in proceedings other than criminal cases, because the it failed to provide for a mechanism through which the abstract decisions of the Constitutional Court would be translated into a concrete remedy for those individuals affected by the application of an unconstitutional law.

The novelty of the 1998 ruling compared to that of 1991, is that the Constitutional Justices through this means – at least provisionally – refrained from overturning the court's judgment comprising the subject of the complaint. They were satisfied with setting a deadline for the Legislature to create the procedural regulations. They deferred to a yet later date any proceedings directed at overturning the court ruling, providing an opportunity thereby for the court itself to bring a decision based on appropriate procedural regulations compliant with the ruling of the Constitutional Court.[41] It must be noted however, that the Constitutional Justices merely reclaimed the same degree of activism that they exhibited in the 1991 ruling. They did not immediately nullify the court judgment, but instead gave a chance to the Legislature, and as a result to the original court, to come to a decision in the matter. However, if the Legislature delays in acting, the threat of overturning the ordinary court's decision continues, without the Constitutional Court's feeling as a result the need to explain on what legal basis it would do such a thing.

2.2.4. "Jurisdiction Alteration" on the Part of the Constitutional Court

Much of the above has revolved around discussion among the Court's various members as to the legally guaranteed jurisdiction of the Constitutional Court and whether that jurisdiction should be exercised in a strict or an extended manner. As we have seen, the extended interpretation also frequently burst open the framework of the given jurisdiction, and in fact resulted in the institutionalization of a new sphere of authority. This is what President Sólyom has somewhat euphemistically termed "jurisdiction alteration".[42] Sólyom himself claims to have borrowed the concept from the Italian Constitutional Court's position on "living law." Sólyom views the transplantation of the exercise of "interpretation in conformity with the Constitution (*Verfassungskonforme Auslegung*)" imported from Germany, as its reverse. In Germany, the Constitutional Court tends to interpret the legal regulations to be examined in light of the demands deduced from the Constitution in order to define an abstract "province of constitutional

---

[41] Parliament did fulfil its legislative responsibility only after the deadline of December 31, 1998 determined by the Constitutional Court in May 1999 enacting the Law XLV of 1999.

[42] Cf. Sólyom (1995).

interpretation." This embraces as a result all the unregulated power of the interpretation of legal regulations to which everyone is subject. A similar kind of extension of jurisdiction activism is evidenced by the Hungarian Constitutional Court deleting the regulations that were to have come into force in the aforementioned austerity package in connection with social rights, where the Court attempted to compensate for the absence of its so-called "institution of temporary action." Such a possibility exists also in Germany, allowing, suspension of the implementation of the examination for constitutional compliance until a decision on the merits.[43]

Two other new forms of constitutional jurisdiction emerged in the wake of a pair of rulings in 1997, one of which (Ruling 4/1997. (I.22.) AB)[44] extended the Constitutional Court's capacity to retroactively examine the constitutionality of international agreements. The other jurisdictional change occurred when the Court deleted a section of its regulation on jurisdiction in order to give itself the power to reject any call for a popular referendum that violated the Court's view of the what the Constitution allowed in that area (Ruling 52/1997. (X.14) AB).[45]

3. WHAT NEXT? (NEGATIVE) LEGISLATOR VERSUS PART OF THE JUDICIARY

There is no doubt that in the Sólyom Era, the President of the Court strove to lead the defense of the Hungarian Constitution in an activist manner, both with respect to the Constitution itself and also in the interpretation of jurisdiction.[46] Stepping down from his position as President and Justice, Sólyom responded to a journalist's inquiry about whether his Court's decisions might later be reviewed and changed by a later Court. Sólyom called attention to two possibilities.[47] First, he said that he thought that the activism of the Sólyom Court would be

---

[43]   Cf. Ruling 43/1995. (VI.30.) AB and Ruling 44/1995. (VI.30.) AB.

[44]   Op. cit. Sólyom/Brunner, at pp. 356–363.

[45]   *Ibid.* at pp. 371–378.

[46]   In this respect it can be compared to the Warren Court in the history of the US Supreme Court, if we follow Bernard Schwartz's categorization, who attempted to group the eras of the Supreme Court based on the role of the Chief Justices. He grouped the sixteen presidencies during the two hundred years into three categories. One is represented by the "super" Chief Justice, in the manner of Earl Warren who directed the Court; the second is associated with a weak-handed Chief Justice, as for example, Warren Burger, who was directed by the Court; finally the third, under the rule of William Rehnquist, still effective as of today, allows for several determinant individuals to direct the Court (for example, William Brennan). Cf. Schwartz (1996).

[47]   Cf. "Farewell to Donáti Street. One on One with László Sólyom, departing President of the Constitutional Court" *Magyar Hírlap [Hungarian Newspaper daily].* 1998 November 28.

moderated by a subsequent Court. Moreover, with respect to the scope of competences, he thought that a more strict interpretation following the letter of the law would become dominant in the new Court. In other words, Sólyom, as he left the bench, believed that the Court that followed his would be less activist in both of these key aspects. The first two years of the new Court's life bear this out. But how can we evaluate the new restraint more accurately?

As seen, the Constitutional Court of Hungary has an exceptionally wide jurisdiction. This is the Kelsenian approach of negative legislation by a constitutional court. But by contrast with this broad power, however it has almost no power to review and annul court decisions or other specific interpretations of law in the context of concrete decisions. The activity of the Hungarian Constitutional Court centers not so much around the review of concrete cases and controversies but rather around the abstract review of legal provisions. This is why the Hungarian Constitutional Court cannot really be characterized as part of the judiciary. According to the original law that outlined the Court's jurisdiction, the most important competence of the Court is regressive abstract norm control. The need to systematically review the constitutionality of the surviving elements of the old legal system existing in parallel with the renewed constitution has made this the main function of the Hungarian Constitutional Court in its first decade.

Arguably, the Hungarian Constitutional court can be freed from all negative political implications about the activist uses of its powers only if it is reconstructed to be more like an ordinary court than like an upper chamber of the Parliament, as it is. The German model would be preferable in this respect, where the vast majority of cases that the Court deals with in any given year are about unconstitutional applications of laws rather than about unconstitutional laws seen in the abstract. Now that the work of building a new legal system on new democratic principles is largely completed, the Court should move away from its initial task of harmonizing all laws with a new constitution and should proceed to the business common in other established constitutional democracies of ensuring that those who make decisions about the lives of citizens also follow constitutional principles in their exercise of official power.

An alternative to the Constitutional Court's decision making in the sphere of fundamental human rights is for these cases to be tried by the ordinary courts as stipulated by paragraph 70/K of the Constitution instead of coming before a revised Constitutional Court. This would require extensive new training of the judges in the ordinary courts. Even though the "new constitution" has been in effect for 11 years now, it is still the case that most ordinary court judges see no relationship between the constitution and their everyday practices of deciding cases. In turn, the Hungarian ordinary courts have not exercised judicial review even though they are authorized to do so in limited ways. It would, therefore, be preferable to invest the Constitutional Court with jurisdiction as regards the real constitutional complaint. In those cases, the decisions would not be limited to cases where the regulations forming the basis of the challenged administrative or judicial decisions are deemed unconstitutional, and the activity of the Constitutional Court would come closer to the activity of the regular courts because the Constitutional Court would be able to ensure that the Constitution is followed in concrete cases.

It is not only the need to strengthen jurisdiction in the field of fundamental human rights that would justify such a change but also that fact that a Constitutional Court based primarily on abstract review can not stand the test of time. At the time of reviewing an old legal system existing in parallel with the new constitution, it was justified to set up a system like that and even complement it with the institution of popular action. However, once the old legal system has been reconciled with the new Constitutional regulations and principles, the Hungarian system can also change over to a norm control based on cases and controversies. Such a change would signal the end of the Hungarian legal "transition" and the birth of a consolidated constitutional democracy.

To return to the start of this chapter, the question remains whether this consolidated constitutional regime, which seems to work, needs a new constitution. Many people thought so in 1995, and the Parliament undertook to draft one during the 1995–1996 Parliamentary session. But it failed because the relevant consensus could not be garnered within the governing coalition. One thing is certain – safeguarding the values of the existing document is more important than changing this constitution for a new one with different values. This is so even if the year 1949 in the legal title of the current constitution conjures unsavory memories. And this is especially so when possible reformers are steered by "revolutionary" or "restorationary" ideas. Of course, the idealistic solution would be to prepare a totally new constitution, following the method of radical continuity.[48] This theory offers a new constitution which would preserve the public law system of the transition and would extend the self-restraining character of the transition to the Constitutional Court too. However the advocates of this idea did not meet with success in their hopes for a "rationalized, newly legitimized" constitution identical with the constitution of the transition. Such a new constitution could have ended the period of transition. But those whose primary aim was stabilization of the democratic changes lost because of the concentration in 1996 of the forces that favored restoration of elements of the old system and a second revolution.[49] It is true that the Constitution of the

---

[48]   This was recommended by Andrew Arató (1994), who developed this idea by accepting the conservative constitutional conception of János Kis (See Kis [1993]). Arató proposes his method for those who worry about the second revolution and argue for a way to develop the old-new constitution through constitutional court decisions. (See Halmai [1994] and Majtényi [1994]).

[49]   In 1996, the concept of the new constitution did not obtain the 2/3 majority of the votes in the plenary session of the Parliament, although the two governing parties did have the 2/3 majority of the mandates. And this happened so because some members of the Socialist Party (MSZP) did not support it. The left wing of the bigger party in the coalition upset

transition builds in an inherent conflict between the Constitutional Court and the Parliament, between constitutionalism and democracy. In long run it enables the establishment of a "constitutional dictatorship" for any force that can receive more than two thirds majority in the Parliament on any issue.[50] Since it takes only a onetime two thirds vote to amend the Constitution and since the Constitutional Court has not entertained the idea that a constitutional amendment may itself be unconstitutional, a constitutional solution can always be imposed by a supermajority over a principled interpretation of the current Constitution. The surprising element of Hungarian politics, however, is that only once has the Parliament overturned a decision of the Constitutional Court by amending the Constitution, and that was in the very first days of the new constitutional system.

Changing this system to create a new "constitutional dictatorship" ought to be avoided even if we have to live under the facade a 50 year old constitution. The Constitution's complete revision which was carried out ten years ago is much more important than the superficial title that the text bears. For the most critical point about the past ten years in Hungary is that, for the first time in Hungarian history, it is a real constitutional state.

---

the approval of the concept, because the declaration of the Republic as a social state and the mechanism of the dispute (interests) settlement were not incorporated.

[50] Arató (1999), p. 10.

9. Slovenia's Constitutional Court within the Separation of Power

Miro Cerar

1. A BRIEF HISTORY OF SLOVENIA'S CONSTITUTIONAL COURT

A constitutional court was first established in Slovenia by the constitution of 1963. Prior to this, the constitutional order of the Socialist Federal Republic of Yugoslavia (SFRY) and – under this – of the Republic of Slovenia required that supervision of the guaranteed general principle of constitutionality and legality should be carried out according to the principle of self-regulation within what was termed the 'assembly system'. However, this supervision proved ineffective. To the extent that it was even carried out, self-regulation through the assembly system related primarily to ensuring the coherence of policy expressed in certain legal acts, and less to the assessment of legality in the proper sense of the word.[1] The Yugoslav Federal Assembly and the assemblies of what were then Yugoslav federal republics therefore set up in 1963 a Federal Constitutional Court and a number of Constitutional Courts for the Republics,[2] which came as quite a surprise and even earned some acclaim abroad, as other communist systems had not yet established any such judicial bodies.[3] In the first instance, the implementation of constitutional courts was accompanied by a debate as to whether the constitutional judiciary was compatible with the then fundamental constitutional principle of the unity of power, although the functioning of the constitutional courts came up to expectations as a factor for ensuring constitutionality and legality[4] – something that was of course fostered by the fact that the functioning of these courts remained within the confines of the communist system and ideology, which were in turn determined by the constitutional order itself.

---

[1] Arne Mavčič, *Zakon o ustavnem sodišču s pojasnili* (Constitutional Court Act with explanatory notes, Ljubljana, Nova revija, 2000), p. 48.

[2] In the two autonomous regions of that time in the Yugoslav Federation (Vojvodina and Kosovo), a constitutional judiciary was established in 1972. In 1991 the Constitutional Courts of Vojvodina and Kosovo were abolished, with the jurisdiction of the Serbian Constitutional Court being extended to the entire territory of the Serbian Republic.

[3] Ivan Kristan, "Ustavno sodišče in parlament" (Constitutional Court and Parliament), *Zbornik znanstvenih razprav*, year 51 (Ljubljana 1991), p. 178.

[4] Arne Mavčič, *Zakon o ustavnem sodišču s pojasnili* (Constitutional Court Act with explanatory notes, Ljubljana, Nova revija, 2000), pp. 48–49.

Wojciech Sadurski (ed.), Constitutional Justice, East and West, 213–245
© 2002 *Kluwer Law International. Printed in Great Britain.*

Moreover, the then jurisdiction of the constitutional courts did not allow these courts to intervene directly in the substance of any regulation (e.g. by abrogating individual provisions), although according to the constitution of 1963, for example, in certain cases the constitutional court determined the substantive meaning of individual regulations that in the court's opinion concurred with the constitution and law.

The new Yugoslav Constitution and Republic Constitutions of 1974 retained the existing Constitutional Courts. Each Constitutional Court in the individual Republics functioned independently, in line with the Republic's Constitution, meaning that the Federal (Yugoslav) Constitutional Court was not directly superior to the Constitutional Courts of individual Republics. In each Republic the position and powers of the Constitutional Court was set out in detail in Constitutional Court Acts, and in some instances even by rules of procedure which defined their organisation and internal operation. The system governing Constitutional Courts in individual Republics was in many aspects similar (e.g. election of Constitutional Court judges by the relevant assembly), although different in certain elements (e.g. the differing number of judges in individual Constitutional Courts). The amended Slovenian Constitution of 1974,[5] which contained numerous provisions on the Constitutional Court, provided that it should be composed of nine judges, who would be elected by the Assembly of the Republic of Slovenia for eight years without the possibility of re-election (article 425 of the Constitution). As a rule the Constitutional Court functioned publicly (i.e. hearings were in open court – articles 418 and 421) and made all its decisions by a majority vote of all its members (article 420). The Constitution itself laid down that decisions of the Constitutional Court were binding and executable, and that if necessary the Executive Council (the then 'government') should ensure execution of the Court's decisions, while the Constitutional Court could also require that measures be taken against the responsible person that did not implement its decision (article 423). Numerous provisions of the Constitution related chiefly to the jurisdiction and procedure before the Court and to the legal consequences of Constitutional Court decisions (articles 408–424), where it would also be pertinent to note that the Slovenian Constitutional Court already held at that time the majority of the 'classical' Constitutional Court powers, yet it could not directly abrogate laws, nor did it hold some of the other significant forms of jurisdiction now held by the present Constitutional Court in line with the new Constitution of 1991 (URS).[6] If we

---

[5] *Ustava Republike Slovenije* (Constitution of the Republic of Slovenia), Uradni list SRS, nos. 44/74, 22/81 and 32/89.

[6] *Ustava Republike Slovenije* (Constitution of the Republic of Slovenia) was adopted on 23 December 1991 (Uradni list RS, nos. 33/91-I, 42/97 and 66/2000).

compare the former system of operation of the Constitutional Court[7] with the current system, we may observe that under the 1991 Constitution, the new powers of the Constitutional Court, that is, those powers which the Court did not possess under the old system, relate primarily to decision-making on the harmony of laws and other regulations with ratified treaties, to the issuing of opinions on the constitutionality of treaties in their ratification procedure and to decision-making on constitutional complaints, on disputes over competence between state bodies, on the unconstitutional activities of political parties and on impeachment charges against the President of the Republic, the Prime Minister and ministers (articles 160, 109 and 119 of the URS).

As mentioned, a central new feature of the Slovenian constitutional order of 1991 is the fact that the Court may now, upon completing the procedure for establishing the constitutionality of a law, directly abrogate an unconstitutional law entirely or in part. The constitutional order of 1974 allowed the Court merely to establish the unconstitutionality of a law, and its validity was terminated only in the event of the Republic's Assembly failing to bring the said law into line with the Constitution within six months of receipt of that decision, which in turn the Constitutional Court had to determine in a special official decision (on the application of the Assembly it could also extend the period for alignment of the law to a maximum of a further six months – article 412 of the 1974 Constitution). None of this, however, was applicable to ordinary regulations (secondary legislation) and other general legal acts, for in the event of the Constitutional Court establishing that they were counter to the Constitution or law, the Court itself directly abrogated or annulled such regulations or acts (article 413).

From the aspect of constitutional control, therefore, the present power of the Constitutional Court as what is termed a negative legislator, in counterbalance to the representative and legislative body of the National Assembly, has been significantly strengthened. With the adoption of the new Constitution of 1991, Slovenia's Constitutional Court started to function according to the provisions of this Constitution, which were specified and – on the basis of the constitution-supplemented by a special law (ZUstS)[8] in 1994, and in 1998 the Court organised its internal functioning in detail through the adoption of its rules of procedure.[9] Despite the fact that there was already an established tradition and continuity

---

[7]   A more detailed analysis of the position of the Constitutional Court in the former system can be found in Ciril Ribičič, "Ustavno sodišče SR Slovenije" (Constitutional Court of the Socialist Republic of Slovenia), in Majda Strobl, Ivan Kristan, Ciril Ribičič, *Ustavno pravo SFR Jugoslavije* (Constitutional law of the SFRY, Ljubljana 1986), pp. 379–382.

[8]   *Zakon o ustavnem sodišču* (ZUstS) – Constitutional Court Act – of 8 March 1994, Uradni list RS, no. 15/94.

[9]   *Poslovnik Ustavnega sodišča Republike Slovenije* (Rules of Procedure of the Constitutional Court of the Republic of Slovenia) of 26 May 1998.

in the functioning of the Constitutional Court in Slovenia, we may observe that its composition, whose members were appointed following Slovenia's independence, that is, from 1991 to 1998, introduced to the work of the Court not only an entirely new system of legal values, which corresponded with the constitutional spirit of the principle of a state based on the rule of law, but also an explicit judicial activism,[10] which in certain cases in fact proved to be politically motivated, and as such had very negative effects on public life (more on this subject below). Since 1998, when there were again major personnel changes to the composition of the Court, such negative activism has at least for the moment no longer been in evidence, with the Court functioning according to well-established legal standards which it set out in the first years of its mandate following adoption of the new Constitution (1991).

2. COMPOSITION OF THE CONSTITUTIONAL COURT AND THE STATUS OF ITS JUSTICES

The Constitutional Court is composed of nine judges elected by the National Assembly on the proposal of the President of the Republic.[11] The Constitution

---

[10] In judicial activism a distinction must be made between activism in the positive sense, where on the basis of constitutional provisions and autonomous expert assessment, the Constitutional Court independently judges the constitutionality of decisions taken by other state bodies, and activism in the negative sense, where in deciding in one or another way, the Court subordinates itself to political or other factors (pressure) or consciously makes a biased decision, for example to the benefit of some specific political option. An analogous distinction, with slightly different argumentation, is presented for example by Cass R. Sunstein, "The Legitimacy of Constitutional Courts: Notes on Theory and Practice", in the *East European Constitutional Review*, Vol. 6, No 1, Winter 1997, pp. 62–63.

[11] The fact that in constitutional debate prior to the adoption of the new Constitution the method of electing Constitutional Court judges was not analysed with any great critical weight or from the aspect of comparative law is pointed out by Igor Kaučič in *"Volitve sodnikov ustavnega sodišča", Zbornik IV. Dnevi javnega prava* ("Elections of constitutional court judges", Portorož 1998), pp. 143 and following. Kaučič offers the generalised view that in this aspect, too, we may observe the Slovenian "syndrome of the assembly system" (*ibid.* 149). The author finds that Slovenia, which in the former system exercised the principle of unity of power (the peak of this "unity" was represented in the formal sense by the republic assembly), is now characterised by an unbalanced parliamentarianism, with an exaggeratedly powerful role played by the legislative body, which is entirely empowered to appoint numerous other important public office holders (for example the National Assembly elects all other judges and appoints ministers on the proposal of the prime minister) (*ibid.*). Moreover, it is worth adding that these and other remnants of the assembly system are to a great extent also a reflection of the genuine enthusiasm for the new parliamentary democracy, in which the representative body of the people was supposed to be the most important regulatory force (Drago Zajc, *"Moč in nemoč slovenske parlamentarne demokracije"* (The power and impotence of Slovenian parliamentary democracy), in

lays down that a "legal expert" may be elected to the Court (article 163 of the URS), while the law supplements this with the conditions of Slovenian citizenship and a minimum age of 40 years (article 9 of the ZUstS). Given that Justices of the Court are elected by the National Assembly by a majority vote of all Deputies (in a secret ballot – article 14 of the ZUstS), each new ruling coalition can impose its will in this. Governmental coalitions since 1992 have been of the politically mixed type, made up of political parties from the 'left' and the 'right' of the political spectrum. Accordingly, the election of individual Constitutional Justices in Parliament has always required a broad consensus of political parties and the formation of different kinds (ad hoc) of alliances, although it must be said that in this context, agreement or compromise within the government coalition is still of key importance.

The President of the Republic proposes to the National Assembly candidates to the Constitutional Court from among persons who respond to the President's public call, but the President may also propose other candidates of his/her own choice (articles 12 and 13 of the ZUstS). To date the President of the Republic has consistently followed the principle of the highest professional expertise of candidates in making the selection, while the practice was also established of the President consulting with representatives of parliamentary parties before submitting proposals – of course within the criteria of "legal expertise" the possibility is not ruled out of the President's greater or lesser political inclination towards various candidates and thus the possibility of political influence on their selection and election. Especially after the aforementioned first composition of the Constitutional Court directly following Slovenia's independence and the adoption of the new Constitution turned out to be extremely inclined towards activism,[12] the question of electing Constitutional Justices became a prominent political issue. The nucleus of Constitutional Court activism was created primarily by a triumvirate of Justices, who in a period of eight years each in turn occupied the position of President of the Constitutional Court.[13] Right up until autumn 1998, when their term in office expired, in most of the more politically prominent decisions of the Court, the majority of votes (five) formed around the aforementioned triumvirate, so that the voting split in these decisions was generally 5:4. In such cases the relatively severe polarisation and confrontation of legal and value-system positions was pointed out by published concurring

Demokracija – vladanje in uprava v. Sloveniji (Democracy – government and administration in Slovenia, Ljubljana: Slovensko politološko društvo 1997), p. 14.

12   Yet some of the Courts of former Communist countries (e.g. Russia and Hungary) are even more 'activist' than the Slovenian Constitutional Court. See Bojan Bugarič: *From Plan to Market: One Way or Alternative Paths?, A Critique of Institutional Reforms in Central and Eastern Europe*, unpublished doctoral dissertation (University of Wisconsin, 1998-I), p. 166.

13   The Constitution provides that the President of the Constitutional Court is elected by the judges from among their own number for a period of three years (article 163 URS).

and dissenting opinions of individual judges. This majority also had a major influence on the adoption of certain decisions that were not just overtly contentious from the aspect of the Constitution and clearly adopted in excess of the Court's powers, but were also overtly in line with the interests of certain specific (chiefly right-wing) political options in Slovenia (e.g. the matter of the "municipality of Koper" and the "1996 electoral referendum" – see below). For this reason it is of course no mere coincidence that all three former Presidents of the Constitutional Court took up ministerial posts in the right-wing government coalition in June 2000 (Ministry of the Interior, Ministry of Education and Sports and a Minister without Portfolio (competent for legislative affairs)). According to some general assessments, since 1998 the composition of the Court has supposedly been rather different ('left-wing') in its political orientation, but in this composition it is for the moment taking decisions within the boundaries of its agreed competence, with a greater (and appropriate) emphasis on judicial self-restraint,[14] so at least thus far it cannot be accused of political orientation of any hue.

As a response to the improper activism of the Constitutional Court, there appeared in legal and political circles certain (isolated) proposals that Constitutional Justices should be elected in the National Assembly by a two-thirds majority,[15] although in wider professional and political circles these proposals did not gain support.[16] This is understandable, since parliamentary decision-making by a two-thirds majority for election of Constitutional Justices would without doubt frequently lead to lengthy impasses in the election of new judges. The highly politicised procedure of electing Justices in the National Assembly is also evident in the fact that in the time since the implementation of the Constitutional Court Act, that is since April 1994, in three cases the National Assembly rejected the election of proposed Constitutional Court judicial candidates, in whom (having satisfied the conditions of citizenship and being 40 years old) it was really not possible to find justifiable fault in terms of meeting the essential qualitative criteria, i.e. legal expertise.[17]

---

[14] Of course the 'right measure' of judicial self-restraint cannot be defined exactly and in advance, yet it is certainly possible to agree with the finding that the principle of restraint in the Constitutional Court requires above all impartiality, but not also neutrality in decision-making ("Der Richter soll unparteilich, aber nicht neutral sein"). See Martin Kriele, *Recht, Vernunft, Wircklichkeit* (Berlin, Duncker und Humblot, 1990), p. 587.

[15] See e.g. Matevž Krivic, *Ustavne sodnike voliti z dvotretjinsko večino* (Electing judges by a two-thirds majority), in the newspaper Delo of 27 January 1996, p. 33.

[16] The National Assembly rejected the proposed Act amending the Constitutional Court Act (published in the *Poročevalec Državnega zbora* – Reporter of the National Assembly, no. 2/1998), which contained the proposed introduction of two-thirds majority election of Constitutional Court judges.

[17] During this period the National Assembly refused to approve proposed candidates for Constitutional Court judge three times (one was even rejected twice, while one candidate who stood again was only elected by a minimum majority, that is with 46 votes for –

The position of Slovenian Constitutional Justices is characterised by the fact that in the *formal legal* sense they are ensured a large degree of independence in their position and functioning. Of course the various constitutional and legal mechanisms guaranteeing such formal independence cannot exert a decisive influence on the personality and value-judgment profile of individual Justices, which in the final instance is always the key factor in decision-making on the basis of broadly open (in the sense of "open texture") constitutional principles[18] and rules. The most important of the systemic factors guaranteeing judicial independence are as follows: the "independent" position of the Constitutional Court *vis-à-vis* other state bodies (article 1 of the ZUstS), whereby individual judges are also independent *vis-à-vis* the constitutional court itself, for they may only be dismissed on their own request, in the event of being convicted of a serious crime or through permanent loss of capacity to perform their office (article 164 of the URS); a relatively long (nine years) term of office (article 165 of the URS), with the legally guaranteed possibility of Justices returning to their former jobs on the expiry of their term (articles 76 and 77 of the ZUstS); enjoyment of the same immunity as National Assembly Deputies (article 167 of the URS); high salaries and official perks – in this regard the President of the Constitutional Court is on a similar footing with the President of the National Assembly, and Constitutional Court Justices with the Vice-President of the National Assembly (articles 71 and 72 of the ZUstS); the guaranteed possibility, in the event of the practical impossibility of Justices resuming their former jobs and obtaining other appropriate employment, of them continuing to receive salary in lieu for one year after the expiry of their term in office (see article 78 of the ZUstS).

In addition, judicial independence is partly reinforced by the fact that the Constitution does not permit re-election to the Court, so judges do not face the temptation to adopt possibly conformist views *vis-à-vis* other bodies of authority in the hope of easing their path to re-election. Further, constitutional and legal provisions exist pertaining to the incompatibility of the office of Constitutional Justice with various other public offices, including, for example, incompatibility with office in bodies of political parties and a general incompatibility with office and work in (other) state bodies and with holders of public authority (see article 166 of the URS and article 16 of the ZUstS). One should also note that in the

---

candidates must secure at least 46 out of 90 votes). In this period the National Assembly elected a total of seven Justices, where except for one instance (68 votes for), their election was not an expression of broad parliamentary consensus (candidates secured the following numbers of votes for: 48, 49, 47, 51, 46, 46) (Source: National Assembly Committee for Elections and Appointments).

[18] See Marijan Pavčnik, *"Razumevanje temeljnih (človekovih) pravic"* (Understanding fundamental (human) rights), in Marijan Pavčnik, Ada Polajnar-Pavčnik & Dragica Wedam-Lukić (eds.), *Temeljne pravice* (Ljubljana, Cankarjeva založba, 1997), p. 98.

initial period following adoption of the new Constitution there was an informal agreement among the Justices whereby during their term in office they would 'freeze' their membership of political parties, if they happened to be members of any party prior to them taking up office.

3. THE CONSTITUTIONAL COURT'S POWERS AND METHOD OF DECISION-MAKING

The new Constitution applies what is termed the *concentrated system* of *a posteriori review* of constitutionality. This means that such review, as distinct from the diffuse or mixed system,[19] is concentrated in one body, i.e. the Constitutional Court. By law this body is defined as the "highest body of judicial authority for the protection of constitutionality and legality and of human rights and fundamental freedoms" (article 1 of the ZUstS), whereby "in its relations with other state bodies it is an independent state body" (article 2 of the ZUstS). In the system of separation of power the Constitutional Court is therefore a kind of hybrid creation *sui generis*, for it combines the judicial function and the function of negative legislator. Of course the question of whether the Court falls (mainly) within the judicial branch of power, or whether it represents a special – fourth – branch of power, is primarily academic, since a realistic assessment of its position must largely be decided by its actual power of influence over the decisions (policies) of other state bodies.

Most of the Court's jurisdiction is directly established by the Constitution, which provides that other, additional, areas of jurisdiction may be provided by law. The jurisdiction or powers of the Constitutional Court may therefore be broken down into the following three basic groups:

3.1. Preventive Review

The influence of the French model of preventive review is reflected only in the power of the Court, on the proposal of the President of the Republic, the government or at least a third of the Deputies in the National Assembly during the process of ratifying a treaty, to express an opinion on the conformity of the said treaty with the Constitution. The National Assembly is bound by such an opinion of the Court (article 160, paragraph 2 of the URS).

---

[19] Regarding the three cited systems of ongoing review of constitutionality see e.g. Ivan Kristan, *Ustavno sodstvo* (Constitutional judiciary), in Franc Grad, Igor Kaučič, Ciril Ribičič, Ivan Kristan, *Državna ureditev Slovenije* (The Slovenian System of State, Ljubljana, Časopisni zavod Uradni list RS, 1996), pp. 198–200.

3.2. "A Posteriori Review"

This form of review encompasses both abstract and concrete review of constitutionality. The Court carries out concrete review if this is requested by any of the regular courts, the state prosecutor, the Bank of Slovenia or the Court of Audit in respect of questions of constitutionality and legality in connection with the procedures being conducted by these bodies. In the same way, the Human Rights Ombudsman may also submit a request for review of a specific (concrete) matter it is dealing with (article 156 of the URS and article 23 of the ZUstS). Yet the main body of work conducted by the Court is in fact its abstract review of constitutionality and legality,[20] which encompasses review of: conformity of laws with the Constitution; conformity of laws and regulations with ratified treaties and with the universal principles of international law; conformity of regulations with the Constitution and laws; conformity of local community regulations with the Constitution and laws; conformity of general legal acts issued for the execution of public authority with the Constitution, laws and regulations (article 160 of the URS).

In the above cases the Court also decides on the constitutionality and legality of procedures according to which such acts have been adopted (article 21 of the ZUstS). Moreover, the Court is not bound simply by the proposal contained in the request or petition, but may also assess the constitutionality and legality of other provisions of the same or another regulation, if such provisions are mutually linked or if this is essential to resolve the matter (article 30 of the ZUstS). It should also be noted that the Court may, if it establishes the unconstitutionality of a regulation or general legal act in the case of deciding on a constitutional complaint, annul or abrogate such regulation or act (article 161, paragraph two of the URS).

3.3. Other Powers

In accordance with the Constitution, the Court also has the power to decide on: constitutional complaints stemming from violation of human rights and fundamental freedoms by individual legal acts (as a rule only after other means of legal protection have been exhausted, and in exceptions earlier, if the asserted violation is obvious and the execution of an individual legal act would lead to irremediable consequences for the complainant – article 160 of the URS and article 51 of the ZUstS); disputes over jurisdiction between the state and local

---

[20] It should be noted that the power of the Slovenian Constitutional Court to decide on *legality* of regulations and general legal acts in the comparative aspect is more an exception than a rule – see Gagik Harutyunyan, Arne Mavčič, *The Constitutional Review and its Development in the Modern World (A Comparative Constitutional Analysis)* (Yerevan, Ljubljana, Hayagitak, 1999), pp. 265 ff.

communities, between local communities themselves, between courts and other state bodies, and between the National Assembly, the President of the Republic and the government (article 160 of the URS); the unconstitutionality of legal acts and the activities of political parties (article 160 of the URS); impeachment charges against the President of the Republic, the Prime Minister and ministers (articles 109 and 119 of the URS); appeals against decisions of the National Assembly confirming the election of Deputies (article 82 of the URS); whether there is any foundation to the view of the National Assembly that a proposer of a referendum has not clearly formulated a referendum request (article 15 of the ZRLI);[21] whether the content of a request for referendum is counter to the Constitution (article 16 of the ZRLI).

The Court may only issue decisions on the basis of an appropriate proposing act. In the case of abstract review of constitutionality and/or legality a written petition may be submitted by anyone who can show a legal interest. The law provides that legal interest in submitting a petition is established if a regulation or general legal act for executing public authority which the petitioner is proposing for assessment, directly infringes upon their rights, legal interests or legal position (article 24 of the ZUstS). In the first few years following adoption of the new Constitution, the Court offered extensive argumentation in its judgments as to whether there existed a legal interest on the part of individual petitioners, but later – probably for the most part as a result of the large number of such petitions – it adopted a restrictive position in its interpretations of the legal interest,[22] and in this way it was able to avoid making decisions on certain politically 'volatile' issues.[23] In contrast to a petition, the lodging of a request for abstract review of norms means that the Court must decide on the content of the request (decision on merit), where the law enumerates the persons eligible to submit a request. Requests for assessment of constitutionality and/or legality

---

[21] *Zakon o referendumu in o ljudski iniciativi* (Referendum and Popular Initiative Act, Uradni list RS, nos. 15/94 and 38/96).

[22] Constitutional Court practice indicates that in its assessment of legal interests within the provisions of the law, the Constitutional Court has additionally taken into account principles whereby the legal interest must be: a) of a personal nature (a personal interest of the petitioner); b) direct and concrete; c) legal; e) actually existing at the time of its assessment. See illustrative examples in Arne Mavčič, *Zakon o ustavnem sodišču s pojasnili* (Constitutional Court Act with explanatory notes, Ljubljana, Nova revija, 2000), pp. 177–188.

[23] For example, in its decision of 8 July 1999 (no. U-I-87/99, pub. OdlUS VIII, 180) the Constitutional Court did not recognise the legal interests of two petitioners (a citizen and a political party) that from different aspects asserted the unconstitutionality and illegality of a government decision of 11 October 1998 in which the government (without the necessary ratification in Parliament) had given the NATO alliance the use of the airspace over Slovenia, which later resulted in flyovers by aircraft conducting military operations in Kosovo.

may therefore be submitted (article 23, paragraph one of the ZUstS) by:[24] the National Assembly; at least a third of the Deputies in the National Assembly; the National Council; the government; representative bodies of local communities, if the rights of local communities are threatened; representative trade unions for the territory of the state, if workers' rights are threatened.

None of these proposers is eligible to submit a request that would relate to an assessment of regulations and general acts they themselves have adopted (article 23, paragraph two of the ZUstS). With regard to the proposers of other proceedings it is provided that such proceedings may be instigated as specified below: *a priori* review of the constitutionality of treaties – President of the Republic, the government or a third of the Deputies in the National Assembly (article 160 of the URS); constitutional complaint – an individual or the Human Rights Ombudsman (article 50 of the ZUstS); disputes over jurisdiction – requests are submitted by the affected body (article 61 of the ZUstS), while petitions may be lodged by a party in the proceedings which led to the dispute over jurisdiction; impeachment charge against the President of the Republic, the Prime Minister or a minister – the National Assembly (articles 109 and 119 of the URS); unconstitutionality of legal acts and activities of political parties – anyone who may demonstrate their legal interest and proposers of abstract review (article 68 of the ZUstS); deciding on the confirmation of election of Deputies – any candidate or representative of a list of candidates who has lodged a complaint with the National Assembly against the decision of an electoral commission (article 69 of the ZUstS).

From the above, we may determine that in the comparative sense, Slovenia's Constitutional Court has a broad range of powers,[25] which in practice leads to a relatively high number of cases that are submitted to it for review. For the moment the Court is managing to resolve at least the majority of cases in reasonable deadlines, although it is now already possible to observe some more serious backlogs of several years, which will grow in the coming years, and may in turn undermine to a certain extent faith in the effectiveness of the Court's work. A perusal of certain data will show that as at 31 December 1998 the Court had 486 matters in hand for assessment of constitutionality or legality of regulations and 446 matters of constitutional complaint, giving a total of 932 matters.

---

[24] This circle also includes proposers of concrete assessments of constitutionality that have been rehearsed above within the presentation of "a posteriori review".

[25] The Slovenian Constitutional Court ranks among those Central and Eastern European Constitutional Courts with powers that are broader for example than those of the majority of Western European constitutional courts or the US Supreme Court (see Stephen Holmes, "Back to the Drawing Board", in East European Constitutional Review, Winter (1993), pp. 21–25) and these powers are exercised in a highly activist or expansive way, see Bojan Bugarič: "*Pravna sredstva za omejevanje pristojnosti ustavnega sodstva*" (Legal Remedies for Restricting the Powers of the Constitutional Judiciary), in: *Zbornik IV. Dnevi javnega prava* (Portorož 1998), p. 93.

As at 30 November 1999 the Court had in hand 413 matters for assessment of constitutionality or legality and 460 constitutional complaints, totalling 873 matters, which indicates that the number of unresolved matters fell slightly from the previous year, but there remains in hand many more matters than the Court could resolve in one year, given its current composition of professional staff.[26] At the end of 1999, in terms of requests for assessment of constitutionality and legality and of constitutional complaints the Court was currently still dealing with 30 matters from 1996 and 128 matters from 1997, while the remaining matters originated in 1998 and 1999. This means that in 1999 the Court was able to decide on all the oldest matters it had in hand at the beginning of 1999 and which dated back to 1994 and 1995, while it accorded priority to matters from 1996 and to certain more recent matters (e.g to disputes over jurisdiction).[27]

In the procedures for assessment of constitutionality and legality of regulations, in terms of the large volume of legislative work done in the years following independence[28] and in view of the number of proceedings instigated, relatively few laws have been abrogated. In the first 11 months of 1999, for example, in 136 cases the Court assessed the constitutionality of laws and in so doing abrogated 9 laws (i.e. some of their individual provisions) and established non-conformity with the constitution in 14 laws – and in these latter cases proposed to the legislator a deadline for removing the irregularities involved. In terms of the total number of laws whose constitutionality was assessed by the Court during this period, the proposer or petitioner was accommodated in 23 cases (16.9%), in regulations they were accommodated in 21.4% of the resolved cases, while the Court abrogated or annulled 44 (16 in 1998) regulations or found that they were not in conformity with ordinary law or the Constitution.[29] As for decisions on constitutional complaints, the data indicates that in the first 11 months of 1999 the Constitutional Court resolved 296 matters, taking 33 constitutional complaints (11% of the resolved matters) for processing. Of these, 13 complaints were rejected, with 20 of the complainants being successful, meaning that out of all resolved matters complainants were accommodated in 6.7% of cases. An interesting point here is that in this period, of the total number of received constitutional complaints (310), 135 were from the field of civil law, 99

---

[26] This assessment, and the statistics supplied, are presented in the *Poročilo o delu Ustavnega sodišča* (Report on the Work of the Constitutional Court) for 1999 of 20 December 1999, no. Su-109/99 (hereinafter: Poročilo US 1999), p. 1. The statistics cover the whole of 1998 and the first 11 months of 1999. All these and other statistics should be seen in light of the fact that the jurisdiction of the Constitutional Court is extended to legal subjects in the context of Slovenia's total population of (only) two million.

[27] Poročilo US 1999, pp. 1–2.

[28] From 1991 to the middle of 2000 the National Assembly adopted a total of 1255 statutes, and in addition to these a large number of other legal acts. (Source: Documentation Service of the National Assembly of the Republic of Slovenia).

[29] Poročilo US 1999, p. 3.

related to criminal law and 76 to legal administration matters and matters arising from labour and social disputes, where the total number of constitutional complaints received was approximately the same as in 1998.[30]

In deciding on constitutional complaints the Court is of course favoured by the fact that the Parliamentary Commission which drafted the new Constitution for the most part avoided 'programmatic' provisions on human rights. In the constitutional debate, for example there was a long period without agreement on how many social and economic rights and in what formulations the Constitution should contain them,[31] but in the end the view prevailed that it made no sense to make constitutional provision for such rights, which would in practice be impossible to protect effectively (e.g. the right to adequate housing or the right to work). The Court has jurisdiction to decide on constitutional complaints (inasmuch as it accepts them for review following prior selection) on all human rights and fundamental freedoms, which are dealt with extensively in chapter II of the constitution. In a number of cases the Court has made reference to the provisions of the European Convention on the Protection of Human Rights and Fundamental Freedoms, and did so even before ratification of the Convention by the Republic of Slovenia.[32] It is interesting to note that in two of its resolutions[33] the Court took the view whereby it distinguished the rights in chapter II of the Constitution, headed "Human Rights and Fundamental Freedoms", from the rights of individuals implicitly or explicitly provided in chapter III of the Constitution, headed "Economic and Social Relations", for the latter (e.g. the right to a healthy living environment) should not in the opinion of the Court rank in the category of "human rights and fundamental freedoms", in respect of which constitutional complaints are possible.[34]

If we now focus on the adoption of decisions by the Constitutional Court, and limit ourselves here to an abstract assessment of the Court, we may see that the Constitution and ordinary law allow the Court various methods of decision-making. The Court, which as a rule decides by a majority vote of all judges (article 162 of the URS),[35] may: *abrogate* an unconstitutional law entirely or in

---

[30] Poročilo US 1999, pp. 2 and 3.

[31] See Miro Cerar, "Die verfassungsrechtlichen Grundlagen der Konstituierung des Staates Slowenien", in Joseph Marko & Tomislav Borić (eds.), *Slowenien - Kroatien - Serbien, Die Neuen Verfassungen* (Vienna, Cologne, Graz, Bohlau Verlag, 1990), pp. 122–123.

[32] See Arne Mavčič, *Zakon o ustavnem sodišču s pojasnili* (Constitutional Court Act with explanatory notes, Ljubljana, Nova revija, 2000), pp. 152–153.

[33] Nos. U-I-30/92 and U-I-91/93.

[34] Such a view from the Constitutional Court is contentious, since several arguments speak in favour of the opposite view. See Marijan Pavčnik, "Razumevanje temeljnih (človekovih) pravic", in Marijan Pavčnik, Ada Polajnar-Pavčnik & Dragica Wedam-Lukić (eds.), *Temeljne pravice* (Ljubljana, Cankarjeva založba, 1997), pp. 91–94.

[35] Exceptions to this majority method of decision-making are provided by the Constitution and ordinary law. For example the Constitution provides that in deciding on impeachment charges the Constitutional Court may decide by a vote of only two thirds of all the judges

part, where the abrogation takes immediate effect (*ex nunc*) or in a period determined by the Court, with the deadline being no longer than one year (article 161 of the URS, article 43 of the ZUstS); annul (*ex tunc*) or abrogate (*ex nunc*) an unconstitutional or illegal regulation or general legal act (article 161 of the URS, article 45 of the ZUstS); merely *find* that a law, regulation or general legal act is unconstitutional or illegal, since it does not regulate a specific issue which it should, or regulates it in a way that does not allow for its abrogation or annulment (article 48 of the ZUstS); in such cases the competent body must remove the established unconstitutionality or illegality within a deadline set by the Court (article 48 of the ZUstS); adopt an *interpretative decision*, with which it explains in a ruling in what way a challenged legal provision should be interpreted in order for it not to contravene the Constitution – this method of decision-making was implemented by the Court on its own initiative, without having any special authorisation for it from the Constitution or ordinary law;[36] in the course of proceedings adopt a decision that until a final decision it entirely or partially stays the implementation of a law, regulation or general legal act, if its implementation could cause harmful consequences that would be difficult to rectify (article 161 of the URS, article 39 of the ZUstS); determine which body must execute a decision and in what way (article 40 of the ZUstS).

In its decision-making the Constitutional Court may of course combine the above methods, or enhance them, from 'milder to harsher' types of decision. This second case is invoked when, for example, the Court first merely finds a certain non-conformity of a law with the Constitution and determines a deadline for its removal, and then upon expiry of the deadline, on the basis of a renewed application for a decision on a matter it finds that the legislator has (still) not

---

on removal from office of the President of the Republic, the Prime Minister or Ministers (articles 109 and 119 of the URS). Further, ordinary law provides that the decision whether to accept a constitutional complaint may be taken by a panel of three Constitutional Court judges in closed session (article 54 of the ZUstS) and that in the event of the panel not accepting the complaint, it is considered as having been accepted if any other three Constitutional Court judges give their consent in writing (article 55 of the ZUstS).

[36] In 1993, when the Constitutional Court first employed this method of decision-making after the model of the German Constitutional Court (decision nos. U-I-25/92, Uradni list RS no. 13/93, OdlUS II, 23; U-I-108/91, Uradni list RS no. 28/91, 52/92 and 42/93, OdlUS II, 67) it transpired for the first time in Constitutional Court history that the minority in separate opinions accused the court of acting contrary to the principle of judicial self-restraint, by supposedly encroached upon the jurisdiction of the legislative branch of power. See Franc Testen, "Tehnike odločanja Ustavnega sodišča v. abstrakni presoji" (Methods of Constitutional Court Decision-Making in Abstract Assessment) in: *Pravna praksa* no. 1 (1999), p. 6; Arne Mavčič, *Zakon o ustavnem sodišču s pojasnili* (Constitutional Court Act with explanatory notes, Ljubljana, Nova revija, 2000), p. 246. To date the practice of adopting interpretative decisions has already become well-established (see Arne Mavčič, id., pp. 246–251).

removed the unconstitutional element, it abrogates the unconstitutional provisions of the law (with either delayed or immediate effect).

The activism, both positive and negative, of Slovenia's Constitutional Court, includes in particular the interpretative decisions, for the adoption of which, as stated, the Court has no explicit constitutional or legal basis. Such decisions have to date been frequently criticised, not simply for the fact that they come controversially close to legislative decisions, but also often because of their actual content. Below I offer a brief illustration of the so-called "referendum decision" of the Constitutional Court, which ranks among the most contentious and politically far-reaching interpretative decisions, and is also a typical example of negative (political) judicial activism. This decision, which over the last two years has clearly marked political events in Slovenia, also sparked numerous legal questions in professional circles, and below there is a brief presentation of such questions, particularly that of the boundaries of decision-making by the Court and the question of compulsory execution of Constitutional Court decisions.

In the spring of 1996 the Social Democratic Party of Slovenia (SDS) collected more than 40,000 signatures in support of its request for a referendum in which voters should decide on the introduction of a two-round majority electoral system (and in this way abolish the existing proportional system). This was the start of the real "referendum race", for at approximately the same time referendum requests for changing the electoral system were also submitted by the National Council (proposal of a combined electoral system) and by two groups of more than 30 Deputies[37] (both groups proposed the introduction of a different kind of proportional system), although later one group of Deputies withdrew its request. Through their requests, which were submitted in advance of the request from the group of voters (although only after the public initiative of SDS had set in motion the collection of voter signatures in support of the party's request),[38] the National Council and one group of Deputies in actual fact desired primarily to prevent the holding of a referendum on the majority electoral system. In a decision[39] the National Assembly resolved to call a referendum only on the basis of the first submitted request, i.e. the request of 30 Deputies for the introduction of a different kind of proportional system, which the National Council and the SDS, by invoking the Constitution and the Referendum and Popular Initiative

---

[37] In accordance with Article 90 of the URS the National Assembly must call a legislative referendum if so requested by at least a third of all Deputies, the National Council or at least 40,000 voters.

[38] Further details in Miro Cerar: "Mechanisms of Direct Democracy in the New Slovene Legal and Political Order: The Legislative Referendum", in: *Conflicts and Consensus: Pluralism and Neocorporatism in the New and Old Democracies*, Samo Koprivnik, Igor Lukšič & Drago Zajc (eds.) (Bled, Slovenian Political Science Association, 1996), pp. 118–119.

[39] A decision concerning calls for a legislative referendum for elections to the National Assembly, Uradni list RS, no. 25/96.

Act (ZRLI), to which the decision referred, challenged before the Constitutional Court. The Court in turn on 14 June 1996 adopted an interpretative decision[40] in which by invoking democratic ideals (e.g. the principle of *in favorem libertatis*) it decided that the law (ZRLI) was not contrary to the constitution, if it was interpreted thus: that referendums are carried out concurrently on all questions that should be the subject of a referendum, contained in all initiatives or requests for the calling of referendums on issues that are governed by the same law, if the initiatives or requests have been submitted prior to adoption of the act regulating legislative referendums, and if all of them satisfy the relevant procedural conditions (from articles 15 and 16 of the ZRLI) and that in the event of a decision being taken on two or more referendums, the National Assembly is bound by the result of the referendum that received the greatest percentage share of votes "for" out of the total number of voters who cast votes in individual referendums.

Even in this decision (which represents a kind of 'introduction' to the later "political referendum decision") the Constitutional Court offered an interpretation of the law which was in fact not an interpretation, but a covert amendment to the law, for there are no provisions in the ZRLI that could be interpreted in such a way. Moreover the solution whereby the proposal receiving the greatest percentage share of "for" votes out of the total number of votes cast on any individual question should be adopted in a referendum, is questionable from the aspect of certain constitutional principles to which the constitutional court has directly referred on several occasions (e.g. the principle of democracy and sovereignty of the people – articles 1 and 3 of the URS) and from the aspect of the provisions of article 90, paragraph four of the constitution,[41] for it allows the possibility of a minority of voters outvoting a majority.[42] Yet to this we must

---

[40]   Decision no. U-I-201/96 (OdlUS V, 99).

[41]   Article 90, paragraph four of the Constitution, which governs legislative referendums, provides: "A proposal is passed in a referendum if a majority of those voting have cast votes in favour of the same". For there to be a positive outcome in a referendum, therefore, a majority vote is required of *all* those citizens who actually *voted* in the referendum. In the National Assembly, which is responsible for calling referendums, at that time and later the belief predominated that on questions falling within the framework of uniform legislative material (on the uniformity of material see e.g. S. Widmer, *Wahl- und Abstimmungsfreiheit*, Disertation (Zurich, Schulthess Polygraphischer Verlag AG, 1989), pp. 97–100), it is not possible to vote at the same time in several referendums, but only in one referendum, in which alternatives (mutually exclusive) are offered. The Constitutional Court also agreed with this argumentation later (see the "Referendum Decision" no. U-I-12/97).

[42]   For example, in the case of the two referendum proposals, the proposal for which the proportion between the "for" and "against" votes would be 90 to 10, would win against the proposal in which the analogous proportion would be 850,000 to 150,000. In line with the proposed criteria of the percentage share, 90 voters would therefore outvote 850,000 voters. The example has been exaggerated, of course, to illustrate the point.

add the fact that this decision by the Constitutional Court, which in its intention was activist primarily in a positive sense (the Court wished to provide equal protection for all referendum proposers before the 'illegal' actions of the National Assembly), was nowhere near as controversial as the later "referendum decision" (see below) although the former generated more intrigue in the political arena.[43]

In the legislative referendum on the electoral system of 8 December 1996, voters decided between four electoral systems (three new proposals and the existing system). The referendum request of the National Council received support in the amount of 14.4%, the request of 30 Deputies received 26.2% and the request of 40,000 voters received 44.5%.[44] This result shows that none of the requests gained sufficient votes (50% or more) in support, so it was clear that the existing proportional system should remain in effect. On 16 December 1996 the proponents of the referendum on a majority electoral system turned to the Court with a constitutional complaint against the report of the state electoral commission, but it was only in the autumn of 1998, just before the term in office of four constitutional Justices expired, that the Court adopted a decision in this matter. It rejected the constitutional complaint, but adopted a decision regarding the aforementioned law (ZNGUIG), which governed the rules for carrying out a referendum on the electoral system. In this "referendum decision",[45] the Court decided that:

(1) article 3, paragraph three of the ZNGUIG was in conformity with the constitution, if it is interpreted in such a way that the proposal is passed for which the majority of those voting on an individual referendum question voted, and;

---

[43] The Constitutional Court would have been acting much more in the spirit of the law (ZRLI) if it had interpreted it in such a way that a referendum be held only on the first request to be submitted, which in this case would have applied to the request contained in the SDS initiative for a referendum on a majority system. However, through its decision, the Court directly stimulated the majority of Deputies in the National Assembly, so that with the adoption of the special Method of Voting and of Determining the Outcome of Voting in a Referendum on the Electoral System Act (ZNGUIG, Uradni list RS no. 57/96) three separate and mutually exclusive referendum requests (for changed proportional, combined and majority systems) were formulated for the electoral referendum in 1996, with the National Assembly determining in line with the Constitution that the referendum request that won would be the one for which the majority of those voting cast votes. Through such a rule on establishing the outcome, which would lead to a diffusion of referendum votes, the parliamentary majority, which was primarily opposed to the majority electoral system, minimised at the outset the possibility of such a system being adopted in a referendum, and this was a politically controversial solution.

[44] Report of the State Electoral Commission of 12 December 1996 (no. 1–1/92–96/R).

[45] Decision of 8 October 1998 (no. U-I-12/97, OdlUS VII, 180).

(2) accordingly, in the referendum the proposal for a majority electoral system won the vote.[46]

Through such an interpretative decision (adopted in a 5:3 vote – one judge being absent), approximately two years after the referendum, the Constitutional Court actually retroactively changed the rules by which the referendum was held and then itself pronounced the "correct referendum outcome".[47] In this way it not only interpreted the law (ZRLI) in an entirely different way from the interpretation of all the Deputies in the National Assembly at the time of its adoption (which is clearly evident from the tape recordings of sessions) and of the public media, which had acquainted citizens in advance with the rules of referendum voting, but also adopted an *unconstitutional* decision, for article 90 of the Constitution provides that a proposal is passed in a legislative referendum "if a majority of those voting have cast votes in favour of the same" (we should not forget that voters chose from several possible proposals in *one* referendum). It is clear, moreover, that by changing the rules retroactively in this way the Court had not simply further exceeded its powers, but had also violated one of the fundamental principles of a state based on the rule of law, that is the principle of legal certainty (the predictability of legal norms). Even if the Court might have had justifiable reservations about the law according to which the referendum was held (the ZNUIG in fact allowed an inappropriate diffusion of referendum votes), it should not have permitted itself to retroactively change the rules of the game in this way. It could, for example, have ordered the referendum to be re-held in line with different rules.

The referendum decision split Slovenia into two camps. For the most part the proponents of the majority electoral system argued that the decision of the Constitutional Court, irrespective of any reservations regarding its correctness,

---

[46] The Constitutional Court thereby changed the 44.5% votes (or 16.9% of the votes of all those eligible to vote in Slovenia) in favour by determining different criteria into as much as a 65% vote in favour of the majority system.

[47] In this the Court also sought support in article 40 of the ZUstS, which states: "Where required, the Constitutional Court determines which body must carry out a decision and in what manner." In point 50 of its explanation of the referendum decision the Court explicitly set out that pursuant to article 40 of the ZUstS it decided that it would itself determine and publish the result of the referendum. The Court referred to article 40 of the ZUstS in a similarly activist way for example in a case where despite the clear provision of article 130 of the Constitution, which states: "Judges are elected by the National Assembly on the proposal of the Judicial Council," the court itself went ahead and proposed to the National Assembly a judge for election (the candidature of the judge in question had already been turned down by the Judicial Council). However, this obvious and entirely impermissible exceeding of powers by the Constitutional Court, in contrast to the referendum decision, was not politically motivated, but motivated by a serious desire to protect the constitutional rights of the individual (decision Up 132/96, OdlUS V, 187).

should be consistently respected and that on the basis of the Constitution and law (article 90 of the URS and article 25 of the ZRLI), and in line with the will of the voters expressed in the referendum, the National Assembly must pass into law the majority electoral system. The opponents of the majority electoral system sought one or another argument that might justify a different approach by the National Assembly,[48] but a legalistic view predominated among lawyers and politicians, whereby it was compulsory for the decision of the Court to be carried out in a reasonable deadline (which the Court itself also made clear in the explanation of its decision). Despite this, two years passed in bitter political dispute on the electoral system. The National Assembly, which can only adopt or amend the law governing the electoral system with a two-thirds majority of all Deputies (article 80 of the URS), debated several times the SDS proposals of a two-round majority system act, which should in fact have signified the carrying out off the will of voters expressed in the referendum, although these proposals were never supported by the required majority. Practically at the last minute the National Assembly then passed a decision that the unconstitutional situation – that is, the non-conformity of the valid electoral system with the referendum decision of the Constitutional Court – should be resolved by a constitutional amendment with which the foundations of the electoral system should be laid down. So on 25 June 2000, a constitutional amendment was adopted by a more than two-thirds absolute majority, when after several months of constitutional debate the amendment gained the support of the great majority of parliamentary parties (it was only opposed by the SDS, which abstained from the vote, and the Slovenian National Party, which only has three Deputies). Article 80 of the Constitution is now amended with a provision according to which elections to the National Assembly are conducted according to the proportional electoral system with certain corrective features (a 4% threshold for election to Parliament and the ensuring of the greatest possible personalisation of elections).[49]

---

[48] Some National Assembly Deputies, for example, who had rejected the passing into law of the majority electoral system, invoked the principle of the free mandate ("Deputies are representatives of all the people and are not bound by any instructions" – article 82 of the URS), whereby they could resist the "instructions" of the people. Such behaviour by the Deputies was of course unconstitutional, for in the Constitution the principles of people's sovereignty and direct democracy (article 3 of the URS) are also realised through the institution of the legislative referendum, the outcome of which is binding for the National Assembly (article 90 of the URS), and for this reason in adopting laws it must abide by a result adopted in an *ex ante* referendum (article 25 of the ZRLI).

[49] In its implementational part the amendment to article 80 of the Constitution goes into greater detail. Since the adoption of the new Constitution in 1991 this is the second amendment to the Constitution (the first amendment was adopted in 1997 and related to the association agreement with the European Union, when the National Assembly lifted the prohibition on acquisition of ownership rights to Slovenian land provided for foreigners by article 68 of the Constitution).

On the one hand such a decision by the National Assembly confirmed the general awareness of the fact that Constitutional Court decisions are binding[50] and that the National Assembly may legitimately deviate from them only in very exceptional cases, and with an appropriate constitutional amendment, while on the other hand the numerous professional (legal) debates have exposed the problem of inadequate self-restraint on the part of the Court (*Quis custodiet custodes?*) and the fact that it too, can act *unconstitutionally*. It should be remembered here that in theory, because of its (exceptional) role as supreme interpreter of the Constitution, the Constitutional Court is often generally ascribed the character of some kind of 'supraconstitutional body'. This is expressed, for example, in the lapidary but very telling finding of the President of the US Supreme Court, Charles Evan Hughes, at the beginning of the 20th century, that "We are under a Constitution, but the Constitution is what the judges say it is."[51] Although such a view, which derives chiefly from the theoretically reflected practice of the US Supreme Court, is held quite broadly, the Constitutional Court must in principle always be regarded and designated as a *subconstitutional* body. Irrespective of the fact that the theoretical and comparative views of the practice of constitutional courts show that *de facto* they often function "supraconstitutionally", such practice and also such a theoretical view which might in some way justify this, should in my opinion be in principle rejected, and this should apply especially to countries in transition or countries with less developed cultures of democracy and law. Inasmuch as we acquiesce with the Constitutional Court being in whatever respect above the Constitution, then of course we are also granting legitimacy to its potential arbitrary actions

---

[50] Article 1, paragraph three of the ZUstS also provides: "Decisions of the Constitutional Court are binding." Here it should be added that of course the actual feasibility of carrying out certain types of Constitutional Court decision is in the final instance always dependent on the legal and political awareness of those holding the other branches and types of power. In addition to the interpretative decisions of the Constitutional Court, in Slovenian practice a particular problem is presented by the carrying out of those decisions of the Constitutional Court whereby the Court merely establishes the non-conformity of certain laws or regulations or their provisions with the Constitution. So for example the National Assembly often does not remove the established non-conformity within the deadline set by the Constitutional Court. The Review of Decisions of the Constitutional Court (1992–2000) of 24 February 2000, drafted by the Legal Information Centre of the Constitutional Court of the Republic of Slovenia, indicates that numerous laws remain untenably in contravention of the Constitution, including for example twelve for which the Constitutional Court already established between 1994 and 1998 that they were partially unconstitutional (i.e. the unconstitutionality of certain individual provisions), where the deadlines for harmonisation with the Constitution have long since passed.

[51] C.E. Hughes: Addresses, New York 1909, p. 139–quoted by Ralf Dreier, *Recht – Moral – Ideologie, Studien zur Rechtstheorie* (Frankfurt am Main, Suhrkamp Verlag, 1981), p. 107.

and at the same time denying that the Court is also simply a (subordinated) part of a state based on the rule of law and of the democratic system. The legal values and interpretative approaches (arguments) of the Constitutional Court must for this reason remain strictly within the bounds of the Constitution. Of course this relates primarily to the question of emphasis and the theoretical orientation of principle, for in practice, given the dynamic nature of law[52] it is impossible entirely to prevent any 'supraconstitutional' (more precisely: unconstitutional) adjudication by the Court.

It should be noted here that constitutional courts must not only be a corrective instance *vis-à-vis* other branches of power, but must also develop the *democratic* (and not some other) spirit of the Constitution.[53] Yet the democratic spirit of the Constitution cannot be developed simply by means of professional legal or other 'esoteric' criteria, which – to a certain extent unavoidably – are determined by constitutional Justices via their professional and personal value views of the cases being handled, and for this reason the Court must constantly preserve the right measure of that legal feeling,[54] which in general meets the level of democratic development of society.[55] In this regard constitutional courts, particularly in new democracies such as Slovenia (can) perform an important role as a legitimating factor of democracy[56] and partly also an educational role. Despite the fact that the Slovenians started to exercise the principle of the state based on the rule of law in individual practical aspects and particularly in theory even under the former system (as part of the SFRY),[57] we have been familiarising ourselves

---

[52] On dynamic (versus static) aspects of the Constitution and of law as such, see Miro Cerar, *(Ir)rationality of the Constitution*, paper at the World Congress on Philosophy of Law and Social Philosophy (New York 1999), pp. 13–15.

[53] Of particular importance for constitutional courts in this respect is the finding that "Good judges recognise that fundamental decisions are best made democratically, not judicially." Cass R. Sunstein, *Legal Reasoning and Political Conflict* (New York & Oxford, Oxford University Press, 1996), p. VIII.

[54] On "constitutional legal feeling" ("Rechtsgefuhl") see Cerar, *(Ir)rationality of the Constitution, op. cit.*, pp. 15–16.

[55] The Constitutional Court should not generate the impression that it desires in its self-understanding to come close to Plato's ideal of philosopher-rulers. Otfried Höffe, *Vernunft und Recht, Bausteine zu einem interkulturellen Rechtsdiskurs* (Frankfurt am Main, Suhrkamp Verlag, 1996), p. 270.

[56] The Constitutional Court does not merely have a "checking function" *vis-à-vis* parliament and other state bodies, but also a "legitimating function", which is expressed in those Constitutional Court decisions with which Acts of Parliament and other state bodies are defined as in accordance with the Constitution. See Alexander M. Bickel: *The Least Dangerous Branch, The Supreme Court at the Bar of Politics* (New Haven, London, Yale University Press, 1986), p. 29 and following.

[57] For the development of the theory of the state based on the rule of law in Slovenia see Miro Cerar, "Rechtsstaatlichkeit in Slowenien" in Rainer Hofmann, Joseph Marko, Franz

with the tradition of the state based on the rule of law in reality (i.e. comprehensively) and consciously internalising this only in the last decade, and for this reason the Court often came to the conclusion in the 1990s that in its explanations, it must set out more broadly than the matter itself would require the doctrine of the state based on the rule of law in the light of cases dealt with.

The fulfilment of the legal educational function by the Court, which is (generally) composed of leading legal experts, is to a certain extent entirely legitimate and even useful, but of course only for as long as the Court and individual judges remain within the understood bounds of their jurisdiction and for as long as this kind of education remains in theoretically legitimate legal frameworks, and does not therefore signify merely the establishing of a certain political or ideological view of law and its basic tenets. To date the Slovenian Constitutional Court has already frequently exceeded these bounds,[58] and frequently individual judges have done so in giving separate opinions. In this regard, too, the Court has to date often exceeded not only its own powers but also the boundary of the prevalent legal feeling,[59] which produced some critical reactions in professional and lay circles, as well as sharp disagreement and tension between certain Justices themselves (which is evident from their separate opinions in individual matters where the Court was distinctly polarised). Yet despite the above it may be reiterated that the working of the Slovenian Court in the time since the adoption of the new Constitution until the present day should to a great extent be assessed positively, while at the same time appropriate (constructive) lessons should be learnt from some of the impermissible and clearly politically motivated, and harmful (for law *and* society), decisions.

Merli & Ewald Wiederin (eds.), *Rechtsstaatlichkeit in Europa* (Heidelberg, C.F. Müller Verlag, 1996), pp. 241–243.

[58] A typical example would be decision no. Up-301/96, OdlUS VII, 98, in which the Court gave in its explanation a historical assessment of the political system in the years immediately following the Second World War.

[59] In the specific period of establishing Constitutional Court practice on the basis of the new Constitution, the Constitutional Court must also establish new approaches that inevitably signify a major intervention in the entrenched legal thinking and legal feeling (for more on legal feeling, sense of justice and related legal phenomena or factors see e.g. the collection *Das sogenannte Rechtsgefühl*, Ernst J. Lampe (ed.), Opladen, Westdeutscher Verlag, 1985). A variance from the prevalent legal feeling may therefore in such a case be entirely justified, but only insofar as it does not lead to an exceeding of the permissible bounds of the (new) constitutional order.

4. THE CONSTITUTIONAL COURT IN THE LIGHT OF PUBLIC OPINION AND WITHIN THE SEPARATION OF POWERS

The constitutional court is an important part of the state based on the rule of law in the broader sense,[60] although at the same time it is not an essential element of such state. This is demonstrated by cases of democratic countries where the state based on the rule of law has been enshrined despite the fact that these countries have no institutionalised constitutional court or any special state body responsible for the abstract assessment of constitutionality of legal and other acts (e.g. the United Kingdom, Switzerland, the Netherlands and Finland).[61] Arguments against the constitutional judiciary and judicial review of constitutionality derive in principle primarily from the fact that neither democracy nor for example the principle of the separation of power require the existence of such a body.[62] Yet today Europe is dominated by opposing arguments, which in the 20th century, and especially in the last few decades have been confirmed by the practice of a 'flourishing' of constitutional courts. Constitutional courts have in recent years developed intensively, particularly in the countries in transition from communism to democracy.[63] In these countries the constitutional courts are becoming established even as the avant-garde of the judiciary (inasmuch as the constitutional courts can be placed in that branch of power) and of the state based on the rule of law.[64] In establishing a state based on the rule of law the ideology of the state based on the rule of law, which is centred on constitutional courts ("das in den Verfassungsgerichten konzentri-

---

[60] Through the concept of the state based on the rule of law in the broader sense it is possible today to combine the substance of the German concept of *Rechtsstaat* and the English "rule of law", for between both concepts, as they are generally exercised in modern democratic systems, there are no essential differences (see e.g. D.N. MacCormick, "Der Rechtsstaat und die rule of law" in *Juristenzeitung* no. 2 (1984), pp. 65–70), although in the historical perspective both concepts are considerably different in many respects.

[61] For the various models of (constitutional) court control of constitutionality around the world see Harutyunyan Gagik, Arne Mavčič, *Constitutional Review and its Development in the Modern World, A Comparative Constitutional Analysis* (Yerevan, Ljubljana, Hayagitak, 1999), p. 28 ff.

[62] See for example Otfried Höffe, *Vernunft und Recht, Bausteine zu einem interkulturellen Rechtsdiskurs* (Frankfurt am Main, Suhrkamp Verlag, 1996), p. 258 ff.

[63] See the abridged overview of historical stages in the development of (constitutional) court control of constitutionality in Gagik & Mavčič, *op. cit.*, pp. 21–27.

[64] Cf. Franz Merli, "Der Rechtsschutz" in Rainer Hofmann, Joseph Marko, Franz Merli & Ewald Wiederin (eds.), *Rechtsstaatlichkeit in Europa* (Heidelberg, C.F. Müller Verlag, 1996), p. 36.

erte rechtsstaatliche Denken"), should therefore be extended and injected into all institutions in the domain of the state.[65] In this way the constitutional court is seen principally as an independent and democratically aware protector against political deviations from the principle of the state based on the rule of law on the part of the government, parliament and other (political) factors.

In the first few years following the adoption in practice of the new Constitution, that is the *actual* adoption, the Slovenian Constitutional Court in general and to a large extent established itself as an independent branch of power, but then, as has already been explained, up until 1998 certain of its 'political decisions' severely dented the Court's image. Yet in view of the fact that on the basis of the new constitutional order the ordinary judiciary in Slovenia has only gradually, and with considerable difficulty, been consolidating its position, thus far the Constitutional Court it has been that element of the judicial branch of power (inasmuch as it may be ranked within that branch) which has kept up with the general trend that has characterised Western Europe over the past twenty years, with the judiciary assuming a very important role in taking decisions of national importance.[66] In this regard the Slovenian Constitutional Court is without doubt a protagonist in the process of emancipation of the Slovenian judiciary.

If we disregard certain explicitly controversial decisions of the Constitutional Court[67] (of course these decisions were also received by a relatively large section of the politically defined public as correct, for this section saw them as a "victory"

---

[65] *Ibid.*, pp. 36–37.

[66] See N.C. Alivizatos: "Judges as Veto Players", in H. Döring (ed.), *Parliaments and Majority Rule in Western Europe* (Frankfurt, Campus Verlag, 1995), pp. 566 ff.

[67] A critique of some such decisions by the Constitutional Court, which may also be labelled as having an impermissibly political character, is presented for example by Janez šinkovec, "Samoomejevanje ustavnih sodišč" (Self-Restraint of Constitutional Courts), in the *Zbornik IV. Dnevi javnega prava* (Portorož 1998), pp. 180–183; Bojan Bugarič: "Ustavno sodstvo in (ali) parlamentarna demokracija: o doktrinah pravnega interesa in političnih vprašanj" (Constitutional Judiciary and (or) Parliamentary Democracy: On the Doctrines of Legal Interest and Political Issues), in the *Zbornik znanstvenih razprav Pravne fakultete Univerze v. Ljubljani*, year 55 (Ljubljana 1995), pp. 61–64; Igor Lukšič: "Političnost ustavnega sodišča" (The Political Nature of the Constitutional Court), in *Teorija in praksa*, no. 6 (Ljubljana 1997), pp. 988–997; Marijan Pavčnik: "Glose k nekaterim ustavnosodnim argumentom" (Notes on Some Constitutional Court Arguments), in *Pravnik*, no. 9–10 (Ljubljana 1999), pp. 547–552; Miro Cerar: "Slovensko ustavno sodišče – med pravom in politiko" (The Slovenian Constitutional Court – Between Law and Politics), in *Uprava in sodstvo v. evropskih povezavah in reforma javne uprave v. Sloveniji – Zbornik IV. Dnevi javnega prava* (Portorož 1998), pp. 125–129.

over their opponents),[68] it would be possible to assess that the functioning of the Court in the eyes of the layperson has been for the most part favourably accepted. Such an assessment cannot in fact be directly supported with empirical data, for surveys of public opinion as a rule do not contain special items on the Constitutional Court, but rather pose questions regarding the "judiciary". In this respect, therefore, it is not possible to determine what 'share' the Constitutional Court holds within the assessment of the entire judiciary in Slovenia. Given the fact that Slovenian public opinion is explicitly unfavourable towards Parliament, the Government and political parties,[69] which in a certain sense create a 'political bloc', whose decisions are assessed and where necessary abrogated by the Constitutional Court (which also in cases of constitutional complaint is 'superior' to all other courts), this position alone is probably

---

[68] This may be illustrated for example by the interpretative decision (no. U-I-121/97, pub. OdlUS VI/1–69), in which in assessing the De-Nationalisation Act the Constitutional Court noted in its ruling that the provision of the Act whereby "land, forests and other property of feudal origin should not be returned is not counter to the Constitution, except where it relates to cases in which those eligible under denationalisation are the Church and other religious communities, their institutions or orders". In the lapidary explanation of this view, the Court recorded that "it would not be constitutionally permissible to equate the nationalisation of property of the Church and religious communities, given their role as socially beneficial institutions and given their position in our legal order, with nationalisation of large estates of feudal origin," and that for this reason there was no violation of article 14 of the Constitution, which would require the same treatment of property acquired by feudal means (covered in more detail by Janez Šinkovec, "*Samoomejevanje ustavnih sodišč*" – Self-Restraint of Constitutional Courts – in: *Zbornik IV. Dnevi javnega prava* (Portorož 1998), pp. 180–181). Since this case involves almost exclusively the question of the property of the Roman Catholic Church in Slovenia, this kind of decision by the Constitutional Court, whereby it exceeded its powers as a *negative legislator* and in fact amended the law, sharply divided public opinion, for rendered somewhat simply, the decision was labelled by those of a more left-of-centre political persuasion as an impermissible political decision, while those of a more right-wing persuasion saw this as legally acceptable and as a just decision. An analogous effect was also produced by the older interpretative decision no. U-I-25/92 (pub. OdlUS II-23), whereby in its assessment of the Denationalisation Act the Constitutional Court determined that it was in contravention of the Constitution if those eligible under denationalisation could not also be legal persons, and the Court itself went ahead and deleted the word "natural", which meant that it extended denationalisation rights to legal persons.

[69] Public opinion polls show that in the period from 1991 to 1998 general trust in these three institutions held the following values: (a) political parties: 12% (1991), 8 (1992), 3 (1993), 5 (1994), 5 (1995), 4 (1996), 6 (1997), 4 (1998); (b) National Assembly: 37% (1991), 20 (1992), 15 (1993), 15 (1994), 10 (1995), 11 (1996), 13 (1997), 9 (1998); (c) Government: 43% (1991) 34 (1992), 13 (1993), 13 (1994), 28 (1995), 29 (1996), 28 (1997), 26 (1998). Niko Toš, "*Zaupanje Slovencev v. demokratični sistem*" (Slovenians' Faith in the Democratic System, Ljubljana, Liberalna akademija, 1999), p. 248.

favourable for the Constitutional Court's popular image. Despite the fact that people's faith in the Slovenian judiciary is not very substantial (although it has been growing again in recent years),[70] it would be possible at least indirectly to conclude that the Constitutional Court enjoys greater trust and distinction than the regular courts.

With regard to public opinion on the work of the Constitutional Court, consideration must of course be given to the fact that particularly in the transition countries (among which Slovenia belonged and partly still belongs) it often happens that the reporting of public media on the decisions of the Constitutional Court is unprofessional, tendentious and politically biased, which renders more difficult the legitimising processes and the formation of a mature legal and political awareness, although of course this does not mean that (proper and professional) critical analysis of Constitutional Court decisions is not needed.[71] Especially in the period from the adoption of the new Constitution up to 1998, in Slovenia the media often reacted strongly to certain clearly controversial decisions by the Constitutional Court, where for example in April 1998 the Court responded to such reporting with a special press release, in which it protested at politically biased reporting in the media on its decisions. According to its statement, this reporting was accompanied by "legal ignorance and lack of familiarity with the foundations of a legal culture".[72] After 1998 such expressly conflicting relations between the media and the Court have been almost imperceptible, although in this time certain decisions have also been subject to major public attention.

For the period following the adoption of the new Constitution it may generally be observed that in expanding its functions and influence within the abstract definition of constitutional jurisdiction, the Constitutional Court has been exceptionally 'successful' vis-à-vis the Parliament, the Government and the ordinary courts. These three branches of power have in this regard been excessively defensive, which would indicate primarily that they have devoted themselves insufficiently and belatedly to a serious study of constitutional concepts, and for this reason they have for the most part dealt with them only when faced with them, in other words in disputes over constitutional law. Such a situation, which was particularly characteristic of the Government and the National Assembly, led to the clear predominance of that understanding of constitutional institutions

---

[70]　General faith in the courts in the years from 1991 to 1998 can be expressed in the following values: 35% (1991), 31 (1992), 25 (1993), 26 (1994), 26 (1995), 24 (1996), 30 (1997), 33 (1998). Niko Toš "*Zaupanje Slovencev v. demokratični sistem*" (Slovenians' Faith in the Democratic System, Ljubljana, Liberalna akademija, 1999), p. 248.

[71]　Albin Igličar: "*Parlament in ustavno sodišče kot dejavnik legitimnosti oblasti*" (Parliament and the Constitutional Court as a Factor of Legitimacy of Authority), *Zbornik IV. Dnevi javnega prava* (Portorož 1998), p. 138.

[72]　The press release was published in the newspaper Delo on 20 and 22 April 1998.

such as had been independently established by the Constitutional Court, something that was facilitated by the acute passivity of the already meagre number of Slovenian scholars of constitutional law, who have thus far barely offered any public response to individual controversial decisions from the Court (the exceptions to this are negligible). In the absence of a broader set of possible or alternative argumentation based on constitutional law, right up until the second half of 1998 the Court often merely confirmed the known idea that a branch of power (including the judiciary) without adequate democratic control and clearly defined boundaries can rapidly be transformed into the arbitrary will of its custodians. As stated, this arbitrary approach was expressed during this period only occasionally (relative to the overall extent of matters handled only in a negligible number of cases), yet because of the political weight and constitutional controversy it has had major public importance and consequences. Towards the end of this period, for example, two clearly politically motivated and constitutionally highly contentious decisions, the aforementioned decision on the electoral referendum and the "Koper" decision,[73] seriously harmed the professional and

---

[73] Decision of 17 September 1998 (no. U-I-301/98, OdlUS VII, 180). In this decision the Constitutional Court established that the urban municipality of Koper was unconstitutional, wherein it referred to its earlier, of course equally contentious or clearly politically coloured decision (no. U-I-90/94), in which for the territory of this municipality it was of the opinion that it "strongly and clearly deviated from the constitutionally provided concept of municipalities". This decision is legally contentious chiefly because the Constitution does not actually define urban municipalities (urban municipalities are covered only in article 141 of the URS, which states: "A town may acquire the status of an urban municipality according to a procedure and under conditions provided by law. Urban municipalities also perform as their own certain tasks provided by law from state jurisdiction which relate to the development of towns."), and for this reason the Constitutional Court's reference to the "constitutional concept of an urban municipality" is an entirely arbitrary improvisation by the majority of the Constitutional Court judges (a more detailed critique of such Constitutional Court references to the actually non-existent "constitutional concept of an urban municipality" is offered by Bojan Bugarič: "Ustavno sodstvo in (ali) parlamentarna demokracija: o doktrinah pravnega interesa in političnih vprašanj" (Constitutional Judiciary and (or) Parliamentary Democracy: On the Doctrines of Legal Interest and Political Issues), in the *Zbornik znanstvenih razprav Pravne fakultete Univerze v. Ljubljani*, year 55 (Ljubljana 1995), pp. 61–64). In its decision of 1998 (no. U-I-301/98) the Court again opposed the legislative decision of the National Assembly, founded on a referendum in which the vast majority of residents of the "municipality of Koper" supported the continued existence of the current urban municipality of Koper. Given that it is generally known that the residents of that area generally support the political parties of the left, there are solid grounds to suspect that the five Constitutional Court judges (centred around the aforementioned nucleus of three) who adopted the decision wished in this way to consciously influence events in favour of breaking up this municipality into smaller units and in this way to weaken the power of the left-wing political option. In all this, of course, there was another legally questionable part of the decision with which the court itself (forcibly) extended the mandate of bodies of the urban municipality of Koper up until the

moral authority of the Court. More recently, that is, from the end of the above period up until early 2000, in its essentially reformed composition the Court has (at least for the moment successfully) clearly been working hard to re-establish itself as a legal *authority* in the authentic sense of the term, and this has been characterised by an appropriate degree of self-restraint, which may be observed, despite the diverse views (professional, value-system etc) of individual constitutional justices, in a major 'depoliticisation' in adopting and justifying decisions.

The reasons for the aforementioned dominance of the Constitutional Court in the period up until autumn 1998 were essentially fourfold. In the first place, the Court and its Justices had extensive legal expertise, and moreover the majority of the judges had considerable personal influence and support in political parties and among other political actors (with some of them also being highly credited for the successful implementation of Slovenian independence and the transition to democracy). Secondly, the low level of trust in other state and political institutions (especially the National Assembly, the government and political parties) automatically raised the expectations and hopes of people in the Court, which could abrogate or annul certain decisions of those institutions. Thirdly, the Court did not face substantial public or intellectual (legal, politological and other) checks and balances. Fourthly, the government, and particularly the National Assembly, owing to their heterogeneous and politically (bi)po-larised composition had in practice great difficulty in uniting in their positions regarding constitutional court decisions. This applied particularly to the National Assembly, where as a rule every (politically) more serious decision by the Court was on the one hand approved, and on the other accepted with dissatisfaction or criticised. Such polarity between the parliamentary coalition and the opposition, as well as in various other diametrical relations between political parties, in fact rendered the National Assembly impotent, and still prevents the adoption of (at least generally) united and professionally reasoned positions regarding Constitutional Court decisions. Moreover, of the four above-listed reasons, to date only the first has in part lost its significance (and of course not in the sense of the expertise of the Court's judges), while all the other reasons remain for the most part salient.

In addition to its relatively broad constitutional and legal powers, the Court is assured a great deal of power by the immanently ideological nature of the Constitution,[74] the high level of abstractness of constitutional provisions and by

---

start of the mandate of bodies of the new (smaller) municipalities which were supposed to be set up in line with the Constitution.

[74] Although in theory it is possible to trace the ideas of and demands for a content-neutral constitution and on its merely procedural function (see e.g. G. Sartori, *Comparative Constitutional Engineering, An Inquiry into Structures, Incentives and Outcomes* (Hampshire, London: MacMillan 1994), p. 202), practically no constitution can be non-ideological or apolitical. The Slovenian Constitution is also an expression of a certain political ideology, or more accurately a combination of various political (ideological) elements. Prevalent among these are the elements of political liberalism, which are evident chiefly in the provi-

that method of reasoning reflected in the (overly) frequent reference by this Court to constitutional (legal) principles, which represents an actualisation of the aforementioned ideological nature. Legal principles provide the Constitutional Court with special power, for through them it is able to rely not simply on explicit constitutional provisions, but also (indirectly) on a doctrine which in the legal sense explains such principles.[75] If by way of illustration we select the *principle of the state based on the rule of law*, we may see that the Court refers in many cases in its decision-making *directly* to this constitutional principle. This means that at the same time it is referring to those (sub)principles which in the development of democratic legal theory have become enshrined within the concept of the state based on the rule of law, but the wording of the Constitution does not explicitly mention them (for example the principle of legal security and the principle of predictability, the principle of trust in the law, the principle of proportionality, the principle of equivalence in contractual payment relations, the principle of fairness, the principle of preventing arbitrariness, the principle of the capacity of a law to have its meaning clear and to be determined, the principle of impermissibility of legal provisions or concepts that cannot be carried out, the principle that it is impermissible to limit evidence in exercising constitutional rights, the principle of clear definition of the right to free discretion, the principle of coherence and non-contradiction of the legal system).[76] Since the formulations of these and numerous other (sub)principles are very open in

---

sions on human rights (e.g. personal rights and freedoms, the right to private property), in the principle of the separation of power, in the guaranteeing of free economic initiative, in the requirement for prevention of unfair trading and monopolies and, of course, in the principle of the separation of the state and religious communities (for more detail see Igor Lukšič, "Politične doktrine v. Ustavi Republike Slovenije" (Political Doctrines in the Constitution of the Republic of Slovenia), in *Teorija in praksa*, no. 3–4 (1992), pp. 305–309). On the other hand, for example, the fundamental constitutional principle of the social state, the constitutionally provided social and cultural human rights and the constitutionally ordered concern by the state for the public good, farm lands, a healthy living environment and so forth reflect other (solidarity, social etc) political preferences, where some of these constitutional principles also represent an ideological antipode to (exaggerated) liberalism, which is to a certain extent rendered relative by the constitutional order of the National Council as the national representative of various public (local and professional) interests.

[75] It is generally typical of legal principles that they offer the interpreter an essentially broader interpretation space than legal rules. Regarding the fundamental differences between legal principles and legal rules see e.g. Ronald Dworkin, *Taking Rights Seriously* (Cambridge, Harvard University Press, 1978), pp. 22–28.

[76] For more detail see Marijan Pavčnik, "Razumevanje temeljnih (človekovih) pravic" (Understanding Fundamental (Human) Rights), in Marijan Pavčnik, Ada Polajnar-Pavčnik & Dragica Wedam-Lukić (eds.), *Temeljne pravice* (Ljubljana, Cankarjeva založba, 1997), pp. 101–102.

meaning (open texture), their interpretation in the majority of cases requires an explicitly value-orientated assessment, such that in this way they express as a rule to the greatest extent subjective (possibly also political) views of individual Constitutional Court judges and of the Court as such. Yet this in no way means that such practice by the Court is in principle contentious, for without the direct application of constitutional principles, owing to the insufficiently formulated constitutional wording it could not in practice perform its office to a satisfactory degree. Of course the already mentioned principle of judicial self-restraint is of key importance here.

Thus far the Court has already formulated numerous constitutional (sub)principles, which have been implemented as abstract value criteria from directly recorded constitutional principles (e.g. from the principle of the state based on the rule of law, the principle of the social state, the principle of the separation of power, the principle of equality or even the principle of democracy).[77] Such a 'constitutional subsystem' is of course essential, but in its very nature it still allows for a wide field of (subjective) value judgments and thereby also the possibility of political interpolation. All of this points to the close link between law and politics, which the Court must rationally separate and gradually render at least approximately harmonised (formally and in their values) in terms of the fundamental predispositions and dispositions of the (constitutional) legal system. Here it should be noted that in studying the interpretative approach of the Court, a very important question is raised of the precedence or effectuation of its decisions. In this connection it is possible to state as beyond dispute the fact that decisions of the Court are binding and that the legal role played by the views and reasoning of individual decisions can be compared with the significance of law of precedent. Yet here it should also be added that for the moment it remains quite unclear in practice which parts of the Court's explanations should have, or rather *can* and *should* actually have, the significance or effect of precedent (*ratio decidendi*), and what this should mean in practice for other state bodies (e.g. for the legislator). This is particularly questionable on the one hand in cases of interpretative decisions by the Court, where the (binding) ruling itself of the decision is imposed as a kind of 'precedent', and on the other hand in cases of (numerous) suggestive explanations from the Court, where it comments broadly on possibilities that are for example 'available' to the legislator, when it will have to replace an unconstitutional legal provision.

---

[77] Regarding pluralism of the concepts of democracy the *legal* reference by the Constitutional Court to the principle of democracy (article 1 of the URS) may be especially questionable, for this involves for the most part a political institution in a legal form. The controversial nature of such practice by the Constitutional Court is pointed out for example by Igor Lukšič: "Političnost ustavnega sodišča" (The Political Nature of the Constitutional Court), in *Teorija in praksa*, no. 6 (Ljubljana 1997), pp. 991–992.

5. CONCLUSION

Given the various inadequacies of the legislator and other state and self-governing local bodies, the Slovenian Constitutional Court is an extremely important and necessary legal instance. In this regard it has to date generally played an important and positive role in the process of establishing a state based on the rule of law in Slovenia, while here through excessive activism and within this context through certain political decisions it has on several occasions also harmed the development of the state based on the rule of law. For this very reason there should be a special undertaking to ensure that the activities of the Court remain within constitutionally permissible boundaries, which also means that it must resist the temptation to become a 'political body'. Only through the appropriate self-restraint of its power[78] will the Court be able to function as an institution of trust, which today and in the future Slovenia will undoubtedly need very much.

Self-restraint of Slovenia's Constitutional Court may sensibly be charted or established primarily on the following orientations: The Court should refer restrictively to general constitutional or legal principles.[79] Of course it must construct or apply the already frequently mentioned "constitutional subsystem", that is, a system of constitutional principles that are not explicitly recorded in the wording of the Constitution, but which are an implicit component of explicitly provided constitutional principles. Here the fact must be considered that many constitutional provisions that regulate individual issues (e.g. the provisions on human rights) are also framed in the form of legal principles. Yet in establishing such a framework of principle as a basis for adopting decisions, the Court should

---

[78] It is worth recalling here the thoughts of the US Supreme Court judge Harlan F. Stone, that "While unconstitutional exercise of power by the executive and legislative branches of the government is subject to judicial restraint, the only check upon our own exercise of power is our own sense of self-restraint." Quoted in W. Lasser, *The Limits of Judicial Power, The Supreme Court in American Politics* (Chapel Hill and London: The University of North Carolina Press 1988), p. 270.

[79] That the application of legal principles on the part of the Constitutional Court is indeed frequent, is shown in abridged form in e.g. decision U-I-197/96, OdlUS V, 176, in which the Court in dealing with the moratorium on the Denationalisation Act, referred to eleven legal principles (here I shall not go into an analysis of this case or into an assessment of whether this was appropriate). This involved the following principles: the principle of fairness, the principle of the state based on the rule of law, the principle of a democratic society, the principle of the separation of power, the principle of equality, the principle of proportionality, the principle of appropriateness, the principle of permanence of laws, the principle of legal security, the principle of trust in the law and the principle of rationality.

not allow itself too broad a space for argumentation, since this could lead to an excessive legal relativism[80] or to an impermissible arbitrariness.

In its practices, the Court should not to an exaggerated extent model itself on the practices of those established constitutional courts which are characterised by strong power in their position and jurisdiction (in practice the Slovenian Court most frequently uses the German Constitutional Court as its role model), for the constitutional and legal powers themselves already provide the Court with a relatively high degree of power.[81]

To the greatest possible degree the Constitutional Court should avoid suggestive explanations of its decisions, whereby it offers the legislator or other body, in a more or less open manner, solutions for settling particular relations (this can in fact represent an impermissible encroachment on the pluralism of possibilities for the legislative or other democratic legal order of social relations).

It should finally be noted that a major contribution towards high-quality work on the part of the Court may be made by a legally aware and critical (professional and lay) public. The absence of ongoing (permanent) public and constructive assessment or critical appraisal of the work of the Court (and of course of all others responsible for the legal branch of government) can lead on the one hand to an overly positive self-perception of Constitutional Court judges and of the Court itself, and this may be reflected in an impermissible feeling of professional and other self-sufficiency or even exaltation ('superiority') on the part of Justices, while on the other hand it can lead to the feeling of impotence in other participants in the democratic process and order *vis-à-vis* the Constitutional Court.

For democracy it is essential that it establishes and preserves between law and politics a *partnership* (in the sense of "checks and balances" between law and politics), which also means that law must establish and maintain a relative autonomy and independence *vis-à-vis* politics, to which particularly on the constitutional level it is closely tied. In this respect it is indeed the Constitutional Court as a legal factor which is the most important partner to politics in Slovenia. If this Court, which often hovers on the boundary between law and politics, decides to adopt a political role,[82] then the legal side will lose a great

---

[80]   The danger of excessive (destructive) legal relativism is shown for example in the theory of legal scepticism, which points out the possibility of a judge deciding entirely at will, for the argumentation methods and the free field of value judgment supposedly offer him sufficient support for his decision to be rationalised or justified at any subsequent point by invoking precedent or a legal standard. See Steven J. Burton, *An Introduction to Law and Legal Reasoning* (Boston, Toronto, Little, Brown and Company, 1985), pp. 188–193.

[81]   As already mentioned, these sweeping powers can easily be transformed into impotence of the Constitutional Court, for in time they may lead towards 'powerful' overburdening of the court and to its incapacity to assess matters in "reasonable deadlines".

[82]   It is especially characteristic of Constitutional Courts in Central and Eastern Europe that they find it "hard to resist" assuming a legislative function in complicated matters such as privatisation, reform of the system of social security, restitution of property or the question

deal of its weight, which is legitimated precisely through the relative autonomy and independence of law *vis-à-vis* politics. For Slovenia this would signify the loss of a protagonist of the state based on the rule of law and a serious undermining of the value of law as such and its subordination to politics. For this reason it is of essential importance for further development that the Court contributes to the continued emancipation of Slovenian law and that to this end it avoids such decisions and their explanation as well as separate opinions that indicate the identifiable political view or preference of individual judges and of the Court as a whole.

---

of constitutionality of political parties, where it is almost impossible to tackle and resolve such matters in an exclusively 'legal' manner. See Bojan Bugarič, *From Plan to Market: One Way or Alternative Paths?, A Critique of Institutional Reforms in Central and Eastern Europe*, unpublished doctoral dissertation (University of Wisconsin, 1998-I), p. 160.

10.   The Rise of Constitutional Adjudication in Bulgaria

Venelin I. Ganev

ACKNOWLEDGMENT

I would like to thank Mila Ganeva, Yonko Grozev, Christian Takov and my father, Iordan Ganev, for the lengthy conversations out of which this paper eventually grew. Research on this project was partially funded by the American Council of Learned Societies, whose financial assistance is gratefully acknowledged.

In an insightful commentary on the wave of constitution-making that swept across the world in the aftermath of World War II, Karl Loewenstein pointed out that technical, legalistic analyses of constitutional provisions "overshadow what may be called the ontology of constitutions, that is, the investigation of what a written constitution really means within a specific national environment [and] how real it is for the common people."[1] It is not unfair to say that in the mushrooming literature on post-communism, precisely the opposite tendency prevails. To be sure, constitutional norms are routinely subject to assiduous textual interpretation, constitutionally established regimes are carefully classified, and similarities and differences with Western models are duly pointed out. And yet, even the most technical studies of the constitutional aspects of political change in Eastern Europe inevitably return to "ontological" questions: is the essence of Western constitutionalism adequately replicated in local contexts? Have the values of liberal democracy been sincerely embraced? Is judicial review real?

These questions are not simply tokens of an epistemological ambition, the ambition to grasp "the true nature" of things. They also reflect a particular "climate of opinion," an intellectual predisposition shared by the preponderant majority of scholars struggling to comprehend the evasive reality of post-communism. And it would not be an exaggeration to assert that, throughout the 1990s, this climate of opinion has been marked by democratic gloom and constitutional angst. Some authors ridicule attempts to "import" constitutional

---

[1]   See Karl Loewenstein, "Reflections on the Values of Constitutions in Our Revolutionary Age," in Arnold J. Zurcher (ed.), *Constitutions and Constitutional Trends Since World War II* (New York: New York University Press, 1951), p. 191.

Wojciech Sadurski (ed.), Constitutional Justice, East and West, 247–264
© 2002 *Kluwer Law International. Printed in Great Britain.*

models from abroad, and predict that pro-reform elites, especially in more "backward" countries like Bulgaria, will never be able to overcome "the overall structural affinity of the respective societies to Soviet-type communism" and erect the edifice of liberal democracy.[2] Other analysts single out the incompatibility between Western and "local" values as the decisive obstacle that renders efforts to "engineer" institutions from above unlikely to succeed. In the absence of cultural underpinnings, "social engineering on the level of institutions [will] hit a massive brick wall."[3] All in all, predictions about the future of post-communist democracies tended to cluster around the view that institutions like the Constitutional Court are simply "legal transplants"[4] offering "no guarantee that the day-to-day practices in which ruling elites engage will be affected by the introduction of new rules."[5] The most likely fate of such "transplants" is rapid and irrevocable degeneration into "mutations", "rickety institutions which continue to exist, but are weak, deformed and cannot fulfil the proper function which they were originally assigned."[6]

My inquiry into recent Bulgarian experiences with judicial review – experiences that have remained largely ignored or persistently misinterpreted – intends to demonstrate the neglected strengths of more nuanced, empirical, analytical studies of legal phenomena in post-communism. Understandable though they are, concerns about the ontology, authenticity and genuineness of constitutionalism may lead astray the analyses of contemporary East European politics. The major issue at stake is not, of course, whether an "optimistic" or a "pessimistic" stance is *a priori* more warranted. More importantly, the dominant approach to the study of post-communism suffers from at least two analytical shortcomings which I will attempt to rectify. Firstly, empirical evidence is systematically misinterpreted in order to make it fit preconceived notions about how successful concrete societies can be in transplanting on their own soil venerated Western models. More often than not, the collection and evaluation of data is guided by the implicit understanding that some countries ("Central European" ones) are culturally endowed to embrace constitutionalism, while others (typically those

---

[2]   See Claus Offe, Jon Elster and Ulrich Press, *Institutional Design in Post-Communist Societies: Rebuilding the Ship at Sea* (Cambridge: Cambridge University Press, 1998), p. 304.

[3]   Francis Fukuyama, "The Primacy of Culture," in Larry Diamond and Marc F. Plattner (eds), *The Global Resurgence of Democracy* (Baltimore: The Johns Hopkins University Press, 1996), p. 321.

[4]   On the notion of "legal transplants," see Alan Watson, *Legal Transplants* (Charlottesville: University of Virginia Press, 1974).

[5]   Cf. Armin Hoeland, "Imposition Without Adaptation? New Opportunities for Old Failure," in Volkmar Gessner, Armin Hoeland and Csaba Varga (eds), *European Legal Cultures* (Dartmouth: Aldershot, 1996), pp. 482–490.

[6]   Robert Sharlet, "Legal Transplants and Political Mutations: The Reception of Constitutional Law in Russia and the Newly Independent States," *East European Constitutional Review*, 7 (Fall 1998), p. 58.

on "South-Eastern Europe" or "The Balkans") are not. Consequently, the former are invariably classified as "advanced," and the latter – as "unconsolidated" democracies. However, the term "unconsolidated democracy" – and cognate terms such as "immature constitutionalism" and "underdeveloped political culture" – is incurably stricken by an analytical malaise which Giovanni Sartori calls "conceptual stretching," in that it is so general and abstract (in effect, it is supposed to encompass more that 2/3 of all political regimes in the world!) that it is almost devoid of concrete analytical content.[7] Observations like those offered by Preuss, Offe and Elster – "the role of the Bulgarian Constitutional Court is unclear" – certainly convey the feeling that something is amiss with the ontological foundations of Bulgarian constitutionalism, and yet their heuristic value, their value as an explanation of the modes of involvement of this particular institution in constitutional debates and practices, is rather limited.[8] Adducing important factual evidence that may eventually allow us to make positive, analytically potent statements about the role of the Bulgarian Constitutional Court is a major objective of this paper.

A second problem also mars the literature on post-communist constitutionalism. All too often, surveys of constitutional practices serve to sustain the illusion of analytical familiarity with post-communist phenomena by denying the social and institutional peculiarity of post-communism as a historical period. In other words, once the premises of "ontological constitutional analysis" are embraced, it is easy to offer a familiar, powerful explanation of the problems East European societies have to cope with. These problems supposedly stem from the "defects" of fledgling democracies and the "unauthenticity" of post-communist constitutionalism. The argument I will develop in the final section of this paper is that, whereas the familiar problems of creating a functioning democracy and constitutionalizing the political process should not be overlooked, there may be other, context-specific, historically unique factors that may in fact pose greater challenges, both for post-communist societies and scholars studying those societies.

The purpose of my remarks on the Bulgarian Constitutional Court, then, are two-fold. On the one hand, I will enrich the universe of facts relevant to the study of post-communist constitutionalism. On the other hand, I will defend an analytical point of view, a theoretical understanding of the problems inherent in the post-communist political condition, that will help us make sense of these facts. Hopefully, my inquiry will provide remedies for some of the empirical shortcomings, conceptual inadequacies and lack of appreciation of historical context that undermine the explanatory potential of traditional approaches to post-communist constitutionalism.

---

[7]   Cf. Giovanni Sartori, "Concept Misformation in Comparative Politics," *American Political Science Review*, 64 (December 1970), pp. 1033–1053.

[8]   Offe, Elster and Preuss, above n. 2, p. 275.

1. JUDICIAL REVIEW: THE CONSTITUTIONAL BACKGROUND

In the paragraphs that follow, I will provide general information about the Bulgarian Constitutional Court: why and how the institution was created, specifics about its structure and functions, and its role in the constitutional system.

Virtually none of the prerequisites believed to be necessary for the emergence of robust judicial review were present in Bulgaria in the early 1990s. *Historically*, the nation had never had any experience with constitutional adjudication, and the establishment of a Constitutional Court was a radical innovation quite at odds with the national political/legal tradition. *Culturally*, Bulgaria was a country where legal rules were just beginning to be recognized as valid constraints on political behaviour. The judicial branch was held in very low esteem, and a legalistic understanding of the nature of the political process was completely lacking. Finally, the social structure of the country was a far cry from the type of society which, according to Max Weber, generates powerful public demand for rational adjudication, namely a predominantly Protestant capitalist society invigorated by a solid bourgeois class. The Court was established only months after the Great National Assembly adopted a new Constitution in 1991, and at that time a knowledgeable observer of Bulgarian politics would have confidently predicted that the Court will be nothing more than an institutional ornament loosely connected to a hastily assembled institutional edifice. Such gloomy predictions were disproved by subsequent developments.

During the public discussions and political bargaining that accompanied the constitution writing process, the structure and function of the Constitutional Court were not among the most contentious issues. The prevailing consensus was that the mechanism of judicial review is an indispensable component of modern democracy. Only a small faction within the ex-communist party (renamed Bulgarian Socialist Party, or BSP) opposed the creation of a Constitutional Court. In his constitutional draft Velko Vulkanov, leader of that faction, envisaged that review of constitutionality of legislation will be entrusted to the Supreme Court, and that the decisions of this court may be overturned by Parliament with a qualified majority.[9] This proposal did not garner enough support within the BSP, the dominant political party at that time, and a chapter establishing a new Constitutional Court was included in the final draft of the Constitution.

It may be argued that the creation of the Court reflects a value orientation rather than immediate self-interest. While the "founders" of the Bulgarian constitution were, for the most part, prone to succumb to opportunistic considerations, and their expectations about the results of the next general elections were at

---

[9]   See Velko Vulkanov, *Na kolene pred istinata* [Kneeling Before Truth] (Sofia: Bulvest 2000, 1996).

times the primary motivational force behind the choice of institutional design (e.g. the design of the presidency)[10] – insofar as the institution of judicial review was concerned, they acted as if behind a "veil of ignorance." None of the major actors involved could form any reasonable expectations about the composition and political "biases" of the newly born institution, and hence it is not unreasonable to assert that the creation of the Constitutional Court points to the existence of an "overlapping consensus." This consensus in turn suggests that within the package of ideas that informed constitution making in Eastern Europe in the 1990s the twin notions that power must be restrained and individual rights need protection were accorded priority over the notion that the unadulterated "popular will" must be ensured unfettered expression.[11]

The appointment procedure is modelled on, albeit not identical to, Art. 159 of the Spanish Constitution.[12] Four of the twelve Justices are elected by Parliament, four are appointed by the President, and four are selected during a joint session of the Supreme Court of Cassation and the Supreme Administrative Court. Every three years, a third of the members are replaced (the order of departure was determined by lot). The mandate is thus for nine years and only lawyers with fifteen years of professional experience are eligible for the job. Justices cannot be re-elected. The Justices cannot be arrested or prosecuted until their immunity is lifted, and the only institution that can authorize the lifting of immunity is the Court itself. So far, there have been no incidents with regards to the Justices' immunity.

In the initial years of the Court's existence, a predictable pattern has emerged. Justices elected by the deputies are most likely to have political connections with Parliamentary parties, while the selection of judiciary (i.e. Justices elected by the Supreme Court of Cassation and the Supreme Administrative Court) have been largely non-political. Arguably, the most interesting aspect of the politics of appointments is that both President (Zhelyu Zhelev, 1991–1997; Petar Stoyanov, 1997–2002) have refused to follow a "party line," i.e. to appoint functionaries of their own party. Instead, they frequently opt to appoint unaffiliated lawyers with whom they have a personal rapport, thus creating a

---

[10] On the design of the presidency, see Jon Elster, "Miscalculations in the Design of the East European Presidencies," *East European Constitutional Review*, 2/4 and 3/1 (Fall 1993/Winter 1994), pp. 95–98, and Venelin I. Ganev, "Bulgaria," in Robert Elgie, ed., *Semi-Presidentialism in Europe* (Oxford: Oxford University Press, 1999), pp. 124–149.

[11] For more on the tension between "popular will" and "constitutional restraints" in a post-communist context, see Venelin I. Ganev, "Emergency Powers and the New East European Constitutions," *The American Journal of Comparative Law*, 45 (Summer 1997), pp. 585–612.

[12] Art. 159 of the Spanish Constitution: "The Constitutional Court shall consist of twelve members appointed by the King. Of these, four shall be nominated by Congress by a majority of three-fifths of its members, four shall be nominated by the Senate with the same majority, two shall be nominated by the Government, and two by the General Council of the Judiciary.".

"Presidential power base" within the Court. It bears emphasizing that the overall goal of the seemingly convoluted procedure was accomplished: the configuration of power within the Court is fairly balanced, and so far the Court has remained "uncaptured" by particular political forces.[13]

The Court has two main functions. First, it offers authoritative and binding interpretations of the Constitution. Second, it evaluates the constitutionality of laws passed by Parliament and Presidential decrees.[14] As to whether laws passed *before* the adoption of the new Constitution fall within the ambit of judicial review, there has been a shift in the Court's position. Initially, the Justices refused to pass judgment on the constitutionality of such laws, arguing that the task of bringing pre-existing legislation in conformity with the Constitution falls within the purview of the legislative branch and has to be completed within three years of the adoption of the new fundamental law. However, when this period elapsed and the Parliamentarians did not so act, the Court issued a new ruling, holding that future evaluations of constitutionality of pre-1991 legislation would be carried out by the Court itself. Thus the scope of judicial review was considerably augmented.

The independence of the Court is generally respected. During 1995–1996, the only period of hostility so far, the Court found itself on a collision course with BSP-dominated government and Parliament. While no dramatic attempts to arrest, dismiss or pressure Justices were recorded, low-visibility strategies for intimidation were in fact employed. For example, an effort was made to move the Court to a new location without obtaining the Justices' consent. The campaign backfired. The Justices, pursuant to a petition filed by the President, declared – not without some gusto – the ministerial decree ordering their own re-location unconstitutional. This line of behaviour was soon abandoned by BSP Prime Minister Videnov and has not been replicated by future governments. Rather than an expression of a culturally embedded aversion to judicial procedures, the conduct of the ill-fated BSP Cabinet stands out as something of an anomaly. At present, the authority of the Court is universally recognized, and its dignity generally respected.

The Court does not possess the prerogative to review *ex ante* the constitutionality of legislative drafts. It cannot initiate the procedure of judicial review on its own initiative – this right belongs to one fifth of the deputies, the government, the President, the Supreme Administrative Court, the Supreme Court of

---

[13] For interesting quantitative analysis of the Court's independence, see Mariela Vargova, ed., *Konstitutzionnijat Sud: Jurisprudentzija* [The Constitutional Court: Jurisprudence] (Sofia: Open Society Institute, 1996); see also Venelin I. Ganev, "The Bulgarian Constitutional Court: Two Interviews," *East European Constitutional Review*, 6 (Winter 1997), pp. 65–71.

[14] Cf. Dimitar Gochev, "Za purvi put Konstitutzionen Sud v. Bulgaria" [A Constitutional Court in Bulgaria – for the First Time], in Vargova, above n. 13, pp. 18–23.

Cassation, and the Prosecutor General. During the first six years of the Court's existence, 63% of the cases were filed by deputies, 17.7% by the Prosecutor General, 13% by the President, 4.5% by the government, and 1.8% by the Supreme Court of Cassation. Obviously, the deputies are much more intensely involved in the process of constitutional adjudication than other entitled political actors. The review of constitutionality is abstract – the Court does not deal with legal disputes between private parties or with concrete controversies.

The two principles – that judicial review should be *ex post* and *abstract*– seem well entrenched, and yet it is possible to conceive of ways whereby the Justices may in practice depart from these principles. For example, when the ordinary Bulgarian courts are confronted with the argument that a particular norm is unconstitutional, they may refer the issue to the Supreme Court of Cassation, which, in turn, may hold the proceedings in abeyance and file a petition with the Constitutional Court.[15] So far, this procedure has not been often used. Nonetheless, on at least one occasion the Court was petitioned by the Supreme Court regarding a controversy that had a tangible impact on dozens of pending cases, namely, whether a legislative act may empower the Council of Ministers to restrict by decree the right of dismissed employees to seek redress in the regular courts. Striking down this legislation as unconstitutional, the Court in effect shaped the outcomes of a number of concrete cases.

Insofar as *ex ante* control is concerned, an argument may be made that this function is fulfilled when requests for authoritative interpretation of constitutional provisions are considered. As a rule, such petitions are filed in the course of legislative work on concrete drafts, and the Court's interpretations usually validate a particular course of action and shut out other options, without explicit references to particular provisions.

After almost a decade of constitutional adjudication in Bulgaria, it seems that two problems in particular need to be addressed, perhaps by means of a constitutional amendment. The first problem is the ambiguity of the constitutional provision describing the conditions under which the Court may issue valid decisions. According to the Constitution, a majority of "more than half of all Justices" is necessary, i.e. seven votes "for" or "against." On several occasions, however, the Justices have been split six to six, or six to five. The practice so far has been that in such cases, the petition asking for a declaration of unconstitutionality is rejected (even if six Justices support it, and only five oppose it). This practice has arguably evolved into a "constitutional convention" and is by now recognized *de facto* as a valid norm within the broader constitutional order. But it would be better if the various hypotheses regarding different majorities are addressed in a clearer and more detailed manner in a legislative and/or constitutional provision.

---

[15]   Cf. Assen Manov, "Konstitutzionnijat sud na Republika Bulgaria" [The Constitutional Court of the Republic of Bulgaria], in Vargova, above n. 13, pp. 14–17.

The second problem concerns cases where an amendment of an existing legal norm is declared unconstitutional. Is the legal validity of the original norm then automatically restored, or do we face a newly created "lacuna" in the legal order, by virtue of the fact that the legislator repealed the old norm, and the Justices invalidated the one intended to replace it? The Court's practice has been consistent. The Justices have repeatedly pointed out that a declaration of unconstitutionality automatically "brings back to life" the original norm. However, the issue triggered heated controversies, and it seems reasonable to suggest that all ambiguities regarding this matter should be resolved by means of an explicit norm.[16]

These ambiguities notwithstanding, the set of constitutional provisions regarding judicial review serves as a reliable institutional basis of the Court's jurisprudence, to the analysis of which I now turn.

2. JUDICIAL REVIEW: CONSTITUTIONAL PRACTICES

In this section, the focus shifts towards an analysis of the Court's impact as a player in the national political process, the scope and significance of its decisions and emerging patterns of relations with other social and political actors. Some analytical questions that may frame current research agendas on post-communist judicial review – such as the nature of the Court's "activism," the problem with "the deficit of democratic legitimacy," and the extent to which its interventions represent a case of "policy distortion" – will be singled out for close, if necessarily brief, consideration.

Over the past seven years, the Court has issued a number of decisions that touch upon a wide spectrum of constitutional issues. The Justices have successfully prevented a government supported by an absolute majority in Parliament from raising taxes by decree, and subsequently forced the same government to amend its budget in order to allocate more money for the judicial branch.[17] The Court has defined the authority of interim governments, delimited the scope of presidential prerogatives and ordered Parliament to re-write its Standing Orders.[18] All parliamentary parties, which otherwise share little in common, are unanimous in their view that conflicts between major institutions should be definitively resolved by the twelve Justices. The Court's assistance in clarifying the ambiguities of various provisions is eagerly sought by politicians. The impact

---

16 For more on this issue, see the excellent exchange between two former Justices, Jivko Stalev and Neno Nenovski, *Konstitutzionnijat Sud i pravnoto deistvie na negovite reshenija* [The Constitutional Court and the Legal Effect of Its Decisions] (Sofia: Civi, 1996).

17 See Decision 17/95, published in *Reshenija I opredelenija na Konstitutzionnija Sud, 1995* [*Decisions and Rulings of the Constitutional Court, 1995*] (Sofia: Akademichno izdatelstvo, 1996), pp. 183–195.

18 See Decision 4/95, *ibid* at pp. 49–76.

of judicial review is palpably felt in various domains of Bulgarian political life. In what follows, I will take a closer look at three decisions which reveal different aspects of the Court's jurisprudence, in particular its comprehensive vision of how the principle of political pluralism should be applied in an ethnically heterogeneous society, its readiness and capacity to stand up to political pressure from hostile majorities, and its role as a guarantor of judicial independence.

2.1. The Constitutionality of the "Movement for Rights and Freedoms": the Court as Visionary

The Bulgarian constitution contains a, now infamous, provision which prohibits the formation of political parties along ethnic lines.[19] In the above mentioned case, the Court offered an interpretation of this provision which effectively obviated its nationalistic, restrictive intent and cleared the way for the formation of political organizations representing all ethnic minorities in Bulgaria.

"The Movement for Rights and Freedoms" (MRF) is a political organization established in early 1990 and supported mainly by ethnic Turks. In the aftermath of the adoption of the prohibitive constitutional provision, a group of legislators asked the Court to declare the MRF unconstitutional. In a widely publicised decision the Court affirmed the constitutionality of the Movement. The Court maintained that the term "political parties formed on ethnic basis" should be interpreted in a very narrow and strict manner, so as not to impinge upon the freedom of association and the principle of democratic pluralism. Furthermore, the Court asserted that Bulgarian Muslims have been the victims of large scale ethnic persecution in the past, and hence the protection of their rights and interests is among the most important task within the context of the new constitutional order. The Justices then concluded that the MRF should be allowed to continue its political activities. Without a doubt, this decision played a major role in alleviating simmering ethnic tensions in Bulgaria, and contributed towards the advancement of the process of ethnic reconciliation.[20]

2.2. The Pirinski Case: The Court Under Assault

Perhaps nothing illustrates the autonomy of the Court vis-à-vis the political branches better than the so called "Pirinski case", decided in 1996. At that time, the ruling Socialist Party had accumulated as much power as any party in a pluralist system can, controlling the legislature, the executive branch, local government and the national electronic media. Georgi Pirinski was Foreign

---

[19]   Art. 11.4: "Political parties formed on ethnic, racial or religious basis ... shall be prohibited.".

[20]   See Decision 4/92, published in *Reshenija I opredelenija na Konstitutzionnija Sud, 1991–1992* [*Decisions and Rulings of the Constitutional Court, 1993*] (Sofia: Akademichno izdatelstvo, 1993), pp. 67–98.

Minister in the Socialist government and in September 1996 was nominated as his party's candidate in the upcoming Presidential elections. At that moment, it was pointed out that Pirinski may not meet one of the eligibility requirements which the Constitution posits, namely that the President be a "Bulgarian citizen by birth." As Pirinski was born in New York, it was unclear whether he obtained his Bulgarian citizenship by birth or by naturalization. (Ironically, the restrictive citizenship law in force in 1948, at the time of Pirinski's birth, was passed by the communists with a view to stripping the children of Bulgarian emigrants of citizenship rights). The Court was asked to step in and clarify the matter. Without referring to Pirinski by name, the Court offered a rigorous interpretation of the relevant constitutional provisions which in effect rendered him ineligible to be President. A torrent of vicious attacks was unleashed against the Court, but to no avail. Invoking the Court's ruling, the Central Electoral Commission refused to register Pirinski as a Presidential candidate, and a unanimous Supreme Court turned down his appeal against the decision of the Commission. The Justices effectively disqualified the candidate of the most powerful party from contesting the Presidency but, more importantly for present purposes, the legitimacy of that decision was generally recognized by state officials and institutions.[21]

2.3. The Law on Judicial Power: The Court as a Champion of Judicial Independence

In 1994, the BSP-dominated Parliament embarked upon a large-scale campaign to cleanse the judiciary from "undesirable elements." A crucial element of the ex-communists' strategy was the retroactive establishment of new eligibility requirements for the country's highest-ranking judges. A newly amended norm in the Law on Judicial Power (passed in June 1994) provided that only judges with 5 years of experience would be eligible to sit on the Supreme Court. In addition, a freshly inserted transitional provision in that law declared that all incumbents who failed to meet the new requirements were automatically dismissed. Given the date of passage, it was clear that only judges affiliated with the *ancien regime* would be able to staff Bulgaria's highest court. The opposition immediately filed a constitutional challenge with the Court. In their decision, the Justices argued that the retroactive effect of the law nullified the constitutional principle that all judges become irremovable after three years in office (Art. 129 of the Constitution) and hence constituted a serious infringement on the principle of the independence of the judiciary. As a result of the Court's decisive intervention, all incumbent judges kept their positions.[22]

---

[21] See. Decision 12/96, published in *Reshenija I opredelenija na Konstitutzionnija Sud, 1996* [*Decisions and Rulings of the Constitutional Court, 1996*] (Sofia: Akademichno izdatelstvo, 1997), pp. 120–140.

[22] For more details on this controversy, see Venelin I. Ganev, "Judicial Independence and Post-Totalitarian Politics," *Parker School of Law Journal of East European Law*, 3 (Fall 1996), pp. 227–233.

With the cleansing operation thwarted, the BSP sought to wield "the power of the purse" and slashed the budget of the judicial branch. Once again, the Justices ruled against the deputies and forced the government to re-work its budget. At this moment, all judges in Bulgaria knew that they could collect their salaries because the Court had intervened on their behalf. The significance of this implicit alliance between judges from different courts should not be under-estimated. As observers of judicial politics are well aware, the relations between a Constitutional Court and the ordinary courts need not be necessarily per-meated by mutual cooperation and respect, as the case of the Czech Republic amply demonstrates. These relations may be tarnished by political tensions, institutional tugs-of-war and, most importantly, personal rivalries. After all, given the demographic potential of most East European countries, the members of all higher courts are recruited from a relatively small pool of top lawyers, who may choose to re-enact their old personal battles in their new institutional roles. In Bulgaria, however, a political momentum developed in 1994–1995 which brought the legal community closer together and erased their differences, and this momentum was created by the Court's resistance to the socialist party's onslaught against the independence of the judiciary.

In their book *Institutional Design in Post-communist Societies*, Offe, Elster and Preuss, who are prone to grieve copiously the "immaturity" of Bulgarian demo-cracy, allege that the "role of the Court is still unclear" and that "it has not yet gained a position of uncontested superiority over the actors of the political game." The evidence they adduce in support of this claim is that on one occasion in 1994 the BSP parliamentary majority defied the Constitutional Court and proceeded to elect a new Supreme Judicial Council[23] even though the Justices had invalidated the dismissal of the old Supreme Judicial Council.[24] It is true that, acting in defiance of the Court, Parliament elected a new Council. What the authors fail to mention, however, is that this decision of the deputies was immediately appealed by the opposition to the Court and the Justices promptly declared it unconstitutional and as a result the BSP's plans for a purge of the judiciary were derailed.[25] Accordingly, a better conclusion to draw from this episode would be *precisely the opposite* of what the distinguished scholars were trying to convey: the story clearly shows that the Justices are ultimately quite capable of "disciplining" defiant Parliamentary majorities.

---

[23] The Supreme Judicial Council is a constitutional organ of self-governance for the judiciary. Among its prerogatives is the power to elect, promote, demote, reassign and dismiss judges. See Art. 129 of the Bulgarian Constitution.

[24] See Claus Offe, Jon Elster and Ulrich Preuss, *Institutional Design in Postcommunist Societies: Rebuilding the Ship At Sea* (Cambridge: Cambridge University Press, 1998), p. 275.

[25] See *Reshenija I opredelenija na Konstitutzionnija Sud* (Sofia: Akademichno izdatestlvo, 1995), pp. 166–171.

According to the Constitution, the Court's decisions are final and cannot be overturned by Parliament. On two occasions, a BSP dominated Parliament re-passed legislation declared unconstitutional (the bills in question sought to block the restitution of property, and to impose various restrictions on the right to own agricultural land), only to be see it invalidated again. The question is whether this mode of legislative behaviour amounts to a "defiance of the Court," and the answer is negative. What usually happens in cases of defiance is a *de facto* refusal to abide by the Court's decisions. In the Bulgarian case, however, no such incidents were recorded – the ambition of legislators to re-pass unconstitutional legislation was not backed up by corresponding acts of executive officials who refused to honour the Court's rulings. The whole incident with the repeated passage of invalidated legislation should be perceived as yet another defeat of the BSP led parliamentary majority.

With a view to elucidating the role of the Court in public debates (as opposed to political struggles), a distinction between the Court as an *arbitrator* and *agenda setter* may perhaps be helpful. Insofar as the Justices' decisions manufacture winners and losers, they invariably generate interest. But the Court's ability to set the agenda for public discussions that transcend concrete constitutional controversies is rather limited. For better or worse, the influence of the Court seems to be confined primarily to elite political circles.

The Court's reputation with the press is generally high (a couple of communist-controlled newspapers excepted), a development that has its origins in the protracted clashes between the BSP government and the free media in 1995–1996. At first, the Justices were asked to interpret the constitutional provision guaranteeing freedom of speech and their comprehensive ruling was greeted favourably by virtually all professional organisations of journalists in Bulgaria. Later, when the BSP passed a fairly restrictive media law – which envisaged, for example, sanctions against journalists who present "a one-sided interpretation of the facts" – the Court struck it down. It should be pointed out that the same pattern of pro-"freedom of speech" rulings transpired after the Socialists were finally thrown out of power in 1997. When the new majority tried to dismiss some journalists perceived as communist holdovers from the national TV and radio, the Court declared such measures unconstitutional. Generally speaking, then the fourth estate is on the side of the Court.

Insofar as the important issue of "democratic legitimacy deficit" is concerned, the Bulgarian experience with judicial review lends credibility to the hypothesis that within the context of a semi-presidential regime (such as the Bulgarian one) the support of a popularly elected President may go a long way towards compensating for this deficit and thus enhances the Court's stature. In other words, when a popularly elected President challenges legislation before the Court, the boundaries between "counter-majoritarian" and "democratic" action become somewhat blurred, because the authority vested in the President is no less democratic than the mandate conferred upon the deputies. At least so far, the support of successive Presidents has been one of the Court's major assets.[26] This circumstance may account for the fact the Court is widely considered as an institution functional to, rather than opposed to, the national democratic process.

Is the Bulgarian Court "activist"? A preliminary discussion regarding the applicability of the term in a post-communist context is perhaps necessary. The pattern of involvement of the Justices in political affairs may be simply an artefact created by virtue of institutional design, rather than a reflection of a particular vision of what "a good democratic polity" should look like. Research on "the activism" of the Bulgarian Court should heed two institutional factors.

Firstly, the Court cannot control its agenda, and specifically it cannot refuse to deal with issues which politicians bring to its attention (i.e. it does not enjoy the discretion to refuse to grant "a writ of certiorari"). Hence, the Court is compelled to be very active, if not activist. The Justices have never declined to fulfil their duties, even when procrastination has been a plausible option. Informal request by politicians to expedite the proceedings (for which the Constitution sets no deadlines) are as a rule met with understanding, especially in situations where the Justices' interpretation of a constitutional provision is a necessary overture to urgently needed political action. A good example would be the Court's interpretation of the constitutional provisions regarding the passage of foreign military planes over Bulgarian airspace. Only days after NATO and Russia requested access to Bulgarian air space and the government asked the Court to specify the conditions under which such access may be granted, the Justices announced their opinion. In short, the Court appears to be destined to partake actively in national politics, and whether or not this participation should be classified as "activism" remains an issue to be resolved in more theoretical and comparative debates.

A second important institutional factor is that ordinary citizens lack the standing to petition the Court. As a result, the scope of issues which the Justices can consider is necessarily circumscribed. In some of its interpretative decisions, the Justices have demonstrated a propensity to tackle broad and general problems (the discussion of the meaning of freedom of speech may serve as a good example). But such lapses into a more activist mood have been rare and, by and large, inconsequential.

In a nutshell, then, it appears that the Court's direct involvement in politics renders constitutional asceticism impossible, while at the same time its institutionalised detachment from society engenders few opportunities for constitutional exuberance.

The Bulgarian Court has overturned various and numerous pieces of legislation. It is perhaps too early to say whether or not this fact should be regarded a case of "policy distortion". We still do not know what strategy the Justices will embrace when exposed to sustained pressure from successive parliamentary

---

[26] For more on this partnership, see Ganev, above n. 10, pp. 134–137.

majorities. One of the distinct peculiarities of Bulgaria's recent politics is that parliamentary majorities change after each successive round of general elections. A logical corollary of this trend is that it is impossible to say whether a Court which invalidates legislation is fighting rear-guard battles against advancing social coalitions, or acts in conformity with the preferences of ascending majorities. In other words, as long as the voters refuse to return to Parliament majorities that oppose the court, and instead propel into power former oppositional forces that have actively sought the Court's intervention, it will be hard to draw a distinction between "policy distortions" and rulings that reflect "the evolving preferences" of the electorate. We will be able to evaluate adequately the extent to which Justices are apt to resort to "policy distortions" only if and when protracted conflicts between the Justices and stable, Rooseveltian-type majorities erupt.

Indisputably, institutional design and the Court's ability to sustain strategic partnerships go a long way towards explaining the relative success of judicial review in Bulgaria. Constitutional arrangements make it virtually impossible for a single political force to colonise the Court, and the implicit alliances which the Justices forged – with the presidency, the rank-and-file judiciary, and the journalist guild – solidified its position. But there is also one conjunctural factor in the story of the Court, a fluke which no serious commentator of Bulgarian constitutionalism should omit: the incredible luck in the choice of first Justices. Granted, this factor is hard to incorporate in parsimonious models that purport to explain the rise of independent courts – and yet without it accounts of the Bulgarian case will be incomplete. What matters most was not professional skills and intellectual brilliance – the single most important quality of the Justices during the crucial first years of judicial review was their loyalty to the new institution. Whatever their personal disappointments and political agendas, the individual Justices appointed to the Bulgarian Constitutional Court – and especially those who found themselves on the losing side – never publicly attacked their colleagues and never questioned the integrity of the process of judicial review. An alternative scenario is not hard to imagine. The fact that it did not materialise cannot be plausibly attributed entirely to factors related to institutional design, constitutional engineering and the democratic vision of the political class. What mattered most was *Fortuna*'s smile and the *virtu* of Bulgaria's first Justices.

If there is one way to summarize the Court's overall contribution to Bulgarian constitutionalism, it would perhaps be fair to say that through their actions, the Justices affirmed the idea and practice of what might be called *constitutionally resolved conflict*. This concept seeks to cover the analytical middle ground between concrete influences in particular cases and the immeasurable general effect on political and social mores. The emphasis falls both on "constitutionally" and "resolved." The former term seeks to distinguish constitutional adjudication from the two other dominant modes of conflict resolution available in a post-communist context: the Round Table model (ad hoc elite bargaining), and electoral competition. And the emphasis on "resolved" is intended to bring into relief the fact that political actors are becoming increasingly accustomed to the idea that once the Court renders its decisions, it is time to "move on" and not re-fight the legislative battles of the past. If it is true that "politics-as-peace stands and falls with legality" (as stipulated by Giovanni Sartori),[27] then one may safely assert that by articulating and implementing the notion of the constitutionally resolved conflict and by persuading other political actors to follow suit, the Court chased the ghosts of war away from Bulgarian politics.

3. IN LIEU OF A CONCLUSION: JUDICIAL REVIEW AND POSTCOMMUNIST POLITICS

The brief history of the Bulgarian Constitutional Court reveals a complex picture, one that cannot be easily straitjacketed in the ready-made categories that usually inform the prevailing genre in the study of post-communist constitutionalism. For example, "the democratic audit" whose main objective is to render a verdict regarding the quality of democratic practices (on the idea of "democratic audit," see Beetham, 1994), is particularly inapt as an analytical strategy.

None of the vices and sickening syndromes itemized in the literature on constitutionalism and the Rule of Law is conspicuously observable in the Bulgarian case. It bears little resemblance, for example, to what Max Weber calls "pseudo-constitutionalism" – a regime where the balance of power is tipped in favour of undemocratic forces, "emergency powers" are constantly invoked to justify encroachments upon basic rights, and the functioning of representative institutions is repeatedly obstructed.[28] It would be equally unjustifiable to apply to constitutional practices in Bulgaria Otto Kirchheimer's powerful metaphor of "the Rechtsstaat as a magic wall." According to the prominent German legal scholar, the core feature of systems hidden behind this wall is the lack of enforcement of basic rules:

"Whether available procedures are put in motion and whether legal rulings once obtained will be enforced or complied with has to be investigated ... Without making such an effort, a rule of law, resting only on the rhetorical availability of legal remedies, somehow resembles a modern house whose glass wall, the major attraction for all visitors, already stands, but whose wooden utility walls no one has bothered so far to build."[29]

---

27 Giovanni Sartori, *The Theory of Democracy Revisited*, Vol. I (Chatham: Chatham House, 1987), p. 246.

28 Max Weber, *The Russian Revolutions* (Ithaca: Cornell University Press, 1995).

29 Otto Kirchheimer, "The *Rechtstaat* As a Magic Wall," in Otto Kirchheimer, *Politics, Law and Social Change* (New York: Columbia University Press, 1969), p. 430.

It is hard to identify on the Bulgarian landscape political forces determined to trample constitutional norms underfoot and the Court has successfully stepped in its constitutionally designed shoes of an "enforcer" of constitutional principles.

The major challenge presented by the Bulgarian case is to comprehend what might be called patterns of "patchy institutionalisation" and to use this knowledge as a starting point for a re-evaluation of the prospects of judicial review in post-communism. "Patchy institutionalisation" simply means that some domains of governance are more amenable to regulation through the creation of legal rules and conventions than others. This – admittedly not very profound – insight may enable us to recognize *both* the fact that various democratic and constitutional procedures, including judicial review, are functioning rather well, and the undeniable reality of Bulgaria's protracted descent into the abyss of economic and social crises in the early and mid 1990s. The Bulgarian experience shows that there is nothing in the creation of a viable Constitutional Court that renders this task inherently more difficult than the establishment of, let us say, an independent Central bank, a functioning system of ordinary courts, corruption-free administration, and efficient bureaucracy. Moreover, I would even venture the opinion that, given the historical peculiarities of post-communism as a historical episode, the task of launching a Constitutional Court may in fact be among the easier ones. My interpretation of post-communism – obviously presented here in a truncated and very stylised form[30] – will explain why much feared massive violations of rights and recrudescence of authoritarian practices did not materialize, and why at the same time most East European societies remained strapped in the clutches of seemingly insurmountable socio-economic malaise. My account rests on a novel understanding of the nature of predatory action and the meaning of "arbitrary power" in the aftermath of the demise of state socialism.

Historically, the independent courts rose as an institution which mediated the large scale process of extraction of resources by powerful agents. During the early modern period, when the major issue was the taxation of the propertied classes, courts regulated the relations between princes and aristocrats. Gradually, with the rise of democracy and the modern taxing state, judicial institutions were entrusted with the more comprehensive authority to monitor the relations between citizens and governments. Thus, historically as well as institutionally, the Courts were designed to hold in check the activities of political elites which either sought to change unilaterally established configurations of power, or to prey upon the population. The rise of the rule of law, then, may be linked to an attempt to restrain particular forms of extraction which affected relatively powerful social groups and were perceived as unjust.

---

[30] For a fuller treatment of the issues raised here, see Venelin I. Ganev, *Preying on the State: Political Capitalism After Communism*, Ph.D. Dissertation, Department of Political Science, The University of Chicago, 2000.

The nature of predatory action under post-communism is entirely different. The object of extraction is the state itself. Power is measured by the ability to hijack state held assets – not the capacity to control the meagre resources of "civil society." The extraction of resources takes place in the administratively defined "space" encompassing the management of state owned enterprises, banks and other agencies possessing residual rights over state property, in other words a "space" which rarely intersects with the proper domain of judicial review. This is a phenomenon which – building upon Benjamin Constant insightful observation that "arbitrary power tends to multiply itself in order to seize new objects"[31] – I have called "the displacement of arbitrariness". Arbitrary power no longer threatens the bodies and property of citizens, but is targeted instead at the material and organizational resources accumulated by the state.[32]

One of the implications of the displacement of arbitrariness is that judicial review will be tolerated by predatory power holders because it does not interfere directly with their strategies for extraction. The Court's greatest strength, then, may have been its irrelevance in the eyes of those who had the power to destroy it. And its chance may have been that the new virtuosos of arbitrariness considered the domain of judicial review as by and large marginal to their strategy for enrichment through extraction from the state. Given the peculiarities of the structural and organizational legacy of state socialism, large-scale looting of the national wealth is perfectly compatible with a half-hearted acceptance of the basic principles of constitutional adjudication. To the extent that it is observable in a post-communist setting, what might be called "judicial heteronomy" – or the negation of "judicial autonomy" – is not an attribute of the relationship between politicians and the Constitutional Court, but a characteristic of the "weakened" post-communist states, a feature of the radically inefficient infrastructure of governance. It is no paradox, then, that at the end of the 1990's Bulgaria emerged as a consolidated, constitutionally governed democracy with a devastated economy and a stolen future.

More than two centuries ago Jean-Jacques Rousseau, yet another famous Western expert hired by an East European nation to help with the designing of a new constitution, described the predicament which he faced: "Now, it is possible to enlighten someone who is mistaken; but how can you restrain someone who is for sale?"[33] It seems to me that the same conundrum has emerged two hundred years later, when East European societies once again embark upon the highway

---

[31] Benjamin Constant, "The Liberty of the Ancients Compared to That of the Moderns," in: *Constant: Political Writings* (Cambridge: Cambridge University Press, 1988), p. 324.

[32] See Venelin I. Ganev, "Bulgaria's Symphony of Hope," *The Journal of Democracy* 8 (October 1997), pp. 149–150.

[33] Jean-Jacques Rousseau, "Considerations on the Government of Poland," in *Rousseau: Political Writings* (Madison: The University of Wisconsin Press, 1986), p. 192.

which is expected to lead them to the much coveted "normality" of the West, a "normality" graced by the institution of judicial review.

The Bulgarian experience shows that we should re-evaluate the conventional way in which the set of related problems related to constitutionalism and the Rule of Law is cast in the context of post-communist studies. More often than not, the issue is formulated in the following way: is it possible to transplant Western institutions and practices in a different socio-cultural setting? It would be better, I would suggest, if the East European experience motivated us to rethink the limits of the idea of the Rule of Law itself. Rather than enlightening uncivilised nations, the challenge seems to be to explain why many of the problems of these industrialized, educated, complex societies cannot be solved even though judicial review is undeniably a fact of life? Debates about the alleged transplantability of institutions and compatibility of "local" and "Western" value orientations are more likely to lead us into an analytical *cul de sac* than an improved understanding of what hopes and expectations should, or should not, be pinned on the rise of constitutional practices. Such approach will make us more knowledgeable about political dynamics in both East and West. It will also help us traverse the uneven landscape of post-communist polities without succumbing neither to facile hopes nor utter despair.

11. The Experience of the Polish Constitutional Court

Leszek Lech Garlicki

1. THE ESTABLISHMENT OF THE POLISH CONSTITUTIONAL COURT

Judicial review was unknown to the Polish constitutions before World War II and naturally it could not be developed in the period of Soviet domination. Thus, when the process of transformation began, in 1980, in Poland there was no tradition of constitutional justice to refer to.[1] And yet the idea of setting up a constitutional court[2] emerged immediately after the establishment of the "First" Solidarity" in the spring of 1981. Without getting into the details of a rather complicated course of events,[3] one should be aware that after Martial Law was imposed in Poland, an amendment to the Constitution (of 26 March 1982) provided for the establishment of two new courts: a Constitutional Court (hereafter 'CC') and an Impeachment Court (*Trybunał Stanu*). This decision was followed by three years of controversy over the final architecture of the Constitutional Court which was finally settled by the Constitutional Court Act of 29 April 1985. In November 1985 judges of the first bench of the CC were appointed and the new CC issued its first judgement in May of 1986.[4]

Thus, the establishment of the CC preceded the final collapse of the Communist system of power. Not surprisingly therefore, the competence and jurisdiction of the CC was the product of compromise and differed from west European models. The most important limitation related to the legal effects of CC judgements, which, in respect of nonconformity of statutes to the Constitution, were not final but were subject to consideration by the Sejm (the only chamber of Parliament at this time) which could reject them by a two-thirds majority. All the same, in

---

[1]   There existed a tradition of administrative courts, and it was not a coincidence that the proposals of the Polish legal doctrine concentrated on reconstruction of such courts (L. Bar, J. Łętowski, S. Zawadzki, M. Wyrzykowski), which eventually led to the establishment of the Supreme Administrative Court in 1980.

[2]   Although its official name is the 'Constitutional Tribunal' (in Polish the word *Trybunał* means a particularly important court), the name Constitutional Court would be more appropriate and comprehensible, hence the use of the term 'CC' in this study.

[3]   Z. Czeszejko-Sochacki, "Przebieg prac nad utworzeniem polskiego Trybunału Konstytucyjnego" ["The Course of Work on the Setting up of the Polish Constitutional Court"], *Przegląd Sejmowy*, 2 (1994), no. 3, pp. 22–75.

[4]   R. Machacek, Z. Czeszejko-Sochacki, "Die Verfassungsgerichtsbarkeit in der Volksrepublik Polen", *Europaische Grundrechte Zeitschrift*, 16 (1989), pp. 269–276.

Wojciech Sadurski (ed.), Constitutional Justice, East and West, 265–282
© *2002 Kluwer Law International. Printed in Great Britain.*

its first years of existence the CC developed an interesting case law concentrating, above all, on relations between statutes and legal acts by the executive, and clearly limiting the freedom of legislative activity of the executive branch.[5] Matters of broader political significance did not appear at that time, partly as a result of a rather short list of actors that could initiate the proceedings before the CC.

Substantive change became possible only after the systemic transformations that began in 1989. The Act of 1985 was amended to remove some of the limitations of the CC's powers and jurisdiction. However, the amendments lacked consistency, for up until 1997, the Sejm retained its power to reject the CC judgements on the unconstitutionality of statutes. A fundamental change to the political context ushered in a sizeable increase in the importance of the CC, as political pluralism led to the public appearance of many controversies, which tried to find their way to the Constitutional Court – more or less successfully. Crucially, however, there was no new Constitution in Poland until 1997, and the constitutional amendments adopted in the meantime did not solve many important questions. Thus, a certain "constitutional deficit" emerged, and the jurisprudence of the CC did much to fill the gap, independently modifying the old constitutional regulations and creating many new rules and principles of constitutional rank. Particularly creative was the interpretation of a clause of "state-ruled-by-law" (Rechtstaat), which appeared in the Constitution in December of 1989, and the interpretation of the principle of equality before the law.[6] All in all, several hundred judgements were issued between 1989 and 1997, often in relation to issues of such importance as relations between the President and the other branches of power,[7] religion as a subject of instruction in public

---

[5]   L. Garlicki, "Constitutional and Administrative Courts as Custodians of the State Constitutions – the Experience of East European Countries", 61 *Tulane L. Rev.* 1285 (1987) and "Constitutional Developments in Poland", *Saint Louis Univ. Law Journal*, 13 (1988), pp. 713–736. For other opinions *see* S. Frankowski, "A Comment on Professor Garlicki's Article", *id.* at 737 *et seq.*

[6]   *See* more M.F. Brzeziński, L. Garlicki, "Judicial Review in Post-Communist Poland: The Emergence of a Rechtstaat?", *Stanford Journal of International Law*, 31 (1995), pp. 13–59; G. Brunner & L. Garlicki, *Verfassungsgerichtsbarkeit in Polen* (Baden-Baden, Nomos Verlag, 1999), pp. 73–76; H. Schwartz, *The Struggle for Constitutional Justice in Post-Communist Europe* (Chicago-London, University of Chicago Press, 2000), pp. 49–74. See also my *Chroniques*, since 1986 published yearly in *Annuaire International de Justice Constitutionnelle* and presenting the jurisprudence of the Polish CC.

[7]   *See*, e.g.: (1) judgement of 26.01.1993 (U 10/92 – parliamentary factions), *Orzecznictwo Trybunału Konstytucyjnego (OTK)* 1993, part I, pp. 19–36 – for German translation *see* G. Brunner, L. Garlicki, above n. 6, at 161–178, for English translation see *A Selection of the Polish Constitutional Tribunal's Jurisprudence 1986–1999*, compiled by J. Oniszczuk (Warszawa, Trybunał Konstytucyjnyk, 1999), pp. 80–90; (2) judgement of 23.11.1993 (K 5/93 – the role of the Senate in the legislative process), *OTK* 1993, part II, pp. 376–392; (3) resolution of 10.05.1994 (W 7/94 – the competencies of the President of the Republic

schools,[8] abortion,[9] "lustration"[10] and the status of the electronic media.[11] The majority of judgements related to less spectacular matters – mainly fiscal, social and economic. Still, many of them had significant financial consequences, and occasionally brought charges that the CC was endangering the budgetary balance of the state.[12] Without any doubt, in that period the position of the CC as an important participant in the process of governing was stabilised. It also became obvious that this organ must be properly situated in the new Constitution.

During the work on the Constitution of 1997 there was, therefore, no doubt as to the preservation of the CC as a separate and independent judicial organ. There was no doubt either that it would not be possible to continue to maintain the limitations to its competence. Thus, although in parliamentary discussions there was an obvious fear of strengthening the CC excessively, the final outcome was positive for the Court, which acquired a position corresponding to western European standards. The most important changes included: the abolition of the Sejm's right to override the judgements of the CC; the introduction of the procedure for the constitutional complaint and granting the CC with the competence to rule on the question of conformity of statutes to international agreements.[13] This did not bring about any major revolution in the functioning of the CC. For, just as the Constitution of 1997 codified – to a large extent – the principles and rules rooted in the jurisprudence of the 1990s, so the judgements

---

of Poland in relation to the National Broadcasting Council), *OTK* 1994, part I, pp. 204–214; *see* G. Brunner, L. Garlicki, above n. 6, at 240–247).

[8] *See* judgements of: 30.01.1991 (K 11/90, *OTK* 1991, pp. 27–72) and of 20.04.1993 (U 12/92, *OTK* 1993, part I, pp. 92–129) – *see* G. Brunner, L. Garlicki, above n. 6, at 119–137 and 179–192; *A Selection ...*, above n. 7, at 45–52 and 90–99.

[9] *See* judgements of: 15.01.1991 (U 8/90, *OTK* 1991, pp. 134–141) and 28.05.1997 (K 26/96, *OTK* 1997, pp. 147–189) – *see* G. Brunner, L. Garlicki, above n. 6, at 113–118 and 273–278; *A Selection ...*, above n. 7 at 43–45 and 184–203; *Global Constitutionalism*, P. Gewirtz and J. Katz Cogan (eds.) (New Haven, Yale Law School, 1999), at 152–175.

[10] *See* judgement of 19.06.1992 (U 6/92), *OTK* 1992, part I, pp. 196–213; G. Brunner, L. Garlicki, above n. 6, at 146–160; *A Selection ...*, above n. 7 at 71–79, see also section III.5 of this study.

[11] *See judgements* of: 2.03.1994 (W 3/94, *OTK* 1994, part I, 154–164 – *see* G. Brunner, L. Garlicki, above n. 6, at 231–239; *A Selection ...*, above n. 7 at 308–314); 10.05.1994 (W 7/94 – see above, n. 7); 7.06.1994 (K 17/93, *OTK* 1994, part I, pp. 84–96 – *see* G. Brunner, L. Garlicki, above n. 6, at 240–247; *A Selection ...*, above n. 7 at 141–145).

[12] Especially in the context of the judgement of 11.02.1992 (K 14/91, *OTK* 1992, part I, pp. 93–148 – see *A Selection ...*, above n. 7 at 57–70) recognising the unconstitutionality of a retroactive introduction of a system of adjusting retirement pensions and wages to the level of inflation.

[13] *See* further, L. Garlicki, "La reforme de la juridiction constitutionnelle en Pologne", *Annuaire International de Justice Constitutionnelle*, XIII (1997) at 11–30. For the French text of the Constitutional Tribunal Act *see*: ibidem, at 839–858; for German text *see* G. Brunner, L. Garlicki, above, n. 6 at 337–356.

issued after 1997 referred broadly to the prior decisions, thus putting an emphasis on continuity.

2. SELECTION AND INDEPENDENCE OF JUDGES

The Constitutional Court is composed of fifteen judges (twelve until 1997), elected by the Sejm for a period of nine years (eight years until 1997). Before 1997, half of the composition of the CC was changed every four years.[14] According to the new Constitution, terms of office of the CC judges are treated individually, which will eventually eliminate the exchange of a large number of judges all at once.

The election of constitutional judges belongs exclusively to the first chamber of the Parliament – neither the second chamber (the Senate), nor the President of the Republic, nor other sections of the judiciary have any role in this decision. There is no doubt that the Sejm, as a political body, considers the elections of the CC judges to be important political decisions. The Sejm elects the judges by an absolute majority of votes with no less than half of the Deputies present. This means that the majority in the Parliament can influence the elections of the CC judges, and give precedence to the candidates of their preference. This is in fact the actual practice. From 1989–2002, twenty nine CC judges were elected: six in November 1989, six in November 1993, six in November 1997, four in November 2001 and the remaining seven nominations resulted from mid-term vacancies in the composition of the CC. In twenty seven cases the elected candidates were put forward by the groups belonging to the then parliamentary majority. Even though in most cases the opposition also proposed some candidates, they never received the required majority. This means that the majority parties, regardless of their political provenence, believed that they did not have to share decisions concerning appointments with the Opposition, and as this political behaviour turned into a custom it became increasingly apparent that each change of political configuration of the Sejm will be reflected in future appointments. Only two exceptions to this rule were observed – in 1995 and in 2001 the elected candidates were nominated by the UW (Union for Freedom), although this party was in opposition at that time. Similarly, in 1993, a judge appointed to the CC on Solidarity's recommendation in 1989 was elected as President of the CC by the SLD – PSL coalition. Such decisions, however, should be considered as exceptional.

---

[14] That is why in November of 1989, in 1993 and in 1997 six new judges were appointed. By coincidence each time the new nominations followed parliamentary elections. Let us remember that in 1989, elections led to the construction of a coalition concentrated around the cabinet of PM Tadeusz Mazowiecki, in 1993 – a coalition was formed by SLD (Democratic Left Alliance) and PSL (Polish Peasant Party), and in 1997 – a coalition of AWS (Solidarity Election Action) and UW (Union for Freedom, which left the coalition in the summer of 2000).

Although the election of the CC judges by the Sejm was perceived, above all, in political categories it did not make the Court's composition excessively political, nor did it polarise the positions of the judges. Three issues should be noted at this point. First, political alterations at the Sejm always make the composition of the CC a product of appointment decisions made by various majorities at various times. Consequently, therefore, a domestic *modus vivendi* must always be found.[15] Secondly, the law requires rather high qualifications for the CC judges (ten years of practice in a law profession, or a position of a professor of law), which eliminate politicians without experience in law. Thirdly, in practice, professors of law are the professionals most frequently appointed to the CC,[16] a fact, which, by its very nature, eliminates the existing divisions and emphasises common thinking patterns and problem solving. Therefore, neither the change of half of the composition of the CC in 1993, nor the appointment of six new judges in 1997, although coming after the elections lost by the previously judgement parliamentary majority, had any effect upon the general lines of the CC's jurisprudence.

Thus, it would be difficult to find any weighty problems ensuing from the fact that the election of a CC judge is – from the point of view of the Parliament – a political decision. Such is the nature of functioning of the Parliament. The threat to the proper functioning of the CC would only appear if the Parliament started to elect active politicians to that body. It could prove excessively difficult for them to detach themselves from their old party connections, and to understand the primacy of law over politics. In practice, however, such instances are rare.[17]

The CC is headed by its President and Vice-President. Until 1997, they were elected by the Sejm, thus making the CC more dependent on the Sejm. The new Constitution abolished this rule and introduced a system where the President and Vice-president of the CC are appointed by the President of the Republic,

---

[15] Which, to a great extent, depends on the Court majority's readiness to compromise. The level of such readiness is reflected by, among other factors, the number of dissenting opinions. If, from that point of view, the period of four years between December 1993 and November 1997 is compared with the period of three years between December 1997 and December 2000 it should be noted that in the first of these the justices wrote 47 dissents in 29 cases, and in the other – 45 dissents in 22 cases.

[16] In the period between 1985 and 2001 thirty six CC judges were appointed, including twenty four professors (five of them with a considerable experience in the profession of practising lawyer or judge), five judges, three prosecutors, two counsellors, and three persons with law experience of other nature. For information concerning the period 1986–1997 *see* G. Brunner, L. Garlicki, *supra* note 6 at 369–376.

[17] Between 1985 and 2001 there were three judges in the CC, who were former MPs. Their political activity, however, ended at least one term before their respective appointments. In addition there were also two judges who were MP at the moment of their election to the CC, while three other judges were deputy-ministers at the moment of their election (two of them had also been MP's in the past).

on recommendation of the CC itself. No later than three months prior to the expiry of the term of office of the President or Vice-president, the CC elects, from among its members, two candidates for a relevant office and submits them to the President of the Republic. It seems that the President is bound by that proposal in a sense that he cannot demand submission of other candidates. However, no problems have appeared in this respect as yet.

Since the choice is made from among the serving judges of the CC, the term of office of the President and Vice-President is determined by the period remaining to the completion of the nine year period for which they were elected as judges. According to the existing provisions, there is no possibility to recall the President or Vice-President, nevertheless, one cannot exclude that – in the case of sharp conflict – the CC would be allowed to apply to the President of the Republic for such recall. There is no doubt, however, that the President of the Republic has no power to take such a step on his own initiative.

The President (and, in his substitution, Vice-President) directs the work of the CC and has several significant powers. Nevertheless, after 1997 he lost three important prerogatives which could exert some influence on the jurisprudence of the CC. Firstly, the President lost the right to decide, at his discretion, which judge would be a rapporteur of the case (the existing law requires that the arriving cases are assigned to the judges in the alphabetical order of their last names). Secondly, the President was deprived of the right to determine the composition of the benches of three and five judges assigned to adjudicate in individual cases.[18] Already in the mid-1990s the practice of several benches sitting in permanent composition was established. However, today the principle of alphabetical order is compulsorily applied in the designation of subsequent benches of judges. Thirdly, a vote of the President is no longer a casting vote when the numbers of votes for and against are equal.[19] Indeed, Article 190 (5) states explicitly that judgements of the CC "shall be made by a majority of votes". Hence, in the event of equality of votes, the adjudication should be postponed.[20]

Independence of judges of the CC is widely guaranteed by law and, generally, it should be stated that the status of a judge of the CC is equivalent to that of a judge of the Supreme Court. Thus, a judge is irremovable[21] and is protected

---

[18] It should be recalled that most cases are decided by benches comprising of three or five judges, and the CC decides cases sitting in full bench only in matters of highest importance (see: Article 25 of the Constitutional Court Act 1997).

[19] Although the provisions have not envisaged such solution, it has been established in the practice of the CC in the early 1990s.

[20] It should be noted that most judgements are made by benches composed of three or five judges, therefore, there is no chance of equality of votes. However, problems may arise when the CC adjudicates in full bench and, due to the absence of one or several judges, the number of the judges has become even.

[21] Unless there is an extraordinary situation, i.e. a judge has been sentenced by a final judgement of a common court for committing an offence, or removed from office of a judge by a decision of a disciplinary court (such court is composed of the judges of the CC).

by immunity (that may be waived by the CC itself), and is entitled to a permanent salary. Judges of the Constitutional Court must not belong to any political party or a trade union, nor hold high public offices (e.g. a seat in Parliament). They are prohibited from engaging in other occupations which would compromise the performance of their judicial duties, although they may be employed as professors at public universities.

The prohibition against re-election to the CC may be considered as an important guarantee of the judges' independence, because it prevents them from soliciting favours of the Parliament and politicians. Following the expiry of the term of office, a judge of the CC, irrespective of his or her age, retires from office. Thereby, he retains the status of a judge and some privileges, but continues to have various obligations and limitations, including the prohibition against the performance of another legal profession. However, there is no obstacle for him to return to an academic career and, in practice, judges do perform some other State functions.[22] This may, obviously, encourage them to seek connections with politics before their leaving the CC, but this is rather a question of personal integrity and character.

In practice, the independence of CC Justices is respected. During the last decade, there were no instances of external pressure, or other threats to their independence, exerted by either politicians or the media.[23] I have no doubt that a judge, if he had really so wished, was able to decide the cases without any external pressure.

3. JURISDICTION OF THE CC – PROCEDURES FOR THE REVIEW OF CONSTITUTIONALITY OF STATUTES

The CC has jurisdiction to rule in respect of several types of matters, including the:

Consequently, such decision is taken within the scope of the judiciary, and with the observance of the due process of law. This has never happened in the history of the CC, however, there were three cases of vacancies due to the death of a judge, and three resignations from office (justified by state of health).

[22] Among the former judges of the CC were an MP (who has served two terms); a Commissioner for Citizens Rights (Ombudsman); and a member of the Monetary Policy Council and the Chairmen of the Legislative Council in the Prime Minister Office. Another former judge became a member of the European Court of Human Rights.

[23] Some problems appeared in the early 1990s when the CC was criticised as an institution for, among others, connections – through its membership – with the pre-1989 period. It is difficult to say whether this situation influenced judicial decisions of the CC (in that period several important cases were considered), but was reflected in one of the dissenting opinions (*see*: Judgement of 7 October 1992, U1/92, *OTK* 1992, part II, pp. 171–172, on abortion).

(a) review of norms, including, among others, examination of conformity of statutes with the Constitution;
(b) examination of constitutionality of the goals or activities of political parties (this may lead to liquidation of a party which has, e.g., violated the prohibitions resulting from Article 13 of the Constitution);
(c) settlement of competence disputes between central constitutional organs of the State (Article 189); and
(d) declaration of temporary incapacity of the President of the Republic to discharge the duties of his office (Article 131).

In practice, only the review of norms has any real significance, since only one judgement has been made so far in respect of constitutionality of political parties (it concerned the details of the statute of one party),[24] and as concerns the other two areas the CC has not yet had an opportunity to rule. It should also be noted that in Poland the CC has no jurisdiction in respect of impeachment (since that is the role of a separate Court of Impeachment) nor in matters concerning elections and referenda (since that is the role of the Supreme Court).

Judicial review of norms relates to:

(a) statutes which are examined for their conformity not only to the Constitution, but also to international agreements ratified on the basis of an accepting statute – the European Convention on Human Rights – being one of such international instruments;
(b) international agreements which are examined for their conformity to the Constitution (no judgement has been made in this respect as yet); and
(c) so-called "sub-statutory" enactments, i.e. any normative acts issued by central organs (above of all, regulations and orders issued by government organs) – they are examined for their conformity to the Constitution, to ratified international agreements, and statutes.

The review of norms relates only to regulations in force. Exceptionally, so-called preventive review is allowed (see *infra* in this section). Moreover, as a rule, a normative act which has lost its binding force may not be challenged before the CC. It is, however noteworthy that in practice the CC has made a distinction between the repeal of an Act and a complete loss of its binding force. It was recognised that if the repealed Act may still be used by courts to adjudicate in individual cases which appeared under that Act, then such Act has not entirely lost its binding force and, therefore, the CC may examine its constitutionality.[25]

The examination of a normative Act is based on the three criteria (Article 42

---

[24] Judgement of 8 March 2000, P 1/99, *OTK* 2000, p. 218 *et seq.*

[25] In 2001 the CC is the issue of constitutionality of some provisions of the Decree of 1944 on Land Reform. The Court found that it had no jurisdiction in this case since the 1944 Degree had lost its binding force. Four judges dissented (judgment of 28 November 2001, SK 5/01).

of the Constitutional Court Act), the: (1) conformity of its contents to the Constitution (international agreement or statutes); (2) observance of the procedure required to issue a given normative Act; and (3) competence to issue a given normative Act.

In Poland, review of norms has mostly an *a posteriori* nature and relates to those provisions which have already come – and remain – into force. Exceptionally, the President of the Republic (and no one else) may initiate a preventive review in relation to:

- international agreements before ratifying them (Article 133(2) of the Constitution) (although such a case has not occurred as yet);
- statutes adopted by the Parliament, before signing them (Article 132(3) and (4) of the Constitution).

As a rule, the President has 21 days to sign a Bill, or he may exercise a veto against it (the Sejm may override a President's veto by a three-fifths majority of votes) or challenge it before the CC, claiming its unconstitutionality. Judgements of the CC are final. If a Bill has been judged as constitutional, the President is obliged to sign it, but if a Bill has been judged as unconstitutional, the legislative procedure (on such a Bill) is discontinued. If, however, the unconstitutionality relates only to particular provisions of a Bill, and the Court does not decide that such provisions are not inseparably connected with the whole Bill, the President has a choice: to sign the Bill with the omission of the unconstitutional provisions or to return it to the Parliament for the purpose of removing the non-conformity.

Preventive review of Bills existed in practice before 1997 and exists under the rule of the present Constitution. In the majority of cases it affects Bills of political significance, to which the head of state has some objections. Therefore, the CC considers such cases sitting in full bench. Between 1 January 1998 and 31 August 2001, the CC considered the substance of 12 applications submitted by the President. Seven bills were judged as constitutional, four as unconstitutional in part, and one – unconstitutional as a whole.

4. *A POSTERIORI* REVIEW

A posteriori review can take one of the following three forms: (1) abstract review; (2) incidental review; or (3) constitutional complaint.

Abstract review is most often used to initiate proceedings before the CC. It related to 42 normative Acts in 1998, 34 in 1999, 46 in 2000 and 50 in 2001. The right of initiative is treated very broadly. It belongs to almost all constitutional organs of the State, and groups of (50) Deputies or (30) Senators, to local government units, trade unions and similar institutions, and also to churches and religious organisations. However, local government units, trade unions and churches may challenge only such normative acts which concern matters relevant to the scope of their activity.

In practice, among the most active initiators are: the Ombudsman (16 applications in 1998, 15 in 1999, 19 in 2000, and 14 in 2001); local government units (respectively, 10, 11, 13 and 15 applications); and trade unions (respectively, 14, 9, 13 and 16 applications). The Deputies are less active (respectively, 2, 3, 4 and 7 applications), while other entitled subjects have very seldom submitted cases to the CC. The preponderance of initiatives stemming from the Ombudsman, local government units and trade unions also determines the character of the cases considered. The number of politically significant cases is relatively small, whereas social, tax and administrative regulations are among the most often challenged.

Incidental review is connected with the initiative of courts. The right of such initiative belongs to any court which has doubts about the conformity to the Constitution (ratified international agreement or a statute) of any legal provision which is to be the basis of the judgement in the case pending before that court (the requirement of relevance). In practice, courts are cautious in applying that procedure, but a growing trend is noticeable. Three judgements were made in accordance to that procedure in 1998, compared to 9 in 1999, 16 in 2000 and 13 in 2001.

This is where the problem of division of competence between the CC and the ordinary courts manifests itself. For, although review of norms falls within the competence of the CC, not always does this court have a monopoly on such decision making. It is a long time since all other courts have been recognised as competent to examine "sub-statutory" enactments, i.e. all regulations whose legal status is below that of a statute. The jurisdiction of the courts and the CC is parallel here, however the effects of their judgements are different. The courts may only refuse to apply a "sub-statutory" provision in a specific case, but this has only an *inter pares* effect. By contrast, the CC decides on the repeal of the provision, i.e. – with an *erga omnes* effect – eliminates it from the legal system. Any court hearing an individual case has a choice, whether to refuse, independently, to apply a "sub-statutory" provision or to refer a relevant question of law to the CC.[26] There are no substantial controversies in this field either in the doctrine or between the courts and the CC.

More complex is the examination of statutes regarding their conformity to the Constitution. The doctrine is dominated by the view that this is an exclusive competence of the CC. Hence, if a court adjudicating in an individual case has any doubts about the constitutionality of a statute, it must refer a relevant question

---

[26]   For example Resolution of a bench of seven judges of the Supreme Administrative Court of 21 February 2000, OPS 10/99, *Orzecznictwo Naczelnego Sądu Administracyjnego* (ONSA) 2000, item 90.

of law to the CC.[27] In the jurisprudence the attitude taken in this respect, particularly in the recent years, is not so unequivocal. In the view of the CC, ordinary courts may not independently refuse to apply statutes claiming their unconstitutionality.[28] The Supreme Court and the Supreme Administrative Court have shared this attitude,[29] but not unanimously, as one may meet with judgements where these courts independently refused to apply a statute without referring a question of law to the CC.[30] This is a serious problem which, in the future, may pose one of the basic threats to the role played by the CC, and to its relations with other courts.

The question of who (only the CC, or also the ordinary courts) is competent to rule on the non-conformity of statutes to international agreements has not been reflected in practice. Arguments presented for or against the CC's monopoly to adjudicate in respect of constitutionality of statutes may be appropriately referred to that question. Additionally, attention should be paid to the consequences of Poland's accession to the EU. As is well known, all courts are recognised as competent to adjudicate on the conformity of national statutes to the Community law, and the CC has no monopoly in this respect. Therefore, it would be difficult not to apply that principle in Poland, yet this would additionally emphasise the role of the ordinary courts and diminish the significance of the CC.

In Poland, the device of the constitutional complaint is framed narrowly,[31] as – in contrast to the German case – it may be lodged not against a decision made by another organ, but only against a legal provision upon which that decision was made. A constitutional complaint may be lodged by anyone (including aliens and legal persons) whose constitutional freedoms or rights have been violated by a final decision taken by a public authority. Hence, a constitutional complaint

---

27 A. Mączyński, "Bezpośrednie stosowanie konstytucji przez sądy" (Direct Application of the Constitution by the Courts), *Państwo i Prawo*, vol. 56 (2000), no. 5 and the references conned therein.

28 See, the judgement of 31 January 2001, P. 4/99, *OTK* 2001, at 71, and the judgment of 4 December 2001, *OTK* 2001 at 1339–1340.

29 *See*, e.g., judgement of the Supreme Court of 20 June 2000, I KZP 13/2000, *Orzecznictwo Sadu Najwyzszego. Izba Karna i Wojskowa (OSNIKW)* 2000, item 66; judgement of the Supreme Administrative Court of 27 November 2000, II SA/Kr 609/98 (not published).

30 *See*, e.g., judgement of the Supreme Court of 26 May 1998, III SW 1/98, *Orzecznictwo Sadu Najwyzszego. Izba Administracji, Pracy i Ubezpieczeń Społecznych* 1998, item 528; judgement of the Supreme Court of 7 April 1999, I PKN 648/98, *Orzecznictwo Sądów Polskich* 2000, item 172; judgement of the Supreme Court of 19 April 2000, II CKN 272/00 (not published); judgement of the Supreme Court of 26 September 2000, III CKN 1089/00 (not published). Also judgement of the Administrative Court in Gdańsk of 21 December 1998, I Aca 999/98, *Orzecznictwo Sądu Administracyjnego w Gdańsku* 1999, item 7.

31 See Brunner's distinction between "echte und unechte Verfassungsbeschwerde" (*See* G. Brunner and L. Garlicki, *supra* note 6, at 49–50).

may be based only on an alleged violation of the constitutional provisions concerning rights and freedoms (other constitutional provisions and provisions of international agreements do not provide such a basis). There is controversy in the judicial practice as to whether or not such complaint may be based exclusively on the alleged breach of the principles constituting the system of government (e.g. the principle of the state ruled by law or the principle of equality[31a]). To this end, an actual breach of any of such rights or freedoms must occur. A constitutional complaint may be lodged only in connection with a final decision in the case, hence, the complainant must first exhaust all available means of appeal. A constitutional complaint is subject to a preliminary examination as to its admissibility; at this stage it is possible to reject a complaint if it is manifestly unfounded.

As constitutional complaints are always lodged against legal provisions, they initiate the procedure to review norms, and the legal effects of the judgements are identical to the effects of those issued under the procedure of an abstract or specific review.

In practice, constitutional complaints have become visible, but they give only a limited chance for success. In 1998, 168 constitutional complaints were submitted for preliminary proceedings, compared to 185 in 1999, 200 in 2000 and 181 in 2001. Nevertheless, more than 80% of complaints were rejected in these proceedings. Judgements on the substance were made in respect of 5 complaints in 1998, 18 in 1999, 27 in 2000 and 26 in 2001. In 13 cases the CC shared the complainant's view and found the contested provisions to be unconstitutional. It is still too early to formulate final opinions, but it is not unlikely that the CC applies too restrictive an approach to the selection of constitutional complaints. At the same time, however, one may notice a considerable growth in the number of cases which have found final conclusions on their substance, and identify at least several complaints which related to matters of great social or political significance.[32]

5. UNCONSTITUTIONAL PROVISIONS

In around one third of submitted cases, the review of norms ended in finding the provision under examination to be inconsistent with the Constitution (international agreement or statute). In view of a relatively large number of rejected applications, this means that, as far as the decisions on the merits are concerned,

---

[31a] In the judgment of 25 October 2001 (*OTK* 2001 at 1142) the Court declared that a complaint based exclusively on the breach of the principle of quality was inadmissible. Five judges, however, dissented.

[32] *See*, e.g., complaint SK 18/99 (8 November 2000, *OTK* 2000, pp. 1255–1281), where constitutionality of the provisions allowing paid education in public establishments of higher education was stated; complaint SK 10/99 (4 December 2000, *OTK* 2000, pp. 1459–1485), where the proceedings in respect of one of the provisions of the Vetting Act were discontinued.

unconstitutionality was found more often than conformity to the Constitution. In 1998, the CC gave 50 judgements in *a posteriori* reviews, in which it found 15 examined provisions to be in conformity to the Constitution, 14 to be inconsistent (wholly or in part) with the Constitution, and in 21 cases the proceedings were discontinued. In 1999–61 judgements were made, in which constitutionality was confirmed in 19 cases, unconstitutionality was found in 28 cases, and in 14 cases the proceedings were discontinued. In 2000, in 84 judgements the CC found constitutionality in 24 cases, unconstitutionality in 28 cases and in other 28 cases the proceedings were discontinued. In 2001, in 94 judgments the CC found constitutionality in 42 cases, unconstitutionality in 34 cases and in the other 28 cases the proceedings were discontinued.

The weight of the provisions found to be unconstitutional varies considerably. However, in each of these years decisions on unconstitutionality of provisions of high political importance can be found. Three examples are worth noting.

The first example relates to the provisions on the so-called 'regulated rent'. Under the Act of 1994, in certain privately-owned houses tenants paid the same rent as those in municipal communal houses, in the amount fixed by local government authorities. When it turned out that, in practice, such rent does not cover all costs of maintenance of the buildings, the Supreme Court formulated the question of law, challenging the conformity of those provisions with the constitutional protection of property. In its judgement of 12 January 2000,[33] the CC shared that position and held that the provision on regulated rent ceased to have effect in relation to privately-owned houses. Aware of the consequences of that judgement for several hundred thousand tenants, the CC postponed its coming into force for 18 months, suggested that within that period the legislator should make a new law, and even indicated the general outline of such regulation. No matter how the legislator meets this obligation, rents will increase considerably, which will have serious social consequences.

The second example relates to the provisions on succession of agricultural holdings. According to the principle applied in Poland since the mid-1960s, agricultural holdings may be inherited only by the successors who currently run those holdings, or have farming qualifications. Other successors were excluded from inheritance. Despite the changes in the system of government, the above mentioned provisions were still in force, causing numerous conflicts, and resulted in the Supreme Court referring a question of law to the CC. In the judgement of 31 January 2001[34] the CC held that the said provisions, as a whole, were inconsistent with the constitutional guarantee of the right of succession, but this decision was limited to successions opened after the publication of that judgement. However, as concerns former successions it was held that the protection of acquired rights, and security and safety of legal transactions have supremacy.

---

[33] P 11/98, *OTK* 2000, pp. 30–56.

[34] P. 4/99, above, n. 28, pp. 42–73.

Thus, the direct effects of determining unconstitutionality of the above mentioned provisions were limited, and – for the future – one of the relics of the old agricultural system was removed.

The third example concerns vetting matters appearing under the Act of 1997. The Act imposes obligation on persons performing superior functions in the State, and those involved in legal professions, to formally declare whether or not they had collaborated with the security services in the period of Communism. Such declaration had no legal consequences (but was subject to publication), making a false declaration, however, deprived the person in question of the office or post held. Any instance of making a false declaration had to be determined in the course of special judicial proceedings resembling those of criminal procedure. The Vetting Act aroused many controversies which, sometimes, found their way to the CC. The first application, made by a group of Deputies, claiming unconstitutionality of the Act was rejected (with one dissenting opinion) because of the expiry of the Parliament's term of office.[35] Subsequent applications were made by the Deputies of the new term of office and by the President of the Republic. In judgements of 21 October 1998[36] and 10 November 1998[37] the CC held (but only by a majority) that the basic regulations of the Vetting Act are in conformity to the Constitution. Among others, the Court rejected the allegations that the Act breached the prohibition against self-incrimination, and that the definition of "collaboration" was insufficiently precise. However, applying an *interpretation conforme* technique, the CC formulated a detailed concept of 'collaboration', thus completing a vague statutory regulation.[38] This allowed the initiation of the vetting process. Nevertheless, subsequent events emphasised numerous defects of the existing provisions. In 2000, when considering a question of law submitted by the Vetting Court, the CC found one of the provisions of the Act to be unconstitutional, and refused at the same time (with four dissenting opinions) to respond to the question of how the presumption of innocence should be applied in the vetting proceedings.[39] On the other hand, the CC rejected (with five dissenting opinions) the constitutional complaint which challenged the rules of publication of declarations confirming the collaboration, and the range of circumstances in which such collaboration had taken place.[40] In consequence, the Ombudsman made his application in the same matter and,

---

[35] Judgement of 12 November 1997, K 27/97, *OTK* 1997, pp. 416–421.

[36] K 24/98, *OTK* 1998, pp. 507–532.

[37] K 39/97, *OTK* 1998, pp. 542–581.

[38] This limited the scope of instances where a declaration of "collaboration" was required and, two years later, a similar attitude was taken in the jurisprudence of the Supreme Court (judgement of 5 October 2000, II KKN 271/00, *OSNIKW* 2001, item 15), excluding instances of "appearances of collaboration".

[39] Judgement of 14 June 2000, P 3/00, *OTK* 2000, pp. 683–704.

[40] Judgement of 4 December 2000, above n. 32.

this time, the CC will certainly be compelled to take a position. Generally speaking, 'vetting matters' demonstrated both the CC's reluctance to interfere in matters of great political significance, and the radical differences in this respect among the judges.

6. LEGAL EFFECTS OF JUDGEMENTS

Legal effects of the judgements are currently arranged in the manner adherent to international standards. Let us remember that until 1997 all of the CC judgements of unconstitutionality of statutes were subject to consideration by the Sejm which had the power to reject them. Such rejection required a two-thirds majority of votes, the same as was necessary to amend the Constitution. When that solution was drafted in 1982, it meant a complete subordination of the CC to the Sejm, as it was not difficult to secure a two-thirds majority of votes in the political circumstances of that period. The change came in 1989 when, due to the pluralistic structure of the Sejm, the votes of the opposition had to be obtained in order to reject the judgement of the CC. At the same time, legal provisions have not specified the effects of a situation where the Sejm was inactive, i.e. failed to accept or to reject the judgement of the CC. Sometimes, in consequence of such a lack of response from the Sejm, judgements of the CC were not executed and unconstitutional statutes still remained in force. It was not until the end of 1993 that the CC ruled that the unconstitutional statute ceases to have effect after six months of inactivity of the Sejm.[41] From then on, the Sejm had to obtain a two thirds majority of votes to reject the judgement. In the practice of 1986–87, the Sejm rejected the judgements of the CC in 8 instances. In view of 72 judgements of unconstitutionality of statutes in the discussed period, the Sejm interfered with slightly more than 10% of all these judgements.[42]

In the course of debates on a new Constitution there was no doubt that the inconclusive character of judgements of the CC could not be maintained, as that substantially departed from the European standards. Nevertheless, those who opposed the strengthening of the CC's position, managed to carry two solutions. The first of them introduced a transitional period (until 17 October 1999) to prolong the power of the Sejm to reject certain judgements of the CC. This has

---

[41] Resolution of 20 October 1993 (W 6/93, *OTK* 1993, part II, pp. 495–509 – *see*: the translations in: G. Brunner and L. Garlicki, above n. 6, pp. 193–201; *A Selection* ..., above n. 7, pp. 299–308.

[42] For more see L. Garlicki: "Das Verfassungsgericht und das Parlament. Die Zurückweisung von Entscheidungen des polnischen Verfassungsgerichtshofs durch den Sejm" in M. Hofmann/H. Kuepper (Hrsg.): *Kontinuität und Neubeginn. Staat und Recht in Europa zu Beginn des 21. Jahrhunderts (FS Brunner)*, Baden-Baden, Nomos Verlag, 2001, pp. 357–364.

been criticised by the doctrine, but during that period the Sejm exercised its power in this field on three occasions.[43] The second gave an opportunity to postpone (for up to 18 months) the commencement of a judgement of unconstitutionality of a statute, thus permitting a temporary preservation of that statute in the system of law (Article 190(3) of the Constitution). The intention of the authors of that solution was to protect a budgetary balance, as they feared that the immediate enforceability of judgements concerning social or taxation matters would destroy the State budget and, therefore they wanted to adjust the State's finances to cope with such a challenge.[44] However, in the practice of recent years there were no judgements with so serious financial consequences, whereas the postponement of commencement of a judgement of the CC was applied mostly to avoid lacunae in the law and to enable the legislator to issue new regulations. As the CC itself decides on the postponement of the commencement (of a judgement), it would be unreasonable to treat such an arrangement as imposing a limitation on the independence of the CC.

Generally, judgements of the CC come into force immediately. A legal provision found to be unconstitutional ceases to have effect on the day of an official publication of the judgement in the Journal of Laws [*Dziennik Ustaw*] Judgements of the CC are conclusive and have universally binding force, whereas the loss of binding force by an unconstitutional provision means that it may no longer be applied by the courts. At the same time, an obligation is imposed on the Parliament to adopt new legislation. Theoretically, one can imagine a repeated adoption of a Bill of similar content. However, this would constitute an infringement of the Constitution. The President would certainly challenge such Bill before signing it, and the CC would not hesitate to invalidate it. But nothing like that has happened as yet.

In practice, various forms of 'interpretative judgements' where the CC, finding a statute to be constitutional also determines its interpretation, are relatively well developed. In the view of the CC, such an interpretation is binding upon other courts, although various conflicts and doubts do arise.[45]

Irrespective of a 'macro' impact of the judgements of the CC on further operation of the examined legal provisions, they also have a 'micro' impact in relation to individual decisions taken in the past on the basis of unconstitutional provisions. According to a general rule, such individual decisions retain legal effect, but may be subjected to a review upon request by their addressees. The scope and consequences of such review are specified by particular judicial procedures which, as a rule, provide an opportunity to reopen the proceedings, whereas

---

[43] *Ibid.* pp. 365–367.

[44] In particular, Judgement K 14/91, above n. 12, was recalled in this respect.

[45] Z. Czeszejko-Sochacki, "Orzeczenie Trybunału Konstytucyjnego: pojęcie, klasyfikacja i skutki prawne (Judgement of the CC: Notion, Classification and Legal Consequences)", *Państwo i Prawo*, vol 56 (2000), no. 12, and literature referred to therein.

civil procedure in particular, puts a considerable accent on protection of acquired rights of the third party. Hence, the enforcement of a judgement of the CC is conferred on common and administrative courts.

7. CONCLUSIONS

During fifteen years of its existence the Polish Constitutional Court has been stabilised and has become a permanent element in the system of law protection. The CC was shaped in 1985–89, during the era of Communist rule and the experiences achieved at that period provided a valuable asset in the reality of a new system of government (1989–1997). At that time the role of the CC manifested itself in several main dimensions.

Firstly, like its counterparts functioning in other "new democracies", the CC contributed (through its jurisprudence) to the creation of foundations of a state ruled by law (*Rechtstaat*), including, among others, transposition into Poland of the constructions and standards typical of western constitutionalism. This has imposed many limitations on the legislator and often has aroused controversies, but, step by step, it has started to bear fruit, and both the Parliament and government have become accustomed to the rules characteristic of a modern state ruled by law.

Secondly, a similar process took place in relation to international law, in particular, the European Convention for Human Rights. Even if the jurisdiction of the CC was subject to various limitations, the Court has greatly benefited from the practice of the European Court of Human Rights.

Thirdly, the characteristic feature of the Polish CC was that, due to the delays in the process of drawing up a new constitution, the jurisprudence of the CC had to fill many gaps and adapt the old text of the Constitution to the needs of the transformation. Hence, even if the results were not always satisfactory, the Constitution of 1997 might be treated as a sign of continuation of the basic outlines of the adjudication policy of the CC, which served as reference for further judgements of the Court.

Fourthly, the nature of the process of systemic transformation determined the nature of matters referred to the CC – they related mostly to economic, taxation and social regulations. Thus, the problem of consequences of the CC judgements for state finances always manifested itself very distinctively. In this context, it was much easier to rule in respect of political and civil rights, however, such matters have been seldom referred to the CC. Moreover, a large proportion of the cases related to resolving of the leftovers of the old system (e.g. vetting, screening of judges, "decommunisation", ownership issues, settlement of trade unions' accounts). It was not easy to reach a consensus on those matters within the CC, as the relatively frequent dissenting opinions testified.

Fifthly, the practical realisation of those tasks required a considerable dose of judicial activism reflected in a relatively high number of judgements of unconstitutionality of statutes. These, in turn, provoked occasional conflicts with the Parliament, although only in a few cases the Parliament managed to exercise its power to reject the judgements of the CC. On the other hand, in respect of matters of the utmost political significance (e.g. abortion, religion, vetting), a cautious, if not a conservative, approach dominated in the CC, irrespective of any changes in its composition.

The experiences presented above provide a background for the present phase of the functioning of the CC, already under the rule of the new Constitution (1997–2001). That period did not bring about any substantial reevaluation and, as already shown, one may speak about the continuation by the CC of the basic outlines of its adjudicative policy. Moreover, there has been no decline in judicial activism, the democratic state-ruled-by-law clause is still applied expansively, and the percentage of judgements of unconstitutionality of statutes remains high. The above is especially interesting in view of the fact that since 1997, for the first time in the past twelve years, a significant majority of the CC judges have been appointed by the judgement parliamentary majority. And although this situation was, to some extent, reflected in the jurisprudence of the CC, and the Constitution was interpreted more conservatively, it did not bring about any review of previous judgements. On the other hand, it helped the CC to improve its coexistence with the Parliament, as the Court supported the majority of important statutes. Time will show, whether this trend will continue after 2001 when, in view of a change of the parliamentary majority, new stimuli to raise the CC's adjudicating activism may appear.

Nevertheless, it does not seem that this may cause any threats to the functioning of the Polish CC, as both the Court itself and the Parliament have learned to shape their mutual relations. All the same, more serious problems may arise concerning relations between the CC and other segments of the judicial power, in particular the Supreme Court. This results from two significant problems, still unresolved. On the one hand, not all the courts are ready to recognise the CC's monopoly on adjudication of unconstitutionality of statutes. If the Supreme Court's tendency to independently refuse to apply a statute was to become established, the role of the CC would be undermined, and its position weakened. On the other hand, it is not clear to what extent the interpretation of statutes fixed by the CC (when adjudicating on their constitutionality) is binding on the ordinary courts. This creates potential conflicts which also endanger the future of a state-ruled-by-law in Poland. It should be noted that in any possible conflict with the Supreme Court, the CC is the weaker side, as constitutional complaints are narrowly framed in Poland. Thus, the CC is unable to impose its position on other courts, and its role is limited to the level of practising persuasion.

12. The Romanian Constitutional Court: In Search of its Own Identity

Renate Weber

1. INTRODUCTION

More than ten years have passed since the Romanian Constitution was adopted and almost the same time has passed since the establishment of the Constitutional Court. This is a Court which possesses both the power to review legislation *in abstracto*, regardless of any particular litigation (the abstract review), the review of laws after their adoption but before their promulgation, and the power to exercise judicial review by means of exception of an Act in the process of deciding a particular case to which this legal act applies (a concrete review). Has this been a long enough period to assess its role over the political and legal life of the country? Has the Romanian Constitutional Court got a place of its own? Are its decisions recognized, accepted and observed by everybody? Has the Court influenced the legislative process or the activity of the judiciary? If yes, what are the sources of this power? If not, what are the arguments against its authority, what are the consequences and how this issue should be addressed? These are just a few of the questions to be answered in relation with the activity of the country's most important institution guaranteeing the observance of the Fundamental Law.

Surprisingly enough, the main issues related to the Constitutional Court's powers on concrete reviews have been raised only after several years of activity. During its first six years or so, the Court's decisions were rather ignored, largely due to the judges' lack of knowledge. At that time only a few legal scholars wrote about it, most often former judges of the Constitutional Court itself. The practice was therefore split: while very few local courts constantly applied its decisions, the vast majority either were not even aware of them or simply considered them as not legally binding except the particular case to which the Act applied. During the last two years however a real debate has finally started involving several tribunals, the Supreme Court of Justice included. The number of articles written by practitioners and legal scholars of various backgrounds analyzing the specificity of the Constitutional Court and its decisions' binding force has increased considerably. And although currently one could speak about a real confrontation between the Constitutional Court and other tribunals, particularly the Supreme Court of Justice, the debate in itself is much better

Wojciech Sadurski (ed.), Constitutional Justice, East and West, 283–308

than the silence and ignorance that have characterized the beginning of this decade. One cannot but hope that clarification will follow either through practice or through constitutional amendments.

On the other hand, when discussing the powers of the Constitutional in relation to *a priori* review and how its decisions have been perceived by the Parliament and the public, one can fairly state that it has been rather mixed. The Court is occasionally regarded as being of a political nature, therefore its decisions are considered politically motivated, whilst in many other instances the members of the Parliament or the Supreme Court of Justice refer to the Court as to the genuine legal protector of the Constitution.

2. WHY A CONSTITUTIONAL COURT?

One of the first questions raised at the beginning of the 1990s, during the drafting of the Constitution, regarded the institution responsible for the constitutionality of laws. The country's history was, among other things, invoked. Since 1866 Romania has constantly had written constitutions whether of a democratic or dictatorial type. However one could hardly speak about a "constitutional tradition" in the sense of observing the country's most important law. This was the case including the 1923 Constitution which at that time was considered quite advanced, since it proclaimed the separation of powers and the supremacy of the fundamental law, and guaranteed fundamental rights. Non-observance of the constitution was true for the inter-war regime, but was most obvious during the Communist regime, which implicitly denied written rules and tolerated frequent abuses perpetrated by the political leadership and its secret police. Many laws contradicted the letter and the spirit of the constitution and were enforced without any real scrutiny.

During the adoption of the 1991 Constitution the issue of the constitutional control was therefore considered the most important means to prevent or challenge parliamentary and governmental abuses and, not surprisingly, it was among the most debated choices of the Constitution. Although the necessity of such scrutiny was never questioned, the debate on which institution should exercise it was more heated than on any other option of the current constitution. Two types of arguments were brought during the debate, based on Romania's own traditions, and the examples offered by other (European) states.

Before 1991, two kinds of constitutional control were known. In the pre-Communist tradition, for a few decades, this concrete control was exercised by the Court of Cassation and Justice. In fact, the Romanian Court's power to check the constitutional compatibility of legislation and government acts was secured at a time when in Europe it was rather unusual to have such control. In the *Bucharest Tram Company Case*, quite famous at that time, the Court ruled that although the Constitution did not mention explicitly, the right to constitutional control of the laws belonged to the judges, this power being originated in the judges' sovereign right to enforce the law, primarily the Constitution. It is to be noted however, that this was only concrete control and did not consider abstract control. During the Communist regime the constitutionality of the laws was theoretically exercised by an autonomous Commission set-up by the country's Great National Assembly. In practice, however, this Commission had no powers of its own, being – as the legislature itself – under the total control of the Communist Party. It was this particular experience that was emphasized after 1991, that 'the mere announcement of the constitutional control over the laws is not enough. It must be accompanied by procedural guarantees: the publicity and contradictory nature of the debates, the right to defense and last but not least the citizen's access to these procedures'.[1] Since this commission was of a political nature, the Romanian inter-war tradition – namely the judiciary nature of the constitutional control – was emphasized.

However, the architects of the 1991 Constitution made a different choice, to a large extent influenced by some European models, establishing a distinct institution of a political and legal nature, the Constitutional Court, which is not part of the judiciary, but a distinct authority. This institution has been granted the right "to adjudicate on the constitutionality of laws before promulgation" [Art. 144(a)] as well as the right "to decide on the exceptions brought to the Courts of law as to the unconstitutionality of laws and (governmental) orders" [Art. 144(c)]. By the time of its establishment the criticism of this option stressed the contradiction of its dual nature and emphasized the dangers that may originate: "it appears as a political-jurisdictional hybrid in a paradoxical logical frame – since it has a political nature it means that we should expect interpretations and decisions determined or influenced by the political factor, which is against the idea of justice; however if it is a jurisdictional body why is it outside the judiciary system, the only one which guarantees and is efficient regarding the impartiality principle?"[2] Although such criticism has its value, it seems that it ignores the legal culture of a country. In a state that abides by the rule of law it may very well be the case that, although of a semi-political nature, either the political factor does not attempt to put pressure on the Constitutional Court or its judges (members) know how to resist to and discourage the political influence whenever it occurs. Their 'duty of ingratitude' towards those who appointed them has been stressed.[3] The opposite may well occur in a country

---

[1] Adrian Vasiliu, 'Curtea Constitutionala, locul si rolul ei in statul de drept' [The Constitutional Court, its Place and Role within the Rule of Law] *Revista Romana de Drepturile Omului* [Romanian Review on Human Rights], 2 (1993), p. 23.

[2] *Ibid*, at p. 26.

[3] Doru Cosma, 'Hotărârea Curții Constituționale nr. 1/1996, accesul la justiție și exigențele art. 6 CEDO' [The Constitutional Court Decision No. 1/1996, Access to Justice and the Requirements of Article 6 of the European Convention of Human Rights], *Revista Română de Drepturile Omului*, 13 (1996), pp. 15–23.

such as Romania, and although according to the Constitution, other laws and practical arrangements, the judiciary is independent, there are a lot of allegations of the courts being directly or indirectly influenced by political factors. The tradition of judicial independence as part and parcel of the legal culture is extremely important.

However, apart from the influence of some European models, one must admit that some local pressure influenced the decision of establishing a Constitutional Court as well. Firstly, one has to note that in 1991 when the Constitution was adopted, the ruling party at that time had more than 70% of the seats in the Parliament (which also played the role of a Constitutional Assembly) thus controlling the entire process.[4] Having in view the very tense political climate at that time one has to admit that the independence of an institution exercising the constitutionality control was not animating the process of constitutional engineering. Secondly, although may seem trivial, it is important to note that all the experts who were members of the Constitutional Drafting Committee (and among whom none was a judge) had in mind the possibility to become judges at the Constitutional Court. Before the adoption of the Constitution only one such member made a declaration in the Parliament that he would not accept to become a constitutional judge.[5] In fact at different moments in time all of them became judges of the Constitutional Court.[6]

3. POWERS AND *SUI GENERIS* PROCEDURES

According to Article 144 the Romanian Constitutional Court was granted two categories of power:
- on constitutional control of laws, parliamentary regulations and governmental orders to:

    (a) adjudicate on the constitutionality of laws, before promulgation;
    (b) adjudicate on the constitutionality of the Parliament internal regulations;
    (c) decide on exceptions brought to the Courts of laws as to the unconstitutionality of laws and (governmental) orders;
- on other issues where specific constitutional provisions must be observed, to:
    (a) supervise the election of the President and confirm electoral results;

---

[4] According to the 1990 Law on Parliamentary Election which also provided for the procedure for the adoption of the Constitution, a majority of two thirds of the Constitutional Assembly was required.

[5] In 1995 however he accepted to be appointed as a judge at the Constitutional Court, although he resigned after a couple of years, before the completion of his mandate.

[6] For example, the requirement of minimum 18 years of either legal activity or academic activity in law faculties for a judge was introduced to suit all the members of the drafting committee.

  (b) consider the circumstances allowing the ad-interim exercise of presidential function;

  (c) give its opinion on the suspension of the President;

  (d) supervise the referendum and confirm its result;

  (e) make sure that the conditions for citizens' legislative initiative are observed;

  (f) decide on complaints related to the constitutionality of a political party.

The Constitution also provides for the mechanism of bringing a law before the Constitutional Court. When it is about the constitutionality of the laws before their promulgation, the complaint may be made by: the President of the country; one of the two Speakers of the two Chambers; the Government; the Supreme Court of Justice; no less than 50 Deputies; no less than 25 Senators; or the Constitutional Court itself on reviews of the Constitution.

In case of constitutional control of Parliament's internal regulations, the complaint may be made by: one of the two Speakers of the two Chambers; a parliamentary group; no less than Deputies; or no less than 25 Senators.

In case of exceptions brought before a court of law, the procedure is provided for by Articles 23–25 of the Law on Constitutional Court No. 47/1992, as amended in 1997. The exception may be raised by: one of the parties of the trial or the court itself.

One of the problems related to the powers of the Court is raised by Law No. 47/1992, which states in its Article 1 that the Constitutional Court is the only authority that has constitutional jurisdiction. This is indeed the case in regard to laws before promulgation or promulgated laws by means of exception, as well as governmental statutory orders by means of exception. It does not, however, apply to government decisions or other acts adopted by ministers or other public authorities which may be controlled only by the ordinary courts of law in concrete cases brought before them.

In terms of the procedure employed by the Constitutional Court it must be mentioned that it changed during the years in order to make the two types of reviews identical. While abstract review has always been decided by the Plenary of the Court, the concrete review was different between 1992 to 1997. The Law 47 of 1992 mentioned that on cases brought by means of exception the Court decided in a panel of three judges as a first level court and in a panel of five judges as an appeal court, the right to appeal being exercised by any of the parties. Since this procedure led to some serious inconsistencies, the Court decided to interpret its own internal regulation as allowing a sort of an extraordinary appeal against its own decisions. Article 26(2) of the Constitutional Court Regulation mentioned that whenever either a panel of three judges or a panel of five judges wanted to have a different legal interpretation than the interpretation of the Plenary of the Court or than the interpretation provided for by a final decision of one of the Court's panels, the Plenary must be asked to decide with a simple majority upon the interpretation which would afterwards become mandatory.

In 1993 several cases were brought before the Constitutional Court challenging the constitutionality of some articles from the Penal Code such as embezzlement, stealing and cheating all regarding the "public patrimony", the punishment in such situations being much more severe than in the case of private property. Initially in eight such cases three different judicial panels ruled on the inconsistency of these provisions with the Constitution. The General Prosecutor appealed and a panel of five brought together all these cases and by means of Decision No. 38 of July 7, 1993[7] overruled the initial decisions. It is interesting to note that out of those five judges only three took this decision, the other two having a dissenting opinion. Briefly, the new decision considered that since "after December 1989 the number of crimes against the public patrimony increased", particularly the criminal activities against the patrimony of those old "state companies", it was not appropriate to give up a higher protection of those forms of property where the State was still the owner. This in fact implied a discriminatory protection of the property based on the ownership: the State versus the private sector including the individuals. Needless to say, the decision proved not to have an understanding of the distinction between the public property and the State's private property. Invoking the provisions of its Regulation, the Plenary of the Court issued the Decision No. 1 of 7 September 1993 striking down the previous one and declaring the above mentioned articles to be abrogated by Article 150 of the Constitution insofar as they applied to other forms of property than exclusively public property.[8]

In 1996 the Court held that it could not rule on any procedural inconsistencies of its own decisions, although the Civil procedure code allows for this option, thus creating the impression that the Court is above any law since there is no other jurisdiction above the Constitutional Court.[9] In fact, following the example of other Romanian institutions, the Court's tendency during the years to give itself more power that the Constitution provided for had become obvious. In response, in 1997 the law on the Constitutional Court was amended and all the cases brought before the Court are to be decided by two thirds of the Plenary of the Court, thus making curbing the Court's practice of deciding twice or even three times on the same issue. Another reason for this amendment was also to eliminate the unfair discrepancy between the *a priori* (abstract) control of the laws done by the Plenary of the court and the *a posteriori* (concrete) control

---

[7] Decision No. 38 of 7 July 1993, *Monitorul Oficial al României* [The Official Gazette of Romania], Part I, No. 176 of 26 July 1993.

[8] Renate Weber, 'O stranie decizie a Curtii Constitutionale' (An Odd Decision of the Constitutional Court), *Revista Română de Drepturile Omului*, 2 (1993), pp. 44–48.

[9] Cosma, above n. 3; 'Constituționalitatea candidaturii Președintelui Ion Iliescu', *Revista Română de Drepturile Omulu*, 13 (1996).

realized firstly by a panel of three judges and in appeal by a panel of five judges.[10]

4. THE JUDGES OF THE CONSTITUTIONAL COURT

The process of appointing the constitutional judges is clearly influenced by the political nature of the Court. Article 141 of the Constitution provides for the conditions of nomination: "The judges of the Constitutional Court must have legal education, high professional capability and at least 18 years of either legal activity or teaching activity in law faculties." Those who meet these requirements may be appointed according to Article 140(2) as follows: three by the President; three by the Senate; three by the Chamber of Deputies. Their mandate is for a nine years period and it may not be prolonged or renewed [Article 140(1)]. Article 143 explicitly mentions that in the exercise of their mandate the judges of the Constitutional Court are independent and may not be removed from office during the mandate. The Constitution also mentions that being a judge at the Constitutional Court is incompatible with any other public or private function with the exception of teaching in law faculties (Article 142).

In fact, the only judges who are simply appointed are those chosen by the President. In the other two cases, their appointment implies a political bargain within each Chamber of the Parliament since they need to be voted. The Law 47 from 1992 mentions that the nominations are made by the Steering Committees of each Chamber with the recommendation of each Legal Commissions. The quorum to take such action is a simple one and the nominee who gets the highest number of votes is appointed [Article 17(4)]. However one must admit that the political agreement has always been applied and the judges were appointed observing the algorithm of the parliamentary structure.

According to Article 140(3) after their appointment the judges secretly elect, with a three year mandate, the President of the Constitutional Court. Neither the Constitution nor the Law on Constitutional Court says anything on the possibility to prolong or renew this mandate, which implies that a re-election is possible but so far the practice has been that after each three year period a new president is elected.

Over the years the political character of the Court has been brought to the public attention due to some decisions when allegations have been made on the political bias of the Court, particularly the President's influence. Such was the case of the decision on the law regulating the restitution of nationalised houses or on President Iliescu's possibility to run for a new mandate in 1996. However

---

[10] Mihai Constantinescu, 'Modificarea procedurii de soluționare a excepțiilor de neconstituționalitate' [On changes brought to the procedure to be used on concrete cases of unconstitutionality], *Dreptul*, 11 (1997), pp. 19–20.

the number and the substance of such claims has considerably decreased in recent years.

5. A SOFT COMPETITION WITHOUT ANY WINNER: THE CONSTITUTIONAL COURT AND THE PARLIAMENT

Article 145 of the Constitution reads as follows:

(1) In cases of unconstitutionality, in accordance with Article 144 letters a) and b), the laws or (governmental) orders shall be returned for reconsideration. If the law is passed again in the same formulation by a majority of at least two thirds of the members of each Chamber, the objection of unconstitutionality shall be removed and promulgation thereof shall be binding.

(2) Decisions of the Constitutional Court shall be binding and effective only for the future. They shall be published in the Official Gazette of Romania.

These provisions must be corroborated with those of Article 51 which says: "The observance of the Constitution, of its supremacy and of the laws is binding."

While the constitutional articles regarding the establishment and the functioning of the Constitutional Court seem to demonstrate its role in checking the power of other public authorities,[11] namely of the Parliament and the Government, Article 145 gives the impression of diminishing its role. If a law is declared unconstitutional before promulgation it is returned to the Parliament for reconsideration. However, if passed in the same way in both Chambers by a two-thirds majority the law is considered adopted and must be promulgated. Which means that in such cases the President, who in principle has the right to veto once any law, may no longer exercise this right. "If the two third majority cannot be obtained the law will be sent for promulgation without the provisions declared unconstitutional, and if the unconstitutionality regards the entire act, the law will no longer be sent for promulgation."[12]

The Constitution does not address this contradiction and this exchange of powers between the Court and the Parliament has not been seriously analyzed by legal scholars. One could however identify some reasonable explanations for this choice. One might be that the Parliament is the representative authority of the people, while the Court is an independent body of a dual nature. Another explanation might be the fact that a two-thirds majority is sufficient to amend the Constitution. Therefore, when the Court decides that a certain law or

---

[11] The Romanian Constitution does not use the term "state powers" but instead it employs the notion "public authorities".

[12] Gheorghiță Mateuț, 'Conținutul jurisdicției constituționale și implicațiile ei asupra procesului penal' [The Substance of Constitutional Jurisdiction and Its Effects on Penal Court Case], *Dreptul* [The Law], 2 (2000), p. 36.

provision is unconstitutional and the Parliament still wants to adopt it, this is an implicit amendment to the Constitution. However there is a strong argument against such a practice: Article 147 requires a referendum to approve any constitutional review. If the Parliament is entitled to pass the laws declared unconstitutional by the Court it implicitly amends the Constitution avoiding the referendum.

One of the main problem regarding the constitutional control of the laws before their promulgation has been to convince those entitled to petition the Court to pay attention to the constitutionality of a law. Generally a law is brought before the Constitutional Court before promulgation on political interests rather than on constitutional grounds. This is the main explanation why in most of the cases there were the political parties' parliamentary groups of Senators or Deputies who exercised this right. The Supreme Court of Justice and the Government exercised this right only in a few cases while the two speakers have not used this right so far. As a result several obviously unconstitutional laws have been passed and are enforced. In general terms every time when a political party feels offended by a certain law or some of its provisions it uses the threat of challenging the law before the Constitutional Court, in order to obtain their removal. By far most such threats have been employed on acts related to the linguistic rights of national minorities, whether they are domestic laws or international treaties requiring ratification.

During its entire activity the Constitutional Court has found less than thirty laws as unconstitutional. According the Constitution and the Law 47 of 1992 the Constitutional Court may only declare a law or a specific provision constitutional or unconstitutional. It may not give recommendation to the Parliament how to rule nor may suspend its enforcement until the Parliament would amend that provision. However it has been the Court's practice to rule on "constitutionality with an interpretation reservation clause"; that is to say that the Court provided for how a law must be interpreted in order to be constitutional. Therefore in most of the cases the challenged provisions were not declared unconstitutional but rather "constitutional in so far as they observe ..." one article or another of the Constitution. Such decisions have been perceived as representing the Court's effort to respond to a political demand which has undermined the credibility of the Court and its perception as an independent institution. In fact they have produced more confusion on those laws, since the interpretation of the laws throughout their enforcement belonged to ordinary persons who were neither aware of these findings nor enough sophisticated to apply. Such was the case of the Decision 49 of 17 May 1994 on the Law on Agricultural Income Tax,[13] regarding the facility offered to former state agricultural enterprises transformed in commercial companies, challenged as violating

---

[13] Decision No. 49 of 17 May 1994, *Monitorul Oficial al României*, Part I, No. 125 of 21 May 1994.

the principle of equality between the different types of property. The court considered that exempting these companies from paying the taxes was constitutional in so far as it did not apply to the land which by virtue of its nature cannot be cultivated or, for example, the Decision No. 72 of 18 July 1995 on the Law on education.[14] Article 9(1) of this law provided that "in primary school religion is a mandatory subject". The Constitutional Court ruled that this provision is constitutional only if Article 29(1) and (6) of the Constitution is observed, namely the right of the parents or of the tutors regarding the education of the children under their responsibility (although by religion it understood only the 15 religious denominations admitted by the authorities, excluding many neo-protestant religions). In the rationale of the decision however, in order to justify the constitutionality of this provision, the Court stated that the "mandatory requirement" regards the inclusion of religion within the school curricula, the religion and the confession remaining in parents' hands to be chosen or not. This rather illogical interpretation which merely wanted to save the law being re-discussed by the Parliament has a very simple explanation: the extraordinary pressure put on the Court by political factors and by media since the most controversial and contested provisions were in relation with education for minorities in their mother tongue. The Court ruled on the constitutionality of every provision regarding the study of or in mother tongue and did not dare to prolong the process of adoption by declaring Article 9(1) unconstitutional. It is interesting to note that in 1998 this law was amended and religion became a "mandatory subject" also in junior and senior secondary school. This time no one challenged this amendment, although the law was sent to the Constitutional Court on other grounds. It is true, however, that nor has this provision been enforced since!

However some decisions regarding the unconstitutionality of laws before promulgation have been very important. Unfortunately their publicity was rather non-existent, the MPs themselves not being interested to draw too much public attention. The media in turn does not pay too much attention to issues that are not considered sufficiently attractive; most often they do not follow nor cover the activity of the Court.

It is a paradox that although almost every Senator or Deputy signed at least one petition addressed to the Constitutional Court on constitutional control of laws, the Parliament as an institution generally has not accepted the idea that the decisions of the Constitutional Court are really mandatory. And although so far the draft laws declared unconstitutional were amended, in several instances the role and the competence of the Court was disregarded. The best example is the Regulations of the two Chambers. In 1994 two Decisions of the

---

[14] Decision No. 72 of 18 July 1995, *Monitorul Oficial al României*, Part I, No. 167 of 31 July 1995.

Constitutional Court[15] declared the unconstitutionality of no less than 39 provisions of the Senate Regulation and 28 provisions of the Chamber of Deputies Regulation. During some heated debates the two Chambers expressed their discontent for what they consider to be the interference of the Constitutional Court with their own activity and decision powers. It took more than three years to bring these two Regulations in line with the requirements of the Court. On the other hand the Law on the status of the Senators and Deputies, which contained a lot of extravagant life time privileges and immunities for the future ex-members of the Parliament and their families, was struck down entirely on procedural aspects, a decision that left many MPs annoyed.

Every time the political parties or members of the Parliament refer to the Constitutional Court it is not due to a genuine interest to find out what is the status of a law but rather as a means to validate their own opinions which most often have nothing to do with the Constitution. MPs' perception that the Constitutional Court should serve their interest was better noted in those instances when the speakers of the Chambers or individual MPs asked for the Court's opinion on issues related to the interpretation of the Constitution without any connection to a particular law, in a procedure which was not within the competence of the Court. However, on each such occasion the Court – in fact either the President of the Court or a group of judges – answered starting by saying that they were not allowed to make any comment since the Romanian Constitutional Court has not such powers but ended by giving their opinion on the issue discussed! Such contradictory behavior was not necessarily politically influenced but rather expressed the need of the Court to show its importance in the sense that its judges are the only ones who can give a professional authorized opinion (although not legally authorized since it contradicts the Court's statute). A sort of childish competition between the Parliament and the Court took place, without any winner, each institution wanting to prove and convince the public on its own legitimacy and credibility.

During the last couple of years this practice has stopped and so did the Court's tradition of recommending a certain interpretation of the law which it considered constitutional. Therefore its decisions on constitutionality have become much clearer. A few laws of a significant interest, such as the Law on Referendums, the Law on Ministerial Responsibility, the Law on Persons' Access to their Securitate Files, and the Law on the Status of Civil Servants were brought before the Constitutional Court by members of the Parliament and the Supreme Court of Justice in an obvious attempt to amend them on grounds other than constitutionality. They were either declared in harmony with the Constitution or the petition was rejected on procedural grounds.

An interesting ruling was the Decision No. 113 of 20 July 1999 on the Law

---

[15] Decision No. 45 of 17 May 1994 and Decision No. 46 of 17 May 1994, *Monitorul Oficial al României*, Part I, No. 131 of 27 May 1994.

allowing the Government to issue statutory orders during the parliamentary vacation.[16] Although the list provided some fifty domains to be regulated by the Government and afterwards submitted to the Parliament for approval, only two were taken to the Constitutional Court, both on mere political grounds. The first one regarded the establishment of an Agency on state territories and the Fund for agricultural development, the second regarded the ratification of the European Charter on Regional or Minority Languages, considered as ignoring and jeopardizing Romania's character as a unitary and national state, its official language, the independence of the judiciary, the administrative autonomy of local authorities and discriminating against the majority. In a well documented decision the Court explained that the provisions of the Charter are in accordance with Romania's Constitution. It is interesting to note that in January 2001, when those who challenged the Charter came into power, they used the same rationale as the Court and invoked the Charter's provisions in order to pass some amendments to the Law on local public administration regarding the use of minority languages.

6. A UNIQUE SITUATION: GOVERNMENTAL EMERGENCY STATUTORY ORDERS

The case of governmental statutory orders is unique in the region. According to the Constitution the laws adopted by the Parliament may only be sent to the Constitutional Court *before* being promulgated in order to be constitutionally screening. Article 114 of the Romanian Constitution[17] provides for a delegation of legislative powers to the Government in two situations: during the parliamentary vacation, based on a specific law, or; in case of emergency. In neither case are the statutory orders sent to the Constitutional Court before being adopted. But they do not escape from a constitutional control, as their review takes place at a later stage: either when the law adopting them is discussed by the Parliament and the control is the same as for any other law before promulgation or by

---

[16] Article 114 of the Constitution, on 'Legislative delegation' states: "(1) Parliament may pass a special law enabling the Government to issue statutory orders in fields outside the scope of organic laws. (2) The enabling law shall compulsorily establish the field and the date up to which statutory orders can be issued. (3) If the enabling law so requests, statutory orders shall be submitted to Parliament for approval, according to the legislative procedure, until expiration of the enabling term. Non-compliance with the terms entails discontinuation of the effects of the statutory order. (4) In exceptional cases, the Government may adopt emergency statutory orders, which shall come into force only after their submission to the Parliament for approval. If Parliament does not sit in a session, it shall obligatory be convened. (5) Statutory orders shall be approved or rejected by a law which must also contain the statutory orders that ceased to be effective in accordance with paragraph (3).".

[17] *Ibid.*

means of exception in individual cases. However, there is a major problem in this respect. These orders enter into force immediately after their publication in the Official Gazette and they have legal effects. Being declared unconstitutional later on and struck down raises a lot of problems in relation with the existing legal effects.

The situation is even more complicated in the case of emergency statutory orders. Article 114(4) states that "In exceptional cases, the Government may adopt emergency statutory orders, which shall come into force only after their submission to the Parliament for approval. If Parliament does not sit in a session, it shall obligatory be convened." In other words, although the Parliament is in session, the Government has an interest to regulate more rapidly and avoid Parliament. The experience of the last decade made very clear the difference between using a right and abusing or misusing it. Until the elections of November 1996, when one political party was in power, more than one third of the total regulations (laws) were passed by the Government through this procedure. The Opposition at that time made very severe reproaches not against the procedure as such but rather in respect of its abuse which was perceived as a means to avoid Parliamentary debates. Moreover, in 1996 the Government issued emergency statutory orders in the field of organic laws (which regulate specific, constitutionally listed domains considered by the Constitution to be of special importance; therefore the adoption procedure is different in that it requires half the votes of the total number of MPs, plus one; such as the law on political parties and some tax exemptions). This time, surprisingly enough, the whole political spectrum accepted this procedure, the explanation being that the Parliament was running out of time.

After the 1996 elections, the new government in power, made up by the former opposition, abused the right to issue emergency statutory orders. In 1997 alone it issued approximately one hundred such emergency statutory orders, in domains regulated either by ordinary laws or by organic laws and in spite of the fact that several political parties represented in the Parliament has expressed their protest. During the last three years although the number has decreased significantly it has still remained very high, difficult to be justified by exceptional cases as the Constitution requires.

The opinions of the Constitutional Court have been rather inconsistent on this aspect, proving that the judges themselves and the Court as a whole do not know how to act in response to political power and the Government's behavior.

On several occasions the Court has ruled on what an "emergency situation" entails. For example, by means of Decision No. 83 of 18 May 1998 in a concrete individual case regarding the Governmental Order No. 22/1997 amending the Law on Public Administration, which at that time was implemented for more than one year, the Constitutional Court decided that the statutory order was unconstitutional since no emergency situation justified its adoption as a governmental order instead of a law debated and adopted by the Parliament.

The aim of the Government was to issue a new regulation, directly enforceable, using a procedure that infringed the constitutional mission of the Parliament, as provided for by Article 58 of the Constitution as the country's exclusive legislative authority. As it was mentioned in the Court Decision No. 65/1995, published in the Official Gazette of Romania, Part I, No. 129 of 28 June 1995, the exceptional situation, on which the constitutional legitimacy of the statutory order is based, is justified by 'the necessity and the emergency to regulate a situation that, due to its exceptional conditions, commands an immediate solution in order to avoid a serious infringement of the public interest'.[18]

In 1999, the Court was asked to review the Law adopting the Emergency statutory order No 36/1997 amending the Law on Education. Among other things, the petition mentioned the unconstitutionality of the emergency order due to the absence of any emergency situation. In the rationale of its Decision No. 114 of 20 July 1999[19] the Court made ample comments on what an emergency situation is, noting that "consideration on what is the public interest must be done in relation with the time when the emergency statutory order was issued and not the time of the parliamentary debate over the law on its adoption or the time when such debate is finalized."[20] The Court took into account the Governmental program, which included special provisions on the acceleration of the reform of the education system, the need to amend the Law on Education before the new school year, and concluded that the emergency was justified. The fact that the emergency statutory order was directed towards a field regulated by organic laws[21] was not discussed.

However, in a more recent decision, the Court decided that the Order abolishing the state monopoly was unconstitutional by a tiny majority in a way that proved the judges' different views on the same matter. By means of Decision No. 15 of 25 January 2000[22] issued in an individual case, the Constitutional Court ruled on the Emergency statutory order No. 23/1999 abolishing the Law No. 31/1996 on state monopoly. This time the decision considered two aspects:

---

[18] Decision No. 83 of 19 May, 1998, *Monitorul Oficial al României*, Part I, No. 211 of 8 June 1998.

[19] Decision No. 114 of 20 July 1999, *Monitorul Oficial al României*, Part I, No. 370 of 3 August 1999.

[20] Due to the provisions on instruction in mother tongue and the possibility to set up universities in minority languages, the parliamentary debates on the adoption of the emergency statutory order amending the Law on Education lasted more than two years.

[21] Article 72 of the Constitution provides for the domains that must be regulated by organic laws, whose adoption procedure requires "the majority vote of the members of each Chamber", unlike ordinary laws which "shall be passed by the majority vote of the members present in each Chamber" (Article 74).

[22] Decision No. 15 of 25 January 2000, *Monitorul Oficial al României*, Part I, No. 267 of 14 June 2000.

the right to issue through emergency statutory orders in fields regulated by organic laws and the emergency situation as such.

On the emergency situation, five judges decided that the emergency order was unconstitutional, mentioning that there were no reasons to abolish the Law on State Monopoly avoiding the parliamentary debates, since no public danger could be identified whose interest would have required such an exceptional procedure. Four judges (including the President of the Court) issued a dissenting opinion stating that, unlike the previous cases, the right to consider a situation as exceptional belonged primarily to the Government. In support of this view they invoked Article 2(3) of the Law No. 47/1992 on the Constitutional Court according to which:

> When exercising the constitutional control, the Constitutional Court shall decide only on legal aspects ... Therefore, it is not within the Court's competence to control the existence or non existence of a *de facto* situation, as in the current court case, on the existence or nonexistence of 'exceptional situations'.

One cannot avoid raising the question if this was just a dissenting opinion, showing a change in the views of some of the judges, or it rather reflected the different ideologies of the judges since the real issue at steak was the elimination of state monopoly. It is true that in time several decisions of the Constitutional Court have proven a clear preference for the protection of state property (transformed into public property), sometime even discriminating against private property. Therefore it is legitimate to wonder if the above decision, having as its effect the persistence of state monopoly, was independent or influenced by such ideology. The answer is not clear yet, and it seems that the Court itself has to clarify its own relation with any ideology, in order to keep itself distant from any political influence, a process that may take quite some time.

On the possibility to regulate by means of emergency statutory orders the Court mentioned its previous constant jurisprudence, according to which "the interdiction for the Government to regulate in fields of organic laws concerns only the statutory orders that are adopted based on a special law enabling the Government to regulate, the interdiction being provided as such by the constitutional text." The Court mentioned however that "the possibility of the Government in exceptional cases, to adopt emergency statutory orders, in a limited manner, even in fields of organic laws, may not be considered as a discretionary right of the Government, and moreover this constitutional power may not justify the abuse of issuing emergency statutory orders. The Executive's possibility to govern by means of emergency statutory orders must be every time justified by the existence of exceptional situations which demand such urgent regulations." At the same time, in a distinct opinion, the former president of the Court disagreed on the issue of the fields that may be regulated by emergency statutory orders and concluded that the Government may not issue such regulations in the fields of organic laws. Among other things, in his opinion he expressed the disappointment regarding Article 114's lack of clarity which has been the source "of a dangerous governmental practice, of doctrinal arguments interesting although neglected, of controversial constitutional jurisprudence". Particularly, due to the fact that in reality "the adoption of emergency statutory orders has transformed itself from an exceptional constitutional solution into a customary rule, which looks like an avalanche beyond any control." It is interesting to note that although this decision was of the utmost importance through its consequences, it passed almost unnoticed and did not provoke any debate on the issues that were addressed. It is true however that the decision as such was published in the Official Gazette almost six months after it was adopted. Since the date of entering into force is the date of publication, it means that the Government was given a long period of time to make the necessary arrangements for the elimination of state monopoly.

7. THE CONSTITUTIONAL COURT AND THE JUDICIARY: AN OPEN CONFRONTATION

The largest part of the Constitutional Court's activity has focused on concrete control, in cases brought by means of exceptions. It is interesting to note how the legal community has built up its own capacity in this respect. In 1993–1994 such cases were brought mainly by some legal scholars. Later on more and more lawyers have raised exceptions on unconstitutionality and more courts send such cases to the Constitutional Court, often even taking the initiative. After the 1997 amendments to the Law on Exceptions practically every case when the issue of unconstitutionality was invoked is to be sent to the Constitutional Court.

Regarding the binding force of its decisions, Article 145(2) of the Constitution states: "The decisions of the Constitutional Court are mandatory and have legal power only in the future. They shall be published in the Official Gazette of Romania." For several years however, the Romanian courts have employed different policies: some applied the findings and the decisions of the Constitutional Court, while others ignored them, not necessarily as a desire to disobey them but rather due to their lack of information and expertise. Many judges have continued to perceive the Constitutional Court as a sort of *sui generis* institution, outside the scope of the judiciary and therefore not to be taken seriously. Not enough efforts were made on behalf of the Constitutional Court itself or the Ministry of Justice as to make the decisions better known by the judges. Nor was enough done to explain what the role and the place of the Constitutional Court was and what is the legal force of its findings. Judges were convinced that the decisions of the Constitutional Court taken in individual cases were mandatory only in those cases and did not apply in others, a view supported by some legal scholars.[23] This explain why so many cases were brought before the Constitutional Court on aspects that were previously decided by the Court. In other words, it has been considered that a specific legal provision could have a dual statute: unconstitutional in some cases and constitutional in others. The Constitutional Court's constant jurisprudence has held that its decisions have an *erga omnes* effect, based on Article 145(2) of the Constitution and that a provision declared unconstitutional may no longer be subject to another concrete review.

More recently several courts, among which the most prominent is the Supreme Court of Justice, have started a crusade against the Constitutional Court and the binding force of its decisions. The starting point was the Decision No. 60 of 25 May 1994 of the Constitutional Court which stated that,

> the final paragraph Article 149 of the Penal Procedure Code is unconstitutional insofar as it is interpreted as allowing the duration of pre-trial detention decided by a court during the trial to be more than 30 days without being prolonged in conformity with to Article 23 of the Constitution.[24]

In other words each court even during the trial may no longer consider the pre-trial detention as automatically prolonged but instead review the detention every 30 days until a conviction sentence is issued. Many courts have enforced this decision and have decided accordingly. Others considered that they were not bound by it. In the summer of 1999 such cases were brought to the Supreme Court of Justice and the contradiction resulting from this split practice was analyzed. The Supreme Court decided that the decisions of the Constitutional Court are not legally binding:

> ... the constitutional provisions do not directly address the judiciary organs which apply the ordinary law but only through the legislative body which has to comply with the Constitution and amend the ordinary laws [sic].

> The decisions of the Constitutional Court have the same status. They represent a reproach to the legislative body and this legislative body must draw its conclusions from this reproach, amending those provisions of ordinary laws that were criticized by the decisions of the Constitutional Court ..." If we apply another rationale it means that the law enforcement judiciary organs, not having a concrete provision in the ordinary law should refer to the constitutional text in order to reject the provisions criticized by the decisions of the Constitutional Court, which is inadmissible.

---

[23] Tudor Drăganu, 'Efectele juridice ale deciziilor şi hotărârilor Curţii Constituţionale' [The Legal Effects of the Constitutional Court Decisions], *Revista de drept commercial* [Commercial Law Review], 3 (1999), p. 34.

[24] Decision No. 60 of 25 May 1994, *Monitorul Oficial al României*, Part I, No. 57 of 28 March 1995.

The judicial organs enforce the ordinary law that applies and not directly the Constitution, the legislative body having the obligation to comply with the Constitution and the constitutional principles by amending the ordinary law in order to observe the Constitution.[25]

The same rationale was employed in other decisions as well:[26]

The judges who have to decide in a case as a first level court, in appeal or recourse may not however periodically review during the trial, each 30 days, the pre-trial detention of the defendant, enforcing directly Article 25(4) of the Romanian Constitution, as it has been stated by several decisions of the Constitutional Court (such as decision no. 546 of 4 December 1997) or as it results from the motivation of other decisions of the same Court.

By doing so, they practically would not anymore be subject only to the penal procedure provisions established by law but to some procedural norms ad hoc set-up by the Constitutional Court by means of interpretation Article 23(4) of the Constitution which set forth the principle that the pre-trial detention of a defendant may not be longer than 30 days.

Not obeying the norms of the Penal Procedure Code, which provide for the maintaining of the pre-trial detention of the defendant, the judges would infringe Article 123(2) of the Constitution according to which they are independent and subject only to the law.

At the same time, applying directly the provisions of the Constitution, they would make justice in the name of other normative provisions than those provided by the law, thus violating Article 123(1) of the Constitution according to which justice shall be rendered in the name of the law.[27]

According to the Romanian legal system the decisions of the Supreme Court of Justice are not binding on other courts. However, being the highest authority in the country it is very likely that many such cases will end up before it, therefore its views are taken into account by judges of lower courts. Currently the courts are split on this issue: some apply the decisions of the Constitutional Court (particularly on the review of the pre-trial detention by the courts each 30 days) while others do not. The immediate result has been that more than 1,000 defendants in pre-trial detention are still in prison, detained in those cases where the courts did not comply with the Constitutional Court's requirement, while others have been released because the courts applied the Constitutional Court's decisions. However there is also a long term consequence, namely the Constitutional Court's powers in relation with the judiciary. Recently the

---

[25]   The Supreme Court of Justice, Decision No. 1613 of 7 May, 1999.

[26]   The Supreme Court of Justice, Decision No. 3277 of 28 September 1999.

[27]   The Supreme Court of Justice, Decision No. 2531 of 17 June 1999.

Bucharest Court of Appeal issued a "non-paper" on this topic, addressed to the judges of Bucharest courts, clearly stating that it considered the Constitutional Court decisions not to be legally binding, a practice that was common during the previous regime, when independence of the judiciary was not an issue. Apart from the fact that such paper itself and the attempt to influence the judges run contrary to the Constitution, the fact remains that it was for the first time when the powers and the competence of the Constitutional Court were openly challenged and judges were instructed not to observe these decisions.

Other reactions have followed. Some legal scholars held up this view, trying to identify its sources in constitutional principles, while others stressed the binding force of all Constitutional Court decisions.

Those supporting the opinion that the judiciary is not legally bound by the decisions of the Constitutional Court stressed their *inter partes* effect, insisting that the lack of an explicit constitutional provision makes impossible to claim their *erga omnes* effect, the general binding force within the Romanian legal system being the exclusive attribute of the law.[28] Two main reasons were invoked: the constitutional principle that a law may be abolished only by the Parliament; and the possibility given to each party to a trial, and to the court itself, to raise the exception of unconstitutionality. The erga omnes effect would simply make this provision inapplicable. "Deciding on the unconstitutionality of a specific legal provision as a result of an *a posteriori* control does not justify ignoring the law as long as that law is still valid."[29] According to this view the only solution is the adoption by the Parliament of a law abrogating the act or the provision declared unconstitutional, a conclusion drawn also from the legal obligation of the Court to send its decisions on unconstitutionality to the Parliament and the Government.

> Therefore, judges are not allowed to directly apply the constitutional provisions ... as they are not allowed to apply the international provisions on human rights, as provided for by Article 11 and 20 of the Constitution, because they have to observe during the trial and for the protection of procedural rights of the parties only the existing legal procedural provisions.[30]

Accepting the possibility that judges "directly apply the Constitution and not being obliged to obey the provisions of the Penal Procedure Code would imply to accept that the judges do not make justice in the name of the law, as required

---

28 Tudor Drăganu, 'Efectele juridice ale deciziilor şi hotărârilor Curţii Constituţionale' [The Legal Effects of the Constitutional Court Decisions], *Revista de drept commercial*, 3 (1999), pp. 30–37.
29 Gheorghiţă Mateuţ, 'Conţinutul jurisdicţiei constituţionale şi implicaţiile ei asupra procesului penal' [The Substance of Constitutional Jurisdiction and Its Effects on Penal Court Case], *Dreptul* [The Law], 2 (2000), p. 45.
30 Ibid, at p. 46.

by Article 123(1) of the Constitution, which is inadmissible."[31] Since the main reason of this situation is the absence of a constitutional provision on the self-executing nature of the constitutional jurisdiction, the conclusion is that either an amendment to the Constitution or to the Law on Judiciary regarding the Courts' obligation to observe the decisions on unconstitutionality of the Constitutional Courts is needed. But even in such a case it is considered that applying the decision is under "the condition of a later approval of the Parliament, thus having legal effects upon this approval and not from the moment when the decisions were adopted in published in the Official Gazette."[32]

Another opinion is that the decision of the Constitutional Court declaring the unconstitutionality of a law is final and mandatory from the date of its publication in the Official Gazette, as provided for by Article 145(2) of the Constitution and Article 25(1) and (3) of the Law 47/1992 as amended and has legal effect only for the future. However, it does not have as a consequence the cessation of a law because the Court may not replace the Parliament. However, those legal provisions declared unconstitutional may no longer be enforced in the concrete case (*ex nunc* effect). Given that the unconstitutional norm is still valid, not being abrogated, the law requires the Court to send the decisions to the two Chambers of the Parliament and the Government in order to take the necessary legislative actions. This is considered to be a reason for a review of a concrete penal case which was decided based on legal provisions declared unconstitutional.[33]

Those supporting the Constitutional Court jurisprudence that its decisions have an *erga omnes* effect emphasize that this is the only solution for observing the principle provided for by Article 51 of the Constitution on its supremacy.[34] In other word the law is mandatory but within the observance of the Constitution.[35]

The Constitutional Court itself gave an answer to all these views in its Decision No. 186 of 18 November 1999.[36] In a concrete control of a provision of the Penal Procedure code, the Court analyzed two aspects:

---

[31] *Id.*

[32] Ibid, at p. 48.

[33] Gheorghe Dumitru, 'Rejudecarea cauzelor în care condamnarea s-a pronunțat pe baza unor prevederi legale declarate neconstituționale pe baza art. 26 alin. 2 din Legea nr. 47/1992' [The review of cases when conviction was based on legal norms declared unconstitutional according to Article 26 para 2 of the Law 47/1992], *Dreptul*, 4 (1996), pp. 51–56.

[34] Article 51 of the Constitution states: "The observance of the Constitution, of its supremacy and of the laws is binding.".

[35] Mihai Constantinescu, Radu Mares, 'Principiul neretroactivității legilor în cazul deciziilor Curții Constituționale' [The principle of non-retroactivity of laws on Constitutional Court decisions], *Dreptul*, 11 (1999), p. 87.

[36] Decision No 186 of 18 November 1999, *Monitorul oficial al României*, Part I, No. 213 of 16 May 2000.

(a) The obligation of the legal courts to directly enforce the provisions of the Constitution. The Court stressed the supremacy of the Fundamental Law as the source of the entire legal system, pointing out that those who refuse to directly enforce the Constitution pretending that they are bound only by the law, base their refusal specifically on the direct enforceability of other constitutional norms, Article 123(1) and (2) and Article 125. "This is to say that the Constitution itself forbids the direct enforceability of the Constitution or that the direct enforceability of the Constitution represents a violation of the Constitution which is illogical." At the same time the Court emphasized that some legal courts used the notion "law" in a wrong way thus concluding that the Constitution is not a law. Article 72 of the Constitution mentions the types of laws within the Romanian legal system: constitutional laws, organic laws and ordinary laws, the courts of justice having the obligation to observe all of them, not being allowed to select only the organic and ordinary ones while refusing to apply the constitutional laws.

(b) On the binding force of Constitutional Court's decision it was stressed that several articles of the Constitutions are relevant: not only Article 145(2), mentioning that these decisions are mandatory, but also Article 51, on the supremacy of the Constitution, and Article 16(1) according to which "Citizens are equal before the law and public authorities, without any privilege or discrimination." If the decisions of the Constitutional Court had no *erga omnes* effect the result would be to consider the same legal provision unconstitutional and therefore inapplicable in one case, but constitutional and enforceable in other cases, a situation that would obviously lead to discrimination.

So far the situation has not changed and although there are some initiatives to amend the Constitution the aspect described above has not been considered an issue.

8. THE CONSTITUTIONAL COURT AND CONSTITUTIONAL AND HUMAN RIGHTS

The Romanian Constitution has an impressive chapter on constitutional rights, civil, political, economic and social rights. In addition, two articles confer a special status to human rights documents.

Article 11 reads as follows:

(1) The Romanian State pledges to fulfil as such in good faith its obligations as deriving from the treaties it is a party to.

(2) Treaties ratified by Parliament, according to the law, are part of national law.

Article 20 states that:

(1) Constitutional provisions concerning the citizens' rights and liberties shall be interpreted and enforced in conformity with the Universal Declaration of Human Rights, with the covenants and other treaties Romania is a party to.

(2) Where any inconsistencies exist between the covenants and treaties on fundamental human rights Romania is a party to, and the internal law, the international regulations shall take precedence.

To these we must add Article 51: "The observance of the Constitution, of its supremacy and of the laws is binding."

It is interesting to note that discussions on the direct enforcement of the constitutional provisions, as well as on the status of international legislation into the domestic one did not take place during the drafting process – when the legal community seemed not to be interested by such 'details' – but afterwards. Although it seems to be evident that the Romanian Constitution adopted the monist principle according to which the human rights international legislation once ratified is included into the domestic legislation and directly enforceable, other opinions have been expressed on the significance of these provisions. Some scholars held that Article 20(1) was worded so as to express Romania's attachment to the Universal Declaration of Human Rights, a fundamental political document in the human rights field.[37] Other scholars consider that the reference to the Universal Declaration has no consequences, because the Declaration is merely a political document and not a treaty in the form provided by the international law.[38] Finally, a third opinion holds that by incorporating the Universal Declaration into the Constitution of Romania and making it compulsory for the interpretation of constitutional provisions relating to human rights, the former has acquired legal power in the Romanian domestic law[39] The most controversial as well as the most important matter, from a practical point of view, regards the precedence of international human rights regulations over domestic laws. The Constitution sets forth the pre-eminence of international law but leaves unsolved the issue of the relationship between international and constitutional legal norms. Could one hold that international regulations should take precedence even when they run counter to the Constitution? An opinion says that the Romanian authorities competent to negotiate and conclude treaties should examine the consistency of such treaties with the Constitution and that

---

[37] Gheorghe Iancu, *Drept constituțional și instituții politice* [Constitutional Law and Political Institutions] (Universitatea Ecologică, 1993), pp. 66–67.

[38] Dan Ciobanu, Victor Duculescu, *Drept constituțional român* [Romanian Constitutional Law] (Editura Hyperion XXI, București, 1993), pp. 87–88.

[39] Ioan Muraru, Mihai Constantinescu, *Drept parlamentar* [Parliamentary law] (Gramar, 1994), p. 203; Genoveva Vrabie, *Organizarea politico-etatica a Romaniei* [Romania's political organization and state structure] (Virginia, 1995), p. 442.

treaties which run against the Constitution should be ratified either with reservations and declarations or after the revision of the fundamental law.[40] According to another opinion,[41] the constitutional text in Article 20 is liable to criticism due to its vague wording. Moreover, the provision relating to the precedence of international regulations is regarded as difficult to enforce, because the Constitutional Court must pronounce only on the constitutionality of laws, not on the consistency between laws and international treaties.[42]

For practical reasons, it is important to explore what was the intention of the Constituent Assembly when Articles 11 and 20 were adopted, in order to understand the competencies of courts in connection with international treaties. Opinions are split in this respect. Some authors and practitioners hold that constitutional provisions moved away from the "traditional solution of enforcing international conventions at the internal level by means of the laws adopted on their basis" and established the "'self-executing' principle, according to which these conventions may be enforced directly, with no need for the screening of the law".[43] This is the most widely shared opinion.[44] Other authors however, hold that in the Romanian legal system the judge does not enforce international treaties directly, as it happens in the United States, for instance, because he is only entitled to enforce the internal laws of the state.[45]

Several practitioners stood up against such interpretation.[46] So far there is no established practice of Romanian courts other than the Constitutional Court in this field. But one must admit that this Court has paid quite a lot of attention from the very beginning to the enforcement of the constitutional rights as well

---

[40] Ioan Muraru, in *Constituţia României comentată şi adnotată* ([he Romanian Constitution with annotation and comments] (Regia autonomă "Monitorul oficial", Bucureşti, 1992), pp. 47–50.

[41] Nicolae Ecobescu, Victor Duculescu, *Drept internaţional public* [Public International Law] (Editura Hyperion XXI, Bucureşti, 1993), p. 59; Nicolae Ecobescu, Victor Duculescu, *Drept internaţional public* [Public International Law] (Editura Hyperion XXI, Bucureşti, 1993), p. 59.

[42] Dan Ciobanu, Victor Duculescu, *op. cit.* For critical opinions on this stand Renate Weber, 'Receptarea dreptului internaţional al drepturilor omului de către sistemul juridic român' [Human rights international law in the Romanian legal system], *Revista Română de Drepturile Omului*, 12 (1996).

[43] Ioan Muraru, Mihai Constantinescu, *op. cit*, p. 203.

[44] See also Doru Cosma 'Rolul instanšelor de judecatš în aplicarea Convenšiei europene a drepturilor omului' (The role of national courts in implementing the European Convention on Human Rights), *Revista Română de Drepturile Omului*, pp. 6–7 (1994).

[45] Nicolae Ecobescu, Victor Duculescu, *Op. cit.*, p. 59. See also Dan Ciobanu, Victor Duculescu, *Op. cit.*, p. 88.

[46] Renate Weber, 'România şi dreptul internaţional al drepturilor omului' [Romania and International Human Rights Law] in Thomas Buergenthal *Dreptul internaţional al drepturilor omului* [International Human Rights] (All, Bucharest, 1996), pp. 221–228.

as to the implementation of international human rights legislation. In 1994, immediately after the ratification of the European Convention on Human Rights, an investigation was conducted by the Human Rights Center in order to assess how prepared were the Romanian authorities to implement the Convention.[47] The Constitutional Court provided the most detailed and clear answers. Among other things, the President of the Court stated that "observance of the Convention is not dependent on the review of the legislation, since the Convention is directly enforceable.".[48] At the same time it was stated that "the logical relation between the European Convention and the Constitution must take into consideration how the European Convention has been interpreted by the European Court case law. Therefore, the Constitutional Court of Romania emerges as a jurisdictional authority which has not only the right but the obligation as well to base its own interpretation of the Constitution in a manner which will ensure the compatibility of domestic legislation with the Convention."[49] Afterwards, the Constitutional Court has been the only one which constantly has referred to the European Convention and stated its direct applicability. The case law based on the Convention encompasses more than 20 cases, some of them notably important for the Romanian legal system.

The first decision that invoked international treaties was the Decision No. 6/1993, when the Constitutional Court ruled out as unconstitutional the provisions of Law no. 58/1992 that stipulated different taxes for three categories of persons (taxes were increased by 30% for incomes resulting from multiple sources). The Court invoked and applied the provisions of Article 26 of the International Covenant on Civil and Political Rights referring to non-discrimination, Article 2 para. 2 of the International Covenant on Economic, Social and Cultural Rights and Article 14 of the European Convention on Human Rights. A few months later, the Court declared the provisions of Article 75 para 1 of the Labor Code unconstitutional by means of Decision no. 59/1994. According to these provisions, complaints filed against decisions to annul labor contracts as well as labor litigation relating to reintegration of managers in their former jobs were to be solved by the administrative body ranking higher in the hierarchy or by a collective leadership body. The Court referred to the violation of Article 16 of the Constitution on non-discrimination and of Article 21 on free access to justice and based its decisions on the provisions of Article 6 pt. 1 of the European Convention, on grounds that the administrative bodies that annulled the labor

---

[47] 'Ancheta Centrului pentru Drepturile Omului: Efectele ratificarii Conventiei europene a drepturilor omului asupra dreptului intern român' [The Center for Human Rights Investigation: the Impact of the European Convention on Human Rights upon Romanian Legal System], *Revista Română de Drepturile Omului*, 5 (1994.).

[48] *Ibid*, at p. 66.

[49] *Ibid*, at p. 67.

contract may not represent an independent impartial tribunal, as the Convention requires.

One of the most notable decisions was the Decision No. 81 of 15 July 1994 on the unconstitutionality of Article 200 para 1 of the Penal code that used to punish by prison terms same sex relations between consenting adults. The Court invoked the provisions of Article 8 of the European Convention, making reference to the European Court of Human Rights' case-law, in particular the Dudgeon, Norris and Modinas cases. However, this decision held that Article 200(1) "was unconstitutional insofar as it applies to sexual relations between same sex adults who freely consent and which do not take place in public nor do generate a public scandal." The Constitutional Court did not define the "public scandal" nor offered any suggestion on what this may be. Therefore, although more progressive, this decision made enough room for abuses. As expected the decision was accepted without any amendment in 1996 when the Parliament changed the Penal Code. Whatever a public scandal means is to be interpreted (and possibly abused) in each individual case.

By means of Decision 45 of 10 March, 1998, the Court referred to Article 3 of Protocol 7 to the European Convention of Human Rights in order to decide in a case regarding the compatibility between the constitutional provision on state responsibility for penal judicial errors and Article 504 of the Penal Procedure Code which limited this responsibility only to two situations, namely when the crime neither existed nor was committed by the defendant. The Court decided that Article 504 is constitutional only insofar as it does not limit State responsibility to those two cases it provided for.

Important was the Decision No. 85 of 3 September 1996 on the initiative of a group of parliamentarians to review Article 41(7) of the Constitution according to which "Legally acquired assets shall not be confiscated. Legality of acquirement shall be presumed." The initiators aimed at replacing this text with a new one stating "The assets whose legal acquirement cannot be proved shall be confiscated," a norm very similar to the existing one during the Communist regime when the presumption of illegality was the rule. The Court declared the initiative unconstitutional due to the fact that it aimed at the suppression of one of the guarantees of the right to property thus infringing the constitutional provisions of Article 148(2) on the limits of constitutional review which states that "No review may be accepted if it has as a result the suppression of the citizens' fundamental rights and liberties or their guarantees." The decision is important particularly since every three to four years Romania faces a new initiative to reintroduce the death penalty.

In spite of these well established practice, having regard to the opinions resulting from the above mentioned decisions of the Supreme Court of Justice and the legal literature supporting these opinions, one may wonder about the future of Article 11 and 20 as well. Since the Constitution is considered as not being directly enforceable, one may question how international treaties will be considered by the highest Court of the country as well as their precedence over some constitutional provisions that – according to the Supreme Court of Justice – may not be taken into account by the courts. So far, with some notable exceptions at the beginning of the 1990s the Supreme Court of Justice has refrained itself from invoking international treaties. And is worth noting that most of the cases when the European Court of Human Rights found that the Romanian State violated various articles of the European Convention were in fact cases decided by the Supreme Court of Justice, its decisions being in violation with the Convention.

9. FINAL REMARKS

Many were either reticent or skeptical about the Constitutional Court by the time of its establishment. As always it is important to see how such an institution works and to draw the conclusions afterwards. Today is quite obvious that the Constitutional Court in spite of some very unhappy rulings, issued some very important and good decisions too, and that their number has increased during the last years. Similarly, its authority has increased. This is probably the main explanation of the recent attitude of the Supreme Court of Justice which fears that will no longer be seen as the highest judicial authority of the country. The way it chose to fight against the theoretical supremacy of the Constitutional Court in relation with the constitutional control may be seen as demonstrating the real powers the Constitutional Court has achieved in practice. However, it is difficult at this moment to predict how this controversy will continue and how it will solved. Therefore, the Parliament should see it as a clear indication that constitutional amendments are if not required at least welcome.

13. The Russian Constitutional Court in an Uneasy Triangle between the President, Parliament and Regions

Klaus von Beyme

1. THE PREDECESSOR: THE COMMITTEE FOR CONSTITUTIONAL CONTROL

The principle of judicial review by constitutional courts was accepted in the second wave of democratization in the 20th century by many countries (Germany 1951, Italy 1956), as well as in the third wave (Greece 1975, Spain 1980, Portugal 1983). Constitutional Courts everywhere in Europe made an important contribution to the consolidation of democracy. Few communist countries had introduced judicial review before the collapse of the system, because this principle was most incompatible with all-encompassing hegemonial claims of 'the Party'. In Poland the Constitution was amended as early as 1982, and the Constitutional Court began its work in 1986.

The Soviet Union during the perestroika only established a Committee for Constitutional Control. Typical of the Soviet ambiguity towards the principle of judicial review which might undermine the control of the party was the contribution of a well-known Soviet scholar to an international conference on judicial review. The first version in 1986 read: 'Why the Soviet Union does not need constitutional review'. The second version for the conference in 1987 read: 'Equivalents of judicial review in the Soviet Union'. The final version in the publication in1988 read: 'Guarantees for Constitutionality of Legislation in the USSR'. This anecdote is telling only when we know the name of the author: it was Vladimir Tumanov,[1] later second President of the Constitutional Court in Russia. By 1988 Tumanov and many other lawyers had opened their minds so far that they preferred a real constitutional court to the half-hearted hybrid which was developed as 'Committee for Constitutional Control'. This Committee got a chance to bud in June 1988 when at the Party convention, a 'socialist legal state' was proclaimed as a major goal of perestroika.[2] In December 1988, a constitutional reform took place which included the new institution into the Federal Constitution. The low rank of this experiment was evident from the

---

[1] Christine Landfried (ed.): *Constitutional Review and Legislation* (Baden-Baden, Nomos 1988), pp. 213ff.

[2] Materialy XIX Vsesoyuznoj konferentsii Kompartii Sovetskogo Soyuza (Moscow 1988), p. 146.

Wojciech Sadurski (ed.), Constitutional Justice, East and West, 309–325
© 2002 *Kluwer Law International. Printed in Great Britain.*

outset because the Committee was inserted at the end of regulations of Parliament. In April 1990 the election of the chairman (S.S. Alekseev) and 25 members, among them one representative from each of the 15 Union Republics, took place.

In June 1989 Gorbachev had failed with a first attempt to get the chairman of the Committee of Constitutional Control elected (V.N. Kudravtsev, Vice-President Lazarev). Many deputies of the Baltic States wanted to postpone the question because they were afraid the Committee might interfere in the process of autonomisation for the budding 'sovereign' Union Republics. They even asked for a veto for each Republic. Moreover, the 'dissidents' thought that the establishment of the Committee was not feasible without prior amendments to the Brezhnev Constitution. When Gorbachev tried to promote the election nevertheless, opposition turned into obstruction. The Lithuanian Deputies left, including the leader of the Lithuanian Communist Party, Brazauskas, later the second President of his country. When the question was discussed again in December 1989 in a committee which had to prepare a law on the 'Committee' under the chairmanship of D.A. Kerimov (Azerbajdzan), two more variations for the new institution were proposed: either a true constitutional court or the transfer of judicial review competences to the Supreme Court of the Soviet Union. Since the profession of lawyers and judges was traditionally underdeveloped and had little reputation, the composition of the Committee showed a trend which persisted in the era of the Constitutional Court: mainly professors of law were chosen.[3] The model for the new Committee which worked out as a compromise was the *Conseil constitutionnel* in France. Its chairman, Badinter, was not by chance the most important foreigner who was consulted.[4] The French model, however, increasingly developed into the direction of a real constitutional court.[5] The same did not happen in the short time of existence of the Russian 'Committee'. It had only time to consider some 40 cases.

The Committee had the competence for abstract control of norms and conflicts in the federal system, but no competences in concrete control of norms and conflicts between state authorities.[6] The work of the Committee was impeded by the fact that the Soviet Union never developed a clear hierarchy of norms and applied the term '*zakon*' (law) also to non-parliamentary acts – contrary to international practice. When Russia finally took over the Western hierarchy of

---

[3]   List in, Konstitutsionnyi sud Rossii: *Spravochnik* (Moscow, Informatsionno-ekspertnaya gruppa ‚Panorama' (2nd edition 1997), p. 36.

[4]   Otto Luchterhand, 'Vom Verfassungskomitee der UdSSR zum Verfassungsgericht Rußlands', *Archiv des öffentlichen Rechts* (1993), pp. 237–288, p. 241).

[5]   Louis Favoreu in Christine Landfried (ed.): *Constitutional Review and Legislation* (Baden-Baden, Nomos 1988).

[6]   Alexander Blankenagel, 'Rechtsstaat UdSSR', *Jahrbuch für Ostrecht*, 1 (1990), pp. 9–31, p. 26.

norms in a constitutional state the 'ukazokratiya', government by decree, blurred again the hierarchy because the executive decree authority was unbroken under Yeltsin's regime.[7]

By the end of 1991 the Committee for Constitutional Control was dissolved. Its former President severely criticized the semi-democratic and ineffective design of the new institution which – according to his view – mainly served the symbolic functions without efficiency.[8] Neither its competences nor its political semi-authoritarian environment of the system – inspite of *glasnost* – made the Committee an efficient instrument of judicial review. Constitutional control was locked in a hierarchical system and remained dependent in the combination with the legislation. Its concept was innovative, however, in so far as it was based on the assumption that the Constitution was no longer only a 'dignified part' of the system for propaganda speeches but was to be implemented and aimed at the restriction for the exercise of power. The Committee – if had lived a normal life – might have developed important functions of conciliation between the state powers. The control of basic rights, however, was at best 'supervision' but hardly real 'control'. Even the President in the amended Soviet system still had more powers to nullify acts which he considered as illegal than the Committee.[9] The Committee was tuned to 'self-purification' of the system. Citizens had a right to carry their grievances to the Committee – but without legal claim for 'judicial review'. At best the Committee might have developed into the function of an *ombudsman* – which was usurped by the 'prokuratura' in the old system. But even this was a first step towards liberalization of the system. Though the prokuratura originally was a repressive instrument of 'revolutionary justice' it had turned to a second function of controlling by 'protests' against legal acts of the administration in case of violations of citizen's rights.

2. THE CONSTITUTIONAL COURT IN THE MAKING: THE FIRST ROUND

The 'Committee of Constitutional Control' was considered as a 'legal planned child of perestroika', whereas the Constitutional Court of the Russian Federation was an 'unexpected illegal child', born out of a constitutional revolution.[10] Its birth started with declaration of sovereignty of the RSFSR (June 12th, 1990). It created a state which after its establishment nobody really wanted. The Russian

---

[7]   Scott Parrish, 'Presidential Decree Authority in Russia 1991–95', in John M. Carey/ Matthew S. Shugart (eds.), *Executive decree authority* (Cambridge, Cambridge University Press 1998), pp. 62–103.

[8]   Cit. in: Otto Luchterhand, 'Vom Verfassungskomitee der UdSSR zum Verfassungsgericht Rußlands', *Archiv des öffentlichen Rechts* (1993), pp. 237–288, p. 247.

[9]   Angelika Nußberger, *Verfassungskontrolle in der Sowjetunion und in Deutschland.* (Baden-Baden, Nomos 1994), p. 228.

[10]   Izvestia, May 26th, 1992, p. 2.

Federation was used to get rid of the Soviet system, but most of the actors did not foresee the consequences of a complete loss of the former Empire.

Only in July 1991 did judicial review become an important factor in the dying Soviet Union. Yeltsin supported the idea as being in tune with his own intentions to de-legitimate the totalitarian system in a favour of his 'legal state', e.g. Russia. The legal fundament was Article 125 of the Constitution of the Russian Federation and the 'Federal Law on the Constitutional Law of the Russian Federation' which tried to implement Article 125 on July, 23rd, 1994. The Russian legal development became possible when the democratic opposition won the elections in Russia in spring 1990. Yeltsin was elected president on May 25th, 1990. He formed a 'constitutional committee' a month later which took up the old idea for a true constitutional court which in 1989 was blocked by the conservative forces of the Soviet Union. The legal formation of the new court was in the hands of the 'Congress of People's Deputies'. When the 'status quo ante-forces' tried in March 1991 to topple Yeltsin and to prevent the establishment of a President of the Russian Federation, the ideal of judicial review received additional momentum. But the conservatives were still strong enough to prevent the election of the judges. The main quarrel of groups in the Congress were waged on the question of individual constitutional complaints. The 5th 'Extraordinary Congress' passed the necessary law. The attempt of a 'coup d'état' in August 1991 interrupted the sessions of the Congress. Only in October 13 of the 15 judges provided got the necessary absolute majority. Parliamentary chairman, Chasbulatov, the representative of the old-regime forces and an opponent of Yeltsin, boycotted the elections for the last two judges, thus clearly exceeding his constitutional powers.[11] The judges were meant to be impartial. De facto, however, they were nominated by the parliamentary groups. Zor'kin, the much disputed first President of the Constitutional Court, came into office with the help of Rutskoj's 'Communists for Democracy'. The independence of the judges was legally protected by strict qualifications (lawyers with ten years of professional work and high 'moral qualities', Art. 12). They had to be at least 35 years old (later 40 years), but not older than 60 years. Some of these qualifications were changed in the second round of reestablishment of the Court after the turmoil of 1993. Most important was the abolition of a 'life time' term according to the American Supreme Court model and the reduction to 12 years (up to an age of 70 years) which followed the German model. The seventy years-clause proved to be embarrassing for the first time when the highly regarded second President, Tumanov, had to leave in late 1996. His mandate was prolonged until a new judge had been elected.

Federalist considerations were amazingly unimportant – contrary to the defunct 'Committee' – but the social composition showed a small minority from

---

[11] Otto Luchterhand, 'Vom Verfassungskomitee der UdSSR zum Verfassungsgericht Rußlands', *Archiv des öffentlichen Rechts* (1993), pp. 237–288, p. 256.

the smaller ethnicities, mostly completely socialized in a Russian environment. The Deputies were still so alienated from the '*Rechtsstaat*' that they showed little interest for the procedure which was dubbed a 'case of lotto' by the Komsomol'skaya Pravda (Oct. 30th, 1992: 1) Threats and attempts on the life of two elected judges showed that certain privileges and many protective measures were necessary. The autonomy of the Court was not guaranteed in a Western manner: the budget was proposed by the President, the Court was, however, independent in setting up its agenda (Art. 11). The law on the Constitutional Court with 89 articles had the length of some constitutions. Its creator, A.S. Pashin, showed a certain perfectionism in the regulations which was quite common in new democracies also elsewhere, e.g. Spain or Portugal.

The decision for a special constitutional court – alien to the American tradition which was fearful of the English 'star chamber' – followed the Austrian-German model. Hans Kelsen invented the model – though it had precedents in the revolutionary Constitution of 1848/49 in Germany (then still including Austria). As in Poland and Hungary, the creation of constitutional judges in Russia was initially entrusted to Parliament. Subsequently however – as in Slovenia – this parliamentary prerogative was curtailed by the right of the President to propose the candidates. Some kind of agreement between the executive and the legislative powers is necessary in most countries, such as Czechia which followed the American solution (the President nominates, the Senate has to approve). The length of the mandate (12 years) followed – like Albania – the German example.[12] This solution is a fair compromise between continuity and adaptation to new political constellations – so difficult in the American model with life-time appointments. But even this apparent preponderance of the President did not prevent conflicts with parliament. The last judge nominated, Marat Baglaj, met with resistance of the Federal Council until 1995, so that the deadlines for the nomination were not met. The independence of the judges may be endangered by the right of the Federal Council to suspend a judge (Art. 18, lin. 2, No. 1 of the Law on the Constitutional Court). The reorganization of the Court after 1993 followed the German example of two chambers (palat) with 9 and 10 judges in order to increase the efficacy of the Court's work,[13] but the plenum has the right to draw any case into its jurisdiction if three judges demand it. This may again endanger efficacy – as well as the rather short deadlines of decisions which were meant to increase trust in the Court. The Russian absolutist tradition knew only complaints and 'humble petitions'. The Russian language

---

[12] See Leszek Lech Garlicki, 'Das Verfassungsgericht im politischen Prozeß', in: Otto Luchterhand (ed.): *Neue Regierungssysteme in Osteuropa und der GUS.* (Berlin: Berlin Verlag 1996), pp. 275–310.

[13] Alexander Blankenagel, 'The court writes its own law', *East European Constitutional Review*, 3/4 (1994), pp. 74–79, p. 77; Nicole Krone, 'Das Verfassungsgericht der Russischen Föderation', *Osteuropa* (1998), pp. 253–267, p. 256.

knows a rather familiar locution: 'otkladyvat' v dolgyj yashchik' (to lay off into a long case). The case was located in the walls of the Kremlin and the *bon mot* hinted at the fact that the deposition of a petition for the Czar was tantamount to eternal non-decision. The Constitutional Court made all the efforts to overcome this tradition of inactivity and ran into trouble. After all, also the rather efficient German Constitutional Court has thousands of cases which wait for decision every year. After the experiences with judicial activism under president Zor'kin's chairmanship the President's competences were restricted in the second round. Public declarations henceforth were possible only after an agreement of the plenum.[14]

The Constitutional Court issues four kinds of action: decisions (opredeleniya), dispositions or orders (postanovleniya), expert reports (zaklyucheniya) and messages (poslaniya).[15] The last two species of judicial activities are problematic because they still invite judicial activism. The competences of the Court are enumerated in Article 125 of the Constitution. They comprise judicial review of legal acts, conflicts between state institutions and constitutional complaints which so far were known only in Germany as a major vehicle of judicial review. Moreover the Court can be asked for a *binding interpretation* of the Constitution – a right which has been abolished in Germany since 1960 because it might prevent innovations – the Court will hardly want to contradict in a decision a former written expertise, even if it has changed its mind. The Court has also an *advising expert function* in cases of impeachments of the President. Rather strange in the light of a strict separation of powers is the right of the Court to *legislative initiative*. In the German model this is formally impossible – but nevertheless in an indirect way the Court has an impact on the legislative power when it excessively regulates the future in its decisions and makes recommendations for legislation even in its '*obiter dicta*' (parts which do not justify the decision but are mentioned in addition).

As in Germany, Russia has both *abstract* and *concrete control of norms*. The *conflict between state authorities* and *disputes between the Federation and its subjects* as well as *conflicts between institutions* within a subject of the Federation are in the competence of the Court. The latter competence is highly disputable because many subjects of the Federation have established their own constitutional courts.[16] The trauma of disintegration after the breakdown of the Soviet Union seems to have inspired this inconsistent remainder of an All-Russian centralism. The *constitutional complaints* are possible only against laws but not

---

[14] Matthias Hartwig, 'Verfassungsgerichtsbarkeit in Rußland. Der dritte Anlauf', *Europäische Grundrechte Zeitschrift* (quoted as EuGRZ), 7–8 (1996), pp. 177–199, p. 181).

[15] M.I. Kukushkin (Red.): Konstitutsionne pravo Rossijskoj Federatsii. Sbornik sudebnykh reshenij (St. Petersburg, Paritet 1997), p. 5).

[16] See the data in M.A. Mityukov, *Konstitutsionnoe pravosudie v. sub'ektakh Rossijskoj Federatsii* (Moscow, Yuridicheskaya literatura 1997).

against court sentences. This restriction is likely to limit the number of complaints from the citizens. Germany has thousands of complaints per annum, but fewer requirements in terms of fees which, in Russia, exceed the income per month of a normal employee. The limitation of the judicial review to laws is an undue restriction. Experience teaches that the citizens feel much more violation of rights by court sentences than by laws.[17] The attempt to protect the citizen's rights by a complaint in front of the Court is possible even before the appeal to higher courts is exhausted. This is another strange consequence of the fact that court decisions are not under the jurisdiction of the Constitutional Court. Some observers were afraid that this inconsistency might increase the number of complaints. On the other hand – again following the German example – fees (not only for abuses) deter the use of this remedy in case of violations of rights.[18]

All important institutions have the right to address themselves to the Constitutional Court. Sometimes it was resented that the General Attorney (*prokuror*) was not mentioned as an important institution. It was suspected that the constitution-makers looked upon this institution 'through American and German glasses'.[19]

The most important cases in the first round related to decrees issued by President Yeltsin. The first challenge concerned Yeltsin's attempt to combine the ministry of domestic affairs with the secret service.

The German practice of *outlawing undemocratic parties* has been introduced in Russia and caused much turmoil. The President's decree to outlaw the Communist Party after the attempted coup d'état of August 1991 was highly disputed. It is certainly an exaggeration that the Russian society expected 'a Russian Nuremberg trial'.[20] The Communist elites were certainly not discredited to the same degree as the Nazi elite. In Nuremberg there was 'no due process' in the eyes of the die-hard Nazis, because foreign law and foreign judges were involved. In Russia individuals were not on trial but an organization. Who was to represent the Party? Gorbachev was still the leader but he declined to go to the Court and the Secretary Kuptsov had to do the job, a decision much resented in Russia which cost Gorbachev a good deal of his residual prestige. Nevertheless it was probably a wise decision as he avoided yet further humiliation. When the CPSU used his colleague Yakovlev as a 'whipping boy', he was merciless attacked as an 'apostate of Communism'. The other side also contributed widely to the

---

[17] Nicole Krone, above n. 13, p. 260.

[18] Vladimir Chetvernin, 'Three Questions to the Authors of the Act', *East European Constitutional Review*, 3 (1994), pp. 80–82, p. 81.

[19] O.V. Brezhnev, 'Konstitutsionnyi sud i organy prokuratury: Osobennosti vzajmoot-noshenii'. *Vestnik Moskovskogo Universiteta*, 5 (1997), pp. 75–82, p. 82.

[20] Yuri Feofanov, 'The Establishment of the Constitutional Court in Russia and the Communist Party case', *Review of Central and East European Law*, 6 (1993), pp. 623–637, p. 623.

transformation of the trial into a soap opera when details were discussed such as the bugging of Yeltsin's sauna and Raissa Gorbacheva's hairdresser by the KGB.[21] The case divided the public on both sides and contributed to ugly scenes which turned the proceedings into political demonstrations. The Court needed 52 sessions with 46 witnesses and 16 experts from May to November 1992.

The sentence was a compromise which upheld the President's decision, but paved the way for a restoration of the Party. The outlawing of the central Party was declared as 'constitutional' because it had behaved like a 'state institution'. But the right of the basic party units to live was not challenged by the majority of the judges. The basic units soon after this decision in February 1993 gathered for the reestablishment of a central Party and treated the putschists of August like heroes in their Party convention.

One of many criticisms of the sentence was that the Court was too slow. This was hardly justified. Such a complicated issue would not have been decided more quickly in Karlsruhe.

One should remember that the outlawing of the Communist Party in West Germany took years. When the sentence was issued, Adenauer was no longer interested in the result because the Party was killed by the five percent-threshold rule and its non-existence caused major troubles in the recently established diplomatic relations with the Soviet Union. Probably the Court was even too quick for political reasons – to avoid turmoil in the new VIIth People's Congress. The decision was worked out in great haste before the question had sufficiently been discussed among the judges. Three dissenting votes by Luchin, Kononov and Evzeev indicated the conflicts within the Court. Luchin, interviewed by the 'Pravda' (Dec. 3, 1992), held that only after the declaration of a state of emergency by Parliament and only after previous warnings of the Communists could such a dissolution of the Party have been justified. Ebzeev[22] later called the sentence a wise decision reconciling the old and the new systems of power.

Until May 1993 the Court has intervened in 12 important conflicts and worked on 1200 constitutional complaints. The Court initially tried to keep an equal distance from both major powers in the state. In the decision on the referendum in April 1993 both sides in the conflict between President and parliamentary majority were criticized on several points and justified on others. In three cases the President's acts were declared unconstitutional:

- The attempt to merge the KGB with the Ministry of Domestic Affairs.
- The decree which outlawed the organizational committee of the right-wing extremist 'National Salvation Front'.

---

[21] Pravda 9.7.1992:2; Sharlet, Robert, 'The Russian Constitutional Court. The First Term', *Transitional Justice, Vol. II Country Studies* (Washington, United States Institute of Peace Press 1995), pp. 738–761, p. 747.

[22] Leonid Nikitinsky,: 'Interview with Boris Ebzeev, Justice of the Constitutional Court of the Russian Federation', *East European Constitutional Review*, 1 (1997), pp. 83–88, p. 84.

- A television speech by Yeltsin in March 1993 in which the President announced a 'special regime' in dealing with Parliament. According to principles of Western judicial review it is highly doubtful that a mere speech can already constitute an illegal action, as long as it has no legal consequences.

The 'speech case' provoked illegal actions from both sides. The President of the Constitutional Court, Zor'kin, criticized the President's announcement on television together with Vice-President Rutskoj and the General Attorney (prokuror) V.G. Stapankov as 'unconstitutional'. Even some of his colleagues thought that their chairman had violated his neutrality and should no longer be involved in judging the case.[23] In Germany this consequence would have been unavoidable, but nothing happened in Russia. Zor'kin continued to mobilize and in March 1993 gave a lecture to the People's Deputies 'on the necessary measures for the preservation of the constitutional order in the Russian Federation' – not quite in tune with his original staunch dogmatism in matters of separation of powers. On May 29th, 1993 Yeltsin met six of the judges whom he considered as 'his group' in the Court (Ametistov, Vitruk, Kononov, Morshchakova, Olejnik and Rudkin). The meeting was supposed to be secret, but hardly anything remained secret in these days of anarchy in summer 1993. The six judges gave as a reason for their political action that they had to see the President in order to promote a legal way to the acceptance of the new Constitution (by the Deputies or by referendum). The President had still no clear majority in the Court and in June had to accept several decisions against his will.

From the foundation in 1991 to autumn 1993, the Constitutional Court took 27 decisions and two expert reports (zaklyucheniya). The most frequent petitioners and plaintiffs were the Deputies (17 cases), the regions (3 times) and the individuals with their constitutional complaints (7 cases). In 9 cases decrees of the President were challenged, in 7 of these cases the Court held that the acts of the President were partly or completely in tune with the Constitution. In two cases the President had acted in an unconstitutional way. Four Laws of the Russian Federation, and in 9 cases of complaints against the Deputies or their speaker, were contested by the Court. In only one case the constitutionality of a parliamentary act was endorsed. In 5 cases the subjects of the Federation were involved and in 6 cases individual citizens complained (the sum exceeds the 27 decisions because in some cases several plaintiffs joined their forces).

On March 5th, the Constitutional Court sent the first time a message (poslanie) to the Supreme Soviet about the 'state of legality in the Russian Federation'. Parliament accepted the Court's deadline and made it mandatory for all the institutions of all levels – without major results of implementation.[24]

Chairman Zor'kin was certainly the judge who excessively used political action

---

[23]   Konstitutsionnyi sud, above, n. 3, p. 62.

[24]   *Ibid.* at 61.

in those days of crisis. 'Zor'kin as a politician'[25] rarely got good marks because he tried to reconcile the President and the Chairman of Parliament, Chasbulatov. Zor'kin commented on TV, met politicians, the patriarch and even foreign diplomats at will. Soon it became a general fear that the Court could not survive so much judicial activism. Yeltsin saw it as a competitor in the political arena. In late September 1993 the liberal judges, Ametistov and Vitruk started a boycott of the sessions, arguing that the Court had turned into a political force. Both judges later joined the sessions again. The Court on October 5th, 1993 decided that in a time of an aggravating legal situation it could no longer review legal norms and would restrict its work to constitutional complaints.[26] Both camps in the Court started to blackmail by challenging the quorum. In January 1994 it became evident that Zor'kin still had followers in the Court. In a vote of 7–3, Zor'kin's capacity as a judge was confirmed by his colleagues. In March – even in a semi-official publication no exact date was indicated – the Court voted 8–4 to warn Zor'kin to take part in a political meeting with Rutskoj and others.[27]

The Court in its present form is the result of the revolutionary events of 1993. Yeltsin had called a Court to his help against the Soviet Union. By 1993 he tried to get rid of the spirits he had invited. One judge, Evzeev[28] called it quite frankly a 'coup d'état'. The ill-famed decree No. 1400 (Oct. 22, 1993) on a 'special regime' violated the Constitution. Yeltsin's administration did not deny this but argued that the President in this crisis was unable to carry out the necessary reforms in the framework of the 'Brezhnev-Constitution'. Yeltsin could not even rely completely on 'his group' in the Court. A critical statement was accepted on a 9–4 majority (Ametistov, Vitruk, Morshchakova, Kononov dissenting). The Court did not accept the President's recommendation to suspend, but continued its work. On October 5th, the head of Yeltsin's office, Filatov, asked Zor'kin to step down from the Chairmanship of the Court. In the next session of the Court some of his colleagues asked Zor'kin to leave. Olejnik blackmailed his chairman by declaring that there was a decree on the President's table to dissolve the Court altogether if Zor'kin did not resign. But still 8 judges recommended Zor'kin not to give in. Finally Zor'kin resigned and the Court's work was suspended because it had played a 'negative role' in the crisis according to Yeltsin. For one and a half year the Court was doomed to inactivity.

---

[25]   Sharlet, above, n. 21, p. 36.

[26]   *Ibid.* at 95.

[27]   *Ibid.* at 95.

[28]   Interview in, Nikitinsky, above, n. 22, p. 85.

3. NORMALISATION OF JUDICIAL REVIEW: THE SECOND ROUND SINCE 1995

On February the 13th, 1995, Vladimir Tumanov was elected with 11 votes as President of the Constitutional Court. Tamara Morshchakova won against Vitruk and Baglaj as a Vice-Chairperson. Tumanov stood for a return to the legal duties of the Court against a political role and in a press conference on July 1996 he was already able to report that the new momentum of the Court had been accepted by most institutions of the system and that there was no threat of the Court becoming 'unemployed'. The criticisms from the part of conservative deputies were opposed by the hint to the fact that many propositions and complaints from Parliament did not contain legal but rather political questions. Tumanov also denied that the decisions of the Court were more in favour of the President than of the Duma.

The new Court in the second round was reorganized and made more efficient. Because of the rule that the President and the Vice-President should not sit in the same chamber (palat), a certain reshuffling had to be organized. Baglaj, President after Tumanov, was transferred to the second chamber.

The most important case at the beginning of the 'second round' was the Chechnya case in July 1995 when the Federal Council and some Deputies from the Duma challenged decrees of Yeltsin. Lukyanov and others took part in the deliberations from Parliament's side, Yurij Baturin – for a while serving on the Security Council – represented the President's side. The Court upheld all four decrees of Yeltsin, but challenged a government action concerning the deportation of citizens living in Chechnya.[29] This decision was criticized as being biased in favour of the President. But on the whole Tumanov managed to demonstrate the 'equidistance' and impartiality of the Court towards the other powers. 'Judicial restraint' became the new device and the Court tried not to interfere in political matters, especially concerning elections.

In 1995, 20 cases were considered in open sessions, 6 in plenary sessions, 8 in the first and 6 in the second chamber. 17 cases were decided upon. Three cases were initiated by the Federal Council, 4 by the Duma, 1 by a group of Deputies, 3 by the federal subjects and 10 by the citizens. The President's decrees were endorsed. The Duma was less successful: the Court agreed only in one case out of three concerning the interpretation of the Constitution. The same success ratio applied to the Federal Council. The subjects of the Federation were successful in 2 out of 3 cases, and the individual complaints on 9 out of 10 occasions.

The work load was increasing by 200 questions for an opinion (obrashchenie) by institutions and citizens of the Russian Federation. The judges in 1995 produced 17 decisions with dissenting votes, most of them concerning the President's decrees and the Chechnya case.

---

[29]   Konstitutsionnyi Sud, above, n. 3, p. 71.

In 1996, 24 cases were considered in 5 plenary sessions, 10 in the first, 9 in the second chamber. Apparently the distribution of the work-load was equalized among the two chambers. 21 decisions have been issued. The plaintiffs were in most cases the individuals (10 cases), and among the institutions: the President (5 cases), the Duma (2 cases), the Federal Council (1 case), the subjects of the Federation (7 cases), other courts (4 cases). The innovation was that for the first time a commercial organization entered the procedure. The cases of Presidential initiative contained only one case which interpreted the Constitution. The decision of the Court was welcomed by the President and the Federal Council, but not by the Duma. The other Presidential initiatives were decided in a fairly impartial way (one case declared 'constitutional' another one 'unconstitutional', in two more cases the President withdrew). The Duma-case was decided in favour of the President. In the four cases brought by federal subjects, 2 endorsed the complainant's view, in one case the act was unconstitutional and in another case the matter was transferred to a procedure of 'mutual agreement'. Individuals held the most favourable record: 10 out of 11 complaints were decided in their favour. In this period conflicts among the judges were still frequent: 13 dissenting votes have been issued in 1996 only. The main dissenter was Vitruk.

There is not yet a statistical service as efficient as in the USA or in Germany. Until 1997 the distribution of issues has been counted as follows:[30]

Interpretation of the Constitution	6
human and citizen's rights	25
separation of powers	10
federal relations	11
constitutional control of the federal subjects	7

The breakdown is less differentiated than the data for the German Constitutional Court. In particular, the policy areas have not really been counted by this merely legal classification. Formalistic typologies prevail in the literature. Social scientists so far have had little interest in the impact of court decisions – contrary to American and, to a lesser extent, the German traditions. There was not a single article on judicial review in 'Polis', the journal of the Political Science in Russia.

In February 1997 a new President of the Court was elected. Several candidates competed, even Zor'kin. He got, however, only seven votes. In the third voting cycle three candidates were left. M.V. Baglaj was elected with 12 out of 19 votes. The rules of 'neutral behaviour' of the judges by 1997 were taken more seriously. Luchin was criticized by the media for opinions which he had written in a book. In Germany, scholarly opinions are normally not recognized to call a judge 'biased' in a certain case. Though the rules of the game were increasingly respected, the Court had many problems with the enforcement of its decisions.

---

[30] M.I. Kukushkin above, n. 15, pp. 662ff.

The 'authorized agent of the President' (polnomochnyj predstavitel' presidenta'), S.M. Shakhraj, moved the problem of control of the acts of regional assemblies. In 42 cases he found unconstitutional decisions and he drew an almost apocalyptic picture of the 'state of the federation'. Apparently little had changed in the illegal behaviour of many regional governors. Since Yeltsin gave them the privilege to be elected by popular vote in 1996 – under the pretext of 'strengthening democracy', in reality to mobilize the heads of the federal subjects for his cause in the struggle with a hostile Duma majority – the unconstitutional behaviour in the regions still increased. The Constitutional Court in the second round of consolidation felt the need to stop the centrifugal tendencies in the Federation. In many cases it had done so only in an indirect way. With the "presidentialisation" of the Russian system, the judges discovered a dogmatic figure taken from the American textbooks: the President had 'implied powers' not directly mentioned in the Constitution, but following 'logically' – as judge Luchin once put it – from the existing articles of the basic law. The liberal Vitruk in a dissenting vote criticized in a case on Chechnya the new doctrine of 'hidden competences' of the President. The dissenters were afraid that the Constitutional Court by such extensions of its jurisdiction would turn from a *law-interpreting* into a *law-creating body*. Others, like Ebzeev, in their scientific work had already promoted the new idea, arguing that the law-creating function of the Constitutional Court was inevitable because no constitution could ever encompass regulations for all cases. This doctrine in the USA was developed in a country where the constitution – according to the deliberate will of some founding fathers – was 'short and obscure'. The unexpected result was that since *Marbury v. Madison* the Court got an unprovided for chance to develop as a third branch of the system. The clumsy amendment procedure in American law-creation strengthened the Supreme Court in addition, whereas Germany has applied excessively both: formal amendments to the constitution and developing law by judicial review. In Russia the situation was different because its Constitution was 'long and less obscure'. Nevertheless judicial review was strengthened because the system developed in other directions than anticipated by the founding mothers and fathers.

In many cases of federalist quarrels the Court decided in favour of the federal subjects and regions. Sometimes the traditional forces in the districts and republics were still stronger than in Moscow. In some cases the regions used a pure parliamentary system which deviated from the semi-presidential scheme of the central institutions. Contrary to the views of the central Government, the Court was more tolerant towards these institutional deviations. The Court argued in some cases that deviations from the scheme of powers in the Federation were acceptable as long as no special federal law had regulated the matter.

The Court could not overlook the fact that new authoritarian tendencies were developing in the center-periphery relations. Udmurtya was one of those authoritarian subsystems. The Republic tried to do away with local government in a shrewd way: by abolishing the most important territorial units which claimed their right to self-government. Towns and cities were elevated overnight to 'municipalities of republican subordination'. The Court's decision in this case was half-hearted, but finally in favour of the higher units. Under the pretext of strengthening the division of powers it opened the door to the erosion of local self-government.[31]

4. CONCLUSION

The first phase of the Court was not a normal life with 'business as usual'. The Court did not consider many cases, but rather focused instead on the draft of Yeltsin's constitution. It was also self-referential in its work on the 'Act on the Constitutional Court'. Chairman Zor'kin ushered the Court into a 'romantic phase', as one of the judges, Ebzeev, dubbed it.[32] This era was characterized by a dogmatic concept of the division of powers which was violated – with best intentions – by the Court itself when it moved to the role of censorship against the rest of the institutions.

The Court was affected by serious non-decisions of the President. One was not to push founding elections early and not to work seriously on the new constitution before the putsch of 1993. For a fair evaluation one must admit that the Court could not be much better than the power game of the early days of non-consolidation.

The main problem was less Parliament, but the President in his quarrels with a hostile parliamentary majority. When the problem was tackled by the President he turned to the holistic approach which had characterized the old regime. An 'All-Russian Congress on Legal Reform' was organized and the President asked 'tutto e subito' in a rather naive maximalistic way: reform of legislation, of the court system, of the executive system and the legal consciousness of the population.[33] None of these reforms was implemented, a situation which did not facilitate judicial review in Russia.

No wonder that the Court was pushed into the direction of overload with the doctrine of law-creation, already developed by Pashin,[34] the father of the court regulations. It was a parallel to the futile competition of the President's *ukazokratiya* versus parliamentary laws. In many cases both were not implemented by the local authorities, especially when they contradicted each other. Only under

---

[31] Blankenagel (1997).

[32] Interview with Nikitinsky, above, n. 22, p. 84.

[33] Friedrich-Christian Schroeder (ed.), *Die neuen Kodifikationen in Rußland* (Berlin, Berlin Verlag 1997), p. 24.

[34] S.A. Pashin, *Kak obratit'sya v. konstitutsionnyi sud Rossii* (Moscow, Juridicheskaya Firma Paritet 1992), p. 7.

Tumanov since 1995 the role-stretching function was reduced and professionalization and de-politization of the Court's work made progress.

Judicial sociology asks for the contribution of social background data on judicial behaviour. This procedure is not very telling in the case of Russia. The personnel of the Constitutional Court certainly meets the conditions of 'high quality lawyers'. If we exclude the three representatives of the President (Savitskij, Mityukov, Shakhray) from the statistical sample because they would distort it by their more political profiles, we get 19 cases[35] and a good picture of normal judicial careers. There is considerable stability: Ametistov had to leave in May 1999, Vedernikov in December 1999. Baglaj was President until February 2000 and served as a judge until May 2001. In the next two years some high profile judges will have to leave for reasons of age, such as Olejnik, Baglaj and Vitruk. But stability prevailed, not even Zor'kin was eliminated from the bench of judges and will serve until 2008.

All of the judges meet the condition of ten years of professional experience. Some are proud to mention pre-professional manual work of the old polytechnic type of education. More than half of the judges studied at MGU in Moscow, some did so after basic instruction in provincial universities. The area between Moscow and the Ural is over represented, the South is under represented. Some of the judges after their studies worked in the Academy Institute 'State and Law', the 'beloved stronghold of most foreign political scientists working in Moscow'. Most of the judges served as professors of law, only Tumanov, however, was an internationally recognized scholar prior to his functions. Quite a few judges have worked in the *prokuratura* or as ordinary judges.

The social profile does not show much variation. There were only two women. The regions and ethnicities are under represented. Siberia and the Far East are lacking. Most of the judges born in former Union Republics or ethnic republics of the former RSFSR mention that they are 'Russian'. President Baglaj was born in Baku, Gadzhiev in Dagestan and Ebzeev in Kirgystan, as member of a small ethnic group from a family which had suffered deportation. All the judges were in the Party with the exception of one woman, mostly until August 1991. Luchin mentioned however that he had left the party twice, the first time in 1968, protesting against the events in Prague. More than half of the judges had some political ambitions and served as Deputies or candidates who failed since 1991. Few judges had administrative experience. All of them are married (one divorced) and have about two children – more than the average Russian family.

Revolutions tend to promote younger people into the top elites. Elite studies in Russia[36] have shown that the age of the top elite when attaining its highest

---

[35] Biographies in, Konstitutsionny sud, above, n. 3.

[36] Olga W Kryschtanowskaja, 'Die Transformation der alten Nomenklatur-Kader in die russische Elite', in, Helmut Steiner/Wladimir Jadow (eds.), *Rußland – wohin? Rußland aus der Sicht russischer Soziologen* (Berlin, Trafo Verlag 1999), pp. 213–243.

office, lowered from Brezhnev (61.8 years) to Gorbachev (54 years), but has decreased only slightly under Yeltsin (53 years). Compared to those figures on political elites, the innovation in the Constitutional Court is remarkable (average age at the first nomination: about 50 years). For the other social background indicators, the elite of judges is in tune with the rest of the political elite: women decreased and a re-ethnisation in favour of Russians took place also in the Court.

What do we know when we know this? Very little. Generally there are few connections between social background and decisions. As in Germany, the middle classes prevail, judges on the whole are more sophisticated and liberal than the rest of the society. Contrary to Germany and the USA religious data are irrelevant which sometimes influence the attitude of judges (e.g. on divorce or abortion and other Weltanschauung's issues). The most important variable in explaining judicial behaviour in Russia is the political background. An analysis of the dissenting votes would probably put some light on the political connections. My impression is moreover that the minority of former penal law specialists and employees of the prokuratura are more conservative than the average constitutional law specialists.

The Constitutional Court of the Russian Federation is an important innovation and since 1995 has functioned in a promising way. There is little evidence that the citizens have the same degree of veneration for the Constitutional Court in Russia as have the Germans. The Court still suffers from the low confidence in the courts of justice. Unlike East Germany, trust in the courts was far below the army, the church and even the media – but above Parliament.[37] Distrust in political institutions was high also in Germany before the consolidation of democracy. But the difference was that the legal system – except the Nazi period – was highly developed and had an old Roman law tradition which was lacking in Russia. Sometimes the court decisions were considered as an alternative to 'selfish political decisions'. This kind of feeling may develop also in Russia. But as long as corruption is suspected everywhere, even the Court is affected by distrust. The Constitutional Court can consolidate its role only when his decisions are also implemented. This problem is, however, the most touchy question of the system.

A non-consolidated democracy has always initially the problem of enforcement of legal sentences. Legally the Court's decisions are binding – but who secures this? It was important that Yeltsin accepted the first decision against his policy when the Court prohibited the combination of the secret service with the ministry of domestic affairs. It was said that Shakhraj had the merit to have convinced the President that this decision could not be ignored.[38] But the federal subjects did not follow this good example. Tatarstan held its referendum inspite of a

---

[37] Stephen White, et al: *How Russia Votes* (Chatham/New Jersey, Chatham House 1997), p. 52ff.

[38] Moskovskie novosti, May 17th 1992: 7.

negative sentence from the Constitutional Court. The problem of center-periphery relations was that the old Soviet system has never developed a mechanism of legal sanctions.[39] The principle of *Bundestreue* in German constitutional law was unknown to Russia. The Soviet Union had inserted even a right to secession into the Constitution, but whoever might have used it was persecuted by penal law – outlawing proclamations of secession – and secret service. This double moral had some consequences in the budding democracy. Chechnya wanted to use the right to secession – but it was no longer recognized by the democrats in Russia. In the case of Tatarstan, Zor'kin tried to invent his own sanctions by mobilizing the media and the federal authorities. An escalation could have been an impeachment against the civil servants and politicians of that Republic which disobeyed court decisions. But 'contempt of court' sanctions have also to be accepted. In Russia the slogan was always present: 'Russia is large and the Czar is far away'. Even Zor'kins campaigns against Tatarstan did not exceed public lamentations without major consequences.

In case Putin's ideas about a 'guided democracy' and a democracy of the strong hand is respecting the Constitutional Court, this institution is likely to help the new President to overcome the centrifugal tendencies in the Federation. The Germans in 1949 had expected that center-periphery litigations would develop a prominent place among the court trials. Surprisingly this kind of procedure plays only a marginal role in Germany. It is likely that the role of this type of conflict will be more prominent in Russia. After all, Federal issues take already the second place after human rights issues – but only because less important citizens' complaints count in numbers, but not in the political weight of the issue. Chechnya has shown that this problem may well be the major challenge for the Constitutional Court of the Russian Federation in the future.

---

[39]   Otto Luchterhand, above, n. 4, p. 279.

14. The Constitutional Court of Ukraine: The Politics of Survival*

Kataryna Wolczuk

The establishment of constitutional courts in the transitional states of Eastern Europe has tended to draw praise and sometime wonder, *viz* Schwartz: '[a]mong the happier surprises in the East Central European world since 1989 are the new Constitutional Courts'.[1] Indeed, the creation of the constitutional review body in a country such as Ukraine, which has no tradition of modern constitutionalism, appears to be a fine example of a successful institutional transplant. After the protracted battle to remove the vestiges of Soviet institutional design, in 1996 the separation of powers was enshrined in the new Constitution, despite the preservation of some Soviet-era institutions, such as the Procuracy. The crowning achievement of the new constitutional order was the creation of the Constitutional Court in 1996, introducing the constitutional review in Ukraine.

Despite the lack of historical grounding, the Ukrainian Court has not shied away from using its powerful prerogatives of invalidating decisions of the legislative and executive branches of power. Yet in doing so, it has tended to limit itself to the confines of legal positivism. With notable exceptions, the Court has generally exercised restraint and largely avoided rulings concerned with rights, which would take it beyond the remits of the Constitution into the wider terrain populated by such concepts as 'the rule of law', 'social justice', 'social state', or 'fundamental rights'. Undoubtedly, the controversies surrounding Ukraine's ties with Europe, including the questions on the exact role of Europe's legal traditions in Ukraine, impacted on the Court's reluctance to embrace the 'culture of rights' developed by Western jurisprudence.

Feeling safer when functioning within the confines delineated by constitutional norms, the Court made the main focus of its attention issues pertaining to the separation of powers. Notwithstanding the positivist inclinations of the judges, this focus was dictated by political expediency. The Court was compelled to

---

* The research for this chapter was made possible thanks to a collaborative research project 'The Quality of Democracy in Ukraine: Representation in and after the March 1998 Ukrainian Elections' funded by the Economic and Social Research Council, UK (Grant No: R000222380).

[1] Herman Schwartz, "The New Courts: an Overview", in Volkman Gessner (ed.), *European Legal Cultures* (Aldershot 1996), pp. 445–451.

Wojciech Sadurski (ed.), Constitutional Justice, East and West, 327–348
© 2002 *Kluwer Law International. Printed in Great Britain.*

respond to political contingencies, when it was drawn in to adjudicate in intra-parliamentary disputes, as well as in stand-offs in executive-legislative relations. At first sight, the Ukrainian Court seems worthy of praise for its role in taming political conflicts, while avoiding the temptation of venturing into the turbulent waters of judicial activism in the form of 'substantive rulings'.[2] Yet, upon closer investigation, neither assertion can be upheld.

Upon becoming a central arena for the on-going conflict between political actors, the Court, hardly unexpectedly, found itself in a highly vulnerable position. Initially, the Court made procrastination and moderation, the main tactics of its 'survival strategy'. The Court endeavoured to refrain from adjudication in the most vexed political issues until the pressures to do so became overwhelming. Despite the frequent invalidation of, at least some provisions of, legal acts, the Court often strived to limit the impact of its rulings by carefully seeking out the middle ground. This strategy, however, began to fail when the presidential offensive on the powers of Parliament curtailed the Court's room for manoeuvre. In fact, the Court only mitigated the worst excesses of the Presidency but did not use its powers to prevent the onslaught on the legislature.

Moreover, while the Presidency was the main initiator of rulings affecting the Parliament (the Supreme Council), the Court became an instrument through which acts of Parliament were challenged by *ad hoc* parliamentary minorities. That this has been resorted to only too often is hardly surprising taking into account the volatility in the factional configuration within Parliament. Because of the relative ease with which a group of deputies (often instigated by the executive) could mount a challenge in the Court to a Parliament's decision, and because of the final nature of the Court's decision, referring cases to the Court turned out to be a more expedient way of invalidating a piece of legislation than the orchestrating of parliamentary campaigns. The cumulative effect of those factors was that while claiming to uphold the separation of powers, the Court became instrumental in eroding legislative power and shifting it to the executive.

1. A PROTRACTED BIRTH: THE FORMATION OF THE CONSTITUTIONAL COURT

As in all post-Communist countries, the notion of embracing the European constitutional traditions in the form of a robust constitutional review was conceived as a means of institutionalising the 'rule of law'. In particular, the endowment of the Constitutional Court in Ukraine with a generous portfolio of powers was viewed as an antidote to the pervasive legacy of 'socialist legality', which was associated with the arbitrary rule of the Communist Party. Moreover, the

---

[2] For a generally positive assessment of the Court's rulings, see Bohdan A. Futey, 'Upholding the Role of Law in Ukraine: Judiciary in Transition', in Theofil Kis and Irena Makaryk (eds.), *Towards a New Ukraine* (Ottawa: Chair of Ukrainian Studies 1999), pp. 59–76.

Ukrainian reformers feared that after the Party's hegemonic role came to an end by 1990, Soviet parliamentarism, according to which the Supreme Council was the fulcrum of the state institutional edifice, would perpetuate the syndrome of arbitrary interference without a system of checks and balances. Yet, these fears were not universally shared. The conservative, left-wing in Parliament opposed the introduction of the principle of the separation of powers and shifting the right of constitutional review from the Supreme Council to the Constitutional Court.

The formation of the Constitutional Court was entangled in the tormented and protracted process of constitution-making. Although the idea of a constitutional review surfaced before independence, it took Ukraine seven years to establish the necessary legislative framework and appoint a Constitutional Court.

The first steps in creating the legislative framework were taken even before independence. As early as October 1990 article 112 on the Constitutional Court was introduced into the 1978 Soviet-era constitution, pursuant to which the Court was to be appointed by the Supreme Council for 10 years and was to consist of 15 judges. At the same time, however, the Supreme Council and its powerful Presidium retained the right of 'constitutional control'. In 1991, Ukraine swept to independence with the Act of Independence in August, which was endorsed by a referendum in December. A 'Law on the Constitutional Court' was adopted in June 1992.[3] Taking into account that these were only the early days of constitution-making, when the form of government was far from decided, the Court was granted far reaching powers, including the power to invalidate acts adopted by the Supreme Council, the executive branch and local self-government. Acts declared unconstitutional would lose their force immediately. The Court was to consist of a chairperson, two deputy heads and 12 judges. Judges were to be appointed by the Supreme Council, though proposed by its chairperson.[4]

However, the actual creation of the constitutional review proved impossible to accomplish. Although a chairman of the Constitutional Court, Leonid Yuz'kov, a distinguished constitutional lawyer, was appointed within one month, the Court did not convene in 1992, because the Supreme Council failed to appoint any judges.[5] The following year, the formation of the Court was entangled with the thorny issue of the re-legalisation of the Communist Party of Ukraine. The left-wing in Parliament set out to challenge the constitutionality of the resolution of the Presidium of the Supreme Council that de-legalised the Communist Party of Ukraine on 30 August 1991 in the aftermath of the aborted

---

[3]   See *Biuletyn Verkhovnoi Rady Ukrainy*, 1992, Fifth Session, No. 54–55.

[4]   On the debates on the 'Law on the Constitutional Court' see *Biuletyn Verkhovnoi Rady Ukrainy*, 1992, Fifth Session, No. 55, 73, 74, and 96.

[5]   The chairman of the Supreme Council proposed candidates for parliamentary approval in November 1992 (*Biuletyn Verkhovnoi Rady Ukrainy*, 1992, Sixth Session, No. 34).

coup in Moscow. While both right and left-wing parliamentarians strived to prevent the potentially undesirable ruling by attempting to control the composition of the Court, none were able to gain an upper hand in the selection process. For the second time, Parliament failed to appoint the judges. The formation of the Court was delayed until after the passage of the new Constitution in 1996.[6]

Following the parliamentary and presidential elections of 1994, constitution-making started afresh. Not only was the exact distribution of institutional prerogatives disputed but so were the very principles underlying the form of government. The hardliners in the Communist Party of Ukraine insisted on the preservation of the system of soviets based on the principle of the 'unity of state power'. In this system, the Supreme Council topped the hierarchy of people's councils. As the Supreme Council embodied state powers in its fullness, there was no need for a constitutional review. In contrast, the moderate right-wing parties, with a strong pro-European orientation, were only too eager to shed Soviet institutional legacies. They favoured a separation of powers, an executive Presidency, and the introduction of a constitutional review. They found a much needed ally in the President, who feared that the affirmation of the supremacy of Parliament would spell an end to his executive prerogatives. After two years of intensive negotiations, punctuated by the adoption of the short-lived Constitutional Agreement in 1995, the Constitution was passed in June 1996. The left incurred a defeat in that the Constitution asserted the principle of separation of powers (art. 6 of the Constitution) and outlined a semi-presidential system of government. Nevertheless, in line with Soviet traditions, the left-wing parties continued to uphold the right of the Parliament to interpret the Constitution.

The new Ukrainian Constitution of 1996 created a president-parliamentary system,[7] which is characterised by the co-existence of two agents of the electorate – the legislature and the President, even though there is no fusion of heads of state and government, something that is found in 'pure' Presidential systems. Instead, there is a duality within the executive branch, in that the Presidency co-exists with the Cabinet of Ministers. Despite the fact that the President was named the 'head of state', the actual powers of the President were those of a chief executive. At the same time, even if the cabinet is responsible to the President, it remains also under control of the Supreme Council. The third

---

[6]   *Biuletyn Verkhovnoi Rady Ukrainy*, 1993, Seventh Session, No. 10.

[7]   Semi-presidentialism is often referred to as a hybrid of ideal types, such as the Westminster model or pure presidentialism. However, Shugart and Carey argue that, rather than being a juxtaposition of elements of parliamentarism and presidentialism, there are several forms of presidentialism, such as premier-presidential or assembly independent systems, which constitute ideal types in their own right. Matthew S. Shugart and John M. Carey, *Presidents and Assemblies: Constitutional Design and Electoral Dynamics* (Cambridge: Cambridge University Press 1992).

branch of power consists of courts of ordinary and specialised jurisdiction. The Constitutional Court belongs to the latter domain, because of its exclusive prerogative of constitutional review. Because of the protracted constitution-making and the divisions between the 'founding fathers' of the Ukrainian constitution, the design of Ukraine's Constitutional Court was the result of eclectic borrowing from different models, rather than a wholesale transplant of any particular design.[8]

2. THE ORGANISATION, POWERS AND COMPOSITION OF THE CONSTITUTIONAL COURT

Once the constitution was in place, the passage of the Law on the Constitutional Court on 16 October 1996 provided the legal basis for the functioning of the Court. The Court consists of 18 judges nominated for 9 years, without the possibility of re-appointment for a second term. The President, Parliament and the Congress of Judges appoint six judges each.[9] The eligibility criteria for judges are the following: at least 40 years of age, higher legal education, at least 10 year professional legal experience and the command of state language, that is Ukrainian (art. 148 of the Constitution). The chairperson is elected for 3 years by the judges themselves in a secret vote. The judges cannot be removed from the Court before the end of the term, apart from in the circumstances outlined in the article 126 of the Constitution, which also apply to judges in courts of general jurisdiction. To secure the financial independence of the Court, the Constitution stated that the expenditure on the Court appears under a separate heading in the state budget (art. 31).

According to the Constitution and the Law on the Constitutional Court, Ukraine adopted what could be defined as the 'European model' of constitutional review: concentrated, abstract, *a posteriori* and final. The prerogative of constitutional review is vested in one body – the Constitutional Court, which is given

---

[8] Amongst the different political actors, the small Christian-Democratic Party of Ukraine was quite influential in shaping the format of the Court. Several of its deputies in Parliament took the initiative in drafting a number of laws concerned with reform of the judicial branch. For example, they proposed that the Court be appointed by the President, Parliament and judiciary. However, their idea that one third of judges be changed every three years was not incorporated into the constitution.

[9] The presidential decree on the appointment of a judge to the Constitutional Court has to be countersigned by the Prime Minister and the Minister of Justice (art. 6 of the Law on the Constitutional Court). Article 7 outlined the procedures of appointment by the Supreme Council, according to which a candidate can be nominated by the chairperson of parliament and at least one fourth of the constitutional composition of the Supreme Council. The Congress of Judges elects the judges to the Constitutional Court in secret voting by a simple majority (art. 8).

sole authority not only to interpret the Constitution, but also rule on the unconstitutionality of laws and normative acts, which results in the invalidation of the Act in question. The Court's rulings are final and are binding on the territory of Ukraine. Apart from special matters, the Court can only consider laws and legal Acts in force. The Court performs abstract reviews, while the consideration of the legality of decisions of bodies of state power and local government falls under the authority of courts of general jurisdiction.

The jurisdiction of the Constitutional Court comprises three categories:[10] 'Constitutionality of laws and Acts' (art. 13.1), 'Official interpretation of the Constitution' (art.13.4) and 'Other matters' (art. 13.2 and 13.3).

2.1. Constitutionality of Laws and Acts (art. 13.1)

The Courts may take decisions on the (un)constitutionality of laws and other legal Acts of the Supreme Council, and the legal Acts of the President, the Cabinet of Ministers and the Supreme Council of the Crimean Autonomous Republic (ARC). The Court can make a finding of unconstitutionality if:

(a) the Act is not consistent with the Constitution; or
(b) the way in which the Act was adopted violated constitutional procedures; or
(c) the body which adopted the Act exceeded its authority.

The Court can invalidate an Act as a whole or certain parts of it. The Act in question loses its force from the date of the adoption of the decision by the Court. Only enumerated entities can challenge the constitutionality of legal instruments, namely the President of Ukraine; at least 45 deputies of the Supreme Council; the Supreme Court of Ukraine; the Authorised Representative of the Supreme Council on Human Rights (the Ombudsperson); and the Supreme Council of the ARC.

2.2. Official Interpretation of the Constitution (art. 13.4)

The Court provides official interpretations of the Constitution and laws of Ukraine. No limits are placed on who may request such an interpretation. The Court's interpretations are binding for ordinary courts. Also, a court of general jurisdiction can ask the Constitutional Court to provide an interpretation of the Constitution or a law related to the case under its consideration. The Constitutional Court has to consider such cases as a matter of priority.

---

[10] For a detailed discussion on the powers of the Constitutional Court see Bohdan A. Futey, 'Comments on the Law on the Constitutional Court of Ukraine', *The Harriman Review*, 10(1) (1997), pp. 15–23.

2.3. Other Matters (art. 13.2 and 13.3)

In addition, within the jurisdiction of the Court lie the prerogatives to issue decisions pertaining to:

(a) the constitutionality of changes to the Constitution. According to article 159, the Court issues an opinion on the conformity of the proposed changes to article 157 and 158 of the Constitution;
(b) the congruence of international treaties, which are in force and those which are tabled in the Supreme Council for ratification, with the Constitution of Ukraine (article 13.2);
(c) the adherence to the constitutional procedure of consideration and investigation of cases on the impeachment of the President (article 111 and 151 of the Constitution);
(d) the constitutionality of acts of the Supreme Council of ACR, which had been suspended by the President of Ukraine (article 137.9 of the Constitution).

The Court can open proceedings only in response to a petition filed by an authorised subject. However, some exceptions are allowed. A case can be considered *sua sponte* if in the process of deliberations on another case, the Court has reason to doubt the constitutionality of a legal instrument (article 61).

2.4. The Composition of the Constitutional Court

The completion of the legislative framework for the constitutional review did not end long-standing controversies. The President swiftly appointed his quota of six judges amongst which, in addition to constitutional lawyers, were two 'legal technocrats' – versed in legal craft but not known for their concern with the end goals to which their skills are used – suspected of pro-Presidential leanings. Because of internal divisions, the Parliament could not compete with the President in terms of decisiveness and the selection of the judges took place in a tense atmosphere reminiscent of events in 1993. The judges finally appointed by the Council were more diverse both in terms of ideological profiles and professional expertise. Finally, the appointees of the Congress of Judges were mostly specialists on procedural issues and no apparent political preferences amongst them were discerned.[11] The fact that one third of the judges was appointed by the judiciary noticeably reduced the perception of political partisanship of the Court's members. In a special session, the judges elected a chairman (for a three year period), Ivan Tymchenko, who was one of the 'legal technocrats'. Prior to his appointment he headed the legal department in the Presidential Administration.

Even before embarking on its first case, the Court found itself pitched against

---

[11] *Den*, 22 October 1996.

the Legislature in a row over its premises. The Cabinet of Ministers allocated the Court housing in one of the 'governmental' buildings, something that – so the Parliament claimed – the Cabinet had no right to do. The building, which had belonged to the Communist Party of Ukraine before the party's delegalisation, was turned over to the Supreme Council following the August coup in 1991. Despite the fact that the Cabinet of Ministers administered the building, the Supreme Council challenged the decision of the Cabinet on the grounds that the Council retained control over the use of the building and threatened to file a case in ... the Constitutional Court.[12] In a press conference, the chairman of the Court, Ivan Tymchenko, assumed the powers of the-still-nonfunctioning Court by announcing that in his opinion the decision of the Cabinet was constitutional.[13]

3. FUNDAMENTAL AND SOCIO-ECONOMIC RIGHTS: AN INCONCLUSIVE RECORD

By early 2000, the activities of the Court have fallen into two broad categories: cases concerned with fundamental and socio-economic rights, and, adjudication in inter-institutional conflicts over competences.[14] The Court's involvement in the first sphere has been limited. To a large extent this inactivity has stemmed from the fact that the Court enjoys only the prerogative of abstract review, although implicit political motives have also played their role.

In the very first year of its existence, the Court obtained over 4,000 petitions from citizens regarding individual cases of infringement of their rights and freedoms by state institutions.[15] The majority of them was concerned with concrete cases, and, as such, they were outside the jurisdiction of the Court. The only way in which citizens can directly interact with the Constitutional Court is by asking for an official interpretation of laws and Constitution, which become binding for ordinary courts. In one of the cases, the Court asserted that the Constitution guarantees the citizen's right to obtain information on him/herself,

---

12 See interview with Ivan Tymchenko, chairman of the Constitutional Court, in *the Ukrainian Weekly*, 2 March 1997.

13 *Den*, 18 December 1996.

14 Between January 1997 and November 1999, that is in the first three years of its existence, the Court heard 40 cases: 18 on the alleged (un)constitutionality of laws and other legal acts, 18 interpretations of the Constitution and laws. Two opinions were given on the proposed changes to the Constitution and justifications for its refusal to open two further cases were also given.

15 Mykola Selianov, 'Problemni Pytannia Formuvania ta Vykonannia Budzhetu Konstytutsiynoho Sudu Ukrainy' [Problematic Questions on the Formation and Implementation of the Budget of the Constitutional Court], *Visnyk Konstytutsiynoho Sudu*, 5–6 (1998), p. 91.

which is collected and stored by the state agencies.[16] In another case, the Court decided that the refusal to hear a case in a court of general jurisdiction violated the right of an individual to have access to the court to protect their rights.[17] This right was – according to the Court – enshrined in articles 55, 64 and 124.2 of the Constitution. Thereby the Court decreed that the court of general jurisdiction had to assume jurisdiction in some cases.[18] State institutions also asked the Court to provide interpretations in cases concerned with the infringement of human freedoms enlisted in the Constitution. For example, upon a petition from the Supreme Court and the Security Services of Ukraine, the Court ruled that members of Parliament have no right of access to files of cases under investigation by the court or security services.[19]

Undoubtedly several high-profile cases in which the Court consistently interpreted the Constitution and/or laws in favour of citizens amounted to a symbolic breakthrough in that it imposed constitutional limits on the exercise of state power vis-à-vis its citizens in Ukraine. By determining that some long-standing practices were unconstitutional, the Court set new standards for politicians and the state apparatus. However, as is the case for all courts with powers of abstract review only, the fact that adjudication in specific cases of application of laws and other legal acts lies within the competence of ordinary courts only, significantly restricts the Court's involvement in adjudication in this sphere. Despite several path-breaking cases, the Court's role has been predominantly educational and symbolic. While ordinary courts are authorised to deal with concrete cases of rights, their inefficiency, inadequate funding and unreformed, Soviet-style approach to the administration of justice renders them grossly ineffective in performing this role. Without a comprehensive overhaul of the court system in Ukraine, the contribution of the Constitutional Court on the protection of constitutional rights cannot be but marginal.

In comparison to fundamental freedoms, the Court's record in the promotion of socio-economic rights, which the Ukrainian Constitution enumerates so extensively,[20] is not only more limited, but also more inconsistent. On the one hand, the Court became the champion of the constitutional right to free medical treatment, but on the other, in a deeply controversial ruling, it ensured the doctrine of the separation of powers to allow the Cabinet to raise utility tariffs, despite protests from the Parliament and the general unpopularity of the decision.

---

[16] Re: K.H. Ustymenko, 30 October 1997 (18/2–3–97). The rulings of the Court are published in the official publication of the Constitutional Court, *Visnyk Konstytutsiynoho Sudu*. They are also available via the Web page of the Supreme Council (http://alpha.rada.kiev.ua/cgi-bin/putfile.cgi).

[17] Re: Residents of the City of Zhovti Vody, 25 December 1997.

[18] Futey, above n. 11, p. 63.

[19] Re: Questions of People's Deputies of Ukraine, 19 May 1999 (N 1–12/99).

[20] See Kataryna Wolczuk, *The Moulding of Ukraine: The Constitutional Politics of State Formation* (Budapest: Central European University Press, 2002).

The Resolution of the Cabinet of Ministers, which specified which services had to be paid for in state health care institutions, was challenged by 66 Deputies of the Supreme Council on the grounds that the Constitution contains the explicit constitutional entitlement to free medial care (article 49). The Court agreed with the Deputies.[22] In its reasoning, the Court decreed that the term of 'medical care' (*medychna dopomoha*) should be understood as 'help the absence of which can endanger a human life'. The Court concluded that the majority of services listed in the Resolution were of such an essential nature for the preservation of human life that they could not only be made available upon payment since the Constitution obliged the state to provide free medical care. The Court went on to instruct the Cabinet on the policy measures to implement the constitutional guarantee:

> The Constitutional Court believes that the way to overcome the critical financial situation in the health services is not with the introduction of an almost unlimited list of paid medial services, but by changing ... the conceptual approaches to realise the constitutional right to free medial services, such as ... the implementation of an appropriate national programme, which would clearly outline the scope of free health services guaranteed by the state [and] the introduction of health insurance.[21]

Even if in this case the Court embarked on the substantive rulings regarding socio-economic policy, it was an exception rather than a rule. In another high profile case concerned with utility tariffs, the Court did not side with Parliament. Although *stricto sensu* the case concerned institutional competences, its economic ramifications for the population were so immediate and tangible, that the Court's decision amounted to an expression of its stance on the state's socio-economic policy. In a dispute over the division of powers, the Court issued a controversial ruling that took away from the Parliament the right to determine the socio-economic policy of the state. By siding with the executive branch, the Court effectively sanctioned its package of austerity measures.

In 1998, the Parliament adopted a law that prohibited the Cabinet of Minister from raising housing and transport tariffs until the salaries of state employees and social benefits, unpaid because of lack of budgetary funds, were paid in full. The rises had been introduced by the executive branch as part of reform measures demanded by the International Monetary Fund (IMF) before the resumption of the \$2.2bn Extended Fund Facility (EFF) programme. President Kuchma successfully challenged the law in the Constitutional Court. The Court argued that in accordance with article 85.5 of the Constitution, the Parliament defines only the "principles of the domestic and foreign policy."[22] The Parliament had defined pricing policy in the Law on Prices and Price-Making of December 1990

---

[21] *Id.*

[22] Re: Communal Services, 2 March 1999 (N 1–18/99).

(adopted before the break up of the USSR and so under the old Soviet Constitution). As in this law the Parliament authorised the Cabinet of Ministers to determine the level of utility tariffs, the Court argued that, in line with the principle of the separation of powers, the Council rescinded the right to determine specific aspects of pricing policy. On similar grounds, the argument that the Supreme Council had the right to determine the principles of social protection of citizens, in accordance with article 92.2, was rejected. Asserting that the Supreme Council exceeded its sphere of authority, the Constitutional Court invalidated the law in question. Following the Court's decision, the government raised the utility tariffs from 1 April 1999.[23] Parliament openly criticised the ruling and accused the Court of the violation of, amongst others, articles 85 and 92 of the Constitution (on the powers of the Supreme Council). The Council condemned the Court's invalidation of its Acts:

> The precedent created by the decision of the Court of 2 March 1999 confirms the imperfection of certain constitutional norms and laws which provides an opening for the non-implementation of laws and other Acts of the Supreme Council as their were intended ... and enables the evidently mistaken decisions of the Constitutional Court to be decisive, despite their rejection by the whole society.[24]

The ruling was challenged by Parliament on the basis that it undermined the authority of Parliament and, secondly contravened the preferences of society. Yet despite the thinly veiled challenge to the constitutional mandate of the Court, the Supreme Council refrained from taking steps to revise the law.

The evidence of the two above cases, which were most directly concerned with socio-economic policy, does provide sufficient reason to argue that, on balance, the Court has not been pre-occupied with socio-economic rights. Notwithstanding the ruling on paid health services, the Court was perfectly aware that the pitiful economic situation would not allow its decisions to be acted on and so too many rulings championing socio-economic rights would only undermine its own position. However, the restraint was also politically motivated. The course of the socio-economic policies of the state was something that put the left-wing in Parliament, which called for greater social protection, and the executive branch, which insisted on austerity measures, at loggerheads. The dearth of decisions defending socio-economic rights reflected as much the underlying desire of the Court to distance itself from the 'economically irresponsible' and 'populist' left-wing in Parliament, as the more or less overt political support for the executive branch in general.

The ruling on the abolition of the death penalty was another example of a decision that closely coincided with the agenda of the executive branch, in spite

---

[23]   *Jamestown Foundation Monitor*, 15 March 1999.
[24]   *Holos Ukrainy*, 17 March 1999.

of the widely known preferences of society and the majority of Deputies. On receipt of a petition from a group of deputies, who had failed to persuade the Parliament to abolish the death penalty, the Court ruled that the provision of capital punishment in the Criminal Code of Ukraine violated the Constitution.[25] The Court argued that article 27 granted the right to life, and other articles of the Constitution did not allow the death penalty as an exception to that article. Yet, taking into account the wide-ranging support for capital punishment in Ukraine both in Parliament and society at large, the Court felt obliged to go beyond the narrow reasoning anchored in legal positivism. Hence, the Court disputed the preventative effectiveness of capital punishment:

> International and national experience show that the death penalty cannot be defended as an effective means in the fight against crime. This type of punishment does not belong to factors that prevent crime. It is supported by criminological research: the level of crimes against human life does not decrease in response to the increase with the court sentences on death penalty. In the last 40 years ..., the number of unlawful killings has increased, despite the use of the highest type of punishment. Hence, from the point of view of prevention of crime, the death penalty cannot be defended.[26]

Moreover, in its reasoning the Court pointed out Ukraine's international obligations stemming from the pledge to abolish capital punishment when it joined the Council of Europe in November 1995.

The Court has also intervened in one of the most sensitive issues of public life in Ukraine – the state language. The ruling was far reaching in its policy ramifications. However, as it was only an interpretation of the Constitution, it is unlikely to be implemented. The decision was delivered by the Court in a case filed by a group of deputies, who asked the Court for an official interpretation of the article 10 of the Constitution: 'the state language of Ukraine is the Ukrainian language'.[27] While Ukrainian was already defined as the state language in the 1989 Law on Languages, the law has not been implemented evenly throughout the country, something that reflected the wide-spread use of the Russian language in public and private life in eastern and southern regions of the country. The Court gave a wide interpretation of article 10:

> [I]ts use is an obligatory medium of communication on the whole territory of Ukraine in the process of carrying out duties by organs of the state and local self-government ..., as well as other public spheres of social life. ... The language of education ... is Ukrainian.[28]

---

[25] Re: The Death Penalty, 29 December 1999 (N 1–33/99).

[26] *Id.*

[27] Re: Use of the Ukrainian Language, 14 December 1999 (N 1–6/99).

[28] *Id.*

By issuing a disposition on the positive action, which the state needed to take, the Court ventured into the sphere of policy-making, whilst also decreeing the place of the Ukrainian ethnic nation in the Ukrainian state:

> The Constitution of Ukraine assigned Ukrainian the status of state language
> ... This fully corresponds to the state-building role of the Ukrainian [ethnic]
> nation, as is pointed out in the Preamble of the Constitution, a nation, which
> historically has lived on the territory of Ukraine, which comprises the absolute
> majority of its population and gave the state its official name.[29]

As the official status and use of Ukrainian and Russian remain a profoundly contentious issue, the ruling provoked an angry reaction from the left-wing in Parliament, as the latter advocates official status as a way of curbing the linguistic and cultural Ukrainisation. The left-wing factions, the Communists and Peasants, protested against the ruling on the grounds that it was a 'political decision', 'supported neither by a majority in the Supreme Council nor by a majority of Ukrainian citizens'.[30] However, the most damning criticism originated inside the court in the form of a dissenting opinion. Judge Petro Myronenko argued that, "Because of its remaining in the tenets of sharp legal positivism and neo-positivism [and] the narrow normative approach to law, the Court adopted a decision which violates the Constitution both in form and content."[31] According to Myronenko, the matter did not lie within the jurisdiction of the Court, as the petition itself was formulated as a political and not legal statement, and hence fell within the competencies of the 'political' (legislative and executive) branches of power. Under the smokescreen of interpretation, the Court created new legal imperative norms, and, as a result, usurped the powers of Parliament. Moreover, by ruling on the obligatory use of a language in spheres of public life, the Court revealed its normativist bias: "Normativists are masters of their 'legal craft', but they are not aware of the limits of normative regulation and remain confident that through legal obligation ... they can solve any problem of the state or social life." Effectively, the Constitutional Court's decision amounted to "the provocative stimulation of the artificial Ukrainization by legal disposition."[32]

Notwithstanding the above cases, the number of rulings that directly intervened in the course of state policies was considerably lower than rulings concerned with the division of powers. In particular, there has been a dearth of rulings on socio-economic issues. This imbalance reflected the demands put upon the Court by a flood of cases on institutional competences. Even if the Court showed a preference for confining itself to the narrow remits of the Constitution, when it ventured into areas affecting policy making, its decisions

---

[29] Id.
[30] RFE/RL Newsline, Part 2, 22 December 1999.
[31] Re: Use of the Ukrainian Language, 14 December 1999 (N 1–6/99).
[32] Id.

was more likely to coincide with, rather than depart from, the policy choices of the executive branch. Therefore, despite its self-restraint, its rulings imposed its values and policy choices upon the Parliament. These early signs of activism may indicate the direction of the Court's future evolution, once it feels more self-assured of its standing among other branches of power.

4. THE DIVISION OF POWERS

As has already been pointed out, the primary area of the Court's activities has been the delineation of the constitutional prerogatives of the state institutions. The drawing of the Court into the long-standing feud between the legislature and executive, which intensified rather than weakened after the passage of the 1996 Constitution, was hardly surprising. The Court was equipped with a powerful tool – the power to invalidate acts of the executive and legislature – something that became sought after as a vehicle to outmanoeuvre political opponents.

The desperate search for a form of government capable of satisfying the diverse agenda of the actors involved in constitution-making, resulted in the creation of a semi-presidential system.[33] While in East-Central Europe parliamentarism became the dominant form of government, in Ukraine, as in other Soviet successor states, systems in which presidents are not only directly elected but also vested with executive powers, commanded favour. So in contrast to parliamentary systems, the popular will is embodied in two agents of the electorate, the Parliament and the President. Each puts forward competing claims to represent the 'sovereign people'. In Ukraine such a form of government was the product of numerous painstaking trade-offs, as the Constitution simultaneously represented a settlement of the intra-elite conflict over institutional resources and a compromise on deeply contested conceptions of statehood and nationhood. The desperate need to reconcile conflicting ideas and interests in a short span of time accounts for the lack of clarity and contradictions in many of the constitutional norms. The overlap in powers between the Parliament and the President, combined with the vagueness of many constitutional norms, such as, for example, the procedures for overriding the presidential veto, opened the way to diametrically diverging interpretations of the Basic Law once the institutions began to exercise, what they believed were, their constitutional prerogatives. At the same time, the lack of congruence between the composition of the legislature and the executive, was further compounded by the lack of a majority in Parliament, which made decisions of the legislature vulnerable to challenges from within.

In this context, adjudication in the inter-institutional conflict became the primary function of the Court. The importance of the adjudication performed by the Constitutional Court was demonstrated by the fact that first, the President

---

[33] Wolczuk, above 20.

and then the Parliament appointed their permanent representatives to the Constitutional Court to defend their institutional interests. As the Court was flooded with cases from both, their prioritisation became a highly politicised issue. Thus, on the second anniversary of the Constitutional Court, Ivan Tymchenko, the chairman of the Court, felt obliged to point out that the Court repels any pressures and, in particular, has no political motives in which cases are given priority, "the only criterion deciding the order of consideration of a matter by the Court is its readiness."[34] This was hardly the case in practice, however.

The Court's initial strategy in the adjudication of inter-institutional conflict has been characterised by procrastination and cautious balancing to minimise the adverse implications for any of the protagonists. The restraint was only too evident in its first ruling in the spring 1997 on the interpretation of the Constitution regarding the combining of parliamentary mandates with posts in the executive branch. According to article 78 of the new Constitution, these posts could not be held concurrently. Parliament had a large contingent of the so-called *sumisnyky*, who were perceived – in particular by the left wing in Parliament – as the President's fifth column. The pressure came from the Socialist chairman of the Supreme Council, Oleksandr Moroz, who obtained a ruling in a city court against *sumisnyky*. Disagreeing with that ruling, the group of Deputies in question filed in a case in the Constitutional Court. The Court ruled that deputies, who were elected in 1994 (that is, while the 1978 Constitution was still in force and before the 1995 Constitutional Agreement), did not have to renounce one of their posts (as this requirement was only introduced by the Agreement), despite the fact that such 'doubling' was explicitly prohibited by the new, 1996 Constitution (article 78).[35] In essence, the Court ruled that some of the Deputies, depending on the time of their election, were not bound by article 78, despite the fact that the Constitution did not envisage any exceptions. This decision can be, at best, interpreted as fence sitting, or, at worst, as politically biased in favour of the executive. It may be argued that faced with a highly political issue and prior to having established its reputation, the Court wisely avoided a head-on collision with any of the branches of powers. On the other hand, this indecisive ruling undermined its credibility, because it immediately sparked off accusations of pro-presidential leanings, repeatedly voiced by the left-wing factions and Oleksandr Moroz in particular. The latter criticised the Court's first ruling and implied that the decision of the city court depriving all *sumisnyky* of a deputy's mandate remained in force.

The principle of the separation of powers became a tool in the hands of the

---

[34] *Den*, 20 October 1998.
[35] Re: On Incompatibility of the Deputy's Mandate, 13 May 1997 (N 03/29–97). See also *Uriadovyi Kurier*, 20 May 1997.

Court to circumvent the prerogatives of the Parliament in line with the more-or-less explicit interests of the executive branch. Amongst the most contentious rulings, the Court contravened the decision of Parliament to set up a powerful Accounting Chamber, which the Parliament aspired to make its agent of control. In two separate decisions in July and December 1997, the Chamber's competences were considerably curtailed in order to – as the Court reasoned – maintain the separation of powers set forth in article 6 of the Constitution.[36] The President also succeeded in making the procedures for the overriding of the presidential veto considerably more difficult for Parliament to meet by getting the Court to decide that each legal revision had to be approved in Parliament by a qualified majority of two-thirds. But it was the Court's decision on factions in Parliament which had particularly far-reaching implications for the executive-legislative relations as it played havoc with the process of the internal structuring of Parliament.

In 1998 the elections were held under the 'Electoral Law' according to which half of the Deputies (225) were elected in single mandate districts using a 'first past the post' formula, and the other half from national party lists in accordance with the principle of proportional representation for those parties which cleared the 4 percent threshold. Although a case questioning the constitutionality of such a mixed electoral law was filed before the elections, the Court refrained from adjudicating on the grounds that it was an internal matter of Parliament.[37] After the elections, the Supreme Council introduced changes to its *Rules of Procedures*, such as that only those parties that cleared the 4 percent threshold could form Parliamentary caucuses. A group of non-affiliated deputies challenged the decision in Parliament. On this occasion, however, rather than refusing to become involved, the Court declared the change unconstitutional on the grounds that it made Deputies elected on party lists 'more equal than others' and discriminated against Deputies elected in single-mandate districts.[38] Such discrimination, the Court argued, violated the constitutional freedom of political activity (article 15). The ramifications of the decision were immediate and far reaching – new factions with very tenuous links to political parties proliferated in Parliament and the structure of Parliament became less politically transparent virtually overnight. The incentive for members of Parliament to develop more stable partisan affiliation was removed. At the same time, the ruling worked in

---

[36] Re: The Constitutional Interpretation of Art. 98 by the Supreme Council, 11 July 1997 (N 1/1909–97), and RE: the Accounting Chamber, 23 December 1997 (N 01/34–97). See also RE: Changes to Art. 98 of the Constitution, 25 March 1999 (N 1–19–99).

[37] Re: Law on Election of Deputies to the Supreme Council of Ukraine, 13 May 1997 (N 03/29–97). On the political implications of the ruling on the 'Law on Elections' see *Zerkalo Nedeli*, 28 February 1998 and *Den*, 3 March 1998.

[38] Re: Formation of Factions in the Supreme Council, 3 December 1998 (N 1–40/98). See also *Uriadovyi Kurier*, 17 December 1998.

favour of President Kuchma for whom the divided and fragmented Parliament presented a weaker opponent. In political terms, the ruling stood in the way of the greater political structuring of Parliament, which is *a sine qua non* for the assertion of its standing on par with the executive.

When the Court adjudicated in the inter-institutional conflict, it did not shy away from using its powers of 'final' constitutional review. In most cases, the Court adopted a decision on unconstitutionality of the Act in question, or, more often, certain sections of it. In the first three years of its existence, only in one out of 18 decisions did the Court rule on the full compliance of the Act with the Constitution. In terms of the origins of cases on (un)constitutionality, the bulk of them were initiated by the President. They were directed against the Parliament, and, to a lesser extent, against another legislative body, the Supreme Council of the Autonomous Republic of Crimea.[39] Even though the President has also had his Acts invalidated by the Court,[40] in the main, the Constitutional Court struck down the Acts of Parliament. Only one case against the President was filed by Parliament as a whole. In all other instances, groups of Deputies challenged the President in the Court.

While Parliament has been on the receiving end of the President's zeal, parliamentary Acts were also successfully challenged on numerous occasions by groups of Deputies. The provision of the Constitution, which allows a group of at least 45 Deputies to file a case, enabled parliamentary factions and *ad hoc* groupings of Deputies to mount repeated challenges to the decisions of parliamentary majorities (often with more or less tacit backing from the Presidency). For example, the rulings on capital punishment and language resulted from petitions from deputies. Taking into account the fragmentation, ideological polarisation and weakness of party discipline in parliamentary caucuses, that such groups seized on any opportunity to revoke the decisions taken by (often

---

[39] See for example a decision on the unconstitutionality of the law of the Supreme Council of ARC on 'On Civic Associations'. The law was suspended by the President, who in accordance with article 137.9 of the constitution, filed a simultaneous appeal in the Constitutional Court to determine the constitutionality of the suspended law. The Court declared that the law was in breach of the constitution on the grounds that the Supreme Council of ARC had no right to adopt such a law; it is a prerogative of the Supreme Council of Ukraine in accordance with art. 92.11 of the Constitution of Ukraine. See Re: Civic Associations in ARC, 3 March 1998 (N 1/5–98). In another decision, the Constitutional Court invalidated the normative act of the Supreme Council of ARC on moving Crimea to a different time zone than the rest of Ukraine. Re: Time Regulation in ARC, 25 March 1998 (N 1–20/98).

[40] See, for example, the ruling on the unconstitutionality of the presidential appointment of the deputy heads of local administration. However, even if the Court denied the president this prerogative, it made its decision prospective, hence the deputy heads appointed by the president stayed in the office. Re: Appointment of deputy Heads of Local Administrations, 24 January 1997 (N 3/690–97).

situational) majorities is hardly surprising. As a result, Parliament's acts have been challenged both from inside and outside the institution. The crippling internal disorganisation of Parliament prevented it from confronting the Court unanimously. In fact the Council never attempted to overthrow the Court's rulings. The futility of an attempt to do so undoubtedly was related to the fact that a majority behind any piece of legislation most often resulted from a coincidence of the diverse motives of the deputies present in the chamber, rather than a co-ordination of positions.

In mounting challenges to Parliament's powers, which provoked anger amongst the Parliamentarians, the Court legitimised its own actions by portraying itself as a new institution, central to the separation of power. This was something – the judges claimed – that Parliament could not appreciate because of its chequered past history. In response to the criticism voiced by the Supreme Council after the first ruling,[41] the Court issued a statement condemning "the continuous ignorance of the principle of the separation of powers as an immovable foundation of the constitutional order." At the same time, the Court implied that the legal culture will improve only with the passage of time: "[U]nderstandably, the legal nihilism, which historically embedded itself in the consciousness of the part of the population and officials cannot be overcome at once."[42] The indictment of the Parliament as an institution debilitated by its past was repeated on other occasions. For example, criticising the reductions in the Court's budget made by Parliament, judge Petro Myronenko described the shortcomings of the Ukrainian legislature:

[L]ike the Parliament of any state, the Supreme Council is inherently bound by the specific-national traits of the historical process in Ukraine. The establishment of political liberalism in Ukraine, as in any post-Soviet states [and] the formation of a genuinely pluralist Parliament is inhibited by various difficulties, the roots of which are in our past.[43]

The legislature's roots in the past became incriminating evidence of its inability to come to respect the new, post-Soviet constitutional order, including the role assigned to the Court. The short life-span of the Court become a legitimising factor, as it portrayed itself as untainted by the distorting legacies of the Soviet-era.

---

[41] In response to the criticism voiced by the Supreme Council after the first ruling (see above).

[42] *Uriadovyi Kurier*, 10 June 1997.

[43] Petro Myronenko, 'Budzhet Yak Chynnyk Sudovoi Nezalezhnosti. Dosvid Konstytutsiynoho Sudu Ukrainy' [Budget as a Factor in Judicial Independence: an Experience of the Constitutional Court of Ukraine], *Visnyk Konstytutsiynoho Sudu*, 5–6 (1998), p. 82.

5. THE CHANGES TO THE CONSTITUTION

The fact that the Court invalidated more Acts of Parliament than of the executive has fuelled accusations of pro-presidential leanings. However, upon examination of the Court's record, these accusations were not fully justified in the first three years of its existence. Rather the overall balance reflected the greater activism of the Presidency in pursuing its political agenda, and the passivity of Parliament as a whole. However, by the fourth year of the Court's existence, its rulings began to bear more clear signs of concession to political expediency.

Neither the conduct nor outcome of the presidential elections in November 1999 bode well for a political truce in Ukraine. Reassured by the renewal of his popular mandate, Leonid Kuchma embarked on a blunt confrontation with Parliament by orchestrating a referendum on the 'redistribution of powers' on the grounds that if the Supreme Council could form a "constructive majority ... the country does not need this Parliament".[44] On 15 January 2000, the President pushed for an expansion of the presidential powers, by decreeing on a nationwide referendum to be held on 16 April 2000. The referendum was to decide whether to give the President the right to dissolve the Parliament if it fails to form a majority within one month after the elections. It would also decide on the following issues: the abolition of Deputies' immunity; the introduction of an upper house of Parliament; a reduction in the number of Deputies from 450 to 300; a vote of no-confidence in the current Parliament, and; the amendment of the Constitution through a referendum (rather than by the Supreme Council). Kuchma's referral to the popular will to circumscribe the legislature, turned into the most stringent test of the Court's ability to withstand political pressures from the executive, which the Court, perhaps wisely from the point of view of its institutional survival, failed to pass.

The decree led to consternation on the domestic scene and the condemnation of Ukraine in the international arena. The Parliamentary factions, ranging from the moderate right-wing Rukh to the left-wing CPU, criticised the idea of the plebiscite and a group of 108 Deputies filed a case on the unconstitutionality of Kuchma's decree. The Council of Europe expressed its concern over the referendum, especially the lack of an adequate legislative basis and the encroachment on the Parliament's powers:

We are concerned about the possible consequences for the separation of powers of an abrupt disruption in the system of checks and balances of the country's institutions. We consider that this referendum will not be valid as it is in contradiction with Ukraine's constitution, which can only be amended with the participation of Parliament. Its modalities and organisation remain unclear. ... There is no legal basis for such a 'popular initiative' in the current

---

[44] *RFE/RL*, 15 December 1999.

Constitution. A valid referendum cannot be organised until a new law on a referendum procedure has been passed by the Verkhovna Rada.[45]

The legal consternation was not alleviated by the Court's ruling of 27 March 2000.[46] The decision sought to square the circle by reconciling the principle of popular sovereignty as expressed in article 5 ("the people are the bearers of sovereignty and the only source of power in Ukraine"), on the one hand, with the doctrine of constitutionalism, according to which the 'popular will' was subject to constitutional limitations, on the other. The Court prioritised the former principle over the latter, although the power of the 'popular will' was somewhat curtailed. Four out of the six questions on the constitutional changes were upheld as suitable for gauging the 'popular will', despite the fact that the Constitution outlines a procedure for the enactment of amendments to the Constitution. (According to article 156, the referendum is one of the procedural requirements for changes to some chapters of the Constitution, but only *after* the Supreme Council has voted in favour of changes by a constitutional majority of two thirds.) The reasoning of the Court was convoluted and perplexing. There was no clear explanation as to why some questions were approved and others rejected. Nevertheless, despite being sketchy and contradictory in its spirit, the ruling struck down the two most dangerous questions which could have allowed for the Constitution to be altered solely on the basis of a referendum (hence by-passing the legislature altogether) and would have granted the President the right to dissolve the Supreme Council. The Court also decided that any changes to the Constitution could only be enacted in accordance with chapter XIII "Introducing Amendments to the Constitution", thereby re-asserting the legislature's exclusive right to amend the Constitution.

Undoubtedly, the exclusion of the two questions eliminated the imminent and gravest threats to the power of Parliament and so was welcomed by Parliamentarians. Serhiy Holovatyi, the most ardent anti-referendum campaigner in the Ukrainian delegation to the Council of Europe, reckoned that:

> The possibility of introducing a new Constitution of Ukraine by using this referendum has been eliminated. That's a blow against those forces that wanted to put Ukraine on the same track as [Belarussian President Aleksandr] Lukashenka. ... By its decision, the Constitutional Court has supported Parliament as an institution.[47]

The ruling, however, did not eliminate the underlying doubts over the referendum. In particular, the Court's insistence that the results of the referendum were

---

[45] Report 'Reform of the Institutions in Ukraine' by the Committee on the Honouring of Obligations and Commitments by Member States of the Council of Europe (Monitoring Committee) of the Council of Europe, Doc. 8666 (14 March 2000).

[46] Re: the All-Ukrainian Referendum Upon People's Initiative, 27 March 2000 (N 1–26/2000).

[47] *RFE/RL Poland, Belarus, Ukraine Report* (31 March 2000).

'binding' for all state institutions was difficult to square with its assertion that change to the Constitution was a prerogative of the Parliament.

The approval of all four questions in the referendum (a result, which was hardly surprising taking into account the involvement of the local state administration in the 'yes' campaign) posed a vexed question on how the results ought to be enacted. Once again the Court was drawn in, when two alternative draft amendment laws were filed simultaneously by the President and parliamentary left-wing opposition. The latter aimed at a more fundamental re-design of the balance of power between the legislature and executive. The Court's decision that the Presidential draft satisfied the criteria of article 157,[48] without announcing its decision on the opposition's draft, revealed overtly political motives for the way the Court prioritised the cases. Under pressure from the Parliament, the Court issued a ruling on the opposition's draft in which it approved only the provisions that coincided with the narrow proposals in the President's draft, on the grounds that other proposed amendments were not directly related to the questions addressed in the referendum.[49] By insisting that only changes initiated in the President's referendum could be incorporated into the Constitution, the Court contravened the Parliament's power to initiate changes to the Constitution at any time. The Court's unjustifiably restrictive stance on the constitutional amendments (even if by that time, a parliamentary majority cobbled together by the Presidential administration, seemed to be willing to rescind its powers), testified to the fact that the Court was acting on the basis of political expediency.

The Court's arbitration on the referendum and constitutional changes evidenced its precarious task of taming the intensifying conflict over competences by subjecting it to constitutional review. Even if the Court tempered the worst excesses of the President's desire to augment his powers by curtailing those of the Parliament, it also provided a seal of approval for the presidential course of action. As a result, the Court's reputation for even-handedness suffered severely and confirmed the widely held belief that, 'the Constitutional Court is dependent to some degree on the President and the Cabinet of Ministers and tends to rule in favour of the executive'.[50]

6. CONCLUSION

The Ukrainian Constitutional Court has mastered the art of navigating the choppy waters of national politics, thanks to – as one author puts it – the

---

[48] Re: Changes to Articles 76, 80, 90, 106 of the Constitution of Ukraine, 27 June 2000 (N 1–38/2000).

[49] Re: Changes to the Constitution upon the Initiative of the People's Deputies of Ukraine, 11 July 2000 (N 1–39/2000).

[50] Serhiy Holovatyi, 'The New Constitution of Ukraine: Developments and Perspectives', in Theofil Kis and Irena Makaryk (eds.), *Towards a New Ukraine* (Ottawa: Chair of Ukrainian Studies 1999), p. 33.

Court's skilful "use of its exceptional powers with the precision of a surgeon". This ability stems from its "extraordinary foresight" in respect of the political repercussions of its decisions.[51] The Court's rulings have been subordinated to the paramount objective of its survival, even if only to ensure the consolidation of constitutional review in Ukraine in the turbulent early days of systemic transformation. The fulfilment of this objective depended – as was seen by judges – on securing the continuous support from the Presidency, the dominant actor in Ukrainian politics. By avoiding bold challenges to the Presidency, the Constitutional Court inadvertently lent its legitimising clout to the President, whose actions were geared to weaken the constitutional basis of Parliament's power. As a result, even if the Court did not undermine the powers of the Parliament by substituting its own value judgements or policy choices, it has become instrumental in circumscribing the powers of the Parliament in the hope of saving its own fortunes by appeasing the executive. In public pronouncements, the Constitutional Court vehemently upholds its judicial independence. Yet, as has been said of the Ukrainian media, even if the Court has the constitutional guarantee of independence, it has the wisdom not to use it.

Undoubtedly the Parliament has contributed to its own predicament, unable so far either to organise itself internally into stable factions or to pursue a consistent legislative agenda which would require the reform of its Byzantine procedures, the violation of which became routine. In addition to the President, parliamentary minorities have successfully mounted legal challenges to the majority. Under such circumstances, it was a foregone conclusion that the executive branch will be the net beneficiary of Parliament's crippling deficiencies, which preventing it from exercising its constitutional powers. Yet, the Court has assisted in turning a *de facto* situation into a *de jure* one.

---

[51]   *Den*, 3 March 1999.

15. The Role and Experience of the Slovakian Constitutional Court

Darina Malová

1. INTRODUCTION

This chapter aims to show that since its foundation in 1993 the Constitutional Court in Slovakia has become a central pillar of the new democratic regime. In a country with only weak constitutional traditions and where democratic consolidation became complicated by national aspirations and nation and state building processes, the performance of the new Constitutional Court has contributed importantly to the stabilization of new democratic regime, promoting the idea of limited government and respect for the rule of law. The achievement of this vital position in the process of balancing and solving political conflicts was a rather unexpected outcome of the institution building process, as the historical, cultural, constitutional and political conditions in which the Court found itself were more likely to constrained the Court's position than encourage the re-emergence of constitutional review in Slovakia.

The Slovak Constitution of 1992 did not impose strong constraints on political actors within the legislative and executive branches of power and so the role of the constitutional jurisdiction in checking political decisions has increased extraordinarily since the establishment of the Constitutional Court. Unclear and contradictory constitutional rules have by and large shaped the Court's agenda. Moreover, the Slovak Constitution attributes to the Court very broad competencies, which have frequently overloaded the Court's docket. In addition, Slovakia's polity has been deeply divided over the nation-state issue, and subsequent political conflicts during 1994–98 between the ruling nationalist coalition, led by the Movement for Democratic Slovakia and the fragmented and weak opposition caused serious concerns about perspectives of liberal democracy in the country. Forty years of communist rule severely undermined the strong legal culture developed during the inter-war Czechoslovakia (1918–1938), and therefore much of the population did not perceive laws and legal order as a 'common good.' On the contrary, there was a widespread popular belief that laws were made to be circumvented. However, strangely enough, even Communist politicians during the final stages of that regime practiced and emphasized 'legalistic', positivist justification of political decisions. Therefore, law schools and profession as such were held in very high esteem, though toughly controlled by the Communist Party. As only a few lawyers joined dissident organizations, restructuring of the rule of law and establishment of judicial

Wojciech Sadurski (ed.), Constitutional Justice, East and West, 349–372
© 2002 *Kluwer Law International. Printed in Great Britain.*

review required the participation of the same staff that participated in the law making of the former regime and so a strong commitment to judicial independence and constitutionalism could not be readily expected. This posed an additional obstacle to the successful institutionalization of constitutional jurisdiction and the rule of law.

I argue that despite unfavorable norms and traditions, which are detrimental to the successful institutionalization of judicial review, the performance of the Constitutional Court in Slovakia has proved to be more balanced than was expected at its establishment. The Court and its decisions have acquired independency, legitimacy, respect, authority and the trust of society. I suggest that the prevailing pattern of judicial review has included emphasis on the procedural, sometimes even technical, argumentation, self-restriction of the Court's mandate, and a cautious 'distribution of victories' between disputants. Finally, the institutionalization of the judicial review in Slovakia has stimulated a productive dialogue between the Constitutional Court and the elected branches of power that has resulted in the amendment of controversial constitutional provisions.

2. TRADITIONS OF PARLIAMENTARY DEMOCRACY AND JUDICIAL REVIEW

Slovakia's political and legal traditions are closely connected with the institutional design of the First Czechoslovak Republic (1918–1938) and the Communist regime (1948–1989). The Slovak Constitution of 1992 based on this institutional background combined two rival ideas. On the one hand, it exhibited a commitment to parliamentary sovereignty and whilst simultaneously incorporating a constitutional jurisdiction. Mainly the French and American constitutional models inspired authors of the 1920 Constitution, however, the Constitutional Court was drafted according to the Austrian model.[1]

A constitutional jurisdiction is usually established in politically fragmented societies, which was a case in the First Czechoslovak Republic (1918–1938) with its multi-ethnic composition, but there the organization and administration of the Government was very unitary and centralist. The regime provided only limited autonomy to Ruthenia,[2] and only in 1938 did it accept the demands of the Slovak political parties, which had asked for autonomy since the foundation of the Republic. The first Czechoslovak Constitution of 1920 "copied foreign models and was a compromise between the wishes of the political parties.[3] The

---

[1]   Richard Walter, 'Středoevropské ústavní soudnictví a ryzí nauka právní. (Central European Constitutional Jurisdiction and the Pure Legal Science), *Právník*, 2 (1994), pp. 136–137.

[2]   The remote and rather backward region in Eastern part of the Czechoslovak Republic, after World War II became a part of the Soviet Union, and now it is a part of Ukraine.

[3]   Ferdinand Peroutka, *Budování státu III (Building of the State, vol. III)* (Praha: Lidové noviny 1991), p. 928.

incorporation of the Constitutional Court resulted more from the hasty Constitution drafting process than from careful consideration on the part of the "Founding Fathers". The Court was competent to examine the constitutionality of laws passed by the Parliament or Parliamentary Assembly of the Ruthenia but it did not play the role of neutral arbiter between equally entitled protagonists, which is a common solution to political conflicts, particularly in federal states.[4]

The first Constitutional Court in Czechoslovakia was formed on November 17, 1921 and was initially granted a ten-year term. The court did not have a pre-legislative supervisory power, i.e. the Court could not comment on constitutionality of proposed or draft legislation. The Constitution established the power of abstract judicial review, and the Court had only one competence – the power to determine the constitutionality of laws. Moreover, the Court did not have an exclusive power to rule over constitutionality of legislation, as such a competency was enjoyed also the ordinary courts. This inconsistency in institutional design stemmed from the attempt to unite several models while drafting the Constitution. In this case judicial review was inspired simultaneously by the Austrian and American models.

The Court had seven members who were appointed by different bodies to ten-year terms. President, on the basis of proposals from both chambers of Parliament and the Cabinet, nominated three out of seven Justices. The President also appointed the Chair of the Court. Two other justices were judges of the Supreme Court and two more were members of the Supreme Administrative Court. During its first term the Court considered only 46 resolutions of the Parliament but no actual laws.

Although the initial term of the Court expired in November 1937, a new Court was not nominated until May 1938, due to political controversies and the poor performance of the Court during its first term.[5] From May 1938 until the end of the First Republic (March 1939) the Court adjudicated upon two laws. Czechoslovakia's inter-war democracy established the idea of constitutional and limited government, however, the dominant practices of strong party government and majority rule limited the institutionalization of judicial review.

After the Communist Party seized power in post-war Czechoslovakia (February 1948), the idea of judicial review was completely abandoned. Nevertheless, during the Prague Spring movement of 1968 – an attempt to democratize the Communist regime – this almost forgotten idea was renewed. It was closely connected with a question of the position of the Slovak nation

---

[4]   Klaus von Beyme, 'The Genesis of Constitutional Review in Parliamentary Systems', in Christine Lanfried (ed), *Constitutional Review and Legislation. An International Comparison* (Baden-Baden: Nomos 1988), pp. 21–38.

[5]   Eva Broklová, *Československá demokracie. Politickš systém ČSR 1918–1938* [Czechoslovak Democracy. Political System in 1918–1938] (Praha: SLON 1992).

within the common state. The new institutional set-up – a federation – was established by the 1968 constitutional amendment (No. 143/1968). Consequently, the Bill on Federation also provided for the institution of the Constitutional Courts. However, the establishment of Constitutional Courts stipulated in the amendment remained on paper only and was not implemented for another 23 years.

Neither the political traditions of the first Czechoslovak Republic nor of the Communist Federation provided a strong impetus for emergence of the idea of judicial review after the collapse of the Communist regime. Despite these legacies, legal experts and leading politicians, after the change of regime in 1989 argued in favor of such an innovation. While many former dissidents understood the judicial review mainly as a mechanism for the protection of the human rights, violated by the former regime, some Slovak nationally-oriented politicians, also supported this move, as they perceived the institution of judicial review as a mechanism protecting Slovakia's position within the Federation. These circumstances may help to explain the unanimous political support for the revival of the old liberal idea of a constitutional jurisdiction in Czechoslovakia. The main political actors believed that constitutional courts had a great role in ensuring that legislation was in line with the new democratic Constitution and its values. Moreover, at the establishment of the new regime and political elite, which was nominated to the Parliament, there was an acceptance of the idea that the majority rule should be constrained by non-representative bodies.

The post-Communist political elite prepared new amendment to the Constitution to provide for the establishment of Constitutional Courts at the level of the Federation and both Republics. This amendment was only partly modeled according to the Czechoslovak traditions. For example, the process of selection of judges was exclusively in the hands of executive and legislative branches of power, as the President has the right to appoint the twelve justices, from candidates nominated by Federal and national Parliaments.

The Federal Constitutional Court's competences were rather broad and based on the concept of abstract judicial review. The Court had power to examine the constitutionality of legal norms passed by the Federal Parliament and Federal Cabinet It could decide over the constitutionality of laws passed by national Parliaments and legal regulations passed by the national governments. The Court also had a power to decide disputes over powers distributed among Federal and national Government authorities. Court had a power to examine citizens' complaints in the case of the violation of basic human rights. The Federal Court was finally established at the beginning of 1992 and functioned only for a year. The Slovak Parliament in December 1991 also passed the law on the establishment of the Constitutional Court in the Slovak Republic, but this body was not founded before the end of the common state.

2.1. The Constitution on the Constitutional Court

Following from the above traditions, Slovak political leaders and legal experts considered the establishment of the Constitutional Court as the inherent body of the new democratic Constitution and a "common good". During the Constitution-writing none of the main political parties questioned the necessity to incorporate the judicial review in the political system. Even many constitutional lawyers, who were members of the Communist Party of Slovakia, favored the institution of the Constitutional Court, because they already endorsed its establishment within the former federation. Also legal experts connected with the national-oriented parties, such as the Movement for Democratic Slovakia (HZDS) and Slovak National Party (SNS) supported creation of the court, as previously it was perceived as the arbiter of Slovakia's interests in the common state with Czechs. The mechanism of judicial review was widely accepted as a vital part of modern democracy.

The set-up of the Court was drafted mostly according to the law passed by the Slovak Parliament at the end 1991, and was very similar to the Federal Constitutional Amendment. During the public debates and party bargaining over the text of the new Constitution there were only a few controversies. One related to the term lengths of justices. While some legal experts were in favor of life-time appointment, some prefer at least ten-year period -according to political traditions. The ruling Movement for Democratic Slovakia (HZDS) pushed for shortening of term to seven years only, the same length which had been set up by the 1968 amendment. HZDS leaders maintained that it was necessary for the first time to "test" the independence of the Court, as it is a new institution. Although the limitation of Justices' term usually undermines it's the Court's independence, especially if parliamentary parties play important role in the nomination of judges, the proposal of the HZDS was passed by the Parliament. This issue was raised again in the Constitutional Amendment of 2001. The revised text of the Constitution proposes extending the term of justices to twelve years, arguing in favor of stabilization of judicial review.

A second debate related to the mode of selection of Justices. The 1992 Constitution instituted a mode of nomination, which stemmed from past practices. The President appoints ten judges to seven year terms from twenty candidates nominated by Parliament. Thus, the judges were selected by the very bodies that they were to control, namely Parliament and President. This pattern does not very much deviate from models typical for Western parliamentary democracies.[6] However, unlike most Western parliamentary democracies[7] the Slovak Constitution does not require any special majority to select its twenty candidates.

---

[6] Alexander von Brünnek, 'Constitutional Review and Legislation in Western Democracies', in Christine Lanfried (ed), *Constitutional Review and Legislation. An International Comparison* (Baden-Baden: Nomos 1988), pp. 219–260.

[7] For example, in Germany, Italy, Spain, Belgium and Portugal the selection of constitutional judges requires an extraordinary parliamentary majority, while in Austria and Switzerland

Article 134 of the Constitution stipulates that only lawyers, above the age of forty, and with at least fifteen years of professional experience are eligible to become judges. The Law on the Constitutional Court passed in 1993 provides for the re-elections of judges for a second term. The Slovak Constitution does not provide opportunity for legal professional organizations and for legal institutions such as the Supreme Court to intervene in the selection of judges. The law on the Constitutional Court remedies this shortcoming, allowing not only Members of Parliament to propose candidates to the Constitutional Court, but also giving this right to the Government, the Chairmen of the Constitutional and Supreme Courts, academic institutions (law schools and the Institute of Law, at the Slovak Academy of Sciences), and the Association of Judges.

2.2. The Independence of the Court

According to Article 124, the Constitutional Court shall be an independent judicial authority vested with the mandate to protect the integrity of constitutional principles. Slovakia's political elite was deeply split over the separation from the Czecho-Slovak Federation, therefore the Opposition opposed the parliamentary mode of selection of judges, fearing the dominant position of HZDS in Parliament. The party-based selection of judges raised doubts about future Court's independence. In particular, the appointment of Milan Čič, a close ally of Vladimír Mečiar, the leader of the Movement for Democratic Slovakia, as the Chairman of the Court caused serious worries among Opposition leaders.

The Court was established in March, 1993. The actual composition of the court was in the end quite balanced in terms of party influence, because HZDS had to accept also candidates of non-governmental parties as a part of bargaining deal with the Opposition over the elections of President. At that time the Constitution required a three-fifth majority to elect President, and the establishment of the Court was not possible without the President, who exclusively has the power to appoint judges.

Article 136 of the Constitution secures the same extent of immunity for the Justices as for MPs. It means that they cannot be arrested or prosecuted until their immunity is lifted, and the only institution that has power to lift their immunity is the Court. After such procedure, in the case of a judge being convicted for a malicious offense upon a disciplinary decision by the Court for misconduct, or if the judge becomes unable to participate in the work of the Court only the President has the right to remove a judge from the Constitutional Court.

According to the first Chairman of the Court, Milan Čič, Justices did not experienced political pressure during the first term. However, the Court's

---

no special majority is prescribed, but a party ratio in the selection of constitutional judges is nevertheless maintained due to political tradition. Ibid, at 225.

decisions, as they were often related to political controversies, have not been immune from attempts by the political parties to question and politicize Court's role. The HZDS-led coalition Cabinet (1994–1998) most often tried to discredit the Court, although did not dare to dismiss or pressure Justices. In 1995, Prime Minister Mečiar decided to "punish" the Chairman of the Court for his independence and took away the car and bodyguard provided by the Government. Only later did Mečiar reverse his decision and returned both items to the Chairman, in a perhaps conciliatory gesture. However, he and his Party did not stop commenting on the Court's decisions. In the same year Mečiar stated that "a situation where the Constitutional Court, by its interpretation of the law either broadens or changes the Constitution cannot be tolerated." He also called the Court "a sick element on Slovakia's political scene." Moreover, HZDS suggested that the procedure of passing Court resolutions by a simple majority should be replaced by either a three-fifths or a four-fifths majority vote, a mechanism which would effectively paralyze the Court. To reach this aim was not possible, as the Government did not have required three-fifths majority in the Parliament. Despite all these attempts to discredit the Court, its authority was and is generally recognized by public opinion, journalists, legal experts and politicians, too.

2.3. Powers and Competence

In five Articles (Art. 125–129), the Constitution defines Court's jurisdiction in a very wide mode, thereby vesting many powers in this new body. The Court enjoys powers to rule over constitutional conflicts between ordinary laws and the Constitution or constitutional statutes; regulations passed by the Government or generally binding rules passed by the ministries or other authorities of the central Government and the Constitution, constitutional statutes, or other laws; generally binding rules passed by local self-governing bodies and the Constitution or other laws; generally binding rules passed by local government authorities and the Constitution, other laws or other generally binding rules, and generally binding rules and international instruments promulgated as fixed by law (Art. 125).

According to the Article 128 the Court enjoys the authority to interpret the Constitution and constitutional statutes. Article 126 stipulates that the Court decides disputes over powers distributed among central government authorities, unless these disputes are to be decided by another governmental authority as provided by law. Article 129 says that the Constitutional Court reviews challenges to decisions that confirm or reject the seat of a Member of Parliament. The Court also decides whether the elections to the National Council of the Slovak Republic and to local self-governing bodies have been held in conformity with the Constitution and the law. The same Article delegates to the Court the power to review challenges to the results of a referendum and gives the Court the final say in dissolving a political party. Moreover, Article 127 states that the Court reviews the challenges to decisions made by central and local government authorities, and by local self-governing bodies in cases concerning violations of fundamental rights and freedoms of citizens, unless the protection of such rights falls under the jurisdiction of another court.

Thus, the Constitution assigns to the Court several different, and broadly defined functions. From the very beginning of its existence the Court had to adjudicate upon the constitutionality of statutes, controversies between the state agencies, to review and interpret division of power between central institutions, to decide over challenges to mandates, to interpret fundamental political institutes such as referendum, amnesty, and at the same time to decide about complaints of individual citizens related to violations of fundamental rights. Since the establishment of the Court, constitutional lawyers have emphasized several shortcomings of unclear constitutional instructions. In particular, the main criticism concerned the Court's competence to examine constitutionality of municipal authorities' decisions, because such competence is also enjoyed by the Parliament. This concurrent competence over the same issue may stimulate actors to appeal to both institutes, and consequently to lead to incoherent jurisdiction, if the Court and Parliament would decide in a different way.[8] The 2001 amendment of the Constitution has changed several relevant constitutional provisions. Many of these changes resulted from the Court's experience and its opinions, as the authors of the amendment served as advisors to the Justices.

2.4. Mechanisms of the Court's Decision-Making

The Court has the power of abstract judicial review, i.e. the Court may examine the constitutionality of any law, statute, or regulation passed by Parliament, Cabinet, or local government without the existence of an actual lawsuit. However, the Court does not have a prior supervision power precedent to promulgation of a law, i.e. the Court cannot comment on constitutionality of proposed legislation.

The Court can be petitioned by one-fifth of all Members of Parliament (30), by the President, the Cabinet, any court, and by the Attorney General. Also citizens can petition the Court directly, but only when their fundamental rights have been violated (Article 130). The Constitution also enumerates cases, which have to be decided by all Justices, the fact that there are ten Justices could complicate the voting procedure, as the Constitution did not define it. Only the Law on the Constitutional Court introduced majority voting rule. This Law also provided rules about the formation and competences of the Constitutional

---

[8]   Ján Drgonec (1994), 'Právomoc Ústavného súdu Slovenskej republiky pri zabezpečovaní súladu právneho poriadku Slovenskej republiky s Ústavou SR'. In: *Právny obzor* č.1, pp. 14–24.

Court's Senates, and which cases fall under their jurisdiction. However, neither the Constitution nor the Court stipulated rules as to how to mediate in such case as where two Senates decide differently in the same case. The 2001 Constitutional Amendment revised this weak point of the decision making rules, and increased the number of the Justices to thirteen, and also included procedures for handling diverse decisions of Senates.

The enforcement of the Court's decision is to a certain extent 'soft'. When the Court finds any contradictions in laws these rules, parts or clauses thereof shall become ineffective. The authorities that passed these rules shall to bring them into conformity with the Constitution not later than six months following the finding of the Constitutional Court. After this period these rules become ineffective. Again, this provision was changed by the 2001 Amendment of the Constitution, which deleted the six months interval and introduced new paragraph according to which the state bodies and corporations are obliged to implement Court's decision "without any delay".

The Court vis-à-vis the Parliament has been designed more in a favor of the principle of parliamentary sovereignty, than judicial review. Therefore, it was unlikely that the constitutional judges may easily exceed their power and give detailed instruction to the legislature in Slovakia. Interestingly, the development of the judicial review in the first seven years of the Court's life has led to a broad reconsideration of the constitutional rules and to substantial amendment of the previous provisions, which were vaguely or even contradictory defined. Thus, the "dialogue" between the legislature and the judicial branch of power, which might seem to be very dramatic in the past, has been productive and stimulated necessary corrections of the Constitution. Whether these changes will lead to an increase of the judicial power remains an open question.

3. JUDICIAL REVIEW: CONSTITUTIONAL PRACTICES

Since the establishment of the judicial review in Slovakia the Court has issued many fundamental rulings embracing a broad scale of constitutional issues. The analysis and evaluation its overall functioning requires summarizing and emphasizing restrictive factors, which were set up by the formal rules. The examination of the Court's competence in the previous section suggests that its agenda would be very broad, which could likely restrain the efficiency of Court's decision-making. Moreover, there were other risky conditions which might undermine successful institutionalization of the judicial review in Slovakia, such as the party mode of the Court's selection, the weak and postponed enforcement of Court's rulings, contradictory and unclear constitutional provisions stipulating its powers. All these perils set up by the formal rules were reinforce by two other elements – the unclear and hastily draft Constitution and a political context characterized by a deep split of the ruling elite over the nation-state issue and foreign policy orientation.

First, I examine Court's jurisdiction over the interpretation of the Constitution, mainly cases where the Justices had to interpret presidential powers. These cases have been selected as the Court's rulings greatly influenced its public perception, and also revealed fundamental weaknesses of the Constitution yet promoted 'dialogue' between the Court and the Parliament. Second, I analyze cases when the Government 'tested' the Court's independence. In the third section, I address the Court's authority in interpreting a new constitutional institution and instrument of direct democracy – the referendum. Then I select the most typical cases of Court's jurisdiction over governmental policies, and finally I will examine Court's rulings related to the protection of fundamental human and minority rights. I would like to prove that the Justices successfully avoided many constitutional traps, provided by the unclear and controversial text of the Constitution, and developed a special mode of judicial review. The Court did not issue any decision that would provide for additional spending from the state budget, and did not take any decisions that would 'distort' governmental policies. In general, the Justices, operating at the forefront of the public interest, tried to maintain their independence and not to follow public expectations.

3.1. The Court in A Trap: Interpreting Ambiguous Constitutional Provisions

The Court's interpretation of the Constitution should be analyzed as a process of mutual learning and teaching between the judicial, executive and legislative branches of power. Because there was weak normative background and no blueprint available for decision-making, the Justices had to find in practice some principles and instruments for reasoning and justification of their findings and rulings. Sometimes, especially when the Court had to decide over politically controversial issues, the Justices struggled with a lack of any normative or procedural guidance. Decisions and interpretations of presidential powers provide a good example of the gradual sophistication in Court's rulings, but also illustrates provisional and temporary nature of Court's decisions, as their validity expire with the change of the Constitution.

The constitutional design of President's position and powers were one of the weakest points of the 1992 Constitution. Until the 1999 Amendment, the Constitution did not precisely stipulate rules regulating the appointment and dismissal of individual ministers, with this authority being divided between the Prime Minister and President in very unclear manner.[9] This constitutional shortcoming came to the fore in 1993, when Prime Minister Mečiar began

---

[9]   Article 111 of the Constitution stated that the President should, on the advice of the Prime Minister, appoint and recall cabinet members. Article 116[4] of the Constitution stated that a motion for the dismissal of a member of the Government might be presented also by the Prime Minister.

dismissing ambassadors and ministers who resisted him. President Kováč petitioned the Constitutional Court to decide whether the President or the Prime Minister had the power to dismiss ministers. The Court ruled that only the President has the power to appoint or dismiss ministers and ministry officials, while the Prime Minister may propose dismissals and appointments to the President. The Court's decision argued that the constitutional provisions allowed the President to preside over Cabinet's meeting and other nomination powers. The Court fell into the constitutional trap that was created by ambiguously drafted institution, which combined elements of semi-presidential and parliamentary model.

The ambiguity of the Constitution led to other ambivalent decisions on presidential powers. Parliament passed two amendments. The first concerned the law on the Slovak Intelligence Service (SIS), according to which the President lost the right to name and recall the Head of the SIS, whilst the second amendment transferred the power to name the Chief of the General's Staff of the Slovak Army from the President to the Cabinet. Both laws were brought before the Constitutional Court, which, in November 1996, ruled that the first amendment was constitutional while the second was not. This decision raised public speculation that the Court was no longer independent, because according to Article 102(g) the President has the right to appoint and remove "the principal officers of national bodies and high officials as defined by law." According to the Law on "Conflict of Interests",[10] the Director of the SIS is a high official, whereas the General Staff is not. The Court's argumentation was rather weak in both cases, as there were no national or international precedents to back up this unbalanced decision. The Court used to anchor its decisions by proclaiming the necessity of the rule of law and the consistency of constitutional rules.

The Slovak Parliament passed an amendment to the Referendum Law which would have shifted the right to screen referendum petitions to Parliament. The Constitutional Court rejected HZDS's proposed amendment to the referendum law, based on Article 95 and Article 102 (m) of the Constitution, which stipulate that "a referendum shall be announced by the President," and that his office is responsible for screening signatures. In this the Court had an easier position, because the Constitution's text provided a more solid base for decision-making and argumentation. Controversies over Presidential powers were also raised about his/her right to attend cabinet's meetings and preside over them, and require reports from the Cabinet and its members. President Michal Kováč never used his right to participate in Cabinet meetings, but he attempted to solicit Cabinet reports, related to the investigation of the abduction of his son. The Cabinet declined to deliver these reports, interpreting Kováč's decision as

---

[10]   This law was passed in summer 1995, proposed by both the HZDS and SDL by a three-fifths majority, which means that the law enjoys constitutional status, so it can be amended only by the same majority.

an attempt to hand out tasks to the ministers and thereby trespassing on the power of the Prime Minister. The Cabinet subsequently petitioned the Constitutional Court to investigate the constitutionality of the President's request. Though the Court ruled in favor of Kováč's request, the President did not press the issue and thus never received the reports from the ministers.

In the short-term perspective all these controversial decisions on President's position exacerbated further political conflicts in Slovakia, but at the end they contributed to the debate over necessity to amendment the Constitution and facilitated political cooperation between democratic forces. Finally, all controversies between the Court and elected branches of government were resolved by the elections and led to a complex re-design of President's office.

3.2. "Testing" the Court's Independence and Enforceability of its Decisions

Slovak politicians in the period 1994–98 used the Constitutional Court as the final arbiter of their political disputes. This development moved the Justices to center of political struggles between Mečiar-led coalition Government and Opposition. The former tried to force the Court to approve and legitimate their political actions, based on the application of the unlimited majority rule and parliamentary sovereignty. The latter's efforts aimed at institutionalization of the liberal idea that the Court's key role is to secure that legislation is consistent with the Constitution.

Mečiar's Movement for Democratic Slovakia (HZDS) several times 'tested' the Court's independency and its ability to limit the HZDS's capacity of achieving an unrestrained majority in Parliament. After the 1994 elections a group of HZDS MPs together with their coalition partners from the Slovak National Party petitioned the Constitutional Court, questioning mandates of members of Democratic Union (DÚ).[11] The Court dismissed the complaint, arguing that approving party member lists is the responsibility of the Electoral Commission, which had already verified the DÚ list. The Justices already understood that it is more legitimate to use procedural argumentation to avoid of accusation of being politically involved in the cases. However, politicians often criticized the Court's rulings, stating that the Justices are politically biased. Despite these verbal attacks the Court's rulings were respected.

Another case when the constitutional court was driven to the center of political struggle was that of the investigatory committees. These committees were conducting investigation over what ruling coalition called a "coup" in the March 1994, when Prime minister Mečiar lost a vote of confidence. The investigation

---

[11] The Democratic Union united three groups of the former members of HZDS and SNS. These parties wanted DÚ seats be distributed according to the requirements of the proportional representation system, which would have also secured a three-fifths majority for the ruling coalition.

committee was established after Parliamentary elections in November 1994 to investigate events from March 1994. A group of Opposition Deputies in Parliament filed a pleading for ruling on parts of a law from the old Slovak Council (44/1989) on the conduct of parliamentary investigations. This law permitted Parliament to establish investigative committees to examine matters of special public significance. Moreover, such committees have the competence, according to the provisions of another law, to compel witnesses to testify.

In the ruling 29/95, the Constitutional Court declared the contested proportions of these laws were inconsistent with several articles of Constitution. The Court's position was that "the Constitution sets out the proportions and boundaries of the separation of powers among individual state authorities. If the National Council of Slovak Republic wishes to ascribe to a certain model relationship the character of legal relationship, it can do so only within the scope and in the manner provided for in the Constitution." Thus, "[the] National Council may not extend its scope of competence beyond the framework given in the Constitution, and restrict the scope of competence of other State authorities, or take over their competencies in a manner, which is not in harmony with the principle of the rule of law."

3.3 Constitutional Jurisdiction and Referendum

Since the 1994 elections the Opposition has had only a limited role in governing the country and often petitioned the Constitutional Court to stop the most destructive pieces of legislation.

As the possibility of amending the Constitution by referendum is not explicitly stipulated by the Constitution, the Opposition based its initiatives on the provisions declaring citizens as the source of the state power (Art. 2.1). According to the Opposition, these provisions imply that citizens have the right to direct legislation, and consequently, also the right to amend the Constitution. Prime Minister Vladimír Mečiar opposed the referendum proposed by the Opposition, but announced that, since the Constitutional Court upheld the constitutionality of amending the Constitution by referendum, MDS would call its own referendum to introduce either a Presidential or Chancellor system.

In April 1997, the Cabinet petitioned the Constitutional Court to interpret the constitutional article related to referendums (Article 93(2) of the Constitution)[12] in an effort to undermine the Opposition's initiative. In turn, the President appealed to the Court, asking it to rule that the Cabinet has a duty

---

[12] Article 93 stipulates: "(1) A constitutional statute on the formation of a union with other states or a secession therefrom shall be confirmed by a public referendum; (2) A referendum may also be used to decide on other crucial issues in the public interest; (3) No issues of fundamental rights, freedoms, taxes, duties or national budgetary matters may be decided by a public referendum".

to administer the referendum. Thus, the Court, which had always been the most publicly trusted institution, was caught in the middle of the political conflict. The Court suspended both petitions using procedural arguments. In the first case, the Cabinet's petition was rejected on the ground that the Cabinet is not entitled to carry out a referendum, only the President and Ministry of Interior have competencies in this area. The Court suspended the second, President's petition, arguing that the President Kováč made a mistake and appealed to the Court as a private person and not as the Head of State.

However, the Court was petitioned for the third time. The Court had to rule over this petition, submitted by the group of MDS Members of Parliament. On May 20, 1997 the Court ruled that a referendum on direct presidential elections was legal and that a change to the Constitution could be the subject of a referendum. The Court said that a constitutional amendment after a referendum had to be approved by the three-fifths majority in Parliament (Article 84, clause 3) to gain legal and constitutional validity. Consequently, the result of any referendum amending the Constitution would only be a "binding" recommendation to the Parliament. The Court, however, decided that the text of a new version of the Constitution concerning direct presidential elections, appended to the referendum question by President Kováč contradicted to the Act on referendum, and consequently Article 100 of the Constitution, which stipulates that "the procedures for holding a referendum shall be defined by law." The Court's decision implied that this constitutional amendment should be a part of the question, not an appendix.

First reactions to the Court's decisions were negative from all quarters. The Opposition and ruling coalition said that the Court's decision was politically biased. The impact of the Court's decision on Slovakia's political life was rather ambiguous. In the long run, this resolution stabilized the constitutional order in Slovakia by preventing possible frequent plebiscitarian changes of the Constitution. However, in the short term perspective, it contributed to the escalation of political tensions between the ruling coalition and the Opposition parties. The Government took an opportunity, provided by the Court's unclear decision, to skip the question on direct presidential elections out of ballots. Interior Minister, Gustáv Krajčí, ordered that referendum ballots omitted this question, thus assuming responsibility for issuing ballot papers with only the three questions about NATO membership. Most of voters refused to cast their vote when presented with a ballot including only three questions. Consequently, Slovakia's referendum was marred by confusion over the ballots. The Central Referendum Commission on 26 May officially announced to Parliament that the referendum was invalidated. According to the Commission the referendum did not comply with rules because four questions should have been included on the ballots.

The issue of referendums continued also in 1998, when the Constitutional Court decided on 9 January that the petition asking for the direct election of the President is still valid. Ivan Šimko (Christian Democratic Movement), the chairman of Petition Committee appealed to the Court which decided that the Minister of Interior violated Šimko's right to directly participate in "the administration of public affairs" (Art. 30(1)). Therefore Šimko used this opportunity and asked President Kováč to announce the referendum once more. President scheduled referendum on April 19, including all four questions. According to public expectations, this referendum was canceled in March, when the Prime Minister Mečiar assumed some presidential powers. This decision only further intensified institutional and political conflicts, which was resolved on July 14, 1998–only two months before the elections – when the Parliament amended the basic law of the country and transferred the power to accept the Cabinet's resignation to the Chairman of Parliament in the case of vacant President's seat.

3.4. Policy Cases: Protecting Private Property and the Rule of Law

The Constitutional Court in 1995 ruled that a law passed by the Parliament, canceling direct sale privatization projects approved by the previous (Moravčík's) Government was unconstitutional. After the 1994 elections a new parliamentary majority, led by Mečiar's party, canceled the Government 's resolution to sell 54 state companies. It implied that all 54 existing contracts between the Government and private companies lost their validity. The Justices ruled on the unconstitutionality of this law on several grounds. First and foremost, they argued that the law violated division of powers between the executive and legislative branches, as the Parliament annulled the resolution of the Government, which can be changed only by the Government. The Justices added that the principle of constitutional equilibrium in a parliamentary democracy means that the legislators do not have the right to dispose freely with individual branches of power in the state, because the legislature is also bound by the Constitution and its constitutive rules (Art. 1). Second, according to the Court's opinion, Parliament's passing this law trespassed into powers which are constitutionally assigned to the judiciary branch of power, because direct sales of the state-owned companies established business contracts between the Government and a private company, and therefore fall under jurisdiction of regular courts (Art. 141 and 142). Third, the law expropriated private property without compensation and this decision was not made in public interest, as it is stipulated by the Constitution (Art. 20). Moreover, the Constitution (Art. 11) states that international conventions and instruments on human rights and freedoms ratified by the Slovak Republic take precedence over national laws, and jurisdictions of respective international courts confirmed that legislatures do not decide about individual cases related to expropriation of private property, but only define conditions for expropriation. Finally, the law canceled the Government 's resolution after the sales, therefore the Justices thought that this law violated rule of law and its ban on retroactivity. This decision of the Court was fully accepted by all main political actors in Slovakia, and indicated the Court's independent position. Following this decision, in five cases property rights were restored.[13]

Under Mečiar's Government, the Constitutional Court ruled on three other cases related to privatization process and protection of property rights. All cases were initiated the by Opposition Members of Parliament under the Article 125 of the Constitution. In the first case, the Court decided the privatization issue regarding the 'golden share', which provides the state with the right to hold a majority share in the privatization of 'strategic' companies. The Justices ruled that the law contradicts to the Constitution, as it violates ownership rights guaranteed to all citizens by the Constitution, and added that the Constitution does not permit expropriation or limitation of ownership by the law. In the argumentation the Court explicitly stated that such possibility was stipulated by the Communist Constitution of 1949. Moreover, the law undermined ownership rights of citizens and other economic actors by providing the state with a privileged position in the privatization.[14]

The second lawsuit concerned with the attempt of Government to limit the restoration of land. The Court ruled against the law which would allow the state to take possession of land if ownership cannot be determined within three months. Again, the Court employed the same argument it did in the previous case, stating that the law violates equality of ownership rights.[15]

The third precarious case relating to privatization concerned the law on large-scale privatization, which cancelled the second wave of the voucher privatization, which was prepared by the previous Government. The law introduced bonds instead of coupons, which could be exchange for shares in privatized companies. To rule on this case the Justices consulted the Governor of the National Bank as the representative of independent institution to provide information about the coupon privatization and also consulted with the Vice-Premier for Economy to explain reasons for the change of privatization method. At the end the Justices decided that this law contradicts to the Slovak Constitution only in one paragraph that required municipalities and housing associations to accept bonds when selling apartments. According to Court's ruling this would be a limitation

---

[13] *Zbierka nálezov a uznesení Ústavného súdu Slovenskej republiky* [Collection of Findings and Rulings of the Constitutional Court of the Slovak Republic], Finding of the Constitutional Court of the Slovak Republic, No. 6/95, File Ref. I. ÚS 16/95, of 24 May 1995.

[14] *Zbierka nálezov a uznesení Ústavného súdu Slovenskej republiky* [Collection of Findings and Rulings of the Constitutional Court of the Slovak Republic], Finding of the Constitutional Court of the Slovak Republic, No. 4/96, File Ref. PL. ÚS 38/95, of 3 April 1996.

[15] *Zbierka nálezov a uznesení Ústavného súdu Slovenskej republiky* [Collection of Findings and Rulings of the Constitutional Court of the Slovak Republic], Finding of the Constitutional Court of the Slovak Republic, No. 5/96, File Ref. PL. ÚS 39/95 of 3 April 1996.

of property rights. In all other aspects this law did not violate any property rights, as citizens did not yet exchange coupons for shares. According to the Court Article 20 of the Constitution merely recognizes the right to protection of property that was acquired in a lawful manner.[16]

The fourth case related to the constitutionality of the law transferring privatization authority from the Government and the Ministry of Privatization to the National Property Fund (FNM). In this way the ruling coalition tried to get rid of the responsibility for unfair and non-transparent privatization. The Opposition argued that law not only moved authority from the Government, but also that the parliamentary ruling majority through its decision has moved privatization out of the effective control of anyone but itself. The Justices ruled in favor of the appeal by the Opposition. Court's ruling declared such transfer of the authority from the Government to the FNM as a limitation of government's fundamental functions, as they are laid down in the Constitution. This transfer represents an inadmissible restriction by the law of the competence granted by the Constitution to the Government as the supreme body of the executive power. In the decision the Court blamed the Parliament that it did not demand that the FMN act in the public interest. The Justices also criticized the legislature for not bringing FNM's legal proceedings to preceding or ex-post evaluation by the competent state agencies. On the other, the court's verdict did not nullify the validity of privatization decisions already made, as the Justices ruled in favor of stability of property rights.[17]

3.5. Interpretation and Protection of Human Rights and Freedoms Granted by the Constitution

The Court's jurisdiction over human rights protection is defined by the notion of "fundamental rights and freedoms" in cases of their violations by governmental authorities, unless the protection of such rights falls under the jurisdiction of another court (Art. 127). The Constitution allows any citizen to appeal to the Constitutional Court where his/her fundamental rights and freedoms are allegedly violated. Those rights and freedoms are defined by the second part of the Constitution. The Slovak Constitution incorporated a slightly amended version of the Bill of Rights adopted by the Czech-Slovak Federal Assembly in

---

[16] *Zbierka nálezov a uznesení Ústavného súdu Slovenskej republiky* [Collection of Findings and Rulings of the Constitutional Court of the Slovak Republic], Finding of the Constitutional Court of the Slovak Republic, No. 11/95, File Ref. PL. ÚS 33/95 of 20 December 1995.

[17] *Zbierka nálezov a uznesení Ústavného súdu Slovenskej republiky* [Collection of Findings and Rulings of the Constitutional Court of the Slovak Republic], Finding of the Constitutional Court of the Slovak Republic, No. 11/96, File Ref. PL. ÚS 1/96 of 14 November 1996.

1991. Two factors have shaped the institutionalization of the Bill of Rights. First, although the Communist regime emphasized social rights, human rights and freedoms were constantly and systematically violated. Consequently, the main target of the anti-Communist Opposition's criticism of the regime focused on these human rights violations. Therefore, when the dissidents came to power, they immediately tried to remedy this and adopted laws guaranteeing and protecting human rights. Second, international organizations, such as the Council of Europe, the Conference on the Security and Cooperation in Europe, and the European Union, pressured post-Communist countries to adopt human rights protection mechanisms in exchange for possible membership in these organizations. The fact that a quarter of the Constitution deals with citizens' rights and freedoms demonstrates how important they were perceived to be. Therefore, it could be expected that the Court's agenda will be excessively shaped by numerous petitions and complains brought to the Court by citizens and/or different companies, corporations and organizations. Even the rough examinations of statistics has suggested that indeed, petitions under the Article 130(c) indeed prevail compared to other complains, as until the end of 1999 the Court received 892 petitions. However, the Justices ruled only on 10 percent of them, i.e. 82 petitions were accepted. The rest of them were rejected on procedural grounds, mostly because the case either did not fall under the jurisdiction of the Constitutional Court or petitions did not fulfill all necessary formal requirements to be considered.

The most frequent decisions are related to the Article 46 of the Constitutions that every person has a right to judicial and other legal protection. Since the establishment of the Court in March 1993 till March 2000, or during the first term of the Court the Justices have considered 56 cases and in 36 cases ruled that the respective rights were violated. The most common infringement (thirty instances) relates to the right to "have his or her case put on trial without unreasonable delay," (Art. 48(2)). Several cases related to political conflicts analyzed in the above sections were brought to the Court under constitutional articles related to political freedoms and liberties, mainly to the Article 30, which provides for free and equal political participation, as the Court ruled that in five cases this right was violated.

Only on a few occasions has the Constitutional Court been petitioned to elaborate on the extent of socio-economic rights, which are broadly declared by the Constitution. Citizens or corporation under Article 130 brought none of these petitions to the Court, i.e. as cases, which would violate fundamental human rights and freedoms. Mostly state institutions or groups of MPs challenge laws on the ground that they violate some socio-economic rights. It has to be stressed that Chapter Five of the Constitution (Articles 35–46) grants economic, social and cultural rights and include the rights to free health care through medical insurance, security for the old, disabled or families deprived of the chief breadwinner; free education; and special protection for pregnant women, children and young people in employment. Cultural rights include those to freedom of scientific research and artistic expression.

One case, which the Justices used as an opportunity to interpret the constitutionally granted the right to work, was brought to the Court as early as 1993. The Constitution states that: "Citizens shall have the right to work. The State shall guarantee, within reasonable limits, the material welfare of those who cannot enjoy this right through no fault of their own. The terms thereof shall be specified by law" (Article 35(3)). A citizen, who was fired, as the employer could not offer her a job suitable for her training, petitioned the Court. First, she brought the case to the regular Court, who justified employer's decision, and than petitioned the Constitutional Court, arguing that the regular Court's decision violated her constitutionally granted right to work. The Justices ruled that this case is not a violation of the right to work, and interpreted the Article 35 of the Constitution, adding; "The right to work may not be construed as the right to be employed in the area for which a person possesses required qualifications."[18]

In another case, the Justices elaborated on the fundamental right to protection of one's health (Art. 40). In this case the Justices deliberated on the Ministry of Health's "Medical Treatment Order," limiting access to free medical care, the Court ruled that the decree contravened the Constitution, which stipulates that the implementation of "the right to free medical care will be determined by law," not by ministerial decree. In its reasoning the Justices states that "the attributes of State governed by the rule of law also include the fact that legal relationship related to fundamental rights and freedoms my be provided for only by law." Therefore, law must lay down the right to free medical care and to the medical supplies, as the fundamental right.[19]

3.6. Minority Rights

The presence of ethnic minorities in Slovakia gives a great significance to constitutional protection of rights and interpretation of the restrictions upon them. The position of the Hungarian minority is especially sensitive because of its size (eleven percent) and because the area in which most of them live was part of Hungary during the Second World War. Articles 33 and 34 relate to the 'Rights of National Minorities and Ethnic Groups'. The former proclaims that

---

[18] *Zbierka nálezov a uznesení Ústavného súdu Slovenskej republiky* [Collection of Findings and Rulings of the Constitutional Court of the Slovak Republic], Finding of the Constitutional Court of the Slovak Republic, No. 8/93, File Ref. II. ÚS 12/93 of 8 July 1993.

[19] *Zbierka nálezov a uznesení Ústavného súdu Slovenskej republiky* [Collection of Findings and Rulings of the Constitutional Court of the Slovak Republic], Finding of the Constitutional Court of the Slovak Republic, No. 19/94, File Ref. PL. ÚS 5/94 of 19 October 1994.

membership of an ethnic minority group "may not be used to the detriment of any individual"; the latter grants minorities "their full development, particularly the rights to promote their cultural heritage with other citizens of the same national minority or ethic group, receive and disseminate information in their mother tongues, form associations, and create and maintain educational and cultural institutions." However extensive these rights may seem, it could be expected that sooner or later political conflicts about details which should be elaborated by the special law, would emerge. Indeed clashes over the use of minority languages and the use of Slovak as official language (Article 6) frequently occurred.

The Court interpreted this constitutional provision in 1996, based on the petition of the group of Opposition MPs, which challenged constitutionality of the State Language Law. Opposition argued that this law contradicts also to the International Pact on Civil and Political Rights and the International Agreement on Abolition of All forms of Racial Discrimination. The Justices declared that the provision which requires all Slovak citizens to use exclusively Slovak when communicating with official bodies is unconstitutional, because it violated the constitutional rights of ethnic minorities to use their own language in official contacts. The Justices interpreted Article 34 as part of legal regime of positive discrimination. The Court maintained that this provision concerns, in particular, the fundamental right to freedom of expression and the right to peaceful assembly. In its reasoning the Court used this opportunity and referred to a missing law on the language of minorities and ethnic groups, which was anticipated by the Constitution. However, the Court refused to strike down the other ten provisions which were also protested. The Chairman of the Court, maintained that several parts of the complaint filed by the Opposition were marred by technical mistakes and therefore had to be dismissed on procedural grounds.[20]

4. JUDICIAL REVIEW: DOMINANT PATTERNS

The Constitutional Court in Slovakia is widely considered as an institution necessary for the further consolidation democracy in the country. Its decisions over presidential powers help to reveal many shortcomings of the Constitution, and thus contributed to the Constitutional amendment, that provided not only for direct elections of President, but also for more clear-cut definition of his competencies. Later amendments of the Constitution even revised those constitutional provisions related to the Constitutional Court.

---

[20] *Zbierka nálezov a uznesení Ústavného súdu Slovenskej republiky* [Collection of Findings and Rulings of the Constitutional Court of the Slovak Republic], Finding of the Constitutional Court of the Slovak Republic, No. 14/97, File Ref. PL. ÚS 8/96 of 29 August 1997.

Legal and political debates concerning the overall performance of the Justices during its first term suggest that they were too involved in interpreting Court's authority and proceedings. It leads to the conclusion that the first term of the Court (1993–2000), the Justices were very active or were forced to be very active, despite the fact that Constitution does not provide the possibility for the Court to act by itself. Maybe, this generally accepted evaluation is too simplistic and needs closer examination. Indeed, the Court was compelled to be very active due to several factors. First and foremost, the Constitution allows ordinary citizens to petition the Constitutional Court. This possibility has prompted many citizens to appeal to the Court, especially when they failed in fighting for justice in ordinary courts, and therefore there are hundreds of petitions submitted by citizens every year. Since the Court had successfully resolved many controversies between the state institutions, citizens have seen the Court as an independent institution and, therefore its public prestige has been rising. Frequent petitions of citizens submitted to the Court support this finding. Notwithstanding the rather restrictive criteria for citizens' approach to the Court, citizens often appeal to the Constitutional Court in seeking justice, even if their case did not fit in Court's competence. Since the Court's establishment almost the half of all complaints were citizens' appeals of lower court decisions. The Court declined to deliberate on nearly one-fourth of these petitions, since basic rights had been violated by the lower courts' decisions only in a few instances. The other half of all petitions to the Court was resolved through a written reply (prípis). Therefore, the Court actually deliberated on only 8 percent of all cases submitted to the Court.

The deeply divided Slovakia's polity, combined with vaguely drafted constitutional provisions, which even increased controversies among political actors have led to a substantial increase of the Court's agenda. Moreover, in many cases the Justices were aware of the "precedential" nature of its adjudication, and therefore used almost every opportunity to redefined and precise own authority and proceedings to elaborate the cornerstone for the judicature in the future. However, many of these rulings in fact limited Court's power. The Justices often used very broad argumentation, attached to the Court's rulings and findings to explain why they cannot deal with issues which politicians, state agencies and citizens have brought to Court's attention. This was the way the Justices chose to limit their agenda, in spite of the constitutional arrangement that does not permit Court's control in this area. Several decisions, especially in the early rulings defined more precisely Court's powers for future adjudication. For example, in the January 1994 the Court ruled that the competence of Court is defined in the Constitution: this definition precludes its competence to take part in the legislative process. Consequently, the Court cannot impose on the Government of the Slovak republic an obligation to initiate draft law. A year later, in 1995, the Justices decided that the Constitutional Court does not have right to take legislative initiative or to act with regard to amending the laws.

The Court has subsequently issued more than ten similar decisions to draw boundaries between general courts, Supreme Court and other state institutions. The Court's 'activism' seemed to decline before the elections of 1998 and toward end of its term. In the former case perhaps the Justices let politicians to solve their conflicts by democratic procedures and in the latter, maybe some of the Justices speculated on the possibility of being re-elected, as the Constitution did not explicitly prohibit such possibility.[21]

Political pressures and public requests to accelerate the proceedings (for which the Constitution sets no deadlines) were not always met with understanding. In particular, the Justices elected to the second Court's term tend to postpone their rulings and leave a space for politicians to reconcile their controversies by themselves. A good example would be the Court's ruling on the constitutionality of the referendum on early elections. First, the Justices were postponing the decision several times, and at the end they ruled that the case did not fall under the Constitutional Court's jurisdiction. To discern a prevailing pattern of behavior of the acting Justices requires detailed comparison not only to their predecessors, but also with other countries.

To answer the question about "policy distortion" by judicature of the Constitutional Court prompts us to look for ways how the Justices carefully judged each case dealing with the governmental policies. Especially, during the rule of Mečiar-led coalition Government the Court ruled over several important issues related to privatization without any fear, and it was clear that the Justices were apparently exposed to the strong pressure from the parliamentary majority. Due to relatively uninterrupted rule of the former Prime Minister Mečiar, the current coalition Government, which often used to request the Court's intervention, is very careful about drafting the legislation and paying attention to governmental bills to prevent their possible challenges by the Opposition at the Court.

Indisputably, the performance of the first Court can be evaluated in terms of the unexpected and unforeseen success of judicial review in Slovakia. Constitutional provisions and the contingent and 'lucky' selection of the Justices in the first Court to develop and maintain its independence. This does not imply that political parties do not exercise influence over nomination of candidates. Party nominations and different explicit or implicit political alliances were rather obvious in both cases of formation of the Court. However, the current fragmentation of party system and a high professional reputation of most of judges limit a possibility to control the Court by a single political force. The internal dynamics of Court's operation helped to consolidate this new institution and increase its public support and authority.

From the very beginning, the Constitutional Court has enjoyed high public

---

[21]   The 2001 constitutional amendment excluded this possibility.

support and prestige among citizens. From 1994 until 1999 Slovakia's citizens considered the Constitutional Court the most credible state institution.

Table 1 Comparison of trust and distrust to the political institutions in Slovakia. The first number indicates trust and the second one distrust.

Institution	Feb 96	Sept 96	Jan 97	July 97	June 98	Nov 98	Jan 99	Mar 00	May 00
Constitutional Court	61:24	59:30	66:22	58:31	68:20	61:22	62:26	44:34	48:41
President	52:43	56:41	56:34	50:46	–	–	–	34:60	31:62
National Council	48:43	44:52	44:48	42:52	43:48	57:28	57:34	35:61	34:62
Government	40:52	36:61	40:56	39:57	36:60	55:33	57:37	61:36	58:37

Source: Institute for Public Affairs Database 1999, 2000.

The closer examination of this data indicates that the Constitutional Court was the only state institution which enjoyed almost equal support among supporters of both, national and liberal political blocks in Slovakia.[22] Public opinion polls indicated that the lowest level of polarization between the respondents was connected with trust to the Court.[23] Surprisingly, the level of the trust in the newly formed Constitutional Court has been decreasing since its establishment. It is difficult to explore whether there is a positive or negative correlation between rather 'invisible' performance of the new Court and its support. The new Justices did not have to rule over cases, which would polarize society.

Although there were a few cases, when the jurisdiction of individual Court's Senates led to contradictory rulings, the Justices usually act as a single and coherent body, proving their commitment to the idea of independent judicial review. In particular, the case of amnesties granted by the former Prime Minister Mečiar and revoked by his successor Mikuláš Dzurinda raised a lot of political controversies and cased an insecurity for investigators and courts acting in respective cases. However, the Justices themselves never became involved in public disputes against their colleagues.

Occasional public attacks on the Justices, questioning the integrity of judicial review have occurred but they originate from politicians and journalists. Political commentators and legal experts stress that the Court's rulings are too technical and legalistic and have paid little attention to "natural rights" doctrine. Some critics expressed dissatisfaction with the mainly self-restrictive interpretation of

---

[22] Zora Bútorová (1998) 'Verejná mienka' [Public Opinion], in Grigorij Mesežnikov & Michal Ivantyšyn (eds.), *Súhrnná správa o Slovensku* [*Global Report on Slovakia*] (Bratislava: IVO 1998), p. 243.

[23] *Id.*

Court's powers and dominance of formal and procedural argumentation of the Constitution.[24]

The new Chairman of the Court nominated in 2000 announced a new "legal doctrine" for the upcoming term of the Court. He stated that the Court will emphasize more the protection of human rights. Actually, during the first year in the office Court has successfully avoided to determine cases related to political conflicts between the ruling coalition and Opposition, which were very often on the agenda of the previous Court.

5. CONCLUSION

The establishment and performance of the Constitutional Court certainly contributed to the acceptance of judicial review in the political system. The Justices and their rulings promoted the institutionalization of political pattern, which relies on constitutionally resolved conflicts. The Court has been a stabilizing factor in the political system during the complicated period of democratic transition and building of new statehood. The Justices have 'resolved' the problem of broadly assigned powers by engaging themselves into re-definition of Court's authority. During their first term, Justices effectively restricted their institutional competence by delineating borders between individual branches of power and regular courts' system. From the very beginning the Court demonstrated a strong inclination toward long and wide ranging opinions included in its reasoning. As the judicial review tradition is weak in Slovakia, the Justices turned to international experience and often backed up their rulings by citing decisions of the European Court for Human Rights, or in similar cases the decisions of other continental courts, mainly the Federal Constitutional Court of Germany and international treaties. In those decisions, where the Justices could not find any 'inspiration' abroad, they often opted for strictly legalistic interpretation of the constitutional text, but without loosing their general commitment to rule of law, constitutionalism and separation of powers.

The analysis of the selected cases has demonstrated that the principle of judicial review was not always fully accepted by main political actors, especially if it threatened the composition of Parliament or could affect electoral results. However, in most of cases, political actors complied with Courts' rulings.

Finally, whatever difficulties emerged during the gradual institutionalization of judicial review in Slovakia, the Justices succeeded in balancing several institutional weaknesses of the Constitution and motivated political actors to direct their conflicts through democratic and constitutional mechanisms.

---

[24] Marek Benedik, Andrea Földesová & Milan Galanda, 'Právny štát, legislatíva, ústavnosť' a súdnictvo' [Rule of Law, Legislative and Judiciary], in Miroslav Kollár & Grigorij Mesežnikov (eds.), *Súhrnná správa o Slovensku* [*Global Report on Slovakia* (Bratislava: IVO 2000), pp. 125–166.

16. Judicial Power vs. Democratic Representation: The Culture of Constitutionalism and Human Rights in the Czech Legal System

Jiří Přibáň

1. A BRIEF HISTORY OF CZECHOSLOVAK CONSTITUTIONAL JUSTICE

Building up the constitutional institutions of the modern Czechoslovak state was strongly marked by the influence of American and French constitutional traditions and republican principles which also dominated in the process of establishment of other independent nation-states in the region of Central and Eastern Europe after the end of the first world war and dissolution of the Austro-Hungarian empire. The first Czechoslovak Constitution was adopted in 1920 and incorporated many checks and balances to be found in the French and American systems of the separation of powers.

Concerning the constitutional justice and judicial review of legislative acts, the Czech constitutional model was nevertheless inspired by Hans Kelsen's design of a constitutional court as a negative legislator in the system of the separation of constitutional and democratic power.[1] Similarly, as in the post-1918 Austrian Republic, the Czechoslovak Constitutional Court was designed by the Constitutional Act as a body with powers to review and declare void Acts of the Parliament on the basis of their inconsistency with constitutional provisions. It consisted of seven members, two delegated from the Supreme Administrative Court,[2] two from the Supreme Court, and two members together with the Chairman of the Constitutional Court were appointed by the President of the Czechoslovak Republic.[3]

The Court was progressive, yet quite limited in its powers because it could not review individual complaints in the field of constitutional and political rights. The seven judges were appointed or delegated for the period of ten years,[4]

---

[1]   Hans Kelsen, 'Wer soll der Hueter der Verfassung sein?' (Who should be the guardian of the Constitution?), *Die Justiz*, 6 (1930–31), pp. 576–628.

[2]   The Supreme Administrative Court also had some very limited power in the field of constitutional justice because it could review individual complaints in the field of constitutional and political rights. For further details, see Vladimír Sládeček, *Ústavní soudnictví (Constitutional Justice)* (Praha: C.H. Beck 1999), p. 12.

[3]   See *The Constitutional Act n. 121 of 1920*, Art. III.

[4]   See *The Act of the Parliament n. 162 of 1920 on the Constitutional Court*.

Wojciech Sadurski (ed.), Constitutional Justice, East and West, 373–394
© 2002 *Kluwer Law International. Printed in Great Britain.*

started to work in 1921 and issued sixty five judgments. The court ceased to exist in 1941 and was not renewed in spite of the fact that it was not abolished until the enactment of the Communist Constitution in 1948.[5]

After the Communist coup in February 1948, one of the first constitutional steps taken was the enactment of a Communist Constitution. *The Constitution of 9th May*, enacted by the Communist Parliament in 1948, transferred the power to review and decide matters of the constitutionality of Acts of Parliament to the Chair Committee of the National Assembly.[6] Article 65 of the 1948 Constitution provided this Committee with the power to decide whether statutes conform to the provisions of the Constitution. Due to the existing system of power and its centralisation in the political bodies of the Communist Party, this provision, nevertheless, did not have any real significance and was just a 'dead letter law'. In 1960, the Czechoslovak Communist regime adopted a new Constitution which kept the principle of legislative power's supervision of constitutionality. However, the power to review the Acts of the Slovak national legislative bodies and other legal regulations and declare them unconstitutional and therefore void was expanded from the Chair Committee to the whole body of the National Assembly.[7]

Attempts to change the Communist system into 'socialism with a human face', usually known as the Prague Spring 1968, lasted only eight months and ended up in the invasion of the Warsaw Pact armies in August 1968. The only outcome of this failure to reform the existing Communist system was a constitutional reform which changed the Czechoslovak socialist republic into a federal system granting the wide autonomy to both the Czech and Slovak republics. *The Constitutional Act n. 143/1968 on the Czechoslovak Federation* enacted a complex change of the Czechoslovak constitutional system and its sixth chapter incorporated the idea of constitutional justice. The Constitutional Court of the Czechoslovak Socialist Republic was to have important powers in the field of constitutional law such as the power to: review statutes and other legislative acts of federal and national legislative bodies; decide disputes between federal and national bodies or Czech and Slovak national bodies; propose legislative changes, protect civil rights and freedoms etc.[8] However, this unprecedented

---

[5]   Vlastimil Ševčík, 'Vyhledy ústavnosti v. novém státě – pokus o analyzující sondu' (Prospects of constitutionalism in the new state – an analytical sketch), *Právník* CXXXIII (1994), pp. 1011–1027.

[6]   The Czechoslovak Parliament was called the National Assembly and later, after the change of the political regime into a Federation in 1968, was transformed into the bicameral Federal Assembly. The Chair Committee of the National Assembly was controlled by the Communist Party leaders and represented an effective instrument of political control in the legislation.

[7]   See Article 41, par. 2 of the Constitution of the Czechoslovak Socialist Republic of 1960.

[8]   See Articles 86–92 of the Constitutional Act n. 143/1968 on the Czechoslovak Federation.

power given to the Constitutional Court coexisted with the principle adopted in the Communist constitutional reform in 1948, according to which the Parliament (transformed into the Federal Assembly in 1968) had the power to declare unconstitutional and void legislative acts and regulations enacted by the executive power.[9] Constitutional jurisdiction was to be shared between the legislative and judicial powers. Nevertheless, this duality in the system of constitutional justice never started to work because the specific law on the Constitutional Court was not adopted and judicial protection of the Constitution therefore did not become a part of the Communist constitutional and legal reality.

Analysing the Czechoslovak Communist constitutional system and its development between 1948 and 1989, it must be emphasised that the real mechanism of state power was never primarily channelled through the constitutional institutions. The real power was exercised and decisions primarily made in the highest bodies of the Communist Party. All levels of constitutional institutions were just to implement policies designed within the Communist Party headquarters. Constitutions and constitutional acts consequently represented just a derivative power structure of secondary importance for the governance of Communist societies.[10]

2. CONSTITUTIONAL JUSTICE AND POST-COMMUNISM

The fall of Communism had paradoxical consequences for the constitutional system of Czechoslovakia. On the one hand, a number of Communist constitutional provisions persisted in the new democratic condition. As if it were enough just to start to *take them seriously* and implement them in the new emerging political reality. On the other hand, the old Communist constitution was perceived as a symbol of the totalitarian past and there was a strong political demand to abolish the old constitutional system. This *new constructivism* was to design and introduce an entirely new constitutional system which would guarantee the principle of the separation of constitutional powers, protect human rights and freedoms, and define new federal relations between the Czech and Slovak Republics based on the principle of equality and fairness.

These two processes – the persistence of pre-1989 constitutional provisions and the fundamental constitutional change, were not typical just of Czechoslovakia and may be detected in any post-Communist political society. In Czechoslovakia, the whole post-Communist situation was more complicated than in other Central European societies because the state was challenged by the Slovak demands for a different form of co-existence between Czechs and

---

[9]   See Article 36, par. 4 of the Constitutional Act n. 143/1968 on the Czechoslovak Federation.

[10] See, for instance, Jiří Přibáň, 'Legitimacy and Legality After the Velvet Revolution', in Jiří Přibáň & James Young (eds), *The Rule of Law in Central Europe* (Aldershot, Ashgate Publishers 1999), pp. 29–30.

Slovaks. This attempt to design *the authentic federation*[11] cost a lot of efforts in the field of the constitutional change of post-Communist Czechoslovakia and did not end up successfully. The *constitutional transformation* of Czechoslovakia therefore consists of a number of failures and only a few real achievements. Two most successful achievements are then: the adoption of a complex catalogue of human rights in *The Charter of Fundamental Rights and Freedoms* and the entirely new system of constitutional justice with the powerful Constitutional Court.[12]

The structure and powers of the Federal Constitutional Court were heavily determined by the legislative proposal drafted by the President of the country Václav Havel. Havel's proposal was subject of criticism in the Parliament, amended by provisions drafted by members of the Parliament, and enacted on April 1, 1991. The statute on the structure and organisation of the Court was adopted by the Federal Assembly in November 1991 and the President appointed the judges in January 1992. If the whole process of the constitutional transformation is determined by the reconstruction of liberal democracy, the adoption of the Charter and legal acts on the Constitutional Court represent *the successful liberal aspect* of this reconstruction. The Court consisted of twelve judges, six from the Czech Republic and six from the Slovak Republic, proposed by the Federal Assembly and national parliaments (each of these three legislative bodies proposed eight candidates), approved by the Federal Assembly and appointed by the President for the period of seven years.[13] The Court had important powers to review Acts of Parliament and decisions of lower courts to decide whether they conform to the constitutional acts and international treaties on human rights.[14]

The Federal Constitutional Court was working between February and December 1992 and made sixteen decisions. After the Parliamentary Elections in 1992, it became obvious that the Federation was speeding up towards the end of its existence and the second half of that year was marked by hectic constitutional activity in all three legislative bodies. While the Federal Assembly was preoccupied with finding the constitutional device for the splitting of the Czechoslovak Federation without referendum, both the Czech and Slovak National Councils were gradually transforming themselves into the Parliaments of the new sovereign states and enacted new Constitutions for these states.

The Czech Constitution was finally adopted in December 1992. It contains a

---

[11] See, Václav Havel, *Summer Mediations* (New York: Vintage Books 1993).

[12] The Charter of Fundamental Rights and Freedoms was adopted by the Federal Assembly of the Czech and Slovak Federal Republic in January 1991. Just a month later, in February 1991, the Federal Assembly also adopted the Constitutional Act on the Constitutional Court of the Czech and Slovak Federal Republic, n. 91/1991.

[13] Article 10 of the Act on the Constitutional Court, n. 91/1991.

[14] See, for instance, Sládeček, *op. cit.*, p. 20.

separate chapter on the Constitutional Court. The Court's powers were significantly inspired by the powers of the former Federal Constitutional Court. It has the power to review and declare void and unconstitutional Acts of Parliament if they are inconsistent with a Constitutional Act or an international treaty on human rights and freedoms promulgated by the Czech Republic. It also is a guardian of legality due to its power to review all other legal acts and declare them void if they do not conform to the statutes of the Parliament.[15] In comparison to the Federal Constitutional Court, the power of the Czech Constitutional Court is strengthened by Article 89, paragraph 2 of the Constitution which states that 'enforceable decisions of the Constitutional Court are binding on all authorities and persons'.

However, legitimacy of the Czech Constitutional Court is different when compared with the former federal constitutional system. The Court consists of fifteen judges, appointed by the President for the period of ten years and subsequently approved by the Senate as the upper chamber of the Parliament. The Czech constitution-makers adopted *the American model* giving the fundamental power to appoint judges to the national President and balancing it with

---

[15] For the powers of the Court, see Article 87 of the Constitution which reads:

(1) The Constitutional Court has jurisdiction: (a) to annul statutes or individual provisions thereof if they are inconsistent with a constitutional act or an international treaty under Article 10; (b) to annul other legal enactments or individual provisions thereof if they are inconsistent with a constitutional act, a statute, or an international treaty under Article 10; (c) over constitutional complaints by the representative body of a self-governing region against an unlawful encroachment by the state; (d) over constitutional complaints against final decisions or other actions by public authorities infringing constitutionally guaranteed fundamental rights and basic freedoms; (e) over remedial actions from decisions concerning the certification of the election of a Deputy or Senator; (f) to resolve doubts concerning a Deputy or Senator's loss of eligibility to hold office or the incompatibility under Article 25 of some other position or activity with holding the office of Deputy or Senator; (g) over a constitutional charge brought by the Senate against the President of the Republic pursuant to Article 65, paragraph 2; (h) to decide on a petition by the President of the Republic seeking the revocation of a joint resolution of the Assembly of Deputies and the Senate pursuant to Article 66; (i) to decide on the measures necessary to implement a decision of an international tribunal which is binding on the Czech Republic, in the event that it cannot be otherwise implemented; (j) to determine whether a decision to dissolve a political party or other decisions relating to the activities of a political party is in conformity with constitutional acts or other laws; (k) to decide jurisdictional disputes between state bodies and bodies of self-governing regions, unless that power is given by statute to another body.

(2) An statute may provide that, in place of the Constitutional Court, the Supreme Administrative Court shall have jurisdiction: (a) to annul legal enactments other than statutes or individual provisions thereof if they are inconsistent with a statute; (b) to decide jurisdictional disputes between state bodies and bodies of self-governing regions, unless that power is given by statute to another body.

the consent of the upper chamber of the Parliament which does not have the primary legislative role within the constitutional system. The procedure of appointment of judges to the Constitutional Court shows the persistence of the influence of the American constitutional model on the Czech constitutional culture. As with the first Czechoslovak Constitution of 1920, the current Czech constitutional system has been inspired by the American model of checks and balances and has incorporated some fundamental elements of the appointment of the Supreme Court judges into the sphere of the Czech constitutional justice.

The Constitutional Court's democratic legitimacy is therefore quite complicated and significantly weakened through the channels of constitutional checks and balances. The will of the people is filtered and 'melted' in several constitutional bodies and procedures: the President of the Republic is elected indirectly at a joint session of the Assembly of Deputies and the Senate by the absolute majority of votes in both chambers and candidates may be nominated by a group of at least ten deputies or senators;[16] the Constitutional Court's judges appointed by the President must be approved only by the Senate which does not have the primary legislative powers commonly given to the democratically elected institutions and its main role is to control the legislation enacted by the Assembly of Deputies. Moreover, the democratic legitimacy of the Court is accompanied by an important constitutional supplement incorporated in the article 85 which formulates the oath of a judge and his/her duty to protect 'the inviolability of natural human rights and the rights of citizens'.[17] The *naturalistic human rights legitimacy* explicitly formulated in the Constitution caused significant academic dispute and represented continuity with the successful liberal aspect of the revolution and post-Communist transformation as mentioned above. It also pre-determined the Court's decision-making culture and activist approach going beyond the limits of formal legalism which will be subject of the following analysis.[18]

3. THE CONSTITUTIONAL COURT – A NEW AND POWERFUL INSTITUTION

The Constitutional Court of the Czech Republic started its work late in 1993 and immediately used the powers provided by the Constitution. Instead of respecting the principle of the sovereignty of the Parliament, the Court was securing its position as a strong and independent agent within the system of separation of constitutional powers. It always sought to become a partner of

---

[16] Article 54, para. 2 and article 58, para. 2 of *The Constitution of the Czech Republic*.

[17] Article 86, para. 2 of *The Constitution of the Czech Republic*.

[18] For further details, see Jiří Přibáň, 'The Constitutional Court of the Czech Republic and the Principle of the Sovereignty of the Law', in Istvan Pogany (ed.), *Human Rights in Eastern Europe* (Aldershot: Edward Elgar Publishing 1995), pp. 135–148.

the legislative power rather than a judicial body applying and extending this power into concrete cases and constitutional disputes.

This struggle for the constitutional position of constitutional courts is typical of most of post-Communist countries of Central and Eastern Europe. In Poland, the Constitutional Tribunal was set up before the fall of the Communist regime in 1985. It was originally designed as a judicial body with very limited powers which should by no means affect the principle of the sovereignty of the Parliament.[19] The position of the Tribunal was originally determined both by the supremacy of the Constitution and the supremacy of Parliament, but, soon after the collapse of Communism, the Tribunal expanded its jurisdiction and shifted its activity into the field of the constitutional review of statutes.[20] This new activity was further expanded by the constitutional changes of October 1992. Fifteen years of the existence of the Polish Constitutional Tribunal are the history of *growing activism* of the Tribunal and the abandonment of its inferior position in relation to the legislative power.

This activism is even more striking in Hungary. The Hungarian Constitutional Court was an outcome of the roundtable talks and dissolution of the Communist regime in 1989–90. Under the presidency of judge Laszlo Solyom, this court rapidly achieved the reputation of one of the most activist constitutional courts in Europe. Its jurisdiction significantly influenced both the legislative and executive powers in spite of the fact that the Hungarian Parliament enjoys more powerful position than others in other Central European post-Communist countries such as Poland and the Czech Republic. However, the principle of the Parliament's sovereignty is limited by broad powers of the Court which were inspired and modelled on the German Constitutional Court.[21] The Hungarian Constitutional Court's decision-making in the field of human rights has profoundly changed and inscribed the 'invisible Constitution' into the legal and constitutional system of Hungary and thus became one of the most important and controversial political institutions in the country.[22]

The Czech constitution-makers, when drafting the provisions concerning the Constitutional Court in 1992, were also significantly inspired by the German Basic Law and constitutional system.[23] This is especially true in the Court's

---

[19] Leszek Garlicki, 'Constitutional Developments in Poland', *St. Louis Law University Journal* 32 (1988), pp. 724–5.

[20] Herman Schwartz, *The Struggle for Constitutional Justice in Post-Communist Europe* (University of Chicago Press, Chicago, 2000), p. 56.

[21] Laszlo Solyom and Georg Brunner, *Constitutional Judiciary in a New Democracy: The Hungarian Constitutional Court* (University of Michigan Press, Ann Arbor, 2000).

[22] For the early stage of judicial activism of the Hungarian Constitutional Court under the presidency of Laszlo Solyom, see Andras Sajo, 'Reading the Invisible Constitution: Judicial Review in Hungary', *Oxford Journal of Legal Studies*, 15 (1995), pp. 253ff.

[23] See, for instance, Pavel Holländer, 'The Role of the Constitutional Court for the Application of the Constitution in Case Decisions of Ordinary Courts', *Archiv für Rechts- und Sozialphilosophie*, 86 (2000), p. 538.

power to review actions of public authorities intruding upon fundamental rights and basic freedoms.[24] The German Constitutional Court radically changed legal culture in the post-war Germany and put an end to the formalist legalism. The sovereignty of statutes of the Parliament was limited by the Court's decisions and its reasoning founded on human rights arguments.[25] The German Constitutional Court attacked the formalist application of legal and constitutional rules and favours broader arguments based on values, the principle of justice and fundamental human rights.[26] The Court participates in shaping the boundaries of the German constitutional system and its landmark decisions are taken as precedents and a part of sources of constitutional law.

Building up the Constitutional Court's position within the framework of the German constitutional system was controversial and opposed by a number of legal theorists before acknowledging its real constitutional power. More than a decade of experience with constitutional justice in the Czech Republic and other Central European post-Communist liberal democracies shows similar reactions and controversies arising among legal professions, academics and in the public. Pavel Hollander, a Czech legal theorist and judge of the Constitutional Court, calls this ambiguous situation the 'paradox of the acceptance and rejection of constitutional courts'.[27] It is typical of the public support and popularity of constitutional courts accompanied by the rejection and hostility among the judiciary, public authorities, legal academics and even the Parliament.

The main conflict between the Constitutional Court and the Supreme Court as the highest body of the ordinary judiciary was about the Constitutional Court's power to review decisions of ordinary courts and therefore its entitlement to review the constitutionality of Supreme Court's decisions. The conflict was whether constitutional court decisions in cassation bind the ordinary courts for future decision-making in the same matters. While the ordinary courts including the Supreme Court stated that they must be exempted from the legal category of 'public authorities', the Constitutional Court ruled in one of its judgments that it has jurisdiction over constitutional complaints against final decisions or other actions by public authorities intruding upon constitutionally guaranteed fundamental rights and basic freedoms. Article 2, paragraph 1 of the Constitution declares that the state authority is exercised through bodies of the legislative,

---

[24]   *Id.*; compare esp. Article 87, paragraph 1d of the Czech Constitution and Article 93, paragraph 1, lit. 4a of the German Basic Law.

[25]   For the importance of human rights, see Dieter Grimm, 'Human Rights and Judicial Review in Germany', in David M. Beatty (ed.), *Human Rights and Judicial Review: A Comparative Perspective* (Hague: Kluwer 1994), p. 277.

[26]   See, for example, the Constitutional Court's decision in the case of the former members of a border guard was published in Karlsruhe, 12 November 1996: Order of 26 October 1996–2BvR 1851/94, 2BvR 1853/94, 2BvR 1875/94 and 2BvR 1852/94.

[27]   See above n. 23, pp. 537f.

executive, and judicial powers, and the definition of the system of courts, laid down in Article 91, para. 1 of the Constitution, also includes the Supreme Court.[28]

Judges of the ordinary courts and some legal academics simply refused to accept a generally binding character of the Constitutional Court in these matters. This ignorance eventually led to a crisis within the system of justice in the famous case of Jehova's Witnesses who refused either to do the military service or work in the alternative public service. The Supreme Court judges refused to accept the ruling and ratio decidendi of the Constitutional Court and virtually put the system of justice into a deadlock.[29] The case may be perceived as a symbolic breaking point in the 'war of the courts'[30] badly damaging both the public and expert reputation of the Supreme Court. This conflict consequently led to the acceptance of the constitutional principle of a generally binding character of the Constitutional Court's decision in the human rights jurisdiction. The case also helped to implement the older judgments of the Constitutional Court in which the Court specified the necessity to accept and respect its decisions by the ordinary courts.

This dispute helped to persuade many judges of the ordinary courts to change their minds and methods of decision-making and respect the precedent-based character of the Constitutional Court's judgments in the sphere of violations of human rights and basic freedoms. The principle of a generally binding force of the Court's judgments in the ordinary courts' jurisdiction, according to which 'ordinary courts must take account of violations of fundamental rights and basic freedoms of citizens, in particular when they have already been designated as such by the Constitutional Court'[31] and 'those cases when the ordinary court does not accord parties the protection of their fundamental rights and basic freedoms, in spite of the fact that the Constitutional Court has already recognized such rights in factually analogous cases, must be considered as a violation of

---

[28] See the Judgment of the Constitutional Court of the Czech Republic, n. 337/97 III US from November 13, 1997.

[29] The dispute may be summarised as the Supreme Court's denial to accept the Constitutional Court's judgment in which the Court ruled that the continuing refusal to do the military or alternative public service for religious or moral reasons had to be considered as one crime continuing in time and not as a series of different crimes. The Constitutional Court therefore interpreted a continuing series of refusals as one criminal act and applied the principle *ne bis in idem* (the impossibility to be punished for the same crime more than once), while the Supreme Court demanded that every act of refusal to start either the military or alternative public service constitutes a distinct criminal act. For details, see the judgment of the Constitutional Court n. 38/1999Pl US.

[30] The expression 'war of the courts' was used for instance in Zdeněk Koudelka, 'Válka soudů aneb dělba moci v soudnictví' (The War of the Courts: on the separation of powers in the system of justice), *Politologický časopis (Political Science Journal)* 7 (1998), pp. 71ff.

[31] The judgment of the Constitutional Court n. 76/95 II US, of September 12, 1995.

the principle of equality of rights',[32] has therefore become a part of the Czech legal system which can be hardly disputed.

4. LEGISLATION VS. JUDICIARY?: COMMENTS ON THE RELATIONS BETWEEN THE PARLIAMENT AND THE CONSTITUTIONAL COURT

Moving our attention to the relation between the Constitutional Court and the Parliament, we can detect a very complex network of mutual tensions and co-operations. In the Czech Republic, more than in other Central European new liberal democracies, the legitimacy of the Court weakens the principle of the sovereignty of Parliament. The abovementioned American model indicates a rather strong and independent judicial body playing an important role in the system of checks and balances and limiting the Parliament in its legislative actions. The judges appointed by the President are subsequently approved only by the Senate which consists of eighty one members elected for six years by the majority electoral system. One third of the Senate, again like in the United States, is renewed every second year. The Senate itself is an important check upon the powers of the lower chamber, the Assembly of Deputies.

The fact that the office of a Constitutional Court judge is ten years, while the mandate of a member of the Senate is only six years and a deputy in the lower chamber only four years, and the President's term is five years, makes the Court a strong and autonomous agent on the constitutional architecture of the Czech Republic. Similarly like in Germany, its primary goal is therefore to find and exercise legal and political *self-restraint*. This self-restraint must determine the Court's relation both to the judiciary and legislature and serve as a counterpoint to its wide constitutional powers.

The relations between the legislative power of the Parliament and the jurisdiction of the Constitutional Court are marked by the duality of approaches. In its judgments, the Court both provides a constitutional support for democratic legitimacy and the concept of the democratic rule of law (democratic *Rechtsstaat*) and regularly challenges Acts of the Parliament and its possible political sovereignty within the system of the rule of law. Let us then divide the analysis of relations between the Parliament and constitutional justice into two following parts: (a) the Court's definition of democratic politics; and (b) conflicts between the Court and legislature.

4.1. The Court's Definition of Democratic Politics

The Court's activism and contributions to the definition of the new emerging liberal democratic system and the rule of law date back to its historically first

---

[32]   The judgment of the Constitutional Court, n. 139/98 III US, of July 9, 1998. For further details see P. Holländer, above n. 23, p. 546.

decision upon the constitutionality of the *Act on Lawlessness of the Communist Regime and Resistance Against It, n. 198/1993*. To the objection that it was unconstitutional to call the Communist regime from 1948–1989 illegitimate, the Constitutional Court responded with a detailed analysis of the principles of the rule of law/Rechtsstaat (a law-based state).[33] The Court correctly refused to perceive the problem of legitimacy in a narrow sense, as a problem of the continuity of the legal system. It refused to call the Communist system legitimate simply because the new liberal regime incorporated its laws and acknowledged its international legal obligations.

The Court refused to understand legitimacy as a mere technical function of legality and concentrated on the wider moral political context. According to its judgment, the new Czech Constitution adopted in December 1992 is not value-neutral and therefore does not regard the principle of legality only as a kind of technique independent of more general values. The Constitution incorporates the leading ideas and values of democratic political society and subjects legality to them.[34]

According to the Court's judgment, the constitutional law-based state must have democratic legitimacy, not only legal legitimacy in its formal sense.[35] The legitimacy of the political regime is derived from democratic political principles, the observance of which characterises all law-based states and the principle of legality itself. The people bear *constitutive* power, while law is the product of *constituted* and institutionalised internal state power.[36] This constituted power, moreover, must not be concentrated in one institution but must be established according to the traditional principle of the separation of powers. (The Court speaks about other values constituting a democratic law-based state, but its analysis is principally focused on the principle of the people's sovereignty and the majority will manifested by constitutional bodies.)

The legitimacy of the law-based state depends upon its democratic nature. It must have democratic elections, its constitutional bodies must make decisions according to the majority will and all laws must have a double democratic background; they must be adopted by democratic parliamentary procedures and those who adopt them (members of Parliament) must be democratically elected. Legality is subject to the legitimation framework of democratic procedures.

The Constitutional Court of the Czech Republic returned to the problem of democratic legitimacy in the constitutional complaint which had sought the annulment of Presidential Decree n. 108/1945Sb., on the Confiscation of Enemy

---

[33] Compare the Court's judgment, n. 19/93Pl.US, para. 21 of the part concerning objections to section 1 to 4 of the Act n. 198/93Sb.

[34] *Ibid*, at para. 24 of the part concerning objections to section 1 to 4 of the Act n. 198/93Sb.

[35] *Ibid*, at para. 25 of the part concerning objections to section 1 to 4 of the Act n. 198/93Sb.

[36] *Ibid*, at para. 29 of the part concerning objections to section 1 to 4 of the Act n. 198/93Sb.

Property and the Funds of National Renewal on the grounds of its unconstitutionality and unlawfulness. It described the decree as an act of political and revolutionary violence, incompatible with the contemporary principles of the law-based state which now bound the Czech Republic. The petitioner demanded the annulment of the decree *ab initio*, on the grounds of its undemocratic character and inhuman substance and for its inconsistency with the Czech constitutional order and international treaties on human rights.[37]

The Court began its judgment by noting the consistency of the decree with the fundamental principles of the law-based state. It then considered whether it may have been legitimate for President Beneš to decree such laws. In this context, the Court emphasised the contrast with the nature of the Nazi political regime, the legal system of which was subject to totalitarian power and served German nationalist and racist interests. The Nuremberg laws from 1935 were taken as examples. In contrast to the German Nazi legislation, the Court referred to the Czechoslovak Constitution of 1920, which defined the democratic and civic character of the Czechoslovak state and subjected its constitutional institutions to democratic legitimacy. In this judgment, the principle of democratic legitimacy is again explicitly superior to the principle of formal legal legitimacy.[38]

The principle of democratic legitimacy was also mentioned in connection with the incorporation of the President's decrees into the post-war Czechoslovak legal order, when these acts were approved by the Provisional National Assembly in its Act n.12/1946Sb.[39] The Court conceived the problem of legitimacy in a way very similar to its approach in its judgment concerning the *Act on Lawlessness of the Communist Regime and Resistance Against It*. A democratic political regime is contrasted with a totalitarian regime, this time the Nazi political regime.

While in democratic pre-war Czechoslovakia the people accepted the law-based state on the ground of general consensus, the Nazi totalitarian state enacted its law by violence and terror. According to the Court, consensus as the concrete expression of the democratic principle of the people's will is a source of legitimation.

The Court continued to define a democratic regime on the basis of citizenship and contrasted the democratic-republican principle of citizenship with the nationalist concept of citizenship as a community of blood and race.[40] The conflict between democracy and totalitarianism is depicted as a conflict between republican and racist values.

---

[37] See the Court's judgment, n. 14/94Pl.US, para. 1 of the reasoning of the Constitutional Court.

[38] *Ibid*, at para. 7.

[39] *Ibid*, at para. 18.

[40] *Ibid*, at para. 22.

4.2. Conflicts between the Constitutional Court and the Parliament

The Constitutional Court naturally did not limit its activity to supplementing democratic legitimacy by way of the new democratic rule of law. Its jurisdiction was designed to become a constitutional watchdog of the Parliament's legislation. The Court's history is thus full of conflicts with the legislative power.

Some legal scholars took a radical position, ignored the 'black letter constitutional provisions' such as Article 89 legislating a generally binding character of the Constitutional Court's judgments, and understood the Court's powers as fully subject to the Parliament's will. According to those views, the legislator is by no means obligated to act within the constraints of the Court's jurisdiction and can ignore its decisions.[41] Theoretically, it would be possible for the legislator to adopt a statute, the content of which was declared unconstitutional by the Court in one of its past judgments. The sovereignty of the Parliament as a ruling principle of the constitutional system could be manifested in ignoring any judicial decisions and their consequences.

This radical position is a reflection of the principle of parliamentary sovereignty and takes judicial power (including the Constitutional Court) only as a mouthpiece of the legislator's will. At the same time, legal theorists defending this position also refuse to acknowledge the fact that the Court's decision would be a source of law and have some law-creating force.[42] In fact, this position seeks to defend an old-fashioned perspective which perceives law only as a system of legal acts enacted by the legislator. This theory has its roots in Rousseau's concept of the sovereignty of the people represented by the legislative body which is typical of the mistrust of courts as bodies representing the 'old regime'.

This theoretical position is outdated not only because it simply keeps to defend the concept of law as a hierarchy of norms issued by the legislator rather than as a complex network of interpretations of normative legal regulations. It is outdated especially because the history of last century proved the inadequacy of formalist approaches in legalism and legalist arguments helped to 'justify' often autocratic and totalitarian policies.[43] Instead of the theoretical approach restricting the legal system to the acts of will and commands of the legislator, recent theoretical streams of legal positivism favour 'ethical legalism', if not explicitly 'supra-positive law' which subjects the system of positive law to the democratic and liberal political values.[44]

---

[41] For this opinion, see esp. Vladimír Mikule and Vladimír Sládeček, 'O závaznosti rozhodnutí Ústavního soudu' (On the binding force of judgments of the Constitutional Court), *Bulletin advokacie (The Bar Association Bulletin)* 8 (1995), p. 46.

[42] See Koudelka, above n. 30, pp. 71ff.

[43] See Přibáň, above n. 10.

[44] For the discussion of ethics in legal positivism, see the legal philosophies of Tom Campbell, Neil MacCormick, and Gustav Radbruch. See especially Tom Campbell, *The Legal Theory of Ethical Positivism* (Aldershot: Dartmouth Publishers 1996); Neil MacCormick, 'The

This opposite approach which builds on the political and ethical foundations of the rule of law and rejects a narrow legal positivism is also echoed in the judicial activity of constitutional courts. The practice of the German Constitutional Court accommodated Radbruch's concepts of supra-positive law, legal principles and justice in law.[45] The Czech Constitutional Court adopted a similar approach when it ruled that:

> A modern democratic written constitution is a social contract, by which the people, representing the constituent power, constitute themselves in one political (state) body and enshrine the relationship of the individual to the whole and the system of state institutions. A document institutionalising the set of fundamental, generally-accepted values and moulding the mechanism and process of the formation of legitimate power decisions cannot exist out of the context of publicly-accepted values, conceptions of justice, as well as conceptions of meaning, purpose, and the manner of functioning of democratic institutions. In other words, it cannot function without a minimum consensus with respect to values and institutions. The conclusion resulting therefrom for the field of law is that, even in a system of enacted law, basic legal principles and customs are also sources of general, as well as of constitutional, law.[46]

This reasoning is an 'extension' of the first judgment of the Court concerning the legality and legitimacy of the Communist regime and clearly shows that, in the judgments of a number of continental European constitutional courts, the interpretive concept of law represented by the theories of Gustav Radbruch or Ronald Dworkin prevailed over the concept of legislative legalism represented by the legal philosophies of H.L.A. Hart or Joseph Raz.

The Constitutional Court is a guardian of the Constitution which functions as a value background and source of principles of the whole legal system. The old metaphysical question of who is going to guard the guardian does not make sense because the contemporary liberal democratic systems of the rule of law lack any sovereign political body. The principle of the sovereignty of the people is rather exercised through different constitutional bodies with mutual checks and balances. Instead of the sovereignty of one political body, we should talk about the sovereignty of the text of the Constitution which is always open to the range of different readings, interpretations and applications within the limits of liberal democratic institutional framework. This perspective was emphasised for instance by the German Constitutional Court already in 1951, when it ruled

---

Ethics of Legalism', *Ratio Juris*, 2 (1989), pp. 184ff.; Gustav Radbruch, *Legal Philosophy* (Cambridge Mass.: Harvard University Press 1950).

[45] See Donald Kommers, *The Constitutional Jurisprudence of the Federal Republic of Germany* (Duke University Press, Durham, N.C., 1997).

[46] The judgment of the Constitutional Court n. 33/97Pl. US, of December 17, 1997.

that the constitutional bodies could not adopt the law with the content which was declared the Court as unconstitutional in its past decision.[47]

In the last decade, the Czech constitutional system experienced several attempts of the legislator to ignore the previous judgments of the Constitutional Court, one of the most important being the case of statutes regulating the salaries of the judiciary. The law n. 268/1998 cancelled the entitlement for an extra supplement to the salaries of some representatives of the constitutional bodies, attorneys, civil servants, judges and members of the Prague stock market board. The law was proposed by the Senate and enacted by the Parliament as a part of austerity measures taken in respect to the economic difficulties and budgeting problems of that time. The controversial supplement was also guaranteed by the law and belonged to the common practice of twelve monthly paid salaries plus two extra salaries paid before the summer and Christmas season. The austerity legislation cancelling one of the supplement salaries had a popular support because it was seen as a contribution to the equal and just distribution of austerity measures and financial burdens of citizens. It even helped to depict the highest representatives of the constitutional power symbolically as 'one of us' and therefore had its ideological value.

The Constitutional Court's judgment was therefore confronted by the democratic will on two different fronts: the will of the democratically elected Parliament and the popular support of the austerity legislation. Yet, the Court ruled that it was unconstitutional to include the profession of judges into the law and removed it from Article 1 of the statute. The Court's reasoning emphasised that the sovereignty of the people is exercised by all branches of the constitutional power, that is, legislative, executive and judicial power. The will of the Parliament cannot be seen as the supreme representation of the will of the people. The Court highlighted the principle of judicial independence as one of the pillars of the democratic rule of law and, to support its ruling, even quoted from Article III of the Constitution of the United States, according to which judges' salaries are guaranteed.[48]

The Court also refused to treat equally the role and constitutional importance of judges and civil servants and justified its ruling on the basis that, unlike other subjects listed in the law, judges play a special role in the protection of the liberal democratic values and the rule of law. It is quite interesting that this part of the judgment was challenged in the dissenting opinion of the President of the Constitutional Court, Zdeněk Kessler, who objected that the Court's decision to discriminate between judges and other representatives of the constitutional power was against the principle of equal treatment.[49]

---

[47] 1 BverfGe 14, 36 (Suedweststaat).

[48] See the judgment of the Constitutional Court n. 13/99Pl. US, of September 15, 1999.

[49] See the dissent opinion n. 3 of judge Kessler in the judgment of the Constitutional Court n. 13/99Pl. US, of September 15, 1999.

This judgment could be just an isolated interpretation of the principle of judicial independence, if the Parliament did not retreat to the same law just a couple of months later. On November 9, 1999, the Assembly of Deputies enacted the Government's austerity law proposal which involved the same subjects and had the same content as the statute from the previous year which was declared by the Constitutional Court as unconstitutional in respect to the profession of judges. The Senate returned the law to the Assembly of Deputies commenting that the lower chamber should respect the Court's judgment, but the Assembly of Deputies ignored both the objections of the upper chamber and the judgment of the Constitutional Court, overruled the Senate's will and enacted the law in its original form.

Similarly, in the disputes between the Supreme and Constitutional Courts, the question of a generally binding character of the Constitutional Court's judgments turned out to be crucial here. Arrogant comments by some deputies of the lower chamber and their disrespect for constitutional and ordinary justice only echoed the theory of the sovereignty of the Parliament and inferior position of judiciary, so typical of the European-Continental legal doctrine of the late eighteenth and early nineteenth century. However, instead of a complex legal doctrine, most deputies manifested only their *political cynicism.*

The sovereignty and cynicism of the Parliament could not, nevertheless, become a solid political strategy. The striking examples of the impossibility to hold this political position are the cases and judgments made by the Constitutional Court in the sphere of democratic elections and free competition among political parties.

In the famous case of the senator for the Civic Democratic Party regarding Dagmar Lastovecka and her campaign during the 1998 Senate elections, the Court specified the limits of a fair campaign and election contest when it ruled that a candidate's media appearance during the forty eight hours period before the elections, which was defined by the election law as a campaign moratorium, did not automatically mean that that person's mandate could be pronounced legally invalid. The Court explicitly stated that this case cannot be taken as a generalisation and that different cases must be treated differently and judges must take into account specific circumstances of individual cases. However, the main consequence of the decision is the impossibility to apply the measures of strict liability of people participating in the elections for any public actions taken during the '48 hours silence period'.[50]

The Lastovecka case meant yet another controversy between the Constitutional Court and the Supreme Court because the Supreme Court, which has jurisdiction in the election matters, applied the principle of strict liability and declared the election void on the basis that Lastovecka gave a TV interview which was broadcast just a day before the elections. The Constitutional Court's

---

[50] See the judgment of the Constitutional Court n. 526/98 I. US, of February 1999.

abolishment of the Supreme Court's decision therefore did not lead to any conflict with the legislator. It rather helped to specify practices and limits accompanying the election campaign and contest. However, conflicts between the Court and the Parliament in the sphere of the election laws and regulations are extremely important for the whole constitutional system of liberal democracy and the rule of law in the Czech Republic.

In this context, the judgment of the Constitutional Court of January 24, 2001, must be seen as truly a landmark decision. The new election law was a part of the 'opposition treaty'[51] between the rightwing Civic Democratic Party and the leftwing Social Democratic Party and its aim was to eliminate smaller political parties from the Parliament and introduce a system with two dominating political parties. In spite of many public and expert criticisms, the law was approved in both chambers of the Parliament. The President and a group of senators sent the complaint to the Constitutional Court with objections mainly to the six following provisions implemented by the new law: (1) introduction of thirty five constituencies instead of the existing eight large electoral regions; (2) new, so called 'modified' d'Hondt's method of the re-distribution of votes (d'Hondt's coefficient would be 1.4 and not the usual 1.0); (3) the lowest number of mandates in a constituency (four mandates); (4) obligatory bails for the elections to the Assembly of Deputies; (5) cuts in the state financial support of political parties: instead of the existing rule of 90Czk (€3) per vote, political parties would get only 30Czk (€1) per vote; (6) new limits for coalitions to enter the Parliament: coalitions of two parties would require 10% of votes, of three parties 15%, of four parties 20% etc. The President's complaint objected to the new law on the basis that it effectively destroys the constitutional principle according to which the Assembly of Deputies as the lower chamber of the Parliament is elected by a proportional election system, while the Senate as the upper chamber is elected by a majority election system.[52]

The law was politically highly controversial. It was perceived as a matter of force which ignored the necessity of political negotiations and wide consent and represented the arrogant political style of the leaders of both the Civic Democratic Party Václav Klaus (the Chair of the Assembly of Deputies) and the Social Democratic Party Miloš Zeman (the Prime Minister of the Government). The enforcement of the law would lead to the chance that a political party with just above 30% of popular vote could form the one-party government. Apart from the opposition parties and the President, there was a strong opposition against the law even among the social democratic senators

---

[51] The 'opposition treaty' was a pact between two major political parties granting the support and stability to the minority government of the social democrats and giving a lot of political control to its rightwing partner, the Civic Democratic Party. It was signed after the elections into the Assembly of Deputies in 1998 and expired with the elections in 2002.

[52] See Article 18, paragraphs 1 and 2 of the Constitution.

and it was finally a ruthless political pressure performed by the social democratic Prime Minister Zeman against the dissenting senators which helped to approve the law in the upper chamber of the Parliament. The subsequent President's veto did not help and was overruled in the Parliament by the majority of votes of the two 'opposition treaty' parties.

The Constitutional Court was therefore in a very difficult position and political implications of its decision were to be enormous in any case. The guardian of the Constitution was expected to act as a strong political agent that could determine the political system and culture of the country for decades. It was confronted with the overtly purposive legislation, the goal of which was to change a political map of Czech society. It also had to provide a complex interpretation of the vague constitutional provision of Article 18, paragraph 1 of the Constitution, according to which 'elections to the Assembly of Deputies shall be held by secret ballot on the basis of a universal, equal, and direct right to vote, according to the principle of proportional representation.'

The judgment of the Court declared five of six objected provisions of the law unconstitutional and therefore void. The only disputed provision which was not annulled by the Court as unconstitutional, was the rule of the arithmetic growth of quorum for coalitions. Politically, it was another significant blow to the 'opposition treaty' parties after they lost the majority in the Senate in the elections in November 2000. Constitutionally and legally, the consequences are even greater. During the process of analysis of the hybrid of the election law, the Court had to come with its own 'constitutional' definition of the proportional election system and its limits. The Court had to use the *creative force* and define the content of the vague constitutional rule concerning the election system into the Assembly of Deputies. This content has a generally binding character and the legislator will have to respect it in the process of adopting a different law regulating the parliamentary elections which will be held in the spring 2002.

The Court decided that the proportionate model of political representation in the legislative body can involve various mechanisms limiting the scale of representation (such as the redistribution of votes, 5% votes clause for political parties to get the mandates in the Parliament etc.), but that these mechanisms enhancing the political integration and stimulating governmental stability must not imperil the principle of representation of the political will of the highest possible number of voters in the elections. The principles of political integration and differentiation are inseparable and the proportionate system can incorporate only those integrative mechanisms which do not avoid the possibility to represent different political programmes and will in the legislative body.[53]

Using the empirical statistical methods and various comparative models, the

---

[53] See the judgment of the Constitutional Court from 24 January 2001, published as n. 42/2000 Pl US.

Court came to the conclusion that the accumulation of the integrative mechanisms in the election law exceeded the limits and continuum of the proportionate system. The law would introduce the model according to which the political party representing the will of less than one third of voters could receive the majority of the seats in the Parliament and therefore form the government. Political parties would have to get more than 10% of votes in the new electoral districts in order to get a minimum of the contested mandates in those districts. According to the Court, this consequence contradicts the constitutional provisions and intention to provide the two chambers of the Czech Parliament with different forms of democratic legitimacy based on the proportionate and majority election system. The only integrative mechanism declared by the Court as constitutional was therefore the arithmetically growing clause for political coalitions which means that a coalition of two political parties must get a minimum of 10% votes, a coalition of three parties 15% etc.

Instead of the Kelsenian negative legislator, the Election Law case proves that the Constitutional Court's position is significantly stronger because it sets up normative limits for the legislative activity of the Parliament. It is a partner of the legislator with the power to limit its will. This time, this fact was widely acknowledged by Members of the Parliament and the legislator respected the Court's judgment in the process of drafting the new election law.[54] Similarly like the Supreme Court in the 'War of the Courts', the Parliament finally had to accept the judgment and reasoning of the Constitutional Court in order to avoid a deep constitutional crisis. Similarly like other constitutional courts, the Czech Constitutional Court also 'reads the invisible Constitution' and its judgments form a fundamental and inseparable part of the Czech constitutional system. In specific circumstances, it can even determine the constitutional limits of legislator's actions.

However, this case is not the first judgment in which the Constitutional Court contradicted the will of the Parliament in the sphere of free and democratic competition among political parties. The Court declared unconstitutional and void Article 85 of the Act n. 247/95 on the parliamentary elections which restricted the entitlement to receive a state financial contribution for the costs related to the electoral campaign to the political parties that received at least 3% of the popular vote.[55] The law on the financing of political parties proposed by the 'opposition treaty' parties and enacted by the Parliament in 2000 was

---

[54] For instance, V. Klaus and M. Zeman both stated that they respected the judgment and would propose a new statute which would conform to the Constitutional Court's reasoning. Yet, Klaus also announced that his political party will continue in its attempt to change the constitutional provisions and introduce the system of a majority rule for the Assembly of Deputies. See *MfDnes*, January 25, 2001.

[55] See the judgment of the Constitutional Court published on November 11, 1999 in the collection of Laws as n. 243/1999.

also abolished by the Court as unconstitutional in its judgment from 27 February 2001. The law would have made substantive changes in the system of state funding of political parties which distinguished between the financial contribution calculated on the basis of received votes and the contribution calculated on the basis of the number of mandates in the Parliament. While reducing the 'ballot contribution', the new law would have doubled the 'mandate contribution'. This new system of state funding would have led to the significant financial problems for non-parliamentary political parties and much greater financial support for the strongest parliamentary parties. The Court ruled that the law introducing such a system causes significant inequality between big and small political parties and introduces the financial discrimination into the political system which is specified by the article 5 of the Constitution as '... founded on the free and voluntary formation of and free competition among those political parties which respect the fundamental democratic principles and which renounce force as a means of promoting their interests.' However, the Assembly of Deputies immediately reacted to the Court's annulment of the law and, just two days after the judgment and before it was even published, enacted the new law which virtually ignored the Court's reasoning and keeps the new system unchanged. This conflict and political and legal tensions arising from it thus remind the analysed 'judges' salary' conflict between the Parliament and the Constitutional Court. However, the new law is likely to be vetoed by the President and will apparently be reported back to the Constitutional Court. The tensions between the Court and the Assembly of Deputies consequently intensified and some politicians turned the Court's decision-making into the political propaganda.[56]

5. CONCLUSION

After a series of the Constitutional Court judgments during the first months of 2001, the tensions and conflicts between the lower chamber of the Parliament dominated by the 'opposition treaty' political parties and the Constitutional Court as a guardian of the Constitution became more intense. The conflicts proceed at two levels: political and legal. At the political level, the conflicts emerged because the 'opposition treaty' civic and social democrats sought to change the political and constitutional system while lacking the support for the changes of specific provisions of the Constitution. They attempted to redraft the

---

[56] For instance, the deputy head of the Civic Democratic Party Ivan Langer attacked the Constitutional Court's decision as a sign of judges' dependence on the President and thus indicated that the Court' decisions favour political forces loyal to the President Havel. However, the new law on financing the political parties was supported by all political parties except the Communists and the Court's judgment may be therefore hardly seen as supporting some political parties or coalitions and discriminating against the others.

rules without redrafting the Constitution itself. The opposition could consequently report all laws changing the political and constitutional system to the Constitutional Court asking to annul them on the basis of their unconstitutionality. Any decision of the Court may be therefore perceived as primarily political because it has to deal with the fundamental political issues and attempts to change rules of the democratic game.

Referring to the political aspects of the Court's decision-making, some 'opposition treaty' politicians also have recently pointed to the weaker democratic legitimacy of the Court in comparison to the Assembly of Deputies.[57] Nevertheless, this political attack on the Court contrasts with its strong public support. At the political symbolic level, the Court is perceived by the public as the constitutional body promoting and defending the human rights principles and culture of constitutionalism more than other institutions of the Czech constitutional system.

However, the legal consequences are more important than the political ones because the recent conflicts between the Assembly of Deputies and the Constitutional Court clearly manifest the constitutional and legal powers of the Court in respect to the legislative power. It is obvious that the Court's decision-making cannot be simplified in the language of the political parties interests or government's policy. If the Parliament refuses to respect the Court's judgments, it risks a deep constitutional crisis. It is in a similar situation to the Supreme Court in the past when it hesitated to accept the Court's judgments and normative power of its reasoning. Finally, the Parliament, similarly like the Supreme Court, will have to accept that its will is restricted by the Court's judgments because it could otherwise initiate never-ending constitutional disputes between the legislation and constitutional justice.

The Constitutional Court's decision-making has fundamentally changed the constitutional system of the Czech Republic, but it also introduced radical changes into the Czech culture of legalism and traditionally strong formalist attitude towards the judicial interpretation and application of law. The Court has introduced balanced techniques of activist reading of the Charter and Constitution and criticised the formalist judicial decision-making. In the field of human rights, especially property rights and principles of due process of law, it abolished the restrictive legislation and strengthened the principles of justice as fairness and equal treatment of all as formulated in the Constitution and Charter which, according to the Court, must have precedence over statutory regulations.[58]

---

[57] For instance, see the Civic Democratic Party deputies' reaction to the Constitutional Court's judgment annulling the legislation which introduced the new system of state funding of political parties. *MfDnes*, 28 February 2001 and 29 February 2001.

[58] See especially a series of the judgments of the Constitutional concerning the process of restitutions and its interpretation of the formal statutory provisions defining the deadlines and procedural duties such as in the Court's judgment n. 48/95 Pl. US.

The Constitutional Court's activism and progressive reading of the human rights catalogue formulated in the Charter of Fundamental Rights and Freedoms cannot avoid conflicts both within the system of justice and broader constitutional framework, but it also provides the Court with a higher public support and political trust. The Court's democratic legitimacy may be procedurally weaker than the legitimacy of the Parliament, yet its current empirical democratic legitimacy is stronger than the empirical legitimacy and public support of both chambers of the Parliament. The Court has thus become both an important agent in the democratic political game supporting its legitimacy and institution fundamentally changing the legal system and legalist traditions deeply entrenched in the Czech legal and constitutional culture.

17. Defending Order and Freedom: The Lithuanian Constitutional Court in its First Decade

Nida Gelazis

"Most people in the postcommunist world have already made a choice between order and freedom, and their choice is order."[1]

1. INTRODUCTION

Order and freedom are not mutually exclusive properties of governance. Indeed, democracy is meant to bring both order and freedom to a society that chooses to govern according to its principles. Yet, in the early years of democratic transition in Central and Eastern Europe, after democracy was thought victorious over the totalitarian state, backpedaling from democratic goals in the hope of regaining order in these reeling societies was not uncommon.

Only a few years after pro-democracy parties ignited the democratization process, in quick succession, voters in Lithuania, Poland and Bulgaria restored ex-Communist party majorities to power. Lithuania seemed particularly torn between choosing a free or orderly society. Somewhat incongruously, the 1992 parliamentary elections, which gave the ex-communist Lithuanian Democratic Labor Party (LDLP) a strong majority, were also used as a referendum for approving the draft constitution that created democratic institutions and a rule-of-law system. And while the LDLP did not challenge the structure of the new democratic regime, the spirit of pluralism and cooperation was dampened since one party essentially controlled all branches of government. Four years later, the electorate ousted the LDLP in favor of the Homeland Union-Conservatives of Lithuania (HU-CL). Although the HU-CL was an offshoot of the pro-democracy Sajudis movement, it did little to open the decision-making process since it quickly formed a coalition with the Christian Democrats and thus formed a new super-majority to replace the political hegemony previously enjoyed by the LDLP. Only after the 2000 elections was the dichotomy between order and freedom seemingly exposed as a sham. With as many as ten parties in Parliament

---

[1]   Charles Gati, 'If Not Democracy, What? Leaders, Laggards, and Losers in the Postcommunist World', in Michael Mandelbaum (ed), *Post-Communism: Four Perspectives* (New York, Council of Foreign Relations Press, 1996), p. 169.

Wojciech Sadurski (ed.), Constitutional Justice, East and West, 395–408
© 2002 *Kluwer Law International. Printed in Great Britain.*

and no clear majority, all the parties have collaborated to create not only a strong, orderly state, but one in which freedom and openness are better served.

The false dichotomy between order and freedom, pitting reform against stagnation, could have been quite damaging to the democratization process. Instead of creating governments representative of a conflicted and evolving civil society, elections gave power to one party and left the Opposition perilously silent during the crucial period of democratic consolidation. It was against this backdrop that the Constitutional Court emerged as a powerful arbiter between feuding political parties, government branches vying for power, and even between the state and society. The Court has provided a forum for the frustrated parliamentary Opposition to voice its protest against decisions passed by the majority. It has mediated between rival branches of government to reestablish the constitutionalized balance of power. Moreover, the Court has upheld international human rights norms despite the electorate's disapproval. In this way, the Court has come to embody the principles of democracy by maintaining order through a consistent interpretation of the Constitution in the constant flux of ideas and passions of a free society.

2. THE INSTALLATION OF THE LITHUANIAN CONSTITUTIONAL COURT

The deep political and ideological conflict which marked the process of constitution-drafting in Lithuania was ultimately overcome through compromise. After months of bickering, the presidential and the parliamentary blocs finally settled on a semi-presidential system. To a great extent, this compromise was forged by making the balance of powers between the major institutions a priority. This system of balancing institutional power included the creation of a constitutional court.

The source of much of the conflict during the period of constitution-drafting was the desire to gain legitimacy, both domestically and internationally, by recreating as closely as possible the institutional structure of the inter-war Republic of Lithuania. In the early 1990s, the public was skeptical of all that might be seen as 'Soviet.' Political or institutional residues from the Soviet period were seen as illegitimate, because they had not been adopted democratically, and dangerous, because they might be used to pull Lithuania back into the USSR. Moreover, creating clear links to the inter-war Republic was an attempt to ease Lithuania back into the international community. Lithuania had been a member of the League of Nations and several countries, such as the United States and Great Britain, had never recognized the illegal occupation of the Baltic States by the Soviet Union.

Although there was good reason to establish clear links to the past, the inter-war Republic was hardly a model for the post-Communist democracy to follow.[2]

---

[2]   Kestutis Lapinskas, 'Lietuvos Konstituciju Istoriniu Teisiniu Sasaju Beieskant' [Searching for Historical Legal Links between Lithuania's Constitutions] paper presented at the con-

Not one, but three constitutions were adopted between 1918 and 1940, which covered the spectrum of possibilities – creating a strong parliamentary system one year, and a strong presidency the next. Nevertheless, in the absence of a guiding state interest or consolidated civil society, harkening back to Lithuania's 'golden past' was a tool for concealing individual preferences and partisan interests.[3] Yet in the process of picking and choosing from the various institutional models available, the new institutional system created by the 1992 Constitution has little resemblance to any of the inter-war regimes.

The Constitutional Court, which was established after the adoption of the 1992 Constitution, was an altogether new institution in Lithuania. As with other constitutional questions, the debate over the creation of a constitutional court was conducted at the level of the political elite, and there were few discussions on this issue open to the general public or in the media. According to Juozas Zilys, the fist chairman of the Constitutional Court, the idea to establish a separate institution for constitutional control first came from the Centre fraction in Parliament in the autumn of 1990.[4] Those in support of establishing a constitutional court looked to foreign models to help determine what type of court to create in Lithuania. Initially, the legal community debated the merits of the French *Conseil Constitutionnel*. Another bloc broke away from the pro-constitutional court supporters and instead advocated a system in which all courts would be responsible for constitutional control. Ultimately neither of these options was constitutionalized. Instead, the constitution-drafters determined that a completely independent institution was necessary to ensure that the Constitution would be implemented accurately and the branches of power would be kept separate and balanced.

In addition to the French model, the German system was investigated when deciding whether to grant citizens the right to petition the Constitutional Court. Following the German example, it was determined that individuals could approach the Constitutional Court indirectly by bringing a case to a lower court that could forward the case to the Constitutional Court if it deemed the case to

---

ference: *Konstitucija, Zmogus, Teisine Valstybe* [*The Constitution, the Individual and the Rule of Law State*] October 24–25, 1997 (Vilnius, Lietuvos Zmogaus Teisiu Centras, 1998), pp. 31–50.

3 '[D]esigners of institutions shy away from accepting responsibility in public for what they are really doing, and that they tend to hide instead behind the often rather fictive notion of imitation or transplantation.' See Claus Offe, 'Designing Institutions in East European Transitions' in Robert E. Goodin (ed), *The Theory of Institutional Design* (Cambridge, Cambridge University Press 1996), p. 213.

4 Juozas Zilys, 'Konstitucinis Teismas Valdziu Sistemoje' [The Constitutional Court within the Governing System] paper presented at the conference: *Lietuvos Respublikos Konstitucija: Tiesioginis Taikymas ir Nuosavybes Teisiu Apsauga* [*The Constitution of the Republic of Lithuania: Direct Effect and the Protection of Property Rights*] February 25–26, 1993 (Vilnius, Teise 1994).

be of a constitutional nature.[5] This decision was perhaps motivated by practicality, that is, to avoid a situation in which the Court was swamped by an unmanageable number of individual rights cases. The Lithuanian Constitution grants citizens a wide array of rights and duties. Beginning with Article 6 ("The Constitution shall be an integral and directly applicable statue, every person may defend his or her rights on the basis of the Constitutions"), the Constitution dedicates three chapters to citizens' rights and the state's obligation to help citizens realize them.[6]

In order to guarantee that the Constitutional Court's power would not supersede that of the representative institutions and would be checked and balanced with the other major state institutions, constitution drafters sought to establish a system that equitably divided the nomination of judges, while reflecting the semi-presidential character of the Constitution. One-third of the nine Constitutional Court justices are replaced every three years. The President, Chairperson of the *Seimas* (Parliament), and Chairperson of the Supreme Court each nominate one candidate.[7] These nominees are then appointed by the *Seimas* to serve nine-year terms. The *Seimas* also appoints the Court Chairperson from among the judges nominated by the President. This concession to the President may be seen as an attempt to depoliticize the court somewhat, since the President, as well as the Constitutional Court justices, may not belong to or participate in any political party.

Special arrangements were made for the first nine years of the Constitutional Court's existence in order to initiate the staggered appointment system. All nine judges were nominated in 1993–each institution nominated three judges. After the judges were appointed, they drew straws to determine the length of their terms. Those with the shortest straws served for only three years, those who chose slightly longer straws served for six years, and the remaining judges served

---

[5] *Id.*

[6] Chapter 2 of the Constitution lists the fundamental rights and freedoms to be enjoyed by individuals in Lithuania including, the right to life, equality, dignity, property, freedoms of speech, thought, religion and conscience, and protection of minority rights. Social and economic rights also occupy a prominent space in the Lithuanian Constitution. For example: Article 39: "The state shall take care of families bringing up children, render them support"; Art. 41: "secondary, vocational, and higher schools shall be free of charge in public schools"; Article 42: "support for culture and science, Lithuanian history, art, and other cultural monuments and objects"; Article 45: "the state shall support ethnic communities"; Article 52 "the state guarantees the right of citizens to old age and disability pension, as well as to social assistance in the event of unemployment, sickness, widowhood, loss of breadwinner, and other cases provided by law"; Article 53: "the state shall take care of people's health and shall guarantee medical aid and services in the event of sickness. The procedure for providing medical aid to citizens free of charge at state medical facilities shall be established by law"; and Article 54 "the state shall protect the environment.".

[7] Article 4 of the Law on the Constitutional Court (no. I-67, 3 February, 1993).

the full nine-year term.[8] The judges subsequently appointed in 1996 and 1999 will serve full nine-year terms.

Constitutional Court judges must be Lithuanian citizens, have impeccable reputations, and at least ten years experience serving in the legal profession (including academics in legal fields).[9] The State and Law Committee of the Parliament decides whether or not candidates nominated by the *Seimas*, President, and Supreme Court Chair meet these requirements. Article 6 of the Law on the Constitutional Court prohibits appointed judges from holding any other elected or appointed office, from being employed in any business, commercial or other private institution or company (with the exception of educational or creative work), and from receiving any remuneration other than their Constitutional Court salary and payment for educational or creative activities. In addition to refraining from participation in political parties or other political organizations, judges may not act as defense counsels or representatives of any company, institution, organization or person.

The immunity of Constitutional Court judges is established in Article 8 of the Law on the Constitutional Court. Judges may not be found criminally responsible, arrested or subject to any other restriction of personal freedom, and their residences and offices may not be inspected or searched without prior consent of the Constitutional Court. Only the Prosecutor General may bring a motion to the Court to institute criminal proceedings against a judge. Judges cannot be prosecuted for their personal views or their position on a Court decision. Criminal cases involving Constitutional Court judges are tried only by the Supreme Court. Judges can be suspended only if court-approved criminal proceedings are initiated by a resolution of the *Seimas* to initiate impeachment proceedings against a judge, or if a judge is deemed to be missing by a court order. An additional guarantee of immunity is the final stipulation of Article 8, which states that "the powers and rights of the Constitutional Court and its judges may not be infringed upon in case of a declaration of war or state of emergency."

The only disciplinary action available to control judges of the Constitutional Court short of impeachment is the reduction of the judge's previous month's salary. This salary reduction may be used against a judge who fails to carry out his or her duties or for nonattendance in court sittings without good reason. Only the Constitutional Court may decide whether or not to initiate disciplinary action against one of its judges and the reduction cannot exceed 50 percent of one month's salary. Thus far, no disciplinary action has ever been taken against a Constitutional Court justice, nor have any impeachment attempts been made.

---

[8] Interview with former Constitutional Court justice, Stasys Staciokas, Vilnius, Lithuania in October, 1996.

[9] Article 5 of the Law on the Constitutional Court (no.I-67, 3 February, 1993).

3. INDEPENDENCE OF JUDGES

It is difficult to find objective evidence that Constitutional Court judges are vulnerable to political pressure. This is in part due to the fact that it is illegal for judges to publicly discuss their opinions on any pending Court case.[10] The Lithuanian News Agency is obliged to report information concerning the sittings of the Constitutional Court by Article 18 of the Law on the Constitutional Court. And because interference in judicial activity by state institutions, political parties, public organizations or citizens is illegal,[11] such interference – if it exists – would be shrouded in secrecy. Moreover, judges seem to be further protected from interference by Article 53, which defends the confidentiality of Constitutional Court deliberations. Therefore, although the arguments and decisions of the Court are published and publicly announced,[12] the judges' individual votes and opinions are unknown.

Despite attempts made to insulate the Court, there is evidence that state institutions consult with the Court prior to serving their petitions. One example of this practice is the case that ultimately abolished capital punishment from the Criminal Code. The initial stimulus for bringing the case to Court was the EU accession requirements for Lithuania presented in the Agenda 2000. Among the political conditions, the EU required that Lithuania abolish the death penalty. In response the Lithuanian Centre for Human Rights (a quasi-state organization affiliated with the Ministry of Justice) conducted a study in 1998 to survey public opinion on capital punishment and determine whether the electorate would support an amendment to the Criminal Code. The survey revealed that 70–80 percent of respondents supported the death penalty.[13] Therefore, finding a political bloc in Parliament to support the bill would have been difficult.[14]

Unwilling to risk the embarrassment that the bill's failure would cause in the EU accession process, a petition was brought to the Constitutional Court by the *Seimas* Legal Committee (composed of representatives from the major political parties as well as independent *Seimas* members). The representative of the *Seimas* group was the chairman of the legal committee Stasys Staciokas, who was also a former justice of the Constitutional Court (1993–1996). The petition requested the Court to investigate the compliance of Article 105 of the Criminal Code (which allows the death penalty to be imposed on persons who have

---

[10] Article 9 of the Law on the Constitutional Court (no. I-67, 3 February, 1993).

[11] Article 17 of the Law on the Constitutional Court (no. I-67, 3 February, 1993).

[12] In addition to the ELTA (the national news agency) reports on Court cases, all the Court's rulings and decisions are available at the Court's web site: www.lrkt.lt.

[13] Constitutional Court Ruling 'On the Compliance of the Death Penalty Provided for by the Sanction of Article 105 of the Republic of Lithuania Criminal Code with the Constitution of the Republic of Lithuania' (Vilnius, 9 December, 1998).

[14] Interview with Lithuanian Centre for Human Rights director, Toma Birmontiene, March 29, 1999.

committed a grave crime) with Article 18 (which deems fundamental rights and freedoms of individuals to be inborn), Article 19 (which states that the right to life of individuals shall be protected by law), and Article 21 (which prohibits torture) of the Constitution.

Contrary to normal practice, in which the petitioner presents his or her arguments and the party concerned defends the alternative position, in this case the party concerned was in complete accord with the petitioner. Moreover, representatives of various government ministries, academics and church leaders were invited to present their own arguments in support of the petitioner's claim that the death penalty was unconstitutional. From among the ten expert witnesses called to the hearing, only one (Dr. L. Labanauskas, President of the Union of Physicians) defended the death penalty as necessary due to the high level of criminality in Lithuania. Other witnesses sited various international human rights conventions, which compelled Lithuania to abolish the death penalty.

The Constitutional Court's lengthy decision begins by pointing out that certain human rights and freedoms are routinely suspended for individuals as punishment for a crime in an effort to deter individuals from committing criminal acts. The Court further indicated that many studies have concluded that capital punishment has not had a deterrent effect, and it has been asserted that the use of violence by the state creates a more violent society.

Due to the fact that Lithuania has never ratified Protocol 6 of the European Convention for the Protection of Human Rights and Fundamental Freedoms, which demands the abolition of the death penalty, the Court could not directly invoke the Convention as a means to abolish the death penalty. Yet, by naming the various international conventions and European countries that have abolished the death penalty, the Court attempted to show that it has become customary for European countries to abolish the death penalty, and conclude that because Lithuania is a part of that community, the death penalty should be seen to contradict the right to life, as guaranteed by the Lithuanian Constitution.

The Court underlined the importance of state sovereignty: "Holding that it is a member of the international community possessing equal rights, the State of Lithuania, of its own free will, adopts and recognizes these principles and norms, the customs of the international community, and naturally integrates itself into the world culture and becomes its natural part." This interpretation of state sovereignty is certainly quite different from what it had been when the Lithuanian independence movement began. In the late 1980s and early 1990s, sovereignty was understood to be the right of each state to self-determination, to be equal with other states in the international arena, and, as a democracy, to follow the will of the citizenry to determine how the state will act. This interpretation of sovereignty was necessary to make a clean and irreparable break from the USSR. Moreover, the Baltic States have used this conservative interpretation of sovereignty as an excuse to resist international pressure to adopt more liberal minority rights standards. Instead, restrictive citizenship and language laws were used to 'punish' the Russian-speaking populations in the region for years of Soviet dominance. Therefore, for the Court to state that sovereignty also includes an element of "integrating with the international community" should be seen as the evolution of Lithuanian attitudes towards international law, which may set a precedent for further liberalization in the field of human rights.

This case reflects the status of Lithuania's democracy in several ways. First, it shows that through ad hoc consultations and coordination of efforts, state institutions have adopted a paternalistic attitude towards governance, in which the political elite makes decisions and finds institutional means to implement them. The result has been that public debate over important issues often occurs only after decisions are made, which results in an increased distance between citizens and the decision-making process. The demands made by the international community, and in particular by the European Union, are to a large extent aggravating this situation. Although it may be difficult to find fault in the result of this process – in this case, the abolition of the death penalty – questions remain over the long-term effects of circumventing the electorate in terms of the durability of the policy and its implementation.

4. JUDGING THE CONSTITUTIONALITY OF STATUTES

The right to petition the Constitutional Court is governed by Article 65 of the Law on the Constitutional Court, which states that in cases concerning laws or other acts adopted by the *Seimas*, the government, a group of one-fifth of *Seimas* members (or 28 MPs), or the courts may petition the Court; in cases concerning the acts of the President, only the courts or a group of one-fifth of *Seimas* members may submit the petition; and in cases concerning government acts, the President, the courts, or a group of one-fifth of *Seimas* members may petition the Constitutional Court.

According to Article 72 of the Constitution, all Constitutional Court decisions are binding. Thus, in order to override a Court decision, the *Seimas* would be forced to initiate constitutional amendment procedures. Chapter 14 of the Constitution deals with constitutional amendment procedures. According to Article 147, amendment proposals may be submitted by one-fourth of all Seimas members or by a petition signed by at least 300,000 eligible voters (roughly 10 percent of the population). Amendments may not be proposed or adopted during a state of emergency or martial law. In order for an amendment to be adopted, it must be passed by at least two-thirds of all members of Parliament in two separate sessions, with a three-month lapse between votes. Amendments to the provisions of Chapters 1[15] and 14 may be made only by a referendum vote.

---

[15]   Chapter I of the Constitution, titled: "The State of Lithuania", sets up the basic guidelines for democracy and the rule of law in the country, the institutional structure of the state and protects the state sovereignty of Lithuania.

Thus far, no Constitutional Court ruling has triggered the *Seimas* to initiate constitutional amendment procedures.

A high proportion of petitions to the Constitutional Court have come from the *Seimas* Opposition, which has given the Court an important power-balancing role, not only between rival political parties, but between institutions as well. While this may be expected of any constitutional court, it was a particularly important role for the Lithuanian Constitutional Court due to the strong party majorities elected in Lithuania during the first eight years the Constitution was put into place.

After the 1992 elections, the ex-Communist LDLP super-majority quickly took the reins of the government and hastily prepared much-needed legislation for Parliament's rubber stamp. With the LDLP controlling 70 of the 141 parliamentary seats, Opposition parties found it difficult if not impossible to significantly influence legislation. Initially, the Opposition parties brought cases to the Constitutional Court on laws that blatantly contradicted the Constitution. Such cases often never had to be ruled upon by the Court, since the majority in Parliament would quickly amend such laws before the Court had a chance to deliberate. One example was the Court's October 13, 1993 Decision Concerning the dismissal of initiated legal proceedings. In this case, a group of Opposition *Seimas* members petitioned the Court to investigate the constitutionality of Part 2 of Article 137 of Chapter IV of the *Seimas* Statute (Standing Orders) which restricted what the Lithuanian media could report on the *Seimas*. The majority hoped to control the content of reports on the Parliament by issuing its own communiqué for newspapers, television, and radio to broadcast. The petitioner argued that this article contradicted Article 25 (freedom of speech) and Article 44 (freedom from censure of the media) of the Constitution. In response, the *Seimas* quickly adopted the law 'On the Alteration of Article 137 of the *Seimas* of the Republic of Lithuania Statute' which eliminated Part 2, and the Court dropped the case.

The success of the Opposition's cases in the Constitutional Court eventually led to more complex petitions in which the Opposition, having failed to influence legislation, attempted to link certain provisions of those laws with constitutional rights. Thus the Constitutional Court became the preferred stage for political battles. For example, the Opposition's attempts to organize referendums in the hope of influencing policy was quickly squelched when on June 15, 1994, Parliament adopted an amendment to the law on referenda, which restricted the power referendum votes had on legislation. This amendment was adopted just as a new referendum initiative 'On Unlawful Privatization, Devaluated Accounts and Shares as well as Transgressions of Legal Protection' was about to be launched by the Opposition. The amendments to the law stipulated that not laws, but only provisions of laws may be brought to a referendum vote. New rules for the procedure of collecting signatures to support a referendum were added, which entailed that all citizens signing a referendum petition were required to submit their passport numbers (at the time, many eligible voters did not yet have Lithuanian passports). The amendments also gave more power to the *Seimas* to determine whether or not to hold a referendum vote. For instance, referenda on economic issues were subject to an examination of the bill's economic consequences, which meant that if the *Seimas*'s review of the bill was unfavorable, it had the power to cancel the referendum vote. The law also stipulated that referenda may be postponed or cancelled if the *Seimas* was debating a bill on the same topic or if the *Seimas* decided to adopt the provisions without holding a referendum vote. The *Seimas* could also dismiss a referendum proposal if it determined that the bill was unconstitutional. Finally, the amendment to the referendum law increased the requirement for voter turnout: a referendum would pass only if at least half of all eligible voters supported the bill. Thus, if less than half of all eligible voters participated in the referendum vote, the referendum would automatically fail.

A group of Opposition *Seimas* Deputies responded by submitting a petition to the Constitutional Court to review the above-mentioned provisions of the amendment to the referendum law. The petitioners' fist point of contention was that the stipulation that referenda could only be held on provisions of laws contradicts Articles 4, 9, 33, and 71.3 of the Constitution, which mention that laws may be adopted by referenda, not simply provisions. Moreover, they argued that the review of economic issues violates Article 4 and 33 of the Constitution as well as Article 6, which states that the Constitution is "integral and directly applicable." The petitioners asserted that the provision that gave Parliament the power to decide whether or not a referendum proposal is constitutional violates Articles 67 and 102 of the Constitution, and that the provision that allowed the *Seimas* to postpone a referendum if it decides to consider a similar law contradicts Articles 4, 9, and 33 of the Constitution. Finally, they contested the requirement that a referendum must win the support of at least half of all eligible voters, arguing that it was disproportionate compared to the relative ease with which laws are passed in the legislature.

The Court's ruling (Case No. 18/94, 22 July, 1994) gave concessions to both the majority party and the Opposition. It stressed that Article 9 of the Constitution established that only "the most important issues concerning the life of the State and the People shall be decided by referendum," which seems to indicate the desire of the Court to side with the majority to some extent in attempting to curb the number of referenda. To that end, the Court let the rather restrictive voting procedures stand, citing that it respects the 'majority principle' of democratic decision-making. At the same time, the Court maintains that state institutions must not limit the sovereignty of the people. It therefore checked *Seimas* power and ruled that any economic or constitutional review of proposed referenda as well as attempts to interfere or delay a referendum are unconstitutional. The referendum law case is typical of the cases brought to the Court by

Opposition MPs. The Court's relatively conservative ruling gave sufficient concessions to the petitioners to encourage the Opposition to continue bringing similar petitions in the future, without inviting retaliation from the ruling party.

Somewhat surprisingly, prior to the 1996 elections, despite decreased public support of the LDLP, the majority did nothing to ameliorate the position of the parliamentary Opposition, nor did it attempt to engineer the electoral laws and spread votes more equitably between parties. On the contrary, electoral laws were revised to make it even more difficult for smaller parties to gain seats in the *Seimas*. The big winners in the 1996 elections were parties with clear ties to the Sajudis movement. The LDLP became a parliamentary minority at the mercy of super-majority Homeland Union-Conservatives of Lithuania (HU-CL) and Christian Democrat coalition, which had been in the Opposition in the 1992–1996 *Seimas*. The LDLP quickly took up the tactics of the former Opposition, by organizing referenda and petitioning the Constitutional Court with even more vigor than the HU-CL. Most of these petitions involved laws and government decrees initiated by the HU-CL, but one case was brought to the Court by the LDLP Opposition to correct a law that had been passed in 1994 by the LDLP majority. The case shows that the LDLP itself may have realized the problem with adopting so many laws so quickly with little debate.

The case was brought to the Court in 1998 by the parliamentary Opposition, headed by former *Seimas* Chairman Ceslovas Jursenas to review the Constitutionality of a number of articles of the Law on Courts of 31 May 1994.[16] The petitioner contended that Articles 14, 251, 26, 30, 33, 34, 36, 40, 51, 56, 58, 59, 66, 69, 691, and 73 of the Law create direct and indirect opportunities for the Minister of Justice to interfere with the activities of courts, which contradicts Article 109 of the Constitution. These articles of the Law govern the appointment and dismissal procedures of judges, court chairpersons and deputy chairpersons. While the Constitution gives the power of appointment and dismissal to either the President or the *Seimas*, the Law makes these appointments and dismissals contingent on the recommendation of the Minister of Justice.

The task of drafting the Law on Courts had been given to the Ministry of Justice in an effort to ensure consistency and efficiency in the process of judicial reform. The Law, which was submitted for quick adoption by the LDLP-led *Seimas* in 1994, created the Department of Courts to safeguard the organizational activities of district and county courts and the Court of Appeals. The Department of Courts was also responsible for training judges and helps with the selection of new judges. As a result, the Ministry's sphere of influence and range of authority were significantly expanded as it became responsible for determining the conditions for the functioning of legal institutions (courts, prosecutors, lawyers, notaries) and for supervising and coordinating their activities. Over time, the Ministry was granted greater authority in drafting proposals for laws related

---

[16] Official Gazette, Valstybes Zinios, 1994, No. 46–851.

to the judicial branch.[17] The Minister of Justice was able to further influence the administrative work of the courts and judges not only through the Department of Courts, but also through the chairpersons and deputy chairpersons of the Court of Appeal, county and district courts, which are appointed and dismissed upon his recommendation.[18]

Minister of Justice Gintaras Svedas, addressed the Court as the party concerned and argued in favor of the law. He asserted that the Ministry of Justice was given this power by the democratically-elected *Seimas* and the President through the law's adoption and promulgation. Moreover, although the Minister of Justice has the power to offer proposals, the *Seimas* or President was under no obligation to comply with the proposal and that the ultimate decision is left to them.

In response to both sides of the debate, the Court sided with the petitioner and reasoned that:

> [The] duty of the state is to create proper work conditions [in] courts. However, this does not mean that in the course of establishing particular powers of the other institutions of power as regards their relations with the judiciary it is permitted to deny the separation of powers established in the Constitution and the essence of the judiciary as all-sufficient power which acts independently from the other powers.

While ensuring the independence of judges and courts, it is of much importance to separate the activity of courts from that of the executive. The Constitution prohibits that the executive interfere with administration of justice, exert any influence on courts or assess the work of courts regarding investigation of cases, let alone give instructions as to how justice must be administered. Supervision of courts and application of disciplinary measures to judges must be organised in such a manner so that the actual independence of judges might not be violated.[19]

The Court also invoked the Universal Declaration of Human Rights, the Convention for the Protection of Human Rights and Fundamental Freedoms, as well as decisions of the European Court of Human Rights that protect the independence of the judiciary. Thus, the Court struck down all the provisions

---

[17] Linas Sesickas, 'Judicial Independence in Lithuania' unpublished report prepared for the 'Monitoring EU Enlargement' Project of the Center for Policy Studies, Central European University Budapest, 2001.

[18] 'The Rules for the Control of Administrative Activity of Courts, with the exception of the Supreme Court,' approved by Seimas on the basis of the Order of the Minister of Justice No. 190, 19 November 1998.

[19] Ruling of the Lithuanian Constitutional Court 'On the compliance of Articles 14, 251, 26, 30, 33, 34, 36, 40, 51, 56, 58, 59, 66, 69, 691, and 73 of the Republic of Lithuania Law on Courts with the Constitution of the Republic of Lithuania' Vilnius, 21 December 1999.

of the law that gave the Minister of Justice the power to propose candidates for appointment to or dismissal from judicial posts. The decision has created a rather large legal vacuum that has yet to be filled by a new Law on Courts. It is anticipated that the new Law on Courts will transfer the power previously held by the Ministry of Justice to recommend judicial appointments to the Council of Judges. But the repercussions of the Court's decision are clear: judicial independence can be subject neither to expedience nor to order in the decision-making process

5. CONCLUSION

The pattern of the Opposition petitioning the Constitutional Court as a means to influence legislation adopted by the parliamentary majority has meant that the Court has adopted the function of mediating between rival political parties. Although in some contexts, this type of political intervention may lead to sanctions brought against the Court by the ruling majority, the Lithuanian Court has not incurred any hostility, and retains a high level of respect among the other branches of power, as well as in the electorate. The Court has been able to maintain good relations with all political parties and institutions in part because of its relatively conservative rulings. Concessions are often given to both parties, and in their rulings the Court takes great pains to write lengthy legal explanations for each decision.

Moreover, as the death penalty case seems to indicate, the Court is not as insulated from political influence as the Law on the Constitutional Court seems to imply. While this sort of behind-the-scenes coordination may allow the Court to continue to play a strong mediating role in politics without fear that other institutions might retaliate against unfavorable court rulings, the government's instrumental use of the Court to sidestep public debate of a highly-charged political issue seems to reflect the Lithuanian government's general mistrust of the democratic process. Nor can it be ignored that in this case the demands of the international community in general, and the European Union in particular, were valued more highly than the will of the people. At best, the Court was able to illustrate in its ruling that the concept of sovereignty today has changed from what it had been during the inter-war period. Certainly Lithuania has taken a positive step in adopting international human rights norms and has shown its eagerness to enter European political structures. However, the Court's complicity with the paternalistic attitude of the government is somewhat troubling.

The referendum law case exemplifies the fine line between order and freedom in a liberal democracy. While the Court allowed restrictions on the use of referenda in order to avoid a situation in which the Seimas is put in a position of competing with the electorate for the prerogative to legislate, it also limited the *Seimas*'s ability to control the content of referendum initiatives. The Court's decision mediated between the parliamentary majority and the Opposition in a way that promoted cooperation in the Seimas and put an end to the Opposition's attempt to conduct parallel legislation through the use of referenda. Thus, while the Opposition argued that the freedom of the electorate to influence policy is restricted by the law, the Court maintained that the Constitutionally prescribed method for legislation must be respected in an effort to maintain order in the legislative process.

The judicial independence case also reflects the Constitutional Court's commitment to protect the letter and spirit of the Constitution by putting an end to a situation in which one branch of power overreached the limits of its competence. And the fact that the case was brought to Court by the party responsible for adopting the unconstitutional provisions of the Law on Courts offers evidence that the ruling elite has recognized the false dichotomy between order and freedom. Although it had been faster and easier to delegate the task of drafting laws to the executive branch, especially when there was no strong opposition in Parliament to challenge them, the constitutionalized power balance must now be restored despite the five-year precedent set by the 1994 Law on Courts. It is hoped that the most recently elected Parliament will continue to legislate in the spirit of cooperation between all elected parties. In this way, public debate will replace efficiency as the guide for decision making and the government will learn to depend on the Constitution to bring order to the regime rather than restrictions to freedom.

Conclusions: Legitimacy of Constitutional Courts: Between Policy Making and Legal Science

Sergio Bartole

1. CONSTITUTIONAL JUSTICE AND DIRECT APPLICATION OF THE CONSTITUTION

The papers collected in this book have different origins: some are works by political scientists and some are the result of legal analyses which adopt the typical reasoning methods of legal studies even when they are testimonies of past or incumbent constitutional judges. It is true that all the authors of the papers offer a survey of the constitutional positions and functions of the constitutional courts of their countries, but at this stage of the research it would be difficult to design different models of constitutional justice adopted in Central-Eastern Europe without the support of other information. The papers we are dealing with, are mainly aimed at offering evaluations and judgements of the legitimatizing factors of judicial review of legislation in the countries concerned, and of the impact of constitutional justice on those political and legal systems: therefore an overall and detailed presentation of the concrete functioning of the constitutional courts is missing. In any case the papers apparently confirm the conclusions I reached in a previuos article devoted to some of the Central – European experiences. Constitutional provisions and parliamentary statutes providing for the establishment of constitutional justice are more concerned with the problems surrounding conformity of the functioning and relations of the superior bodies of the State with the constitution, than with the questions of the protection of individual rights and liberties and of access of the citizens to the constitutional courts.[1]

I have the feeling that in some of the systems of constitutional justice described in the papers the exigencies of the protection of individual rights and freedoms attracted space and attention only with some difficulties and efforts as far as the existing rules were pliable to new purposes. For instance, even if the Ukrainian ordinary judges do not have the power of requesting the Constitutional Court to decide on the conformity of a law with the constitution, they have obtained from that body opinions about the interpretation of the constitution which are

---

[1] I elaborated this point in S. Bartole, "Modelli di Giustizia Costituzionale a Confronto": alcune recenti esperienze dell'Europa centro – orientale, in *Quaderni costituzionali* (1996), pp. 229–241.

Wojciech Sadurski (ed.), Constitutional Justice, East and West, 409–432
© 2002 *Kluwer Law International. Printed in Great Britain.*

useful to them in light of deciding the cases with which they are dealing. Therefore they are in the position of being able to read the legislative rules concerning human rights and fundamental freedoms according to a correct interpretation of the constitution. In Armenia access of citizens to the Constitutional Court was envisaged on the basis of the theory that legislation providing for the establishment of that body necessarily implies an individual power of access to the judicial review of legislation:[2] eventually the Court gave up on this idea but it was an interesting example of the problems which are confronting constitutional justice in the new democracies. Moreover in Hungary the Court derived its quasi-normative power of establishing remedies for the effective protection of individual rights from the provisions concerning individual constitutional complaints. In Slovenia constitutional justice ensured the enforcement of the European Convention for the protection of human rights and the fundamental freedoms even before its ratification by the Parliament of that country, and the Convention was used by the Polish Constitutional Court as a source for transplanting principles and standards of western constitutionalism into Poland. These results are very similar to the results which Czech constitutional justice achieved through the implementation of theories of natural rights which are at the basis of its judicial activism and of its rejection of traditional legal formalism.

The trends I have described are strictly connected with a typical feature of all the new constitutions. It is a general principle of law supported by the common opinion of legal doctrine: that the provisions of the constitution can be directly applied and enforced to social relations without the need for implementing intermediate ordinary legislation. In the past the idea was generally accepted that compliance with constitutional rules was a matter of interest for the superior bodies of the State as far as they were concerned with the relations and the activity of the top organs of State, and specially with the functioning of Parliament because it is in charge of the legislative implementation of the constitutional choices in the field of human rights and fundamental freedoms. To-day protection and implementation of constitutional rights and freedoms are immediately derived and judicially enforced on the basis only of constitutional rules without any legislative intermediation. Therefore, today constitutional rules, as was the case in the past, are immediately applied to the relations between the superior authorities of the State, but, in contrast to the past, the constitutional provisions are direclty complied with even when they are dealing with the relations between the citizens and the citizens and the authorities.

For this reason judges, public authorities and citizens immediately refer to the constitution when they are dealing with social relations or have to decide a case.

---

[2] The studies aimed at reforming the Armenian legislation in view of ensuring individual claims direct access to constitutional justice are mentioned by G. Haratunian, "Democratic Processes and Present – Day Tasks of the Constitutional Court of the Republic of Armenia", *26 Review of Central and East European Law* (2000), pp. 259–266.

Sometimes the constitutional rule provides for the complete and exhaustive settlement of a case, sometimes it only concurs in the finding of the rationes decidendi of a case, and sometimes the interpretation of ordinary legislation is inspired by the constitutional rule. Antal Adam correctly emphasizes the fact that in deciding an individual constitutional complaint the Hungarian Constitutional Court is confronted with two different questions: on one side, it has to review the conformity of a legislative provision to the constitution, and, on the other side, it has to find a remedy for the violation of a fundamental right by an act of a public authority. As Halmai reminds us, the Court does not help in dealing with the practical problem of following – up of its decisions as far as its statements display binding effects even on the concrete activity of the Supreme Court.

This connection between the decisions of the constitutional judge and those of the other judges can explain the frequent use of "interpretative" decisions. If when making a decision stating the unconstitutionality of a law the judges have sometimes to fill the resulting lacuna by directly applying the relevant constitutional provisions, the decision of rejecting a constitutional complaint can imply that the judges shall implement the relevant legislative rule in the light of a connected constitutional provision. It happens frequently that the constitutional judge refuses to declare the unconstitutionality of a legislative rule when this rule can be construed in conformity with the constitution notwithstanding the fact that the expressions used by the legislator could be misleading and suggest a discrepancy with the constitution. Therefore the judges stick to the interpretation of the legislative and constitutional rules adopted by the Constitutional Court, and directly apply the constitution in settling concrete cases. We have many examples of this practice and they cover both the field of abstract judicial review of legislation and the concrete one, both of the a priori judgement and of the a posteriori one. For instance, in the paper on Slovenia by Miro Cerar this phenomenon interests all the functions of that Court, and Renate Weber explains that the Romanian Court often refuses to declare the unconstitutionality of legislative rules whose interpretation can be elaborated in conformity with the constitution. Obviously this kind of decision has a special practical relevance when a Court is required to deal not with a draft of law, but with a concrete case concerning a law which is in effect, or its implementation by an act of a public authority. It may be useful to remind the reader of the special utilization of the power requiring the opinion of the Court on the interpretation of constitutional rules which is given to ordinary judges. These developments do not prevent the possibility that in other legal orders – for instance in Bulgaria – the body entrusted with the functions of constituional justice could be helpful even when it has to express its advise about the interpretation of constitutional rules with regard to the drafting of a bill of law and selects between different alternatives the solution which is apparently more in conformity with the constitution.

Leaving aside the problems concerning the exercise of consultative functions of the Constitutional Courts, it is evident that the consequences of e direct applicability of constitutional provisions do not fall in the framework of the pure Kelsenian model of constitutional justice. According to this model the judicial review of legislation should be restricted to the judgement of the conformity of the legislative rules with the constitution and should not deal with the practical implementation of those rules in the context of social relations. But the provisions of the new constitution can be directly enforced in concrete cases and this feature has deeply conditioned the work of the Constitutional Courts, even outside the constitutional judgements incidentally initiated by initiatives of the ordinary judges in view of the decision of cases falling in their competence or by individual complaints submitted by citizens. The Courts are necessarily confronted with the question of the correct interpretation of the constitutional rules in view of their direct implementation even without the intermediation of executive legislative rules. If they are read in connection with the exigencies of practical social relations, the peculiarities of the constitutional rules are especially evident: they are very frequently principles, they are phrased in very general terms and not in an all – or – nothing fashion. Therefore when the problem of their direct application to concrete cases of social life arises, they have to be integrated. The old theory of law entrusted this integration to the competence of the legislator, whilst the modern doctrine is ready to include this in the remit of ordinary judges when they are deciding concrete cases. A kind of delegation of normative power is implied by the open structure of the statements of the new constitution to the State's bodies which are in charge of their implementation. Frequently it happens that all the operational potentialities of the constitutional rules may be expressed only through the work of the judicial bodies. These integrative developments have a quasi – normative relevance and imply an activity which we could qualify as creation of law. Actually the creation of law is the task that Constitutional Courts claim to fulfill when they consider the practical effects of their interpretation of the constitutional rules which can be directly applied to the cases of social life. As a matter of fact the ConstitutionaL courts try to substitute for ordinary judges in completing and integrating the open texture of constitutional provisions and to comply with the delegation of power which those provisions imply. In this way the Courts enter into fields of activity which are completely different from those envisaged by the Kelsenian theory of constitutional justice.

2. MODELS OF CONSTITUTIONAL JUSTICE AND SEPARATION OF POWERS

The new concept of the normative force of constitutional rules, which is at the basis of the described trends of jurisprudence of the new Constitutional Courts, could have suggested to drafters of the constitutions of Central Eastern Europe a different approach to the problems of constitutional justice. If the constitutional provisions are no longer aimed at governing only the activity of the superior bodies of the State, but also the relations between the citizens and between the citizens and the authorities, a convenient rationalized solution could have been the adoption of arrangements closer to the American model of judicial review of legislation. Actually, according to this model all the judges are allowed to judge upon the conformity of legislative rules with the constitution, and may directly apply the constitutional rules to the relations of social life when the case requires it. When there is not a discrepacy between the constitution and the legislative rules, the provisions of the constitution are indirectly implemented through legislative rules, and when there is a disrepancy, it is the constitution which is directly applied, because the judge is bound not to apply a legislative rule which is unconstitutional, even if he does not have the power of depriving it of its legal force (or of stating with general effects that it is null and void). Such an arrangement would have emphasized the connection of judicial review of legislation with the judicial function and its relevance in the choice of the rule which has to be applied in the case pending before the judge.

Notwithstanding the general trend in favour of the European model of constitutional justice there are countries in Central Eastern Europe which offer food for thought about the convenience of adopting the American model of judicial review of legislation. First of all, we have to remember that between the two World Wars the Romanian Court of Cassation reviewed the conformity with the constitution of legislation and of normative acts of the Cabinet: can current practice draw inspiration from that experience?[3] Secondly, Estonian constitutional justice allows all the judges the power not to apply legislative rules which he considers unconstitutional, but requires a successive judgement of the special section of the Supreme Court to grant erga omnes effects to the decision.[4] And in Poland the Supreme Court recently twice refused to apply legislative rules which were supposed to be unconstitutional, without asking for a decision of the Constitutional Court on the matter. While in Estonia the mixed nature of constitutional justice is the result of a conscious choice of the legislator, the refuse of the old jurisprudence of the Romanian Court of Cassation and the criticism of the strange initiatives of the Polish Supreme Courts are largely shared by the doctrine of both the countries and, therefore, the central role of unitarian constitutional justice is generally accepted.

In any case common acceptance of the direct and immediate applicability of constitutional rules in Central Eastern Europe is altering the functioning of the

---

[3] The Romanian Supreme Court of Justice tried to revive old theories of judicial review of legislation before the advent of the new constitution: M.Criste, "Un controle juridictionnel des lois en Roumanie?", in *Revue francaise de droit constitutionnel* (1992), pp. 179–183.

[4] See C. Tribe, "Constitutionalism in Estonia, Latvia and Lithuania", *Iustus Forlag, Uppsala* (2001), p. 107, where a further elaboration of the place of the Estonian model in the doctrine of constitutional justice is nevertheless missing.

classic centralized model of constitutional justice. But the choice of the centralized model is strongly based in the European experience, as Sadurski says, and is supported by other practical reasons which are connected with the transition process from communism to liberal democracy.

First of all it is worthwhile underlining that recent constitutional engeneering considers the functions of constitutional justice as autonomous functions, which have to be entrusted to a separate body which has to be suitable both from the organizational point of view and with regard to the professional suitability of its membership. That is, those functions are not seen by the drafters of the new constitutions as an extension of the judicial function which is obviously included in the competence given to the ordinary judges. Therefore, if they are thought as distinct functions with their own characteristics, which conceptually preexist the body to which they will be given, the functions of constitutional justice cannot be conceived as an additional and eventual manifestation of the judicial function which is perceived only in presence of cases requiring their exercise, as in Marbury v. Madison.[5]

For that reason it is understandable that, following this cultural approach, the Constitutional Courts, even if the relevant provisions are placed in the chapters of the constitutions dealing with judicial power, take an autonomous and separated standing not only from the other powers of the State, that is the Parliament, the Head of the State, the Cabinet, but also from the bodies of t judicial power, that exercise functions which – from many points of view – can be assimilated to judicial functions both because of the nature of their material and of the relevant procedural rules.

These conceptual explanations are to be taken in consideration in conjunction with practical and constitutional considerations. Exigencies of coherence and certainty of law require that the decisions of constitutional justice display general effects and, consequently, a legislative rule which is declared unconstitutional, not only should not be applied to the case at stake but also should be deprived of its effects with regard to all the subjects of the relevant legal order. In the American system of law this result is secured on the basis of the principle of stare decisis. It is generally accepted that the Supreme Court is bound by its previous statements holding that a legislative rule is unconstitutional. Therefore the inferior judges are refrained from not following the jurisprudence of the Supreme Court, at least if the cases at stake are similar to the case decided by the Supreme Court itself. The machinery functions because there is a connection between the Court and the other judges, whose decision can be appealed before

---

[5]   The idea underpinning *Marbury v. Madison* is that the judicial power of reviewing the legislation belongs to the judges as a part of their power of identifying the law which has to be applied in cases pending before them: "it is, emphatically, the province and duty of the judicial department, to say what the law is"; see quotations and comments in L. Tribe, *American Constitutional Law* (II ed., New York 1988), pp. 23–32.

that higher authority and are directly affected by the developments of its jurisprudence.

In European countries the principle of stare decisis does not legally bind the judges, it does not have the dignity of a constitutional principle, even the judicial bodies de facto comply with it in view of the continutity and the coherence of their jurisprudence.[6] For that reason the result of the deprivation of the legal effects of the legislative rules declared unconstitutional has to be obtained by different means, that is by concentrating all the functions of constitutional justice in one central body of the State and affording its decisions general effects erga omnes.

Such a solution also ensures the correct and adequate exercise of the other functions of the Constitutional Courts in the frame of a system that increasingly becomes more similar to a system of general constitutional justice aimed at ensuring effective compliance with the provisions of the constitution not only with regards to the limits of the legislative functions but also with regards to the guarantee of human rights and fundamental freedoms. This approach implies that the superior bodies of the State, and also (not only in the federal legal orders) the autonomous territorial entities are given rights of access to constitutional justice to guarantee the compliance with the rules concerning the relevant relations (I mean conflicts between the State's powers, criminal trials affecting the Head of the State, judgements on the inability of the Head of the State to exercise his own functions, electoral cases, judgements of the admissibility of the referenda, cases on the conformity to the constitutional principles of the organization and functioning of the political parties, and so on). Moreover we have to keep in mind that – as I remarked in a previous contribution – in Central – European constitutions the initiative of the judgements on the conformity to the constitution of the legislative rules is frequently entrusted to the superior bodies of the State, which are therefore allowed "to check" the activity of the Parliaments, by requesting the intervention of the Constitutional Courts.

Shapiro correctly reminded us of the attention paid by those new constitutions to the principle of the separation of powers, even with regard to the definition of the relations between the Head of the State and the Cabinet which he thinks should fall in the remit of executive power, but in Europe are arranged according to a dualistic approach and, therefore, a clearly stated division of roles and functions.[7] If the constitutions divide and distribute the functions amongst the superior bodies of the State, conflicts – Shapiro underlines – can arise between

---

6   An interesting presentation of this point was made by M. Kriele, "Das Prajudiz im Kontinental – Europaischen und Anglo – Amerikanischen Rechtskreis", *Università degli studi di Ferrara, Facoltà di giurisprudenza, La sentenza in Europa*, Padova (1988), pp. 62–80.

7   A discussion on this point is presented by A. Barbera & C. Fusaro, *Il governo delle democrazie* (Bologna 1997), pp. 85–103, in dealing with the evolution of the parliamentary governments and the advent of the semipresidential governments.

theose bodies. The model of general constitutional justice I have just described, is actually aimed at solving and settling these conflicts. We frequently find in the jurisprudence of the new Courts of Hungary, Slovakia and Ukraine, for instance, decisions dealing with conflicts between the powers of the State, and the calling of referenda did not arouse constitutional cases only in Slovenia. As a matter of fact, those decisions were not always able to give a definitive solution to the conflicts concerning the definition of the relations between the bodies concerned, which often have a political nature.

But these partial failures can be easily explained: the relations between the bodies at the top of the State are based not only on the principle of separation of powers but also on the functioning of the machinery of checks and balances which cannot be completely reviewed by the Constitutional Courts. Actually the decisions of the Courts regarding this matter had an indirect relevance in view of the political settlement of conflicts in Slovenia, Slovakia and Ukraine through the revision of the constitution. In any case it is evident that, from many points of view, a central body of constitutional justice is the natural judge of this kind of case which cannot be entrusted to the ordinary judges as long as the constitutional law has the special characteristics which it has in Europe.

Recently Louis Favoreu underlined that at the basis of the choice of establishing a central body of constitutional justice is the intent of avoiding the entrusting of the relevant functions to the ordinary judges.[8] The framers of the new constitutions do not trust them because they were apparently too closely connected with the old communist regimes, but they also rationalize this choice with the exigency of selecting the membership of the new bodies according to peculiar criteria which assign special relevance to professional capabilities not present in the ordinary judges. The adopted solution, suggested many years ago by Hans Kelsen,[9] provides for the appointment of the constitutional judges mainly by political bodies, whose discretion is limited by the requirement of the membership of the persons who are appointed to special professional categories qualified by legal knowledge and experience. Frequently in this way, because of the political nature of the actors of the relevant procedures, the appointments or elections of the constitutional judges are affected by political interests and are obtained only through political compromises. An interesting exemple is offered by Hungary, where the Parliament elects the constitutional judges on the basis of proposals submitted by a special parliamentary committee where a representative for each parliamentary faction is present. Political exigencies slowed the process of formation of the new body in Ukraine. Both the Czech Republic and the Russian Federation preferred to look at the American model which balances the choice of the Head of the State with the consent of one of

---

[8] L. Favoreu, *Les Cours constitutionnels* (Paris 1992), pp. 8–10.

[9] H. Kelsen, 'La Garanzia Giurisdizionale della Costituzione', in H. Kelsen, *La giustizia costituzionale*, C. Geraci (ed.) (Milano 1981), pp. 143–206.

the parliamentary assemblies. More prudent are apparently the constitutions of Rumania and Bulgaria which divide the powers of appointing or electing the constitutional judges between some superior bodies of the State, for instance the Parliament, the Head of the State and the judiciary: in this regard the practice in Bulgaria followed the Italian experience[10] underlining the neutral nature of the intervention of the President who is concerned with avoiding the appointment of lawyers directly connected with one or other of the political parties.

3. THE PROBLEM OF LEGITIMACY

The practice of the selection of members of the new bodies of constitutional justice shows the presence and the influence of political criteria, even if the rules concerning the professional requirements are complied with. The recourse to those criteria plays an important role in establishing a connection between the Courts and the political representative organs, at least an indirect link which is getting weaker by the day because of the differences between the terms of office of the members of the political representative bodies of the State and the Constitutional Courts. As a matter of fact the political factor of the election or the appointment of the judges raises the question of the legitimacy of the new bodies with regard to the exclusively technical legitimacy of the ordinary judges. At the same time it does not have a direct and immediate relevance and does not put them on an equal footing with the organs of the State which solely have democratic legitimacy. Therefore, if – on one side – their legitimacy can be questioned, as frequently happens,[11] in connection with their interference in the State's democratic decision making processes, the political factor itself – on the other side – can apparently put in danger their independence, which is a crucial factor in their legitimacy.

It is not surprising that the legitimacy of the new Courts of Central Eastern Europe has been also questioned: actually the problem is getting more and more serious as a result of their activism, which apparently is evidence of their tendency to enlarge the scope of the sphere of competence reserved to them.

The problem of legitimacy arises not only with regard to the body entrusted with the task of constitutional justice but also – as the American experience confirms – with the functions that are exercised by that body according to the relevant rules or to the enlargement of its role envisaged by the body itself. The

---

[10]   The Italian practice in this matter is correctly explained by G. Zagrebelsky, *La giustizia costituzionale* (Bologna 1977), pp. 72–76.

[11]   Recent useful discussions of the debate concerning the relations between judicial interpretation of the Constitution and the policy -making activities of the other bodies of the State are presented in A. Scalia, *A Matter of Interpretation* (Princeton 1997), and S.M. Griffin, *American Constitutionalism: From Theory to Politics* (Princeton 1996).

problem can be dealt with from two different points of view: on one side, we can adopt a static approach looking at the question of the legitimacy of the membership of the Court and the procedures for its election or appointment, but, on the other side, we can choose a dynamic approach analysing the results of the activity of the Court. It is from this last point of view that the legitimacy of the Court can be questioned with regard to its interference both with the legislative activity and with the effective content of the constitution and of the constitutional laws. The point is very delicate because it is commonly accepted that the legitimacy of the Constitutional Courts is based on their subordination to the constitution just as the ordinary judges are subordinated to the law. But this statement of principle has to be bypassed: even if we do not accept the paradoxical conversion of the question of the legitimacy of the Court into the question of the legitimacy of the constitution, as was proposed by Wojciech Sokolewicz,[12] it is evident that when the Courts are substituiting themselves not only for the ordinary legislator but also for the constitutional legislator, it is difficult, if not contradictory, to found the legitimacy of the Court on the constitution.

The contradiction or paradox can be solved if we develop the topic of possible duplication of the point of view we adopt when looking at the problem of the legitimacy of constitutional justice. If we adopt both a static approach and a dynamic one, it could be easy to reconsider – without neglecting the activism of the Courts – the old doctrine which bases that legitimacy on the constitution.

It is true that when we say that the body entrusted with the task of constitutional justice is legitimatized by its subordination to the constitution, we do not look at the criteria and the procedures adopted for the formation of that body as factors legitimatizing the body itself, but we see them as instrumental elements aimed at insuring the professional skills of its membership, and – therefore – its independence in dealing with the constitution without external interferences. It follows that adequate criteria and procedures of election or appointment have to be integrated by rules ensuring the independence of the members of the Courts. The judges have to be protected against pressing or compelling influences of other powers of the State, their present and future personal position and financial situation cannot depend on the decision of other bodies, and the Courts have to be provided with all the necessary means for the exercise of their functions.

But the question is still open. How can we imagine that the constitution itself is at the basis of the legitimacy of the Courts if these bodies are de facto allowed to manipulate that act, that is if we recognize that the Courts are in the position

---

[12] W. Sokolewicz, 'Constitutional Tribunal – The Polish Variation of Judicial Review', in *Giustizia Costituzionale e Sviluppo Democratico nei Paesi dell'Europa Centro – Orientale*, G. de Vergottini (ed.) (Torino 2000), pp. 243–271.

of changing and integrating its meaning day by day according to the changing social and political exigencies with which they deal?

The papers published in this book confirm that the Courts of Central Eastern Europe share the destiny of the Courts of Western democracies and have displayed a great deal of activism. We can offer only some examples, from amongst the materials at our disposition, without any pretence of being exhaustive. First of all the doctrine of human dignity set out by the Hungarian Constitutional Court, which elaborated from that doctrine a set of new rights which are not expressly provided for by the constitution deserves to be underlined. But it is not always the case that constitutional jurisprudence displays an integrative and additional role with regard to the text of the constitution: expressly stated provisions have sometimes been rephrased by the Courts with the aim of limiting or thwarting their meaning and content. This is the case of the Bulgarian constitutional provision which prohibits ethnic political parties: the Bulgarian Court construed the prohibition in a restrictive way allowing the Movement for rights and freedoms to declare itself tutor and protector of the Muslim Bulgarian citizens, who have Turk ethnic origins. Many developments touched the relations between the superior bodies of the State. In Slovenia the Court was accused of having reformed the constitutional provisions concerning the referenda, in Romania the emergency powers of the Cabinet were redefined, in Slovakia the Court frequently decided to reshape the presidential powers, and – eventually – in the Czech Republic constitutional jurisprudence deeply affected electoral legislation. And we cannot forget that in Lithuania the Constitutional Court elaborated a doctrine of the State's sovereignty that was completely different from the doctrine which was adopted at the time of the proclamation of independence, but we will return to this development in the following pages.

All these developments have to be taken into account in dealing with our question. If effectiveness is a necessary character of sources of law and – therefore – we can say that the explicit mention of a source in the constitution does not offer sure evidence of its effective existence, when it is not underpinned by a practice or custom of unchanging compliance,[13] the same has to be said about the constitution. A constitution which is not effective, is not a constitution, it exists and is legally relevent only if it is the object of continuous observance. When we say that the legitimacy of the Constitutional Courts is based on the constitution, we are referring to the effective constitution and not only to the historical written document.

Constitutional Courts are therefore subordinated to the constitution as it was shaped by the historical experience of its compliance, by the meaning given to it on a daily basis by the State's bodies and by the citizens. If we say that the Court takes part in this process, our statement cannot be accused of being

---

[13] This point was elaborated by C. Esposito in the entry 'Consuetudine (dir. cost.)' for *Enciclopedia del diritto, IX* (Milano 1961), pp. 456–476.

autoreferential. First of all, when the constitutional judges are pushed by their activism to a creative jurisprudence, that implies an integration and an enrichment of the meaning which can be derived from the constitution on the basis of an interpretation respectful of the text and of the original intent of the framers: they are not bypassing the great guidelines stated by the authors of the constitution and elaborated by their jurisprudence itself. Even the frequently criticized jurisprudence of the American Supreme Court in dealing with the issue of abortion has its roots in the precedents concerning the right to privacy and in a similar fashion the developments in the matter segregation are connected with the doctrines of equality of treatment. Moreover the Courts, aiming to up-date the constitutional principles, are anxious to get compliance with their decisions, that is, to strengthen their effectivity. Changes and integrations of the meaning of constitutional provisions can be received in the jurisprudence of the Courts as far as there are clear indications that they will be welcomed by the citizens and by the superior bodies of the state. If these indications are missing the Courts are not in a position to innovate; otherwise – as happened in the new democracies of Central Eastern Europe – they are in danger of being contradicted by a revision of the constitution by the political parties represented in Parliament which bypasses their decisions.

If we adopt this point of view, we can explain two different phenomenons which play a relevant role in the development of the jurisprudence of the old and new Courts. These bodies try frequently to distinguish the constitutional provisions which can be revised from those which cannot be revised, and put limits not only on the constitutional legislator but also on the Constitutional Courts which are not allowed to give up the bounds which can be derived from them. Besides, it is easier to understand the special connection between constitutional jurisprudence and the social conscience which is at the same time – as Rousseau underlined[14] – a source of inspiration for the Courts and a factor of the effectiveness of their jurisprudence.

The relationship between the Constitutional Courts and the constitutions has a circular nature: the Courts are legitimized through the subordination to the constitution and the constitution develops new meanings through the work of the Courts. But that subordination is, in the long term the recognition of a starting point of a further process and the Courts are entrusted with the task of elaborating the constitution. Confronted with the constitution, on one side, and with the social conscience, on the other, the Courts use the social conscience as a litmus paper for giving constitutional provisions meanings which are more fitted to the modern-day content of those provisions in view of social developments. The link which connects the constitution to constitutional jurisprudence is – as far as the social conscience is taken into account – the only guarantee of certainty which can be given by the Courts. The social conscience displays a

---

[14]   D. Rousseau, *La justice constitutionnelle en Europe* (Paris 1992), pp. 140–156.

double role, being – on one side – the barometer of the acceptance of decisions of the Courts by the State's community and, on the other side, the source of the novelties which constitutional judges receive from concrete social exeperience. Therefore we cannot say that the constitution is what the Courts say. The constitutional jurisprudence is always tested by its acceptance or otherwise by the social conscience, and in case of a rupture the only remedy is a possible revision of the constitution, according to which the choices not accepted by the social conscience will be declared unconstitutional.

4. PRIMACY OF THE CONSTITUTION AND EUROPEAN CONSTITUTIONAL HERITAGE

The reference to the social conscience has in the experience of Central Eastern European Courts a special meaning in so far as it was also their task to conform the relevant legal orders to the common principles of liberal Western democracies. They frequently made significant efforts to bring about a coherent and complete internal implementation of the European constitutional heritage, which has played an essential role in shaping the destiny of the new democracies, and was not the object of a vocal emphasis only.

We have to remember the part played by the Courts in removing the death penalty. In Lituania, following an initiative of the Legal Committee of Parliament, the Court decided that, according to the principles of international law, the criminal rules providing for the death penalty did conflict with the right to life guaranteed in the constitution. The Hungarian chapter states that the Court of Solyom was ready to declare unconstitutional an amendment to the constitution in order to enforce its decision that the death penalty was not in conformity with the constitution and that Parliament did not have the power of freely legislating in the matter. For the ukrainian constitutional Court too, the death penalty was not only in contradiction with international practice, but also with some articles of the constitution (especially the article concerning the right to life) and with the Ukraine's commitments as a member of the Council of Europe. Moreover, even if a report concerning Albania is missing in this book, we cannot forget that that Constitutional Court adopted a similar decision.[15]

Another field that is addressed by interesting decisions of the new Courts is that of the 'purge legislation'. In Hungary some of the relevant rules were declared unconstitutional: the Court found a breach of the right to privacy and of the right of concerned people to free access to relevant personal information; and in Poland the constitutional judges had to deal with the matter twice, on

---

[15] F. Abdiu, 'Le Probleme de la Peine de Mort', in *Quaderni del Dipartimento di scienze giuridiche, L'attuazione della costituzione albanese* (Trieste 2001), pp. 183–189.

one side stating the unconstitutionality of the relevant legislation notwithstanding the interpretative efforts to put it in agreement with the constitution, and on the other side declaring the unconstitutionality of a rule even without analysing its possible conflict with the constitutional principle of the presumption of innocence. In Bulgaria rules providing for the retroactivity of new requirements for the progression of the career of judges were declared unconstitutional because of the conflict with the principle of the independence of the judiciary, but they favoured the oldest judges frequently connected with the previous regime.

Many of these decisions are not easily accepted by the electors when the increasing number of crimes apparently requires the introduction or the keeping of the death penalty, or when there is a poor understanding of the extension of the guarantee of the rule of law to persons linked to the communist totalitarian governement. People can feel that the Courts conflict with the social conscience and opinion: therefore our interpretation of their role is in danger of being contradicted. It could be reasonable to have reservations about the anti-majoritarian justification of this jurisprudence, which is apparently imperilling the implementation of democratic principles which require that public decisions have to be adopted in conformity with the will of the people. But we can bypass all possible objections keeping in mind the fact that, even in the short term, there are conflicts between constitutional jurisprudence and the public opinion: day by day it is increasingly evident that the Courts give effect to basic decisions adopted by the people when they supports the fall of the old regimes and accept the fundamental principles of Western democracies. When the Courts are interpreting the social conscience, they do not look at the transient opinions of the people, but at the guidelines which are at the basis of the new constitutional orders. They implement the deeply rooted choices of the electors.

In actual fact the new democracies established after the fall of communist totalitarian regimes unconsciously accepted the principles which are part of the European constitutional heritage that require compliance with the rule of law, the separation of powers, the safeguarding of human rights and fundamental freedoms in a democratic framework that allows the people to freely express its will. It is true that this choice sometimes implies the adoption of decisions which are not easily accepted by people eager to complete as soon as possible the transition from the old regime to democracy. The rejection of the death penalty is apparently in conflict with the desire to establish quickly social peace and order and combat crime that originates in the economic problems of the transition itself. Legislative programs which are aimed at the purge of the people connected with the totalitarian government and at the establishment of a regime of transparency by the opening of the old archives are certainly implemented with some difficulties when the principles of the rule of law have to be complied with.

Sadurski correctly reminds us of the largely shared opinion that liberal democracies do not always offer practical means for a quick engagement of the process of transition requiring as it does a centralization of power and a change of the political, administrative and judicial personnel which is not easily implemented in complete compliance with human rights and fundamental freedoms. It is difficult to accept the idea that freedom and democracy is more readily established with a transient and partial disregard of the principles which are at their basis. There is always the danger of the development of illiberal policies which once engaged are difficult to stamp out.. Therefore it is understandable that the Courts adopted the guidelines I previously described.

It is equally difficult to democratically reconcile interventions by the courts in the form of governments adopted by the States concerned. It is true that there are precedents of international practice aimed at implementing the principles of the European constitutional heritage and at averting developments in the relations between superior bodies of the State that conflict with the exigencies of constitutional reforms supported by international institutions and authorities. In the case of Belarus the decision of the President of the Republic purporting to reduce the independence and the powers of Parliament was strongly crticized in the international fora. Analogously the calling of a referendum to change the balance of powers in Ukraine was judged innadmissible by the Council of Europe. And again the Council of Europe, monitoring the situation in Croazia, submitted detailed proposals for a conversion of the presidential regime into a parliamentary government with the aim of increasing the accountability of Executive power before the legislative assemblies.[16] In all these cases new arrangements concerning the machinery of parliamentary inspection of the cabinet and of t public administration were supported and the importance of political participation, democratic representation and the separation of powers was underlined.

Following the same line of reasoning we can understand some decisions of the Ukrainian and Slovakian Courts and we can object to the criticism of some commentators who did not apparently appreciate the efforts made by these constitutional judges in defining the separation of powers between the Head of the State and the Cabinet and underpinning the accountability of the Cabinet before the Parliament. But the jurisprudence of the Slovakian Court apparently conflicts with the mentioned principles and values as far as it gives preferential treatment to the role of the President in the relations with the Meciar Cabinet which was not supposed to be politically and constitutionally trustworthy. And it was evident that the efforts of the Ukrainian Constituional Court in finding compromise solutions was motivated by the desire to avoid irritating the Head

---

[16] See the Opinion of the European Commission for Democracy through Law on the Amendments of 9 November 2000 and 28 March 2001 to the Constitution of Croatia prepared for the parliamentary Assembly of the Council of Europe and adopted at the 47the Plenary Meeting of the Commission (Document CDL – INF (2001) 15).

of State. In both cases political convenience apparently coexisting with compliance with constitutional principles, when political convenience did not quite obviously bypass them.

When the Courts are dealing with issues connected to the form of government, they are in danger of being perceived as players in the constitutional conflicts that have also a political dimension. They may lose the trust of public opinion in their neutrality, not only because they can arouse the impression of being less independent than their constitutional legitimacy requires, but also because the people see them in the same sceptical light as they view the behaviour of the political actors. This can very easily happen in countries where diffidence about policy – makers draws inspiration from the diffidence about the communist regimes. Moreover we have to keep in mind that lawyers are traditionally seen as instruments of the holders of the power.

The point deserves a lot of attention. The commentators who react with criticism to the decisions of the Courts concerning the relations between the superior bodies of the State, and are preoccupied by the interference of constitutional jurisprudence with politics, accuse the Courts of usurping the role of the policy – makers and envisage the advent of a third Chamber. It is a suggestion which is a product of the realistic approach of those political scientists who try to classify the institutions of State and the functions de facto exercised by them according to criteria which are completely different from those adopted by legal science. This approach is not easily accepted by a lawyer, at least as far as he is convinced that the principle of effectivity implies a full correpondence between the functions entrusted to the bodies and the institutions of the State by the constitution and the functions which are in fact exercised by the same bodies and institutions.

But the same approach may deserve attention if we consider that, as far as their effective role in the constitutional systems is concerned, the Constitutional Courts can be seen as the most important point of emergence of the contribution of the community of the jurists, that is of the holders of legal knowledege and of its historical continuity with the social life. Actually the role of jurists in society has always had a peculiar character and a special relevance, both when they found only in the Universities a meeting point to work together (as happened in continental Europe in the Middle Ages), and when they had the chance of displaying a collective effort (as in France in the Council of State at the time of the advent of administrative law, or in the Supreme Court of the United States of America during the presidency of Marshall in the past and of Warren in recent times).

In the present century a new chance has been apparently offered to the legal community by the establishment of constitutional justice: it is an hypothesis which deserves to be elaborated. On one side, it is evident that the Constitutional Courts are the bearers of a traditional knowledge, of a legal and institutional continuity, and they may therefore display a conservative role (as happened with the Supreme Court at the time of the New Deal and is happening to the Court of Karlsruhe concerning the European developments), but, on the other side, the growing and various social demands are frequently satisfied through constitutional jurisprudence and the legal developments which are elaborated by it. The constitutional cases are occasions for bringing the past face to face with the present and for making an effort to give – as far as it is possible – new meanings to constitutional provisions according to legal doctrines more responsive to social exigencies. We can remember the input given by the Italian Constitutional Court to the understanding of the role of the constitution in the Italian legal system, and the new doctrine of the rights elaborated by the French Constitutional Council on the basis of a previously unthinkable use of the preamble of the French constitution.

The Central – Eastern Courts have complied with this task by enforcing the principles of the European constitutional heritage, acting as intermediaries between the new constitutional democracies of Central-Eastern Europe and the principles and values of the Western legal tradition, whose implementation was required by the new constitutions and by the international engagements of the concerned States. The legal culture and the experience which the new Courts referred to, mostly have their origins outside the recent national traditions of those States and are related to the developments of the European society at large. Certainly it is a paradox that these constitutional choices have been made when these countries delivered themselves from communist totalitarian regimes and refused the doctrine of the so called limited sovereignty reinstating their national sovereignty. But there is no doubt that those choices were the result of international obligations which imply a new limitation of sovereignty and, therefore, of the newly acquired independence of the ex-communist States. Actually at the very moment of the apparent reestablishment of the old doctrine of unconditioned and unlimited sovereignity the countries of Central – Eastern Europe accepted to be bound by the principles commonly accepted in the European (or – perhaps – international) order, which are at the core of the European constitutional heritage. This obligation was complied with in many ways: such as by asking for international cooperation in drafting the new constitutions and constituional laws, or by accepting the subordination to monitoring procedures managed by international organizations in the frame of international agreements, or entering into the processes of association with the European Union with a view to accession to it.

All these events have actually introduced a new concept of State sovereignty as was correctly pointed out by the Lithuanian Constitutional Court. The constitutional judges, realizing this novelty, are faithful to the traditional task of legal science which has to read the new lines of development of the legal systems under the coverage of the explicit provisions of the constitutions and to go along with their consequences in agreement with the traditional criteria of a scientific experience which has its roots beyond the contingencies of politics.

5. THE CHOICE OF LEGAL HERMENEUTIC METHODOLOGY

The task which confronted the new Constitutional Courts and was generously taken on by them as a duty to be complied with, obliged the new constitutional judges to adopt legal hermeneutic methodologies completely different from the traditional ones. Adopting the principles of the European constitutional heritage as yardsticks of judicial review of legislation implies a not easy interpretive effort which goes beyond the formalistic exegesis of the legal texts. It is necessary to discover and understand both the guidelines that underpin the developments of the legal systems of Western democracies, and all the engagements deriving from the international instruments in the field of human rights and fundamental freedoms, which are also connected with these developments. A further step implies the elaboration of the follow – up of those guidelines and engagements in the internal constitutional orders of the state concerned.

Therefore it is understandable that the Polish Constitutional Court is greatly appreciated for having given a substantial contribution to the establishment of the rule of law in Poland filling – before the advent of the new constitution – the lacunas and shortcomings of the previous constitutional order. Moreover the commentators explicitly recognize that the Hungarian Constitutional Court gave up the traditional legal formalism substituting the concept of the secret constitution carefully worked out by its distinguished chairman Prof. Solyom for the old positivist ideal – types. In this way it was able to elaborate a trustworthy yardstick for the judicial review of legislation going beyond the written constitution and its possible reforms or revisions. And study of the jurisprudence of the Czech Constitutional Court, yields the understanding that it rejected the narrow approach of legal positivism in looking for a concept of law which is larger than the traditional concept of positive law and attentive to liberal and democratic political values. The judges of the Czech Court consciously declared their will to look for a table of values commonly accepted, to an idea of justice generally shared, that is to a bundle of fundamental legal principles and customs which are the sources of the law in general, and of the constitutional law in particular. This explains how, drawing inspiration from the Slovenian experience, but not only from it, it was said that the Constitutional Courts wanted to be the vanguard of judicial power, as far as they are a part of it, or of a State's government founded on the principles of the rule of law.

It is understandable that a jurisprudence inspired by these guidelines was not easily to accepted. The model of judicial power which is still commonly accepted even in the new legal systems is inspired by the principle of the separation of powers, and is the model elaborated by Montesquieu according to which the judge is the mouth of the law, and is not allowed to add something to the explicit statements of the legislator. But, even in the frame of this conception of judicial power, the judges, and the Constitutional Courts in particular, are qualified not only by their exclusive and direct relation with the law, but also –

as Pasquino and Ferejohn underline – by the peculiarities of their way of proceeding by comparing ideas and opinions in their internal decision – making process and in the context of the constitutional and social relations.

It is true that constitutional jurisprudence apparently flows from the independent (or – better – unconditioned) and inescapable choices of a superior body, whose decision are binding on all the subjects of the concerned legal order. Sometimes the Constitutional Courts resemble an oracle, or at least this is the idea frequently received by the Parliament in dealing with constitutional justice. It happens that the legislative Assemblies have the feeling that the activity of the Courts is characterized by a great deal of arbitrariness and they often react by approving again the laws declared unconstitutional or by refusing to comply with the Courts decisions, even if such a move conflicts with the principles and the rules of the constitutional legality. These are supposed to be exceptional events, but the reports published in this book offer some interesting examples: a law of the Czech Republic which assimilated the status of the judges to that of other public officials; in Bulgaria we have the precedent concerning laws with limitations of agricultural properties; and the example of the Slovenian case, where the Parliament refrained from implementing a decision of the Court on the results of a referendum about electoral legislation, and – the reaction of the polish Assembly to the decision of the Court which, in the frame of the old constitution, stated that a law declared unconstitutional by the Court loses its force after the publication of the decision even if the legislator does not abrogate it.

In all these countries the resistance of the Parliaments failed: the decisions of the Court are commonly accepted as the last word in the matter concerned. And when this particular role of the Court was contested, they provided for a revision of the constitution. In Slovenia the Parliament avoided complying with the obligation flowing from the decision of the Court that the proposal for majoritarian electoral legislation had the support of the majority of the electors; the Assembly bypassed the obstacle by introducing in the constitution a rule providing for a proportional electoral system. The Polish Court explicitly suggested that only by adopting a revision of the constitution, the Parliament is allowed to provide for the continuity of the laws declared unconstitutional by the Court itself And this is substantially the choice made, with some difficulties, by the Romanian Parliament with regards to procedural provisions which mostly resemble those of the revision of the constitution. It is true that in this last case we have perhaps an example of a legitimate breach of the efficacy of the constitution which does not imply the adoption of a law ranking at the same position of the constitutional laws in the hierarchy of the sources of law, but the derogation of the Court decision is evident.

When a decision of the Constitutional Court is adopted, even it has to be qualified as a final decision, as there is always space for a revision of the constitution (or even for a special power of breaking its efficacy). Therefore the decision takes place in the context of the dialogue between the superior bodies of the state. It could happen that the Parliament reacts with a contrary move if the interpretation given to the constitution by the constitutional judges or their efforts of up – dating the previous interpretation does not satisfy public opinion or the political parties. This is the reason why the choice made by the Slovenian Parliament is not appreciated by all the commentators because, instead of implementing the will of the people, it was apparently adopted against the preferences expressed by the referendum. It is a typical inconvenience of representative democratic regimes that the parliamentary mandate is unlimited and members of Parliament elected by the people are allowed to adopt decisions conflicting with the opinions of the people the only restrictive feature being that they can be deprived of their seat at the next election, if in the meantime the people does not change its mind and accept and share their choice.

Therefore the decisions of the Courts are taken in the frame of a process which develops according to the ways of deliberative democracy, both when the process started before the adoption of the decision and when it flows from the decision itself. The Court is in this way one of the institutions of deliberative democracy: its contribution to the democratic process is not a mere declaration of the will of the framers of the constitution, but is the result of an interpretive effort connecting the statements of the constitution with the social conscience. Actually the social dialogue starts outside the Court and before its decision, and is aimed at influencing it. But the impact of this dialogue on the Court has to comply with the times and modes of the decision-making process of this body which is formally open in different ways as far as its rules allow only the partecipation of the subjects who initiated the judgement, or of the counterparts or, but not always, of third parties. The same acts which are the result of the exercise of the right to access to the Court offer elements of knowledge and the judges can profit by them in view of the decision which has to be taken. But the structure of the internal deliberative process of the Courts is also influenced by the rules providing for the existence of internal minor structures (senates or sections), for filtering the questions which are submitted to the Court, and eventually for appeals from one minor structure to the plenary meeting of the body. When they are not included in the constitution, all these rules are not always adopted by the Court or by its internal organs, and there are countries where their approval falls in the competence of the parliamentary legislator. The choices in the matter are different: even if the independence of the body entrusted with the functions of the constitutional justice is common throughout the states, the different countries have a different approach to dealing with the competence of the constitutional judges to provide for the internal organization of their activity and with the guaranties of stability and the amending procedures of those provisions.

As a matter of fact the role of the Courts in the frame of deliberative democracy mainly depends on the rules concerning access to its judgements and their initiative. The choices in this matter are not left to autonomous decisions of the Courts, because they are determinative in designing the "predictive or coordinating" functions which Ferejohn and Pasquino attributes to them.

Serious attention is not always paid to the fact that the choices concerning access to the Courts are conditioned – at least as far as judicial review of legislation is at stake – by the concept of the constitution adopted by the legislator. It was recently said that the preventive character of judicial review of legislation entrusted to the Constitutional Council favours the certainty of law, because it impedes a new submission of the same question after the decision of the Council or after the expiration of the deadline for access to the judgement of this body. Actually there is no further chance of contesting the conformity to the constitution of a law when the Constitutional Council decided on the same question or the time for the submission of the question to the Council passed.[17] The remark is correct and interesting, but it is not satisfying. Even when the right of access is given not only to some organs and institution of the State, but also to the parliamentary factions or to a substantial number of parliamentarians, the relevance of the question is circumscribed to the relations between the superior bodies of the State.

First of all the exercise of the right of access can have political implications as far as – for example – the members of the French Parliament are in the position of blackmailing the Cabinet and threatening a legal action before the Constitutional Council when they dislike a draft – law supported by the Cabinet itself. Moreover the limitation on the number of subjects allowed access to the Council apparently implies that the constitution is a source of law which displays effects at the level of the superior bodies of the State: apparently only these bodies are interested in compliance with the constitution and only they can take the initiative as regards questioning conformity of the laws to the constitution. It is true that the Constitutional Council tried to go beyond this restricted view, adopting – for instance – the Italian model of interpretive decisions which are specially fitted to taking into consideration the practical aspects of the implementation of the law submitted to its judgement and the possible, consequent interpretation. But these efforts of the French constitutional judges did not imply a direct revision of the rules concerning t access to the review of legislation, even if the ideas underpinning the described developments of the jurisprudence of the Council are aimed at an enlargement of the scope of application of the constitution to affect private relations.

As I underlined in the opening pages of this paper, the efficacy of the provisions of the new constitutions does not interest only the relations between the s.c. constitutional bodies of the State, but also the relations between private subjects. In both cases they can be applied directly and immediately, without the intermediation of the legislator and even when this intermediation is missing. From this

---

[17] Rousseau, *op. cit.*, pp. 79–81.

point of view direct access to the courts by private subjects is of great relevance (or of the submission incidenter tantum of a question concerning the constitutionality of a law by the judge of a pending case). This solution is evidently excluded when the review of the legislation has a preventive nature and access to it is restricted to only some bodies or institution of the State.

At this stage of our work it would be possible to deal with the traditional issue of the models of constitutional justice by identifying, alongside the traditional American model of juducial review of legislation, a possible, unique European model of Verfassungsgerichtbarkeit. But a study in this direction would go beyond the purposes of this book, which is essentialy aimed at dealing, on one hand, with the legitimacy of the bodies entrusted with the task of the constitutional justice and, on the other side, with the impact of the constitutional jurisprudence on the functioning of the new constitutional systems as far as the relations between the superior bodies of the State and the relations between private and public subjects are concerned. And the final observations will be devoted to these items.

6. FINAL THOUGHTS

It is worthwhile now to summarize the thoughts that the essays in this book suggest, which are also at the basis of the considerations I have developed.

First of all it was evident that without a reference to the constitution and to the functions affecting the constitution which they display, the question of the legitimacy of the Constitutional Court does not have any meaning. This question has to be dealt with not in an abstract way, but by looking at concrete practice, and the solution depends on the theory of the constitution which is accepted by the judges and the organs of the State. Therefore the topic of the effectiveness of the constitution is immediately relevant, but effectiveness of a constitution means effectiveness of the interpretations of the constitution which are accepted and of the meanings which are given to the constitutional provisions.

These meanings are the terms of reference of the research concerning the effectiveness of the constitution: when these meanings are frequently changing and do not have continuous observance, the effectiveness of the constitution is in danger, even if the same constitutional text is always in force.

It follows that the effectiveness of the constitution depends on the Constitutional Court which is in charge of its observance. This is true even for those commentators who think that there are other factors that are relevant in the matter, such as public opinion, political parties and the behaviour of the superior bodies of the State. The enlargement of the functions of the constitutional judges implies that the impact of their jurisprudence affects not only the compliance with the provisions of the constitution concerning the traditional issues of human rights and fundamental freedoms but also the relations between the powers of the State. Therefore the effectiveness of the constitution depends on the ability of the Court to obtain legitimacy by interpreting and enforcing the constitutional provisions regarding the functioning of the superior bodies of the state when it is putting its feet in the political conflict and is especially in danger of being contested by the political actors. In fact the Court has to be able to keep in touch not only with the developments of the social conscience but also with the changing evolution of political life, without subordinating its jurisprudence to the contingent exigencies of the political parties.

Looking at the problem of the legitimacy of the Court only from the point of view of its establishment and of the appointment of its members does not have any meaning, because the problem of legitimacy arises with regard to the activity of the Court. At the moment of its establishment or of its installation the question is that of identifying the technical and professional capabilities which will allow the Court to obtain the required legitimacy through its activity and to guarantee the effectiveness of the constitution which it has to interpret and implement.

Moreover we cannot confuse the problem of the legitimacy of the Courts with the problem of the reasons of their establishment in the new constitutional orders. Leaving aside the high symbolic value of the adoption of constitutional justice in the new democracies, it is important to remember the exigency of guaranteeing the effectivity of the rigidity of the constitutions, the extension of the rule of law to the relations between the s.c. constitutional organs, the safeguard of human rights and of fundamental freedoms provided for by the constitution, the design of an anti – majoritarian machinery aimed at protecting the minorities, and so on.

It is evident that the problem of legitimacy and of the effectiveness of the constitution can – at least partially – be identified with the problem of the legitimacy of the Constitutional Court and viceversa. There is a circular process which is at the basis of the effectiveness of the constitution and of the legal order flowing ftom it. The role of the Constitutional Court is essentially an intermediate one in this process and emphasizes the responsibility of legal science, which has to provide for the professional capabilities which guarantee the efficacy of that intermediation.

If the Courts are not the only factor in the development of the constitutional system, great relevance has to be given to the the dialogue which takes place between the Courts themselves, on one side, and the public opinion and the s.c. constitutional organs, on the other side, both in view of the ability of the latters of elaborating the messages of the former and of the potential capacity of the Courts of taking note of the changes of public opinion and of the policies of the superior bodies of the State. This dialogue is possible only in the framework of a free and democratic society: totalitarian or authoritarian regimes do not allow or favour it because their are missing the requirements of deliberative democracy which make possible that dialogue. In order to achieve a successful process it is the responsibility of the courts to gain the trust of the holders of the right or power of access to constitutional justice and to offer them reasons for submitting to them their claims and initiatives. It is also the responsibility of the Courts to leave open space for the exercise of political powers and for the reaction of public opinion. From Ely to Sunstein American legal literature has many suggestions in this direction: it is very eager to stimulate the Supreme Court not to identify the effectiveness of the constitution only with the success of its jurisprudence and to connect it with the overall developments of the democratic deliberative process.

These positions cannot be read as an evidence of the mistrust of the role of the Courts in settling constitutional cases and conflicts, but are the expression of the right exigency of ensuring a balanced development of constitutional systems and of avoiding a government of judges, of which all the democratic doctrines are afraid.

Obviously when the open texture of the constitutions leave considerable space to the interpretive functions of the Courts, we can say that in some way the role of these bodies depends on the drafting of the constitutions: ambiguous texts imply a kind of delegation of normative functions to the judges. Therefore in the new democracies, which are frequently in danger of internal political conflicts and failures in the implementation of democratic and liberal principles, the study of the interventions of the Constitutional Courts has to be attentive to the changes in democracy and toits expansion and development not only with regard to the guarantee of human rights and fundamental freedoms but also with regard to the functioning of the goverment and to the relations between the superior bodies of the State.

Bibliography

Ackerman, Bruce, 'The Rise of World Constitutionalism', *Virginia Law Review* 83 (1977), pp. 771–97.

Ackerman, Bruce, *We the People*, vol. 1 (Cambridge, Mass.: Harvard University Press 1998).

Alexander, Larry, ed., *Constitutionalism: Philosophical Foundations* (Cambridge University Press, Cambridge 1998).

Allan, J, 'Turning Clark Kent into Superman: The New Zealand Bill of Rights Act 1990', *Otago Law Review*, 9 (2000), pp. 613–632.

Angiolini, V., *La 'manifesta infondatezza' nei giudizi costituzionali* (Padova: Cedam 1988).

Anzon, A., B. Caravita, M. Luciani & M. Volpi (eds), *La Corte costituzionale e gli altri poteri dello Stato* (Torino: Giappichelli 1993).

Arató, Andrew: Civil Society, Revolution and Constitution (Civil társadalom, forradalom és alkotmány), in Új Mandátum, *Budapest. Preface* (Előszó) (1999).

Arató, Andrew: End Play of the Constitutional Drafting (Alkotmányozási végjáték), in *Beszélő, 12* (1996).

Avril, Pierre & Jean Gicquel, 'La Constitution est-elle devenue 'ringarde'?', *Le Monde*, 1 July 1999.

Avril, Pierre & Jean Gicquel, *Le Conseil constitutionnel* (Paris: Montchrestien, 1998).

Barile, P., E. Cheli & S. Grassi (eds), *Corte costituzionale e sviluppo della forma di governo in Italia* (Bologna: Il Mulino 1982).

Beatty, David M., ed., *Human Rights and Judicial Review* (Kluwer: Dordrecht, 1994).

Beaud, Olivier, 'Le Souverain', *Pouvoirs*, n° 67, 1993, pp. 31–45.

Beaud, Olivier, *La puissance de l'État* (Paris: PUF, 1994).

Beer, Lawrence, *Constitutional Case Law of Japan, 1970–90* (Seattle: University of Washington Press 1996).

Beetham, David, 'Key Principles and Indices for a Democratic Audit,' in David Beetham (ed.), *Defining and Measuring Democracy* (London: Sage Publications, 1994), pp. 25–43.

Bell, John, *French Constitutional Law* (Oxford, Clarendon Press 1992).

Bell, John, *French Legal Cultures* (London: Butterworths, 2001).

Benedik, M., Földcesová. A, & Galanda, M., 'Právny štát, legislatíva, ústavnosť a súdnictvo' [Rule of Law, Legislative and Judiciary], in Miroslav Kollár & Grigorij Mesežnikov (eds), *Súhrnná správa o Slovensku* [*Global Report on Slovakia* (Bratislava: IVO 2000), pp. 125–166.

Beyme, Klaus von, 'The Genesis of Constitutional Review in Parliamentary Systems', in Christine Lanfried (ed), *Constitutional Review and Legislation. An International Comparison* (Baden-Baden: Nomos 1988), pp. 21–38.

Beyme, Klaus von, *The Legislator: German Parliament as a Centre of Political Decision-making.* (Aldershot, Ashgate 1998).

Beyme, Klaus von, *Transition to Democracy in Eastern Europe.* (Basingstoke: Macmillan 1996).

Bhardwaj, R (ed), *Constitution Amendment in India*, 6th ed (New Delhi: Northern Book Centre 1995).

Bickel, Alexander, *The Least Dangerous Branch* (Indianapolis: Bobbs-Merrill 1962).

Billing, W., *Das Problem der Richterwahl zum Bundesverfassungsgericht*. (Berlin, Duncker & Humblot 1969).

Blankenagel, Alexander, 'Rechtsstaat UdSSR', *Jahrbuch für Ostrecht*, 1 (1990), pp. 9–31.

Blankenagel, Alexander, 'The court writes its own law', *East European Constitutional Review*, 3/4 (1994), pp. 74–79.

Blankenagel, Alexander, 'Totgesagte leben länger: Die Osteuropa-Disziplinen im Dschungel der Wissenschaften', *Osteuropa* 12 (1997), pp. 1041–1049.

Blanquer, Jean Michel, 'Bloc de constitutionnalité ou ordre constitutionnel', in *Mélanges offerts à Jacques Robert* (Paris: Montchrestien, 1998), pp. 227–238.

Blasi, Vincent, 'Constitutional Limitations on the Power of State to Regulate Goods in Interstate Commerce', in Terrance Sandalow & Eric Stein (eds.), *Courts and Free Markets* (Oxford: Oxford, University Press 1982), pp. 247–281.

Bon, P., 'Le Tribunal constitutionnel espagnol', in *Cahiers du Conseil Constitutionnel, no. 2*, 1997, pp. 38–53.

Bozóki, András (ed.), *Transcript of the Transition. Round Table Negotiations in 1989. I-IV.* Magvető (A rendszerváltás forgatókönyve. Kerekasztal-tárgyalások 1989-ben) (1999).

Brünnek, A. von, 'Constitutional Review and Legislation in Western Democracies', in Christine Lanfried (ed), *Constitutional Review and Legislation. An International Comparison* (Baden-Baden: Nomos 1988), pp. 219–260.

Brennan, F., *The Wik Debate: Its Impact on Aborigines, Pastoralists and Miners* (Sydney: University of New South Wales Press 1998).

Brewer Carias, Allan-Randolph, *Judicial Review in Comparative Law* (Cambridge, Cambridge University Press, 1989).

Brezhnev, O.V., 'Konstitutsionnyi sud i organy prokuratury: Osobennosti vzajmootnoshenii', *Vestnik Moskovskogo Universiteta*, 5 (1997), pp. 75–82.

Brilmayer, Lea, 'A Reply', *Harvard Law Review* 93 (1980), pp. 1727–33.

Brilmayer, Lea, 'The Jurisprudence of Article III: Perspectives on the 'Case or Controversy' Requirement', *Harvard Law Review* 93 (1979), pp. 297–321.

Broklová, E. *Československá demokracie. Politickš systém ČSR 1918–1938* [Czechoslovak Democracy. Political System in 1918–1938] (Praha: SLON 1992).

Brown, L. Neville & John S. Bell, *French Administrative Law* (Oxford: Clarendon Press, 5th ed. 1998.

Brzezinski, Mark F., 'Toward Constitutionalism in Russia. The Russian Constitutional Court', *International and Comparative Law Quarterly*, July (1993), pp. 673–690.

Brzezinski, Mark, Herbert Hausmaniger & Kim Scheppele, 'Constitutional 'Refolution' in the Ex-Communist World; the Rule of Law', *American University Journal of International Law and Policy* 12 (1997), pp. 87–116.

Burdeau, Georges, Francis Hamon & Michel Troper, *Droit constitutionnel*, vol. 26 (Paris: L.G.D.J. 1999).

Bútorová, Z. 'Verejná mienka' [Public Opinion], in Grigorij Mesežnikov & Michal Ivantyšyn (eds.), *Súhrnná správa o Slovensku [Global Report on Slovakia]* (Bratislava: IVO 1998), pp. 233–268.

Cameron, J, 'Dialogue and Hierarchy in *Charter* Interpretation: A Comment on *R v. Mills*', *Alberta Law Review*, 38 (2001), pp. 1051–1068.

Campbell, T.D., *The Legal Theory of Ethical Positivism* (Aldershot: Dartmouth Publishers 1996).

Campbell, T., K. D. Ewing & A. Tomkins, eds, *Sceptical Essays on Human Rights* (Oxford: OUP 2001)

Cappelletti, M., *La giurisdizione costituzionale delle libertà* (Milano: Giuffrè 1955).

Carlassarre, L. (ed), *Le garanzie giurisdizionali dei diritti fondamentali* (Padova: Cedam 1988).

Carré de Malberg, Raymond, *Contribution à la théorie générale de l'Etat* (Paris: Sirey, 1920–1922 [reprint Paris: CNRS 1985]).

Carré de Malberg, Raymond, *La loi, expression de la volonté générale* (Paris: Economica, 1984 reprint).

Catelani, E., *La determinazione della 'questione di illegittimità costituzionale' nel giudizio incidentale* (Milano: Giuffrè 1993).

Cayla, Olivier, 'Le Conseil constitutionnel et la constitution de la science du droit', in *Le Conseil constitutionnel a quarante ans* (Paris: L.G.D.J., 1999), pp. 106–141.

Cerri, A., *Corso di giustizia costituzionale* (Milano: Giuffrè 1997).

Chantebout, Bernard, *Droit constitutionnel et science politique* (Paris: A Colin 1997).

Cheli, E., *Il giudice delle leggi* (Bologna: Il mulino 1996).

Chetvernin, Vladimir, 'Three Questions to the Authors of the Act', *East European Constitutional Review*, 3 (1994), pp. 80–82.

Chevalier, Jacques, *L'Etat de droit* (Paris: Montchrestien 1992).

Choper, Jesse, *Judicial Review and the National Political Process* (Chicago: University of Chicago Press 1980).

Clark, David S., ed., *Comparative and Private International Law: Essays in Honor of John Henry Merryman on His Seventieth Birthday* (Duncker u. Humblot, Berlin 1990

Constant, Benjamin, 'The Liberty of the Ancients Compared to that of the Moderns,' in Constant, *Political Writings* (Cambridge: Cambridge University Press, 1988).

Conseil constitutionnel a quarante ans (Paris: L.G.D.J., 1999).

Constitution of the Italian Republic and the Legal Instruments Governing the Constitutional Justice System, and the Organization and Operation of Constitutional Court (Rome: Corte Costituzionale 1997).

Corte Costituzionale (ed), *Effetti temporali delle sentenze della Corte costituzionale* (Milano: Giuffrè 1989).

Corte Costituzionale (ed), *Il principio di ragionevolezza nella giurisprudenza della Corte costituzionale* (Milano: Giuffrè 1994).

Corte Costituzionale (ed), *L'opinione dissenziente* (Milano: Giuffrè 1995).

Corte Costituzionale (ed), *Le sentenze della Corte costituzionale e l'art. 81, u.c., della Costituzione* (Milano: Giuffrè 1991).

Corte Costituzionale (ed), *Strumenti e tecniche di giudizio della Corte costituzionale* (Milano: Giuffrè 1988).

Corte Costituzionale, Judgments no. 185–1998 and 43–1997.

Corwin, Edward S., *The President: Office and Powers*, 4th ed. (New York: New York University Press 1957).

Costa, Jean-Paul, *Le Conseil d'Etat dans la société contemporaine* (Paris: Economica, 1993).

Costanzo, P. (ed), *Organizzazione e funzionamento della Corte costituzionale* (Torino: Giappichelli 1996).

Crisafulli, V., *Lezioni di diritto costituzionale*, vol. 2, *La giustizia costituzionale* (Padova: Cedam 1984).

Czeszejko-Sochacki, Zdzislaw, Leszek Garlicki & Janusz Trzciński, *Komentarz do Ustawy o Trybunale Konstytucyjnym* (Wydawnictwo Sejmowe, Warszawa 1999)

D'Amico, M., *Giudizio sulle leggi ed efficacia temporale delle decisioni di incostituzionalità* (Milano: Giuffrè 1993).

D'Amico, M., *Parti e processo nella giustizia costituzionale* (Torino: Giappichelli 1991).

D'Orazio, G., *La genesi della Corte costituzionale* (Milano: Comunità 1981).

Dahl, Robert A., 'Decision-making in a Democracy: the Supreme Court as a National Policy-maker', *Journal of Public Law*, 6 (1957), pp. 279–295.

Decisions of Ordinary Courts', *Archiv für Rechts- und Sozialphilosophie*, 86 (2000), pp. 537–53.

Dicey, A, *Introduction to the Study of the Law of the Constitution*, 10th ed (London: Macmillan 1959).

Drago, Guillaume; Bastien François and Nicolas Molfessis (eds.), *La légitimité de la jurisprudence du Conseil constitutionnel* (Paris: Economica, 1999).

Drgonec, J., 'Právomoc Ústavného súdu Slovenskej republiky pri zabezpečovaní súladu právneho poriadku Slovenskej republiky s Ústavou SR' [The Power of the Constitutional Court in Harmonizing Legal System of the Slovak Republic with the Constitution of the SR], *Právny obzor*, 1 (1994), pp. 14–24.

Duhamel, Olivier & Jean-Luc Parodi (eds.), *La constitution de la cinquième République* (Paris: FNSP 1985).

Elster, Jon, 'Miscalculations in the Design of the East European Presidencies,' *East European Constitutional Review*, Vol. 2 (4)/Vol. 3 (1) (Fall 1993/Winter 1994), pp. 95–98.

Ely, John Hart, *Democracy and Distrust* (Cambridge, Mass.: Harvard University Press 1980).

Emerson, Thomas I., *The System of Freedom of Expression* (New York: Random House 1970).

Epp, Charles R., *The Rights Revolution* (University of Chicago Press, Chicago 1998).

Epstein, Richard, *Principles for a Free Society: Reconciling Individual Liberty with the Common Good* (Reading, Mass.: Perseus Books 1999).

Fallon, Richard H., 'The Supreme Court, 1996 Term – Foreword: Implementing the Constitution', *Harvard Law Review* 111 (1997): 54–152.

Favoreu, Louis (ed.), *Le Conseil constitutionnel et les partis politiques* (Paris: Economica, 1988).

Favoreu, Louis, 'Dualité ou unité de l'ordre juridique: Conseil constitutionnel et Conseil d'Etat participent-ils de deux ordres juridiques différents?', in *Conseil constitutionnel et Conseil d'Etat* (Paris: LGDJ-Montchrestien, 1989), pp. 145–190.

Favoreu, Louis, 'L'apport du Conseil constitutionnel au droit public', *Pouvoirs*, n° 13, 1980, pp. 17–26.

Favoreu, Louis, 'La légitimité du juge constitutionnel', *Revue Internationale de droit comparé*, 1994, pp. 557–581.

Favoreu, Louis, 'Le Conseil constitutionnel et la cohabitation', *Regards sur l'actualité*, n° 135, 1987, pp. 3–22.

Favoreu, Louis, 'Synthèse', in Guillaume Drago, Bastien François et Nicolas Molfessis, *above*, pp. 385–400.

Favoreu, Louis, *Droit constitutionnel* (Paris: Dalloz, 1999).

Favoreu, Louis, *La politique saisie par le droit* (Paris: Economica, 1988).

Feofanov, Yuri, 'The Establishment of the Constitutional Court in Russia and the Communist Party case', *Review of Central and East European Law*, 6 (1993), pp. 623–637.

Fiss, Owen, 'Introductory Remarks, Symposium', 19 *Yale J. Int. L.* 219 (1994).

Freund, Paul, *Supreme Court and Supreme Law* (Cambridge, Mass.: Harvard University Press 1954).

Fromme, Friedrich K., 'Wer bestimmt?', *Frankfurter Allgemeine Zeitung*, 14 February 1996, p. 1.

Fukuyama, Francis, 'The Primacy of Culture,' in Larry Diamond & Marc F. Plattner (eds.), *The Global Resurgence of Democracy* (Baltimore: The Johns Hopkins University Press, 1996), pp. 320–327.

Futey, Bohdan A., 'Comments on the Law on the Constitutional Court of Ukraine', *The Harriman Review*, 10(1) (1997), pp. 15–23.

Futey, Bohdan A., 'Upholding the Role of Law in Ukraine: Judiciary in Transition', in Theofil Kis & Irena Makaryk (eds.), *Towards a New Ukraine* (Ottawa: Chair of Ukrainian Studies 1999), pp. 59–76.

Gabriel, Oscar W. (ed.): *Politische Orientierungen und Verhaltensweisen im vereinigten Deutschland* (Opladen, Leske & Budrich 1997).

Ganev, Venelin I., 'Bulgaria,' in Robert Elgie (ed.), *Semi-Presidentialism in Europe* (Oxford: Oxford University Press, 1999), pp. 124–149.

Ganev, Venelin I., 'Judicial Independence and Post-Totalitarian Politics,' *Parker School of Law Journal of East European Law*, Vol. 3, No. 2 (Fall 1996), pp. 227–233.

Ganev, Venelin I., 'The Bulgarian Constitutional Court: Two Interviews,' *East European Constitutional Review*, Vol. 6, No. 1 (Winter 1997), pp. 65–71.

Ganev, Venelin I., 'Emergency Powers and the New East European Constitutions,' *The American Journal of Comparative Law*, Vol. XLV, No. 3 (Summer 1997).

Ganev, Venelin I., 'Bulgaria's Symphony of Hope,' *The Journal of Democracy*, Vol. 8, No 4 (October 1997), pp. 135–151.

Garlicki, Leszek, 'Constitutional Developments in Poland', *St. Louis University Law Journal* 32 (1988), pp. 713–736.

Garlicki, Leszek Lech, 'Das Verfassungsgericht im politischen Prozeß', in Otto Luchterhand (ed.): *Neue Regierungssysteme in Osteuropa und der GUS* (Berlin: Berlin Verlag 1996), pp. 275–310.

Garlicki, Leszek, ed., *Konstytucja Rzeczypospolitej Polskiej: Komentarz* (Wydawnictwo Sejmowe, Warszawa 1999)

Gati, Charles, 'If Not Democracy, What? Leaders, Laggards, and Losers in the Postcommunist World', in Michael Mandelbaum (ed), *Post-Communism: Four Perspectives* (New York, Council of Foreign Relations Press, 1996).

Genevois, Bruno, *La jurisprudence du Conseil Constitutionnel – Principes directeurs* (Paris: S.T.H., 1988).

Gicquel, Jean, *Droit constitutionnel et institutions politiques* (Paris: Montchrestien, 15th ed. 1997).

Ginsberg, Thomas, *Growing Constitutions: Judicial Review in New Democracies* (Dissertation, University of California, Berkeley 1999).

Gochev, Dimitar, 'Za purvi put konstitutzionen sud v. Bulgaria', in Mariela Vargova (ed.), *Konstitutzionnijat Sud: jurisprudentzija* (Sofia: Open Society Institute, 1996), pp. 18–23.

Grassi, S., *Il conflitto di attribuzione tra Stato e regioni e tra regioni* (Milano: Giuffrè 1985).

Gray, John, 'From Post-Communism to Civil Society: The Reemergence of History and the Decline of the Western Model', *Social Philosophy and Policy* (1993), pp. 26–50.

Griffin, Stephen M., *American Constitutionalism: From Theory to Politics* (Princeton: Princeton University Press 1996).

Grimm, D., 'Human Rights and Judicial Review in Germany', in David M. Beatty (ed.), *Human Rights and Judicial Review: A Comparative Perspective* (Hague: Kluwer 1994), pp. 267–95.

Groppi, T., *I poteri istruttori della Corte costituzionale nel giudizio sulle leggi* (Milano: Giuffrè 1997).

Grudzińska Gross, Irena (ed.), *Constitutionalism & Politics* (Bratislava: Slovak Committee of the European Cultural Foundation 1994), pp. 271–88

Habermas, Jürgen, *Between Facts and Norms*, trans. William Rehg (Polity Press, Cambridge 1996).

Halmai, Gábor & Kim Lane Scheppele, 'Constitutional Protection for Homosexuality in Hungary', *East European Human Rights Review*, 1 (1997).

Halmai, Gábor, "Establishing a State Governed by the Rule of Law in Hungary", *Review of Central and East European Law*, 22 (1996), pp. 347–64.

Halmai, Gábor, "Kell-e nekünk új alkotmnány?" [Do We Need a New Constitution?], 2000 (1994, no. 7), pp. 7–11.

Hartwig, Matthias, 'Verfassungsgerichtsbarkeit in Rußland. Der dritte Anlauf', *Europäische Grundrechte Zeitschrift* (quoted as EuGRZ), 7–8 (1996), pp. 177–199.

Hausmaniger, Herbert, Mark Brzezinski & Kim Scheppele, 'Constitutional 'Refolution' in the Ex-Communist World; The Rule of Law' *American University Journal of International Law and Policy* 12 (1997), pp. 87–116.

Havel, V., *Summer Mediations* (New York: Vintage Books 1993).

Hiebert, J, 'A Hybrid-Approach to Protect Rights? An Argument in Favour of Supplementing Canadian Judicial Review with Australia's Model of Parliamentary Scrutiny', *Federal Law Review*, 26 (1998), pp. 115–138.

Hiebert, J, *Limiting Rights* (Montreal: McGill-Queens University Press 1996).

Hiebert, J, 'Why Must a Bill of Rights be a Contest of Political and Judicial Wills? The Canadian Alternative', *Public Law Review*, 10 (1999), pp. 22–36.

Hiebert, J, 'Wrestling with Rights: Judges, Parliament and the Making of Social Policy', *Choices*, 5(3) (1999) (Institute for Research on Public Policy), pp. 1–36.

Hoeland, Armin, 'Imposition Without Adaptation? New Opportunities for Old Failure,' in Volkmar Gessner, Armin Hoeland & Csaba Varga (eds.), *European Legal Cultures* (Dartmouth: Aldershot, 1996), pp. 482–490.

Hogg, P & A. Bushell, 'The *Charter* Dialogue Between Courts And Legislatures (Or Perhaps The *Charter Of Rights* Isn't Such A Bad Thing After All)', *Osgoode Hall Law Journal* 35 (1997), pp. 75–124.

Hogg, P & A. Thornton, 'Reply to "Six Degrees of Dialogue"' *Osgoode Hall Law Journal*, 37 (1999), pp. 529–536.

Hogg, P, *Constitutional Law of Canada*, 3rd ed (Scarborough: Carswell 1992).

Holländer, Pavel, 'The Role of the Czech Constitutional Court: Application of the

Constitution in Case Decisions of Ordinary Courts', *Parker Sch. J.E.Eur. L.* 4 (1997), pp. 445–65.

Holmes, Stephen, 'Back to the Drawing Board', *East European Constitutional Review* 2 no. 1 (1993), pp. 21–25.

Holmes, Stephen, *Passions and Constraints: on the Theory of Liberal Democracy* (Chicago, University of Chicago Press, 1995).

Howard, A.E. Dick (ed.), *Constitution Making in Eastern Europe* (Washington, D.C.: Woodrow Wilson Center Press 1993)

Jouanjan, Olivier, 'La forme républicaine, norme *supra* constitutionnelle?', in *La république en droit français* (Paris: Economica, 1996), pp. 267–287.

Katz, Stanley, 'The Politics of Law in Colonial America: Controversies Over Chancery Courts and Equity Courts in the Eighteenth Century', in Donald Fleming and Bernard Bailyn (eds.), *Law in American History* (Boston: Little Brown 1971), pp. 257–286.

Keith, K, 'Concerning Change': The Adoption and Implementation of the New Zealand Bill of Rights Act 1990', *Victoria University of Wellington Law Review*, 31 (2000), pp. 721–46.

Kelsen, H., 'Judicial Review of Legislation. A Comparative Study of the Austrian and the American Constitution', *The Journal of Politics*, 4 (1942), pp. 183–200.

Kelsen, H., 'La garantie juridictionnelle de la Constitution (La Justice constitutionnelle)', in *Revue du droit public et de la science politique en France et à l'étranger*, 45 (1928), pp. 197–257.

Kelsen, H., 'Wer soll der Hueter der Verfassung sein?' (Who should be the guardian of the Constitution?), *Die Justiz*, 6 (1930–31), pp. 576–628.

Kelsen, Hans, *Théorie pure du droit* [translated into French by Ch.Eisenmann from the second edition of *Reine Rechtslehre*] (Paris: Dalloz, 1962).

Kenney, Sally J., William M. Reisinger & John C. Reitz (eds), *Constitutional Dialogues In Comparative Perspective* (London: Macmillan 1999).

Kinley, D., *The European Convention on Human Rights: Compliance Without Incorporation* (Aldershot: Dartmouth 1993).

Kirhheimer, Otto, 'The *Rechsstaat* as a Magic Wall,' in *Politics, Law and Social Change: Selected Essays of Otto Kirchheimer* (New York: Columbia University Press, 1969), pp. 428–452.

Komesar, Neil K., 'Taking Institutions Seriously: Introduction to a Strategy for Constitutional Analysis', *Univ. of Chicago Law Review* 51 (1984), pp. 366–446.

Kommers, D., *The Constitutional Jurisprudence of the Federal Republic of Germany* (Durham, N.C.: Duke University Press 1997).

Kommers, Donald, *Judicial Politics in West Germany.* (London, Sage 1976).

Konstitutsionnyi sud Rossii, *Spravochnik* (Moscow, Informatsionno-ekspertnaya gruppa 'Panorama': 2nd edition 1997).

Koudelka, Z., 'Válka soudů aneb dělba moci v. soudnictví' (The War of the Courts: on the separation of powers in the system of justice), *Politologickš časopis (Political Science Journal)* 7 (1998), pp. 71–4.

Kresák, P., *et al.*, *Rozhodovacia činnost' Ústavného súdu Slovenskej republiky* [Decision Making of the Constitutional Court of the Slovak Republic] (Bratislava: Kalligram 1999).

Krone, Nicole, 'Das Verfassungsgericht der Russischen Föderation', *Osteuropa* (1998), pp. 253–267.

Kryschtanowskaja, Olga W., 'Die Transformation der alten Nomenklatur-Kader in die russische Elite', in Helmut Steiner & Wladimir Jadow (eds.): *Rußland – wohin? Rußland aus der Sicht russischer Soziologen* (Berlin, Trafo Verlag 1999), pp. 213–243.

Kukushkin, M.I. (Red.), *Konstitutsionne pravo Rossijskoj Federatsii. Sbornik sudebnykh reshenij* (St. Petersburg, Paritet 1997).

Lacharrière, René de, 'Opinion dissidente', *Pouvoir* 13 (1980), pp. 132–150.

La Fave, Wayne, *Search and Seizure: A Treatise on the Fourth Amendment* (1978) (St. Paul: West 1996).

Lambert, Edouard, *Le gouvernement des juges et la lutte contre la législation sociale aux Etats-Unis; l'expérience américaine du contrôle judiciaire de la constitutionalité des lois* (Paris: Giard 1921).

Landfried, Christine (ed.), *Constitutional Review and Legislation. An International Comparison.* (Baden-Baden, Nomos 1988).

Landfried, Christine, *Bundesverfassungsgericht und Gesetzgeber* (Baden-Baden, Nomos 2nd edition 1996).

Landfried, Christine, 'Judicial Policy-Making in Germany', *West European Politics* (1992), pp. 50–67.

Lapinskas, Kestutis, 'Lietuvos Konstituciju Istoriniu Teisiniu Sasaju Beieskant' [Searching for Historical Legal Links between Lithuania's Constitutions] paper presented at the conference: *Konstitucija, Zmogus, Teisine Valstybe* [*The Constitution, the Individual and the Rule of Law State*] October 24–25, 1997 (Vilnius, Lietuvos Zmogaus Teisiu Centras, 1998).

Lauvaux, Philippe, *Le parlementarisme* (Paris: PUF, coll. Que-sais-je? 2nd ed. 1997).

Lavroff, Dimitri Georges, 'Le Conseil constitutionnel et la norme constitutionnelle', in *Mélanges Gustave Peiser* (Grenoble: P.U.G., 1995), pp. 347–362.

Lazarev, L.V., 'Konstitutsionno-pravovye osnovy organizatsii i deyatel'nosti konstitutsionnogo suda Rossijskoj federatsii', *Sovetskoe gosudarstvo i pravo*, No. 6 (1996), pp. 3–12.

Lochak, Danièle, 'Le Conseil constitutionnel, protecteur des libertés?', *Pouvoirs*, n° 13, 1991, pp. 35–47.

Loewenstein, Karl, 'Reflections on the Values of Constitutions in Our Revolutionary Age,' in Arnold J. Zurcher (ed.), *Constitutions and Constitutional Trends Since World War II* (New York: New York University Press, 1951), pp. 191–224.

Luchaire, François, 'Le Conseil constitutionnel est-il une juridiction?', *Revue du droit public*, 1979, pp. 27–52.

Luchaire, François 'Souvenirs du 16 juillet 1971' in *La Liberté d'association et le Droit – Centenaire de la loi du 1er juillet 1901* (Paris: Conseil Constitutionnel, 2001), pp. 17–22.

Luchterhand, O., 'Vom Verfassungskomitee der UdSSR zum Verfassungsgericht Rußlands', *Archiv des öffentlichen Rechts* (1993), pp. 237–288.

Luciani, M., *Le decisioni processuali e la logica del giudizio incidentale* (Padova: Cedam 1984).

Ludwikowska, Anna M., *Sadownictwo Konstytucyjne w Europie Srodkowo-Wschodniej w Okresie Przeksztalcen Demokratycznych* (TNOiK, Torun 1997)

McAdams, A. James (ed), *Transitional Justice and the Rule of Law in New Democracies* (Notre Dame: University of Notre Dame Press 1997).

MacCormick, D. Neil & Robert S. Summers, *Interpreting Precedents: A Comparative Study* (Dartmouth: Aldershot, 1997).

MacCormick, N., 'The Ethics of Legalism' *Ratio Juris*, 2 (1989), pp. 184–93.

Majtényi, László, Whose is the constitution. Is there a need for a new constitution in Hungary? in *Kritika. 3. (Kié az alkotmány? Szükség van-e Magyarországon új alkotmányra?)* (1994).

Mandel, M, *The Charter of Rights and the Legalization of Politics in Canada*, revised ed (Toronto: Thompson Educational Publishing 1994).

Manfredi, C & J. Kelly, 'Six Degrees of Dialogue: A Response to Hogg and Bushell' *Osgoode Hall Law Journal*, 37 (1999), pp. 513–536.

Manov, Assen, 'Konstitutzionnijat sud na Republika Bulgaria,' in Mariela Vargova (ed.), *Konstitutzionnijat sud: jurisprudentzija* (Sofia: Open Society Institute, 1996), pp. 14–17.

Materialy XIX Vsesoyuznoj konferentsii Kompartii Sovetskogo Soyuza. (Moscow 1988).

Mathieu, Bertrand & Michel Verpeaux (eds.), *La constitutionnalisation des branches du droit* (Paris: Economica-PUAM, 1998).

Mayer, Jacob-Peter (ed.), *L'Ancien Régime et la Révolution* de Alexis de Tocqueville (Paris: Gallimard 1985).

Mendelson, Wallace, *Justices Black and Frankfurter, Conflict in the Court* (Chicago: University of Chicago Press 1961).

Meunier, Jacques, *Le pouvoir du Conseil constitutionnel. Essai d'analyse stratégique* (Paris-Brussels: L.G.D.J.-Bruylant), 1994.

Mihalicz, Csilla, 'Interjú Sólyom Lászlóval, az Alkotmánybíróság volt elnökével.' ('Interview with former President of the Constitutional Court, László Sólyom'), *Buksz* Winter (1998), pp. 435–43.

Mikhailovskaia, Inga, 'Constitutional Rights in Russian Public Opinion', *East European Constitutional Review*, 4, no. 1 (1995), pp. 70–76.

Mikule, V. & V. Sládeček, 'O závaznosti rozhodnutí Ústavního soudu' (On the binding force of judgments of the Constitutional Court), *Bulletin advokacie (The Bar Association Bulletin)* 8 (1995), pp. 35–51.

Mityukov, M.A., *Konstitutsionnoe pravosudie v. sub'ektakh Rossijskoj Federatsii* (Moscow, Yuridicheskaya literatura 1997).

Morabito, Marcel, *Histoire constitutionnelle de La France – 1789–1958* (Paris: Montchrestien, 2000, 6th ed.).

Morton, F.L., 'The Charter Revolution and the Court Party', *Osgoode Hall Law Journal* 30 (1992), pp. 627–52.

Myronenko, Petro, 'Budzhet Yak Chynnyk Sudovoi Nezalezhnosti. Dosvid Konstytutsiynoho Sudu Ukrainy' [Budget as a Factor in Judicial Independence: an Experience of the Constitutional Court of Ukraine], *Visnyk Konstytutsiynoho Sudu*, 5–6 (1998).

Neuborne, Burt, 'Judicial Review and Separation of Powers in France and the United States', *N.Y.U. Law Review* 57 (1982): 363–342.

Nikitinsky, Leonid, 'Interview with Boris Ebzeev, Justice of the Constitutional Court of the Russian Federation', *East European Constitutional Review*, 1 (1997), pp. 83–88.

Nußberger, Angelika, *Verfassungskontrolle in der Sowjetunion und in Deutschland.* (Baden-Baden, Nomos 1994).

Occhiocupo, N. (ed), *La Corte costituzionale tra norma giuridica e realtà sociale* (Bologna: Il Mulino 1978).

Offe, Claus, 'Designing Institutions in East European Transitions', in Robert E. Goodin (ed), *The Theory of Institutional Design* (Cambridge, Cambridge University Press 1996).

BIBLIOGRAPHY

Offe, Claus; Jon Elster & Ulrich Preuss, *Institutional Design in Postcommunist Societies: Rebuilding the Ship at Sea* (Cambridge: Cambridge University Press, 1998).

Onida, V. & M. D'Amico, *Il giudizio di costituzionalità delle leggi* (Torino: Giappichelli 1998).

Osiatynski, Wiktor, 'Rights in New Constitutions of East Central Europe', *Columbia Human Rights Law Review* 26 (1994): 111–166, p. 151

Parrish, Scott, 'Presidential Decree Authority in Russia 1991–95', in John M. Carey & Matthew S. Shugart (eds.), *Executive decree authority* (Cambridge, Cambridge University Press 1998), pp. 62–103.

Pashin, Sergej, 'A Second Edition of the Constitutional Court', *East European Constitutional Review*, 3/4 (1994), pp. 82–85.

Pashin, S.A., *Kak obratit'sya v. konstitutsionnyi sud Rossii* (Moscow, Juridicheskaya Firma Paritet 1992).

Pasquino, P., 'Constitutional Adjudication and Democracy: Comparative Perspectives: USA, France, Italy', *Ratio Juris* 11 (1998), pp. 38–50.

Pasquino, P., 'L'origine du contrôle de constitutionnalité en Italie. Les débats de l'Assemblée constituante (1946–47), *Cahiers du Conseil Constitutionnel*, mars 1999.

Pasquino, P., 'Lenient Legislation. Constitutional Adjudication in Italy' (paper presented at the conference: Constitutional Adjudication and Democracy, Rome, Constitutional Court, June 1999).

Peroutka, F. *Budování státu, III. [Building of the State, vol. III]* (Praha: Lidové noviny 1991).

Perry, Michall, *The Constitution, the Courts and Human Rights* (New Haven: Yale University Press 1982).

Pfeffer, *The Liberties of an American* (Boston: Beacon Press 1956).

Philip, Loïc & Louis Favoreu, *Les grandes décisions du Conseil Constitutionnel* (Paris: Dalloz, 2001, 11th ed.).

Philippi, K.J., *Tatsachenfeststellungen des Bundesverfassungsgerichts* (Cologne, Heymanns 1971).

Pisaneschi, A., *I conflitti tra i poteri dello Stato* (Milano: Giuffrè, 1992).

Pizzorusso, A.; G. Volpe, F. Sorrentino & R. Moretti, *Garanzie costituzionali. Artt. 134–139*, in Giuseppe Branca (ed), *Commentario della Costituzione* (Bologna: Zanichelli 1981).

Pizzorusso, A.; R. Romboli, E. Rossi (eds), *Il contributo della giurisprudenza costituzionale alla determinazione della forma di governo italiana* (Torino: Giappichelli, 1998).

Pokol, Béla, 'A magyar parlamentarizmus' (*'Hungarian Parliamentarism'*), Cserépfalvi, Budapest (1994).

Ponthoreau, Marie-Claire, *La reconnaissance des droits non écrits par les cours constitutionnelles italienne et française. Essai sur le pouvoir créateur du juge constitutionnel* (Paris: Economica-PUAM) 1994.

Preuss, Ulrich K., Politik aus dem Geist des Konsenses. Zur Rechtsprechung des Bundesverfassungsgerichts *Merkur* (1987), pp. 1–12.

Přibáň, J., 'Legitimacy and Legality After the Velvet Revolution', in Přibáň, J. & J. Young (eds), *The Rule of Law in Central Europe* (Aldershot, Ashgate Publishers 1999), pp. 29–55.

Přibáň, J., 'The Constitutional Court of the Czech Republic and the Principle of the

Sovereignty of the Law', in Istvan Pogany (ed.), *Human Rights in Eastern Europe* (Aldershot: Edward Elgar Publishing 1995), pp. 135–148.

Pugiotto, A., *Sindacato di costituzionalità e 'diritto vivente'* (Padova: Cedam 1994).

Radbruch, G., *Legal Philosophy* (Cambridge Mass.: Harvard University Press 1950).

Robert, Jacques & Dominique Rousseau, 'Neuf années au Conseil constitutionnel. Débat entre Jacques Robert et Dominique Rousseau', *Revue du droit public*, 1998, pp. 1748–1770.

Rohr, John A., *Founding Republics in France and America – A Study in Constitutional Governance* (Lawrence: University Press of Kansas, 1995).

Romanow, R, et al, *Canada ... Notwithstanding: The Making of the Constitution 1976–1982* (Toronto: Carswell/Methuen 1984).

Romboli, R. (ed), *Aggiornamenti in tema di processo costituzionale* (Torino: Giappichelli 1990, 1993, 1996).

Romboli, R. (ed), *La giustizia costituzionale a una svolta* (Torino: Giappichelli 1990).

Romboli, R. (ed), *La tutela dei diritti fondamentali davanti alle Corti costituzionali* (Torino: Giappichelli 1994).

Romboli, R., *Il giudizio costituzionale incidentale come 'processo senza parti'* (Milano: Giuffrè 1985).

Rose, Richard, 'Russia as an Hour-Glass-Society. A Constitution without Citizens', *East European Constitutional Review*, 4 no. 3 (1995), pp. 34–42.

Rosenberg, Gerald, *The Hollow Hope* (Chicago: University of Chicago Press 1991).

Rousseau, Dominique (ed.) *La démocratie continue* (Paris-Brussels: L.G.D.J.-Bruylant, 1995).

Rousseau, Dominique & Frédéric Sudre, *Conseil constitutionnel et Cour européenne des droits de l'homme* (Paris: S.T.H., 1990).

Rousseau, Dominique, *Droit du contentieux constitutionnel* (Paris: Montchrestien, 1999, 5th ed).

Rousseau, Jean-Jacques, 'Considerations on the Government of Poland,' in: *Political Writings* (Madison: The University of Wisconsin Press, 1986).

Rousseau, Jean-Jacques, *Du Contrat social ou principes du droit politique*, 1762 (Paris: Flammarion [Gf Philosophie], 2001).

Roussillon, Henri, *Le Conseil constitutionnel* (Paris: Dalloz, 1996, 3rd ed).

Ruggeri, A. & A. Spadaro, *Lineamenti di giustizia costituzionale* (Torino: Giappichelli 1998).

Russell, P., 'Standing Up for Notwithstanding', *Alberta Law Review*, 29 (1991), pp. 293–309.

Sadurski, W., 'Conventional Morality and Judicial Standards', *Virginia Law Review* 73 (1987), pp. 339–97.

Saitta, A., *Logica e retorica nella motivazione delle decisioni della Corte costituzionale* (Milano: Giuffrè 1996).

Sajo, Andras, 'How the Rule of Law Killed Hungarian Welfare Reform', *East European Constitutional Review* 5 no. 1 (1993), pp. 31–41.

Sajo, Andras., 'Reading the Invisible Constitution: Judicial Review in Hungary', *Oxford Journal of Legal Studies*, 15 (1995), pp. 253–67.

Sandulli, A.M., *Il giudizio sulle leggi* (Milano: Giuffrè 1967).

Sartori, Giovanni, 'Concept Misformation in Comparative Politics,' *American Political Science Review* 64 (1970), pp. 1033–1053.

Sartori, Giovanni, *The Theory of Democracy Revisited*, Vol. I (Chatham: Chatham House, 1987).

Scheppele, Kim; Mark Brzezinski & Herbert Hausmaniger, 'Constitutional 'Refolution' in the Ex-Communist World; the Rule of Law', *American University Journal of International Law and Policy* 12 (1997), pp. 87–116.

Schlinck, Bernhard, 'German Constitutional Culture in Transition', in Michel Rosenfeld (ed.), *Constitutionalism, Identity, Difference, and Legitimacy: Theoretical Perspectives* (Durham: Duke University Press, 1994), pp. 197–222.

Schmidhauser, John, *The Supreme Court as Final Arbiter of Federal State Relations* (Chapel Hill: University of North Carolina Press 1958).

Schneider, Hans-Peter, 'Richter oder Schlichter? Das Bundesverfassungsgericht als Integrationsfaktor', *Aus Politik und Zeitgeschichte* B 16 (1999), pp. 9–19.

Scholz, Rupert, 'Das Bundesverfassungsgericht: Hüter der Verfassung oder Ersatzgesetzgeber', *Aus Politik und Zeitgeschichte* B 16 (1999), pp. 3–8.

Schroeder, Friedrich-Christian (ed.), *Die neuen Kodifikationen in Rußland* (Berlin, Berlin Verlag 1997).

Schwartz, Bernard, *'Decision: How the Supreme Court Decides Cases'* (Oxford University Press, New York 1996).

Schwartz, H., *The Struggle for Constitutional Justice in Post-Communist Europe* (Chicago: The University of Chicago Press 2000).

Schwartz, H., 'The New Courts: an Overview', in Volkman Gessner (ed.), *European Legal Cultures* (Aldershot 1996), pp. 445–51.

Schwarze, Jürgen, *European Administrative Law* (London: Sweet and Maxwell, 1992), pp. 261–277.

Schweisfurth, Theodor: 'Der Start der Verfassungsgerichtsbarkeit in Rußland', *EuGRZ* (1992), pp. 292ff.

Selianov, Mykola, 'Problemni Pytannia Formuvania ta Vykonannia Budzhetu Konstytutsiynoho Sudu Ukrainy' [Problematic Questions on the Formation and Implementation of the Budget of the Constitutional Court], *Visnyk Konstytutsiynoho Sudu*, 5–6 (1998).

Sesickas, Linas, 'Judicial Independence in Lithuania' unpublished report prepared for the 'Monitoring EU Enlargement' Project of the Center for Policy Studies, Central European University Budapest, 2001.

Ševčík, V., 'Všhledy ústavnosti v. novém státě – pokus o analyzující sondu' (Prospects of constitutionalism in the new state – an analytical sketch), *Právník* CXXXIII (1994), pp. 1011–1027.

Shapiro, Martin, *Courts: A Comparative and Political Analysis* (University of Chicago Press, Chicago 1981)

Shapiro, Martin, 'Fathers and Sons: The Court, The Commentators and The Search for Values', in Vincent Blasi, *The Burger Court* (New Haven, Yale University Press 1983), pp. 218–238.

Shapiro, Martin, 'Introduction to Charles Warren, "The Charles River Bridge Case"', *Green Bag* 2d, 3 (1999), pp. 75–78.

Shapiro, Martin, 'The Supreme Court and Economic Rights', in M. Judd Harmon (ed.), *Essays on the Constitution of the United States* (Port Washington, N.Y.: Kennikat Press 1978), pp. 74–99.

Shapiro, Martin, 'The Supreme Court's 'Return' to Economic Regulation', *Studies in*

American Political Development (New Haven: Yale University Press 1986) vol. 1, pp. 91–141.

Sharlet, Robert, 'Legal Transplants and Political Mutations: The Reception of Constitutional Law in Russia and the Newly Independent States,' *East European Constitutional Review*, 7 no. 4 (1998), pp. 59–68.

Sharlet, Robert: 'Chief Justice as Judicial Politician', *East European Constitutional Review*, 2 no. 2 (1993), pp. 32–38.

Sharlet, Robert: 'Russian Constitutional Crisis', *Post-Soviet Affairs*, 4 (1993), pp. 314–336.

Sharlet, Robert: 'The Russian Constitutional Court. The First Term', *Transitional Justice, Vol. II Country Studies* (Washington, United States Institute of Peace Press 1995).

Shugart, Matthew S. & John M. Carey, *Presidents and Assemblies: Constitutional Design and Electoral Dynamics* (Cambridge: Cambridge University Press 1992).

Shul'zhenko, Yu.L.: *Konstitutsionnyj kontrol' v. Rossii* (Moscow, Rossijskaya akademiya nauk: Institut Gosudarstva i Prava 1995).

Siegan, Bernard, *Economic Liberties and the Constitution* (Chicago: University of Chicago Press 1980).

Sieyès, Emmanuel Joseph, *Ecrits politiques* (Paris: Editions des archives contemporaines, 1985).

Simpson, B, *In the Highest Degree Odious: Detention Without Trial in Wartime Britain* (Oxford: Oxford University Press 1994).

Slattery, B, 'A Theory of the *Charter*', *Osgoode Hall Law Journal*, 25 (1987), pp. 701–747.

Snowiss, Sylvia, *Judicial Review and the Law of the Constitution* (New Haven: Yale University Press 1990).

Sólyom, László & Georg Brunner, *Constitutional Judiciary in a New Democracy: The Hungarian Constitutional Court* (Ann Arbor: The University of Michigan Press 2000).

Sólyom, László, 'Az Alkotmánybíróság hatáskörének sajátossága'. ('Idiosyncrasies of the Constitutional Court's Jurisdiction'), in, 'Emlékkönyv Benedek Ferenc 70. születésnapja alkalmából.' (*'Memorial Volume in Commemoration of Ferenc Benedek's 70th Birthday'*), Pécs (1995).

Sólyom, László, 'The First Year of the Constitutional Court', *Acta Juridica Academiae Scinetiarum Hungaricae* 1–2 (1991).

Sólyom, László, 'The Hungarian Constitutional Court and Social Change', *Yale Journal of International Law* 19 (1994), pp. 223–237.

Spagnoli, U., *I problemi della Corte* (Torino: Giappichelli 1996).

Stalev, Zhivko, & Neno Nenovski, *Konstitutzionnijat sud i pravnoto deistvie na negovite reshenija* (Sofia: Civi, 1996).

Starck, Christian (ed.), *Bundesverfassungsgericht und Grundgesetz.* (Tübingen, Mohr, 2 vols. 1976).

Starck, Christian, *Das Bundesverfassungsgericht im politischen Prozeß der Bundesrepublik.* (Tübingen, Mohr 1976).

Sterett, Susan, *Creating Constitutionalism?* (Ann Arbor, University of Michigan Press 1997).

Stone, A., 'Constitutional Politics and Malaise in France' in J.T. Keeler & M.A. Schain (eds), *Chirac's Challenge* (New York: St. Martin's Press 1996).

Stone Sweet, Alec, *Governing with Judges* (Oxford: Oxford University Press 2000).

Stone, A., *The Birth of Judicial Politics in France* (Oxford: Oxford University Press 1992).

Strashun, Boris/Sobakin, Vadim: 'Defending the Russian Constitutional Court Act', *East European Constitutional Review*, 1 (1995).

Strong, Frank, Substantive *Due Process of Law* (Durham, N.C., Carolina Academic Press 1986).

Sunstein, Cass R. *One Case at a Time: Judicial Minimalism on the Supreme Court* (Cambridge: Harvard University Press 1999).

Tarnopolsky, W, *The Canadian Bill of Rights*, 2nd ed (Toronto: McClelland and Stewart 1975).

Teitel, Ruti, 'Post-Communist Constitutionalism: A Transitional Perspective', *Columbia Human Rights Law Review* 26 (1994): 167–190.

Teitel, Ruti, 'Transitional Jurisprudence: The Role of Law in Political Transformation', *Yale Law Journal* 106 (1997), pp. 2009–2080.

Thayer, James B., 'The Origin and Scope of the American Doctrine of Constitutional Law', *Harvard Law Review* 7 (1893), pp. 129–56.

Tóth, Gábor Attila, Sólyom, Lászlóval, az Alkotmánybíróság elnökével beszélget. 'A 'nehéz eseteknél' a bíró erkölcsi felfogása jut szerephez' ('In 'difficult cases' a judge's moral concepts comes into play'. Attila Gábor Tóth in a conversation with László Sólyom, the President of the Constitutional Court. *Fundamentum*, 1 (1997).

Tribe, L, *American Constitutional Law* vol. 1, 3rd ed (New York: New York Foundation Press 2000).

Troper, Michel, 'Comment décident les juges constitutionnels', *Le Monde*, 13 February 1999, also published in *Revue française de droit constitutionnel* (1999, n° 37, pp. 325–328).

Troper, Michel, 'Justice constitutionnelle et démocratie', *Revue française de droit constitutionnel*, 1990, pp. 31–48.

Troper, Michel, «La notion de principes *supra* constitutionnels», *Revue internationale de droit comparé*, n° spl., journées de la société de législation comparée, 1993.

Troper, Michel, 'La signature des ordonnances. Fonctions d'une controverse', *Pouvoirs*, n° 41, 1987.

Troper, Michel, 'Le problème de l'interprétation et de la théorie de la supralégalité constitutionnelle', in *Mélanges Eisenmann* (Paris: Cujas, 1975)..

Troper, Michel, 'Preface' in Jacques Meunier, *above*, pp. 7–11.

Tumanov, Vladimir: 'Guarantees for Constitutionality of Legislation in the U.S.S.R.', in Christine Landfried (ed.), *Constitutional Review and Legislation* (Baden-Baden, Nomos 1988).

Tumanov, Vladimir: 'Sudebnyi kontrol' za konstitutsionnost'yu normativnykh aktov', *Sovetskoe Gosudarstvo i Pravo*, 3 (1988).

Tushnet, M, 'Policy Distortion and Democratic Debilitation: Comparative Illumination of the Countermajoritarian Difficulty', *Michigan Law Review* 94 (1995), pp. 245–301.

Vargova, Mariela (ed.), *Konstitutzionnijat sud: jurisprudentzija* (Sofia: Open Society Institute, 1996).

Vedel, Georges, 'Le précédent judiciaire en droit public', *Revue Internationale de droit comparé*, n° spl. *Journées de la société de législation comparée*, vol. 6, 1984.

Vedel, Georges, 'Préface aux actes du Colloque de Rennes', in Drago *et al.*, *above*, p. IX-XV.

Vedel, Georges, 'Schengen et Maastricht. A propos de la décision n° 91–294 DC du 25 juillet 1991', *Revue française de droit administratif*, 8 (1992), pp. 173–180.

Vedel, Georges, 'Souveraineté et *supra* constitutionnalité', *Pouvoirs*, n° 67, 1993, pp. 79–97.

Viala, Alexandre, *Les réserves d'interprétation dans la jurisprudence du Conseil constitutionnel* (Paris: L.G.D.J., 1999).

Vitruk, N.V. et al: *O konstitutsionnom sude Rossijskoj federatsii. Kommentarij* (Moscow, Yuridicheskaya literatura 1996).

Vulkanov, Velko, *Na kolene pred istinata* (Sofia: Bulvest 2000, 1996).

Walker, Edward W.: 'Politics of Blame and Presidential Powers in Russia's New Constitution', *East European Constitutional Review*, 3 no. 1 (1994), pp. 116–20.

Walter, R., 'Středoevropské ústavní soudnictví a ryzí nauka právní. [Central European Constitutional Jurisdiction and the Pure Legal Science], *Právník*, 2 (1994).

Wasby, Stephen, The Impact of the U.S. Supreme Court (Homewood, Ill. Dorsey Press, 1970).

Wasilewski, Andrzej, 'Przedstawianie pytań prawnych Trybunalowi Konstytucyjnemu przez sądy (art. 193 Konstytucji RP)', *Państwo i Prawo* vol. 54, no 8/1999, pp. 25–39.

Watson, Alan, *Legal Transplants* (Charlottesville: University of Virginia Press, 1974).

Webber, J, 'Beyond Regret: Mabo's Implications for Australian Constitutionalism', in Duncan Ivison et al (eds), *Political Theory and the Rights of Indigenous Peoples* (Cambridge: Cambridge University Press 2000).

Webber, J, 'Constitutional Poetry: The Tension Between Symbolic and Functional Aims in Constitutional Reform', *Sydney Law Review* 21 (1999).

Webber, J, 'Constitutional Reticence', *Australian Journal of Legal Philosophy* 25 (2000).

Webber, J, 'Tales of the Unexpected: Intended and Unintended Consequences of the Canadian Charter of Rights and Freedoms', *Canterbury Law Review* 5 (1993).

Webber, J, *Reimagining Canada: Language, Culture, Community, and the Canadian Constitution* (Montreal: McGill-Queen's University Press 1994).

Weber, Max, *The Russian Revolutions* (Ithaca: Cornell University Press, 1995).

Wechsler, Herbert, 'Toward Neutral Principles of Constitutional Law', *Harvard Law Review* 73 (1959), pp. 1–37.

Weiler, P, 'Rights and Judges in a Democracy: A New Canadian Version', *University of Michigan Journal of Law Reform* 18 (1984), pp. 51–92.

Westle, Bettina, *Kollektive Identität im vereinten Deutschland.* (Opladen, Leske & Budrich 1999).

White, Stephen et al: *How Russia Votes* (Chatham/New Jersey, Chatham House 1997).

Wolczuk, Kataryna, 'Constituting Statehood: The New Ukrainian Constitution', *The Ukrainian Review* 45(3) (1998).

Zagrebelsky, G., *La giustizia costituzionale* (Bologna: Il mulino 1988).

Zifcak, Spencer, 'Hungary's Remarkable, Radical, Constitutional Court', *Journal of Constitutional Law in Eastern and Central Europe* 3 (1996): 1–56

Ziller, Jacques 'Le contrôle du pouvoir réglementaire en Europe', *Actualité Juridique, Droit Administratif*, n° 9/199.

Zilys, Juozas, 'Konstitucinis Teismas Valdziu Sistemoje' [The Constitutional Court within the Governing System] paper presented at the conference: *Lietuvos Respublikos Konstitucija: Tiesioginis Taikymas ir Nuosavybes Teisiu Apsauga* [*The Constitution of the Republic of Lithuania: Direct Effect and the Protection of Property Rights*] and February 25–26, 1993 (Vilnius, Teise 1994).

Zines, L, *The High Court and the Constitution*, 4th ed (Sydney: Butterworths 1997).

Index of Names

Law and Philosophy Library

1. E. Bulygin, J.-L. Gardies and I. Niiniluoto (eds.): *Man, Law and Modern Forms of Life.* With an Introduction by M.D. Bayles. 1985   ISBN 90-277-1869-5

2. W. Sadurski: *Giving Desert Its Due.* Social Justice and Legal Theory. 1985   ISBN 90-277-1941-1

3. N. MacCormick and O. Weinberger: *An Institutional Theory of Law.* New Approaches to Legal Positivism. 1986   ISBN 90-277-2079-7

4. A. Aarnio: *The Rational as Reasonable.* A Treatise on Legal Justification. 1987   ISBN 90-277-2276-5

5. M.D. Bayles: *Principles of Law.* A Normative Analysis. 1987   ISBN 90-277-2412-1; Pb: 90-277-2413-X

6. A. Soeteman: *Logic in Law.* Remarks on Logic and Rationality in Normative Reasoning, Especially in Law. 1989   ISBN 0-7923-0042-4

7. C.T. Sistare: *Responsibility and Criminal Liability.* 1989   ISBN 0-7923-0396-2

8. A. Peczenik: *On Law and Reason.* 1989   ISBN 0-7923-0444-6

9. W. Sadurski: *Moral Pluralism and Legal Neutrality.* 1990   ISBN 0-7923-0565-5

10. M.D. Bayles: *Procedural Justice.* Allocating to Individuals. 1990   ISBN 0-7923-0567-1

11. P. Nerhot (ed.): *Law, Interpretation and Reality.* Essays in Epistemology, Hermeneutics and Jurisprudence. 1990   ISBN 0-7923-0593-0

12. A.W. Norrie: *Law, Ideology and Punishment.* Retrieval and Critique of the Liberal Ideal of Criminal Justice. 1991   ISBN 0-7923-1013-6

13. P. Nerhot (ed.): *Legal Knowledge and Analogy.* Fragments of Legal Epistemology, Hermeneutics and Linguistics. 1991   ISBN 0-7923-1065-9

14. O. Weinberger: *Law, Institution and Legal Politics.* Fundamental Problems of Legal Theory and Social Philosophy. 1991   ISBN 0-7923-1143-4

15. J. Wróblewski: *The Judicial Application of Law.* Edited by Z. Bańkowski and N. MacCormick. 1992   ISBN 0-7923-1569-3

16. T. Wilhelmsson: *Critical Studies in Private Law.* A Treatise on Need-Rational Principles in Modern Law. 1992   ISBN 0-7923-1659-2

17. M.D. Bayles: *Hart's Legal Philosophy.* An Examination. 1992   ISBN 0-7923-1981-8

18. D.W.P. Ruiter: *Institutional Legal Facts.* Legal Powers and their Effects. 1993   ISBN 0-7923-2441-2

19. J. Schonsheck: *On Criminalization.* An Essay in the Philosophy of the Criminal Law. 1994   ISBN 0-7923-2663-6

20. R.P. Malloy and J. Evensky (eds.): *Adam Smith and the Philosophy of Law and Economics.* 1994   ISBN 0-7923-2796-9

21. Z. Bańkowski, I. White and U. Hahn (eds.): *Informatics and the Foundations of Legal Reasoning.* 1995   ISBN 0-7923-3455-8

22. E. Lagerspetz: *The Opposite Mirrors.* An Essay on the Conventionalist Theory of Institutions. 1995   ISBN 0-7923-3325-X

Law and Philosophy Library

23. M. van Hees: *Rights and Decisions*. Formal Models of Law and Liberalism. 1995
ISBN 0-7923-3754-9

24. B. Anderson: *"Discovery" in Legal Decision-Making*. 1996 ISBN 0-7923-3981-9

25. S. Urbina: *Reason, Democracy, Society*. A Study on the Basis of Legal Thinking. 1996
ISBN 0-7923-4262-3

26. E. Attwooll: *The Tapestry of the Law*. Scotland, Legal Culture and Legal Theory. 1997
ISBN 0-7923-4310-7

27. J.C. Hage: *Reasoning with Rules*. An Essay on Legal Reasoning and Its Underlying Logic.
1997 ISBN 0-7923-4325-5

28. R.A. Hillman: *The Richness of Contract Law*. An Analysis and Critique of Contemporary
Theories of Contract Law. 1997 ISBN 0-7923-4336-0; 0-7923-5063-4 (Pb)

29. C. Wellman: *An Approach to Rights*. Studies in the Philosophy of Law and Morals. 1997
ISBN 0-7923-4467-7

30. B. van Roermund: *Law, Narrative and Reality*. An Essay in Intercepting Politics. 1997
ISBN 0-7923-4621-1

31. I. Ward: *Kantianism, Postmodernism and Critical Legal Thought*. 1997
ISBN 0-7923-4745-5

32. H. Prakken: *Logical Tools for Modelling Legal Argument*. A Study of Defeasible Reasoning
in Law. 1997 ISBN 0-7923-4776-5

33. T. May: *Autonomy, Authority and Moral Responsibility*. 1998 ISBN 0-7923-4851-6

34. M. Atienza and J.R. Manero: *A Theory of Legal Sentences*. 1998 ISBN 0-7923-4856-7

35. E.A. Christodoulidis: *Law and Reflexive Politics*. 1998 ISBN 0-7923-4954-7

36. L.M.M. Royakkers: *Extending Deontic Logic for the Formalisation of Legal Rules*. 1998
ISBN 0-7923-4982-2

37. J.J. Moreso: *Legal Indeterminacy and Constitutional Interpretation*. 1998
ISBN 0-7923-5156-8

38. W. Sadurski: *Freedom of Speech and Its Limits*. 1999 ISBN 0-7923-5523-7

39. J. Wolenski (ed.): *Kazimierz Opalek Selected Papers in Legal Philosophy*. 1999
ISBN 0-7923-5732-9

40. H.P. Visser 't Hooft: *Justice to Future Generations and the Environment*. 1999
ISBN 0-7923-5756-6

41. L.J. Wintgens (ed.): *The Law in Philosophical Perspectives*. My Philosophy of Law. 1999
ISBN 0-7923-5796-5

42. A.R. Lodder: *DiaLaw*. On Legal Justification and Dialogical Models of Argumentation. 1999
ISBN 0-7923-5830-9

43. C. Redondo: *Reasons for Action and the Law*. 1999 ISBN 0-7923-5912-7

44. M. Friedman, L. May, K. Parsons and J. Stiff (eds.): *Rights and Reason*. Essays in Honor of
Carl Wellman. 2000 ISBN 0-7923-6198-9

Law and Philosophy Library

45. G.C. Christie: *The Notion of an Ideal Audience in Legal Argument*. 2000
ISBN 0-7923-6283-7

46. R.S. Summers: *Essays in Legal Theory*. 2000
ISBN 0-7923-6367-1

47. M. van Hees: *Legal Reductionism and Freedom*. 2000
ISBN 0-7923-6491-0

48. R. Gargarella: *The Scepter of Reason*. Public Discussion and Political Radicalism in the Origins
of Constitutionalism. 2000
ISBN 0-7923-6508-9

49. M. Iglesias Vila: *Facing Judicial Discretion*. Legal Knowledge and Right Answers Revisited.
2001
ISBN 0-7923-6778-2

50. M. Kiikeri: *Comparative Legal Reasoning and European Law*. 2001
ISBN 0-7923-6884-3

51. A.J. Menéndez: *Justifying Taxes*. Some Elements for a General Theory of Democratic Tax
Law. 2001
ISBN 0-7923-7052-X

52. W.E. Conklin: *The Invisible Origins of Legal Positivism*. A Re-Reading of a Tradition. 2001
ISBN 0-7923-7101-1

53. Z. Bańkowski: *Living Lawfully*. Love in Law and Law in Love. 2001
ISBN 0-7923-7180-1

54. A.N. Shytov: *Conscience and Love in Making Judicial Decisions*. 2001
ISBN 1-4020-0168-1

55. D.W.P. Ruiter: *Legal Institutions*. 2001
ISBN 1-4020-0186-X

Volumes 1–55 were published by Kluwer Academic Publishers.

56. G. den Hartogh: *Mutual Expectations*. A Conventionalist Theory of Law. 2002
ISBN 90-411-1796-2

57. W.L. Robison (ed.): *The Legal Essays of Michael Bayles*. 2002
ISBN 90-411-1835-7

58. U. Bindreiter: *Why Grundnorm?* A Treatise on the Implications of Kelsen's Doctrine. 2002
ISBN 90-411-1867-5

59. S. Urbina: *Legal Method and the Rule of Law*. 2002
ISBN 90-411-1870-5

60. M. Baurmann: *The Market of Virtue*. Morality and Commitment in a Liberal Society. 2002
ISBN 90-411-1874-8

61. G. Zanetti: *Political Friendship and the Good Life*. Two Liberal Arguments against Perfectionism. 2002
ISBN 90-411-1881-0

62. W. Sadurski (ed.): *Constitutional Justice, East and West*. 2002
ISBN 90-411-1883-7

Printed in the United States
145360LV00001B/18/P